Contemporary
ETHICAL
ISSUES

THIRD EDITION

Contemporary ETHICAL ISSUES

THIRD EDITION

A Personalist
Perspective

WALTER G. JEFFKO

Humanity
Books

an imprint of Prometheus Books
59 John Glenn Drive, Amherst, New York 14228-2119

Published 2013 by Humanity Books, an imprint of Prometheus Books

Cover design by Jacqueline Nasso Cooke
Cover illustration by Joost van Roojen

Inquiries should be addressed to
Humanity Books
59 John Glenn Drive
Amherst, New York 14228–2119
VOICE: 716–691–0133
FAX: 716–691–0137
WWW.PROMETHEUSBOOKS.COM

17 16 15 14 13   5 4 3 2 1

Library of Congress Cataloging-in-Publication Data

Jeffko, Walter G.
    Contemporary ethical issues : a personalist perspective / By Walter G. Jeffko. — Third edition.
        pages cm
    Includes bibliographical references and index.
    ISBN 978-1-61614-731-0 (pbk.) • ISBN 978-1-61614-732-7 (ebook)
    1. Ethical problems. 2. Personalism. I. Title.

BJ1031.J44 2013
171'.3—dc13

                                                                        2013002221

Printed in the United States of America

CONTENTS

PREFACE TO THE THIRD EDITION

It is with great pleasure that I present this third edition of *Contemporary Ethical Issues*. Besides numerous revisions and updates throughout the book, the single most important reason for a new edition is a whole new chapter on the ethics of war, which is an expansion and update of my latest Harrod Lecture, "The Moral Treatment of Civilians in War," delivered at Fitchburg State University on October 19, 2010. Two noteworthy features of this chapter are, first, a narrative of John Macmurray's service in World War I and how his war experience led him to pacifism, which he was forced to rethink as he grappled with the horrendous evils of Hitler's Nazism in World War II; and, second, an extensive critique of Michael Walzer's influential and controversial concept of supreme emergency, which, he argues, justifies directly attacking and killing enemy civilians in warfare.

I now highlight the other significant changes in this edition. In chapter 1, I analyze more fully my definition of value and how it relates to fact and to science. I also state more carefully the relation between science and technology. In chapter 2, the principles of double effect and intentionality are further refined. In chapter 3, I explain how the Roman Catholic Church has changed its moral position on suicide in relation to St. Augustine's argument against suicide.

Chapter 4, on abortion, has several changes. The fallacy of affirming the consequent is replaced with a novel interpretation of the genetic fallacy in connection with my criticisms of the immediate animation theory. Information on fetal viability is updated. I refine my own theory of personalization, which I now call the *viability-mutuality* theory. I replace Roger Wertheimer's somewhat dated and confusing classification of moral positions on abortion with a simpler classification that is more coherent, more contemporary, and more clearly connects with my own position. Abortion statistics are updated. Regarding the legal dimension of abortion, I add a fourth condition for making a claimed immoral act illegal, taking into account Rawls's theory of political liberalism. Finally, I comment on the recent so-called personhood amendments proposed by some state legislatures.

In chapter 5, on euthanasia, the physician-assisted suicide issue is updated. Chapter 6 has several revisions. In the theory of retributivism, the concept of punishability is introduced. Also under retributivism, I argue why punishing the innocent is morally worse than not punishing the guilty. I revise the various criticisms of the utilitarian theory of punishment. Death penalty statistical trends are updated. The relation between the Bible Belt and the "death penalty belt" is briefly explored. Five additional Supreme Court decisions on the death penalty—four of them recent—are discussed. A new section is added, "The Death Penalty in Decline," referring specifically to the United States.

In chapter 7, I recast and expand my critique of Macmurray concerning his notion of the materiality of personhood and introduce the term *person-body* to characterize his position. Statistics on the growing inequality of wealth and income in the United States—especially since the Great Recession of 2008— are updated in connection with my enlarged critique of libertarianism. In this context, I explain why the distinction between distribution and redistribution of wealth and income is arbitrary and artificial.

In chapter 8, I comment on the increasing influence of libertarianism on the Republican Party in connection with Rawls's brief critique of the former. In a new section, "Liberalism and Two Political Controversies," I further comment on and update the same-sex marriage issue, and I defend the Obama administration's position on the issue of religious liberty versus a woman's right to contraception with respect to a provision in the Patient Protection and Affordable Health Care Act (a.k.a., Obamacare).

In chapter 9, I briefly develop a view of animal rights that is analogous to human rights. This analogous concept of rights likewise applies to the human conceptus-fetus for its entire period of gestation. I have dropped the expression, stated several times in the second edition, that only persons have rights in the strict sense.

Chapter 10, on affirmative action, has four changes. I comment on the Supreme Court's recent important decision on employee tests in the workplace, *Ricci v. DeStefano*. As background for this case, the *Griggs v. Duke Power Co.* decision is discussed for the first time. The reverse discrimination argument is recast. And I refine my response to the antimerit argument.

In chapter 11, I update important statistics on global warming and explain why that term is preferable to *climate change*. I also briefly examine the newly emerging practice of rotational-grazing.

There are many minor stylistic changes. Several typos were corrected. Perceived mistakes were corrected or deleted. I made several major deletions, mostly of material I deemed too closely tied to the second edition.

I thank my longtime friend and Macmurray colleague, Harry Carson, for his supportive and discerning remarks after he read portions of the manuscript. Once again, I thank my wife, Catherine, for her loving support throughout this project. And I especially thank my dear and devoted friend, Catherine Hill, for her meticulous production of the entire manuscript.

PREFACE TO THE SECOND EDITION

I am pleased to present this preface to the second edition. As would be expected, the new edition has many updates, for example, commentary on recent Supreme Court decisions. More important, it has numerous changes in wording and substance. There are three new chapters and several major deletions. I have scrutinized every word of the original edition and made whatever changes I deemed desirable or necessary. Perceived mistakes were corrected. I spared myself no mercy. The overall aim was not only to update but also to improve. Although the basic plan of the book remains the same—it is principally based on my Harrod Lectures and influenced by John Macmurray—after almost ten years my thinking has evolved on many of its issues. Other issues have been added. In a sense, the new edition is a new book. I now indicate its important changes.

The most important changes to the new edition are its three additional chapters. The original volume had eight chapters; the present edition has eleven. Chapter 11 is all new. It is an update and heavy revision of my latest Harrod Lecture delivered on October 30, 2001, "Ethics and the Environmental Crisis." The other two additional chapters are the result of expanding and subdividing two chapters of the original edition.

Chapters 1 and 2 of the present edition are an outgrowth of the original chapter 1. The new chapter 1 parallels the original chapter through the section on instrumental and aesthetic value. The major change in this chapter is replacing the idea of person as relational agent with person as *communicative* agent. The word *relational* in this context now strikes me as redundant and noninformative. However, most of the changes to the old chapter 1 are in the new chapter 2, which is exclusively devoted to moral value. Chapter 2 thus parallels the last section ("Moral Value") of the original first chapter, but in a much more expanded and revised form. As such, chapter 2 is the second additional chapter of the new edition. The most important change in this chapter consists of replacing the traditional principle of double effect with what I call the principle of intentionality. This change required me not only to compare intentionality with double effect but also to two other related doctrines: doing/allowing and voluntary/involuntary. The upshot of this change is that intentionality is the main procedural principle for applying the principle of community, both of which constitute the subject matter of chapter 2. I also clarify my value theory in relation to the conventional distinction between teleological and deontological theories.

The third additional chapter results from subdividing the original chapter 6, "Privacy, Private Property, and Justice." The new chapter 7 corresponds to the old chapter 6 through the section on Plato's organic society. I now give a more careful analysis of Plato's intermediate part of the soul, the "spirited" part. A new section has been added in chapter 7 on the spirituality of personhood in relation to self-consciousness. This section responds to recent questions about whether science has solved the "mystery" of consciousness and to what I think is an incoherence in Macmurray's conception of personhood. Chapter 8, "The Personalist Society, Community, and Justice," is the third additional chapter. It is a much expanded and revised version of the last section of the original chapter 6, "The Personalistic Society." (Throughout the new edition, I changed the word *personalistic* to *personalist*.) There are two major additions in chapter 8. First and foremost is my treatment of John Rawls's theory of political liberalism, which I interpret as a model for the economic and political structure of a personalist society. In the first edition, I did not mention this theory at all, which was an unfortunate omission. Second, I take some of his remarks on the family to address the controversial issue of same-sex marriage.

There are other important substantive changes throughout the book. In chapter 3 on suicide, I give more attention to some of its definitions. In chapter 4 on abortion, I address the issues of the abortion pill RU-486 and embryonic stem-cell research. I also present a more detailed account of fetal growth, and a clearer definition of moral status. On euthanasia in chapter 5, I have changed my mind on one significant point in connection with the Terry

Schiavo case. I now hold that direct-passive euthanasia can be morally right in the absence of the legalization of direct-active euthanasia, providing it is voluntary or nonvoluntary (but not involuntary). More consideration is given to the concept of persistent vegetative state (PVS) and its difference from coma. Chapter 6 on the death penalty has a whole new section on Supreme Court decisions, since the Court has handed down so many key rulings on the issue, several of them since the book's original edition. I also take up in more detail the question of deterrence and indicate recent death penalty trends. At the same time, I deleted my critical analysis of Ernest van den Haag's wager for the death penalty. It does not deserve the attention I gave it in the first edition. On the moral treatment of animals in chapter 9, I deleted the long section on the concept of human nature. It now seems to me that this concept is wholly unnecessary to explain the difference between humans and animals, since my conception of person already serves this purpose. In chapter 10, there are three major changes. First, I have changed my mind on the ethics of affirmative action. I now hold that strong affirmative action (preferential treatment based on race, ethnicity, or gender) is prima facie immoral, but not intrinsically immoral, as I held in the first edition. Second, my supporting argument for this changed position is much longer and more carefully developed than the corresponding argument in the original edition. And third, I restructured the last section on other arguments. Several arguments from the first edition have been dropped, and one new argument has been added. Of the arguments I kept, I almost completely recast my response to them. Besides these major and significant changes, there are many minor ones too numerous to mention.

One final point. For many years, I have perceived a conflict between the rational requirements of philosophy and the authoritarianism (or so I think) of my Roman Catholic Church. From a theological standpoint, this conflict has led me to adopt positions on moral and doctrinal issues that characterize me as a liberal Catholic. I see my personalist philosophy as perfectly compatible with liberal Catholicism and more broadly with a liberal interpretation of Christianity. This observation does not alter the fact that I present this volume as an expression of autonomous philosophy. Its positions and arguments must ultimately stand the test of reason. As a philosopher, I reject fundamentalism and fideism as incompatible with philosophical reason. Both of these religious positions, in my view, sow the seeds of intolerance and, in some cases, fanaticism.

There are two people in particular I wish to thank for the completion of this book. I thank my wife, Catherine, for her constant emotional support for a project that proved much more daunting and time-consuming than I originally anticipated. I thank my longtime friend and secretary, Catherine Hill, for her unstinting devotion to the preparation and production of the entire manuscript. Without these two persons, this volume never would have seen the light of day.

PREFACE TO THE FIRST EDITION

This volume is based principally on rewritten, expanded, and updated versions of seven lectures (the Harrod Lectures) delivered at Fitchburg State College, Massachusetts, between 1979 and 1997. These lectures address a series of contemporary ethical problems from a personalistic perspective influenced by the Scottish philosopher John Macmurray (1891–1976). I utilize key elements of his thought in developing my own viewpoint, and I relate Macmurray's ideas to a wide variety of important philosophers, ethicists, and behavioral scientists. In doing so, I apply his thought to issues that he himself did not address.

Although my attitude toward Macmurray is basically sympathetic, this does not mean that I accept everything he says. Far from it. My attitude is not that of a disciple or follower. Some of his ideas have to be developed further; others have to be critically modified; still others have to be rejected altogether. Nevertheless, I find what he says important today, and one of my main intentions is to make that importance manifest. In this regard, Humanity Books has performed a valuable service in reissuing several of Macmurray's major works.

The book is divided into eight chapters. In the opening chapter, I develop the anthropological and ethical theory that forms the basic framework for the subsequent chapters. The main ideas of this framework are as follows: person as relational and rational agent, and reason as the standard of value; three basic modes of value—instrumental, aesthetic, and moral; reinterpretation of the principle of double effect based on a distinction among an action's motive, intention, and consequences, and between prima facie and intrinsically immoral actions; and the principle of community as the supreme moral or ethical standard. The next seven chapters are devoted to the issues developed in the Harrod Lectures: suicide, abortion, euthanasia, capital punishment, privacy, the treatment of animals, and affirmative action. I present these issues in their original chronological order.

The Harrod Lecture Series was inaugurated in June 1978 by the former president of Fitchburg State College, Vincent P. Mara, to honor Walter F. Harrod. At that time, Professor Harrod had recently retired from the college, where he had taught with distinction for twenty-nine years and was highly esteemed by colleagues and students alike. The purpose of the lectures is to display the academic interests and diversity of the faculty. The annual series consists of two to four lectures, which are selected anonymously by a committee comprising students, faculty, and administrators. The lectures are delivered by the faculty members to the college community and are open to the general public. They are subsequently published in booklet form by the Fitchburg State College Press.

The Harrod Lectures are expected to blend scholarship with a nontechnical style. I have tried to retain as much of their original style as possible and have modified it only in the interest of philosophical rigor. I have written this book primarily for students and other nonspecialists who want a rational approach to ethical issues. As a result, the book emphasizes the connection between ethics and logic, and when a technical term is used, especially a logical fallacy, I provide a brief explanation of it. At the same time, since the book has a philosophical form—a major component of which is logical or rational argumentation—and since I discuss and critically evaluate the views of many philosophers, it may also appeal to professional philosophers. Since my book covers much of the same ground as a textbook, it may be used as one when an instructor desires a different approach from that of standard textbooks, which are generally neutral toward the different viewpoints they present. Or it may be used as a companion to a textbook.

I would like to thank those who have helped me in the conception and preparation of this book. After reading my original Harrod Lectures, Harry Carson encouraged me to adapt them to a wider audience in one volume. Over the years, James Colbert has provided me with valuable insights and comments on my Harrod Lectures and on the book proposal itself. Dean Shirley Wagner of Fitchburg State College was instrumental in releasing funds for the support of this project and in rearranging my teaching schedule to allow me more time for research and writing. John Howie encouraged me with his favorable comments on one of my Harrod Lectures. I thank my countless students whose interest in, and critical comments on, much of the book's material required me to put it in a form that led to both the Harrod Lectures and this volume. I especially thank Catherine Hill for her dedication and editorial assistance in typing the entire manuscript. Finally, I am grateful to my wife, Catherine, whose love and emotional support were a constant source of inspiration throughout this lengthy project.

1

PERSON, REASON, AND VALUE

A CRISIS OF VALUES

That there exists a crisis of values today can hardly be denied. Our society is rife with moral chaos. At one extreme, we have the proliferation of the radio/TV talk show mentality, the growing opinionization of news, and more recently the rise of the Internet blogosphere and social media, where morality and values are basically expressions of unreflective personal opinion. At the other extreme, there are those who dogmatically assert what is right and wrong for everybody with no rational basis for doing so, as exemplified by the radical religious right, whether Christian or non-Christian. Many others flounder along somewhere in the middle, not sure what or who to believe. What is lacking, on both a national and an international level, is a common set of rationally justifiable values, rooted in community, that would bind us together and overcome this crisis. Instead of true community, we have a society that has become increasingly fragmented. Today's emphasis is on diversity without unity; the assertion of individual or group rights without any corresponding vision of, and responsibility to, the larger community. The events of 9/11, the Iraqi War, the emergence of international terrorism, the government's failure to respond adequately to the victims of Hurricane Katrina, the growing crisis of global warming, the growing divide between the two major political parties in the United States primarily caused by the increasing extremism and dogmatism of the political right, and our nation's severe maldistribution of wealth and income, are all rooted in a fundamental clash of values and how they are grounded.

In philosophy, too, this crisis of values reigns supreme. There is little agreement among philosophers on what value is or what constitutes an adequate standard of value. On the one hand, there are those who hold that value is simply a matter of what the subjective evaluator believes is right or wrong, good or bad. On the other hand, there are those who say that value is entirely in the object or act evaluated and exists independently of the evaluator. Philosophical theories of value, then, tend to be either subjective or objective, with little attempt to integrate or synthesize them.

At the basis of this split between subjectivism and objectivism is the controversy concerning the relation of reason to value. Although there is a long tradition in Western philosophy going back to Plato and Aristotle that holds that reason is the specific or essential difference between humans and animals, it is often held that this power or capacity does not apply to values. Subjective theories in particular deny that value is the product of reason. Emotivism holds that value is merely the expression of an individual's feelings of approval or disapproval. What emerges is a dualism between subjective feelings and objective reason. According to this view, reason knows and determines facts, as in science, but reason cannot determine what is valuable or disvaluable. Again, in some versions of existentialism, value is totally a matter of what one freely chooses. On this view, free choice has no rational basis and is purely arbitrary and subjective. Finally, in cultural (or ethical) relativism, the subjective beliefs of the majority or those in power determine what is right and wrong for all members of a society, through a pattern of mores and folkways that is supposed to preserve the existing social order but is seen as having little or nothing to do with rationality.

In objective theories, reason has an ambivalent status. In the intuitionism of G. E. Moore, the goodness or value inherent in objects and acts is a single and indefinable quality that is intuited but not rationally analyzable. In fideism, the laws of God, which are the standard of value, are based on faith, not reason. By contrast, reason is the standard of value in both natural law ethics and Immanuel Kant's deontological ethics. Each, however, has a serious flaw. Natural law ethics' objectivism does not take subjectivity seriously. It exalts nature at the expense of human reason and personhood. It too easily infers or derives the good from the natural, a procedure critics call the *naturalistic fallacy*.[1] The role of reason is largely passive: to observe and conform itself to an order of goods and precepts that are fully constituted in nature independently of the subjectivity of human personhood. Kant's objectivism, however, does seem to take subjectivity seriously. His three formulations of the categorical imperative are really three objective moral principles produced by the a priori structure of reason: the principle of universalizability, the principle of respect for persons, and the principle of autonomy of the will. The problem, however, is that Kant's subjectivity is legalistic. Reason's categorical imperative formulates these principles as absolute and exceptionless moral *laws*. Kant does not make a distinction between laws (or rules) and principles, where the former is subordinated to the latter. Had he done so, and had he interpreted his three formulations of the categorical imperative as principles rather than as laws, his concept of subjectivity would have been more adequate.

Finally, we are left with utilitarianism, which is probably the most prevalent philosophical theory of ethics and value, at least in Anglo-American philosophy. And interestingly, utilitarianism (in some versions, anyway) seems to weave a synthesis of subjectivity and objectivity in which reason plays an important role. The principle of utility—the greatest happiness for the greatest number of people—has both a subjective and an objective dimension. Subjectively, happiness excludes pain and includes the feelings of pleasure and well-being; objectively, it involves the satisfaction of human needs. Moreover, each individual must rationally calculate, in a given situation, what constitutes the greatest happiness for the greatest number of people.[2] The major difficulty with utilitarianism, however, is that the principle of utility is grounded in an inadequate theory of human nature and personhood. Jeremy Bentham, for example, has a one-dimensional view of human nature: humans by nature are fundamentally pleasure-seeking and pain-avoiding beings. "Nature has placed mankind under the governance of two sovereign masters, *pain* and *pleasure*. . . . The *principle of utility* recognizes this subjection."[3] Although John Stuart Mill's theory of human nature is more subtle and complex than Bentham's, it is still too closely associated with pleasure.

In this opening chapter, I develop a value and ethical theory that is different, in one way or another, from all the above theories—one that synthesizes objectivity with subjectivity within the context of reason as the standard of value and that grounds reason in the nature of human personhood.[4] I call my theory *transobjectivism* to distinguish it from other types of objectivism and from relativism and subjectivism. To proceed in an orderly fashion, I first sketch a theory of personhood. Then I briefly develop a concept of reason as the standard of value and apply it to instrumental and aesthetic values. In chapter 2, I apply reason to moral value.

PERSON AS COMMUNICATIVE AGENT

The fundamental proposition of a personalist anthropology is contained in John Macmurray's stark statement: "We are not organisms, but persons."[5] What he means is that the wholeness of human personhood cannot be reduced to the category of organism—or any other category of reality, for that matter—and that organicity is a subordinate but essential dimension of personhood. In short, as (human) persons we are more than rather than other than organisms. As persons, we are only partially organisms. But what, then, is a person, if not an organism as such? To answer this question, three interrelated dimensions of personhood must be briefly developed: mutuality, agency, and reason. The first two are considered in this section. The combination or synthesis of mutuality and agency yields the idea of person as communicative agent. Reason is taken up in the next section, when I connect it with value. The full form (or definition) of personhood that emerges is: a person is a communicative and rational agent whose self-realization or fulfillment is achieved in community.

THE MUTUALITY OF THE PERSONAL

The mutuality of the personal, to borrow a term from Macmurray,[6] is the concrete context for agency and reason. It denotes a relational theory of personhood that differs sharply from *individualism* and from an organic interpretation of the person. The latter view I call *organicism*.

For mutuality, the relations among persons are constitutive of person-hood. The unit of personal existence is not I in isolation, but You and I as inherently related to each other. The primary human reality is the field of persons-in-relation. This field by definition includes all persons and is the inclusive context for all aspects of individuality, experience, and culture.

As all-inclusive, the mutuality of the personal includes both *direct* and *indirect relations*. In direct relations, persons are acquainted to one degree or another; they know one another. Indirect relations lack this element of knowledge or acquaintance, yet the persons involved are still related to one another. Three types of indirect relations may be distinguished: economic, political, and ontological. I am economically related to the Japanese who built and exported my automobile. I am politically related to all Americans whom I do not know personally. And I am ontologically related to all other humans, since we share the same common human nature.

In contrast to the mutuality of the personal, individualism holds that a human being is fully constituted as a person in himself or herself, independent of relations with other persons. The solitary I is the unit of personal existence. Sociality, culture, and community are external to personhood rather than constitutive of it. René Descartes' cogito and the social contract theories of Thomas Hobbes, Jean-Jacques Rousseau, and John Locke are major examples of individualism. So also is Henry David Thoreau's naturalism.

Unlike individualism, organicism holds that humans are inherently related to one another and to the rest of nature. However, it reduces these relations to a biological level. By organicism, I mean any philosophy that holds that the concept of organism, or any related concept such as animal, is adequate to represent and understand human nature. Consequently, it holds that the concept of person is a legal, moral, religious, or poetic concept, but not one that has any rational or ontological (being-constituted) meaning. Correspondingly, organicism maintains that all of reality is nature. It thus includes all those forms of naturalism that are not connected with individualism. Since organicism reduces human nature to a biological level, human personhood and individuality are submerged in a web or network of organic relations. Whereas individualism exalts individuality at the expense of relationality, organicism exalts relationality at the expense of individuality.

Marxism, behaviorism, ethology, sociobiology, psychobiology, and some environmentalist philosophies such as deep ecology are all important examples of organicism. So also are theories that hold that genes and DNA are the sole determinants of human nature.

Unlike individualism and organicism, mutuality does full justice to both relationality and individuality. The mutuality of the personal is the essential context for individuality; it is only in and through the interpersonal context that individual persons can exist in the first place and subsequently grow. Both relationality and individuality are essential dimensions or "poles" of personhood; neither by itself constitutes a person's total reality. A person cannot be reduced to a web of relations; mutuality does not imply a fusion of selves. Each self or person has its own identity and individuality. Still, relationality is primary and individuality is secondary, in the sense that persons are constituted as individual persons within the inclusive field of persons-in-relation. The mutuality of the personal is similar to Martin Buber's concept of I-Thou and to the theory of intersubjectivity developed by Gabriel Marcel and existential phenomenology.

However, this view raises a serious objection: personal individuality cannot be fully constituted, or brought into existence, by relationality alone; relationality cannot be a sufficient condition of individuality. As Norris Clarke, the well-known contemporary Thomist, writes: "metaphysically this [view] will not work. We cannot literally bring into being another person that was not there before simply by relating to the thing that is there with attentive love. . . . The being to which we relate must already be of the type that *can* respond to such an invitation by intrinsic powers already within it."[7]

Clarke's objection is valid, but it does not apply to my position. For the mutuality of the personal, relationality is a necessary condition for individuality, but not a sufficient condition for it. Besides relationality, what is needed to constitute personhood is God's creative activity: God creates a field of persons-in-relation within which are constituted individual persons who then grow and develop in both their individuality and their relationality.

In its full implications, then, the mutuality of the personal is theistic and metaphysical. In this regard, Macmurray's distinction between *self* and *other* is helpful.[8] Self denotes any human person considered as I. Other, which is correlative to the self, denotes any and all reality excluding the self, to which the self is related. The other includes three realms: persons, biological reality, and material reality, in descending order of inclusiveness. In turn, persons include not only finite, human persons but also God, the infinite, universal person. Just as an individual person is necessarily related to a personal other, the whole field of persons-in-relation is necessarily related to a universal personal other who creates the world or universe. God, as personal, both transcends and is immanent in the world. Thus, an authentic personalism implies theism, although the axiology (theory of value) and ethics to be developed in this chapter and the next can be viewed as either standing on its own, independent of God, or open to the existence of a theistic god.

THE AGENCY OF THE PERSONAL

The relations among persons consist of action rather than pure thought, that is, thought in Descartes' sense of the term. Action by its nature is interaction. Action cannot occur in a vacuum; the self needs an other with which to interact. Action, therefore, is inherently relational. Thought, in contrast, is a private and inward activity. In reflection, the self withdraws from active relations with others into itself and its world of ideas. In this sense, thought is individualistic. Action expresses the relational aspect of mutuality; thought expresses its individual aspect. This does not mean, of course, that thought has no relation to the other. Such a statement would be absurd. It does mean, however, that in action the other is given immediately and directly, whereas in thought the other is given derivatively and indirectly. Moreover, in view of the relational character of action, it has a collective dimension. It involves not only a singular agent interacting with a singular other—whether personal or nonpersonal—but more significantly a plurality of agents in concert.

From this analysis we may conclude that the self (or person) is primarily agent and secondarily thinker; action is primary and thought is secondary. This is what I mean by the phrase *the agency of the personal*. To develop it further, we must explain three specific meanings of primary and secondary in this context. First, the self exists as agent rather than as pure (Cartesian) thinker; the self's being lies fundamentally in its agency and only partially and derivatively in its thinking capacity.

Second, action in comparison with thought is a much more inclusive activity of the self. In thought, the mind alone is active; in action, both mind and body are active. Action is not blind. It contains a cognitive element that is essential to its constitution. In action, not only are we aware that we are acting, but also, to some extent at least, we know what we are doing. This knowledge or cognition in action is thought (or thinking) at its original and basic level. I call it *prereflective* or *primary* thought, to distinguish it from thought that is withdrawn from action and thus constitutes an activity distinct from action.[9] This latter thought I call *reflective* or *secondary* thought. Prereflective thought involves *intention*, which may be defined as what the agent knowingly and self-consciously aims at in action. In addition, action includes sense perception and free choice. To act is to choose between alternative courses of action: to voluntarily do this and not that. Without free choice, action would become (animal) behavior, as it does in behaviorist psychology.[10] This power or capacity of free choice in action Macmurray calls *absolute freedom*. It is absolute in that it constitutes an essential difference between action and behavior.[11] Again, to perform an action requires a *motive*. By motive, I mean a disposition of the agent to act in a certain manner or direction that is rooted in feeling and originates and sustains the intention. Intention is closely connected with the knowledge element of action, and motive is connected with its emotion or feeling element. Motive and intention are quite different elements of action, and this distinction has considerable moral significance.

Consequently, besides bodily or physical movement that produces consequences, action also includes knowledge-intention, sense perception, free choice, and motive-feeling, all of which are integrated with movement to constitute one continuous activity. When we think in the sense of reflective thought, we exclude at least bodily movement. What else is excluded depends on how pure the thinking becomes. Action, then, is a fully concrete activity of the self in which all its basic capacities are employed, whereas (reflective) thought consists of an activity that excludes some of the self's powers and withdraws into an activity that is less concrete and less existential. In this respect, agent and person are coextensive terms; persons-in-relation are agents-in-relation.

The third meaning of primary and secondary refers to the relation between action and reflective thought. It means that all reflective thought arises from action—from some problem in action—and, correspondingly, its ultimate purpose is to return to action in order to reconstitute and improve action, wherein reflective (secondary) thought is either verified or falsified. However, this is a large and complex subject that cannot be treated here.[12]

Clearly, there are similarities between the agency of the personal and pragmatism, but there are differences too. Pragmatism is largely an epistemology; it refers to the third meaning of the primacy of action over thought. The first two meanings, however, denote the agency of the personal as an ontology of the self, as a theory of the self's being.[13] So, too, does the agency of the personal differ from Marxism. The latter's conception of persons as agents is reducible to biological and economic categories of being.

Of all philosophies, the ontological aspect of the agency of the personal most resembles the action philosophy of Maurice Blondel.[14] His action theory is basically an ontology of the self as agent. However, it does not seem that Macmurray was familiar with Blondel's thought. For Blondel, the core of the self is the will-willing (*la volonté voulante*), which is oriented toward God, the transcendent, infinite, and absolute being. Will-willing expresses itself in the will-willed (*la volonté voulue*), which are particular activities of volition. These acts of volition include both thought and action. Indeed, Blondel says that thought is a form of action in the sense that thought is an activity; it is something that the self does. However, he does not thereby distinguish between action and activity. On this point, he differs from my view and Macmurray's. For the agency of the personal, activity is a generic term that refers to thought (i.e., secondary or reflective thought) and action as two very different types of activity. Thus, thought is not action; it is not a form of action. Blondel simply confuses action with activity.

Moreover, unlike the agency of the personal, Blondel's action philosophy appears to be a version of individualism. It is concerned with the self's relation to God rather than the self's relation to others. His action theory is not situated within anything resembling the mutuality of the personal. Furthermore, it places much greater importance on will than does the agency of the personal. Blondel makes will an all-inclusive category of the self's being. In my view, however, will is only one aspect of the self's being and agency. Will is primarily the self's power or capacity of free choice in action; it denotes what we have called absolute freedom. This view of will likewise differs from the traditional Scholastic position. In Scholasticism, will is the mind's capacity to decide, prior to action, which action is to be performed. Thus, will is not in the action itself; it precedes an action. For the agency of the personal, will is closely connected with an action's intention. It is what the agent wills in action.

As mentioned above, persons as agents are communicative agents. Before I close this section, I briefly address the issue of communication. Two basic modes of action must be distinguished: *interpersonal* and *nonpersonal*. In interpersonal action, the self interacts with another person. In nonpersonal action, the self interacts with a nonperson, either animate or inanimate. Interpersonal action generally involves some degree of communication. For this reason, interpersonal action may also be called *communicative action*. Moreover, since a person as agent has more being than a nonperson, interpersonal or communicative action is a fuller expression of action than is nonpersonal action.

Communication is the intentional transference of a meaning from self to personal other, from speaker to listener. Meaning is embedded in primary thought and can have an intellectual, emotional, or actional (practical) end or purpose. The speaker can communicate a thought, a feeling, or a practical result (e.g., when a quarterback completes a pass to his intended receiver). Communication occurs in both the direct and indirect relations of persons. Thus, we have a distinction between *direct* and *indirect communication*. Teaching and conversations are major expressions of direct communication. In indirect communication, the focus is on communications media: journalism, film, video, TV, recordings, the Internet, and so on. However, this is a large subject that cannot be treated here.[15]

PERSON AS RATIONAL AGENT

Reason as Self-Transcendence

Mutuality and agency constitute the context in which reason exists and functions. Therefore, reason is primarily communicative and actional in character. Although I accept, as Macmurray does, Aristotle's definition of reason as the specific or essential difference between humans and animals, the definition as it stands is purely formal. It does not tell us what reason is: all those characteristics, and their common essence, that distinguish human persons from animals. For this definition to be valid, it must include the whole range or content of reason, and not just thought or intellect, as Aristotle apparently held. A fortiori, reason cannot be identified with reasoning (or logic), the capacity to correctly draw conclusions from premises, which is only one aspect of thought itself.

Since agency is inclusive of our existence as persons, reason is primarily our capacity to act and to communicate. It therefore derivatively includes our capacity to feel and to think. As we have seen, the nature of action includes both feeling and thinking elements. Moreover, feeling and thinking may become disengaged from action and exist by themselves as reflective modes of reason, as modes of secondary reflection. Three modes of reason, then, may be distinguished: actional/communicative, emotional, and intellectual.[16] Basically, however, reason is the capacity by which the agent-self determines how it should act toward the other, and if the other is personal, how it should communicate with the other.

In this context, reason may be defined as *self-transcendence*: the self's capacity to synthesize objectivity (primarily) with subjectivity (secondarily).[17] *Objectivity* denotes the self's capacity to act/communicate, feel, and think in terms of the nature or reality of the other. *Subjectivity* denotes the self's capacity to act/communicate, feel, and think from (or for) itself, that is, freely, in the sense of absolute freedom. As a synthesis, one is the condition for the other. For example, the self's loving actions toward the personal other are constituted by a free, subjective response to the other's objective needs and nature, which is why Macmurray always held that genuine love is wholly rational.

In this synthesis, objectivity is the primary element and subjectivity is the secondary element. This means that it is the nature or reality of the other that determines the kind of response from the self rather than vice versa, although the self's subjectivity, as free, initiates the response. In love, the other's objective needs and nature determine how the self responds, and not the other way around. Reason, then, as self-transcendence, is the self's capacity for the synthesis of objectivity (primarily) with subjectivity (secondarily). As such, reason is the capacity for an objectivity that does not exclude subjectivity but includes, subordinates, and is partially constituted by it.

This definition of reason can be illustrated further by the nature of science, which everyone will agree is a rational activity of some sort. One of the hallmarks of science is its objectivity. Science provides us with a method or procedure for knowing the nature or reality of the other independently of our own personal beliefs, biases, or prejudices. Earth is round whether we like it or not or believe it or not. But science also involves subjectivity. To think scientifically is to think independently, employing a rigorous methodology that itself is a subjective construction, instead of believing something on the basis of custom, tradition, authority, or guesswork. Moreover, science's objectivity is the primary element in this synthesis. The scientific method does not determine the nature of the other. Rather, it discloses the other as it really is. The purpose of science, then, is to provide us with a subjective method that is indispensable for knowing the objectivity of the other. One can guess or arbitrarily believe that Earth is round, but until one verifies this belief scientifically, it lacks true objectivity. Although the belief happens to be in conformity with the objective nature of the other, the self has not comprehended this conformity.

The foregoing definition of reason implies some form of realism.[18] Indeed, Macmurray always considered himself a realist. In idealism, subjectivity determines objectivity; subjectivity is primary and objectivity is secondary. The Anglo-American personalism of the late nineteenth and early twentieth centuries is usually called personalist idealism. The personalism being developed here can be called personalist realism. Macmurray's personalism is much closer to the French personalism of the first half of the twentieth century, and especially to the personalism of Emmanuel Mounier, than it is to personalist idealism.[19] However, Macmurray seems to have been unaware of this movement. The personalist thinker that most influenced him was Martin Buber.[20]

Reason and Irrationality

At this point, it may be objected that reason cannot constitute the human differentia because human beings in general are more irrational than rational. Or, as Paul Weiss expressed it:

> Few today, to be sure, accept the structures which Aristotle took to express the essential, intelligible nature of man. He thought it was a combination of genus and species, "rational animal." But if it is of the essence of man to be rational, it will be hard to see how one can say that the infantile, the senile, and the idiotic belong to the human family.[21]

Human irrationality, however, does not invalidate reason as the differentia of the human, so long as one's conception of reason is broad enough to include it. In this connection, four terms must be distinguished: reason, rationality, irrationality, and nonrationality. Reason is bipolar. Its positive pole is rationality, and its negative pole is irrationality. Since rationality is the positive fullness of reason, it is defined in terms of rationality. By contrast, irrationality, as the negative pole of reason, is the privation of rationality that ought to be present, just as blindness is the absence of sight that ought to be present. To speak of irrationality, then, implies that it should be replaced by rationality, that an irrational act should not occur, even if it does.

Moreover, reason not only includes irrationality; reason is also partially constituted by it. If we could not act irrationally, if we did not have the choice between acting rationally and irrationally, then the term *rational* would lose all meaning and become indistinguishable from nonrational. Since humans are free, finite, and fallible agents, their capacity to act irrationally is an essential aspect of human reason. Nevertheless, irrationality is a subordinate aspect of reason. Rationality ought to predominate over irrationality, keeping the latter in check; we should always act rationally rather than irrationally. In this sense, the negative is in and for the sake of the positive. In sum, reason in its positive fullness is rationality; but reason also includes, subordinates, and is partially constituted by its own negative, irrationality.[22]

Finally, the irrational should be distinguished from the nonrational. Only a rational being can be irrational. A nonrational being is one that lacks reason. Hence, it can be neither rational nor irrational. Whereas nonrationality is the total absence of reason, irrationality is the privation of rationality.

Reason and Value

Because I used science as a major example of reason, it may be wondered how my definition of reason can apply to values. It is often held that science determines facts but not values. However, this statement is not entirely true. Certainly science determines facts or, perhaps more accurately, discovers facts. And it is also true that there are certain kinds of values that science cannot determine. Nevertheless, science and value are deeply connected. This connection is an important first step in overcoming the so-called fact-value dualism.

At the outset, I proposed reason as the standard of value. This implies that value has a rational content. I define value as the *actualizing* of objectivity (primarily) with subjectivity (secondarily).[23] Value is in the relation between self and other; it exists neither exclusively in the self nor exclusively in the other. It exists in both together, in the self's activity of synthesizing them. I call this theory transobjectivism, since objectivity is the primary determinant of value. However, it is a form of objectivism in which objectivity includes, subordinates, and is partially constituted by subjectivity. Therefore, transobjectivism goes beyond conventional objectivism, which excludes subjectivity as a determinant of value. A fortiori, transobjectivism differs from subjectivism and relativism. In subjectivism, objectivity is missing altogether; in relativism, it is at best inadequate and at worst totally absent. Therefore, for transobjectivism, values may still be regarded as objective rather than either subjective or relativistic, in terms of this conventional triadic distinction. Values are not solely created by the self, independently of the nature of the other. Nevertheless, since subjectivity is secondary, values are not objective in the sense of completely existing, or being fully constituted, independently of the self's free choices in action. Values are not merely discovered, like the unwrapping of a gift. They are lived by.

Since the self exists as agent, the foregoing synthesis occurs originally and primarily on the level of action. Valuation, then, is inherent in the nature of action.[24] This level of actional (or practical) valuation, as I call it, generally involves the following three steps or phases: First, the agent-self discriminates the other into a system of possibilities for action. This discrimination is determined primarily by the objectivity of the other. Second, the self evaluates and arranges each possibility on a scale or in a hierarchy of best to worst. Third, the self chooses the possibility that he or she evaluates as the best one.

To be sure, the self's characterization of the chosen possibility as right or good does not imply that the characterization is true. Since choice-in-action is inherently free, the self can always err and choose the wrong possibility. If the wrong possibility is chosen, the self acts irrationally, fails to synthesize subjectivity with objectivity, and affirms disvalue (i.e., what is truly or objectively wrong or bad). Conversely, if the self makes the right choice, the self acts rationally, synthesizes subjectivity with objectivity, and affirms (positive) value (i.e., what is truly or objectively right or good). In the former case, actional valuation needs reflective valuation—valuation on the level of reflective thought—for its rectification. In the latter case, it needs reflective valuation for its full justification. Reflective valuation explicates our practical value choices and carries the activity of rational valuation, begun on the level of action, to a higher level. The distinction between actional and reflective valuation corresponds to morality and ethics, respectively.

Reference has been made to the *fact-value dualism*. In contemporary ethical theory, it is connected with the naturalistic fallacy. As we saw at the outset, this fallacy denotes the procedure of inferring values from facts, goods from nature, or ought statements from is statements. Its status as a fallacy is controversial. Many contemporary ethicists accept its validity. Not surprisingly, natural law advocates reject it.[25] It appears that the naturalistic fallacy is based on a confusion between the levels of actional and reflective valuation. As we have seen, in actional valuation, value is inherent in action. But in action, value contains fact as a constituent element. Every situation in which action occurs has a factual or existent basis to be evaluated. Therefore, in action, fact and value are united in one integral experience. The fact-value dualism and the naturalistic fallacy, however, presuppose that fact and value are separate. Consequently, the dualism and fallacy cannot apply to actional valuation.

Instead, the dualism and fallacy arise on the level of reflective valuation. First, we sharply distinguish the concepts of fact and value. This distinction is perfectly legitimate, since concept formation is essential to thought. However, we then make the mistake of reifying these concepts, by interpreting fact and value as two mutually exclusive and incommensurable realities. This mistake creates a false dualism between fact and value. It also produces the natural-istic fallacy. However, this fallacy is valid on the level of reflective valuation, so long as we do not reify the concepts of fact and value. Since the concept of value is more inclusive than the concept of fact, value cannot be logically derived from fact; the greater cannot be validly inferred from the lesser.

The foregoing analysis also indicates why my definition of value cannot apply to fact *by itself*. First, since fact, in its original existence, is an element of value in action, my definition of value ipso facto includes value's factual element. Second, since the concept of fact by itself is the product of secondary thought, and since secondary thought intentionally withdraws the self from its relation to the other in action, my definition of value cannot apply to fact alone because the definition presupposes that self and other are concretely and intentionally interrelated in the actualizing of subjectivity and objectivity. A fact per se, as the product of secondary thought, is an instantiation of objectivity only.

In the next section and in chapter 2, I apply the foregoing definition of reason and value to its three basic modes: instrumental, aesthetic, and moral. Since they have a rational content, they are three different expressions of self-transcendence, three different syntheses of objectivity (primarily) with subjectivity (secondarily).

From the standpoint of the rational agent, the three modes of value are derived from three aspects of action: means, end, and interrelation of ends. As Macmurray expresses it: "The means chosen must be efficient, the end to be realized must be satisfactory, and the action as a whole must be moral, that is to say, compatible with the community of action as a whole."[26] The means corresponds to instrumental value, the (isolated) end to aesthetic value, and the interrelation of ends (or action as a whole) to moral value. I first consider instrumental and aesthetic value.

INSTRUMENTAL AND AESTHETIC VALUE

On the level of actional valuation, instrumental value refers to the means aspect of action, where the other is used by the self as a means to achieve its ends or purposes. Therefore, the other is valued only for its efficiency or usefulness. As such, instrumental value refers primarily, though not exclusively, to technology and to the material other. I say "not exclusively" because the biological and personal other can be valued instrumentally too. When we do, however, we value only a part or an aspect of their whole being. By contrast, instrumental value denotes the total value of technology, and of the material other considered merely as raw material. On the level of reflective or secondary thought, technology expresses itself in science; science is the reflective or theoretical counterpart of technology.

However, technology is not merely the application of science. From a broad historical perspective, and especially from the standpoint of the primacy of the self-as-agent (the agency of the personal), science is the reflective expression of technology, taking technology in a broad sense, for example, Heidegger's view (which is supported by anthropological evidence) concerning the historical primacy of homo faber (man the maker) over *Homo sapiens*.[27] Therefore, if we look at science from the standpoint of the agency of the personal, my definition of value can apply to science in a *derivative* sense, just as secondary thought is derived from action. In particular, through technology science actualizes the synthesis of subjectivity and objectivity. In this respect, science has instrumental value. Through technology, science creates an abundance of instrumental values for human society. However, science and technology are limited to instrumental value. Although both give us the means to achieve our ends or purposes, they are utterly unable to evaluate the worth of those ends themselves insofar as the ends are part of the interrelation of ends.

We are so dazzled by the brilliance of science and technology that many of us have become blind to their limitations. To be sure, one of the most outstanding features of the modern and contemporary world is the tremendous development of science and technology. They have given us untold knowledge of, and control over, nature. They have been of immeasurable benefit to humankind. Their extraordinary success, however, has a downside. In many quarters, there is an obsession with technology that is expressed in the maxim "Can implies ought." Reflectively, this obsession is expressed in the doctrine of *scientism*, which holds that only science is knowledge and which characterizes much of naturalism and organicism.[28]

On the side of the other, then, instrumental value involves the other-as-means. This denotes its objective dimension. Correlatively, on the side of the self, instrumental value involves the self-as-user. This denotes its subjective dimension. To take a simple example, I use a marker as a means to the end of writing on the whiteboard. The value of the marker-as-means is not the marker as such, to the exclusion of its actual or potential use by the self. Nor is the value of the marker exclusively in the way the self uses it independently of its objective nature. For the marker to have value, it must be used rationally, in accordance with its nature or objective reality. The self must write with it on a whiteboard rather than on paint or wallpaper. It is the nature of the marker that determines how I ought to use it. Accordingly, instrumental value may be defined as a synthesis of the other-as-means (primarily) with the self-as-user (secondarily).

Quite obviously, this synthesis is a limited one. First of all, since the other is valued solely as means, the synthesis excludes the other considered both as an end in itself and as an interrelation of ends, that is, the end and the interrelation-of-ends aspects of action. By the same token, the self-as-user has a limited relation with the other, because the relation is purely instrumental. Consequently, it excludes both a personal and an aesthetic relation with the other.

Whereas instrumental value is value-as-means, aesthetic value is value-as-end. Aesthetic value is intrinsic value. A beautiful object is valued for its own sake, for what it is in itself, apart from any instrumental considerations. On the level of actional value, aesthetic value refers to the end aspect of action. In this aspect of action, the self abstracts his or her object from its concrete relations with the rest of the other and treats the object as a self-contained and self-sufficient whole. Similarly, the self abstracts its own self from its concrete relations with the rest of the other and completely focuses on the object of beauty. Aesthetic value, however, is not limited to art. It is also an important value in nature, a view held by some environmentalist thinkers.[29] This issue will be addressed in chapter 11. Persons, too, have aesthetic value, insofar as a person is abstracted from his or her concrete relations with other persons and with the rest of reality and considered only as an isolated end in itself.

On the side of the other, then, aesthetic value involves the other-as-isolated end. This is its objective dimension. On the side of the self, aesthetic value involves the self-as-appreciator, which is its subjective dimension. To appreciate something is to experience its beauty, and this experience of beauty is neither wholly in the other nor wholly in the self, neither exclusively objective nor exclusively subjective. It is in the synthesis between them. This is clearly the case in art. Take a simple example of a landscape painting. It is a depiction or representation of objective nature in the form of the other-as-isolated end. At the same time, it is not exclusively objective; it is not a snapshot or a photographic reproduction of the other. The painting also and necessarily embodies the emotional subjectivity of the artist, which is why each artist's painting of the same landscape will be somewhat different. Still, the expression of each artist's emotional subjectivity in the painting should be determined by the objective reality of the landscape. Beauty is not merely in the eye of the beholder. It is there primarily because there is a beautiful object to behold. In sum, then, aesthetic value is a synthesis of the other-as-isolated end (primarily) with the self-as-appreciator (secondarily).

It is clear that this synthesis is also a limited one. As we have seen, it abstracts both self and other from their relations with the rest of reality. Nevertheless, aesthetic value involves a more inclusive synthesis of subjectivity and objectivity than does instrumental value. Since the means is for the sake of the end, the other-as-end contains more reality than does the other-as-means. Similarly, the self-as-appreciator includes more of the self than does the self-as-user. The self-as-appreciator deeply engages the self's emotions or feelings, which necessarily include a cognitive element. By contrast, the self-as-user engages mostly cognition, to the exclusion of emotion and feeling; the emotions expressed are superficial. For these reasons, aesthetic value is higher than instrumental value. Instrumental values are for the sake of aesthetic values, which ought to be preferred over the former when the two are in conflict. For instance, technology and monetary wealth should be used to promote and preserve the natural environment, not ravage and pollute it.

Since instrumental and aesthetic values involve a limited synthesis of subjectivity and objectivity, both are incomplete or partial expressions of rationality. Thus, neither one can count as the primary or highest mode of value. What is needed is a third mode of value that refers to the interrelation-of-ends aspect of action, that produces an all-inclusive synthesis of subjectivity and objectivity, and that, consequently, is both a complete expression of rationality and the primary mode of value. This mode is moral (or ethical) value, which will be developed in the next chapter.

Before we develop it, however, a serious objection arises that must be answered. It is often held that reason or rationality is inherently instrumental. Reason applies only to the means aspect of action; it cannot be applied to our ends, much less the interrelation of ends. As Bertrand Russell expresses it: "'Reason' has a perfectly clear and precise meaning. It signifies the choice of the right means to an end you wish to achieve. It has nothing whatever to do with the choice of ends."[30] More recently, Herbert Simon writes: "Reason is wholly instrumental. It cannot tell us where to go; at best it can tell us how to get there. It is a gun for hire that can be employed in the service of any goals we have, good or bad."[31] This limited conception of reason seems to have its roots in David Hume. In an oft-quoted statement, he says that "it is not contrary to reason to prefer the destruction of the whole world to the scratching of my finger. . . . It is not contrary to reason for me to choose my total ruin. . . . It is as little contrary to reason to prefer even my own acknowledged lesser good to my greater [good]."[32] According to this view, then, science and technology are rational, and so are logic and mathematics, insofar as they are instrumental and are components of science. But aesthetic, moral, and religious rationality is impossible. Likewise, philosophy as a substantive discipline cannot be rational, especially metaphysics. Philosophy, as rational, is reduced to method: logic, linguistic analysis, and philosophy of science. With respect to axiology, only instrumental values are rational. Aesthetic and moral values are incapable of rational justification.

To be sure, instrumental rationality is an important and essential mode of reason. It is probably even its most evident mode. But the restriction of rationality to instrumentality is arbitrary and contrary to the nature of reason. Since humans are by nature rational beings, reason must include, in one way or another, all distinctively human activities, not only instrumental ones.

That being the case, the above position appears contradictory and impaled on the horns of a dilemma, for if one asserts that all rationality is instrumental, this assertion is either nonrational or rational. If it is nonrational, then one makes an arbitrary assertion without any supporting, justifying reasons. Such an assertion is incompatible with the nature of philosophy and rationality. Hence, it offers no good reason why it should be accepted. If, however, it is a rational assertion, then it contradicts itself: The activity by which one asserts that all rationality is instrumental cannot itself be an activity of instrumental rationality, since it is the ground of instrumental rationality. The reasons and arguments that one gives to justify this assertion cannot be instrumentally rational. Ultimately, too, this assertion trivializes reason. If, as Hume says, I cannot rationally choose between destroying the world and pricking my finger, if the difference between them is only a matter of subjective, nonrational feeling, then it really does not matter much whether means can be rational. Within the total context of human experience and activity—that is, the entire field of the interrelation of persons—the rationality of the means derives its ultimate value and significance from the ends and interrelation of ends, and their value and significance, in turn, are determined and justified by their rationality.

Some instrumentalists will object that any attempt to extend rationality beyond instrumentality is simply begging the question. When I define reason as the synthesis of objectivity (primarily) with subjectivity (secondarily) and apply this definition to the fields of ends and interrelation of ends, such application cannot be justified without at the same time assuming that it is legitimate to do so, which is the very point at issue. There is no possible answer I could give, it will be charged, that would not involve circularity. The charge is true, but it is also one that applies to the instrumental theory. If the instrumentalist were asked why rationality must be limited to instrumentality, what could he possibly say that would be noncircular? The question is not, of course, whether instrumental rationality as such is valid. Everyone who grants the validity of rationality grants that. The question is whether instrumental rationality covers the whole content of rationality. So if a critic were to ask an instrumentalist to justify the claim that reason is wholly instrumental, I suppose he would say something like the following: only instrumental rationality is valid, because it is certainly rational to efficiently and effectively achieve our ends, but there is no way to rationally determine our ends, much less any possible arrangement of the interrelation of ends. And why not? Because rationality is inherently instrumental—which is obviously circular. The instrumentalist is in the same boat as the noninstrumentalist, and for good reason. Since reason is fundamental to our nature or essence as persons, no one can explain and justify a theory of reason without employing reason. There is no possible nonrational standard that could serve as the premise for inferring reason as the conclusion. Since reason is a fundamental or bedrock human characteristic, it constitutes the most fundamental premise (i.e., level) of distinctly human activity. Therefore, the charge of circularity, whether directed toward an instrumentalist or a noninstrumentalist, is not a legitimate criticism if it implies the fallacy of petitio principii (begging the question). This fallacy applies to an argument in which premise and conclusion are essentially the same but should be different—for example, we must have law and order, because law and order are necessary. An argument, consisting of premise (or premises) and conclusion, and the various fallacies invented by logicians to characterize different kinds of arguments are products of secondary thought. But reason, as a bedrock or foundational human activity, is not an argument. It is a fundamental mode of our existence as persons.

Moreover, because human reason is fundamental, it is also universal or inclusive: no aspect of distinctively human nature falls outside of reason. Therefore, an adequate theory of reason must apply to all essential human activities, not only to some. In this respect, the instrumentalist theory fails. It explains only one mode of rationality.[33]

Since I have just considered reason as it applies to means (instrumental value) and to isolated ends (aesthetic value), we must now turn in chapter 2 to reason as it applies to the interrelation of ends (moral value).

2

MORAL VALUE, INTENTIONALITY, AND COMMUNITY

I now apply reason to moral value. As we have seen, moral value—as distinct from aesthetic value and instrumental value—refers to the interrelation-of-ends aspect of action, which is action in its wholeness. This statement means that the field of morality consists of interpersonal action, or the relation among persons. When two or more persons are related, either directly or indirectly, their actions have moral quality: they are moral-type actions, they are morally right or morally wrong. When I consider the moral treatment of animals in chapter 9, I will extend the field of morality to include persons' actions and relations with sentient animals.

From the standpoint of persons as rational and communicative agents, there are two main principles of morality: the principle of intentionality, and the principle of community. The first is a reinterpretation and modification of the traditional principle of double effect. Like double effect, it is a procedural principle and thus requires a substantive principle to determine what is morally right and wrong, good and bad. This principle is community. Accordingly, the chapter is divided into two major sections. In the first, I address several issues related to the principle of intentionality. In the second section, I develop community as the supreme moral standard.

THE PRINCIPLE OF INTENTIONALITY

Because my principle of intentionality modifies double effect, I first explain this traditional principle. I then analyze and weigh the various moral elements of action, which are either implied or suggested by double effect. This procedure forms the framework for articulating the principle of intentionality and comparing it with double effect. Finally, I compare intentionality to two other traditional moral doctrines that are relevant to several issues in this volume: doing/allowing, and voluntary/involuntary.

Double Effect

The principle of double effect has its origins in the thought of Thomas Aquinas. Subsequent Catholic moralists developed it into a formal principle with several rules. Although historically the principle is largely associated with Roman Catholic thinking, it is not inherently Catholic or theological. Some non-Catholics support the principle. Ultimately, it is a principle of moral philosophy that must be evaluated on its own rational merits or lack thereof. Double effect is usually formulated as a general statement and four rules.[1] There have been several formulations and versions of double effect. My formulation of it is as follows.

General Statement: In actions that have two conflicting effects or consequences, one good and the other bad (or evil), such actions are morally permissible if they meet the following four rules.

Rule One: The good effect must directly flow or follow from an action whose intention is good. The good effect must be willed or aimed at by the agent. The intention consists of the end and means aspects of action. The end must be good and the means must be at least morally indifferent. Neither end nor means can be bad.

Rule Two: The bad effect cannot be willed or aimed at either as the end or means of the action. The good effect cannot be achieved by means of the evil effect. It must be merely foreseen and allowed by the agent as an incidental by-product or side effect of his action.

Rule Three: The good effect must be proportionate to the bad effect.

Proportionate means approximately equivalent. Ideally, the good effect should outweigh the bad effect, but the good effect is morally sufficient if it only equals the bad effect. The bad effect can override the good effect only if the bad effect is greater than (or outweighs) it.

Rule Four: The bad effect cannot be desired or wanted in any way. It must be regretted or at least tolerated. Otherwise, the action would become immoral by having a bad motive.

These four rules can be illustrated by a simple example. A man runs into a burning building to rescue a child and puts his own life at risk. His action is morally justified by double effect. The good effect of saving the child, if achieved, directly flows from a good intention. The man's end is to save an innocent child (good) by means of running into the building (indifferent). Rule One is satisfied. By running into the building, the man does not will or aim at his own death or injury, but merely permits or allows it with some foreseen degree of probability. The good effect is not achieved by means of the evil effect but rather in spite of it. He cannot rescue the child if he gets killed beforehand. So Rule Two is satisfied. Moreover, since the man is risking his life to save another person's life, there is proportionality between the good and bad effect, and hence Rule Three is satisfied. This rule would be violated, however, if he ran into the building to save something of lesser value than a person. Finally, Rule Four is met, since the man is not looking for an excuse to die or to commit suicide while appearing to onlookers as a hero. He does not want or desire to die. His motive is love or caring for the child.

Not all actions are as easily resolvable by double effect as this one. I do not have space to discuss all the criticisms that have been leveled against the principle. One of its major burdens is that in its application, it must always make a real, significant distinction between an action's bad side effect and its means. Critics charge that this is often not the case. As a result, say critics, proponents of double effect frequently engage in hairsplitting. Consider the following example well-known to moral philosophers.[2]

Suppose a group of explorers is caught in a cave that is rapidly filling up with water. There is one small opening out of the cave. The first explorer to climb out is fat, gets stuck in the opening, and no one can dislodge him. The explorers caught inside will soon die by drowning. So, too, will the fat man, since even his head is still inside the cave. Happily, one of the explorers has a stick of dynamite that can be placed in his appropriate anatomical aperture, dislodge him, and kill him.

In my view, it is not rational to claim in the example that there exists a real, significant distinction between the action's means and its foreseen, indirect side effect. If one claimed there were, he would have to argue something like this: The means is placing the dynamite stick in the man's posterior, which dislodges him by blowing him to pieces (morally indifferent); and the foreseen, indirect bad effect is his death. This is hairsplitting at its worst. In fact there is no indirect effect at all. There is only end and means. Not all actions have an indirect effect. In this example, if the dynamite stick is used, the end is saving the lives of all explorers caught inside the cave by means of killing the fat man. But according to double effect, one cannot use a bad means to achieve a good end, and killing the man is bad because it is murderous. Therefore, the dynamite stick must not be used and all must perish inside.

Most people, I think, would reject this moral conclusion as irrational. I certainly do. Reason tells us that, of course, we ought to use the dynamite stick. Double effect, it seems, has a serious flaw: it cannot always make a real, significant distinction between an action's means and its indirect or side effect.

This flaw reveals another defect of double effect: the absolutist or inflexible quality of Rules One and Two, which *always* prohibit the use of a bad means. I argue later that this prohibition is incompatible with moral rationality. Nevertheless, there is a noteworthy element of truth in the first two rules: What we intentionally do is morally more important than what we indirectly foresee as a side effect or by-product of our action, ceteris paribus. To develop this truth, I turn now to the moral elements of action.

Moral Elements of Action

Based on my analysis of action in chapter 1 and upon the preceding analysis of double effect, I single out three main moral elements of action: intention, motive, and consequences. As a start, Macmurray tells us that "the moral rightness or wrongness of an action resides in its intention. [Its morality] . . . is independent of success or failure. The man who attempts to kill his neighbour and fails is morally guilty of murder, though not legally."[3] I use Macmurray's moral emphasis on intention to construct the principle of intentionality. This principle will gradually unfold in what follows.

I agree that intention is of great moral importance, as double effect holds. I disagree, however, that we can reduce the total morality of an action to its intention. Both motive and consequences have moral significance as elements of action. If a person succeeds in killing his neighbor, his action as a whole is morally worse than if he fails. The achieved or successful consequence is an aggravating factor of the intention's immorality; it adds to the wrongness of the action. Nevertheless, consequences cannot completely determine the morality of an action, as the ethical theory of *consequentialism* holds. Utilitarianism is usually regarded as the principal type of consequentialism.

Further reflection on the principle of double effect yields a distinction between *direct intention* and *indirect intention*. There are, then, four basic moral elements of action: direct intention, indirect intention, motive, and (actual) consequences. I must now explain direct and indirect intention and consider what weight to assign to each of the four moral elements.

The direct intention is simply intention as I defined it in chapter 1: what the agent knowingly aims at and wills in action. It consists of end and means. Direct intention corresponds to what double effect simply calls *intention*. However, we must emphasize that the direct intention is *in* the action and does not wholly precede the action as a purely mental activity. This point is not made clear by double effect. As an illustration of direct intention, if someone intends to murder another, the would-be victim is the end, and the murder weapon (a gun, for example) is the means. As he aims his loaded gun at his victim, he starts executing his direct intention. Of course, if the murder is premeditated the man's direct intention will be preceded by much deliberation and planning. The planning will involve actions such as purchasing the gun and ammunition that have their own direct intentions that ultimately culminate in the direct intention of aiming the gun at the murder victim. The murder as a whole is a continuum of action. And the deliberation that goes into the crime, which precedes it, is an activity of secondary reflection that is connected with and passes over into the action's direct intention of committing the crime. Still, most murders are not premeditated, but are "crimes of passion" whose direct intention is not preceded by deliberation. For example, if a man comes home early from work one day and finds his wife in bed with her lover, and then immediately goes to his gun cabinet and kills them both, and the act is not a truly compulsive one, his action has a murderous direct intention. He knowingly and willingly aims the gun at both of them and pulls the trigger from a powerful motive of jealousy and anger. In sum, then, the direct intention is in the action, and is not a purely mental activity that precedes it.

End and means here must not be confused with aesthetic and instrumental value, respectively. Aesthetic value denotes the end as end, the end as *isolated* end; instrumental value denotes the means as means. By contrast, the end and means elements of the direct intention denote end and means insofar as they are elements of the interrelation of ends, elements of interpersonal action. For example, potential murder weapons are evaluated in terms of their efficiency, and that is obviously a major factor in the murderer's choice of weapon. From the standpoint of the rest of us, however, we are far more interested in the moral import of the weapon as the means element of the interpersonal action of murder. Similarly, if the murderer views his action from the perspective of committing the perfect crime in a stylistic sense, then he is viewing it aesthetically, not morally. Again, the rest of us will evaluate his end morally, in its interpersonal significance, as the direct killing of an innocent person.

Every action as action has a direct intention. Otherwise, it would be an instance of behavior. In addition, however, many actions have an indirect intention: what is foreseen but unwilled in the action. It is appropriate to call it *intention*, because it is generated (indirectly) by the direct intention. Aquinas is mistaken in calling the indirect intention "accidental." In double effect's full development by his followers, they drop the word *accidental* and characterize what I call indirect intention with words such as "incidental by-product," or "side effect," which is merely "permitted" or "tolerated," but always *unintended* although "foreseen." Sometimes they call it "the indirect voluntary." Double effect does not call the side effect *indirect intention* for two reasons: first, double effect restricts intention to what I call direct intention; and second, it does not distinguish between *indirect intention* and *indirect consequences*. I briefly consider both of these points.

Double effect restricts intention to direct intention, because it identifies the concepts of will and intention. According to double effect, what is intended must be both willed and foreseen. Since the indirect side effect that is permitted is only foreseen but not willed, it is not intended. This analysis, I think, is mistaken. I agree that the indirect side effect is not willed, but it does not follow that it is completely devoid of intentionality. If it were, the indirect side effect would be accidental, which is Aquinas's mistake. The agent would then not be morally responsible for his indirect consequences, which is clearly false. That is why some proponents of double effect dropped the word *accidental*. Nevertheless, for double effect to be internally consistent, it should characterize the indirect element of action as intentional in some sense. Bentham was correct in distinguishing between *directly intentional consequences* and *obliquely intentional consequences*.

Furthermore, it is a mistake for double effect not to distinguish between an action's indirect intention and indirect consequences, since the former may not be realized in action. If a person runs into a burning building to save a child's life, he may escape death and injury, and so his action has no indirect consequence although it still has an indirect intention. For he foresaw that when he willed to save the child's life he could die or be seriously injured. An action has an indirect intention when an agent foresees that when she begins to execute her direct intention there is a significant degree of probability that something might happen that she does not want or will to happen, regardless of whether it actually happens. If it does happen, her action has indirect consequences; if it does not happen, her action lacks indirect consequences, but still has an indirect intention. We must always distinguish between intention and consequences, whether the intention is direct or indirect.

These distinctions can be illustrated by another murder example. Let us assume that a murderer is going to fire a gun in a fairly crowded area. He foresees that he might miss his mark and kill someone else instead. Of course, he does not want or will this to happen. If it does happen, obviously it will produce different consequences than if the direct intention had been successful. Thus, we must distinguish between an action's direct consequences and its indirect consequences. The former is produced by the direct intention and the latter by the indirect intention. Direct consequences are both willed and foreseen, whereas indirect consequences are foreseen but unwilled. There are also truly accidental consequences, which are both unwilled and unforeseen. Suppose the murderer has a heart condition that is unknown to him. As he begins to aim his gun at his victim and execute his murderous intention, he is struck by a massive heart attack and falls down; the gun fires wildly, and the bullet lands harmlessly in the ground somewhere. No one is killed or injured. The action has no direct or indirect consequences, but it still has a murderous intention. However, our murderer dies of cardiac arrest. His death is an accidental consequence of his action.

Finally, a murderous action must have a motive, a reason that someone intends to commit murder—the emotion (or emotions) in which the intention is rooted and that supplies and sustains the intention's energy. Typical motives of murder are greed, jealousy, power, revenge, hatred, and fear. We must not confuse motive with the end of direct intention, as some authors do. The relation among all these moral elements is illustrated in Figure 1.1.

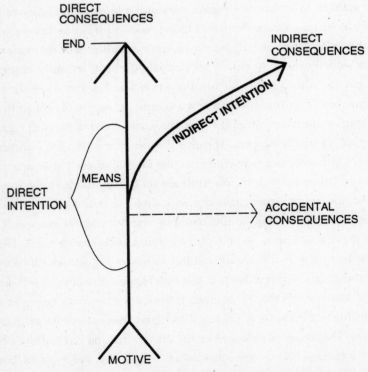

FIGURE 1.1: RELATION OF MORAL ELEMENTS

In determining the weight of each element, both Macmurray and the principle of double effect are helpful. When Macmurray says that the morality of an action resides in its intention, and when double effect identifies intention with direct intention, both positions suggest that the direct intention is the *primary* moral element of action. I now justify this claim.

Of all the moral elements of action, it is the direct intention that constitutes the core difference between action and behavior. Behavior, like action, has consequences and motive, although behavior does not have action's higher rational motives. Similarly, behavior produces deterministic consequences, unlike the intentional consequences of action. Again, the difference underscores the primary importance of intention. Finally, there would be no indirect intention without direct intention; the former is a by-product or side effect of the latter. There is good reason for the law to say that murder, as a form of direct killing (killing that is part of the direct intention) is morally worse than vehicular homicide, which is a form of indirect killing (i.e., killing that belongs to the indirect intention). In sum, then, the direct intention is the primary moral element of action, and indirect intention, motive, and consequences are its secondary moral elements. I now consider what this means in practice by developing my principle of intentionality and comparing it with double effect.

Intentionality Stated and Compared with Double Effect

Reinterpreting and modifying double effect is nothing new. Philippa Foot, following Bentham's lead, distinguishes between direct and oblique intention. Warren Quinn distinguishes between direct and indirect agency. I do something similar in distinguishing between direct and indirect intention. Contrary to double effect, I argue that it is occasionally the case that a morally right action has a bad direct intention.

As a beginning, I distinguish two types of bad direct intentions: *gravely bad* and *significantly bad*. A gravely bad direct intention is so fundamentally bad that it corrupts the action as a whole, regardless of whatever goodness the action's other moral elements may possess. A significantly bad intention is bad in itself and therefore is usually bad enough to make an action immoral, but not so bad that it always corrupts the action as a whole. A gravely bad intention produces a type or class of action called *intrinsically immoral*, for example, slavery. An intrinsically immoral action is one that is always immoral— universally and necessarily immoral. In Kant's language, it can be expressed in a synthetic a priori judgment. A significantly bad intention produces a type or class of action that is *prima facie immoral*, for example, breaking a promise. A prima facie immoral action is one that is immoral in general, immoral in most situations, but not immoral in exceptional or extraordinary situations. In exceptional situations, the badness of the significantly bad direct intention is outweighed and overridden by the goodness of the action's other moral elements.[4] The situations in which a significantly bad direct intention can be overridden by the goodness of an action's other moral elements must be restricted to exceptional cases, since the direct intention is the primary moral element of action and the other elements are secondary. Likewise, if the direct intention is good, we must still evaluate an action's other moral elements. The goodness of the direct intention does not guarantee the moral rightness of the action as a whole. We must apply the third rule of the principle of double effect to see whether the goodness of the direct intention is proportionate to the badness of the indirect intention. Then, too, we must morally evaluate the action's motive, as well as its actual consequences if the direct or indirect intention is successful. Bad consequences aggravate an already bad intention; good consequences enhance the goodness of a good intention. Finally, direct consequences have greater moral importance than indirect consequences, and accidental consequences have no moral significance at all, since they are not connected with an action's direct intention.

By contrast, a good direct intention is one that, first and foremost, has a good end and a good (or at least indifferent) means. However, in exceptional cases, a direct intention is good when it has a good end paired with a bad means. In these cases, the goodness of the end outweighs the badness of the means. I speak more on this momentarily.

In applying the distinction between intrinsically immoral and prima facie immoral action, we must bear in mind that we are not always dealing with a single or individual act. Action also has a social or collective dimension. In this regard, we can speak of a continuum of action, or a practice. In this case, end and means are distinct actions themselves and not merely elements of a single action, for example, a society that justifies slavery as a means of promoting its economic well-being. This society is using an intrinsically immoral action as a means of achieving an end it believes is good. The society is mistaken in its belief, but even if it were not, even if a society in this situation had a truly good end, it would never be morally justified institutionalizing slavery, since slavery constitutes an intrinsically immoral practice and ought never to be paired with a good end, no matter how good it is.

I must now qualify my statement that consequences are a *secondary* moral element. The statement refers to consequences in general in relation to the direct intention in itself. It does not take into account the difference between direct and indirect consequences and the fact that a direct intention naturally (but not always) produces direct consequences, and an indirect intention naturally (but not always) produces indirect consequences. Since an indirect intention is secondary in relation to direct intention, and since accidental consequences have no moral significance at all, it is principally indirect consequences that are referred to when I speak of consequences as a secondary moral element of action. Direct consequences are secondary only in relation to the direct intention as such, but not in relation to the action as a whole. Direct intention is primary in relation to direct consequences for two reasons: first, of all the moral elements of action, it is direct intention which constitutes the core essential difference between action and behavior; and second, sometimes a direct intention does not produce direct consequences, either wholly or partially. Nonetheless, since direct consequences are so closely connected with direct intention, they must be regarded as morally primary in relation to motive, indirect intention, and indirect consequences.

I now formally state the principle of intentionality: *The morality of an action is determined primarily by its direct intention/consequences, and secondarily by its indirect intention/consequences and by its motive.* The principle consists of five rules, which modify and replace double effect's four rules.

Rule One: If the direct intention/consequences are good, the action is morally right, unless the badness of the indirect intention/consequences and/ or motive outweighs (is greater than) the goodness of the direct intention/ consequences in which case the action is morally wrong.

Rule Two: If the direct intention/consequences are gravely bad, the action is intrinsically immoral and thus always morally wrong.

Rule Three: If the direct intention/consequences are significantly bad, the action is prima facie immoral and hence morally wrong in general; but the action is morally right in exceptional cases, that is, in those instances in which the goodness of the indirect intention/consequences and/or motive outweighs the badness of the direct intention/consequences.

Rules Four and Five apply to a continuum of action, where end and means are distinct actions.

Rule Four: If a direct intention has a good end and a bad means, the direct intention is gravely bad if the means is an intrinsically immoral action, regardless of how good the end is. Hence, the action as a whole is intrinsically immoral and always impermissible.

Rule Five: If a direct intention has a good end and a bad means, the direct intention is significantly bad if the means is a prima facie immoral action. We must then weigh the goodness of the end against the badness of the means to determine if the action as a whole is morally permissible. If the end outweighs the means, which it does only in exceptional cases, the action as a whole is morally permissible; if the means outweighs the end, which it does in most cases, the action as a whole is morally impermissible.

There are two major differences between intentionality and double effect. The first difference is intentionality's distinction between a gravely bad and a significantly bad direct intention, and its corresponding distinction between an intrinsically immoral and a prima facie immoral action. The second difference is that, for intentionality, an action whose direct intention has a bad means can occasionally be morally permissible. This claim is likewise rejected by double effect.

Doing/Allowing, Voluntary/Involuntary

Besides double effect, there are two other important traditional moral theories that are related to the principle of intentionality: the doctrine of doing and allowing, and the theory of voluntary/involuntary acts. I first take up doing and allowing.

1. The doctrine of doing and allowing asserts that doing bad (or harm) is morally worse than allowing bad (or harm), ceteris paribus.[5] With respect to the end-means distinction, doing uses an *active means* and allowing a *passive means*. The doctrine is closely allied to double effect, which usually speaks of the direct, intentional effect as "performed" or "done," whereas the side effect is "merely allowed." However, there is not a necessary connection between the two doctrines. One is not a corollary of the other. The principal difference between them is that for double effect, the (direct) intention can be equally constituted by allowing or by doing. For example, double effect would hold that a person who starves herself to death commits suicide just as much as a person who shoots himself in the head with a gun, since both equally have a (direct) intention to end their lives. By contrast, the doctrine of doing and allowing is apparently driven to the absurd conclusion that only the person who shoots himself commits suicide and that his action is morally worse than the person who starves herself to death, even though her manner of killing herself is surely worse because she causes herself prolonged and unnecessary pain and suffering, whereas the other person instantly ends his life by putting a bullet through his head. Because of this example and many others like them, I reject the doctrine of doing and allowing. It is false to claim that doing bad is always worse than allowing bad. Sometimes doing bad is worse than allowing bad. But sometimes the reverse is true, as in the above example. Since I have replaced double effect with the principle of intentionality, intentionality a fortiori replaces the doctrine of doing and allowing.

I now compare these three principles by applying them to Judith Jarvis Thomson's trolley car example.[6] In this hypothetical case, a person is driving a trolley car whose brakes have failed. There are five workers on the track who are about to be killed by the runaway car. Fortunately, just before the workers is a spur leading off to the right. On this spur is one worker. So if the driver steers her trolley car to the right onto the spur, she will kill one person rather than five. Our moral reason tells us that steering the trolley car to the right is the morally right thing to do in this tragic situation. But the traditional doctrine of doing and allowing says no, because *steering* is doing something, while just letting the trolley car go straight ahead on the main track is doing nothing and only allowing something to happen that is not the driver's fault, since she did not cause the trolley car's brakes to fail. It is most unfortunate, of course, that five people have to die, but it would be a greater tragedy to have the one worker die by the driver *doing* something to cause his death. Therefore, the driver acts immorally by steering right and killing one person, but does not act immorally by allowing her runaway car to go straight ahead thus killing five people.

The principle of intentionality rejects this moral conclusion. For whatever the driver does, she performs an action that has a direct intention. Since she has a free choice between steering right and going straight ahead, whatever she chooses to do she ipso facto aims and wills to do. Consequently, her willed choice becomes unified with the movement of the car. Furthermore, however she chooses, her choice has a motive. Both alternatives constitute a course of action in which the driver performs a physical activity integrated with sense perception, free choice, direct intention, and motive—key elements of action. She is no mere bystander or spectator if she allows the car to go straight. She is a willing participant in the physical activity of the car heading toward the workers. The only important difference between the two actions is that in the one characterized as "doing," only one person will be killed; and in the other characterized as "allowing," five persons will be killed. For intentionality, the direct intention that kills one person versus the other one that kills five persons is the morally right action—just the opposite of what doing and allowing concludes.

The foregoing analysis implies that sometimes, but not always, the distinction between doing and allowing is not psychologically or physically valid—or at least not clear. This is another reason why the moral doctrine of doing and allowing fails. Doing and allowing will come up later, especially in the euthanasia issue.

Double effect applied to this example reaches the same conclusion as intentionality, but its reasoning differs. For double effect, the driver's end is to save the lives of the five workers on the main track by means of steering right onto the spur. The end is good and steering right is indifferent. As a foreseen but unwilled side effect of steering right, one worker is killed. Since the bad side effect of killing one worker is far outweighed by the good direct effect of saving five lives, double effect's Rule Three of proportionality is satisfied.

Once again, however, the rationality of this analysis depends upon whether there is a real, significant difference between the means (steering right) and the indirect effect (killing the one worker on the track). In my view, there is not, and so double effect ultimately fails as applied to this case.

2. I turn now to the Aristotelian-Thomistic theory of the voluntary/involuntary. Unlike the doctrine of doing and allowing, this theory seems wholly consistent with the principle of intentionality.[7] The theory is a significant part of several ethical issues, including suicide, euthanasia, and the death penalty, not to mention the law. The direct intention produces *voluntary* acts: actions based on knowledge and will. In a voluntary act, we know that we are acting, we know what we are doing, and we freely will to do it. Voluntary acts are normal (or normative) for human persons. By contrast, *involuntary* acts lack knowledge or will (or both). They are acts that persons do not normally perform. Traditionally, they are divided into four classes: *coerced* acts, *compulsive* acts, *insane* acts, and *invincible-ignorance* acts.

A coerced act lacks (free) will[8] because it is caused by extreme external force, as in the case of a shotgun wedding. A compulsive act lacks will because of extreme internal force in the form of an uncontrollable powerful emotion or drive determining one's behavior, for example, a psychoneurotic who cannot help washing his hands a hundred times a day and hates doing it. An insane act can stem from either temporary or permanent insanity. It can lack both knowledge and will. By insanity, I take what is probably the most important definition of it: the M'Naghten rule, based on the famous M'Naghten case in England in 1843. An insane act is one in which a person either does not know the nature and quality of what he is doing, or else he does not know right from wrong. An invincible-ignorance act obviously lacks knowledge. But its ignorance cannot be reasonably overcome in a given situation, and so a person is not responsible for her ignorance. For example, suppose a nurse mistakenly gives a patient a lethal overdose of a poison from the same bottle containing his regular medication not knowing that a terrorist in the hospital has made a perfect, undetectable switch of replacing the medicine capsules with the poison. There is no evidence of the switch. Although in a physical sense she causes the patient's death, she is not culpable for it. In contrast are *vincible-ignorance* acts, in which the ignorance should be overcome in a given situation. In these acts, a person is responsible for his ignorance, and so vincible-ignorance acts are voluntary acts.

There are two other classes of acts that should be added to the list of involuntary acts. First, there are truly accidental acts, in the sense in which we have described them. They are involuntary because they are wholly unintentional, as are all involuntary acts. Second, there are acts that are the product of *brainwashing*. Such acts are involuntary because a person who is brainwashed performs compulsive acts that have been conditioned into her by the systematic and skilled use of coercive means. Brainwashed acts, then, are a kind of hybrid of compulsive and coerced acts. In my terminology, involuntary and accidental acts are not actions at all but instances of behavior.

In between voluntary and involuntary acts are two other kinds of acts: the *indirectly voluntary* (or the *voluntary in cause*) and *diminished-voluntary* acts. The indirect intention produces an indirectly voluntary act, for example, vehicular homicide. If one drives a car recklessly, he ought to foresee that he might kill someone, even though he does not will to do so. But he voluntarily drives recklessly, which causes the death of another. A diminished-voluntary act has a significantly reduced direct intention. The idea of diminished voluntariness is crucial in evaluating most suicides, which are committed in a moment of despair, and in determining whether juveniles and mentally retarded persons should receive the death penalty.

THE PRINCIPLE OF COMMUNITY

The principle of intentionality is only a procedural principle. It does not tell us what is good or bad, right or wrong. To determine this, we need a substantive moral principle. Following Macmurray, I call this principle community. However, Macmurray's conception of community has some difficulties that must be resolved before community can be accepted as the supreme moral principle or standard. In this section, I first formulate the principle of community within the context or framework of personal and impersonal relations. Then the main ideas of the principle are developed, and I explain to what extent my version of the principle departs from Macmurray's views.

After briefly comparing community to feminist ethics and communitarianism, I conclude the chapter by connecting community with reason.

Personal and Impersonal Relations

Since the field of morality is the field of interpersonal action and relations, the principle of community refers to the good or well-being—what Macmurray calls the "harmony"[9]—of persons, the good of each and every person, in both their relational and their individual aspects. Consequently, the field of interpersonal action and relations implicitly and derivatively includes *intrapersonal* action and relations. Since the self is as much a person as another, how one treats oneself has moral significance.

I now formulate *the principle of community: an action is morally right if it promotes a personal relation of persons, either interpersonal or intrapersonal, and it is morally wrong if it directly intends an absolute impersonal relation of persons.* Later, we will extend the principle to include our dealings with sentient animals. If persons act in accordance with this principle, they achieve community as a moral value, indeed, as the inclusive moral value. Let me now analyze the key words of this principle.

First, the word *promotes* refers primarily to an agent's direct intention. In addition, however, the agent must evaluate an action's other moral elements. As we have just seen, in a particular situation, the badness of these moral elements could outweigh and override a good direct intention. Therefore, an action promotes a personal relation only if it is good after all its moral elements have been evaluated, in accordance with the principle of intentionality. If an agent directly intends an absolute impersonal relation, the action is ipso facto immoral; there is nothing else in the action that could make it morally right.

Second, relation has two meanings. In its ordinary sense, it implies a continuum of action, a series of actions, as in friendship, slavery, marriage, a business relation, and so forth. In another sense, relation denotes a singular or individual action, that is, an act. Since the later chapters are concerned mainly with issues of life and death—suicide, abortion, euthanasia, the death penalty—the latter meaning is more appropriate in those instances when a person, or some being, is killed. Thus, for example, I ask whether suicide constitutes an absolute impersonal act. Both these meanings of relation are legitimate, since the ontological core of a relation is action.

And third, to speak of absolute impersonal relations implies that some impersonal relations are *relative*. The principle of community, then, suggests three types of relations (which can occur in either of the two meanings of relation): personal, relative impersonal, and absolute impersonal. *Friendship*, I contend, is the archetype or fullest expression of a personal relation. To continue my analysis of the principle of community, I explain the nature of friendship and then explain the difference between absolute and relative impersonal relations.

If we now consider community as the inclusive moral value, its core consists of the relations of friendship among its members. Friendship denotes a relation of two persons in which both treat each other as whole persons and not as mere functions or objects. Specifically, this means that they love each other and treat each other freely, equally, and justly. *Love* is the motive of friendship, and *freedom*, *equality*, and *justice* are its three constituent values. Freedom and equality are its primary or dominant values, and justice is its secondary or basic value. The fruition of friendship is twofold: *communion* and *peace*. Communion is the fulfillment of communication. It is symbolized by Macmurray's oft-stated remark: "We belong together and are glad of it." Peace is the positive harmony that flows from the achievement of friendship and community. It is much more than the mere absence of strife, conflict, violence, or war.

Love is a positive motive, in contrast to negative motives such as fear, hate, and selfishness, not to mention indifference or apathy. In love, the self cares for another person for his or her own sake and for itself only for the sake of the other. Love is altruistic or heterocentric.

Freedom, as a constituent value of friendship, has two aspects. First, it is neither coerced nor coercive. It is not imposed on its members from without by social pressure. Nor does one member impose it on the other. It is mutually voluntary. Second, each friend acts fully himself or herself with the other and desires the other to act in the same manner. There is mutual self-expression and self-revelation, the fullness of communication. Neither friend is inhibited with the other; neither is under any constraint to play a role or act out a part. Friends are spontaneous and honest with each other.

In this context, freedom should not be confused with the absolute freedom discussed earlier. Absolute freedom is free will: the power or capacity of free choice in action. The rational exercise of absolute freedom is a necessary condition of freedom in friendship, the freedom I have just described. In turn, freedom in friendship is the fulfillment of what Macmurray calls *relative freedom*.[10] By relative freedom, he means the extent to which a person or society is actually free, the degree to which persons use their absolute freedom to either increase or decrease their actual freedom. He calls it relative because how free anyone is in the concrete is relative to certain conditions, the most important of which is the interpersonal. And this interpersonal condition is fulfilled in friendship.

Just as absolute freedom denotes subjectivity, relative freedom is connected with objectivity. That is, when the self exercises its absolute freedom, it can act either rationally or irrationally. The self acts rationally if it acts objectively. In this case, it directly increases its relative freedom and indirectly strengthens its absolute freedom. In a word, the self acts autonomously. *Autonomy* is the rational exercise of absolute freedom. And freedom in friendship is the fulfillment of autonomy. Conversely, if the self acts irrationally, it acts unobjectively. As a result, the self directly decreases its relative freedom and indirectly weakens its absolute freedom. In this case, the self acts heteronomously. *Heteronomy* is the irrational exercise of absolute freedom.

Equality in friendship means *intentional* equality: friends treat each other as equals, with the same consideration that each expects from the other. Its basis is ontological equality, the fact that all persons share in the same common human nature and personhood. Intentional equality overrides whatever factual inequalities exist between them, whether the inequalities be social, economic, psychological, physical, and so on.

Finally, justice means that we give the other his or her due as a matter of right and reciprocal duty or obligation. In this respect, justice is friendship's secondary or basic value. Freedom and equality transcend justice but include it. Indeed, justice is the basic or minimal level of morality in all interpersonal and intrapersonal relations and actions. If an action fails in justice it is ipso facto immoral; an unjust action cannot be morally right. In friendship, justice guarantees that personal intimacy will not lead to taking liberties with the other. It establishes minimal conditions for self-respect and respect for the other. It safeguards the identity and integrity of self and other.

To carry my analysis of community further, it is necessary to point out four difficulties in Macmurray's theory of community. First, he holds that friendship is the only type of personal relation. "To create community is to make friendship the form of all personal relations."[11] Second, since friendship is a direct relation of persons, it follows that all personal relations must be direct relations; he denies that indirect relations can be personal ones. "All indirect relations are . . . necessarily impersonal."[12] Third, the basic reason that Macmurray limits a personal relation to a direct relation is his insistence that personal acquaintance is a necessary condition of a personal relation.[13] It cannot be a sufficient condition of a personal relation, of course, since personal acquaintance is a sufficient condition of all direct relations, impersonal as well as personal. And fourth, he maintains that community, regardless of its size, consists entirely of friendship. "The structure of a community is the nexus or network of the active relations of friendship between all possible pairs of its members."[14] The fourth proposition, however, is incompatible with his view that, in principle, the size of community has no limits; indeed, its inherent ideal is universality. "The inherent ideal of the personal . . . is a universal community of persons in which each cares for all the others."[15]

Macmurray, I think, is correct on the last point. For community to be a supreme ethical standard, it must be universal; it must include everyone. As a moral principle, community must be universal. If it is less than universal, then we are forced to divide humanity into a community in-group and a noncommunity out-group. In this dichotomy, members of the community in-group would have personal relations with one another and absolute impersonal relations with members of the noncommunity out-group. But absolute impersonal relations are a violation of community, are forbidden by the principle of community. To justify this statement, let me now explain the nature of impersonal relations and, in the process, address the four difficulties just mentioned.

An impersonal relation of persons is constituted by a direct intention to treat a person, including oneself, as a function, not as a whole person. It must not be confused with a nonpersonal relation (or action), mentioned in chapter

1, in which the other is a nonperson. Because we live in an institutional society, a functional treatment of persons is often necessary, and it is morally justifiable, providing the impersonal relation is subordinated to a personal relation. When this occurs, there exists a *relative impersonal* relation: the self's treatment of someone as a function is subordinated to his or her treatment of that person as a whole person. Justice is the essential, constituent value of a relative impersonal relation. Moreover, since it is for the sake of a personal relation, a relative impersonal relation promotes the principle of community. But when the self treats a person only or merely as a function, and when the impersonal relation is directly intended for its own sake, there exists an absolute impersonal relation. Slavery is an extreme example of such a relation. Since an absolute impersonal relation is constituted by a direct intention not to treat a person as a person, and since such treatment is directly intended for its own sake, such a relation must be excluded from community; it must be regarded as a violation of community. Likewise, an absolute impersonal relation fails in justice; it is an inherently unjust relation.

Since an absolute impersonal relation, as absolute, is ipso facto morally wrong, it might seem that such a relation consists of intrinsically immoral action having a gravely bad direct intention. However, this is not always the case. The direct intention of an absolute impersonal relation can be either gravely bad or significantly bad. An absolute impersonal relation has a gravely bad direct intention in an intrinsically immoral type of action, for example, slavery. An absolute impersonal relation has a significantly bad intention in a prima facie immoral type of action insofar as this type of action is immoral, for example, lying in general. In exceptional situations when a prima facie immoral type of action becomes morally right, the goodness of a particular action's motive and/or indirect intention/consequences outweighs the badness of the direct intention and transforms what is otherwise an absolute impersonal relation into a personal relation that may include a relative impersonal component. The significantly bad direct intention continues to exist in these exceptional situations that are morally right, since every action must have a direct intention and since these particular actions are still instances of a class of actions that is prima facie immoral, for example, lying, stealing, promise-breaking, and so on. However, in these exceptional situations the significantly bad direct intention is overridden by a personal relation with which it is paired. For example, although it is always bad to lie, it is not always morally wrong to lie. I briefly address the relation between the right and the good at the end of the chapter.

Since a personal relation can coexist with a significantly bad direct intention, this suggests that friendship is not the only type of personal relation in the constitution of community. There are two reasons why this is so. First, as Macmurray himself recognizes, friendship is a special and relatively rare personal relation, at least in the sense in which I have just described it. "It [friendship] is, perhaps, even rarer than we are apt to think."[16] However, because of its specialness, there are direct, personal relations other than friendship. Second, even in indirect relations, it is possible to have a personal relation. This becomes essential in larger communities and a fortiori in a universal community, where many—indeed, most—of the relations are indirect. Macmurray's insistence that a personal relation be based on personal acquaintance, if true, would restrict community to a very small size indeed.

To fully justify these statements, I need to spell out the minimal conditions or elements of a personal relation, either interpersonal or intrapersonal. First, a personal relation must be constituted by a direct intention to treat a person as a whole person, and not merely as a function. Second, love is the motive of the relation. Third, justice must be a constituent value of the relation, and equality must be present if the relation is interpersonal. And fourth, we must treat ourself and the other with as much freedom as the relation will allow. Freedom as a constituent value of friendship is the full reality of freedom. But short of that there are lesser degrees of freedom that are appropriate for a personal relation. In these lesser degrees we must not subordinate the other to ourself, and we must intend others' political, social, and economic freedom.

Such personal relations, it seems, can exist in both direct and indirect relations. Take a teacher-student relation, for example, which is typical of many personal relations. On one level, the relation is impersonal. Teacher and student treat each other as functions within an institutional setting of authority and responsibility. At the same time and on a higher level, this impersonal relation is subordinated to a personal relation: teacher and student ought to, and normally do, care for and treat each other as persons. Nevertheless, this personal relation is far from being a friendship, and in most cases it probably will not be, because of the institutional constraints of their relative impersonal relation. Moreover, personal relations can be indirect. For example, a personal indirect relation exists if a person is motivated by love to help poor, hungry, and otherwise needy people through various relief and charitable organizations, when it is not feasible or possible for a person to help others directly, as is often the case.[17]

In fairness to Macmurray, it might be argued that at least some of the foregoing difficulties can be resolved if we apply, as he would, his concept of the logical form of the personal. This concept, according to Macmurray, is a fundamental category by which personal reality can be adequately represented and understood. The form states that personal reality is a positive that includes, subordinates, and is constituted by its own negative. Earlier, I applied it to the relation among reason, rationality, and irrationality. If we apply the form to the present context, the positive fullness of community consists of friendship, and its negative aspect consists of relative impersonal relations.[18]

However, there are difficulties with this application that have much to do with the difficulties of Macmurray's form; it has probably proved to be the most controversial idea of his philosophy. It does not seem to make sense to call relative impersonal relations negative, since they are for the sake of personal relations, which are positive. It would make sense to call only the absolute impersonal relations negative. But they are excluded from community. Moreover, this interpretation of Macmurray still denies (1) that indirect relations can be personal and (2) that there can be personal relations other than friendship. I have tried to show that both of these denials are mistaken. In the last analysis, there are certain problems of both coherence and adequacy with Macmurray's conception of community that cannot be overcome within the context of his thought. Therefore, if Macmurray's concept of community is going to serve as an adequate and supreme moral standard, it must be appropriately modified. I have tried to do this in my preceding formulation and development of the principle of community.

Since community is the supreme moral standard, it subordinates the principle of intentionality. Community determines the goodness and the badness of the various moral elements of action that come under intentionality, which is a necessary procedural principle. Intentionality determines how the principle of community applies to particular actions and relations.

Feminism and Communitarianism

The principle of community can also resolve a controversy raised by feminist thinkers such as Carol Gilligan.[19] She makes a distinction between two basically different kinds of ethics. The first is an ethics of justice and rights, which is traditional and created by men. It emphasizes universal principles of justice that treat everyone equally. It is associated with Kant and his followers, notably Lawrence Kohlberg and John Rawls.[20] The second is an ethics of care and responsibility, which is characteristic of women. It is grounded in interpersonal relationship and mutual interdependence and emphasizes love and compassion in meeting people's somewhat different needs. What is needed, says Gilligan, is a "marriage" between these two ethics.[21]

The principle of community is one form of such a marriage or synthesis. On the one hand, it incorporates traditional Kantian ethics by emphasizing the values of justice and equality. On the other hand, the principle of community incorporates female ethics by grounding itself in the mutuality of the personal and by intending a personal relation of persons in which love (or caring) is the motive and in which the value of freedom meets the full needs of both self and other.[22] The ethics of community, then, transcends the opposition that feminists postulate between the male ethic of justice and the female ethic of caring.

Likewise, my ethics of community bears a resemblance to the recent, influential communitarian movement, as represented by social scientist Amitai Etzioni.[23] It includes such noted philosophers as Alasdair MacIntyre, Michael Sandel, and Michael Walzer. Communitarianism tries to transcend the ideological opposition between liberalism and conservatism. To some extent it has succeeded, drawing praise from such luminaries as former president Bill Clinton, former vice president Al Gore, former vice presidential candidate Jack Kemp, and political pundit William Bennett. Communitarianism criticizes a version of individualism: the recent emphasis on individual rights without a correlative emphasis on the individual's responsibility to the common good of the community. This notion of responsibility, of course, is nothing new. In Western thought it goes back at least to Plato and Aristotle. Still, it is a much-needed corrective to a one-sided emphasis on individual rights, as represented, for example, by the American Civil Liberties Union (ACLU). However, as I see it, communitarianism has a major defect. Since its fundamental distinction is between the individual and community, it is based on an organic model of society rather than on a personalist model. A number of personalist thinkers have distinguished between the person and the individual. A person, as such, is more than an individual member of society. Here Macmurray would make a distinction between community and society.[24] As a person, a human being is a whole unto itself, oriented toward other personal wholes in the community and ultimately to God, the infinite, absolute person. As an individual, a human being is a member of society, conceived as an economic and political structure. Ironically, perhaps, communitarianism does justice to the individual-society distinction but not to the higher and more inclusive person-community distinction. Its philosophy of community is really a philosophy of the individual's proper relation to society. It is not a philosophy of community in a personalist sense. A more extensive analysis and critique of communitarianism's concept of community will be developed in chapter 12.

Community and Reason

Community, we have seen, is the supreme moral standard. If a person acts in accordance with the principle, he or she achieves it as the inclusive moral value. If persons in general act in accordance with this principle, then society becomes a true community, that is, a personalist society rather than either an organic or an individualistic society. And if everyone in the world were to habitually act in accordance with this principle, they would achieve universal community, or a global personalist society.

Since community is the supreme moral principle or standard, and since acting in accordance with it achieves community as the inclusive moral value, and since moral value is its highest mode, constituting the fullness of both value and reason, community achieves an all-inclusive synthesis of self and other, of subjectivity and objectivity. It achieves an inclusive synthesis within the self. Because community can be achieved and maintained only in action/communication, community includes the whole self-as-agent, who synthesizes thought and feeling in action/communication. Moreover, because the underlying motive of community is love, community depends on the self's free responses to the other. Community is thus an affirmation of the self's subjectivity. Likewise, community achieves an inclusive synthesis of the other. In community, all persons are related as whole persons. In addition, the personal other ultimately includes God, the infinite and universal personal other, who is the creator of human persons and nature. In this context, God is the ground of the unity of community, in the sense that all of us can think of our common relationship to one another by virtue of our common creation by, and relationship to, God. In this sense, too, God is the head of community. All of us love one another as an expression of our love of God. Furthermore, community involves a harmonious relation between persons and nature. On the side of the other, then, community involves a synthesis of the whole other: the wholeness of human persons with God and with nature. Finally, the whole other is synthesized with the whole self as a communicative and rational agent to achieve an all-inclusive synthesis. In this synthesis, objectivity is primary and subjectivity is secondary. It is the nature of the whole other—human persons, God, and nature, considered as an interrelation of ends—that determines the type of response by the self that is essential to constitute community. The principle of community, then, is at once the supreme moral principle and the supreme rational principle. As such, community is the self-realization of persons.

Clearly, my conception of community has a religious orientation. Nevertheless, community can be achieved as a moral reality that is independent of religion. At the same time, since God may be regarded as the ground of the unity of community, genuine religion must be seen as a positive force in community's achievement. Still, the essence of community is moral or ethical; indeed, I defined the principle of community without any reference to God and religion. Although genuine religion necessarily includes morality, the converse is not true. Genuine morality need not imply religion, just as it need not exclude religion either.

Not everyone is religious, or believes in the existence of God (or the

Gods). And for those who are religious, there are many diverse religions throughout the world. From the standpoint of philosophical reason, it is imperative that a conception of community not depend on any particular religion or religious viewpoint. Otherwise, community could not be, philosophically speaking, either the supreme moral principle or the supreme rational principle. Macmurray was a devout Christian, and his conception of community bears the influence of his interpretation of Christianity. Nonetheless, since community is inherently and ideally universal in the sense explained, it obviously cannot be only for Christians. Indeed, when Macmurray the philosopher developed his conception of community as a *moral* reality, he did so independently of specifically Christian language and doctrines.

Throughout this chapter, I have been using the terms *value, good,* and *right* without explicitly distinguishing and connecting them. Let me close the chapter by briefly addressing this issue. It is often said that the right and the good are the two major ethical concepts and that value is closer in meaning to good than to right. In my theory, good and value have the same basic meaning and are distinguished from right.

It is also said that the nature of an ethical theory is determined by how it defines and connects the good and the right. The resolution of this problem generates a basic distinction between *teleological* and *deontological* ethical theories.[25] In teleological theories, the good is prior to the right. The good is defined independently of right, and the right is defined as maximizing the good. Utilitarianism, consequentialism, and natural law ethics are major teleological theories. By contrast, in a deontological theory, the right is prior to the good. This means that the good cannot be defined independently of the right, or the right cannot be understood as maximizing the good. Kant's ethics is the most famous example of a deontological theory.

By these definitions, my ethical theory has elements of deontological and teleological ethics, and so I regard my theory as some sort of synthesis of them. It is deontological in the sense that the inclusive moral good of community cannot be defined independently of the right of justice. As we have seen, community necessarily includes justice. Although the achievement of justice is surely a good, justice itself is defined in terms of each and every person as such possessing rights and reciprocal duties. Within this definition, a person who acts justly acts rightly. In sum, the moral good of community is partially defined by the right of justice.

In another sense, my theory may be regarded as teleological. Although the right is not *defined* as maximizing the good, it is certainly the case that the right of justice maximizes the good of community. Indeed, community cannot exist without justice. My theory is also teleological in the sense that the good of community transcends, and is more inclusive than, the right of justice. As we have explained, freedom and equality in their fullness, as the two primary constituent values of community, go beyond justice (while they still retain a necessary element of justice). In this respect, the good has a certain priority over the right. The right is a necessary condition for the (moral) good. Macmurray's (modified) form of the personal can be applied: The good includes, subordinates, and is partially constituted by the right.

3

SUICIDE AND THE
RIGHT TO DIE

In some quarters, it appears that suicide is viewed as a private action not worthy of serious moral consideration. In a majority of ethics textbooks and anthologies, it is passed over in silence, or else the emphasis is on suicide prevention. After all, there is no point in moralizing about suicide after someone has taken his or her life; nothing can be done for that person. What can and should be done is to identify the complex causes of suicide so that its incidence can be reduced. Thus, we need psychology, sociology, and psychiatry, but not ethics.

There is truth in these views, but it is only a partial truth. Suicide is indeed a private action in the sense that it is intrapersonal. For that reason, however, it is a moral-type action. In addition, it is moral because it has important interpersonal consequences; the family and friends of someone who commits suicide are profoundly affected by the action. In this respect, suicide is a public act. Furthermore, the reason we want to prevent suicide is that we have already made the value judgment that suicide is immoral. Indeed, most of the Western religious and philosophical tradition has condemned suicide as intrinsically immoral, the most notable exception being David Hume. However, this condemnation is not shared by many Eastern cultures. Ludwig Wittgenstein expresses the dominant Western attitude when he proclaims that "if suicide is allowed then anything is allowed. If anything is not allowed then suicide is not allowed. This throws a light on the nature of ethics, for suicide is, so to speak, the elementary sin."[1]

In recent years, however, a backlash has developed against this position, especially in psychiatric circles. Some even go so far as to say that a right to suicide is as basic as the right to life and that there are no valid moral rules prohibiting suicide.

In addition to various moral viewpoints on suicide, there is considerable controversy on what suicide is and how it should be defined, or whether a universal and objective definition is even possible.[2] It is my view that an adequate definition of suicide must be not only universal and objective but also morally neutral, since we want to avoid begging the question of suicide's morality before an ethical analysis of it begins. Finally, because of its interpersonal nature, I postpone until chapter 5 the question of (physician) assisted suicide, when I take up the euthanasia issue.

Taking all these points into consideration, my first aim in this chapter is to survey and critically evaluate the various definitions of suicide that have been proposed, as a prelude to formulating an adequate definition of it. Next, I examine and critically evaluate the major arguments against and in favor of suicide. Finally, I develop my own ethical position on suicide.

DEFINITIONS OF SUICIDE

The first definition of suicide is the literal definition: any killing of oneself, any self-killing. A moment's reflection, however, reveals that this definition is woefully inadequate because it is too broad and simplistic. Its most obvious difficulty is that it includes all accidental self-killings as well as intentional ones.

This difficulty leads to the standard or conventional definition of suicide: any self-killing that is intentional rather than accidental. This definition, too, raises problems. There are many instances of self-killing involving intentional activity that may not be suicide. Did Socrates commit suicide when he drank the hemlock? Does a pilot who decides to crash-land his ailing plane in a nearby nonpopulated area rather than bail out over a populated area, and who faces almost certain death, commit suicide? Does a person who engages in a dangerous lifestyle and is killed commit suicide? Does a person who runs into a burning building to save another's life and is killed in the process commit suicide? Does someone who smokes heavily and dies of lung cancer commit suicide? Did the Buddhist monk who torched himself as a moral and religious protest against the Vietnam War commit suicide? Did Samson commit suicide when he brought the temple down on himself?

There are those who would say that these questions cannot be answered with reference to intentionality, for intention is too subjective. What is needed, they say, is a "scientific" definition: one based on objective, observable behavior. Émile Durkheim proposed this sort of definition. According to him, "the term suicide is applied to all cases of death resulting directly or indirectly from a positive or negative act of the victim himself, which he knows will produce this result."[3] One obvious problem with this definition is the last clause, "which he knows will produce this result." What counts as knowledge here? The answer appears to be certainty and a fairly high degree of probability. But what degree of probability? The statistical probability that a heavy smoker will die of lung cancer is significantly higher than that for a nonsmoker. Would Durkheim classify all heavy smoking as suicidal behavior? Again, one may plausibly argue that a person who runs into a burning building to save another's life and is killed fits into Durkheim's definition, because he indirectly kills himself by performing a "positive" act, and he knows in advance that he may be killed. Yet it seems odd to call his action a suicide, especially since, under normal conditions at least, he does not want to die. Finally, a terminally ill patient who refuses extraordinary medical care and who subsequently dies also seems to fit Durkheim's definition, and it is certainly arguable that this action should not be classified as suicide. Durkheim's definition, then, appears to be too broad.

Nevertheless, Ronald Maris proposed an even broader definition, an omnibus definition. "Suicide occurs when an individual engages in a life-style that he knows might kill him . . . and it does [kill him]. This . . . omnibus definition of suicide . . . includes various forms of self-destruction, such as risk-taking and many so-called 'accidents.'"[4] It is not clear why this definition should not include all sorts of hazardous occupations—firefighter, police officer, FBI agent, soldier, and so on. Yet it seems absurd to say that someone who chooses one of these careers and is killed in the line of duty is committing suicide. Since Durkheim's definition is too broad, so is the omnibus definition.

Dissatisfied with the foregoing definitions, Tom Beauchamp, a contemporary ethicist and authority on suicide, goes on to formulate his own definition:

> An act is a suicide if a person intentionally brings about his own death in circumstances where others do not coerce him to the action, except in those cases where death occurs through an agent's intentional decision but is caused by conditions not specifically arranged by the agent for the purpose of bringing about his own death.[5]

Elsewhere, he simplifies this rather complex definition. "The death of person A is a suicide only if (1) A's death is intentionally self-caused by A and (2) A's self-caused death is noncoerced."[6]

However, Beauchamp's two stated conditions are really three. First, a self-killing must be intentional; second, it must be self-caused; and third, it must be noncoerced. Based on Beauchamp's definition, Socrates' death is not a suicide. Although he intended to kill himself, he was coerced to perform the action by the Athenian court. By the same token, Socrates' death was not self-caused: He did not specifically arrange the conditions of his death; they were arranged for him by the court. Hence, his death was caused by the court rather than by himself. Taking another example, Beauchamp tells us that "an act is *not* a suicide if the person who dies suffers from a terminal disease or from a mortal injury which, by refusal of treatment, he passively allows to cause his death—even if the person intends his death."[7] This individual does not cause his death; his death is caused by his terminal illness. But in the famous and controversial case of Captain Oates, Beauchamp concludes that he did commit suicide. Oates walked into an Antarctic blizzard, thus killing himself, because his serious illness was hampering the safe progress of his expedition party. Based on Beauchamp's definition, Oates not only intended his death but ultimately caused it. According to Beauchamp, the blizzard was merely the proximate cause of his death, and hence not its real cause. Nor did his illness cause his death. The real cause of his death was his action of walking into the blizzard. Finally, a soldier who jumps on a grenade does not commit suicide, since he does not intend his death. He intends to save his comrades.[8]

In my view, Beauchamp's definition is superior to the others we have examined. However, his distinction between a killing that is self-intended and one that is self-caused is potentially troublesome and requires further analysis. In some cases, the distinction works, in others it does not. And even when it technically works, it is sometimes trivial. I now explain.

If we provisionally define suicide in terms of direct intention, Beauchamp's distinction will be adequately covered by such a definition, and so Beauchamp's distinction becomes unnecessary. This definition would enable us to make three salient points. First, if an agent's direct intention to kill himself is successful and thus produces the direct consequence of death, his death is obviously self-caused. In this type of action, Beauchamp's distinction is trivial and unnecessary.

Second, if an agent's direct intention to kill himself fails and produces no direct consequences, he is still alive, and so the element of self-caused death is inapplicable. In this type of action, the distinction does not work, because from a definitional standpoint, the action should still be regarded as suicide (i.e., attempted suicide). Beauchamp apparently limits the definition of suicide to successful suicides. This is a mistake. Since an adequate definition of suicide is needed as a prelude to its moral analysis and evaluation, and since a person who directly intends to take his own life and fails is as morally responsible for his action as another person who succeeds in his direct intention to kill himself (since the morality of an action is determined primarily by its direct intention), attempted suicides should be included within the definition.

Third, a self-caused death is not always directly intended, for example, a motorist who kills herself by driving negligently. Beauchamp would apparently say her death is not a suicide, and I agree. In this type of action, Beauchamp's distinction is helpful. But in other cases in which he claims that a self-caused death does not imply a self-intended death, the distinction is troublesome, as in the death of Socrates. Beauchamp's claim that Socrates' death was not self-caused but caused by the Athenian court seems to indicate a defect in his notion of causality. By drinking the hemlock, Socrates was in fact the immediate cause of his death; he died literally by his own hand. That does not mean the court did not play a causal role in his death. Socrates and the court had different causal roles in his death. Indeed, if we define suicide in terms of direct intention, it follows that since Socrates' death was successfully self-intended, it was ipso facto self-caused. It does not follow, however, that Socrates committed suicide, for he did not take his life on his own authority but on the authority of the Athenian court.

The word *authority* suggests the final definition to be considered, the traditional, Scholastic one: "Suicide . . . [is] the direct killing of oneself on one's own authority."[9] I think that this definition is basically sound, but it needs to be amended in two ways. As I amend it, I will be formulating my own definition of suicide. First, although the element of direct killing in the definition is valid, I base its validity on my notion of direct intention. Therefore, I use this concept in constructing my definition. At the same time, the Scholastic phrase "on one's own authority" appears superior to Beauchamp's element of "noncoercion." I retain the older, more established phrase. It seems that Beauchamp's term "noncoercion" is supposed to replace the Scholastic phrase, "on one's own authority." However, the two terms are not equivalent in meaning. I now explain why the Scholastic term is preferable to Beauchamp's.

The deaths of Samson and Socrates are two examples of persons who took their own lives not on their own authority but on the authority of another: in Samson's case, the authority of a divine command, and in Socrates' case, the authority of the Athenian court. Samson's action must be understood in the context of the Judaic-Christian religion. In this context, an action that obeys a divine command or commandment is morally and religiously authentic only if it is a *free* response to God; the response must be a voluntary act. Samson could have freely chosen to disobey God. Being virtuous, he freely chose obedience. Hence, his action was not coerced.

A similar analysis applies to Socrates. In Plato's *Crito*, the setting is Socrates' imprisonment awaiting his execution. His friends come to visit him and describe their plan to help him escape. Socrates rejects the idea and explains to them all his moral reasons for accepting the state's unjust verdict. In doing so, he articulates a model of a free or voluntary action: an act that is performed because a person gives himself rational moral reasons for doing so.

The second way that the Scholastic definition needs to be amended is that an adequate definition of suicide should make a reference to motive. This reference is needed to ensure a morally neutral definition and to prevent the definition from becoming culturally relativistic. For example, if a culture disapproves of suicide, it might not classify as suicide a self-killing that springs from a noble or sacrificial motive. In contrast, a culture that approves of the same act would be inclined to classify it as suicide.

Accordingly, I define suicide as any self-killing that is directly intended on one's own authority, regardless of the moral quality of the motive. Let me now apply my definition to several of the foregoing examples. In the pilot example, certainly no one coerces him to perform his action; it is done on his own authority. His direct intention is to crash-land his plane in a nearby unpopulated area, not to kill himself. His indirect intention is that he foresees but does not will his death. Therefore, when he is killed in the crash, he dies by indirect intention; his death is an indirect consequence of his action. Hence, it is not a suicide. Some people might not classify his action as suicide because of its noble motive. However, according to my definition, the goodness or badness of the motive has no bearing on whether an action is a suicide, but only on whether a suicide is morally right or morally wrong.

Neither is the death of Socrates a suicide, but for different reasons. Socrates' self-killing may be characterized as a means to an end. The end consists of upholding his moral principles, which he believed would have been violated had he fled the state and not accepted the court's verdict and sentence. Therefore, he killed himself by direct intention. However, since he did not take his own life on his own authority but on the authority of the state, his death should not be classified as an act of suicide, but as an act of capital punishment in which Socrates served as his own executioner. Once again, it does not matter that Socrates had a noble motive. Furthermore, it does not matter whether the means chosen are active or passive. If someone kills himself by putting a bullet through his head, or if someone else kills herself by starvation, both acts are suicides, because both are equally constituted by a direct intention to end one's life.

In the Captain Oates case, I agree with Beauchamp that his death should be classified as suicide. His end is to kill himself by means of walking into a ferocious blizzard. Thus, he kills himself by direct intention, and he does this on his own authority.

Let me provide a few more examples before I close this section. A prisoner of war is about to be tortured to make him divulge vital information concerning his army's strategic battle plans. He knows that if he is tortured long enough, his captors will probably get their way, so he decides to end his life. His death is a suicide, because he dies by direct intention. The end of his action is to spare the lives and injuries of his comrades, by means of taking his own life. His action is performed on his own authority. It is not coerced by his captors, who want to keep him alive. By the same token, the Buddhist monk who immolated himself to protest the Vietnam War committed suicide.

However, based on my definition, Samson did not commit suicide, because his action was commanded by God. Thus, it was done not on his own authority but on the authority of God. On this point, I agree with Saint Augustine and Saint Thomas Aquinas.[10] Therefore, according to my definition, if God orders someone to directly intend her own death, the action should not be classified as suicide. However, this situation is so speculative and so difficult to verify that I do not consider it further. Instead, I turn to the question of suicide's morality.

ARGUMENTS AGAINST SUICIDE

In this section, I examine and critically evaluate six arguments against suicide. The first argument is theological (or religious). According to Augustine, suicide is intrinsically immoral, because it is a violation of God's commandment: "Thou shalt not kill."[11] The soundness of the argument rests on the truth of three presuppositions: (1) God exists, (2) God has revealed Himself through the Bible, and (3) we humans can adequately interpret the Bible on our own. Since the latter two presuppositions are theological, I do not comment on them further. However, the first presupposition is philosophical as well as theological. In Western thought, God has long been an object of philosophical reason. Augustine held this view, and he offered several arguments for God's existence. Although I agree that the existence of a theistic God can be rationally justified, this difficult and complex issue lies outside the scope of this book. Consequently, I put these three presuppositions aside and analyze the argument's internal coherence (or lack of it).

In his exegesis of the commandment, Augustine concludes that there are three types of homicide but only one type of self-killing that falls outside the commandment.[12] The three homicide exceptions are capital punishment; a nation waging a just war; and killing another by divine command, as in the case of Abraham, who was ordered by God to slaughter his son, Isaac. The one self-killing exception involves killing oneself by divine command, as in the case of Samson. However, Augustine does not classify this type of self-killing as suicide, so his absolute prohibition against suicide still stands.

Since there are three exceptions in which killing others is morally permissible but only one exception in which self-killing is morally permissible, Augustine appears to view self-killing as morally worse than killing others. And if we discount the one exception in which self-killing is morally permissible, we are left with a moral view of suicide that is so bad that it is classified as murder. "Whoever kills a man, either himself or another, is implicated in the guilt of murder."[13]

However, Augustine's views are open to criticism. First, it is inconsistent to hold that self-killing is worse than killing others, other things being equal. Such a view violates the fundamental equality of persons; it values self more highly than others. Second, a classification of suicide as murder expresses a Pickwickian definition of suicide. It ignores the fundamental distinction between suicide and homicide. It represents an attempt to condemn suicide as intrinsically immoral without giving a serious ethical analysis and justification of such a sweeping judgment, for in this view, murder is already intrinsically immoral. By classifying suicide as murder, one is spared the otherwise necessary task of determining whether there are any relevant moral differences between them. Our standard of a morally neutral definition is not satisfied. I conclude, then, that Augustine's argument lacks coherence and is incapable of establishing his conclusion that suicide is intrinsically immoral.

A corollary of this argument, in traditional Roman Catholic theology, is that everyone who commits suicide ipso facto goes immediately to hell, because such an act is a mortal sin (versus a venial sin). A mortal sin is one that gets the perpetrator into hell if it is not forgiven by a priest before death in the Sacraments of Confession or Last Rites (also called Extreme Unction, now called the Anointing of the Sick). Since this forgiveness—formally called absolution—is impossible in the case of suicide, suicide is a hell-bound act. That is why Roman Catholics who committed suicide were denied burial in a Christian cemetery.

This argument, however, is open to the following response. Anyone who believed that if she committed suicide she would go straight to hell and did it anyway would be insane—at least temporarily insane when she committed suicide. But an insane act is an involuntary act and not justly punishable. Therefore, if God sent people to hell for committing suicide, He would be acting unjustly. But since the Christian-theistic God is supposedly perfect and thus perfectly just, He cannot commit injustice. Therefore, since God cannot commit injustice, God cannot send suicide victims to hell. Consequently, either God sends suicide victims to hell, which contradicts his perfect essence and thus is metaphysically impossible; or else He does not send them to hell, in which case the traditional Roman Catholic position is mistaken. The Church's traditional doctrine is impaled on the horns of a dilemma.[14] In recent times, the Roman Catholic Church has considerably moderated its moral position on suicide. The Church now emphasizes the profound gap between suicide's "objective" morality and the degree of subjective responsibility of a person who commits suicide. Since a mortal sin is one that not only contains grave matter but must also be a fully voluntary act, and since we cannot really know a person's state of mind when he commits suicide, any person committing suicide has the possibility of salvation, of making it into heaven. "We should not despair of the eternal salvation of persons who have taken their own lives. By ways known to him alone, God can provide the opportunity for salutary repentance. The Church prays for persons who have taken their own lives."[15] There's no point, of course, in praying for persons in hell.

The second argument against suicide is a philosophical one, even though it presupposes that God exists and that He is our creator. It is philosophical because proponents of this argument contend that these two presuppositions can be rationally justified. According to this argument, since God creates us, only God can take away our life. In effect, God owns us; we are His property. God has absolute dominion over us. Suicide violates God's ownership of us, His property rights in us. As a consequence, suicide is intrinsically immoral; it is never morally permissible. This argument is a common and influential one and was developed by such major philosophers as Aquinas, Kant, and Locke.[16] To analyze it in some detail, let us now examine Aquinas's and Kant's versions of the argument.

Aquinas's version is based on a master/slave analogy. He writes:

> Life is God's gift to man, and is subject to His power, Who kills and makes to live. Hence, whoever takes his own life, sins against God, even as he who kills another's slave, sins against that slave's master, and as he who usurps to himself judgment of a matter not entrusted to him. For it belongs to God alone to pronounce sentence of death and life.[17]

One would think that Aquinas would have said that the fundamental sin in killing a slave, as in directly and unjustly killing anyone, is that of murder. Or is it his view that a slave is not a person? Such a view would certainly be anti-Christian. In any case, he says that the killing of another's slave is wrong because it violates the master's property rights in the slave. Hence, he implies that killing a slave is morally equivalent to vandalism or malicious destruction of property. This view presupposes, of course, a moral acceptance of slavery, which is implied by his usage of the master/slave analogy in constructing the argument.

However, Aquinas's moral acceptance of slavery is both false and anti-Christian. And since this acceptance is a premise of his argument, the argument is unsound and incompatible with his own Christian religion. It is false, because if anything is intrinsically immoral, slavery certainly is.[18] Slavery is an absolute impersonal relation constituted by a gravely bad direct intention on the part of the master. Slavery is inherently incompatible with personhood. The master intentionally denies the personhood of the slave by treating him or her as a mere thing or function for its own sake and by owning the slave as a mere external possession or piece of property. Such treatment and ownership completely violate the three essential values of a personal relation and of community: freedom, equality, and justice. Therefore, persons cannot be owned by anyone, not even by God, and slavery is intrinsically immoral. I say "not even by God" because, since He creates us as persons, His intention is not to own us as slaves. Slavery violates the principle of community and Rules Two and Four of the principle of intentionality.

Slavery is anti-Christian for similar reasons. The concept of person is essential to Christianity and, therefore, to Aquinas's thought. But since slavery is morally incompatible with personhood, it is inherently anti-Christian. Historically, Christianity developed the notion of person to explicate its two central doctrines of the Incarnation (one person, Jesus Christ, having two natures, human and divine) and the Trinity (one divine nature existing in three persons, Father, Son, and Holy Spirit).[19] It is understandable, then, for Aquinas to hold that person denotes the highest mode of being. *"Person* signifies what is most perfect in all nature—that is, a subsistent individual of a rational nature."[20] By this definition, God is the supreme person, and among creatures, only angels and humans are persons. As a Christian, Aquinas cannot, with consistency, have such an august view of human personhood and, at the same time, morally accept slavery.

I can now summarize my critique of Aquinas's argument against suicide. A basic premise of the argument is that we are related to God as a slave is related to his or her master. I have just explained why this premise is false and anti-Christian. Therefore, the premise is totally incapable of supporting the argument's conclusion, that suicide is intrinsically immoral. The argument fails to establish that the conclusion is either true or Christian.

However, within Aquinas's Christianity, I accept the two presuppositions on which his argument rests: God exists, and God creates us. Unlike Aquinas, though, I draw the following two conclusions from these presuppositions. First, we have a prima facie moral duty to God, but not an absolute duty, to preserve our life and develop our personhood. Second, since God creates us as persons, we have a limited right to dispose of our life under certain conditions. Both conclusions are developed further in a later section.

Kant is even more explicit than Aquinas that God owns us as His property. In addition, Kant appeals to the sentinel metaphor:

We have been placed in this world under certain conditions and for specific purposes. But a suicide opposes the purpose of his Creator; he arrives in the other world as one who has deserted his post; he must be looked upon as a rebel against God. So long as we remember the truth that it is God's intention to preserve life, we are bound to regulate our activities in conformity with it. We have no right to offer violence to our nature's powers of self-preservation and to upset the wisdom of her arrangements. The duty is upon us until the time comes when God expressly commands us to leave this life. Human beings are sentinels on earth and may not leave their posts until relieved by another beneficent hand. God is our owner; we are His property; His providence works for our good. A bondman in the care of a beneficent master deserves punishment if he opposes his master's wishes.[21]

It is extraordinary that Kant sees no contradiction between this argument and his second formulation of the categorical imperative: treat every person, including yourself, as an end and never merely as a means. How can God treat us as ends if we are his property? According to the categorical imperative, we must treat property merely as a means. But to treat a person as an end is precisely to exclude treatment of him or her merely as a means. Since God creates us as persons, even He must treat us as ends and never merely as means. Consequently, we cannot be God's property, and Kant's argument is thereby contradicted and invalidated by one of the most important and influential principles of his own ethics. Nevertheless, as we shall see, Kant uses this formulation of the categorical imperative as the basis of another argument against suicide.

The third argument, held by Aristotle and Aquinas, concludes that suicide is always wrong, because it is an injury against the community. Aquinas writes: "Every part, as such, belongs to the whole. Now every man is part of the community, and so, as such, he belongs to the community. Hence by killing himself, he injures the community."[22]

There are two difficulties with Aquinas's argument. First, it is based on an organic conception of society rather than on a personalist conception. He says that the relation of an individual person to society (or to the community) is a relation of a part to a whole. Likewise, the relation of an organ to an organism is a relation of a part to a whole. Therefore, the community is like a social organism, which includes and submerges all individual persons as its various "organs" and "members." However, the organic conception of society is false, because it interprets personal reality as if it were merely biological reality. If put into practice, it produces some form of totalitarianism, under which individual persons are completely subordinated to the state and have no inherent rights vis-à-vis the state. By contrast, in a personalist society, which is required by the principle of community, persons are related to one another in two different ways: as persons and as functions. In the first case, there are personal relations; in the second case, there are relative impersonal relations. In the latter case, the individual is related to society as a part to a whole, insofar as society is a system of institutions, especially economic and political institutions and, above all, the state. But on a higher level of personal relations, as in friendship, persons are related to one another as whole persons. On this level, the part-to-whole relation fails. Persons as such are related to one another in a way that transcends the functional and impersonal relations of institutional society. They are related to one another not as parts to a whole but as a field of autonomous and equal wholes. As we saw in chapter 2, there is a difference between community and society, and this argument against suicide fails to take into account that important distinction.

The second problem with the argument is that, even if the organic conception of society were true, it could not prove what Aquinas claims it proves. As Hume and others have pointed out, it proves that someone injures the community only if one is a "healthy" and contributing member of society.[23] If someone contributes nothing to society, then society is not injured if that person commits suicide, just as we do not harm our organism if we remove a vestigial organ like an appendix. And a fortiori, if someone were a harmful member of society, for example, a serious criminal, it seems to follow that one ought to commit suicide to avoid committing any further injury to the community, just as a surgeon removes a diseased limb or organ for the sake of the life and health of the whole organism. Ironically, Aquinas uses this very argument to justify the death penalty.[24]

Aristotle's version of this argument is presented in the context of the question whether a person can treat himself unjustly:

> The law does not expressly permit suicide, and what it does not expressly permit it forbids. . . . He who through anger voluntarily stabs himself does this contrary to the right rule of life, and this the law does not allow; therefore he is acting unjustly. But towards whom? Surely towards the state, not towards himself. For he suffers voluntarily, but no one is voluntarily treated unjustly.[25]

What is different about Aristotle's argument in comparison to Aquinas's is the doctrine that a person cannot treat himself unjustly, since he voluntarily consents to such treatment. Therefore, justice is wholly inapplicable to intrapersonal action; it applies only to interpersonal action. That is why Aristotle says that suicide is an injustice against the state (i.e., society). However, justice and morality apply intrapersonally as well as interpersonally. In the *Social Contract*, Rousseau maintains that it would be immoral for anyone to voluntarily consent to being a slave. Such an act, he says, is "absurd and inconceivable; . . . null and illegitimate."[26] The apparent implication, with which I agree, is that voluntary slavery would be an action of injustice against oneself. By the same token, committing suicide can be an action of injustice against oneself. This point is developed in a later section.

The fourth argument is based on self-love and was developed by Aquinas and Kant. Aquinas's version is sometimes called the natural law argument, for he connects self-love with the natural inclination to self-preservation, in the sense that self-love ought to imply self-preservation. Hence, suicide is a violation of self-love and of the natural law, since it is contrary to the natural inclination of self-preservation. As he puts it:

> Everything naturally loves itself, the result being that everything naturally keeps itself in being, and resists corruptions so far as it can. Wherefore suicide is contrary to the inclination of nature, and to charity whereby every man should love himself. Hence suicide is always a mortal sin, as being contrary to the natural law and to charity.[27]

Kant's version of the argument emphasizes that since self-love implies self-improvement, it is contradictory to use self-love to destroy one's life:

> A man who is reduced to despair by a series of evils feels a weariness with life but is still in possession of his reason sufficiently to ask whether it would not be contrary to his duty to himself to take his own life. Now he asks whether the maxim of his action could become a universal law of nature. His maxim, however, is: For love of myself, I make it my principle to shorten my life when by a longer duration it threatens more evil than satisfaction. But it is questionable whether this principle of self-love could become a universal law

of nature. One immediately sees a contradiction in a system of nature whose law would be to destroy life by the feeling whose special office is to impel the improvement of life.[28]

Aquinas's and Kant's argument is essentially this: Since one ought to love oneself, and since self-love always implies self-preservation (and in Kant's case, self-improvement), it is always immoral to commit suicide. Therefore, suicide can never be based on the motive of self-love; suicide is necessarily an action of self-hatred. However, this claim is implausible. It is true in most cases that self-love implies self-preservation, but not in all cases. If someone is in the last stages of cancer, and life has nothing more to offer this person than excruciating pain and suffering, and the person still has the capacity to make a rational decision, then her choice to end her life could very well be motivated by self-love. She could reason thusly: the good of my personhood is better affirmed and achieved by choosing to end my life instead of choosing to continue it, because I can no longer enjoy any of the goods associated with personhood, except the good of exercising my rationality to end my life, and because I will be avoiding the evils associated with my low quality of life— evils for myself and for my loved ones, who must indirectly bear my pain and suffering. Such reasoning, I contend, is based on both self-love and love for others. In this case, self-love becomes a moment or element in a higher and greater love: altruistic love. This is also the case in my previous POW example. By killing himself to save his comrades, he is both transcending and affirming his self-love. He is transcending it, because his primary motive is altruistic love. But self-love is still a secondary motive, since he thinks enough of himself and cares enough for himself to decide that his life is worth sacrificing for his fellow humans.

Critics often misunderstand Aquinas's argument, however, because they misinterpret his concept of natural inclination. They mistakenly interpret it as purely descriptive and empirical, as if he were saying that all persons, in fact, do incline toward self-preservation.[29] If that were true, no one would commit suicide, and the argument would be obviously invalid. In truth, Aquinas's natural inclinations are prescriptive. In his view, they tend toward the good of the human being and are the basis for corresponding moral laws or precepts. Therefore, everyone ought to act in accordance with their natural inclinations. However, since humans have free will, they can and sometimes do act contrary to them. When they do, they violate the natural law and thus act immorally. In the natural inclination toward self-preservation, the good it tends toward is the basic good of life itself. We always ought to aim at this good and never violate it, according to Aquinas. But since this natural inclination is not a blind animal instinct, it is sometimes disobeyed, as when suicide is committed. Aquinas's natural laws are not scientific laws of nature, such as the law of gravity.

It is my view that both Aquinas's and Kant's versions of this argument can show that suicide is prima facie immoral but not intrinsically immoral, as their authors claim. In most cases, life is a basic good, but not in all cases. Yes, one ought to love oneself, and in most instances, self-love ought to imply self-preservation. But I deny that self-love ought to imply self-preservation in all instances. I develop this point later.

The fifth argument against suicide is unique to Kant. It is based on the second formulation of his categorical imperative, his so-called principle of respect for persons: always act so as to treat humanity, whether in your own person or in that of another, as an end and never merely as a means. From this principle, he writes:

> According to the concept of necessary duty to one's self, he who contemplates suicide will ask himself whether his action can be consistent with the idea of humanity as an end in itself. If, in order to escape from burdensome circumstances, he destroys himself, he uses a person merely as a means to maintain a tolerable condition up to the end of life. Man, however, is not a thing, and thus not something to be used merely as a means; he must always be regarded in all his actions as an end in himself. Therefore, I cannot dispose of man in my own person so as to mutilate, corrupt, or kill him.[30]

According to this argument, then, suicide is intrinsically immoral, because it always treats oneself merely as a means; it can never treat oneself as an end. Crucial to this argument is understanding what Kant means by treating a person (whether another or oneself) as an end. The answer is found in his concept of personhood and value. A person is a rational and autonomous being, having intrinsic or unconditioned value. Consequently, persons are to be treated accordingly, as ends in themselves. Things (or nonpersons) lack rationality and autonomy. They have instrumental (or relative) value. As a result, things are to be treated merely as means to ends. So if it were the case that a suicide could treat himself as a rational and autonomous being, the suicide would be treating himself as an end. But contrary to what Kant says, in some cases this appears to be possible, as in the previous cancer patient and POW examples. It seems, however, that the vast majority of suicides, especially those involving adolescents, are committed in a state of severe depression, so the resulting action does not possess sufficient rationality and autonomy to count as treating oneself as an end. At the very least, these suicides have diminished voluntariness. I conclude, then, that Kant's argument establishes that suicide is prima facie immoral but not intrinsically immoral.

The sixth argument is proposed by the well-known contemporary rule utilitarian R. B. Brandt. Unlike in all the previous arguments, Brandt wants to establish only that suicide is prima facie immoral. Indeed, he characterizes the view that suicide is intrinsically immoral as "absurd."[31] Brandt's argument is that a rule such as "suicide is prima facie immoral" is more likely to promote the principle of utility than the absence of this rule. In his words:

> Suppose it could be shown that it would maximize the long-run welfare of everybody affected if people were taught that there is a moral obligation to avoid suicide—so that people would be motivated to avoid suicide just because they thought it was wrong. . . . In other words, it might be a good thing in its effects for people to feel about suicide in the way they feel about breach of promise or injuring others, just as it might be a good thing for people to feel a moral obligation not to smoke, or to wear seat belts.[32]

Brandt has some misgivings about his argument, for he goes on to say that it does not consider those suicides that would really promote the principle of utility. Consequently, his argument does not specify the types of situations in which suicide is morally permissible. This is surely a weakness of an argument trying to establish that suicide is prima facie immoral. Nevertheless, the argument as a whole is telling if one accepts the principle of utility, as many contemporary Anglo-American philosophers do. This is probably why Brandt says that it will appeal to the "modern mind" and to "some contemporary philosophers." And even if one does not accept the principle of utility as the supreme moral principle, Brandt's argument still has a certain appeal and persuasiveness, since he has set himself a more modest task than his philosophical predecessors by not trying to establish that suicide is intrinsically immoral.

My overall conclusion is that the collective strengths and weaknesses of the arguments against suicide suggest that suicide is a prima facie immoral action that has a significantly bad direct intention. It remains to be seen whether this conclusion should be modified by the arguments in support of suicide, to which I now turn.

ARGUMENTS FOR SUICIDE

In this section, I present and critically evaluate four arguments in favor of suicide. The first is by David Hume. In the first part of his famous essay "On Suicide," Hume attacks versions of arguments that are similar to Aquinas's three arguments.[33] Then he constructs a positive argument in support of suicide. It is a utilitarian argument based on the premise that there is a reciprocal obligation between individuals and society: since we receive many benefits from society, we have an obligation to make a similar contribution to society. Based on this premise or principle, he develops a lengthy argument by describing several cases that do not satisfy this principle and, as a result, justify suicide:

> A man who retires from life does no harm to society; he only ceases to do good; which, if it is an injury, is of the lowest kind. All our obligations to do good to society seem to imply something reciprocal. I receive the benefits of society and therefore ought to promote its interests, but when I withdraw myself altogether from society, can I be bound any longer? But, allowing that our obligations to do good were perpetual, they have certainly some bounds; I am not obliged to do a small good to society at the expense of a great harm to myself; why then should I prolong a miserable existence, because of some frivolous advantage which the public may perhaps receive

from me? . . . But suppose that it is no longer in my power to promote the interest of society; suppose that I am a burden to it; suppose that my life hinders some person from being much more useful to society. In such cases my resignation of life must not only be innocent but laudable. . . . [Finally,] a man is engaged in a conspiracy for the public interest; is seized upon suspicion; is threatened with the rack; and knows from his own weakness that the secret will be extorted from him: Could such a one consult the public interest better than by putting a quick period to a miserable life? This was the case of the famous and brave Strozi of Florence.[34]

Hume's passage contains four cases that are progressively more compelling with respect to the moral rightness of suicide. Each one serves as a paradigmatic example of a type of situation in which suicide is morally permissible. In the first example, a person has nothing to contribute to society, because she has dropped out of society. Therefore, she does society no harm by killing herself. The obvious objection is that she could still do harm to herself. In the second example, a person may commit suicide if the harm done to himself by his continued existence outweighs any slight good his continued existence can do for society. This example is sounder than the first one, since it takes into account the good of the individual as well as the good of society. In the third example, not only is someone miserable and a noncontributing member of society, but she is also a positive burden on society. Therefore, in this case, suicide is "laudable." Fourth, if a spy is captured by the enemy and threatened with torture that he fears will break him into divulging critical secrets that will be harmful to his society, then perhaps he even has a duty to commit suicide.

Except for the first example, Hume has presented a strong case for the moral justifiability of suicide. Notice, too, that Hume's and Brandt's arguments complement each other. Brandt says that suicide is prima facie immoral without specifying the situations in which it is morally right. Hume's argument specifies these situations and in doing so presupposes that suicide is prima facie immoral. In most cases, Hume apparently believes that people will be able and willing to contribute to society in a way that satisfies the reciprocity principle. Therefore, although Hume's argument is explicitly an argument for suicide, it is implicitly much more of an argument against suicide. It tacitly supports the tentative conclusion I reached at the end of the previous section: suicide is prima facie immoral.

The next three arguments go beyond Hume by trying to establish a broader scope for the permissibility of suicide. They are all presented by psychiatrists. The first one is by Thomas Szasz:

> A man's life belongs to himself. Hence, he has a right to take his own life, that is, to commit suicide. To be sure, this view recognizes that a man may also have a moral responsibility to his family and others, and that, by killing himself, he reneges on these responsibilities.[35]

The basic premise of Szasz's argument is his first sentence: "A man's [person's] life belongs to himself [herself]." However, this premise is atheistic; it presupposes that God does not exist (and thus cannot create us). Indeed, Szasz is a confirmed atheist. The premise presupposes that we are not created by God, because if God exists and creates us, our moral duties to Him are sufficient to render it false to say that our lives simply belong to ourselves. That does not mean, of course, that our lives "belong" to God either. We have seen that this is not the case. The falsity of this proposition, however, does not imply the truth of Szasz's proposition. Since we are persons, and since we are persons created by God (as I hold, anyway), I have sketched a middle ground between our lives belonging to God and their belonging to us. Essentially, the word *belonging* is inappropriate. Furthermore, unlike Szasz, most people are not atheists. Therefore, they would probably find his premise weak or unacceptable. That does not mean, of course, that it is false. But it is false if theism is true, as I claim it to be.

Szasz's argument is quite different from Hume's, because Szasz claims that a person has a basic right to commit suicide. Such a right would be quite foreign to Hume's thought. Whereas Hume starts from the position that suicide is wrong unless it falls outside the reciprocity principle, Szasz starts from the position that suicide is permissible unless it falls outside of a person's right to end his or her life. Szasz's argument specifies this right's limits. If a person has responsibilities to family and to others, the right has been exceeded, and that person ought not to take his or her life.

It may be objected that most of us do have moral responsibilities to others. Most people are not hermits. In the concrete, then, Szasz's right to commit suicide, even with its atheistic premise, does not extend very far; it may not justify any more suicides than Hume's argument. Therefore, although Szasz may want to establish the position that suicide is morally right in general, or prima facie right, his argument is utterly incapable of doing so. Even if we accept its atheistic premise, the most that the argument could establish is that suicide is morally right in exceptional cases when a person has no responsibilities to others. But again, this implies that suicide is wrong in general, that it is a prima facie wrong.

The next argument is by Jerome Motto. It, too, asserts that a person has a right to suicide, but it is a right based on the person's pain.

> From a psychiatric point of view, the question as to whether a person has the right to cope with the pain in his world by killing himself can be answered without hesitation. He does have that right. . . .
>
> I use two psychological criteria as grounds for limiting a person's exercise of his right to suicide: (a) the act must be based on a realistic assessment of his life situation, and (b) the degree of ambivalence regarding the act must be minimal.[36]

By pain, Motto apparently means emotional pain rather than physical pain. First of all, he says that there are two types of situations in which the moral permissibility of suicide is a foregone conclusion and, therefore, not part of his argument: "Altruistic self-sacrifice for what is perceived as a noble cause; and the severe, advanced physical illness with no new therapeutic agents anticipated in the foreseeable future."[37] He then goes on to say that "our most difficult problem is more with the person whose pain is emotional in origin and whose physical health is good, or at most constitutes a minor impairment."[38] Such a person, he says, has a right to commit suicide to cope with his or her pain, provided the two limiting criteria are satisfied. By the first criterion, he means that the patient's assessment of his or her life situation must agree with the psychotherapist's assessment of it. "If I am working with a person in psychotherapy, one limitation I would put on this right to suicide would be that his assessment of his life situation be realistic as *I* see it."[39] Obviously, this criterion is open to the objection that it gives too much power and authority to the therapist. It gives the therapist the power of life and death over the patient; in effect, it allows the therapist to play God. This criterion, I submit, is a violation of the patient's autonomy. The second criterion—that a person must have minimal ambivalence about ending his or her life—is obvious to the point of being trivial. What therapist would give his or her blessing to a suicide when the patient's mind was undecided? Still, the second criterion is meant to limit the power and authority of the therapist in advising or not advising a patient to end his or her life.

In spite of these two limiting criteria, it appears that Motto's argument goes beyond Szasz's. Motto does not say that a person in emotional pain does not have a right to commit suicide if he or she has responsibilities to others. Even so, the moral right of suicide is the exception rather than the rule, considering the number of persons who could satisfy the conditions of this argument. Even if the argument were sound, it would still basically leave intact my tentative conclusion that suicide is prima facie immoral.

But aside from the objections already raised against Motto's argument, it has another serious flaw. Motto's basic claim is that the fact of pain establishes a moral right to commit suicide. It appears that Motto commits the naturalistic fallacy. What is needed is an intervening argument or premise to explain why it is legitimate to infer this right from this fact. Until that is done, one may question whether his argument has any validity at all.

The last argument, and by far the most radical, is offered by European psychoanalyst James Hillman. It may be called an existential argument, since it is rooted in existentialism. Some existentialists tend to glorify and romanticize suicide. As Camus puts it: "There is but one truly philosophical problem, and that is suicide."[40] Out of this universalization of Hamlet's dilemma—to be or not to be—Hillman develops his argument. It is presented in two parts. The first part is a statement about the nature and value of death:

> Death is the only absolute in life, the only surety and truth. Because it is the only condition which all life must take into account, it is the only human a priori. Life matures, develops, and aims at death. Death is its very purpose. We live in order to die. Life and death are contained within each other, com-

plete each other, are understandable only in terms of each other. Life takes on its value through death.[41]

In the second part of his argument, Hillman identifies death and suicide:

> Suicide is no longer one of the ways of entering death, but *all death is suicide*, and the choice of method is only more or less evident, whether car-crash, heart-attack, or those acts usually called suicide.[42]

It may be wondered whether these strange utterances constitute an argument at all. Literally, he seems to be saying this: since death is the perfection of life, and since all death is suicide, suicide is the perfection of life. If so, however, then everyone ought to commit suicide as soon as possible, thus rendering the human race extinct. This interpretation of Hillman is a reductio ad absurdum of his argument.

What he probably means is something like the following: Life and death are correlative; each has meaning and value only in relation to the other. Therefore, unless a person seriously reflects on death or suicide as a possible choice, that person cannot appreciate the meaning and value of life itself. Suicide is not just a choice for sick or troubled "souls"—to use Hillman's term for the core of personhood. It is a possible authentic choice for any soul. The possibility of suicide is a necessary condition for affirming the meaning of life. There are no valid moral rules or principles that can determine whether suicide is morally right or wrong. Each person must make his or her own choice whether to live or to die.

Even with this more moderate interpretation, however, his argument contains a latent reductio ad absurdum, for if no suicide is ruled out a priori as immoral, it is logically possible that every soul could decide that suicide is its authentic choice. And if every soul did in fact make that choice, the human race would become extinct. An argument for suicide that places no inherent moral limits on the right to suicide is not rationally defensible.

It may also be objected that the first part of Hillman's argument commits the fallacy of equivocation on the word end. The fallacy of equivocation is committed when a key term in an argument is used in two different senses. In the statement that death is the very purpose of life, let us stipulate that end is a synonym for *purpose*. We may then reformulate the first part of his argument in the following syllogism:

> Major premise: The end of a thing is its perfection.
> Minor premise: Death is the end of life.
> Conclusion: Death is the perfection of life.[43]

In the major premise, *end* means final stage of growth and development, as in Aristotle's example that the end of an acorn is an oak tree. In the minor premise, *end* means final event. Thus, *end* is used in two senses. This equivocation produces the absurd conclusion.

Finally, how should the second part of his argument be interpreted? If he means it literally, that death and suicide are identical, then the term *suicide* is so broad as to be meaningless. Consequently, his entire argument is rendered meaningless. However, there is no indication in what I have cited, or in any of his contextual material, that Hillman makes any distinction between death and suicide.

Hillman's argument is so devoid of rationality that it is incapable of justifying any act of suicide. Therefore, I conclude that the four arguments examined in support of suicide have not altered my tentative position that suicide is prima facie immoral. I now consider whether this position should be made firm in light of the ethical theory developed in chapter 2.

COMMUNITY, JUSTICE, AND SUICIDE

The principle of community applies to intrapersonal actions as well as to interpersonal ones. Thus, it requires us to always have a personal relation with ourself. As previously noted, we may not freely consent to become slaves. If we did, we would have an absolute impersonal relation with ourself. More broadly, we may not allow others to exploit or manipulate us or to otherwise violate our rights. In all these relations, a person is consenting, by his own absolute freedom, to unjust treatment by another. Such consent consists of a direct intention to reduce one's own personhood to that of a thing or function. In these relations, persons lack proper love and respect for themselves and treat themselves in an unjust and heteronomous manner. By contrast, a personal relation with oneself means that the self's motive is self-love (including self-respect) and that the self directly intends the values of autonomy and justice.

It is possible, then, to treat oneself unjustly, thereby having an absolute impersonal relation with oneself. Since justice is the minimal condition of morality and the basic value of a personal relation and of community, if suicide is ever morally permissible, it must be an act of justice toward oneself. Therefore, let us now inquire if one can ever treat oneself justly in committing suicide, or if committing suicide is always and necessarily an act of injustice against oneself. To state it another way: Is suicide always an absolute impersonal act against oneself? Can it ever constitute a personal relation with oneself?

To speak of justice is to speak of the moral domain of rights and their reciprocal or correlative duties. Essential to the constitution of personhood are rights. These rights are sometimes called moral, human, or natural rights. They are contrasted with legal rights, or entitlements, although in many cases the latter are expressions of the former. Since I am not presently concerned with legal rights, I simply use the term *rights*, without any qualification. Rights are inherent and universal: All persons by their very nature possess them. They are not conferred upon us by others or by states. On the contrary, everyone and all states have a duty to recognize and respect them and not to deny or violate them.[44]

If anything is a right, it is the right to life. Indeed, it is the most basic right, for without life, no other rights can be exercised and enjoyed. Therefore, all persons have a duty to respect everyone's right to life, *including their own right to life.* Since I am as much a person as another, I have a duty to respect my own right to life, just as I have a duty to respect another's right to life. In this regard, the right to life is not waivable. Therefore, I may not commit suicide. Suicide is immoral, because it violates one's own right to life. It thus commits an act of injustice against oneself. Suicide constitutes an absolute impersonal act against oneself, thereby violating the principle of community.

The foregoing argument seems to imply that suicide is intrinsically immoral. However, this is not the case, for not every instance of suicide is a violation of one's own right to life. Consequently, not every act of suicide is an injustice, or an absolute impersonal act, against oneself. All rights have their limits, including the right to life. For example, if someone is threatening my life with deadly force and the only way I can prevent him from killing me is by killing him, I do not violate his right to life. This self-defense homicide simply falls outside my unjust assailant's right to life. Similarly, there are situations involving suicide that fall outside the limits of my own right to life in relation to myself. When these limits are reached and exceeded, we may speak of the *right to die.* This right also applies to interpersonal relations involving euthanasia (including assisted suicide), as discussed in chapter 5.

Suicide, then, as I defined it earlier, is a prima facie immoral action, which has a significantly bad direct intention. It is bad in itself to directly intend one's own death, whatever else might be the case about a particular action that has this direct intention. But it does not follow that each and every instance of suicide is immoral, that suicide is an intrinsically immoral action, which has a gravely bad direct intention. There are exceptional situations in which the goodness of a particular action's other moral elements outweighs and overrides the badness of the direct intention. In these situations, a person's right to life with respect to himself or herself has exceeded its limits, and suicide is morally permissible and an exercise of that person's right to die.

There are two types of exceptional situations. In the first, one's quality of life is so low that one is incapable of ever enjoying one's personhood again. In the second, there is a direct and irresoluble conflict between a person's own life and the life (or lives) of others. In these two situations, a person has the right to die, whether it be in the form of suicide, assisted suicide, or euthanasia. These two types are represented, respectively, by the terminally ill cancer patient and by the POW examples previously described. The cancer patient can never again enjoy her personhood (at least not in this life, which is the only concern here), and there is no way for the POW to resolve the conflict between his life and the lives of his comrades. I conclude, then, that suicide is prima facie immoral and that it is morally permissible in these two types of situations. The range of suicide's moral impermissibility and the range of its moral permissibility accord with Rules Three and Five of the principle of intentionality.

Let us now consider some possible objections to my argument. Conservatives sometimes argue that the right to die is invalid, because death is merely an inevitable fact. This fact by itself cannot constitute a right to die. One cannot have a right to do what will happen anyway. My answer is that this objection is based on an elementary confusion between two very different facts of death: the fact of death as such, and the fact that one can choose the conditions of one's death. The right to die is connected with the second fact; this right denotes the morally permissible conditions under which one can terminate one's own life instead of letting nature take its inevitable course. Interestingly, these same conservatives insist on an almost absolute right to life. But life as such is as much a fact as death as such. Nevertheless, no one seriously argues that the fact of life rules out the validity of the right to life.

Conservatives also argue that since the right to life is the most basic right, life is the most basic good. As the most basic good, it must always be intended; it can never be directly violated as it is in suicide. I agree that in general, life is the most basic good. But I deny that basic in this context implies universality and necessity. I deny that life must always be intended no matter what, irrespective of the quality of life. Within the context of morality and personhood, what counts is not the mere organicity of life but a meaningful and significant life. The bare biological life of a person ceases to be a good if it is permanently contrary to either the exercise or the enjoyment of personhood. To say that life is the most basic good in the sense of being a universal and necessary good is to commit the naturalistic fallacy, for in this case, one directly infers the good of life from the mere biological fact of life.

The foregoing analysis implies that the right to life has both a range of waivability and a range of nonwaivability. The latter, of course, is much broader than the former, since suicide is prima facie immoral. Within its nonwaivable range, one has a duty to respect one's right to life by not committing suicide. Within this range, suicide is immoral, because it violates one's right to life. Hence, suicide is an unjust and absolute impersonal act against oneself, which violates the principle of community. Moreover, one has a moral duty to God to preserve one's life and not to commit suicide within the right to life's nonwaivable range. Within its waivable range, the right to life is waived by a person's autonomous consent. If it is waived, the right to die takes effect, and suicide is morally permissible. If the self chooses to exercise its right to die, the self treats itself justly and autonomously and achieves a personal relation with itself. Thus, the principle of community is promoted, and the self does not have a duty to God to preserve its own life.

Finally, an immoral suicide is irrational, and a moral one is rational. An immoral suicide is deficient in objectivity and subjectivity. It is not based on a realistic assessment of one's life situation, taking into consideration all relevant factors, and it is heteronomous rather than autonomous. These deficiencies are clearly the case in adolescent suicide, for example. A rational suicide possesses adequate objectivity and subjectivity. It is based on a realistic assessment of one's life, and it is autonomous.

4

ABORTION, PERSONHOOD, AND COMMUNITY

O f all the controversial moral issues today, abortion is perhaps the most intractable and divisive. More than in any other issue of life and death, there is fundamental disagreement on what kind of being is destroyed. There is no consensus on the ontology of the fetus, no consensus on what kind of being it is. But how one views the fetus has an important bearing on one's moral and legal position on abortion.[1] For example, at one extreme, the pro-life or right-to-life movement, spearheaded by the Roman Catholic Church and the religious Right, holds that the fetus is a person from the moment of conception. Therefore, all abortion is murder, since it involves the direct killing of an innocent person. On the legal level, this movement not only wants a reversal of *Roe v. Wade*,[2] it also wants an almost total ban on abortion, including a constitutional amendment to prohibit it. At the other extreme, the most radical elements of the pro-choice or abortion-on-demand movement do not see abortion as a moral issue at all—unless the law interferes with a woman's reproductive rights, her right to control her own body. Abortion as such is morally neutral, like an appendectomy. It is essentially a medical issue. This moral trivialization of abortion is based on the ontological premise that the fetus is an insignificant form of life. Especially in the first trimester, it may be regarded as merely a piece of protoplasm, tissue, or unborn vegetating matter. As Thomas Szasz writes: "[Abortion] during the first two or three months of gestation [is morally equivalent] to removal of a piece of tissue from the woman's body."[3] Legally, if this moral view had its way, it would extend abortion on demand into the second and third trimesters of pregnancy.

The ontological question, then, is the fundamental question of the abortion issue. It is explored in the first section. Then I develop a moral position on abortion, which is partially based on my ontological conclusions. Next, I examine to what extent, if any, my moral position ought to be legalized. Finally, I address two controversial issues related to abortion: the abortion pill RU-486, and embryonic stem-cell research.

ONTOLOGY OF THE FETUS

Regarding what kind of being the fetus is, ontology must take biology into consideration but also go beyond it.[4] This procedure is especially important in addressing the crucial question of personhood: whether the fetus is a person, and if so, when that personhood begins? In this section, I first examine the fetus from a biological standpoint and then take up the issue of personhood.

Biology of the Fetus

Unlike with suicide, there is no serious dispute concerning the definition of abortion. A modified version of Joel Feinberg's definition may be accepted: abortion is the direct killing of a fetus, either by causing its death in the womb or by removing it from the womb before it is viable, that is, before it can survive outside the mother's womb.[5] This definition has two elements that need further comment. First, since abortion is direct killing, the fetus is killed by direct intention. This rules out so-called indirect abortions, which I discuss later. Only direct abortions, which constitute the vast majority of abortions, are real abortions. Second, the word *fetus* has two meanings. In a broad sense, as contained in the definition of abortion, it denotes a human offspring at any stage of gestation, the average length of which is about nine and one-half lunar months. In this sense, *conceptus* is a synonym for fetus, and I sometimes use the former term for clarity. In a narrower sense, *fetus* denotes a conceptus from about eight weeks of gestation until birth. I use *fetus* in both senses, and it should be clear from the context which meaning is intended.

The end of the eighth week of gestation is important for two reasons. First, by that time, the fetus has developed the basic structure or morphology of its species. It unmistakably looks like a human being, despite its tiny size. Second, brain waves are generally detectable. Prior to eight weeks of gestation, the conceptus is called a *zygote, morula, blastocyst,* or *embryo,* depending on its stage of development. To explain these distinctions, we begin with the process of fertilization. Fertilization occurs when two gametes, one a female ovum (or egg) and the other a male sperm, fuse to form a new cell, the zygote. A gamete is a mature germ cell (a haploid cell) containing a single set of twenty-three chromosomes. Chromosomes are the carriers of all hereditary material in units of DNA and subunits of genes. The zygote is a diploid cell: it has forty-six chromosomes in twenty-three pairs, one set from each parent. Fertilization lasts about twenty-four hours. When it is completed, its process of fusion, by which a male sperm penetrates the female ovum and mingles with it, results in conception, which creates the zygote. Fertilization can occur either naturally or artificially. In the latter case, it takes place by one of several artificial reproductive technologies (ARTs)—also called assisted reproductive technologies. The technology that is relevant here is in vitro fertilization (IVF). In this procedure, a female ovum is fertilized by a male sperm in a petri dish under laboratory conditions, thus producing a zygote. IVF duplicates natural fertilization and conception.[6]

Whether naturally or artificially created, the zygote at the time of conception is a unicellular, microscopic *organism.* It is appropriate to call the zygote an organism for two reasons. First, it has all the genetic information or material that the human individual will ever have, whether in utero or ex utero. Second, because of this fact, the zygote has the potentiality to grow and develop into a human person like the rest of us.

Upon conception, the zygote immediately begins a process of cell division. First it divides into two cells, then four cells, then eight, and so on. After the zygote divides into eight cells, it looks like a mulberry and is called a morula. (At this stage, it can be implanted into the mother's uterus if it has been created artificially.) The morula continues to grow and develop by cell division, which includes cell multiplication and cell differentiation. After two or three days, it starts to develop a central cavity, and is now called a blasto-cyst. At about five days, the blastocyst has acquired about one hundred cells and can now be used for embryonic stem-cell research if created artificially. As the blastocyst continues to grow and develop, it leaves the woman's fal-lopian tube, down which it has been traveling since conception, and enters her uterus. The blastocyst then begins attaching itself to her uterine wall, a process called *implantation*. This process lasts from about six or seven days to thirteen or fourteen days. When implantation is completed by fourteen days, the blastocyst becomes an embryo. For the sake of accuracy, then, many biolo-gists typically refer to zygote, morula, and blastocyst as *pre-embryos*. Because the embryo's uterine environment is so rich and fertile, gestational growth and development now take a quantum leap, as it were. The embryo exists from two weeks to eight weeks of gestation. By eight weeks, the embryo is so advanced in its structural growth that it is now called a fetus in the narrow sense of the term. All these biological distinctions indicate that gestational growth and development are qualitative and not merely quantitative processes. This sug-gests that a fetus at eight months, or even at two months, is a somewhat dif-ferent kind of being than it is at conception.

Nevertheless, because of the continuity of fetal growth, certain constants exist throughout gestation. The most basic constant is that the fetus is a human being at conception in a significant sense of the term. To justify this statement, I need to distinguish the terms *life* and *human life* from *human being*. In the strict sense, life denotes anything that is biological or that has a biological aspect, for example, viruses, amoebas, apes, human organs and parts such as a heart or nose, human sperm and ova, a human fetus, and a human person ex utero. With the term *human life*, we start narrowing the field of biological reality. It excludes all life that cannot be subsumed under the category of human, for example, rep-tiles, insects, birds, nonhuman mammals, amoebas, viruses, and so on. What it includes, however, is still quite broad, for example, human parts and organs, human sperm and ova, a human fetus, and a human person ex utero.

Among nonphilosophers, the ontological question is often posed as follows: is the fetus, even from the moment of conception, life (or human life)? The answer is obviously yes. But the answer is as trivial as it is true, for it is inconsequential in determining the morality of abortion. The answer has virtually no bearing on why the fetus ought to be preserved and protected rather than aborted. Viruses and insects are also life, and a human appendix and tonsils are also human life, and no one claims that to destroy them raises moral questions. If the fetus were merely life, or even human life, abortion would be primarily a medical and legal problem: Is abortion safe? Is it legal?

However, the term *human being* is far more significant than *life* or *human life. Human being* is a synonym for *human organism.* As we have seen, from the moment of conception, the zygote is an organism. And since it is an organism inside a human mother and has a human genetic code, it belongs to the human species. If born, it will be a child and not a cat, dog, and so forth. Even at conception, the fetus is no mere appendage, part, or organ of the mother. It contains all the genetic material that will eventually develop into the complete human person. It rapidly develops its own morphology. At the end of the first month, it has a backbone and head. A rudimentary digestive tract is present, and so are incipient arms and legs. The tube that produces the future heart has been formed, and the organism as a whole is pulsating regularly and propelling blood through microscopic arteries. The embryo has its own independent circulatory, hormonal, and nervous systems. Teleologically, the fetus possesses its own immanent potentiality for growing and developing into a human person. In all biological respects, except for its home (the womb) and its source of nourishment, the fetus is distinct from the mother. Although it is *in* her, it is not part *of* her, as her nose and heart are. These considerations rule out any view of the fetus as a mere piece of tissue, protoplasm, or bit of unborn vegetating matter—expressions that are popular with the most radical abortion-on-demand proponents. Such views can be maintained only by conveniently ignoring the biological evidence. From the moment of conception, then, the fetus is a human being (or human organism). By contrast, *human being* cannot be applied properly to either the unfertilized ovum or to the spermatozoon. Neither gamete is an organism; neither by itself possesses the total genetic material or immanent potentiality that will develop into a human person. Some authors deny that the pre-embryo is an organism because it lacks structure. However, for all the above reasons, the lack of structure is not enough reason not to call it an organism.[7]

At this juncture, however, there are two interrelated problems. First, many authors on abortion argue that just because it may be proper to call the fetus a human being, it does not follow that it is a person.[8] And second, there are different legitimate meanings of human being. Mary Anne Warren distinguishes two meanings of human being: genetic and moral.[9] A *genetic human being* denotes the human organism only insofar as it contains its full genetic code. A *moral human being* is a human being in the full sense of the term, as when we say in the Jeffersonian sense that all humans (and not only men) are endowed with the inalienable rights of life, liberty, and the pursuit of happiness and are full-fledged members of the moral community. According to Warren, only moral human beings are properly called persons. She then goes on to specify five primary criteria of personhood: consciousness, reasoning, self-motivated activity, communication, and self-awareness.[10] By these criteria, she obviously denies that any fetus (or neonate) is a person. When abortion opponents argue that abortion is wrong because (1) the fetus is a human being and (2) it is wrong to kill innocent human beings, this argument, according to her, is fallacious; it commits the fallacy of equivocation on the term *human being*. In premise (1), human being means only a genetic human being. In premise (2), human being means moral human being.

Warren, in my view, convincingly demonstrates that there are different legitimate meanings of human being and that *human being* and *person* are different terms. Indeed, Macmurray suggests a similar distinction between human being and person, although he does not develop it nor apply it to the abortion issue. "My reason for this preference [of 'person' to 'human'] is that the term 'human' tends to carry a biological reference. . . ."[11]

Nevertheless, Warren's distinction between genetic and moral human being is inadequate for three reasons. First, on her view, a moral human being (a human person) does not exist until sometime after birth. Therefore, all fetuses and neonates are merely genetic human beings. This term is too simplistic to cover all human organisms from conception through early infancy. There are two problems here: (1) "genetic human being" does not sufficiently reflect the qualitative growth and development of the fetus for the entire period of gestation, and (2) the term fails to reflect the significant differences between fetushood and infancy. I address the second problem later. Regarding the first problem, we have seen that, at about two months of gestation, the conceptus has attained the basic structural plan of its species and is now called a fetus in the narrower sense. I propose to call a fetus beginning at nine weeks or so a *morphological human being.* From conception to the end of the eighth week, the conceptus is merely a genetic human being. A morphological human being is qualitatively and ontologically higher than merely a genetic one, higher in the sense of more inclusive.

Second, Warren's *moral human being* excludes all merely genetic and all merely morphological human beings from the moral community, for only moral human beings are persons. In her view, only persons belong to the moral community; only persons have moral status.[12] Although I agree that genetic or morphological human beings as such are not persons, I argue later that they still have significant moral status and hence are members of the moral community.

Third, her concept of personhood is also too narrow, if only because it excludes all neonates. Why neonates should be called persons, and when a human being becomes a person, are indeed the most crucial and difficult questions of the abortion issue.

Before I attempt to answer them, I want to emphasize that the personalism expressed in this volume agrees with Warren on two points: (1) some humans may not be persons, and (2) some persons are not humans. Since I have just analyzed the first proposition, I need only comment briefly on the second one. There are several actual or possible kinds of nonhuman persons. As noted earlier, God is a person—at least the God of theism. If extraterrestrial intelligent beings exist, they may be persons. The angels and devils of the Christian tradition are persons. However, their actual existence is a theological issue, not a philosophical one. Finally, some animal rights advocates claim that some higher mammals besides humans may be persons. This claim is investigated in chapter 9. In brief, personalism makes a fundamental distinction between *human being* and *person.*

In sum, I distinguish three ontological terms relevant to the abortion issue: genetic human being, morphological human being, and human person. These three terms represent real qualitative growth and development within a spectrum of continuity and identity. One does not cease to be a genetic human being in becoming a morphological human being. Nor does one cease to be a morphological human being in becoming a human person. A human person, therefore, is secondarily a morphological human being and tertiarily a genetic human being, just as a morphological human being is secondarily a genetic human being. But the reverse is not true. A genetic human being in itself is neither a morphological human being nor a human person, and a morphological human being in itself is not a human person. What we have are three modes of being that constitute a hierarchy of inclusiveness and may be represented by three concentric circles. Hence, the higher includes the lower, and the lower excludes the higher.

Within the context of this triadic distinction, we must now determine when, or at what point, a human being becomes a person. Of course, it may be said that both occur simultaneously, since an ontological difference does not necessarily imply a temporal difference. Pro-life advocates would likely argue that all three of my ontological categories occur at once, that a genetic human being at conception is ipso facto both a morphological human being and a human person—which is why they would say that my distinctions are trivial. To resolve these problems, we need to explore the various theories of *personalization*, that is, theories concerning when personhood begins.[13]

Theories of Personalization

The earliest theory of personalization is *immediate animation*. It holds that personhood begins at conception. Hence, a genetic human being is ipso facto a person. This theory is the implicit position of the pro-life movement and the explicit position of the Roman Catholic Church. Proponents of this position believe that immediately upon conception, God infuses a spiritual soul into the zygote, which animates the zygote and makes it a person. Quite apart from this traditional ensoulment theory, however, contemporary proponents of immediate animation offer four reasons that the newly conceived zygote is a person.

First, and most basically, the zygote has all the genetic material it will ever have, regardless of its stage of growth and development. Since it is certainly a person when it becomes an adult, it must be a person as a zygote. In both cases, the human being has a full genetic code. As John Noonan expresses it:

The positive argument for conception as the decisive moment of humanization [i.e., personalization] is that at conception the new being receives the genetic code. It is this genetic information which determines his characteristics, which is the biological carrier of the possibility of human wisdom, which makes him a self-evolving being. A being with a human genetic code is man [i.e., a person].[14]

Stephen Schwarz offers three additional reasons for immediate animation.[15] He begins his analysis by making a sharp distinction between being a person and functioning as a person; the former is a necessary (but not a sufficient) condition of the latter. Thus, one can be a person without functioning as a person, for example, a sleeping adult or a newly conceived zygote. He then goes on to present three arguments, or "indications," for the personhood of the zygote.

First, there is a continuity of being between the zygote and the adult. "The adult now sleeping is the same being who was once an embryo and a zygote. There is a direct continuity between the zygote at F and the child at E, through to the adult at A."[16]

Second, there is a continuity of essential structure between the zygote and the adult. The zygote has the same essential physical structure as the human being in all its late stages of development. "Thus the zygote has, in primitive form, the physical basis of his basic inherent capacity to function as a person. In the adult this same basis exists in developed form."[17]

Third, there is a continuity of capacities between the zygote and the adult. "The zygote has the capacity to acquire what is needed to learn to function as a person."[18]

All four arguments in support of immediate animation have serious difficulties. In addition, the phenomenon of identical twins represents a formidable objection to the ensoulment theory. This phenomenon occurs when one fetus divides into two fetuses, usually ten to fourteen days after conception. Based on the ensoulment theory of immediate animation, it would seem that one person splits into two persons. But that is impossible, for the spiritual soul that constitutes personhood is, precisely as spiritual, simple and indivisible. To this objection, it is sometimes replied that prior to twinning, two souls are actually present. But this answer contradicts the ensoulment theory, according to which only one soul is needed to animate a body. And prior to twinning, there is only one actual body. More than one soul per body would pose insuperable problems for personal unity and identity.[19]

Noonan's genetic argument maintains that the genetic code is a sufficient condition of personhood. But is it? This claim is implausible. It violates the ordinary, commonsense meaning of personhood. In ordinary language and experience, the concept of human person denotes a set of structural and functional characteristics in addition to the genetic criterion. The zygote's genetic code, then, seems to be merely a necessary condition of human personhood. Furthermore, when the genetic argument is linked with the ensoulment theory, the claim is made that the zygote's genetic code is a sufficient condition for God's creating a soul and infusing it into the zygote. But this claim, too, seems implausible, for the ensoulment theory has its roots in the *hylomorphism* of the Roman Catholic Church's pre-eminent theologian and philosopher, Thomas Aquinas. Following Aristotle's hylomorphism, Aquinas held that the soul is the *form* of the body. Therefore, Aquinas concluded that the fetus must develop a recognizable human body as a sufficient condition for God's infusing it with a soul. Although Aquinas did not pinpoint when this ensoulment occurs, it is clear that it occurs sometime considerably after conception.[20] Aquinas, then, denies that God infuses a personal soul into a formless, microscopic, unicellular zygote. Otherwise, the soul could not be the form of the body.

It is an irony that so many immediate animationists are traditional, conservative Catholics and reject Aquinas's ensoulment theory. Of course, it could be objected, even by an immediate animationist, that just because Aquinas held a position, that does not make it true. However, Aquinas is closer to a plausible conception of personhood than is immediate animation, because of his insistence on structural characteristics of personhood.

Schwarz's three arguments go far beyond Noonan's genetic argument. Let us evaluate each one. His continuity of being argument holds that unless the zygote is a person, there is no continuity of being between the zygote and the adult person. This argument is fallacious. One can say, as I have, or as Warren says, that continuity of being is guaranteed by the fact that at conception the zygote is a genetic human being and continues to be at least a genetic human being for its entire life, whatever else it becomes. No one, especially the immediate animationists, disputes the fact that the human organism from conception until death retains its full genetic code. There is no need to resort to the highly dubious claim that the zygote is a person in order to account for this continuity.

Indeed, if one argues that the zygote is a person because the adult is a person, one commits a version of the *genetic fallacy*. In this fallacy, one reasons that the present nature of something and the nature of its origin are the same because there is some continuity between them. This fallacy has two versions, what I call *forward reasoning* and *backward reasoning*. In the first, one infers what something is now from the nature of its origin. For example, since the original humans 6 million years ago were vegetarians, it is natural and good for us today to be vegetarians. In the second version, one infers the nature of an origin from what something is now. This is the version of the fallacy committed by some immediate animationists when they reason that because we are now persons, the original zygotes we come from are persons. What this fallacy does is to deny the reality of change, of growth and development, of evolution as a process that continually creates new and qualitatively higher and different kinds of beings.

Schwarz's second argument is equally unsound. His claim that the zygote has the same essential structure as any human being at a later stage of development appears to be based on a version of the scientifically discredited theory of *preformation*. According to this theory, the original zygote contains a morphological human being in miniature, with a full complement of microscopic limbs, organs, and structures. Fetal growth and development, then, are quantitative rather than qualitative. It was because of preformation that the Roman Catholic Church, centuries ago, abandoned Aquinas's position in favor of immediate animation. As the science of biology progressed, however, preformation was replaced by the theory of *epigenesis*, according to which the original zygote is an undifferentiated organism that develops all of its organs and structures through a gradual and complex process of growth, cleavage, differentiation, and organization. Fetal growth is as much qualitative as it is quantitative.

Schwarz's third argument, that the zygote is a person because it has the capacity to acquire personal function, simply confuses the important distinction between *capacity* and *potentiality*. In truth, the zygote has the potentiality to acquire personal function. It does not follow that it has the capacity for personal function, as, for example, a sleeping adult has. To speak, as Schwarz does, of the zygote's "capacity to acquire what is needed to learn to function as a person" is to so qualify the term *capacity* that it becomes virtually indistinguishable from potentiality. Later in the chapter, I further develop the distinction between capacity and potentiality. In any event, Schwarz holds that the zygote is a potential person only with respect to functioning as a person. It is an actual person with respect to being a person.[21]

There is still another objection against immediate animation. Since scientists routinely create zygotes by IVF, are they creating persons in laboratories? Some immediate animationists say yes, others say no. Those who say yes reason as follows. Whether zygotes are produced naturally or artificially, God is the principal and ultimate cause of creating persons, because only He infuses a spiritual soul into the zygote, which constitutes its personhood. Parents by natural procreation and scientists by IVF are merely instrumental causes acting under God's principal causality. The difficulty with this argument, however, is precisely the difficulty with the ensoulment theory at conception, which I reviewed earlier.

Other immediate animationists reject this argument. They hold that persons are created by God only by natural fertilization and conception, only by heterosexual intercourse. The problem with this view is that since IVF duplicates this natural process, what difference should it make to God how zygotes are produced? What matters is that the entity is a zygote and this is the moment when immediate animation states that personhood begins. This view is inconsistent with the basic premise of immediate animation. It also seems to turn God into an illogical and moral monster who arbitrarily discriminates against all IVF zygotes by denying them personhood. Furthermore, many of these zygotes will eventually be born and become full-fledged persons like the rest of us, thus compounding the irrationality of this position.

At this point, a distinction can be made between theoretical and practical immediate animation. So far I have been discussing the former view.

Practical immediate animation holds that because of the difficulties with the theory of immediate animation and, indeed, with all other theories of personalization, it cannot be known with certainty exactly when personhood begins. Nevertheless, the newly conceived zygote *may* be a person. Hence, for all practical purposes, we must assume that it is a person, since we must not kill what may be a person. Germain Grisez, a noted conservative Catholic moralist, articulates the full form of this argument ("embryo" here includes a newly conceived zygote):

> In being willing to kill the embryo, we accept responsibility for killing what we must admit *may* be a person. There is some reason to believe it is— namely the *fact* that it is a living, human individual and the inconclusiveness of arguments that try to exclude it from the protected circle of personhood.
>
> *To be willing to kill what for all we know could be a person is to be willing to kill it if it is a person.* And since we cannot absolutely settle if it is a person except by a metaphysical postulate, for all practical purposes we must hold that to be willing to kill the embryo is to be willing to kill a person.[22]

This rather complex argument is actually two interconnected arguments, in which the conclusion of the first argument (contained in paragraph one) is a premise of the second argument (contained in paragraph two). To facilitate a critical evaluation of the argument, I formally restructure it and slightly amend its wording:

Premise one: The zygote-embryo is a living human individual.

Premise two: All arguments against the personhood of the zygote-embryo are inconclusive.

Conclusion: Therefore, the zygote-embryo may be a person.

Premise one: The zygote-embryo may be a person.

Premise two: To kill what may be a person is morally equivalent to killing what is a person.

Conclusion: Therefore, to kill the zygote-embryo is morally equivalent to killing a person.

The argument as a whole fails on premise one of the first argument. All this premise shows is that the zygote-embryo is a genetic human being. From that fact, it does not follow that the zygote-embryo is a person, or even that it may be a person. Genetic humanhood is a necessary condition of human personhood, but not a sufficient condition for it. In view of this fact, and in view of all the foregoing difficulties with the immediate animation theory, I must now issue a flat denial: The newly conceived zygote is certainly *not* a person. Personhood does not begin at conception.

Let us turn now to the second theory of personalization: *mediate animation*. It holds that personhood begins when the developing embryo acquires a recognizable human form and organization. In terms of modern biology, this occurs when the embryo becomes a fetus in the narrower sense—at about two months of gestation. For mediate animation, then, a morphological human being is ipso facto a person. Historically, mediate animation is essentially the position of Aristotle and Aquinas. One of its leading contemporary proponents is the well-known Catholic philosopher Joseph Donceel.[23] Hylomorphism is the philosophical basis of mediate animation: the soul is the form of the body. Specifically, Donceel holds that since the brain is the most important organ of the human body with respect to the human differentia of rationality, a person does not exist until the brain is sufficiently developed to permit the detection of brain waves.

Donceel argues that mediate animation is the authentic Catholic position. Not only was it Aquinas's view but it was also more broadly the Church's traditional position—until it was abandoned in favor of the false theory of preformation. Consequently, Donceel recommends that the Church return to its traditional roots and embrace hylomorphism again. Today, he claims, the Church's doctrine has been infected by Cartesian *dualism*. For Descartes, soul and body are two independent, though interacting, substances or entities. Dualism, it may be said, undermines the unity of the self or person. In effect, one self becomes two selves: a bodily self and a spiritual or mental self.[24] Because of dualism's substantial separation of soul and body, later Cartesians viewed the soul in utero as the efficient cause of the body rather than as its formal cause, as hylomorphism holds.

Another reason for the Catholic Church's support of immediate animation, according to Donceel, was its long-standing opposition to evolution. Immediate animation and preformation tacitly deny in utero evolution. However, the Church has dropped its opposition to evolution, and since mediate animation recognizes the existence of fetal evolution, Donceel argues that the Church should adopt mediate animation to show its acceptance of evolution.

In my view, Donceel has effectively shown that mediate animation is philosophically and scientifically superior to immediate animation. It overcomes the identical twin and in vitro fertilization objections. It rejects preformation and accepts evolution. It comes closer than does immediate animation to a plausible conception of personhood by making personhood dependent on form or structure and minimal brain function. However, its obvious weakness is that a two-month-old fetus, like a zygote, lacks any rational function, or capacity for rational function, usually associated with personhood.

The third theory is based on *quickening*. It holds that personhood begins when the mother first starts experiencing the fetus's movements in her body, usually somewhere between twelve and sixteen weeks. According to this view, the fetus is now "alive" and thus a person. Again, the major problem is one of function. Random, sporadic movements of the fetus are far below the level of rational functioning constitutive of personhood.

The fourth theory is that personhood begins with *viability*.[25] In general, viability begins at twenty-six weeks. Nearly all healthy babies born prematurely at twenty-eight weeks survive. The earliest point of viability is believed to be between twenty-three and twenty-four weeks. The likelihood of survival before twenty-three weeks is very low, primarily because the fetus's lungs are too underdeveloped for it to breathe on its own. However, on October 24, 2006, a baby named Amillia Taylor was born at twenty-one weeks and six days. She survived and is doing well. Amillia holds the world record for the youngest preemie.[26]

This theory is quite popular. Proponents emphasize the greater independence of a viable versus a nonviable fetus. Still, a viable fetus, like a newborn infant, is almost totally helpless and dependent on an adult person or persons for its survival. And a viable fetus's capacity to breathe on its own is certainly not a rational function constitutive of personhood. Nevertheless, viability may be, to borrow Feinberg's term, a *superficial characteristic* of personhood, a clue or indication of what really constitutes personhood.[27] We shall see.

The fifth theory is that personhood begins *at birth*. This is the position of traditional Anglo-American law and of the US Supreme Court in *Roe v. Wade*. It is also Macmurray's position. Macmurray holds that personhood begins at birth, because birth is the beginning of mutuality. As he expresses it:

> The baby is not an animal organism, but a person, or in traditional terms, a rational being. . . . He can live only through other people and in dynamic relation with them. In virtue of this fact he is a person, for the personal is constituted by the relation of persons. His rationality is already present, though only germinally, in the fact that he lives and can only live by communication. His essential natural endowment is the impulse to communicate with another human being.[28]

Macmurray specifically denies that personhood begins *after* birth.[29] However, he is unconcerned with the status of the fetus and is silent on the subject.

The at-birth theory has several strengths. First, the newborn infant (or neonate) has more function than a fetus: It breathes, it cries, it sucks, it enters into a variety of social relations. Second, the beginning of personhood can be determined with precision. Third, most people would be against establishing personhood any later than birth on moral grounds, to avoid the moral permissibility of infanticide. However, as critics such as Warren emphasize, a newborn is still not a person in a commonsense meaning of the term: it lacks actual rational function.

The sixth and final position is that personhood begins sometime *after birth*. In this view, personhood consists of some minimal level of actual, rational function. Michael Tooley, for example, holds that self-consciousness must be present for personhood to exist.[30] Warren, we have seen, lists five criteria of personhood. Moreover, only persons have rights in the strict and full sense. Therefore, prior to the possession of these functions, infants and a fortiori fetuses are not persons and do not have any rights, including the right to life. On that basis, Warren and Tooley hold that infanticide and full-term abortion are morally permissible.

The major objection to the after-birth theory is that it permits infanticide. Unlike abortion, society virtually condemns infanticide; it draws a sharp moral line between the infant and the fetus. As we have seen, traditional Anglo-American law holds that personhood begins at birth. However, just because society finds a practice morally unacceptable does not prove that the practice is really or objectively morally wrong. Philosophy is based on reason, not majority opinion or social custom. I have already rejected ethical relativism, and we certainly want to avoid committing the fallacy of argumentum ad populum. According to this fallacy, something is true because it is supported by the people, by majority opinion. But this reasoning is obviously fallacious. For example, the vast majority once believed that Earth was flat, and that there was nothing wrong in denying women the right to vote. Still, it may be objected that the after-birth theory is counterintuitive and wrongheaded. If so, this theory's wrongness must be established by rational argument, as I will try to do shortly.

In any event, the strength of the after-birth theory is that it is the only one that appears to be consistent with an ordinary, commonsense view of personhood, which consists of some capacity of rational function. A dilemma is thus reached in the abortion debate. The earlier we establish the beginning of personhood for the purpose of protecting the unborn and the newborn, the more we adopt a concept of personhood that contradicts its ordinary, commonsense meaning. Conversely, the later we establish the beginning of personhood, the more we approach its ordinary, commonsense meaning precisely at the expense of counterintuitively permitting both late abortion and infanticide. Is there any way out of this dilemma? Is it really a dilemma? Or is it instead based on certain misconceptions?

To answer these questions, we must have some idea of what personhood is. In chapter 1, I developed three essential aspects or dimensions of human personhood: mutuality, agency, and reason (rationality). From an ontogenetic standpoint, mutuality is the original dimension, for it is the necessary, concrete context in which the agency and rationality of individual persons emerge and become operative. On this ontological foundation, I now develop a version of the viability theory as my own theory of personalization. I call it the *viability-mutuality* theory.

I begin with Macmurray's views. As we have seen, Macmurray holds that mutuality begins at birth. This is true if we speak of operative mutuality. But a distinction must be made here between *operative* mutuality and the *capacity* (or capability) for mutuality. Since a viable fetus is one that can survive if born, a viable fetus has the capacity for mutuality, which becomes operative at birth. In this sense, the capacity for mutuality is actual and not merely potential. Prior to viability, a fetus has only the potentiality for mutuality, since it lacks the capacity to survive outside the womb. Therefore, since mutuality is the original dimension of personhood, and since the capacity for mutuality begins at viability, I conclude that *personhood begins at viability*.[31] To further justify this conclusion, I must now exhibit some important differences between the mother-infant and mother-fetus relation.

Birth is the beginning of operative mutuality, because, at birth, the infant begins a *communicative* relation with primarily its mother and also with others. Prior to birth, the fetus has a *parasitic* relation with its mother.[32] The fetus lives in the mother and is biologically attached to her. The mother is the host organism. Through the umbilical cord, she provides the fetus with nourishment, and her womb provides the fetus with shelter. And if the mother dies, the fetus ipso facto dies, unless it is viable and can be saved. By contrast, mother and infant are not organically attached; the infant lives neither in nor on the mother. To be sure, the infant is quite helpless and completely dependent on his mother—or a mother substitute. He can make only a few random movements and reflexes. He has no actual power of locomotion and purposive behavior. Nevertheless, from the moment of birth, the parasitic relation is replaced by a mutual or communicative one. It is not merely that the umbilical cord is broken and the infant becomes a biologically separate being capable of breathing on its own. These are merely superficial characteristics of personhood. More significantly, these biological phenomena are necessary conditions for the infant to enter into a network of communicative relations: first and foremost with her mother, who holds, fondles, and nurses her, as the infant emits stimuli such as crying, which call for a communicative response from the mother; second, with the father and other family members and friends who visit her, hold her, and exult in her presence; third, with the hospital staff, who care for many of her needs; and, finally, with the larger society, which now requires that she be given a legal name, thus symbolizing society's recognition that she is a person. The neonate has much more individuality than the fetus. As a result, there is a basic difference between the way the mother cares for her fetus and the way she cares for her infant. When she is pregnant, she goes to her obstetrician or gynecologist to take care of primarily herself. After the infant is born, she takes her baby to a pediatrician to take care of him.

Consequently, although a viable fetus has an operative parasitic relation with its mother, it has the capacity for a communicative relation, unlike a previable fetus, which lacks such a capacity and merely has a potentiality for a communicative relation. All viable fetuses, therefore, are persons, but no previable fetuses are persons. To be on the safe side, I fix the beginning of viability at twenty-one weeks of gestation. I stipulate, then, that personhood begins at twenty-one weeks of gestation, while recognizing, of course, that in virtually all cases, it actually begins later. But in this case, we truly do not want to kill what might be a person. Prior to twenty-one weeks, a previable fetus is only a genetic human being for the first eight weeks of gestation and then only a morphological human being from nine weeks to viability.

However, just because a previable fetus is not an actual person, it does not follow that it is an insignificant being. First of all, it is a potential person and the only kind of being that is known for certain to be a potential person. Second, it is an actual human being—either genetic or morphological. For both reasons, a previable fetus is worth protecting and nurturing even though its ontological status is lower than that of persons.[33] Moreover, a morphological human being is higher than a merely genetic human being, just as a person is higher than a morphological human being. What bearing this ontology has on the morality of abortion is now considered.

MORAL IMPLICATIONS

The moral question of abortion can be posed as follows: At what stage of fetal development, if any, and for what reasons, if any, is abortion morally justifiable? In response to this question, we must first distinguish five major moral positions on abortion: conservative, extreme conservative, moderate, liberal, and extreme liberal. The *conservative* position holds that all abortion is immoral, except to save the mother's life. For the *extreme conservative* position, all abortion is immoral, even to save the mother's life. This position might be called the Roman Catholic view, but it is shared by others, both non-Catholic Christians and non-Christians. The *moderate* position holds that abortion is morally permissible before viability for rape, incest, or if the mother's or child's physical or mental health would probably be gravely impaired. Upon viability, abortion is permissible only to save the mother's life. For the *liberal* position, all abortion is morally permissible before viability. Upon viability, it is permissible only to save the mother's life or health. Finally, the *extreme liberal* position holds that abortion is morally permissible at any stage of gestation and for any reason whatsoever. In the concrete, however, there are variations of these positions, especially the non-extreme ones.[34]

I now explain the official moral view of the Catholic Church on abortion as perhaps the most important version of the extreme conservative position. It is structured by the double effect principle. The Roman Catholic Church does not permit abortion under any circumstances—not even to save the mother's life—unless the abortion is indirect. However, as we have seen, indirect abortion falls outside the definition of abortion, so the official Catholic position is that all (direct) abortion is immoral; abortion, regardless of the stage of gestation, is an intrinsically immoral action. In Catholic theology, there are at least two situations involving indirect abortion: a cancerous uterus and an ectopic pregnancy. Here the action's intention is to give the mother essential, life-saving medical care, which she has a right to receive. The end is to save her life by means of the necessary surgery. The indirect consequence of the action is the death of the fetus. In contrast, in direct abortion, abortion is part of the action's intention: it is either the means or the end of action. All such abortion is impermissible, says the Church, including abortion as a means of saving the mother's life, even if it is medically certain that by doing nothing, both mother and fetus will die. If we abort the fetus to save the mother, we commit murder. But if we do nothing, we do nothing immoral, since both mother and fetus die from a tragic natural event. Such reasoning is based on the doing/allowing doctrine carried to its ultimate extreme.

I now develop my own moral position as a variation of the moderate position. To begin with, I apply the principle of community to abortion. Clearly, it can be applied to viable fetuses, since they are persons. A fortiori, the mother and others affected by an abortion are persons. Although previable fetuses are not actual persons, they are potential persons, and they are actual human beings. Accordingly, it seems a reasonable extension of the principle of community to bring them analogously under the principle. Such a subsumption implies that previable fetuses have less moral status than persons do. In a similar vein, R. M. Hare has argued that the Golden Rule and other equivalent moral principles can be logically extended to fetuses on the grounds that they are potential persons.[35]

An explanation of the term *moral status* is in order here. Moral status denotes a type of moral value. It is the moral value that higher kinds of beings have insofar as they are higher beings. I distinguish at least three kinds of higher beings: persons, previable fetuses, and sentient animals. Within each class, all individual members possess moral status equally. But the classes as such do not share moral status equally. Since persons are higher beings than previable fetuses and sentient animals (see chapter 9), persons possess a higher moral status than do the other two classes of beings. The *moral status of persons* is equivalent to the more traditional term "dignity of persons" or to Kant's view that all persons as persons have "intrinsic," "unconditioned," or "absolute" value. Nevertheless, all beings with moral status belong to the global moral community and are worthy of greater consideration and protection than are beings without moral status.

Since viable fetuses are persons, it follows that aborting a viable fetus is murderous and, therefore, immoral, with one exception. If a viable fetus constitutes a serious threat to the mother's life, and the only way to save the mother is to kill the fetus, abortion is morally permissible. Although such cases are rare, they can occur. As Jonathan Bennett observes:

> A woman in labor will certainly die unless an operation is performed in which the head of her unborn child is crushed or dissected; while if it is not performed, the child can be delivered, alive, by post-mortem Caesarian section.[36]

The obvious objection here is that even a viable fetus that is a threat to the mother's life is as innocent as one which is not such a threat. And since, according to my view, both are persons, the definition of murder is equally satisfied in both cases: the direct killing of an innocent person.

My reply to this objection is a version of the self-defense argument. Based on the principle of self-defense, the mother has a right to use whatever force is necessary, including deadly force, to protect and preserve her life against any person who constitutes an imminent and serious threat to her life. It does not matter whether the threatener has intention or not, is sane or insane, impulsive or premeditative—or a viable fetus. Nor does it matter if the threatener is aggressive or nonaggressive, innocent or noninnocent. What matters is the nature of the threat itself, that it is lethal. Therefore, although mother and viable fetus, as persons, have an equal right to life in the abstract, the mother's right to life takes precedence over the fetus's right to life in this concrete situation. The fetus, as a matter of fact, is threatening the life of the mother, and the mother has a right to defend herself against all deadly threats. Otherwise, we would be forced to conclude that the mother must do nothing and allow herself to die, to be killed by her fetus. We would then imply that the fetus's right to life takes precedence over the mother's right to life. But this conclusion is unreasonable. It exhibits defects in the doctrines of double effect and doing/allowing.

Consequently, although the viable fetus in this situation is innocent—as Feinberg observes, it did not choose to threaten its mother, it did not ask to be born[37]—its innocence does not alter the fact that it is a lethal threat to the mother. And this threat, I submit, overrides the fetus's innocence, so that its abortion is morally permissible and nonmurderous. That the fetus is a lethal threat has greater moral importance than its innocence. As a result, the fetus is not treated unjustly. Hence, no absolute impersonal act is committed against it, and the principle of community is not violated.[38]

Unless the mother's life is at stake, however, aborting a viable fetus is morally impermissible. Outside this exception, aborting a viable fetus is an absolute impersonal act and therefore a violation of community. Still, in view of this exception, the abortion of a viable fetus is a prima facie rather than an intrinsically immoral type of action. As such, its direct intention is significantly bad, not gravely bad. Therefore, its morality is governed by Rules Three and Five of the principle of intentionality.

I turn now to the morality of aborting previable fetuses. It is more complicated than the morality of aborting viable fetuses for three reasons. First, since a previable fetus is not a person, the moral conflict of abortion is not between beings of equal moral status. A previable fetus has less moral status than its mother and any others with whom its life may be in conflict. Therefore, it might seem, as some have argued, that the interests of persons always (or at least in most cases) override those of the fetus, and that an abortion-on-demand policy ought to be the norm for the entire period that the fetus is not a person. Warren, for example, holds this view:

> Neither a fetus' resemblance to a person, nor its potential for becoming a person provides any basis whatever for the claim that it has any significant right to life. Consequently, a woman's right to protect her health, happiness, freedom, and even her life, by terminating an unwanted pregnancy, will always override whatever right to life it may be appropriate to ascribe to a fetus, even a fully developed one. . . . Thus . . . the laws which restrict the right to obtain an abortion, or limit the period of pregnancy during which an abortion may be performed, are a wholly unjustified violation of a woman's most basic moral and constitutional rights.[39]

Since Warren holds that all fetuses are genetic human beings and not persons, it follows for her that the rights and interests of the mother, as a person, always take precedence over those of the fetus, regardless of its age.

Since I have concluded that viable fetuses are persons, Warren's argument is fallacious as it applies to them. However, her argument is unsound even when it is applied to previable fetuses, because of the second reason that the morality of aborting previable fetuses is more complicated than that of aborting viable fetuses: although previable fetuses have less moral status than persons do, *they still have a significant moral status.* For Warren, however, they have no moral status, since they are not persons, not moral human beings, and thus not members of the moral community. By contrast, I contend that since previable fetuses do have significant moral status, there always exists a moral conflict in abortion situations between the previable fetus and its mother—and any others whose good or well-being is affected by abortion. In some cases—indeed, in many cases—this conflict ought to be resolved in favor of the fetus; in other cases, it ought to be resolved in favor of the mother.

The third reason that the morality of aborting previable fetuses is more complicated concerns my distinction between a morphological human being and a genetic human being. Depending on its stage of gestation, a previable fetus will be merely a genetic human being or a morphological human being. The latter has a higher moral status than the former. This difference in moral status likewise has a bearing on the morality of aborting previable fetuses.

I now attempt to translate these three reasons into a moral position or policy. Since a previable fetus has significant moral status, there must be serious reasons for having an abortion. Even more serious reasons must exist for aborting a fetus after two months, when a genetic human being becomes a morphological one. In both cases, less serious reasons are required than in the case of aborting a viable fetus. There are four reasons that morally justify abortion for the entire previable term of twenty-one weeks. A fifth reason justifies abortion only in the first eight weeks.

1. Since the abortion of a viable fetus is morally permissible if it is a serious threat to the life of the mother, the abortion of a previable fetus is a fortiori morally permissible if the mother's life is at stake. In the case of a previable fetus, however, we can add another argument to the self-defense argument. A previable fetus has less value (i.e., less moral status) than the mother. Consequently, if a previable fetus constitutes a serious threat to the life of the mother, her greater moral status than that of the previable fetus outweighs and overrides it, and so in this situation abortion is morally permissible.

2. If the previable fetus is a serious threat to the physical or mental health of the mother, abortion is morally permissible. The threat must be serious enough so that if the pregnancy is allowed to continue, it is likely that the woman will not have the physical or mental capacity to raise the child, and there are no feasible alternatives open to her. The situation becomes even more severe if the woman has a family to care for. Hence, if she is forced to bear and raise the child, her ability to exercise, much less enjoy, her personhood will be greatly diminished, to the detriment of the well-being of the child.

3. In the case of rape or incest, abortion is morally permissible. True, a woman can condone the existence of such offspring if she so chooses; that is her right. If she does, however, and the previable fetus is allowed to become viable, she cannot then change her mind and decide to abort it, for it is now a person with an inherent right to life.

4. If the fetus has a serious predictable deformity, abortion is morally permissible. Since the fetus is a potential person, we have to ask what that potential is and what will be the consequences for others if the fetus is allowed to be born. More specifically, we must ask such questions as: Will the deformity adversely affect the family's community in a serious way? What impact will the infant have on the mother's health? Will he be such a physical and financial burden on the family that other children are deprived of such goods as education, suitable clothing, and even an adequate diet? If the infant must be cared for by a social agency, what will be the cost in relation to quality of life? When all these sorts of questions are answered, the fetus's potential content of personhood may be low enough, and its adverse consequences on mother, family, and society serious enough, to justify abortion.

5. Abortion is morally permissible if severe overpopulation exists, either in a family or in a society. In this situation, the fetus, if allowed to be born, would be a serious burden on the community of a family or of a society. Overpopulation on a societal level involves both a dense population rate and poverty. On the family level, overpopulation involves the issues of adequate housing and financial support for all members of the family. However, the state does not have the right to impose abortion on families; abortion is a decision for parents or individuals to make. Overpopulation is not as serious a reason for having an abortion as the other four reasons, so it is a morally justifiable reason for abortion only when the fetus is merely a genetic human being, or for the first eight weeks of gestation.

Earth's growing overpopulation contributes to massive poverty that exacerbates the abortion problem worldwide. The world's population has grown exponentially since about 1800, when it passed the one billion mark. Today, Earth's population is over seven billion and is expected to reach nine billion by 2050. Ninety percent of the population growth is in the poorest countries, which often do not have contraceptive devices and information. As a result, abortion is used as a means of birth control, and in a wider sense, population control. Under these conditions, abortion is morally permissible in lieu of contraception. Of course, contraception is morally better than abortion. But in the absence of contraception, it is better for women to have abortions than for them to subsequently contribute to world poverty and to put additional burdens on Earth's limited and dwindling natural resources.[40] In this context, there is a practical contradiction in the Roman Catholic Church's absolute opposition to both contraception and abortion. If one is serious about reducing abortion rates, one ought to favor contraception. The one thing on which abortion opponents and proponents agree is that preventing abortions is better than performing abortions. An ounce of prevention is worth a pound of cure. More broadly, the social problem of abortion cannot be effectively tackled unless it is seen as enmeshed in a cluster of other problems such as overpopulation, contraception, sex education, social welfare legislation, realistic alternatives to abortion, sterilization, premarital sex, and so forth. The social problem of abortion is only part of a whole nexus of problems. In particular, we must eliminate as far as possible those untoward pregnancies that create the situations in which abortion is considered an appropriate or feasible alternative and preclude the use of abortion as a primary means of birth control. Society must address not only the morality and legality of abortion but its causes as well. Many immoral abortions can be prevented by eliminating their social causes; it is not enough to moralize about abortion, much less to pass restrictive or repressive abortion laws. The United Nations estimates that meeting the needs of the 201 million women worldwide who do not have access to contraception could prevent annually 52 million unwanted pregnancies, 22 million abortions, 1.4 million infant deaths, and 142,000 pregnancy-related deaths. In the words of Lester Brown: "Filling the family planning gap may be the most urgent item on the global agenda. The benefits are enormous and the costs are minimal." [41]

In terms of my moral spectrum, I have developed a variation of the moderate position. There is no moral justification, in my view, for performing anywhere near the 1.2 million abortions performed annually in the United States.[42] But neither is there any moral justification for the pro-life position, or the Roman Catholic position, or any position close to them. In my own terminology, abortion is prima facie immoral. It has a significantly bad direct intention and is governed by Rules Three and Five of the principle of intentionality. As we have seen, when the abortion of a viable fetus is morally impermissible, it constitutes an absolute impersonal act. By comparison, when the abortion of a previable fetus is morally impermissible, it is analogous to an absolute impersonal act. It is analogous, because the previable fetus is not an actual person but a potential person, although it is an actual human being. In either case, abortion is a violation of the principle of community.

Before I turn to the legal question, I consider two other noteworthy approaches to the morality of abortion. The first is developed by Don Marquis. In two well-reasoned articles, he argues that all theories of abortion based on the ontological or moral status of the fetus are mistaken, because they are irreconcilably at odds with each other and thus incapable of resolving the moral issue of abortion.[43] For him, abortion is prima facie immoral for the same reason killing adults and children is prima facie immoral: it deprives fetuses of a "future like ours" (FLO), a future having the same kind of experiences, activities, projects, and enjoyments. There are four exceptions in which abortion is morally permissible: (1) rape, (2) the first fourteen days of gestation when the fetus is not yet an "individual," (3) a threat to the woman's life, and (4) an ancephalic fetus. I comment only on his main position concerning why abortion is prima facie immoral.

Marquis' moral position seems to be a development of Hare's view that abortion is wrong in general because the fetus is a potential person. I partially agree with Marquis. One reason killing adults, children, and fetuses is morally wrong is that it deprives all of them of a meaningful future. But that is not the only reason such killing is wrong. In effect, what Marquis does is to take Aristotle's distinction between actuality and potentiality, and focus exclusively on future potentiality. However, since actual being is prior to and grounds potential being, the fundamental reason why killing adults, children, and viable fetuses is wrong is that they are actual persons. As a result, they have a high moral status. Although the ontological and moral status of previable fetuses is not as high as that of persons, it is still significant because of the fact that they are the only nonpersons who have an FLO. Therefore, their actual being and corresponding moral status are high or significant enough to justify calling their killing prima facie immoral. Actual being and potential being are reciprocal; one cannot separate them, as Marquis does.

The second approach to the morality of abortion is virtue theory. This is Rosiland Hursthouse's approach. She develops a virtue theory based on Aristotle's idea of eudaimonia, which she interprets as human "flourishing" or "living well." This theory leads her to a moderate position on abortion.[44] While there is nothing wrong with this approach to abortion or to any other moral issue for that matter, it does show the limitation of virtue theory in general. Virtues, as moral habits, are subjective dispositions that enable persons to *do* what is right and good, and not merely know them. Virtues are gradually cultivated by a person performing a series of actions of the same kind, for example, courage. But they presuppose that we already *know* what is right and good. This knowledge is provided by an ethical theory consisting of a system of values (or goods), principles, and rules, whose practical dimension is a system of virtues. No ethical theory can be complete without an account of virtue. By the same token, no virtue theory by itself can constitute a complete or comprehensive ethical theory. In a sense, virtue theory is question begging. To say that justice is a virtue does not tell us what justice is; it only tells us that we must have the power to act justly, which is trivial and question-begging. In the first two chapters, I did not speak of virtue at all, but this omission was due to space limitations. These few remarks on virtue partially correct this omission.

ABORTION AND THE LAW

Just because an action is immoral, it does not follow that it should be made illegal. There are at least two problems in translating morality into legality. First, society has to consider the enforceability of a law. And second, in a diverse and pluralistic society such as the United States, moral controversy on issues such as abortion is inevitable and substantial, and to some extent we must accommodate differing moral views. This is especially the case in a society that claims to be democratic. Moral and religious fanaticism must be avoided. We must be careful that the moral views of one group are not imposed on the rest of society, when reasonable people disagree on an issue.

It would be undesirable, even impossible, then, to make every immoral action illegal. Therefore, the question is: What kinds of immoral acts ought to be illegal? I provisionally accept Aquinas's answer, which appears to be reasonable:

> Human law is framed for a number of human beings, the majority of whom are not perfect in virtue. Wherefore human laws do not forbid all vices, from which the virtuous abstain, but only the more grievous vices, from which it is possible for the majority to abstain; and chiefly those that are to the hurt of others, without the prohibition of which human society could not be maintained: thus human law prohibits murder, theft and such-like.[45]

Implied in this passage are three conditions for making an immoral action illegal: (1) the action must be seriously immoral, (2) the majority in society must agree that the action is seriously immoral in order to ensure the law's enforceability, and (3) the action must primarily harm others. However, to prevent a possible tyranny of the majority under condition (2), another condition must be added: (4) a moral position, in the form of a proposed law, cannot conflict with the basic rights of persons, especially human rights; and if the society in question is a constitutional democracy such as the United States, a moral position cannot conflict with the constitutional and civil rights of its citizens. If a moral position does, it cannot be translated into public law; it must remain a privately held belief.

Since a viable fetus is a person, the first and third conditions of my moral position are satisfied with respect to viable fetuses. Moreover, the second condition is approximately satisfied, because most reasonable people probably agree that a viable fetus is either a person or some kind of significant being whose killing would be seriously immoral. Consequently, restrictive abortion laws applying to viable fetuses as permitted by *Roe v. Wade* are reasonable. In *Roe*, the Court fixed the beginning of viability at twenty-four weeks, or the beginning of the third trimester of pregnancy. Although the Court denied that a viable fetus is a person, it claimed that it is *potential life*, an unfortunate term that probably roughly means sufficient potentiality of personhood worth protecting legally. In any event, the Court ruled that in the last trimester the various states may prohibit abortions except when it is necessary to preserve the mother's life or health. Admittedly, the word *health* is vague. In my view, it is too broad to constitute a valid reason for the legalization of aborting a viable fetus, even though late-term abortions are extremely rare.[46] The health hazard should be specified as serious. However, since my moral position permits abortion from twenty-one weeks on *only* if the mother's life is at stake, it is more restrictive than *Roe v. Wade*. Since *Roe* is the landmark Supreme Court decision on abortion that establishes a woman's constitutional right of abortion within the limits it specifies, the fourth condition is not satisfied, and so the elements of my moral position that differ from *Roe* must take a backseat to it. I address the problem of morality and the law in greater detail in chapter 8.

Two of the four foregoing conditions cannot be satisfied with respect to my moral policy on previable fetuses. The third condition cannot be satisfied, since "others" means other persons, and the previable fetus is not a person. The first condition, though, is satisfied. Abortion is prima facie immoral, regardless of the fetus's stage of previability. But the second condition is not satisfied, for it is doubtful that a majority agree with my moral position. Moreover, the fourth condition is not satisfied, since my moral position is considerably more conservative than *Roe*. Most of the moral controversy pertains to earlier, previable stages. Indeed, the earlier the stage, the stronger the controversy becomes, primarily because there are such sharply divided views on the ontological status of the fetus at its earliest stages. For this reason, it was not unreasonable for *Roe* to conclude that all abortion during the first trimester ought to be legal. The Court did not think it was its place to settle difficult philosophical and theological disputes, especially those concerning personhood. Moreover, during this period, as the Court emphasized, abortion is safe (indeed, safer than childbirth) but thereafter becomes increasingly hazardous to the mother. The Court was vague about what kind of laws the states may pass pertaining to the second trimester. It ruled that the states may regulate abortion to the extent that such regulation reasonably relates to the preservation and protection of maternal health. However, since the Court's ruling has been interpreted in practice as prohibiting many second trimester abortions, the ruling does not seem unreasonable in relation to majority opinion.

I am not saying that *Roe* is perfect—far from it. Its ontological foundation is weak, and some of its specific rulings and key concepts are vague. Although its constitutional basis has been strongly criticized by conservatives, a thorough evaluation of this point is beyond the scope of this chapter.

Despite its flaws, *Roe v. Wade* represents a reasonable legal position on abortion in the light of our four conditions. On such an important moral and legal issue as a woman's right to have an abortion, justice probably requires one uniform federal standard. A woman's moral right to abortion should not depend on the will of fifty different state legislatures. It is morally unjustifiable that a woman in one state should have more of a legal right to abortion than a woman in another state. Abortion rights should not depend on geographical accident.

Nevertheless, after *Roe*, the Court has been moving in the direction of returning abortion rights to the various states. In *Webster v. Reproductive Health Services*,[47] the Court upheld the constitutionality of a Missouri law that requires doctors to test for the viability of a fetus at twenty weeks and sharply restricts the availability of publicly funded abortion services. In doing so, the Court invited state legislatures to experiment with new laws designed to limit access to abortion. The Court also criticized *Roe*'s emphasis on viability and its division of pregnancy into trimesters.

However, testing for viability at twenty weeks is a little too early, although one may certainly question whether twenty-four weeks is too late. I have fixed viability at twenty-one weeks. As a matter of law, these differences can be fine-tuned to reflect the best and latest available evidence. Moreover, as I have explained, *Roe*'s trimester framework seems reasonable enough as a legal policy. Although it is true that *Roe* should have provided a sounder justification for the importance of viability, its trimester framework is far more rational than fifty potentially different sets of state abortion laws. Abortion rights ought not to be put on the same level as speed-limit laws.

Three years after *Webster*, in 1992, the Supreme Court handed down another major decision on abortion, *Planned Parenthood v. Casey*.[48] As in the Webster decision, the Court wanted to return abortion to the states. It ruled that states are free to restrict abortion, so long as abortion laws do not place an "undue burden" on women—Justice Sandra Day O'Connor's standard. Using this standard, the Court made the following rulings on a Pennsylvania law: (1) it could impose a twenty-four-hour waiting period before a woman has an abortion; (2) it could require doctors to tell women about other options; (3) it could demand parental notification for minors, although states must provide a "judicial bypass," allowing minors to seek permission from a judge in lieu of parental notification; and (4) it could require doctors to provide statistical information about abortion patients. The Court ruled, however, that Pennsylvania could not force a woman to notify her husband about an abortion.[49]

Casey, like *Webster*, chipped away at *Roe* but did not overturn it. The standard of undue burden is far more vague than anything proposed by *Roe*. It is so vague that it is unclear how much it challenges *Roe*. As things now stand, *Roe* is still the basic law of the land on abortion.

Opponents of *Roe* and of abortion in general want to make abortion illegal for two reasons. First, of course, they believe abortion is immoral. Second, they think its illegality will significantly reduce the total number of abortions. The second reason is false. An important new study on abortion trends conducted jointly by the Guttmacher Institute and the World Health Organization (WHO) reached four conclusions: (1) the number of abortions worldwide decreased from about 46 million to 42 million between 1995 and 2003; (2) abortion rates declined more in developed countries where it is generally safe and legal than in developing countries where it is mostly illegal and unsafe; (3) abortion rates in 2003 were approximately equal in developed and developing regions; and (4) half the 42 million abortions were performed by unskilled persons or in unhygienic conditions.[50] It is common knowledge that abortion in the first trimester is inherently safe (safer than childbirth), providing it is legal, and that making it illegal will substantially increase abortion's fatality and major injury rate for women. Consequently, there is no good (much less compelling) reason to make abortion illegal in the first trimester of pregnancy, regardless of one's moral views on abortion.

I now comment on a late-term abortion procedure that is politically controversial: partial-birth abortion. The term *partial-birth abortion* was coined by opponents of the procedure that physicians call intact dilation and extraction. In the procedure, a fetus is removed feetfirst. Then an incision is made in its head to suck out its brain. The skull collapses and the head is removed from the birth canal. This extreme procedure is used rarely; it accounts for only about 450 to 2,000 abortions annually in the United States. On the political and legal level, it is interesting to note that the main debate has not been whether the procedure should be used at all, but whether it should be performed only if the mother's life is at stake (opponents) or performed to protect her health as well as her life (proponents). Hence, so-called opponents of partial-birth abortion do not absolutely oppose it.

Partial-birth abortion is the least used of three methods of performing late-term abortions (i.e., those occurring after twenty weeks of pregnancy). The other two methods are "classic" dilation and extraction, in which a fetus is scraped out with serrated forceps and thus dismembered and killed, and the injection of a fetus with a fatal solution and its postmortem delivery. Most late abortions take place between twenty and twenty-four weeks. Since all three procedures appear to be equally gruesome, it is puzzling that conservatives have focused only on so-called partial-birth abortion, especially since it is the least common. In my view, there is no moral difference among them, and there should be no legal difference either. Still, if late abortions are performed for serious medical reasons, they should occur as close to twenty weeks as possible. After twenty-one weeks, I support abortion only to save the life of the mother.[51]

In June 2000, the US Supreme Court struck down the constitutionality of state laws that prohibit partial-birth abortions. In *Stenberg v. Carhart* (5–4), the Court ruled that in some extreme cases partial-birth abortion may be the most medically appropriate method of abortion. The ruling specifically invalidated a Nebraska statute and rendered unconstitutional similar statutes in thirty other states.[52] The Court gave two reasons for declaring the Nebraska statute unconstitutional. First, it lacked any exception for the preservation of the health of the mother, in violation of *Roe v. Wade*. Second, the statute was so vague it could be interpreted as including a ban on most second trimester abortions, thus imposing an undue burden on women in violation of the standard set forth in *Planned Parenthood v. Casey*.

Congress showed its displeasure with the *Stenberg* decision by passing the Partial-Birth Abortion Ban Act in 2003. This federal law prohibited partial-birth abortion except if a woman's life were at stake. There was no provision for her health. The law did not take effect, however, because it was declared unconstitutional by lower federal courts.

The law's status changed on April 18, 2007. In *Gonzales v. Carhart* (5–4),[53] the Supreme Court upheld the constitutionality of the federal act. Justice Samuel Alito, who replaced Justice O'Connor, proved to be the swing vote. O'Connor had voted with the majority in the *Stenberg* case. Justice Ginsberg, writing for the minority, denounced the decision as having ancient, discredited notions on women's place in the family and under the Constitution. In a concurring opinion, Justices Scalia and Thomas said they would not be satisfied until *Roe v. Wade* was overturned. Justices Alito and Roberts (President Bush's two appointees) did not sign the opinion. It remains to be seen if the increasingly conservative Court will impose further restrictions on abortion. The immediate reaction of both supporters and critics of the decision runs the risk of committing the slippery slope fallacy. This limited ruling is far from sufficient evidence for either predicting or fearing the eventual overturn of *Roe*. Nevertheless, since *Roe* permits third-trimester abortions to preserve the pregnant woman's health and does not prohibit any method of late-term abortion, the *Gonzales* decision does chip away at *Roe*, as the previously mentioned decisions did. There is some medical evidence that intact dilation and extraction is the safest late-term procedure in some cases, but the evidence did not sway the majority.

A recent development on the political right is an attempt by some state legislatures to pass so-called personhood amendments to their state constitutions. Essentially, these amendments aver that the life of a human person begins at conception. In effect, these bills would legalize the immediate animation theory. Specifically, they would outlaw virtually all abortions, including those resulting from rape and incest; the abortion pill RU-486; all IVF; and even some methods of birth control, such as IUDs and the "morning-after pill." These bills are plainly unconstitutional; they are a blatant violation of *Roe v. Wade*. Happily, none yet have been passed into law. On Election Day 2011, Mississippi's personhood bill—Amendment 26—was soundly defeated by the voters, in one of the most conservative states in the nation.[54]

THE ABORTION PILL AND
EMBRYONIC STEM-CELL RESEARCH

In closing this chapter, I address two issues related to abortion: the abortion pill RU-486, and embryonic stem-cell research. I take up the abortion pill issue first.

1. In one sense, RU-486 adds nothing to the morality of abortion. It is another *means* of early abortion, to be used within seven weeks of a woman's last menstrual period. As a means of abortion, only its safety and effectiveness are relevant, not its morality. Since RU-486 is a technological product, it embodies instrumental value, not moral value. In this regard, it is no abortion panacea. It has a 5 percent failure rate. It can have side effects such as cramping, nausea, and severe bleeding. In Europe, it accounts for about 20 percent of abortions. RU-486's generic prescription name is mifepristone. After much controversy, the FDA gave its final approval to mifepristone on September 28, 2000.

Reaction to the FDA's decision was swift, strong, and predictable. Some abortion opponents denounced the decision for advocating baby poison, the intentional killing of people, and do-it-yourself abortion that has no place in a civilized society. By contrast, one abortion proponent hailed the decision as the most significant advance in women's reproductive healthcare since the birth control pill. Opponents expressed fear that mifepristone will increase abortions. Their fear was unfounded. RU-486 has been legal in Europe for over eighteen years with no increase in abortion rates. Indeed, in France the abortion rate has slightly declined since 1988 when RU-486 first became available. Abortions have likewise declined in the United States.

As noted above, the *Webster* and *Casey* decisions have chipped away at *Roe v. Wade* and partially returned abortion rights to the states. Since mifepristone is a means of abortion, its usage is apparently subject to the same state laws that regulate and prohibit surgical abortion. The FDA's decision does not override state abortion laws. Since these laws now differ significantly from state to state, women's access to mifepristone depends on what state they live in and can travel to. However, a right as important as abortion ought not to depend upon geographical location.

Perhaps the most important moral consequence of mifepristone is that it gives women the opportunity to have a more private early abortion. Instead of having surgical abortions in special clinics, which are routinely picketed by antiabortion protesters and are sometimes the objects of violence, women can now have abortions in the privacy of their physician's office and at home. The physician can be an obstetrician-gynecologist or a family practitioner. Moreover, as we saw earlier in this chapter, a seven-week embryo is a genetic human being and not yet a more developed and ontologically higher morphological human being. Therefore, other things being equal, it is better to have an abortion before rather than after eight weeks. Thirty-three percent of women have abortions within the first seven weeks.

Mifepristone-induced abortions are called medical abortions as distinguished from conventional surgical abortions. Medical abortion involves three stages. First, a woman in her doctor's office takes three pills of mifepristone, which counteracts the effect of progesterone, a hormone necessary to maintain pregnancy. Mifepristone causes the uterus to shed its lining and dislodges the embryo. Second, thirty-six to forty-eight hours later, the woman returns to her doctor's office to take two tablets of a second drug, misoprostol, a hormone-like substance that induces contraction of the uterus and expels the fetal tissue. Third, about fourteen days after her original visit, the woman returns to her doctor to ensure that she is not pregnant and has no fetal remains in her uterus. The doctor must provide surgical intervention if anything goes wrong, either to complete the abortion or to stop heavy bleeding. The latter occurs in 1 to 2 percent of all cases. Medical abortion costs about the same as surgical abortion.[55]

2. I now turn to the more controversial issue of human embryonic stem-cell (ESC) research. ESCs are the body's so-called master cells. They are primordial or progenitor all-purpose formative cells that can develop into virtually any type of mature body cell. They live indefinitely providing they have adequate nutrition, and so can produce an endless supply of cells of various types. Because of their versatility, they have the potential for developing treatments and cures for such critical or serious diseases as cancer, Parkinson's disease, juvenile diabetes, Alzheimer's disease, spinal-cord injuries, heart disease, osteoporosis, and arthritis. ESCs have enormous instrumental value.

Before I proceed, a word about terminology is in order. From the standpoint of biology, it is inaccurate and misleading to use the word *embryonic* to denote ESC research. As noted earlier, the embryo in the strict and proper sense of the term does not begin until implantation is complete, about fourteen days into gestation. A four- or five-day-old blastocyst is not yet an embryo. Consequently, many scientists prefer the term *pre-embryo* in this context. In what follows, I use pre-embryo to denote a zygote, morula, or blastocyst. Embryonic stem-cell research, then, should really be called pre-embryonic stem-cell research. The difference is not merely verbal. By calling a pre-embryo an embryo, we create the impression that the entity being destroyed is more advanced and developed than it actually is. Nonetheless, since embryonic stem-cell research is the accepted public term, I use it with the above caveat.

At present, there are at least five ways or methods of harvesting human ESCs. In addition, there are two techniques that are highly experimental because they have been used only on mice but hold much promise for humans. The first way uses the surplus pre-embryos from fertility clinics, which have been created by in vitro fertilization (IVF). Couples always produce more fertilized eggs than they need, since the pregnancy success-rate of IVF is only 24 percent, and only 78 percent of this figure result in live births. As we saw earlier, when an artificially created zygote grows to an eight-celled morula, it can be transferred to a woman's uterus. Other morulas are frozen for later insertion into the woman, and still others are discarded. Those pre-embryos destined for destruction by fertility clinics are often acquired by ESC research institutes. These pre-embryos are grown into a hundred-celled, five-day-old blastocyst. The inner cells of the blastocyst are its stem cells. They are extracted from the blastocyst thus killing it, and are placed in their own laboratory dish where they are nurtured under specialized conditions to grow into the different kinds of cells that make up the human body's approximately 220 various tissues. For instance, pancreatic islet cells may one day provide a cure for diabetes; muscle cells might repair or replace a defective heart; nerve cells could someday be used to treat Parkinson's disease, spinal-cord injuries, and strokes. Since these treatments and cures are a long way off, widespread research is needed to develop them.

More than 400,000 frozen pre-embryos exist in clinic tanks throughout the United States. Since many of them will be discarded, it is commonly argued that they should be allowed to grow into blastocysts for ESC research so that they can do some good instead of being wasted. This procedure, however, has serious scientific limitations. The freezing process makes it harder to extract stem cells. Moreover, the reason the morulas were frozen in the first place is that they were the weakest ones created. For both reasons, they may not produce high-quality stem cells.

The second way of harvesting ESCs occurs outside fertility clinics. It is based on IVF in ESC research institutes. The institute advertises for egg and sperm donors. The donated material is then mixed by IVF. The fertilized eggs are grown and their stem cells harvested in the manner just described.

However, the second way involves a terminological problem that must be clarified. The accepted medical definition of IVF refers to artificially created zygotes for the purpose of pregnancy and birth and not for the purpose of ESC research. The definition has two elements. First, as noted earlier, IVF denotes a laboratory procedure in which sperm are mixed with an unfertilized egg in a Petri dish to achieve fertilization. Second, the resulting zygote is then transferred into a woman's uterus to begin pregnancy or frozen for future pregnancy use.[56] The definition, therefore, basically operates within the context of fertility clinics. However, in my present discussion of IVF within the context of ESC research, I use the term IVF as denoting only the first element of the definition. It seems arbitrary to restrict the definition of IVF to situations involving the use of artificially created pre-embryos for pregnancy and birth purposes.

Although both methods are similar because they are based on IVF, they have important differences. First, the genetic material used in the second method is superior to that of the first. However, egg donors in the second method have become scarce or even nonexistent, because they are not paid for their services. In 2006, the National Academy of Sciences recommended that women not be paid for eggs donated for ESC research, and in 2005 Massachusetts made such payments illegal. In contrast, women are paid about $5,000 per person for eggs donated to fertility clinics.

Second, the two methods have a somewhat different direct intention. Although all methods of harvesting ESCs have the same ultimate end—cultivating stem cells that will eventually cure patients of a wide range of critical or serious diseases—they differ in their means. In the first method, the means involves the destruction of pre-embryos that were created for pregnancy and birth reasons. Since these pre-embryos were not used for these reasons, they are slated to die anyway. In the second method, the means involves the destruction of pre-embryos created in order to be destroyed for their stem cells. Many people who approve of the first method condemn the second on the grounds that its means cheapens procreation and parenting, and commodifies pre-embryonic life. It is this difference that accounts for the fact that women egg donors are paid in the first method but not in the second.

However, I find this distinction morally unimportant in this context. In both methods, researchers employ a means whose common element is what is morally important: the removal of stem cells from the blastocyst, which removal ipso facto kills it. The fact that in the first method frozen embryos will eventually die anyway is distinct from an agent's own action and direct intention in the destruction of these beings, for which he is as morally responsible as are researchers who destroy the same kinds of beings in the second method. In my view, the morality of both means is basically the same. Whether they are morally right or wrong will be discussed momentarily.

The morality of both methods differs from the morality of President Bush's decision in August 2001 to provide federal funds for adult stem-cell research, and ESC research on sixty-four (later increased to seventy-eight) existing stem-cell colonies, called *lines*. Since the blastocysts that produced these ESCs had already been destroyed, researchers who use them cannot be accused of having a direct intention to kill pre-embryos. The difficulty here is that these ESCs proved to be very scientifically inadequate. Only twenty-one lines were usable, and these were neither genetically diverse nor entirely safe.

The third way of harvesting ESCs also falls outside of fertility clinics. It is a form of therapeutic cloning, or what scientists call *somatic cell nuclear transfer* (SCNT). In this procedure, the nucleus from a cell of a patient's body (e.g., a skin cell) is removed and fused with an enucleated donor egg cell, that is, an egg cell whose nucleus has been removed. The new cell is then stimulated to fertilize on its own. The pre-embryo is placed in a Petri dish where it grows into a blastocyst that is then destroyed for its stem cells. The value of this procedure is that the stem cells identically match the patient's DNA so that his body is less likely to reject any tissue developed from them compared to the first two procedures. As with the second procedure, however, donated eggs are scarce because women are not paid for their services.

The fourth way is a variation of therapeutic cloning that has been recently developed by Harvard University researchers. It involves the cloning of fertilized eggs discarded by fertility clinics. Scientists had long believed that such cloning could not produce stem-cell lines. Kevin Eggan of the Harvard Stem Cell Institute proved otherwise. His team showed that this type of cloning works with a unicellular zygote whose chromosomes are removed and replaced by the DNA of a mature body cell. The modified cell grows into a blastocyst which is then destroyed for its stem cells. This procedure, say supporters, has the benefit of being able to use the many thousands of genetically defective fertilized eggs discarded by fertility clinics, which are stuck at their zygote stage, and transforms them into healthy pre-embryos. Moreover, it avoids a disadvantage of the second method: women who donate their eggs for ESC research must first undergo hormonal therapy to stimulate their egg production. Such therapy, however, poses health risks for women.

It must be emphasized that most people (including myself) make a sharp distinction between therapeutic cloning and reproductive cloning. The former has widespread support, but the latter has been strongly denounced in the United States and worldwide. They are two different moral issues because they are constituted by very different direct intentions with respect to their ends. In therapeutic cloning, the end is to cure critically or seriously ill patients; in reproductive cloning, the end is to create a child that is genetically identical to the DNA donor. In a hypothetical scenario of reproductive cloning, a woman would have one of her eggs enucleated and filled with the DNA extracted from one of her bodily cells. The new cell would then be coaxed to grow to the blastocyst stage and inserted into her uterus. At present, however, reproductive cloning is very unsafe and ineffective for humans. Even if it were safe, it raises ethical issues that are beyond the scope of this book.

The fifth way for harvesting ESCs is called *altered nuclear transfer*. In this procedure, a gene known as CDX2 is removed from a patient's cell before it is fused with an enucleated ovum. The removed cell guarantees that the pre-embryo lives only long enough to produce the desired stem cells before it dies. This method is favored by some ethical and religious conservatives who reason that since the pre-embryo dies on its own, ESC researchers have no direct intention to kill it. Critics counterargue that this procedure is unethical, since it is based on a direct intention to so severely cripple the pre-embryo that it dies exactly when you want it to die. I see no significant moral difference between this method and the first two, for all are based on an agent's direct intention to destroy the pre-embryo.

The last two methods are recent and have been performed only on mice. The sixth procedure does not entail the destruction of pre-embryos. Separate research conducted by the MIT-affiliated Whitehead Institute for Biomedical Research, the Harvard-affiliated Massachusetts General Hospital, and Japan's Kyoto University have developed a procedure that reprograms mature body cells to regress to an ESC-like stage. In this procedure, a skin cell is removed from a mouse. Then a virus that is engineered to have four specific genes is inserted into the cell nucleus. The viral genes activate the same four genes in the new reprogrammed cell. This activation causes the new cell to regress to the ESC stage. Although conservatives have praised this new technique because it does not involve the destruction of pre-embryos, scientists caution that it will take years to adequately develop it for use on humans.

The seventh procedure is cloning with a fertilized mouse egg obtained by IVF. In this technique, a mouse pre-embryo having defective chromosomes is stopped by chemical means from developing further. Its genetic material is then removed and replaced with the DNA from a skin cell on the mouse's tail. Since the new cell is healthy, it grows and divides normally. When it reaches the blastocyst stage, it is destroyed to harvest its stem cells. However, much work is needed before this technique can be applied to human pre-embryos.

In addition to embryonic stem cells, there are adult stem cells and umbilical-cord stem cells. The former exist in many major tissues; they are found in the blood, skin, and brain. Umbilical stem cells consist primarily of blood cells, but others can be developed into bone, cartilage, heart muscle, brain, and liver tissue. Both types of stem cells have considerable instrumental value. However, they are not nearly as versatile and useful as ESCs. Adult stem cells can produce only a limited number of mature cell types. And an umbilical cord is too short to contain enough cells to treat adults. From the standpoint of science, there is no substitute for ESCs.[57]

I now make some generalizations about the morality of ESC research. There is little doubt that ESC research, as represented by the above seven methods, has enormous instrumental medical value. However, only the sixth method does not entail the destruction of pre-embryos. Therefore, most ESC research is opposed by immediate animationists, since they believe that a blastocyst is a person, or some equivalent being, regardless of the terminology they use. For them, killing a pre-embryo by removing its stem cells is as murderous as abortion. However, we have seen good reason to reject immediate animation. In my view, personhood does not begin until viability. A blastocyst is solely a genetic human being. Its moral status is not nearly as great as the moral status of a person. Nevertheless, since blastocysts have some moral status, it is immoral to destroy them at will, or without good reason. From my personalist standpoint, the central moral conflict in ESC research is whether it is morally permissible to destroy genetic human beings for the future good of human persons. I conclude that it is.

The good of human persons here is substantial. The research will eventually (probably) yield treatments and cures for a host of life-threatening diseases and other serious ailments. Through this research, society is promoting personal relations with the patients who will be saved and helped by the resulting cures and treatments. In this respect, ESC research is morally justified by the principle of community.

ESC research is also justified by Rule Five of the principle of intentionality. Let us recall this rule in part: If a direct intention has a good end and a bad means, the direct intention is significantly bad if the means is a prima facie immoral action. ESC research has a direct intention whose end, as specified above, is good but whose means is bad since it involves killing genetic human beings. However, the direct killing of a genetic human being is a prima facie immoral action, not an intrinsically immoral one. ESC research, then, has a significantly bad direct intention rather than a gravely bad one. Since the end of ESC research involves a substantial (future) good for persons, and since the moral status of persons is far greater than that of genetic humans, the goodness of the end outweighs and hence overrides the badness of the means. In contrast, ESC research would be morally impermissible if conducted for frivolous or unnecessary reasons. For then the badness of the means would outweigh the goodness of the end, and both the principles of community and intentionality would be violated.

On the political level, the major controversial question is whether public funds should be used for ESC research. Immediate animationists say no, for they do not want the government's money (to which they contribute) to promote activity they believe is immoral. This is why in 2006 President Bush vetoed a bill that would have authorized federal funds for such research. But this opposition is unjustified. It does not satisfy the four conditions we specified for making an immoral act illegal. Specifically, it does not satisfy the second condition. The vast majority of American citizens are not immediate animationists and so do not believe that ESC research is murder or the moral equivalent thereof. Most polls taken after Bush's veto disagreed with his decision by a two-to-one margin. Consequently, if the majority of Americans want federal funding for this research, immediate animationists have no (moral) right to use their ethical and ontological position as a basis for opposing government funding, unless they can translate their moral/ontological position into important and relevant values of a constitutional democracy, which I doubt can be done (at least effectively or convincingly), as we shall see in chapter 8. President Bush's veto seems to have been based on a version of immediate animation. At the time, his press secretary, Tony Snow, said that Bush considers ESC research "murder." Under hard questioning from journalists, Snow retracted his statement, explaining that he overstated the president's position. Still, the murder comment is consistent with Bush's staunch antiabortion stance. Furthermore, since a woman has a constitutional right to abortion-on-demand during the first trimester, the Supreme Court in *Roe* declared the immediate animation theory unconstitutional as a matter of public law. Therefore, anyone who is opposed to the *legality* of ESC research based on immediate animation, or on any theory holding that the pre-embryonic blastocyst is a person, is running afoul of constitutional law.

On June 20, 2007, President Bush vetoed a similar measure, declaring: "Destroying human life in the hopes of saving human life is not ethical." The United States is "a nation founded on the principle that all human life is sacred."[58] These statements assume that *human life* has the same meaning whether the term denotes a five-day-old blastocyst or a human adult (or child).

It does not. A blastocyst is only a genetic human life (or being); an adult or child is a human life in the fullest sense of the term—a human person (or a moral human being). Bush commits the fallacy of equivocation on *human life*. In doing so, he confirms reports that he thinks ESC research is murderous and that he is some sort of immediate animationist. I agree with Mr. Bush that a blastocyst, as a genetic human being, has significant moral status, but its moral status is not nearly as important as that of a child and adult, who are persons.

EUTHANASIA
A Reinterpretation

E uthanasia has important similarities to, and differences from, suicide and abortion. Many of the arguments for and against suicide in chapter 3 also apply to euthanasia. The basic difference between the two issues is that suicide is an intrapersonal act, whereas euthanasia is interpersonal. In euthanasia, someone's death is caused or brought about by another. In this respect, euthanasia includes assisted suicide—sometimes called allocide. In assisted suicide, another person supplies the means of death, which the patient then self-administers. In euthanasia, the other administers the means of death, as in a lethal overdose of a drug. In both acts, another person plays a causal role in the death of a patient. For this reason, assisted suicide, like euthanasia, is an interpersonal action. Although the other's causal role is different in both acts, this difference need not concern us here.[1]

There are two similarities between euthanasia and abortion, and one basic difference. First, infanticide is viewed in some quarters as an extension of the abortion issue,[2] and the moral question of infanticide is generally recognized as a dimension of the broader issue of euthanasia. Infants whose life and death are controversial usually have serious medical conditions and low quality of life, similar to adult cases of euthanasia. Second, in both euthanasia and abortion, the question of personhood is crucial. For example, is an anencephalic infant—literally, an infant without a brain—a person? Is an irreversibly comatose adult, or an adult in the most advanced stages of senility, a person? They are certainly human beings in a biological sense—or in my terminology, morphological human beings. But as I illustrated in the previous chapter, a human being is not necessarily a person. The major and obvious difference between euthanasia and abortion is that euthanasia involves the death or killing of a postnatal human, whereas abortion is the killing of a prenatal human being.

There are three questions concerning the euthanasia issue that need to be examined: How should euthanasia be defined? Are euthanasia patients always, or even generally, persons? And most important, what are the moral and legal statuses of the conventional types of euthanasia? In the first section, I briefly examine the problem of definition. Then I critically evaluate the conventional types of euthanasia and, in doing so, address the issue of personhood. Since I conclude that the conventional types of euthanasia have serious difficulties, in the last section I develop my own personalist theory of euthanasia.

DEFINITIONS OF EUTHANASIA

Although there is some problem in defining euthanasia, it is not a major one.[3] Literally, euthanasia comes from two Greek words that together mean good death. This literal definition suggests two key elements of euthanasia. First, the reason for calling death good is that the patient is usually seriously suffering from an incurable or terminal illness.[4] As a result, proponents of euthanasia see death as a blessing or at least relief from a life that has little or nothing to offer except pain and suffering. Second, the patient's death is caused or brought about by another from the motive of mercy or compassion, which I regard as a form of love. From these two elements, we derive the traditional definition of euthanasia as mercy killing: the active, intentional, compassionate killing of a patient who is seriously suffering from a terminal illness, for example, injecting a lethal overdose of a drug into a dying cancer patient. As such, mercy killing is a form of homicide that clearly distinguishes it from suicide. Indeed, some critics call it murder. By contrast, some proponents call it nonharmful killing.[5]

There are some students of euthanasia who think that this definition is adequate.[6] Although it is sound as far as it goes, there are three reasons that this definition should be expanded.

First, it excludes persons who are seriously suffering from a nonterminal illness or, indeed, from no illness at all. R. M. Hare describes the following poignant case:

> The driver of a petrol lorry was in an accident in which his tanker overturned and immediately caught fire. He himself was trapped in the cab and could not be freed. He therefore besought the bystanders to kill him by hitting him on the head, so that he would not roast to death. I think that somebody did this, but I do not know what happened in court afterwards.[7]

If a bystander had killed the driver, he would have committed euthanasia, regardless of one's moral views of the action.

Second, the traditional concept of mercy killing does not specifically include seriously defective infants about whom life-and-death decisions are made. An anencephalic infant is not seriously suffering in the sense of feeling intense pain, although one could say that it is suffering from a very grave defect. As long as such deaths are brought about from the motive of mercy, they ought to be classified as euthanasia.

And third, mercy killing does not include individuals who exist, as the medical profession puts it, in a persistent vegetative state (PVS), as in the famous Karen Quinlan and Terri Schiavo cases. Because of advances in medical technology, many people who would have died of natural causes can be kept alive artificially, sometimes indefinitely. Or else a decision can be made to withhold or withdraw treatment, thus bringing about or hastening the patient's death. Again, these individuals are not suffering in the strict sense, even though they are suffering from a very low quality of life and their condition is hopeless. And if medical treatment is withheld or withdrawn and they die, it may not be proper to say that they were killed or that this action was a form of homicide, as in mercy killing. Rather, it is usually said that they were allowed to die.

In view of these considerations, I define euthanasia as follows: an action that directly or indirectly intends, from the motive of mercy, the death of another who is seriously suffering from a hopeless condition that produces a low quality of life. I use this definition when I develop my own theory of euthanasia. I now turn to a critical examination of the conventional types of euthanasia.

CONVENTIONAL TYPES OF EUTHANASIA

In euthanasia literature, two basic distinctions are made with respect to types of euthanasia. Euthanasia can be either active or passive, and it can be either voluntary or involuntary. Active euthanasia is virtually identical to mercy killing. It is defined as the direct, intentional killing of a patient, such as by injecting her with a lethal drug overdose. In passive euthanasia, a person refrains from performing actions to prolong a patient's life by either withholding or withdrawing medical treatment, such as by disconnecting a mechanical respirator from a PVS patient. The difference between active and passive euthanasia is often expressed in terms of the distinction between killing the patient and allowing the patient to die. It rests on the faulty doctrine of doing and allowing, examined in chapter 2.

Voluntary euthanasia has a patient's consent; the patient wants to die. Involuntary euthanasia lacks the patient's consent; a patient has not expressed his or her desire and intention to die. In the concrete, these two pairs of distinctions generate four types of euthanasia: active/voluntary, active/involuntary, passive/voluntary, and passive/involuntary.

The validity of the active/passive distinction is seriously disputed. Although the voluntary/involuntary distinction is regarded as basically sound, it is inadequate as it stands. I first critique the active/passive distinction.

Proponents of the active/passive distinction support it on moral grounds. Since active euthanasia directly kills a patient whom they consider a person, they always oppose active euthanasia on the grounds that it is a form of unjustifiable homicide or even murder. In contrast, since passive euthanasia merely allows the patient to die a natural death, proponents of the distinction view it as morally permissible in a wide variety of situations. This moral position is well entrenched. It is supported by the American Medical Association, by many religious groups, and by US law. Active euthanasia is illegal in all states of the United States.

I argue, however, that the active/passive distinction, as denoting two basic and mutually exclusive types of euthanasia, is both conceptually incoherent and morally indefensible. The very definition of active euthanasia is incoherent. To avoid circularity, active euthanasia is not defined as active killing, but as intentional killing. In this context, *intentional* means direct intention, not indirect intention. Therefore, active euthanasia denotes the direct intentional killing of a patient. The problem is that this definition sometimes applies to passive euthanasia. The direct intentional killing of a patient can involve withholding or withdrawing medical treatment, as illustrated by the famous case of Elizabeth Bouvia:

> In September 1983 Elizabeth Bouvia, a twenty-six-year-old cerebral palsy victim, checked into the Riverside (California) General Hospital and informed the staff that she wished to die of starvation while they made her comfortable by administering painkillers. (Lacking use of her limbs, she maintained this was the only means of suicide available to her.) The hospital refused this request, and a court battle ensued.[8]

Bouvia later changed her mind and began eating. Nevertheless, if the hospital had acceded to her request and starved her to death, the act would have been a directly intentional killing, even though it also would have been an act of passive euthanasia by withdrawing (or withholding) food. Consequently, passive euthanasia sometimes involves the direct intentional killing of a patient. That being the case, active euthanasia cannot be defined as having the element of direct intentional killing and passive euthanasia defined as lacking this element—which is exactly how they are defined. I conclude, then, that the active/passive distinction is conceptually incoherent.

In light of this difficulty, sometimes the withdrawal of medical care is referred to as an active means, as in the following appeals court decision regarding Claire Conroy. The appeals court reversed the decision of the lower court, which had permitted the removal of her nasogastric tube:

> If the trial judge's order had been enforced, Conroy would not have died as the result of an existing medical condition, but rather she would have died, and painfully so, as the result of a new and independent condition: dehydration and starvation. Thus she would have been *actively* killed by independent means.[9]

It is incoherent (or contradictory), on the one hand, to define passive euthanasia as the withdrawal or withholding of medical means and to imply that this definition does not denote the direct intentional killing of a patient because that is how active euthanasia is defined, and, on the other hand, to say that the withdrawal of food and water is an active means presumably because it does constitute the direct intentional killing of a patient.

This incoherence is produced by the doing/allowing doctrine. However, if one rejects this doctrine, as I did earlier, the incoherence can be easily corrected. I replaced doing/allowing with the principle of intentionality. This principle suggests that a distinction between direct and indirect euthanasia should replace the active/passive distinction as two basic types of euthanasia. Nevertheless, in this context the active/passive distinction retains an element of truth: it denotes two different *means* of performing euthanasia, either direct or indirect. I explain these distinctions later.

Because of its conceptual incoherence, the active/passive distinction cannot support the moral weight it was designed to support: the moral doctrine that active euthanasia is always impermissible but that passive euthanasia is often permissible. The most articulate and forceful critic of this doctrine is the well-known moral philosopher and euthanasia expert James Rachels. He argues that the distinction is morally irrelevant. That is, there is no moral difference in the bare distinction between active and passive euthanasia, because the distinction between killing and letting die is morally insignificant.

In a seminal essay, he constructs two situations that, he argues, are parallel to the active/passive distinction.[10] In the first situation, Mr. Smith stands to gain a large inheritance if his six-year-old cousin dies. One evening, while the boy is taking a bath, Mr. Smith sneaks into the bathroom and drowns him by pushing his head underwater until he is dead. Then he arranges everything to make the death look like an accident. In the second situation, Mr. Jones also stands to gain a large inheritance if his six-year-old cousin dies. Like Mr. Smith, he plans to drown his cousin in the bathtub. However, just as he enters the bathroom, the child slips in the bathtub, hits his head, and falls underwater. Since Jones had planned to kill the child anyway, he stands by and does nothing as he watches the child die. According to Rachels, the first situation is parallel to active euthanasia, because Mr. Smith kills the boy. The second situation is parallel to passive euthanasia, since Mr. Jones merely allows his cousin to die. But both actions are equally wrong, says Rachels. Both stem from the same motive of greed, and both have the same end or intention—the death of an innocent child. It makes no moral difference that in one case someone actively kills a child, and in the other case he passively lets him die. In both cases, the agent is morally guilty of murder. Rachels concludes that the bare difference between killing and allowing to die is morally irrelevant and, therefore, so is the distinction between active and passive euthanasia. If anything, passive euthanasia is sometimes worse, for it often involves a slow and long-suffering death, whereas active euthanasia is quick and painless. As he puts it: "The doctrine that says that a baby may be allowed to dehydrate and wither, but may not be given an injection that would end its life without suffering, seems so patently cruel as to require no further refutation."[11] There is no rational justification, he says, for the view that active euthanasia is always wrong and passive euthanasia is often right. Rachels obviously rejects the doing/allowing doctrine.

Not surprisingly, Rachels's rejection of the active/passive distinction has been widely criticized, since the distinction is so deeply ingrained in philosophy, religion, and law.[12] Nevertheless, it is my view that Rachels has successfully discredited the traditional doctrine that active euthanasia is always impermissible and that passive euthanasia is sometimes permissible. It does not follow, however, that his own position is entirely correct. In the active/passive controversy, Rachels and some of his critics agree that one must choose between the traditional position, which Rachels criticizes, and the position he defends, which he calls an "alternative" view and critic J. P. Moreland calls a "radical" view.[13] No other legitimate positions are recognized. However, this is not the case. There are elements of truth and error in both positions. Consequently, I will develop a third position later in the chapter.

For now, we must complete our analysis of the active/passive distinction by examining the related distinction between ordinary and extraordinary means. Paul Ramsey's description is widely cited:

> Ordinary means of preserving life are all medicines, treatments, and operations, which offer a reasonable hope of benefit for the patient and which can be obtained and used without excessive expense, pain and other inconveniences.
> Extra-ordinary means of preserving life are all those medicines, treat-

ments, and operations which cannot be obtained without excessive expense, pain, or other inconveniences, or which, if used, would not offer a reasonable hope of benefit.[14]

Supporters of the active/passive distinction hold that ordinary means must always be employed, but extraordinary means may sometimes be withheld or withdrawn. To salvage the distinction, however, it must be applied with more flexibility than in the traditional theory. Antibiotics, for example, are generally considered ordinary means. But antibiotics may be extraordinary means for a pneumonia patient who also has terminal cancer that has metastasized to the liver and brain. And what may be extraordinary means in a small rural hospital may be ordinary means in a large metropolitan medical center. Again, cost is relative to the patient's ability to pay, although some would question the moral relevance of the cost factor altogether. However, with medical costs in the United States soaring at a rate that has far exceeded the general rate of inflation and is expected to rise even more steeply in the future, a distinction between ordinary and extraordinary means within the context of cost-benefit analysis becomes critical in bringing these runaway costs under control. A disproportionate percentage of national wealth is spent on medical care in the last year of life, to the detriment of other important public goods. In any event, unless we accept the ordinary/extraordinary distinction (or a similar distinction), there will be no general—and therefore rational—moral policy for determining when medical treatment is required and when it is not. Cases will be decided on an ad hoc and sometimes inconsistent basis. Accordingly, I keep the ordinary/extraordinary distinction and incorporate it into my direct/ indirect distinction later on.

Compared with the active/passive distinction, the conventional distinction between voluntary and involuntary euthanasia is basically sound, though inadequate. The distinction is sound, because there is a real difference between a patient giving consent and not giving consent to die, and this difference is morally important. The distinction is inadequate, because there is ambiguity in the term *involuntary*. There can be two reasons that the consent of the patient is lacking: (1) The patient is unwilling to give consent but has the capacity to give it. This unwillingness may take the form of outright refusal—

"I do not want to die." Or it may involve simply not giving permission to die. (2) The patient lacks capacity to give consent. If a patient is terminated under the first condition, involuntary euthanasia is committed. If a patient is terminated under the second condition and has not given consent in the past through a living will, *nonvoluntary* euthanasia is committed. Nonvoluntary euthanasia includes neonates and severely senile and PVS adults. Since consent of the patient is lacking, it must be given by another (by proxy). Consent should be given by someone who knows and loves the patient: a parent, a spouse, or some other close and competent next of kin. Finally, voluntary euthanasia occurs when a patient gives consent to die and he or she is terminated. Consent can be given either in the present, if the patient has capacity to give it, or in the past through a living will, if the patient presently lacks capacity to give it.[15] These three types of euthanasia will be incorporated into my direct/indirect distinction.

I turn now to the question of personhood. I have already stated that, in my view, personhood begins at viability. I now contend that it continues throughout postnatal life, regardless of the quality of life of the individual human being. There are two reasons that I hold this view. First, viable fetuses are counted as persons not because they exercise personal function, but because they possess the capacity to do so, that is, the capacity for mutuality. Analogously, certain adults, such as the severely senile and those in PVS, should not be denied personhood just because they are presently incapable of exercising personal function, since they did so in the past. Second, personhood does not end with death. In my view, a person is immortal. At death, a person's organicity ceases to exist but not his or her personhood as such. By the same token, personhood cannot cease to exist because of a biological abnormality or defect. However, the immortality of personhood cannot be justified here.[16] In any case, I would not make the second reason a basis for public law, since it rests on such a distinctive ontological position.

Just because all postnatal humans are persons, though, it does not follow that euthanasia is never morally permissible. Since suicide and the abortion of viable fetuses are sometimes morally permissible, it would be odd if euthanasia were not sometimes morally permissible too. Indeed, I argue that euthanasia is morally permissible in a broader range of cases or situations than is suicide and the abortion of viable fetuses. To justify this position, I must now develop my distinction between direct and indirect euthanasia and connect it with the principles of community and intentionality.

DIRECT AND INDIRECT EUTHANASIA

The difference between direct and indirect euthanasia is partly based on the distinction between direct and indirect intention. Direct euthanasia is the directly intentional killing of a patient by either an active or a passive means. It is a form of direct killing. The end of the action is to kill the patient, and the means, whether active or passive, intends to cause the patient's death. An indisputably lethal overdose of a drug intends to cause the death of a patient (active means), and so does permanently withholding or withdrawing a patient's feeding tubes (passive means). In order to show the continuity and similarity between my own position and the traditional, conventional position, I propose a distinction between direct-active euthanasia and direct-passive euthanasia. In both cases, the end is the same: to kill the patient. They differ only in their means to achieve this end.

Aside from the question of voluntariness, the central moral question of euthanasia is whether direct euthanasia is ever morally right. If the answer is affirmative, then on moral grounds, the means chosen should be as quick and painless as possible. We should not worry about the distinction between active and passive as such. Instead, we should be concerned with ending a patient's life as quickly and painlessly as possible. Clearly, this involves an active means.

It may be objected that my definition of direct euthanasia is somewhat circular, since the word *direct* appears in both the definiendum (subject) and definiens (predicate) of the definition. The objection is valid, but this slight logical irregularity will have to be tolerated in the interests of avoiding the much more serious problems of logical incoherence and moral unjustifiability, which would exist if we retained the active/passive distinction in its traditional, conventional form. For these reasons, the direct/indirect distinction is intended to replace the active/passive distinction. Moreover, since direct euthanasia is a form of direct killing, the same irregularity exists in the definition of direct killing: killing someone by direct intention. However, the notion of direct killing is clear enough and morally important enough to retain.

Indirect euthanasia has both a direct intention and an indirect intention. The end of the action's direct intention does *not* consist of killing the patient. Rather, the action's end consists of allowing the patient to live out the rest of his or her life with as much dignity as possible, instead of employing expensive and invasive technology that does little or no good because the patient's condition is severe and hopeless and his or her quality of life is low. The means involved are a combination of active and passive ones. On the one hand, we actively administer ordinary means of medical care such as food and water to avoid directly killing the patient by starvation or dehydration. We also administer medicine to avoid killing the patient by infection and to make him or her as comfortable as possible. On the other hand, we passively withhold or withdraw extraordinary means of treatment. By doing so, our end is not to kill the patient, and the withdrawal or withholding of such means is not intended to cause the death of the patient and, in fact, very often does not. The above choice of active and passive means is designed to fulfill the direct intention of indirect euthanasia just described. However, by withholding or withdrawing extraordinary means, we may very well be shortening the patient's life, but we will not be certainly causing the patient's death. Consequently, in indirect euthanasia, the indirect intention may be characterized as the increased probability of the patient's death. For this reason, indirect euthanasia may be called a form of indirect killing. Because of the lack of certainty of death, it also can be spoken of as allowing the patient to die.

There is some similarity between indirect euthanasia and the traditional, conventional category of passive euthanasia, but the two also differ, since some passive euthanasia is direct. Indirect euthanasia includes all those instances of passive euthanasia in which extraordinary means are withheld or withdrawn and ordinary means are actively administered. Moreover, indirect euthanasia also includes some instances of active euthanasia. For example, if a terminally ill patient's pain can no longer be managed by normal doses of painkillers but only by doses that are borderline lethal, and if a nurse or physician administers such a dosage to relieve his pain and he dies, his death should be regarded as indirect euthanasia. In this instance, the caregiver's direct intention is not to kill the patient (which would be the case if the dose were grossly lethal) but to relieve his pain. The foreseen and unwilled consequence of this dosage is the possible death of the patient. Although under our supposition the patient does die, his death was far from certain.

Likewise, there is similarity and difference between direct and active euthanasia. Direct euthanasia includes all instances of active euthanasia in which the agent's end or direct intention is to kill the patient, but it also includes all instances of passive euthanasia in which ordinary means such as food and water are withheld or withdrawn.

A perfect example of indirect euthanasia is the celebrated case of Karen Quinlan. One night in April 1975, while attending a party, Quinlan became unconscious. It was soon learned that her condition was permanent. The exact cause of her coma is still unknown. On the night she became unconscious, she consumed alcohol and Valium, but not in dangerous amounts. That night it is known that she stopped breathing for two fifteen-minute periods, and during this time her brain suffered massive damage because of oxygen depletion. She was quickly put on a respirator to help her labored breathing. In spite of her extensive brain damage, the lower brain, including the brain stem, was basically intact. Her brain showed patterns of electrical activity, and she had a discernible pulse. She could not be considered dead by any legal or medical criteria. Her prognosis, however, was very poor. Medical opinion was agreed that her condition was that of permanent or persistent vegetative state (PVS).

It is important here to distinguish between coma and PVS. A coma is a deep or profound state of unconsciousness. It is characterized by immobility and by a total lack of function, except for cardiovascular function. Although an individual in a coma is alive (she is not clinically brain-dead), she is completely unable to react or respond to her environment. By comparison, a patient in PVS retains some lower, minimal consciousness, and is sometimes said to be "awake," since she has a noncognitive sleep-wake cycle. However, she is wholly devoid of self-awareness and awareness of her surroundings, and lacks higher cognitive activity such as speaking, thinking, and understanding, but exhibits reflex activity such as eye-blinking to light, turning one's body in the direction of a loud noise, and occasional grimacing, crying, or laughing.

The higher, cerebral brain is essentially destroyed, but the brainstem, the seat of respiration and circulation, is intact. Consequently, individuals in PVS may continue to live for years. When PVS lasts for at least twelve months, it is considered permanent (or irreversible). In contrast, a coma rarely lasts for more than two to four weeks. A patient in a coma will either die; progress to PVS, as Karen Quinlan did; or to a less severe physical, intellectual, or psychological disorder that requires special care. For these reasons, it is PVS rather than coma individuals who are the subjects of euthanasia and included in my definition of euthanasia.[17]

Karen Quinlan's parents were convinced that she would not want extraordinary measures used to continue such a permanently low quality of life. They consulted with their parish priest, and he assured them that withdrawing the respirator was permitted by the doctrines of the Roman Catholic Church. As a result, they requested the hospital to discontinue the respirator. The hospital refused and told them that since Quinlan was over twenty-one, they were no longer her legal guardians. In September 1975, her father, Joseph Quinlan, asked the Superior Court of New Jersey to appoint him as her legal guardian so that he would have the express power to authorize the discontinuance of all extraordinary means of sustaining her life. On November 10, 1975, Judge Robert Muir ruled against Mr. Quinlan, who then appealed the decision to the New Jersey Supreme Court. On March 31, 1976, the court ruled in favor of Mr. Quinlan and appointed him Karen's guardian.[18] Shortly thereafter, Quinlan's respirator was turned off. For more than nine years, she lived in a nursing home. She breathed spontaneously and received high-nutrient feedings and regular doses of antibiotics to ward off infections. At times, she made reflexive responses to sound and touch. She died in June 1985. Who knows how long she would have lived on the respirator.

The end of Mr. Quinlan's direct intention consisted of allowing his daughter to live out the rest of her life in dignity, recognizing that her medical condition was both severe and hopeless. The means involved were a combination of active and passive: the application of ordinary, active means, and the withdrawal of extraordinary, passive means. Although the withdrawal of the respirator increased the probability of her death, Mr. Quinlan's direct intention in doing so was not to cause her death, nor did it in fact cause her death, since she lived for more than nine years thereafter. However, even if Quinlan had died shortly after the removal of the respirator, it would have been her medical condition, not the removal of the respirator, that would have been the primary cause of her death. In the words of the New Jersey Supreme Court: "The ensuing death of [Karen Quinlan] would not be homicide but rather expiration from existing natural causes."[19]

Mr. Quinlan's indirect intention was the foreseen but unwilled consequence that Karen Quinlan's life would probably be shortened by removing the respirator. That there was a significantly increased probability of her death off the respirator was the main reason that the hospital had refused Mr. Quinlan's initial request to discontinue it. When Quinlan was first put on the respirator, the medical experts thought that she could not survive without its assistance, although no one was willing to predict exactly how long she might live without it. So when the court finally granted Mr. Quinlan permission to withdraw the respirator, he knew, based on available medical knowledge and opinion, that he might be shortening her life.

Indirect euthanasia can be justified by the principle of community as applied to the principle of intentionality. The direct intention is good: allowing the patient to live out the rest of his or her life in dignity and to die with dignity, under the conditions specified. The direct intention is good because, in accordance with the principle of community, it treats the patient as a whole person rather than as a mere medical function; it constitutes a personal relation between agent and patient. Moreover, the agent acts from the motive of mercy, or love, as it would appear that Mr. Quinlan did toward his daughter. Since the indirect intention of not employing extraordinary means increases the probability of the patient's death, it must be regarded as bad. But its badness, in my view, is outweighed by the direct intention's goodness. Indirect euthanasia, then, satisfies Rule One of intentionality.

Direct euthanasia as such is more serious than indirect euthanasia as such and thus requires greater moral justification. Direct euthanasia is a form of direct killing, whereas indirect euthanasia is at worst indirect killing and at best merely allowing the patient to die. In this respect, the distinction between doing and allowing has some truth, insofar as the distinction is subordinated to and is a component of the principle of intentionality. It is on this point that my position differs from Rachels's.[20] However, a key term here is *as such*. Consequently, it does not follow from my position that every instance of direct euthanasia is worse than every instance of indirect euthanasia when all the moral elements of a particular action are considered; much less does it follow that direct euthanasia is always morally wrong. In order to determine in some detail the morality of both direct and indirect euthanasia, we must now connect them with voluntary, nonvoluntary, and involuntary euthanasia. This connection yields six types of euthanasia: direct-voluntary, direct-nonvoluntary, direct-involuntary, indirect-voluntary, indirect-nonvoluntary, and indirect-involuntary. In turn, the direct types can be subdivided into active and passive, as previously indicated.

Although indirect euthanasia can also use an active or a passive means, I will not subdivide the indirect types into active and passive, since indirect euthanasia in general is relatively noncontroversial. I morally evaluate each of the six types and their appropriate subtypes and comment on the question of legalization.

Direct-Voluntary

I begin with direct-voluntary euthanasia, because most of the moral controversy concerns direct-active-voluntary euthanasia. As direct, its end is to kill the patient, regardless of how one characterizes the end, for example, relieving the patient of her suffering. It achieves this end by an active means. And as voluntary, it has the consent of the patient, either in the present or in the past through a living will. In contrast, the previously mentioned Elizabeth Bouvia case would have been an example of direct-passive-voluntary euthanasia if the hospital had granted her request and starved and dehydrated her to death.

James Rachels describes a "perfect" or "central" case of direct-active-voluntary euthanasia:

Albert A., a hospital patient, was dying of cancer, which had spread throughout his body. The intense pain could no longer be controlled. Every four hours he would be given a painkiller, but over many months of treatment he had built up a tolerance for the drug, until now it would relieve the pain for only a few minutes each time. Albert knew that he was going to die anyway, for the cancer could not be cured. He did not want to linger in agony, so he asked his doctor to give him a lethal injection to end his life without further suffering. His family supported this request.[21]

Albert A.'s doctor denied his request. To grant it would have been illegal.

Nonetheless, this example, I contend, is a paradigm for the moral rightness of direct-active-voluntary euthanasia, because it meets the following six conditions: (1) the patient is seriously suffering; (2) death is imminent; (3) the patient's condition is hopeless or irreversible; (4) quality of life is low; (5) the means are as quick and painless as possible, which is a necessary condition for the motive of mercy; and (6) the patient requests to be killed. Of course, the sixth condition applies to direct-voluntary euthanasia by definition. I add the condition for the sake of emphasis and because it is contained in the above example. In any case, under these six conditions, direct-active-voluntary euthanasia promotes the principle of community and thus overcomes the badness of direct killing as such. It consists of a personal act, a personal relation of persons: the agent treats the patient as a whole person; the agent's motive is mercy, which is a mode of love; the patient's right to die is respected, thus satisfying justice; the patient's autonomy is respected; and the patient is treated as an equal, capable of making a rational decision.[22] Under these conditions, a killing is nonharmful, for the continuation of a person's life would cause him more harm than his death.

Proponents (like myself) of direct-active-voluntary euthanasia, then, put strict limits on its moral permissibility.[23] Their position, however, is often distorted by opponents, who interpret them as holding that this type of euthanasia is morally right in general, as if it were prima facie right, such as truth-telling, for example. This interpretation is false and commits the straw man fallacy.

Notice that the fifth above condition is absent from direct-passive-voluntary euthanasia. A passive means could not be the quickest and most painless means to die. Hence, on the grounds of the prevention of needless cruelty, direct-active-voluntary euthanasia is always morally better than direct-passive-voluntary euthanasia, ceteris paribus. However, it is a widely held view that direct-passive euthanasia is sometimes morally right and that direct-active euthanasia is always morally wrong. This position is both irrational and cruel. It confuses the end and the means of the direct intention. Once it has been determined that it is morally right to directly kill a patient (end)—which is exactly what has been decided by someone who advocates direct-passive euthanasia—then it logically and morally follows that an active means should be used, since only an active means can be the quickest and most painless means, thus guaranteeing that the motive of mercy is present, which is required by the very essence or definition of euthanasia. This is precisely the point on which Rachels is correct. Once again, the falsity of the doctrine of doing and allowing is revealed.

In my view, direct-active-voluntary euthanasia includes physician-assisted suicide. Therefore, insofar as the former is morally right, so is the latter. However, it is sometimes held that these two acts are distinct—indeed, mutually exclusive—for the causal role of the other is different in both acts. Although this view is reasonable, I am more concerned with the moral conclusions that can be drawn from it. First, the moral rightness of physician-assisted suicide need not imply the moral rightness of direct-active-voluntary euthanasia. This conclusion logically follows. However, sometimes it is argued that whereas physician-assisted suicide is morally acceptable, direct-active-voluntary euthanasia is not.[24] This conclusion, of course, I must reject. In any event, no one would argue that the moral rightness of direct-active-voluntary euthanasia does not imply the moral rightness of physician-assisted suicide, and that is my main point. Still, most opponents of direct-active-voluntary euthanasia also oppose physician-assisted suicide, because they see no moral and causal difference between them. This view is mistaken.[25]

In a similar vein, most of the major moral arguments against direct-active-voluntary euthanasia are the same arguments against suicide that I critically evaluated in chapter 3. Consequently, I will not repeat them here. Suffice it to say that, since these arguments could not establish that suicide is intrinsically immoral, neither can they establish that direct-active-voluntary euthanasia is intrinsically immoral. Direct-active-voluntary euthanasia (including physician-assisted suicide) is morally right under the above enumerated conditions.

Since direct-active-voluntary euthanasia is sometimes morally right, it would seem to follow that it should be legal. In fact, it is illegal in all states of the United States. However, direct-passive-voluntary euthanasia is legal. The legal status of physician-assisted suicide has proved to be more complicated. In the spring of 1996, two important federal court decisions were handed down. In March, the US Ninth Circuit Court of Appeals, in *Compassion in Dying v. Washington*,[26] struck down a Washington State law prohibiting doctor-assisted suicide. In an 8–3 decision, Judge Stephen Reinhardt, speaking for the majority, held that there is a constitutionally protected liberty interest in determining the time and manner of one's death—a right to die—that applies to mentally competent, terminally ill adults who wish to hasten their deaths by obtaining medication prescribed by their physicians. In April, the US Second Circuit Court of Appeals, in *Quill v. Vacco*,[27] ruled that similar statutes in New York are unconstitutional because they violate the equal protection clause of the Fourteenth Amendment.

Both decisions substantially extended the constitutional right to die beyond the Supreme Court decision, *Cruzan v. Director, Missouri Department of Health*.[28] In that decision, the Court ruled that terminally ill patients, or patients in PVS with living wills, have a right to die by refusing food and water. The Court legalized direct-passive-voluntary euthanasia without legalizing direct-active-voluntary euthanasia. Later in the chapter, I will say more about this important decision, when I comment on the Terri Schiavo case. In effect, the Court said that it was all right to directly kill a patient, as long as one did not employ the most painless and quickest means. The *Compassion* and *Quill* decisions may be regarded as attempts to partly correct this moral error. The two decisions implicitly affirmed the principle that it is sometimes morally right to directly end one's own life by using an active means provided by another. I would go one step further and affirm that it is sometimes morally right to directly end *another's* life by using an active means.

On June 26, 1997, the US Supreme Court ruled on the *Compassion* and *Quill* decisions. In a pair of 9–0 decisions, *Washington v. Glucksberg* and *Vacco v. Quill*,[29] the Court upheld the constitutionality of state laws prohibiting physician-assisted suicide and denied that there exists a general right to suicide (physician-assisted or otherwise) under the equal protection clause of the Fourteenth Amendment. However, it left the door open to future claims of terminally ill patients suffering from excruciating and intractable pain. The Court suggested that at least some of them may have a constitutional right to physician-assisted suicide and invited the states to experiment with laws permitting it if they choose to do so. It encouraged moral debate on the issue as vital to a democratic society. In effect, the Court said it was up to individual states to decide if they wanted to legalize physician-assisted suicide.

In 1994, Oregon became the first state to legalize physician-assisted suicide by approving the state's Death with Dignity Act. It went into effect on October 27, 1997, after the Ninth Circuit Court of Appeals lifted an injunction against the law. Since then, about thirty persons a year, mostly cancer patients, have ended their lives with a lethal dose of drugs prescribed by their doctors. The Bush administration, however, challenged the Oregon statute. In *Gonzales v. Oregon*,[30] it argued that a federal law, the Controlled Substances Act, allowed the federal government to prohibit physicians from prescribing lethal doses of drugs to their terminally ill patients. On January 17, 2007, the Supreme Court ruled against the Bush administration and upheld the constitutionality of Oregon's law. Justice Anthony Kennedy, writing for the majority, reasoned that the plain intent of the federal law applies to physicians only insofar as it prohibits them from using their prescription-writing powers to engage in illegal drug dealing and trafficking, but does not extend to physicians in their legitimate professional activity of prescribing medication to their patients. The ruling was limited, however. It did not address the issue of a constitutional right to die. It did not deny that Congress could pass legislation overriding state laws that permit physician-assisted suicide. In 2008, Washington became the second state, and on December 31, 2009, Montana became the third state to legalize physician-assisted suicide.[31]

A major argument against the legalization of direct-active-voluntary euthanasia is the wedge or slippery slope argument. It holds that even if this type of euthanasia is morally unobjectionable in itself, it should not be legalized, for legalization would lead to all sorts of morally bad consequences. There are two versions of the argument: logical and empirical. In the logical version, legalization of voluntary euthanasia would necessarily lead to the legalization of such serious evils as involuntary euthanasia, widespread infanticide and disposal of the elderly, elimination of socially undesirable groups and individuals—and to the ultimate horror of all, Nazism. To prevent these evils from happening, then, there must be an absolute ban on direct-active-voluntary euthanasia. The empirical version of this argument is not as extreme. Not all the foregoing evils would necessarily follow from the legalization of direct-active-voluntary euthanasia, but some of them would *probably* follow, because of the general deterioration of respect for persons that the legalization of direct-voluntary euthanasia represents. Sometimes the empirical version is presented as a probable abuse argument: if direct-voluntary euthanasia is legalized, the likelihood of the law being abused by medical personnel, family members, and other interested parties is so great that its abuse outweighs any of its possible benefits.

The following is a typical example of the logical version of the argument, by Bishop Joseph Sullivan of the Roman Catholic Church:

> Once a man is permitted on his own authority to kill an innocent person directly, there is no way of stopping the advancement of that wedge. There exists no longer any rational grounds for saying that the wedge can advance so far and no further. . . . That is why euthanasia under any circumstances must be condemned. . . .
>
> If voluntary euthanasia were legalized, there is good reason to believe that at a later date another bill for compulsory euthanasia would be legalized. Once the respect for human life is so low that an innocent person may be killed directly even at his own request, compulsory euthanasia will necessarily be very near. This could lead easily to killing all incurable charity patients, the aged who are a public care, wounded soldiers, captured enemy soldiers, all deformed children, the mentally afflicted, and so on. Before long the danger would be at the door of every citizen.[32]

The argument is unsound, because it is based on a false premise: that there are no rational grounds for distinguishing between direct-active-voluntary euthanasia and the chain of evils of which the bishop speaks. It is false, because supporters of this type of euthanasia have supplied the rational grounds, as I and others have done. Therefore, since rational grounds do exist, and since direct-active-voluntary euthanasia is morally right on those grounds, there is no good reason not to legalize it.

An empirical version of the argument is presented by the highly respected British moral philosopher Philippa Foot. She writes:

> Legalizing active euthanasia is . . . another matter. Apart from the special repugnance doctors feel toward the idea of a lethal injection, it may be of the very greatest importance to keep a psychological barrier up against killing. It would be hard to devise procedures that would protect people from being persuaded into giving their consent. . . . Active voluntary euthanasia might change the social scene in ways that would be very bad. As things are, people do, by and large, expect to be looked after if they are old or ill. . . . It might come to be expected that someone likely to need a lot of looking after should call for the doctor and demand his own death.[33]

Foot concludes that direct-active-voluntary euthanasia should not be legalized, even though she thinks that it is morally right in some cases.

However, Foot's fearful predictions are based on speculation, not on hard evidence. Consequently, the main question that must be asked of the wedge argument is this: what is the evidence that the claimed evils and abuses will in fact follow from legalization? There is plenty of evidence that they will not follow. All societies permit killing in some circumstances although they prohibit it in general. In the pre–*Roe v. Wade* era, antiabortionists used the same argument against legalization of abortion, although their dire predictions have been falsified and were even contradicted at the time by nations that had permissive abortion laws.[34] A good law will hold abuse to a minimum, but it is unrealistic to expect that abuses will never occur. Anything humans create is sometimes abused. Opponents have not proven that in countries where it is legal—for example, the Netherlands—abuse outweighs its benefits.

Direct-Nonvoluntary

I must distinguish between active and passive versions of this type of euthanasia, as I did with direct-voluntary euthanasia, since direct-active euthanasia is morally better than direct-passive euthanasia. However, direct-active-nonvoluntary euthanasia is not as morally justifiable as direct-active-voluntary euthanasia, for two reasons: (1) since it is nonvoluntary, it lacks the patient's consent; and (2) some of the cases in which it arises do not involve a medical condition in which death is imminent. One important class of individuals who are included in this type are seriously defective infants. In my view, euthanasia is morally justifiable only in those cases involving the most severe defects, one of which has already been mentioned: anencephaly. In this condition, the infant's brain is either substantially or totally absent. In some cases, death is a virtual certainty. The individual is so extremely retarded that he or she has minimal control over bodily movements and functions. There is never hope for improvement by any known medical means.

Another defect or condition almost as severe is spina bifida accompanied by hydrocephaly (which it almost always is) and myelomeningocele. Spina bifida is a birth defect that involves an opening in the spine. The open vertebrae often allow the membrane covering the spinal cord to protrude to the outside. Sometimes the membrane forms a bulging, thin sac that contains spinal fluid and nerve tissue. This condition is called myelomeningocele and is very severe. Hydrocephaly literally means water on the brain. When the flow of fluid through the spinal canal is blocked, the cerebrospinal fluid within the brain cannot escape. Pressure buildup from the fluid can cause brain damage. If it is not released, the infant will die. Treatment for these three interrelated conditions is long, complicated, costly, risky, and painful, and has a marginal chance of success. The initial opening of the spine must be closed. In myelomeningocele, the sac is removed and the nerve tissue inside is placed within the spinal canal. Then the whole area is covered with normal skin. Since the danger of infection (meningitis) is great, treatment with antibiotic drugs is necessary. Because of nerve damage, especially in extreme cases, a child with spina bifida is likely to require orthopedic surgery to correct deformities of the legs and feet. The bones are thin and brittle, and fractures are common. The child is almost always paralyzed to some extent below the waist. Again because of nerve damage, he or she will have limited sensation in the lower body. The child will have no control over bladder and bowels. The lack of bladder control may lead to infection of the bladder, urinary tract, and kidneys, because the undischarged urine can be a breeding ground for microorganisms. Surgery may help—somewhat. Treatment for hydrocephaly involves surgically inserting a thin tube or shunt to drain fluid from the skull to the heart or abdomen, where it can be absorbed. The operation is necessary to save the infant's life, but it is risky. Mental and physical damage is frequent. Many operations may be required to place the shunt correctly and get it to work properly. Hydrocephaly is the condition of spina bifida that is treated first.[35]

Despite the severity of these defects, however, unless death is imminent, direct euthanasia is morally impermissible. And to employ passive means of death here would be even worse than active means. If death is imminent, active means should be used if a decision is made to terminate life.

One defect in which direct-nonvoluntary euthanasia is clearly morally wrong is Down's syndrome complicated by duodenal atresia. About one out of every thousand children is born with Down's syndrome. It is a genetic defect characterized by mental retardation and various physical abnormalities that are relatively minor in nature. These include a broad skull, a large tongue, and an upward slant of the eyelids. The last feature has led to the name mongolism for this condition. IQs are generally in the range of 50 to 80. Those with the defect can be taught simple tasks. They are capable of playful activity. Despite their condition, they lead happy lives and are capable of both giving and receiving affection.

Sometimes, however, Down's syndrome occurs with a condition called duodenal atresia, which is a form of intestinal blockage. The duodenum is the upper part of the small intestine, into which food from the stomach empties. In duodenal atresia, the duodenum is closed off so that food cannot pass through and be digested. Unless the condition is corrected, the baby will starve to death. Happily, the condition is easily corrected through surgery that is relatively simple and inexpensive. It is considered ordinary medical care. When normal children are born with the condition, the operation is unhesitatingly performed. Unfortunately, some parents do not want a mongoloid child, so they refuse to consent to surgery, and the baby slowly and painfully starves and dehydrates to death. Despite its cruelty, the practice is fairly widespread, since it does not involve an active means.[36]

The most recent and famous case of direct-nonvoluntary euthanasia is that of Terri Schiavo. In early 2005, her case raised a level of national controversy on euthanasia not seen since the Karen Quinlan case of the 1970s.

Terri Schiavo was a forty-one-year-old Florida woman at the time of her death on March 31, 2005. She had been in PVS since February 26, 1990. She died of starvation and dehydration after a Florida state court ordered on March 18 that her feeding tube be removed in accordance with the long-standing wishes of her husband and legal guardian, Michael Schiavo. Although she had no living will or similar document, Florida state courts repeatedly ruled that Michael presented sufficient evidence that she would not have wanted to live in her condition.

Terri Schiavo's Roman Catholic parents opposed the removal of her feeding tube and asked the courts to replace Michael with them as her legal guardians. Their case was dismissed. In February 2000, Judge George W. Greer of a Florida state court ruled, for the first time, that Schiavo's feeding tube should be removed. After much legal wrangling, it was removed in April 2001. Two days later a different judge in a new case ordered the tube reinserted. In October 2003, a state court ordered the tube removed a second time. Subsequently, the Florida state legislature passed "Terri's Law," and her tube was reinserted six days later. In March 2005, a federal court ruled that Terri's Law was unconstitutional, and on March 18 her tube was removed for a third time. On March 21, Congress, bowing to intense pressure from religious conservatives, passed a law that again transferred her case to the federal courts. On March 24, the US Supreme Court refused to hear her case, and Terri Schiavo died on March 31.

Schiavo's euthanization was bitterly opposed by a large number of vocal and well-organized religious conservatives. They raised two issues that I want to briefly discuss. First, they disputed the court's claim that Schiavo was in PVS. Part of their reasoning was that she was not completely unconscious. She did exhibit some activity that they wrongly interpreted as involving higher cognition and higher consciousness. They confused PVS with coma. The overwhelming opinion of medical experts was that Terri Schiavo was in PVS. According to medical evidence and testimony, she had been in a permanent vegetative state since February 26, 1990. This finding was supported by an autopsy after her death, which revealed massive destruction of her brain. Most of her brain cells had been destroyed. Her PVS was precipitated by a potassium deficiency brought about by an eating disorder (probably bulimia) causing her heart to stop and depriving her brain of oxygen for a prolonged period (anoxia).[37]

A second important issue raised by opponents of Schiavo's euthanization was their claim that all direct-passive-nonvoluntary euthanasia is immoral and ought to be unconstitutional. Many of them characterized her death as murder. In this regard, they challenged the constitutional right to die standard set forth by the Supreme Court in the *Cruzan* decision previously noted. Because of its importance to the Schiavo case, I now give this decision more attention than earlier in the chapter. In *Cruzan*, the Court ruled that two classes of individuals have a constitutional right to die by refusing food, water, and medical treatment. First, there are terminally ill patients who are competent to give consent. Second, there are incompetent patients in PVS. The second class of patients includes two subclasses of individuals: (a) patients who have left a living will or other legal document expressing their desire not to continue living in such a condition, and (b) patients who have no living will or similar document but whose legal guardians and/or next-of-kin can present clear and convincing evidence to the courts that the patient would not want to live in this condition. Thus, the Court implied there is a constitutional right to die in cases of direct-passive-voluntary and direct-passive-nonvoluntary euthanasia under the above conditions.

On a moral level, I think the *Cruzan* ruling is correct as far as it goes, but it does not go far enough. I agree with the Court that direct-passive euthanasia of patients in PVS is morally permissible in its voluntary and nonvoluntary modes. However, as I previously indicated, in these cases it would be morally better to use quick and painless active means rather than prolonged passive means: direct-active euthanasia is morally superior to direct-passive euthanasia. As we have seen, though, active means of euthanasia are illegal throughout the United States and are presently unconstitutional. I regard this complete prohibition of active means to be morally mistaken, but unless or until our laws are changed to allow direct-active euthanasia, I reluctantly support direct-passive euthanasia in both its voluntary and nonvoluntary modes in cases like Terri Schiavo's. In her case, it is morally better to perform euthanasia with a passive means than not to perform it at all. Since the patients at issue are in PVS, there is no evidence they are in pain when food and water are withdrawn, although such an unnecessarily prolonged manner of death compared with an active means must be regarded as cruel. Family, friends, and hospital staff who love the patient and care for her are forced to see her body slowly die and wither away under their watchful eyes. And since a patient in PVS still retains some minimal degree of lower sensory and reflex consciousness, we cannot be absolutely sure she is not in pain as she slowly starves and dehydrates to death, although there is no observable evidence that the patient is suffering. For all these reasons, once it has been determined that in a case of direct euthanasia it is morally right to directly intend the death of the patient, it is morally preferable to use active means over passive means. There is no doubt that active means are both quick and painless.

In sum, then, direct-nonvoluntary euthanasia is prima facie immoral, governed by Rules Three and Five of the principle of intentionality, but its active version is always morally better than its passive version, ceteris paribus.

Direct-Involuntary

In this type of euthanasia, a patient is directly killed against his or her will. Consequently, it is the most difficult of the six types of euthanasia to morally justify. Indeed, in my view, it is never morally justifiable; it is intrinsically immoral. Hence, the distinction between active and passive means has no moral importance here, except that a passive means would aggravate its already intrinsic immorality. Were it not for the presumed motive of mercy, we would call this type murder. However, if the means were passive, mercy could not be present, and then this type would be murder—indeed, murder by torture. Direct-involuntary euthanasia violates the principle of community; it is an absolute impersonal act. It has a gravely bad direct intention. It is prohibited by Rule Two of intentionality. Virtually no one advocates this type of euthanasia; it is morally noncontroversial. Yet many opponents of euthanasia focus their attention and arguments against direct-active-involuntary euthanasia. In doing so, they commit the straw man fallacy.

Indirect-Voluntary

Morally, this is the least objectionable type of euthanasia. In my view, its indirectness and its voluntariness guarantee its moral rightness. It is noncontroversial. A model example would be the Karen Quinlan case with a living will. It is morally justified by the principle of community and Rule One of intentionality. Another example, previously noted, is a patient whose pain cannot be managed by normal, safe doses of drugs. Consequently, with the patient's consent, her doctor gradually increases the doses of painkillers to borderline lethal levels, and she dies. This type of example, too, is justified by Rule One.

Indirect-Nonvoluntary

The Karen Quinlan case perfectly exemplifies this type of euthanasia. As indirect, it is morally justifiable. In this context, so is its nonvoluntariness, for a proxy must fulfill two criteria: he or she must be acquainted with the patient well enough to know what the patient would likely request in this situation, and he or she must act from a merciful or loving motive. It would seem that Mr. Quinlan met both of these criteria. Indirect-voluntary and indirect-nonvoluntary constitute the range of morally noncontroversial euthanasia. They are morally justified as indicated under indirect-voluntary euthanasia.

Indirect-Involuntary

Here we have a moral conflict: As indirect, it is morally right; as involuntary, it is morally wrong. In the context of indirect euthanasia, it is always wrong, in my view, to refuse a patient's request not to employ extraordinary means. However, the converse is not necessarily true. It may sometimes be morally permissible to overrule a patient's request to continue extraordinary means, for the request may be unreasonable. For example, suppose someone in Karen Quinlan's condition requests in a written document that she be kept on a respirator indefinitely. If that same respirator were needed to save another patient's life who was suffering from a serious respiratory ailment but who was otherwise normal, then the respirator should be transferred to the second patient—against the first patient's will. Since extraordinary means may sometimes be scarce, situations like this can arise, especially if the first patient is wealthy. However, not every request for medical care is reasonable, and scarce medical resources should not be allocated on the basis of wealth. This type of euthanasia, then, is prima facie immoral and is regulated by Rule Three of intentionality.

6

THE DEATH PENALTY AND PURPOSES OF PUNISHMENT

There is a major difference between the death penalty and the other issues of life and death that we have examined. In the death penalty, the person executed is judged to be guilty. Moreover, unlike the abortion and euthanasia issues, there is no reasonable doubt that the individuals killed are persons. Nevertheless, public opinion has been strongly in favor of the death penalty. According to recent polls, Americans support the death penalty by a two to one margin. It must be the case, then, that the guilt or noninnocence factor, in the public mind, carries the whole moral weight of the death penalty issue. The fact that the state is executing a *person* is considered morally insignificant by supporters of capital punishment.

Majority opinion, however, is no criterion of truth or moral rightness. To say that it is commits the ad populum fallacy, as discussed in a previous chapter. Public opinion on this issue is also fickle. In the 1960s, a majority of Americans were opposed to the death penalty. By contrast, in 1994, 80 percent of Americans supported the death penalty. Since then, this figure has slowly declined and by October 2011 stood at 61 percent. Moreover, American opinion conflicts with that of most Western European nations and world democracies, which have long since abolished capital punishment. Unfortunately, most Americans seem to base their support of capital punishment on unreflective emotion, especially on revenge or vengeance, rather than on knowledge and a thoughtful evaluation of the issue. Psychiatrist Louis Gold has observed that "the average American appears to have only a limited concept of the issue, has done very little reading on the subject, and has not taken much time to think it through in an objective manner. Most folks accept the idea in a traditional sense without an intelligent appraisal of its significance."[1]

The chapter is divided into two broad sections. Since one's attitude toward the death penalty is significantly determined by one's theory of punishment in general, in the first section I examine and critically evaluate the two major philosophical theories of punishment: retributivism and utilitarianism. I find both theories inadequate as they stand. I argue that the personalism expressed in this volume requires a synthesis and modification of retributivism and utilitarianism. I call this synthesis the personalist theory of punishment. Then in the second section I apply retributivism, utilitarianism, and the personalist theory to the death penalty. In the process, I discuss several recent Supreme Court decisions on capital punishment.

I defend two positions in this chapter. First, the death penalty is morally justifiable in the *abstract* for the most serious crime: premeditated murder. Second, the death penalty in the *concrete*, that is, here and now and in the foreseeable future, is morally unjustifiable and ought to be abolished.

PUNISHMENT IN GENERAL

We begin with a definition of punishment. Among philosophers, there is no serious dispute concerning how it should be defined. Differences among definitions are mostly semantic, and the main elements of an adequate definition are agreed upon. To some extent, my definition reflects key ideas developed earlier, for example, the concepts of direct intention and person. Accordingly, I define (criminal) punishment as follows: the deprivation of a good or right to which a person is normally entitled, because the person has been judged guilty of a serious violation of a society's law, by a person or persons who are authorized by the state to directly intend the deprivation. Since punishment involves depriving a person of a good or right especially by direct intention, it requires moral justification. In Western philosophy and civilization, retributivism and utilitarianism are the two detailed answers to the question: why do we punish, or, more precisely, why ought we to punish?

Since retributivism is the older theory, I examine it first. In what follows, I use the word *offender* for *criminal*.

Retributivism and Revenge

Retributivism has fallen on hard times. Most criminologists and social scientists oppose it. So do many philosophers. It is considered unfashionable, archaic, a thing of the past. Yet some of the greatest philosophers favored it: Aristotle, Aquinas, Kant, and Hegel, to name a few. Recently, however, there has been a modest resurgence of interest in retributivism among philosophers. Suddenly, it is not quite as unfashionable as it used to be.

Since the unpopularity of a view does not imply its falsity any more than its popularity implies its truth, it is important to ask why retributivism is so unpopular among intellectuals. The basic reason seems to be that its critics identify it with revenge, and revenge, according to them, is simply not a morally valid purpose of punishment. I completely agree that revenge is a morally invalid purpose of punishment, but I deny that revenge and retribution are identical purposes of punishment. Indeed, there is sufficient difference between them to conclude that retribution is the basic and indispensable purpose of punishment. To show this, I explain the theory of retributivism and why it ought to exclude revenge (or vengeance).

In general, retributivism is based on a conception of a human person as a rational and social being. Such a conception was elaborated in chapter 1, where I explained three dimensions of personhood: mutuality, agency, and reason. In order for humans to develop their rational nature as persons, they must live in a society of persons. In turn, society requires a state and a system of law that the state administers and enforces. There are at least two reasons that the state is necessary to society. First, it is necessary for the very survival of society. In the memorable phrase of Hobbes, without the state, we would have "the war of all against all." There would be "continual fear, and danger of violent death; and the life of man [would be] solitary, poor, nasty, brutish, and short."[2] Second, the state and its laws are necessary instruments for establishing and promoting justice; they constitute an order of justice. This does not mean, of course, that every law is actually just, but it ought to be. Justice is the essence of law. As Augustine puts it, an unjust law is no law at all.[3] Or in Macmurray's words: "The law and the State [are] . . . a necessary system of devices for achieving and maintaining justice."[4]

Because a system of law represents an order of justice, the state distributes both goods and burdens among its members. The distribution of goods is the subject of distributive justice; the distribution of burdens belongs to retributive justice. Besides paying taxes, the main burden is the duty or obligation to obey the law if the whole system of law is going to work. If some members obey the law and some do not, then the latter gain an unfair advantage over the former. Those who refuse obedience shift their burden to the law-abiding members. They take the goods of society without any corresponding burden, while the law-abiding members take on a double burden. This provides a further incentive to violate the law. Why assume the burden of obeying the law if those who do not obey it are treated exactly the same as those who do? Obviously, under such conditions the whole system of law will rapidly break down, and with it, society itself.[5] To prevent the dissolution of society, then, the laws of society must be enforced, and those who violate its laws must be punished.

For retributivism, then, punishment is for the sake of justice. Retributivism aims at restoring or rectifying an order of justice that an offender has broken. Unless it can be shown that a particular law is unjust, a violation of the law is ipso facto unjust. Or as Hegel puts it, punishment is "the righting of a wrong."[6]

Within this background theory of retributivism, the essence of retribution as a specific purpose of punishment consists of three propositions.[7] The first two propositions concern the conditions under which a person is punishable; the third is concerned with the degree or kind of punishment a person deserves. The first proposition simply asserts that a person must be guilty of committing a crime. This means that a person must both actually and voluntarily violate a law. Since a person by nature is a rational being, normally he or she voluntarily chooses to violate a law. In those exceptions when criminal activity is not voluntary (as in insanity) or involves diminished voluntariness, the burden of proof is on the accused to show that this is the case. Diminished voluntariness still involves some degree of freedom and thus entails a correspondingly diminished degree of responsibility and culpability. The first proposition obviously rules out punishment of the innocent. A person can be either objectively innocent, because he or she did not commit the crime at all, or subjectively innocent, because he or she did not voluntarily commit it. Conversely, for a person to be guilty, he must be objectively guilty and subjectively guilty. Objective guilt means that a person actually committed the crime for which he is accused. Subjective guilt means that he freely willed to do it and hence performed a voluntary act. A rational conception of guilt includes both elements, and accords with our definition of reason in chapter 1 as the synthesis of objectivity (primarily) with subjectivity (secondarily). Objective guilt is primary because a person must obviously first commit a crime before he can be judged morally responsible for committing it. The first proposition also rules out not punishing the guilty. I address this issue later.

The second proposition is that a person must be found guilty in accordance with fair procedures of justice. The presupposition is that society has a developed sense of justice, as any society ought to have. We see it in many features of our own society: the Bill of Rights, the principle that a person is innocent until proved guilty beyond a reasonable doubt, the emphasis placed on the defendant's rights, and the exclusionary rule. These two propositions together establish the concept of *punishability*. It defines who is worthy or deserving of punishment and who is not.

Punishability, however, does not tell us *how* an offender should be punished, what kind or degree of punishment is deserved. Thus, there is a third proposition of retributivism: The offender deserves a punishment that fits the crime. Still, there are two somewhat different interpretations of this proposition: the principle of equality and the principle of proportionality.[8] These two principles have a bearing on the difference between retribution and revenge.

The principle of equality is expressed in the biblical *lex talionis*: an eye for an eye, a tooth for a tooth. It is favored by Kant.[9] It states that we must always aim at penalties that are equal to, or the same as, their corresponding crimes. However, critics say that it is often impossible, unreasonable, or immoral to make punishment equal to a crime. For example, what is the equal punishment for treason, rape, assault and battery, libel, child sexual abuse, or theft of a large sum of money by a poor person? What punishment could Hitler or Stalin have received to equal the enormity of their crimes? As Sir William

Blackstone once remarked: "Theft cannot be punished by theft, defamation by defamation, forgery by forgery, adultery by adultery, and the like."[10]

Critics of the principle of equality adopt the principle of proportionality: the offender deserves a punishment that is proportionate to the crime. Proportionality sometimes implies equality. Indeed, equality should be intended if there is no countervailing reason that it should not be intended. However, there are many cases in which countervailing reasons do exist, cases in which equality of punishment is either physically impossible or morally unjustifiable. In these cases, proportionality denotes a reasonable relation, or an approximate similarity, between a crime and punishment, while it avoids the two extremes of excessive and lenient punishment. One is reminded of Aristotle's view that virtue is a mean between two extremes of vice.

The principle of proportionality also requires that punishment be uniform for the same crime, taking into consideration any relevant differences among cases. I call this requirement the principle of uniformity. For example, one cannot give a white person a more lenient punishment than a black person for the same crime, other things being equal. The obverse of uniformity is that all the relevant circumstances of a particular case must be considered and weighed by a judge before sentencing is pronounced. However, mandatory sentencing rules out this important judicial function and is, in my view, a violation of retributivism. Mandatory sentencing appears to be a usurpation of judicial function by the legislative branch of government. The principle of uniformity, then, is a corollary of the principle of proportionality.

When it comes to the type or amount of punishment an offender deserves, retribution adopts the principle of proportionality, whereas revenge applies the principle of equality. As we have seen, if the state always aims at equality of punishment, it will sometimes be necessary to inflict cruel and barbaric punishments, as the *lex talionis* implies. Plucking out someone's eye, or pulling out someone's tooth, is hardly a humane form of punishment. By contrast, the principle of proportionality is much more flexible. It enables the state to avoid aiming at equality of punishment when equality implies cruel or inhumane punishment.

There are three other important differences between retribution and revenge.[11] First, retribution is disinterested, whereas revenge is self-regarding.[12] Retribution is administered by a neutral or impartial legal authority—by a judge, for example. Revenge is typically administered by an injured party outside the framework of the law. "Taking the law into your own hands" expresses this aspect of revenge. Second, the motive of retribution is the rational and ethical desire to achieve justice. Hence, retribution is often called retributive justice. Or in Hegel's words, "punishment is inherently and actually just."[13] The motive of revenge, in contrast, is the purely emotional and unethical desire to get even by directly intending to cause the offender pain and suffering. It has a sadistic quality. For example, some people are opposed to execution by injection, because they believe that it is too painless. "It's too lenient. They've got to go out painfully."[14] Third, retribution views the offender as a person and treats him or her accordingly. Revenge views the offender as something subhuman, especially when the most serious of crimes, such as murder, is involved. Some retentionists, for example, refer to capital criminals as "uncontrollable brutes," "mad animals," and even "germs." But as Sissela Bok correctly observes: "To question someone's humanity or personhood is a first step to mistreatment and killing."[15] Because of this difference, retribution is much more concerned with such things as protecting the rights of the accused and the criminal, the necessity of assuming that the accused is innocent until proved guilty, giving the accused a fair trial, and the concepts of due process and equal protection of the law. By contrast, the spirit of revenge is the spirit of the lynch mob.

For retributivism, then, retribution and not revenge is the proper function or purpose of punishment. Revenge violates the principle of community by producing an absolute impersonal relation on the part of the punisher toward the punishee. Retribution promotes the principle of community by establishing a relative impersonal relation of persons. The relation between the state and the punishee is essentially impersonal, since it is institutional and functional. However, in retribution, the impersonal relation is for the sake of a personal relation. The punishee is recognized and treated as a person. His rights are respected, and he is treated humanely and with dignity. He is treated justly. He is given as much freedom as circumstances allow. Legal equality is present. The principle of equal justice under law belongs to the essence of retributivism.

The reasonable doubt principle (or rule) as part of proposition two raises a question. Conservatives in particular often criticize the rule because they claim that it sometimes results in the guilty being acquitted. The reply usually given is that the rule is needed as a safeguard against punishing the innocent and that it is worse to punish the innocent than to acquit the guilty. But why is punishing the innocent worse?

One answer, I think, lies in the concept of human rights. And human rights, I would argue, constitute an essential component of justice within a personalist theory of retributivism. Article 11 of the Universal Declaration of Human Rights states: "Everyone charged with a penal offense has the right to be presumed innocent until proved guilty according to law in a public trial at which he has had all the guarantees necessary for his defence." [16] A corollary of this right, I contend, is the reasonable doubt rule. For if we have a criminal justice system with a rule that specifies a lower standard of proof for convictions than the reasonable doubt rule, then we directly intend the design and establishment of a system in which more innocent persons will be found guilty and punished than in a system that has the reasonable doubt rule. With a lower standard than reasonable doubt, we create a system in which the violation of human rights is built into it. But this is not the case in a criminal justice system that practices the reasonable doubt rule. It is the highest *practical* standard of proof. If practiced consistently, the rule adequately protects the innocent without unduly acquitting the guilty. As bad as it is to occasionally acquit those persons who may or would have been found guilty under a lower standard of proof and who are actually guilty under proposition one of retributivism, this is not as bad as an act, practice, or institution that violates some defendants' human rights in a criminal justice system that has a lower standard of proof for convicting the accused than it needs to have and should have. The lesser bad is to be tolerated when the only way to prevent it is the creation of a system that violates human rights. It is not a violation of anyone's human rights to acquit a defendant who is de facto guilty under proposition one and who might have been found guilty under a lower standard than the reasonable doubt standard, providing that all the relevant rules of justice under an ethically sound retributivism have been followed. The foregoing analysis also implies that intentionally punishing the innocent is a violation of human rights.

I conclude that retribution is the primary and indispensable purpose of punishment (since it is required by justice), that retribution and revenge are morally incompatible, and that revenge is a morally impermissible purpose of punishment. Retribution, however, is not the only valid purpose of punishment. To show this, I turn now to the utilitarian theory.

Utilitarian Theory

The utilitarian theory of punishment has its roots in Jeremy Bentham. The principle of utility holds that pleasure is the supreme good (and, indeed, the only intrinsic good) and pain the ultimate evil. Therefore, Bentham begins with the premise that punishment as such is an evil, since it inflicts pain in one form or another. He writes: "All punishment in itself is evil. . . . It ought only to be admitted in as far as it promises to exclude some greater evil."[17] In other words, punishment is morally justifiable only if it produces good (or pleasurable) consequences for society and/or for the criminal that outweigh its evil (or painful) consequences. The utilitarian view sharply contrasts with retributivism, which holds that punishment as such is just, since it is the righting of a wrong. In what follows, I give a loose interpretation of Bentham.

Bentham distinguishes three types of good consequences of punishment: prevention, deterrence, and reform.[18] In prevention, punishment stops offenders from committing the same crime again or from committing other crimes by incapacitating them, for example, through incarceration. Prevention involves "disabling" the offender by restricting his "physical power." Prevention is a good consequence for society, since, if it works, it protects society from the harmful consequence of any future crimes that the offender might or will commit. Deterrence works through fear. A punishment may deter others from committing the same type of crime that an offender has just committed. Likewise, punished offenders can be deterred from committing future crimes. Deterrence operates by setting an "example" to people. Deterrence, too, is a good consequence for society. It protects society from all those crimes that otherwise would have been committed. Finally, a punishment may reform (or rehabilitate) offenders by providing them with a set of socially and occupationally desirable skills while they are incarcerated, so that they may become useful and productive members of society. If successful, reform produces good consequences for both society and the criminal.

Utilitarians in general still follow Bentham's triad. For the utilitarian theory, prevention, deterrence, and reform are the only legitimate purposes of punishment. A particular punishment can serve any of these three purposes in combination. Minimally, it must serve one of them. Ideally, it serves all three. If punishment serves none of them, it is morally impermissible, an action of pointless revenge. Moreover, punishment is morally impermissible even if it does serve some of these purposes but its good consequences are outweighed by the evil consequences of the punishment as such. The utilitarian theory has no use for the retributivist idea of punishing for the sake of justice, since this idea attempts to justify punishment independently of the utilitarian formula of good versus bad consequences. As a result, for the utilitarian theory, retributivism is based on revenge. Utilitarianism sees no difference between retribution and revenge; they are identical purposes of punishment.

There is obvious truth in the utilitarian theory. Punishments ought to deter and prevent crime, and they ought to reform the offender. At the same time, the theory has many critics. I now discuss six common criticisms (which seem fair to me). First and fundamentally, the utilitarian theory is wholly indifferent to the ethical concept of punishability. Its sole concern is to devise a system of punishments that produce good social and/or personal consequences as determined by the principle of utility, as when a punishment prevents and deters crime, and reforms the offender. The theory presupposes that a society has already decided, by whatever standards, that a person should be punished. But it does not judge the moral adequacy of these standards themselves. The utilitarian theory simply accepts them as a given. In this sense, it is concerned only with *how* we should punish offenders and not with *why* a person ought to be punished in the first place. Therefore, the first two propositions of retributivism fall completely outside the purview of the utilitarian theory.

The other five criticisms are more specific and fall within the generality of the first. The second criticism is that the utilitarian theory cannot adequately protect against punishing the innocent. Deterrence by itself is wholly indifferent to the guilt or innocence of the person punished. Deterrence can be equally effective in punishing the innocent as in punishing the guilty. For retributivism, however, it is simply unjust to directly intend the punishment of innocent persons. Such an intention seems gravely bad, producing an intrinsically immoral type of action, prohibited by Rule Two of the principle of intentionality. But the utilitarian theory, say critics, cannot provide a justification for this basic moral truth. Retributivism does. Punishing the innocent violates the first, and fundamental, proposition of retribution.

It might seem that punishing the innocent would be a problem only for act utilitarianism, for cannot a rule utilitarian hold that the principle of utility is promoted by the simple rule that it is always wrong to punish the innocent? Apparently not. Sophisticated rule utilitarian Richard Brandt explains why, and under what conditions, it is sometimes permissible to punish the innocent:

> He [the rule utilitarian] is not in the position of the act-utilitarian, who must say that an innocent man must be punished if in *his particular* case the public welfare would be served by his punishment. The rule-utilitarian rather asserts only that an innocent man should be punished if he falls within a class of cases such that net expectable utility is maximized if *all* members of the class are punished, taking into account the possible disastrous effects on public confidence if it is generally known that judges and prosecutors are guided by such a rule.[19]

It appears that Brandt has impaled himself on the horns of a dilemma, for either the rule to punish the innocent is publicly known or it is not publicly known. If publicly known, the rule is immoral if only because of the disastrous effects such knowledge will have on public confidence; if not publicly known, the rule is immoral if only because of the conspiratorial deceit (or cover-up) perpetrated by high-ranking legal authorities. Moreover, the apparent converse of the view that it is sometimes permissible to punish the innocent is that it is sometimes permissible to acquit the guilty on irrelevant social and moral grounds—a practice that includes jury nullification. It is forbidden by retributivism.

Third, the utilitarian theory cannot rule out punishing the guilty excessively. Again, if the sole purpose of punishment is deterrence, an excessive punishment can deter as well as a nonexcessive one, maybe even more so, if it scares the living daylights out of some would-be offenders. However, an excessive punishment by definition is unjust, since it violates the principle of proportionality. An offender deserves a punishment that is proportionate to his or her crime. Proportionality excludes excessiveness, regardless of the latter's deterrent effect.

Fourth, prevention by itself could lead to similar abuses. Without a controlling idea or theory of justice, prevention could include the preventive detention of innocent persons based on groundless fear and suspicion. One of the most notorious examples in US history was the incarceration of Japanese Americans on the West Coast soon after the outbreak of World War II.

Fifth, without the ethical control of retributive justice, reform can likewise be abused. Some critics charge that it is not uncommon for an offender to serve a long and indefinite prison sentence only to satisfy some vague standard of rehabilitation that has nothing to do with the crime; if he had been sentenced in accordance with strict retribution, he would have long since paid his debt to society and been released.[20]

Sixth and finally, there are cases in which it makes moral sense to punish even when the utilitarian purposes have little or no application. For example, take some highly publicized cases of accused Nazi war criminals who have been discovered decades later. Typically, they are accused of committing hundreds, even thousands, of murders and other atrocities. The evidence against them is usually strong, sometimes overwhelming, and certainly strong enough to try them. But they are old men now. They have become socially integrated and may even be model citizens. They are harmless, so there is nothing to reform or prevent. And what or whom will be deterred by punishing them? Not another Third Reich, not a regime or movement similar to the Third Reich, and not even violent crimes committed by current Nazi and Nazi-like thugs. It is unlikely, then, that punishment will have much, if any, deterrent effect. Yet from the standpoint of retributivism, none of this matters. Murders committed many years ago are as unjust as murders committed today. The enormity of the crimes demands justice in the form of some kind of proportionate punishment. The infliction of proportionate punishment as the performance of justice is itself a consequence of sufficient moral weight to justify punishing these individuals.

However, these criticisms are denied by some rule utilitarians. William Shaw especially rejects the criticism that utilitarianism permits punishment of the innocent.

. . . There are conclusive utilitarian objections to a legal (or quasi-legal) system that instructs or permits its officials to frame innocent people whenever those officials deem it necessary for the benefit of society. The potential for abuse is so great that the contention that utilitarians would favor and attempt to design such a system is preposterous.[21]

I agree that such a system is morally corrupt. Unfortunately, not all utilitarians rule out punishment of the innocent, as I showed in my citation from Brandt. But there is a deeper point here. Why is it wrong to punish the innocent? Utilitarians like Shaw ultimately appeal to the principle of utility: in the long run, a society that has a legal system that permits punishment of the innocent would produce less happiness (or pleasure) for the greatest number of people than a society whose legal system prohibits punishment of the innocent. From my personalist standpoint, this reason is inadequate. The fundamental reason punishing the innocent is wrong is that it violates the principles of community and intentionality, and it violates human rights. Community is violated because the state establishes an absolute impersonal relation with the punishee by committing an act of injustice against him, since it violates his inherent moral and human right not to be punished if he is innocent. The state violates his moral status as a person. Intentionality is violated because the state's direct intention to punish an innocent person is gravely bad and produces an intrinsically immoral action, prohibited by Rules Two and Four of intentionality. And we have seen how it violates human rights.

Personalist Theory of Punishment

The utilitarian theory by itself fails as an adequate theory of punishment primarily because it does not and cannot establish the concept of punishability. But neither is traditional retributivism perfectly adequate as it stands, although it is far more adequate than the utilitarian theory. Each theory needs the other; both must be synthesized within a larger framework or theory that I call personalist. According to the personalist theory, retribution is the primary and indispensable purpose of punishment, since it is grounded in justice; the utilitarian purposes are ancillary and, to some extent, necessary purposes. There are three reasons that I call this synthesis personalist. First, retributivism itself, I contend, is personalist. It is based on the personalist themes of the inherent rationality, sociality, and freedom (free will) of human persons and of justice as an intrinsic moral good (or value). The utilitarian theory is nonpersonalist, because it is not specifically based on any of these themes. Second, the utilitarian purposes acquire a personalist character by being synthesized with retributivism; they are given a personalist foundation. And third, the personalist nature of retributivism is enriched by the utilitarian purposes. Let me now sketch this synthesis.

For the utilitarian purposes to acquire moral legitimacy, they must be grounded in retributivism. That is, it makes moral sense to speak of prevention, deterrence, and reform only if a person (1) is guilty, (2) is found guilty according to fair procedures of justice, and thus (3) deserves a punishment proportionate to his or her crime. However, the third proposition needs the utilitarian theory to make complete sense. What constitutes a proportionate punishment in each and every case must take into consideration prevention, deterrence, and reform. The third proposition is partially determined by the utilitarian purposes; they help fill in its content.

The first two propositions of retribution stand alone and are entirely independent of any utilitarian considerations. And even the third proposition cannot be totally determined by the utilitarian purposes. As we have seen, there are some cases in which there is no apparent utilitarian benefit in punishing, even though punishment is morally required. There are still other cases in which retribution would forbid the state to punish persons excessively, even if such a punishment would have significant utilitarian benefit. Several years ago, Beijing executed eight thieves as part of a national campaign to deter theft and crime in general in China. Let us assume that these punishments have a significant deterrent effect. They are still prohibited by retribution, because they are excessive and hence violate the principle of proportionality. Singapore's caning of Michael Fay for vandalism is another notorious example of deterrence out of control.

For the personalist theory, then, an ideal punishment would integrate retribution with prevention, deterrence, and reform. Short of this ideal, retribution ought to be integrated with some of them. When this occurs, the principle of community is promoted, since the state enhances the personal relations between punishers and punishees, already begun by retribution itself.[22]

THE DEATH PENALTY

It is time to apply the foregoing theory of punishment to the death penalty. I first apply the five possible purposes of punishment individually: revenge, retribution, prevention, deterrence, and reform (or rehabilitation). Revenge, reform, and prevention can be examined briefly and are discussed together. Deterrence and retribution require detailed analyses in their application to the death penalty and are developed in separate sections. Since the Supreme Court has shown a remarkable interest in the death penalty, I then briefly discuss nineteen of their major cases, all but one since the 1970s. Finally, I apply the personalist theory. Throughout the discussion, proponents of the death penalty are called *retentionists*, and opponents are called *abolitionists*.

Revenge, Reform, and Prevention

We have seen that revenge is a morally invalid and impermissible purpose of punishment. Therefore, it has no place in a society's criminal justice system. Revenge is a mark of an uncivilized society. A fortiori, revenge has no morally valid application to the ultimate punishment, the death penalty. It is fallacious for a retentionist to conclude that the death penalty is morally permissible, based on the premise that the state has a moral right to express society's revenge toward the most serious crimes and criminals. Since the premise is false, the truth of the conclusion does not follow. A false premise cannot imply a true conclusion. The state has no business executing offenders to satisfy a public lust or outcry for vengeance, even if it is the will of the majority—indeed, especially if it is the will of the majority. A just society cannot be ruled by the tyranny of the majority.

However, conservative moralist Walter Berns disagrees. According to him, punishment in general and capital punishment in particular are morally justified as an expression of society's anger. "Punishment arises out of the demand for justice, and justice is demanded by angry, morally indignant men; its purpose is to satisfy that moral indignation and thereby promote the law-abidingness that . . . accompanies it."[23]

I agree that punishment ought to be grounded in justice, but it is false to say that justice is grounded in anger. Anger is an accompaniment of injustice. Persons with a developed sense of justice are naturally angry when injustices are committed. Nevertheless, the ground and framework of justice is not institutionalized anger, but a system of persons' inherent moral or human rights and reciprocal duties within the field of interpersonal acts and relations. Berns's morality of anger is a version of revenge or vengeance.

However, the opposing argument of abolitionist-utilitarians is also fallacious. According to this argument, the death penalty is morally impermissible because (1) it is necessarily based on revenge, since (2) the death penalty cannot be justified by prevention, deterrence, or reform. We shall see whether the second premise is true. Even if it is true, the conclusion—that the death penalty is morally impermissible—would not follow, since the first premise is false. It is false because it identifies revenge and retribution. Therefore, the fact that the death penalty is unjustifiable by revenge (indeed, no punishment is justifiable by revenge) does not imply that it is unjustifiable by retribution.

Reform cannot possibly apply to the death penalty. A criminal cannot be reformed by being executed. Despite this obvious truth, it is disputed by some retentionists. According to Louis Pojman, the death penalty can reform, since "the criminal may be given time to repent of his or her offense before execution."[24] And if the criminal repents, some reform does occur. Such repentance, however, is wholly independent of the death penalty's direct intention; it is incidental to the act. Moreover, reform, as it is usually understood, is much broader than the criminal's repentance. It involves rehabilitating the criminal to the point where he can be of benefit both to society and to himself. A presupposition of reform, then, is that the criminal live instead of being executed. And for those who think that murderers are unreformable, such a view is not supported by the evidence. Consider, for example, the following two death-row inmates:

To Jesse Tafaro, 37, an eight-year resident of Death Row, life in a 6-by-9-foot cell is empty. A Zen Buddhist, Tafaro eats his vegetarian meals, reads, paints, and listens to music in his cell. Twice a week he exercises for two hours in the prison yard. . . . James McRae . . . [was] convicted in the 1973 shooting death of Margaret Mears, 63. He reads classic literature, including Shakespeare, and is one of the top basketball players in the prison.

He is soft-spoken, polite and self-possessed. "I try to alleviate the misconceptions about Death Row prisoners," said McRae. "To bring a realization of our humanity. We breathe, smell and taste. We didn't spring from the earth. We're not monsters with fangs." [25]

Consider the sensational cases of Karla Faye Tucker and Tookie Williams. Tucker and boyfriend David Garrett were sentenced to death in 1984 for the June 14, 1983, pickax murder of Jerry Lynn Dean and Deborah Thornton in Houston, Texas. Garrett died in prison the next year, but Tucker's case became a worldwide controversy. One reason was that Texas had not executed a woman since 1863. The more important reason was that, after spending fourteen years on death row, she was apparently rehabilitated.

At the time of the murders, Tucker was a twenty-three-year-old prostitute and drug addict. She expressed no remorse for the killings and even bragged that she experienced sexual pleasure with every blow of her pickax. While in prison, however, she became a born-again Christian, and repented her crimes. She was involved in a prison-run program counseling young people to avoid crime. She married a prison minister, and was an active evangelist, writing articles and making antidrug videotapes. She appeared on Pat Robertson's Christian cable TV show, *The 700 Club*. Her appeal for clemency was supported by Pope John Paul II, Robertson, Bianca Jagger, Jesse Jackson, the National Council of Churches, the European Parliament, prison guards, former prosecutors, the detective who arrested her, one of her jurors, and even the brother of the woman she murdered. Nearly 2,400 people sent letters to Governor George W. Bush asking that her death sentence be commuted to life in prison. The Texas Parole Board voted 16–0 against commuting her sentence, and she was executed on February 3, 1998. On the basis of rehabilitation alone, I think her life should have been spared. [26]

Stanley Tookie Williams, 51, was executed in San Quentin prison in California on December 13, 2005, for the robbery murders of four people in Los Angeles in 1979. He was the cofounder of the violent Crips street gang.

Although he admitted a violent past, he maintained his innocence of the slayings and became an antigang crusader during his long stay on death row. He wrote several children's books with an antigang message, and donated the proceeds of his royalties to antigang community groups. He was nominated for the Nobel Peace Prize and the Nobel Prize in Literature by some of his many supporters, which included celebrities Jesse Jackson and Sister Helen Prejean, author of *Dead Man Walking*. The US Supreme Court and Governor Schwarzenegger rejected his appeals for clemency. Most of his supporters wanted his death sentence commuted to life in prison so he could continue his antigang writing and crusade; some thought him innocent. Reverend Jackson denounced Schwarzenegger for choosing "revenge" over "redemption."[27] From the standpoint of reformation, Williams's execution was the waste of a future good life. More will be said about rehabilitation later.

In its application to the death penalty, prevention appears to be the opposite of reform. Whereas it is physically impossible to apply reform to the death penalty, prevention seems to apply perfectly, for it is absolutely certain that an executed criminal will never again commit a crime—or do anything else again, good or bad. However, the death penalty's perfect prevention is an illusion. It is based on a confusion between the death penalty's incapacitative and preventive effects. In truth, the death penalty perfectly incapacitates the offender, since it kills him or her, and thus makes it impossible for an offender to ever act again. But it does not follow that the death penalty is a perfect prevention.[28] To be that, it must be the case that each executed offender would have committed at least one other serious crime had he or she been imprisoned instead of being executed. However, this is impossible to know with certainty. Only God could have such absolute precognition. The death penalty (like all punishments) is imperfectly preventive: we know only with some degree of probability that a convicted murderer eligible for the death penalty will murder again or commit some other serious crime. As we shall see, the degree of probability in most murder cases is quite low. The death penalty, then, combines perfect incapacitation with imperfect prevention.

This combination of the death penalty raises a question about its severity. Would a less severe punishment of long-term imprisonment, or life imprisonment, which is only imperfectly incapacitative, be sufficiently preventive?

If so, the death penalty may be too severe, that is, excessive. And if excessive, it would violate proportionality and therefore fail to meet the requirements of retribution. We shall see. Moreover, since the death penalty is irrevocable, the state cannot correct an error when an innocent person is executed. In both respects, prevention is connected with retribution. I take this issue up again when I apply the personalist theory to the death penalty.

We are left, then, with deterrence and retribution. In their application to the death penalty, they generate its two most important questions: Does the death penalty deter the crimes it is supposed to deter—principally murder? Is the death penalty ever a morally valid expression of retribution, and are there any crimes for which only the death penalty is a proportionate punishment? I answer the deterrence question first.

Deterrence and Murder

Whether the death penalty is an effective deterrent has long been vehemently debated. Part of the problem is that the question is often improperly formulated. Sometimes retentionists speak as if the deterrence of capital punishment should be compared with the alternative of no punishment. But this is an illogical and unfair comparison, for criminals are not going to go unpunished if they are not executed. Instead, they will be given long-term prison sentences, whether life or less than life. Moreover, we must be clear about which classes of crimes are to be deterred by the death penalty. In recent history, murder is the chief capital crime. Taking both points into consideration, the deterrence question should be formulated as follows: is the death penalty superior to long-term imprisonment as a deterrent for the crime of murder?[29] There are two ways that this question can be answered. The first is through statistical data. The second is based on so-called common sense.

The first way has been adopted by criminologists and other social scientists. For decades they have studied criminal homicide rates in various jurisdictions, both in the United States and abroad, to see whether murder rates vary with the abolition or retention of the death penalty. More specifically, death penalty expert and abolitionist Hugo Adam Bedau lists six propositions that such investigations have tried to verify or falsify (or confirm or disconfirm): (1) death penalty jurisdictions should have a lower annual rate of murder than abolition jurisdictions; (2) jurisdictions that abolished the death penalty should show an increased annual rate of murder after abolition; (3) jurisdictions that reintroduced the death penalty should show a decreased annual rate of murder after reintroduction; (4) given two contiguous jurisdictions differing mainly in that one has the death penalty and the other does not, the latter should show a higher annual rate of murder; (5) police officers on duty should suffer a higher annual rate of criminal assault and murder in abolition jurisdictions than in death penalty jurisdictions; and (6) prisoners and prison personnel should have a higher annual rate of criminal assault and murder from life-term prisoners in abolition jurisdictions than in death penalty jurisdictions.[30]

Most of the evidence to date fails to verify or confirm all six hypotheses. For example, one of the most comprehensive studies on deterrence ever undertaken was conducted some years ago by the British Royal Commission. After four years of studying homicide rates in the United States and Europe, it concluded that there is no clear evidence that the abolition of capital punishment led to an increase in the homicide rate or that its reintroduction led to a fall.[31] Thorsten Sellin, a foremost authority on the deterrence question, reached the following two conclusions: "executions have no discernible effect on homicide rates," and "from an inspection of the data . . . it is impossible to conclude that the states which had no death penalty had thereby made the policeman's lot more hazardous."[32]

In contrast, a sophisticated econometric study by Isaac Ehrlich reached the startling conclusion that each execution saves eight innocent people. "On the average the tradeoff between the execution of an offender and the lives of potential victims it might have saved was on the order of 1 for 8 for the period 1933–1967 in the United States."[33] However, Ehrlich's study has been widely criticized by other scientists.[34] Since its validity and conclusions are seriously disputed, it does not seem that his study can be given much weight. Accordingly, I cannot agree with Jeffrey Reiman, who contends that "the advent of Ehrlich's research, contested though it may be, leaves us in fact with research that tends to point both ways."[35] Precisely because it is so contested, the research cannot point both ways equally. If we take into consideration the large body of evidence amassed prior to Ehrlich that fails to show that the death penalty deters and the extensive and serious criticisms of Ehrlich's study itself, it seems reasonable to conclude that the death penalty most probably is not a superior deterrent to long-term (including life-term) imprisonment. As Bedau succinctly puts it, "The deterrence achieved by the death penalty for murder is not measurably any greater than the deterrence achieved by long-term imprisonment."[36]

More recently, two distinguished researchers, John Donahue and Justin Wolfers, have reached similar conclusions in two scholarly studies they copublished: "We are led to conclude that there exists profound uncertainty about the deterrent (or antideterrent) effect of the death penalty; the data tell us that capital punishment is not a main influence on homicide rates. . . . It is entirely unclear even whether the preponderance of evidence suggests that the death penalty causes more or less murder."[37] Their other study reinforces this conclusion: "The view that the death penalty deters is still the product of belief, not evidence. The reason for this is simple: over the past half century the U.S. has not experimented enough with capital punishment policy to permit strong conclusions."[38]

Against this conclusion, Ernest van den Haag, a prominent retentionist scholar, offers the following argument: Although it may be true that the statistical evidence in general fails to establish that the death penalty is a deterrent, it does not follow that the death penalty is not a deterrent, as abolitionists claim. The death penalty could still be a deterrent, even though there is insufficient (or even little) evidence to show that it is. Therefore, says Van den Haag, the evidence is "inconclusive," and it is "uncertain" whether the death penalty is or is not a deterrent.[39]

I agree with Van den Haag as a point of logic that the evidence does not conclusively prove that the death penalty is not a deterrent. Indeed, by the very nature of the case, how can one prove a negative, that is, that something does not exist? How can one prove, for example, that the Loch Ness monster does not exist or that ghosts do not exist? The usual reply, of course, is that there is no credible evidence that they do exist. But using that as a basis to infer that they do not exist is to commit the fallacy of argumentum ad ignorantiam, which is precisely Van den Haag's charge. According to this fallacy, something is the case because no one can prove that it is not the case; or conversely, something is not the case because no one can prove that it is the case.

However, this logical fallacy is unimportant in the present context. On the one hand, there exists a massive body of evidence that fails to confirm that the death penalty is a superior deterrent to life imprisonment for the crime of murder; on the other hand, there is no substantial, much less comparable, body of evidence to confirm that it is such a deterrent. Consequently, the overwhelming preponderance of the evidence *fails* to establish that the death penalty is a deterrent instead of establishing that it is a deterrent. But Van den Haag's (and other retentionists') characterization of the evidence as inconclusive without further qualification suggests that the evidence points equally in both directions. This is not the case. In light of the statistical evidence, it is much more probable that the death penalty is not a superior deterrent to long-term (and life-term) imprisonment for murder than that it is such a deterrent. In my view, the degree of probability is high enough to give retentionists the burden of proof to show why, on the basis of deterrence, convicted murderers ought to be executed, especially because a death penalty policy is bound to execute some innocents.[40] Statistical evidence does not support a death penalty policy. The statistical approach to deterrence favors abolition, though by itself it does not *justify* abolition. Such a justification would depend on an entire theory of punishment.

Let us turn now to the commonsense approach to the deterrence question. This retentionist approach consists of the following "commonsense" argument: Since human beings fear death more than anything else, they must fear the death penalty more than any other penalty, and so the death penalty is a greater deterrent than any other penalty. No one has expressed this argument more eloquently than noted Victorian judge and historian of the law James Fitzjames Stephen:

> No other punishment deters men so effectually from committing crimes as the punishment of death. This is one of those propositions which it is difficult to prove, simply because they are in themselves more obvious than any proof can make them. It is possible to display ingenuity in arguing against it, but that is all. The whole experience of mankind is in the other direction. The threat of instant death is the one to which resort has always been made

when there was an absolute necessity for producing some result. . . . No one goes to *certain inevitable* death except by compulsion. Put the matter the other way. Was there ever yet a criminal who, when sentenced to death and *brought out to die*, would refuse the offer of a commutation of his sentence for the severest secondary punishment? Surely not. Why is this? It can only be because "All that a man has will he give for his life." In any secondary punishment, however terrible, there is hope; but death is death; its terror cannot be described more forcibly.[41]

This argument can be criticized on two counts. First, the type of punishment an offender would prefer or fear the most *after* he has been convicted and sentenced may be quite different from the type of punishment that may or may not *deter* him before he commits a crime. Obviously, an offender who has been sentenced to death and who is in a position to prefer some less severe penalty was not deterred from committing his crime even by the supposed fear of the death penalty. By this argument, then, it would seem that the state should institute death by torture for those offenders who have not been deterred by the death penalty as such. However, even proponents of this argument would reject such cruel and inhumane punishment, which would necessarily be an exercise of revenge.

Second, in general, murderers do not expect to get caught. And even if some think that they might be caught, they know that the probability of their being executed is very low. Only 2 percent of known murderers in the United States receive death sentences and many fewer still are actually executed.[42] It is difficult to see how a penalty that is applied so infrequently and randomly can have any significant deterrent effect. But even when the United States executed a record 199 persons in 1935, executions had no discernible effect on homicide rates. How many annual executions must occur before any deterrent effect is detectable or measurable? Apparently, many more than the United States could possibly tolerate or that any reasonable person or civilized society would ever tolerate.

Another difficulty with the commonsense argument is that it fails to take into account the various types of murders. It has been estimated that as many as 90 percent of murders are crimes of passion, and the murderer is not thinking of punishment. Many of these murderers are actually insane, although not necessarily in the legal sense. How could the death penalty effectively deter these murders? Of the remaining 10 percent, some are professional contracts, where the murderer does not expect to get caught and in fact usually does not. Or else they are murders committed by terrorists, who are already committed to dying and do not care if they are executed. Indeed, many would probably jump at the chance to become an instant martyr for their cause. Moreover, many murders are followed by suicide. Consequently, there does not appear to be any statistically significant type of murder that could be deterred by the death penalty. For all the above reasons, the commonsense argument fails.

The deterrence question, however, is a double-edged sword, for it raises the opposite question: Does the death penalty *incite* murder? This question refers to the so-called brutalization effect of the death penalty. There is some evidence that it does, but the evidence is far from conclusive. In one study, the authors conclude that each execution produces two murders within a month after the execution and that these murders are real additions and not merely a shift in their timing.[43] Similarly, another author points out that the publicity surrounding the death penalty may incite murder in two types of unbalanced (though not necessarily insane) people.[44] First, there are those individuals who have repressed self-destructive impulses. Executions provide them with a psychological opportunity to act out their impulses, which generally takes the form of murder and suicide. The second group of individuals wants to imitate the executioner or the murderers who are executed. These individuals are particularly dangerous, and capturing them may cost additional lives. Bedau observes that the death penalty may incite some persons who are afraid to commit suicide to commit murder instead, in the hope that the state will execute them. The death penalty may also incite others who reason that if it is all right for the state to execute people, then it is all right for them to kill too.[45] Van den Haag claims that no serious evidence exists to support the view that murders increase immediately after executions. Indeed, he cites a study that argues the contrary thesis that they drop immediately after executions.[46]

From 1999 to 2012, there have been some significant changes in facts related to the death penalty in America that further disconfirm the claim that the death penalty is an effective deterrent vis-à-vis long-term imprisonment. In the last few years, the following four phenomena have declined: the murder rate, death penalty sentences, executions, and prisoners on death row. In 1999, there were ninety-eight executions in the United States (one-third of them in Texas), the highest number since the death penalty was reinstated in 1976. By 2006, this figure dropped to fifty-three, and in 2008 it fell to thirty-seven. In 2011 and 2012, it rose to forty-three each year. (Nevertheless, the United States is the fifth leading nation in the world in number of executions, after China, Iran, Saudi Arabia, and Iraq.) Since the murder rate generally has declined while executions and death penalty sentences have likewise declined, this correlation is additional evidence that the death penalty is not a superior deterrent to long-term imprisonment for the crime of murder.[47]

There are many more recent facts that count against the deterrent effect of the death penalty. Since 1977, 82 percent of executions in the United States have occurred in the South, which also has the highest murder rate of any region in the United States. By contrast, the Northeast, which has accounted for less than 1 percent of America's executions, has the nation's lowest murder rate. The murder rate has been declining in New York City since 1990, five years before the state restored the death penalty. In 2001, Texas had a 7.6 percent increase in homicides, while it executed three times as many persons as any other state. In general, abolition states in the United States have lower homicide rates than retentionist states. In 1999, for example, the average of murder rates per 100,000 population in retentionist states was 5.5, while in abolitionist states the average was 3.6. According to another study, for 2010 the average murder rate in death penalty states was 4.6, and for abolition states it was 2.9. When the United States is compared to Western European abolitionist nations, the picture is similar. The United States has a homicide rate that is more than three times greater than the following abolitionist nations: Sweden, Netherlands, France, Italy, Great Britain, and Germany. In comparing the United States with Canada, the situation is the same. The death penalty in Canada was abolished in 1976. In 2001, its number of homicides was 23 percent lower than in 1975. In general, Canada's homicide rate has been three times lower than in the United States.[48]

I conclude, then, that on the basis of deterrence alone, the death penalty is unjustifiable.

Retribution and the Death Penalty

With respect to the five possible purposes of punishment, we are left with retribution. Are there any crimes for which the death penalty is the only proportionate penalty? To answer this question, we must first give a kind of "phenomenology" of the death penalty: a detailed description of it in order to comprehend its essential nature.[49] The death penalty is a complex action that has five key elements that constitute the severity of the death penalty.

First, the death penalty is the killing of a person. This might seem to be an obvious and trivial statement were it not for the fact that some retentionists deny that capital criminals are persons in any legitimate or significant sense. However, it is one thing to say that they are bad persons or that they are persons who have committed seriously immoral acts; it is quite another thing to deny that they are persons at all. Moreover, a denial of their personhood implies a denial of the possibility that, while on death row, they may become at least partially reformed and may continue to reform in the future. At the same time, it must be recognized that some capital criminals may not be reformable, and still others are probably unreformable. But to make the blanket judgment that all capital criminals are subhuman or subpersonal makes it impossible to rationally determine who is reformable and who is not.

Second, the death penalty is a direct form of killing: the state's direct intention is to execute the offender. The end of the action is to kill the offender, and the means is whatever method of execution is employed. And as we have seen, direct killing is worse than indirect killing, other things being equal.

Third, the death penalty is premeditated killing. Premeditation is an aggravating moral factor of direct killing. Premeditated murder is worse than unpremeditated murder, since in premeditated murder the badness of its direct intention is aggravated by all the planning and deliberation that goes into the direct intention. Worse still, the death penalty is one of the most premeditated forms of killing. The state informs the offender well in advance of the execution exactly where and how he will be killed. Or else we leave the criminal on death row indefinitely while a lengthy appeals process is exhausted, partly to minimize the risk of executing the innocent. And then there are the stays of execution, which are almost like dying several deaths.[50]

Fourth, there is often cruelty and barbarism involved in the means of execution. Until fairly recently, electrocution was the leading method of execution in the United States. It was not considered a cruel way to kill someone. Sometimes, however, there are technical glitches, as in the following case: "Prison officials could not explain yesterday why it took 10 minutes and three jolts of electricity to execute convicted murderer John Louis Evans III in what his lawyer called 'a barbaric ritual.'"[51] Lethal injection has now become the number one method of execution in the United States. It is often touted as painless, but doubts remain. An eyewitness to one execution by injection reported that "there were two series of apparently involuntary efforts to breathe" and a "churning of . . . stomach muscles."[52]

And fifth, there is the finality of the death penalty: It is irrevocable and perfectly incapacitative. In its finality, the death penalty is not merely an unusual punishment but a unique one as well. If a judicial error is made and an innocent person is put to death, the punishment cannot be revoked and the victim cannot be compensated. If, however, an error is not made, the death penalty is still perfectly incapacitative: a person who is executed will never do, experience, or enjoy anything else again in this world.

These five features of the death penalty, then, indicate that it is a highly premeditated form of direct killing possessing considerable psychological horror and sometimes a certain amount of physical pain. Its direct intention must be regarded at least as significantly bad. But is it gravely bad? If so, the death penalty would be intrinsically immoral and hence always impermissible.

I shall not answer this question immediately. But on the basis of retribution alone it seems reasonable to conclude that the death penalty is a proportionate punishment for premeditated murder, provided that the method of execution is as quick and painless as possible. This probably means lethal injection, as long as it is administered in a technically efficient manner by competent personnel. If the state's method of execution were more painful than necessary, its direct intention would contain an element of revenge and thus be immoral. On the basis of retribution, then, the state has a moral right to execute premeditated murderers. But does it have a duty to execute all premeditated murderers? Kant apparently thought so. "Anyone who is a murderer . . . must suffer death."[53]

On retribution alone, it seems difficult to dispute Kant's contention, for otherwise the state would be selective in choosing which premeditated murderers to execute. Either this selectivity would be arbitrary and capricious or it would be based on nonretributive criteria. And even if the state decided to execute only the worst premeditated murderers, this rough standard would be inconsistent with the retributive idea that the death penalty is a proportionate punishment for premeditated murder as such. I conclude that on the basis of retribution alone, the state is morally required to execute all convicted premeditated murderers. Since I regard this conclusion as morally wrong— indeed, morally outrageous—it reveals a serious defect in retribution when it is applied by itself to the death penalty. As we shall see, however, this conclusion does not follow from the personalist theory of punishment.

I make one final point before we leave this section. As noted above, 82 percent of executions in the United States since 1977 have occurred in the South. The top five Southern states—Texas, Virginia, Florida, Missouri, and Oklahoma—have accounted for 66 percent, and the top eleven execution states are in the South. This striking fact has led some observers to speak of the South as the Death Penalty Belt, an oblique reference to the fact that this region is also called the Bible Belt. Is this remarkable correlation merely a coincidence or is there a causal connection between the two belts? One can make a reasonable or plausible case for a causal connection. The South is dominated by religious and political conservatives. Political conservatives support the death penalty much more than do political liberals. More importantly, religious conservatives, both Catholic and Protestant, place much theological weight on the Old Testament *lex talionis*: "life for life, eye for eye, tooth for tooth, hand for hand, foot for foot, burn for burn, wound for wound, and bruise for bruise."[54] This passage taken by itself, especially if accepted literally, as conservative Protestant fundamentalists do, supports the death penalty for murder and perhaps for all forms of negligent homicide. But we have seen good reason to reject the *lex talionis*: It is an expression of revenge rather than genuine retribution. Moreover, Christians who support the death penalty on this basis conveniently ignore Jesus's apparent repudiation of this law: "You have heard that it was said, 'An eye for an eye, and a tooth for a tooth.' But I say to you, do not resist him who is evil; but whoever slaps you on your right cheek, turn to him the other also."[55] I do not know how this passage can be reconciled with the death penalty.

The Supreme Court and the Death Penalty as Retribution

Since the death penalty, according to retribution, is a proportionate punishment for premeditated murder, it is an excessive punishment for less serious crimes—which, I contend, includes *all* other crimes. In *Coker v. Georgia* (1977),[56] the US Supreme Court correctly ruled that capital punishment is excessive for the crime of rape. Likewise, in *Locket v. Ohio* (1978),[57] it ruled that the death penalty is excessive for crimes in which someone did not fire the fatal shot or directly intend the death of the victim. However, in *Tison v. Arizona* (1987),[58] the Court appears to have partially overruled the Locket decision. By a five-to-four decision, it ruled that accomplices to a crime that results in murder may be executed if their participation in the crime was major and if they displayed a reckless indifference to the value of human life. The *Tison* decision, in my view, exceeds the legitimate bounds of retribution.

The *Coker* decision, however, raised the question whether laws that permit the death penalty for the rape of a *child* are constitutional. For although the victim in the *Coker* case was sixteen years old, she was an adult under Georgia law because she was married. So did the Supreme Court intend to prohibit the death penalty in all cases of rape, including children, or only in cases involving rape of an adult? On June 25, 2008, the Court answered this question. In *Kennedy v. Louisiana* (5–4),[59] the Court ruled that laws permitting the death penalty for the rape of a child are unconstitutional. The decision overturned such laws in Louisiana and five other states. With respect to the issue of retribution, Justice Anthony Kennedy, writing the majority opinion, made a distinction between inflicting the death penalty for (direct) intentional first-degree murder and inflicting it for all non-homicide crimes, implying that the death penalty is excessive punishment for the latter, even the rape of a child. Citing the Court's concern for "evolving standards of decency," Justice Kennedy noted that of the thirty-six states that have the death penalty, thirty bar the execution of child rapists.

As we have seen, retribution requires that punishments be uniform for the same crime, other things being equal. Consequently, it is a serious violation of retribution for the state to use the death penalty as an instrument of racial discrimination, as has been the case in the United States. In *Furman v. Georgia* (1972),[60] the Court ruled that the death penalty was unconstitutional in practice, because it was being imposed in an arbitrary and capricious manner. Juries had been allowed to inflict the death penalty without any explicit guidelines or standards. One result of this practice was that blacks were receiving the death sentence much more frequently than whites. The various states reacted to this ruling in one of two ways. Some states enacted laws making the death penalty mandatory for certain crimes, thus leaving no discretion to juries in imposing the death penalty. In *Woodson v. North Carolina* (1976),[61] the Supreme Court subsequently declared mandatory death sentences unconstitutional. Other states took a different tack. They enacted laws that required that juries be supplied with standards for imposing the death penalty, but not to the point where any specific crime made the death penalty mandatory. Georgia, for example, passed a law specifying ten aggravating circumstances, any one of which constituted a capital crime. If a jury found beyond a reasonable doubt that one of these circumstances existed, it had the option of imposing the death penalty.

The second route was eventually accepted by the Court in *Gregg v. Georgia* (1976),[62] the landmark decision on the death penalty. The Court ruled that the death penalty as such is constitutionally permissible, because it is not a cruel and unusual punishment as prohibited by the Eighth Amendment. Consequently, executions, which had been put on hold awaiting the Court's decision (there had not been an execution in the United States since 1967), were resumed with the execution of Gary Gilmore by a Utah firing squad on January 18, 1977. *Gregg*, however, reaffirmed *Furman*'s concern that the death penalty be administered in a nondiscriminatory way.

Over the next decade, the Court's concern about discrimination in imposing the death penalty apparently diminished. In *McCleskey v. Kemp* (1987),[63] it upheld Georgia's death penalty statute, despite statistical studies showing, among other things, that Georgia defendants convicted of killing whites were eleven times more likely to be sentenced to death than those who killed blacks, and that of the eleven defendants executed in Georgia between 1973 and 1979, nine were black, and ten of them had white victims.[64]

The discriminatory application of the death penalty has long been one of the favorite arguments of abolitionists. Many appear to hold that this argument by itself is sufficient reason to abolish the death penalty. However, this is a mistake. The discrimination argument cannot be a primary argument for abolition; it cannot be an argument against the death penalty as such, for it shows only that the discriminatory application of the death penalty is unjust and should be abolished. It does not show that the death penalty as such is immoral. If the death penalty could be applied in a uniform and nondiscriminatory manner, then the argument would logically imply retention instead of abolition. For the state to retain the death penalty, however, retribution requires that the state have the direct intention to apply it nondiscriminatorily. If it does not, the death penalty violates retribution, even for premeditated murder. The reason is simple. As we have seen, under retribution, proportionality of punishment implies uniformity of punishment: Different persons must receive the same punishment for the same crime in similar circumstances. If a state executes a black person for premeditated murder and does not execute a white person for the same crime only because of their racial difference, the principle of uniformity is violated. But so is the principle of proportionate punishment. For if a state determines that the death penalty is a proportionate punishment for premeditated murder and executes a black person but not a white person for that crime, then the white person receives a lenient, or less-than-proportionate punishment, which violates retribution. Therefore, under retribution, if a state cannot cease its discriminatory application of the death penalty, it should abolish it altogether.

In the *McCleskey* case, the Court ruled that intent and not statistics must be the basis for proving discrimination. Unfortunately, the Court made a fallacious distinction between intention and statistics. As we have seen, the direct intention is *in* the action; it is not a purely mental act that precedes the action. Consequently, after an action is performed, be it individual or institutional, the nature and quality of its direct intention can be inferred from the action itself. In the *McCleskey* case, the cited statistics exhibit a pattern of institutional action that is so glaring and extreme in its racial discrimination that this pattern must be the result of a direct intention to discriminate. There is no other way to explain it.

In 1986, the Court issued the first in a series of decisions on the question of subjective guilt and innocence. In *Ford v. Wainwright*,[65] it held that the cruel and unusual punishment clause of the Eighth Amendment prohibits executing the insane. Although the Court did not formally define insanity, it ruled that for a person to be eligible for the death penalty he must be sane enough to be conscious of the punishment and understand why he is receiving it. The correctness of the ruling seems obvious. Since an insane act is an involuntary act, for which therefore a person is not culpable, it is irrational to punish him at all, let alone to inflict upon him society's ultimate punishment.

On June 28, 2007, the Court, invoking the Ford decision, overturned a very controversial Texas death penalty sentence. In *Panetti v. Quarterman* (5–4),[66] the Court ruled that lower courts had erred when they sentenced Scott Louis Panetti to death for the 1992 murder of his wife's parents. Mr. Panetti is a psychotic person who has been hospitalized fourteen times for schizophrenia, manic depression, hallucinations, and persecution delusions. The Court held that the lower courts had not demonstrated that Panetti exhibited sufficient understanding of why he was sentenced to death. On the basis of the evidence, it is indisputable that he is clinically insane.

In 1988 and 1989, the Court took up the all-important issue of juvenile executions. At that time, several states permitted executing fifteen-year-olds. In *Thompson v. Oklahoma* (1988),[67] a plurality of four justices ruled that the execution of a person who was fifteen years old at the time of his or her offense is unconstitutional because it is a violation of the Eighth Amendment ban on cruel and unusual punishments. In effect the Court said that executing a fifteen-year-old is excessive punishment and thus a violation of retribution's principle of proportionate punishment.

However, the Court's decision left in limbo the question of inflicting the death penalty on sixteen- and seventeen-year-olds. Nineteen of the thirty-eight states that had death penalty statutes permitted execution of sixteen- and seventeen-year-olds. More than seventy juveniles were on death row. The United States was virtually alone among the nations of the world in permitting the execution of juvenile offenders. Many criminologists and ethicists are opposed to the execution of sixteen- and seventeen-year-olds for three reasons: (1) juveniles are less culpable than adults, (2) juveniles are more capable of rehabilitation than adults, and (3) juveniles are less likely than adults to be deterred by the death penalty.

Underlying all three reasons is a juvenile's basic immaturity. There is much scientific evidence that the areas of the brain that regulate practical reasoning, impulse control, and decision making are underdeveloped at that age. Therefore, the actions of juveniles in general are acts of diminished voluntariness having a significantly reduced direct intention. A juvenile's culpability in committing criminal acts is likewise reduced, since in general he is not fully subjectively guilty for committing them. That being the case, juveniles do not deserve society's ultimate punishment, the death penalty. Under retribution, the death penalty ought to be reserved for those adults who are fully subjectively guilty for committing premeditated murder. Likewise, mentally retarded persons have a diminished capacity for voluntariness and are significantly less culpable than normal adults. As we shall momentarily see, the Court has ruled that it is unconstitutional to execute the mentally retarded.

Despite these facts and considerations, the Supreme Court ruled in *Stanford v. Kentucky* (1989),[68] in an opinion authored by Justice Antonin Scalia, that the Eighth Amendment of the Constitution does not prohibit the execution of a person who committed his or her crime at the age of sixteen or seventeen. The Court reasoned that since it could find no national consensus against executing sixteen- and seventeen-year-olds, the various states must decide if they want to execute juveniles. This reasoning is fallacious. In a constitutional democracy like the United States, questions concerning the fundamental rights of persons—and what could be more fundamental than the right to life—ought not to be determined by the majority opinion of this or that state. This point will be taken up again in chapter 8. In *Stanford*, then, the Court said it was all right to execute sixteen- and seventeen-year-olds. In *Thompson* a year earlier, it said just the opposite in executing fifteen-year-olds. In my view, the *Thompson* and *Stanford* decisions are wholly inconsistent.

In June 2002, the Court issued two major decisions on the death penalty. On June 20, in *Atkins v. Virginia*,[69] the Court ruled, 6–3, that it is unconstitutional to execute the mentally retarded. Twenty states had laws permitting the execution of mentally retarded persons. The laws generally considered such a person as having an IQ below 70. At issue in the case was a Virginia statute that sentenced to death Daryl Renard Atkins, who had a measured IQ of 59. At the time, it was estimated that 5 to 10 percent of the 3,700 prisoners on death row were mentally retarded. Therefore, this decision spared from 185 to 370 prisoners from death. By the same token, of the approximately 800 prisoners executed between 1977 and 2002, 40 to 80 were mentally retarded.

On June 24, in *Ring v. Arizona*,[70] the Court ruled, 7–2, that juries and not judges must determine the presence or absence of the aggravating factors that make a convicted murderer eligible for the death penalty. Five states had laws permitting judges to make these critical determinations. The Court ruled that such laws are unconstitutional because they violate the Sixth Amendment guarantee of trial by jury. At the time of the decision, the lives of at least 168 death row inmates were spared.

Because of the inconsistency between the *Thompson* and *Stanford* decisions, and because the Court ruled that executing the mentally retarded is unconstitutional, it decided to re-examine the issue of executing sixteen- and seventeen-year-olds. On March 1, 2005, in *Roper v. Simmons*,[71] the Supreme Court ruled, in a 5–4 decision, that executing sixteen- and seventeen-year-olds is unconstitutional, thus overturning its *Stanford v. Kentucky* ruling of 1989. The majority opinion was authored by Justice Anthony M. Kennedy. As a reason for reversing the earlier decision, Kennedy cited evolving standards of decency in determining what constitutes cruel and unusual punishment. He observed that the United States is virtually alone in the world in executing juveniles. The ruling spared seventy-two juvenile murderers in nineteen states. Thus, the Court implied that sixteen- and seventeen-year-olds, like fifteen-year-olds and the mentally retarded, have a capacity for diminished voluntariness, which makes them ineligible, in the Court's view, for receiving society's ultimate punishment. Similarly, in *Miller v. Alabama* (2012),[72] the Court ruled that *mandatory* life sentences without parole for juvenile offenders are unconstitutional.

On June 12, 2006, the Court handed down a pair of decisions that could have far-reaching consequences for the death penalty in America. The first decision is *Hill v. McDonough*.[73] In a 9–0 ruling, the Court held that in cases of lethal injection, a death row inmate can challenge whether the chemicals to be used in his execution will cause him unnecessary pain and suffering, which would constitute cruel and unusual punishment in violation of the Eighth Amendment. An inmate can question the chemical mix even after all his appeals have been exhausted. For every state in the union except Nebraska, lethal injection is the principal method of execution; in Nebraska it is electrocution. The ruling supports my view that retribution, as opposed to revenge, requires that an execution be as painless as possible. The other decision is *House v. Bell*.[74] By a 5–3 margin, the Supreme Court ruled that a death row inmate can present new evidence, especially DNA evidence, that tends to prove his innocence even though it does not conclusively exculpate him.

In *Baze v. Rees* (2008),[75] the Court decided to further address the constitutionality of lethal injection. By a 7–2 margin, it ruled that Kentucky's lethal injection protocol presented only "minimal risk" of harm to its recipients and thus does not constitute cruel and unusual punishment prohibited by the Eighth Amendment. Therefore, *any* method of execution that involves only a minimal risk of harm is constitutional. For a method of execution to violate the Eighth Amendment, it must present at least a "substantial" or "objectively intolerable" risk of serious harm to its recipient. In *Wilkerson v. Utah* (1878),[76] the Court held that the Constitution prohibits torture as a form of punishment and likewise prohibits all torturous methods of execution, such as disemboweling, beheading, quartering, dissecting, and burning alive. All such methods constitute excessive and unnecessary pain, and the infliction of pain for its own sake. Hence, in my view, they are motivated by revenge, not genuine retribution, and I think the Court was saying the same.

The Death Penalty in Decline

Notwithstanding the growing number of conservative justices on the Court over the last several years, it is clear that the Court has substantially restricted the range of the death penalty and tightened up its requirements for imposition. Although support for the death penalty among Americans remains relatively high at about 61 percent, this is considerably down from the all-time high of 80 percent in 1994. There is an unmistakable trend in America away from capital punishment which is almost certain to continue.

On January 2, 2007, the New Jersey Death Penalty Study Commission recommended to the governor and state legislature that the state's death penalty be abolished. Its report concluded that "there is no compelling evidence that the New Jersey death penalty rationally serves a legitimate penological intent."[77] In December 2007, New Jersey became the fourteenth state to abolish the death penalty and the second since *Gregg* in 1976. After *Gregg*, there were only twelve abolition states for twenty-eight years. Since 2004, five states have abolished the death penalty. In 2004, New York ended executions by a state court decision, thus becoming the thirteenth abolitionist state. In March 2009, New Mexico became the fifteenth state; and in March 2011, Illinois became the sixteenth state to end executions. On April 25, 2012, Connecticut became the seventeenth abolitionist state. As I write, Maryland is about to become the eighteenth.

There are two main reasons for declining support of capital punishment in America: (1) mounting evidence that innocents are wrongly convicted and sentenced to death, and (2) growing unease that the whole death penalty system does not work well. Famed defense attorney Barry Scheck and his Innocence Project have gained national recognition by freeing several death row inmates on the basis of DNA evidence. Since the project began in 1992, 289 prisoners convicted of various crimes have been exonerated by DNA evidence after serving a collective 3,800 years.[78]

The resurgence of sentiment against the death penalty was reinforced by a stunning report issued by the JusticeProject on June 12, 2000: *A Broken System: Error Rates in Capital Cases, 1973–1995*.[79] The report's overall conclusion is that the death penalty system in the United States is essentially "broken." The study showed that of the 4,578 appeals of capital cases between 1973 and 1995, 68 percent of the death penalty convictions were overturned by a state or federal court for a variety of reasons amounting to serious miscarriages of justice: incompetence of defense attorneys, such as falling asleep during the trial, lack of experience in capital cases, or failure to subpoena witnesses who would have probably been helpful to the defense; police or prosecutorial misconduct in suppressing evidence that would have been helpful to the defendants; bias on the part of judges or juries—for example, judges who tell the news media what they think of the defendant during the trial;

judges who give faulty instructions to juries; coerced confessions; prosecutors who keep African Americans off juries when a black defendant is on trial; and police who plant informers in jail to listen to conversations between defendants and their attorneys.

Even more important than the 68 percent of death penalty convictions that were overturned were the report's findings concerning what happened to these cases afterward. Seventy-five percent of the cases were given lesser sentences after retrials, either in plea bargains or by order of the judge; and an astounding 7 percent were found not guilty on retrial. Only 18 percent were given the death penalty on retrial, but many of these defendants had their convictions overturned again in the appeals process.

On a collateral issue, the report found no evidence that the death penalty deters murder, thus supporting the preponderance of the evidence cited earlier in this chapter. During 1973–1995, the murder rate for the nation as a whole was 9 per 100,000. In death penalty states, the murder rate was 9.3 per 100,000.

Not surprisingly, then, the study concludes that "our 23 years of findings reveal a capital punishment system collapsing under the weight of its own mistakes." Because of these mistakes, the requirements of retribution, in my view, are not being satisfied by our capital punishment system.

The Personalist Theory and the Death Penalty

As we have seen, retribution by itself justifies the death penalty for premeditated murder, but only for premeditated murder, providing a person is executed as painlessly as possible, and providing the principle of uniformity is satisfied. The moral justifiability of the death penalty for premeditated murder, however, is true only in the abstract, only if we consider the bare relation between retribution and the death penalty. In the concrete, the personalist theory requires that retribution be synthesized with the utilitarian purposes of punishment. In this synthesis, retribution is modified and justice is tempered with mercy. As a result, the death penalty is wholly unjustifiable, for several reasons.

First, when the combination of retribution and prevention is applied to the death penalty, prevention modifies retribution to the extent that the death penalty becomes an excessive punishment even for premeditated murder. Because of the death penalty's finality—which includes its irrevocability, its noncompensability if an error is made, and its perfect incapacitation—we must ask whether a less severe punishment of long-term imprisonment would adequately protect society. If the answer is yes, then the less severe punishment would satisfy prevention. If it satisfies prevention, the death penalty would be too severe, or excessive, and therefore a violation of retribution. But it does seem that society can be adequately protected without resorting to the death penalty. There are a growing number of supermax prisons for the worst offenders.[80] It is a well-established fact that convicted murderers rarely murder again. According to Bedau, fewer than one in five hundred convicted murderers murders again.[81] With respect to felonies in general and homicide in particular, murderers have the lowest recidivism rate among all classes of offenders.[82] They are among the best parole risks.[83] Former governor of Ohio Michael DiSalle employed eight convicted murderers in his executive mansion. This is strong evidence, too, of their reformability. Of course, if we execute all premeditated murderers, as I have concluded that retribution by itself requires, this will eliminate all risk of repeat murders—but only those murders committed by premeditated murderers. However, I now argue that the moral, social, and economic costs of such a death penalty policy far outweigh the slight risk that would be eliminated.

My second reason favoring abolition, then, concerns the enormous costs of a death penalty policy. As we have seen, it is virtually certain that some innocents will be put to death. And if we execute all convicted premeditated murderers, the number of innocents executed may be significant. Then there are the harmful psychological effects on the prison population. Executions and the very existence of a death row have a depersonalizing effect not only on those executed and their executioners but also on inmates and staff in general, even custodians. The time shortly before and after an execution is particularly disturbing to all the inmates and guards.[84] Finally, there are the financial costs. One of the standard retentionist arguments is that the death penalty is a tax-saving device, based on the commonsense premise that it is cheaper to execute a criminal than to lodge him or her for life. However, in the concrete, this premise is false, for it is far more expensive to maintain a criminal justice system that has the death penalty than a system that does not.

There are several large expenses in maintaining a death penalty system. First, the trial process is more expensive. Most criminal cases, including murder cases, are resolved by guilty pleas that avoid the expense of a trial. All death penalty cases, however, require a jury trial. And the trials are longer, more complex, and more expensive than other trials, including noncapital murder cases. Second, the appeals process is lengthier and more expensive in a death penalty system. That, in turn, leads to more retrials in capital cases and thus more expense. Third, in most capital cases, appellate review is carried out by state supreme courts. In noncapital cases, this review is done by intermediate courts and is less expensive. Fourth, there is the additional expense of a death row, or maximum-security unit of a prison. According to one corrections administrator, the expenses of "administering the unit add up to a cost substantially greater than the cost to retain them in prison for the rest of their lives."[85] And fifth, many defendants who go through the death penalty process of trial, appeals, possible retrial, and so on will ultimately avoid the death penalty anyway, so society must bear the double expense of the death penalty process and life imprisonment. On average, it costs three times as much money to execute an offender as it does to lodge him in prison for the rest of his natural life.

The third reason favoring abolition concerns the combination of retribution and deterrence. As we have seen, long-term imprisonment most probably deters premeditated murder as effectively as the death penalty. The small probability that the death penalty deters a few would-be murderers not deterrable by long-term imprisonment is offset by a similar degree of probability that the death penalty incites a few murders that otherwise would not have been committed.

Fourth, and finally, there is the combination of retribution and reform. Where there is life there is hope. By not executing even premeditated murderers, those who are reformable can be reformed, and the numbers are high, as we have seen. On the basis of the evidence, Karla Faye Tucker and Tookie Williams were reformed enough to have had their death sentences commuted to life in prison. That they were executed instead is a waste of all the good they would have done.

For all these reasons, the death penalty is excessive even for premeditated murder and thus fails, in the concrete, to meet the personalist requirements of punishment. Hence, the death penalty is unjustifiable here and now and in the foreseeable future. It ought to be abolished. Since the death penalty is excessive, retribution for premeditated murder is satisfied by long-term (including life-term) imprisonment. Such imprisonment is proportionate punishment for premeditated murder.

Still, the death penalty is not absolutely impermissible; it is not an intrinsically immoral action, which has a gravely bad direct intention. There is one exception in which the death penalty is morally justifiable: if it could be shown with a high degree of probability that for every premeditated murderer executed, at least an equal number of innocent persons would be saved.[86] In this context, innocent persons must be given greater moral weight than guilty persons. Therefore, in this one exception, the goodness of the innocent lives that would be saved would outweigh the badness of the guilty lives that would be lost, and so Rule Three of the principle of intentionality would be satisfied. Since, however, it is impossible to show the truth of this exception here and now, and since its truth will most likely not be shown in the foreseeable future, abolition remains intact.

Yet my position is open to a serious objection. The principle of community forbids all absolute impersonal acts and relations. But it would seem that any instance of the death penalty, including the above exception, constitutes an absolute impersonal act. Robert Gerstein, for example, argues that the death penalty is always wrong, because of "its dehumanizing character, its total negation of the moral worth of the person to be executed."[87]

My answer to this objection is that in all instances of the death penalty, *excluding the above exception*, the state has an absolute impersonal relation with the person executed. But in my one exception, the state would have a relative impersonal relation with the punishee. If it were the case that for every premeditated murderer executed an equal or greater number of innocent persons would be saved, then the punishee would be treated as a person rather than as a mere function, thing, or means. First of all, the punishee would be treated justly. The powerful deterrent effect of capital punishment would synthesize with retribution in such a way that it would concretely affirm what retribution in the abstract has already affirmed, namely, that the death penalty is a proportionate punishment for premeditated murder. If the state were not to execute murderers under this hypothetical condition, it would fail in its fundamental duty to adequately protect society from premeditated murderers. This failure would be an act of injustice toward innocent members of society. And second, since premeditated murder involves rational planning and voluntary decision making, the crime is a free action. Therefore, in being executed, the punishee is being treated as a free and responsible person who is being held proportionately accountable for his or her crime. For both reasons, the death penalty, in this one situation, would promote the principle of community. The death penalty, then, is a prima facie immoral action, which has a significantly bad direct intention.

Since, however, this one exception is not only hypothetical but also extremely improbable, it should not be taken too seriously.[88] The concrete reality of the death penalty is that it constitutes an absolute impersonal act and is thus a violation of the principle of community. The state's right in the abstract to inflict the death penalty for premeditated murder is overridden by more serious moral considerations. As Jeffrey Reiman expresses it: "Refraining from executing murderers will contribute to the advancement of civilization and may, in the long run, reduce the incidence of murder."[89] Under present and foreseeable conditions, the death penalty must be viewed as an abuse of state power. By abolishing the death penalty, the state can set an example in raising the standard of public morality. There is no moral justification for the government to be in this sordid business of premeditated killing. More than 110 nations worldwide have abolished the death penalty in law or in practice. The United States can take a significant step in restoring its global moral leadership by joining their ranks.

7

PRIVACY, PRIVATE PROPERTY, AND JUSTICE

Unlike the previous issues, which have preoccupied me since the 1970s, I first became interested in privacy as a philosophical issue during the Senate confirmation hearings of Robert Bork. As is well known, Bork proved to be a controversial nominee, and his candidacy for the Supreme Court was ultimately rejected by the Senate. There were several reasons that Bork was controversial, one of which involved his views on privacy. It was alleged by his critics that he denied a constitutional right to privacy, a view that they considered outrageous. Although he subsequently denied the charge in the simplistic way in which it was presented, it was widely felt—rightly or wrongly—that Bork was not sufficiently sensitive to the right to privacy.

It is not my purpose to take sides in the Bork controversy.[1] Nor is it my intention to explore the issue of a constitutional right to privacy. My purpose is to explore the relation between privacy and personhood strictly as a moral and philosophical issue. As I reflected on the nature of privacy, however, I realized that it could not be separated from the crucial moral and political issue of private property and distributive justice. In turn, different theories of privacy and private property reflect the broader issue of defining and reconciling the individual and relational dimensions of personhood.

In the first section, I examine the relation between privacy and personhood. I argue that persons have a general right to privacy. Then I take up the issue of private property and distributive justice. I sketch two antithetical types or models of society, whose differences are determined by their correspondingly different reconciliations of the individual and relational dimensions of personhood. As a result, they have very different attitudes toward privacy, private property, and the distribution of wealth. In chapter 8, I develop a third type of society, which is a synthesis of the first two.

PERSONHOOD AND PRIVACY

Privacy and Self-Consciousness

As we saw in chapter 1, for the mutuality of the personal, relationality is the primary or inclusive dimension of personhood, and individuality is secondary but necessary. That is, persons are constituted as individual persons in their inherent relatedness to one another. Relations are not merely external to personhood. Interpersonal relatedness normally takes the form of communication. Essential to the growth of persons is the growth of both individuality and relationality in their growth as rational and communicative agents. To explain this dual process of growth, Macmurray introduces the idea of "the rhythm of withdrawal and return."[2] Although the newborn infant is an individual person, it has not yet achieved any significant individuality in a psychological and functional sense. In order to develop its individuality, the child must withdraw from the relation of persons. The child must contrast and even oppose herself to the family to which she belongs. But since relationality is primary, the withdrawal cannot last indefinitely; it cannot exist for its own sake. The individual's withdrawal exists for the sake of its return to the relation of persons to enrich the content of communicative relationality and to give individuality meaning and purpose. Then the process starts all over again and continues throughout life in various relational contexts. The rhythm of withdrawal and return is an ongoing process or pattern of personal growth.

A distinction should be made, then, between original individuality and acquired individuality. The former denotes the fact that each person is an individual person. The latter denotes the personal growth and identity that is achieved in the withdrawal phase. What gives rise to the first instance of withdrawal in the child's life is her emerging self-consciousness. And central to self-consciousness is a sense of privacy. Self-consciousness as such consists of an inward and private domain of experience. In its full form, the privacy of self-consciousness discloses our own individual self, which is distinct from all other selves and is the ground, source, and unity of all our thoughts, feelings, and actions as ours and no one else's. A sense of privacy, then, is constitutive of self-consciousness. And since self-consciousness is an essential characteristic of personhood in the sense just explained, and since persons are beings with rights, I conclude that self-consciousness is the ground of the right to privacy.

I define the right to privacy as a person's right to think, feel, speak, and act in a manner that other persons and institutions, and especially the state, have no right to infringe on. Since the right to privacy is grounded by self-consciousness, it is a natural right. All persons have it simply by being persons. It is not a right conferred on us by the state or by society. It is a right that the state and others have a duty to recognize and respect. In addition, it is a basic or primary right; it is not derived from any of our other rights.

In earlier chapters, I spoke of human or moral rights. All of our basic (or primary) rights, like the right to privacy, have three essential attributes: they are human, moral, and natural (rights). Basic rights are human rights in the sense in which the Universal Declaration of Human Rights speaks of rights. All humans, as persons, possess these rights. In this respect, basic rights are worldwide or global in scope; they are not restricted to any particular nation, region, or culture. Second, basic rights are moral; they have a moral content. They denote a realm of justice in which everyone has a duty to respect each and every person's rights. Third, basic rights are natural; they belong to the very nature of personhood. They are not *constituted* by social recognition or legal conferral, although every society has a duty to recognize, promote, and institutionalize these rights. In doing so, however, societies do not thereby create these rights; they realize them. Finally, the right to privacy is a general right. It is not limited to a specific institutional context, for example, the right to own private property, or the Fourth Amendment right to home privacy.

I now critically examine three views of privacy that differ markedly from mine. The comparison will enable me to further develop my own view and to see how well it stands up to opposing theories.

Some time ago, the excellent journal *Philosophy and Public Affairs* published a series of articles on the right to privacy. The first article is by Judith Jarvis Thomson.[3] She denies that there exists a right to privacy as such. According to her, privacy consists of a cluster of rights that intersect with two other clusters of rights: property rights and rights over the person. The last cluster includes the right not to be looked at and the right not to be listened to under certain conditions. Rights over the person she characterizes as ungrand, in contrast to the grand rights such as the right to life, the right to liberty, and the right not to be hurt or harmed.

Thomson's view of the right to privacy differs from mine in two respects. First, she claims that the right to privacy is derivative; it is derived from either property rights or rights over the person. By contrast, I claim that it is a basic or primary right, not derived from other rights. Second, she claims that it is a cluster of rights. I claim that there is one basic, general right to privacy— which manifests itself, to be sure, in different contexts.

As is so characteristic of her philosophical strategy, Thomson gives a number of ingenious examples to support her position. I discuss two of them here. In the first example, she tries to show how the right to privacy is derived from property rights. Suppose a man owns a pornographic picture that he does not want anyone else to see, so he locks it up in his wall safe. However, we have heard about the picture and want to see it, so we focus our x-ray device on the safe, look in, and see the picture. Thomson says that the man's right to privacy has been violated, and I agree. However, her reasoning is that his property ownership rights have been violated. He owns the picture and the wall safe, and if he does not want anyone else to see the picture, that is completely within his property rights. But he does not have any special or distinctive right to privacy with respect to the picture that is not reducible to his property rights in owning it.

I disagree with her, and so does Thomas Scanlon. In a companion piece to Thomson's, Scanlon argues that privacy rights are at least partially independent of property rights and therefore are not reducible to them.[4] In Thomson's wall safe example, although Scanlon agrees with her that the man's right to privacy is violated, its violation does not depend on his ownership of the pornographic picture. Suppose, Scanlon says, that the picture belongs to someone else who has instructed the man to lock it up in his safe, or that the safe is empty, or that the man has mistakenly taken someone else's picture, thinking that it was his own. In all three cases, anyone who used an x-ray device to look into the man's wall safe would violate his privacy rights. Of course, Thomson could reply that the man's right to privacy in these three cases is reducible to his ownership of the wall safe. Not so, according to Scanlon. Suppose the man lends the wall safe to a friend, and someone uses an x-ray device to see whether anything is in it. The man's privacy rights are not violated, although his friend's are.

Continuing his criticism of Thomson, Scanlon offers the following example to further emphasize the independence of privacy rights from property rights:

> Suppose . . . that each person was assigned a plot in the common field to use as a place to bury valuables. Then anyone who used a Thomson device on my plot without my consent and without special authority would violate a right of mine, and would do so even if all he discovered was that I didn't have anything buried there. But I don't *own* the plot. I can't sell it; I can't build on it; perhaps I can't even use it for any other purpose.[5]

Scanlon holds that anyone who uses an x-ray device on my plot, just as anyone who uses such a device in the wall safe examples, violates a person's conventional "zone" (or "territory") of privacy.

Scanlon's criticism of Thomson's attempt to derive privacy rights from property rights is, I think, sound. However, his own position is as different from mine as is Thomson's. For one thing, he agrees with Thomson that there are many rights to privacy and that there is no one overarching privacy right. I claim that there is. Scanlon also holds that our rights to privacy consist of two elements: (1) a group of special interests that members of a society have in being free from certain kinds of intrusion, and (2) the conventions and laws that are established by that society to protect those interests.

In effect, Scanlon says that the right to privacy is a conferred right, conferred on us by our society. This view is the result of his social contract theory of morality. On the contrary, I hold that it is a natural right that ought to be supported and strengthened by all societies and governments.

Let us now turn to Thomson's second example, in which she tries to reduce privacy rights to rights over the person. Suppose a married couple is having a quiet fight in their home behind closed windows. Suppose someone across the street uses an amplifier on their house so he can hear what they are saying. According to Thomson, the couple's right to privacy is violated, and I agree. However, I disagree as to why it is violated. She says that it is violated because a certain right over the person—the right not to be listened to under certain conditions—is violated. So in this case, she tries to derive the right to privacy from a right over the person, a right that she calls an ungrand right. I hold that the right to privacy is a primary right, not derived from a more basic right or rights.

In a third article, Jeffrey Reiman criticizes both Thomson and Scanlon by arguing, as I have, that privacy is a primary right.[6] It is primary because it is intimately connected with personhood as such. Privacy protects a fundamental interest of all human beings, even those in solitary confinement—namely, a human being's interest in becoming and remaining a person. It does this through the medium of social practice and ritual. The content of privacy consists of a set of social practices that range from not asking nosy questions, to not looking into other people's windows, to not entering a room without first knocking, to not knocking down a closed door without a warrant, and so on. The point of these social practices is that "privacy is a social ritual by means of which an individual's moral title to his existence is conferred."[7] Privacy enables an individual to think of his existence as belonging to him and to him alone. It is both the precondition and the confirmation of personhood. The social ritual of privacy is an essential element by which persons are created out of prepersonal infants, and it demonstrates respect for persons already developed. Since Reiman believes that the creation of persons is an ongoing social process, these two dimensions of privacy eventually merge. "Privacy is a condition of the original and continuing creation of 'selves' or 'persons.'"[8]

Since the right to privacy, according to Reiman, establishes our existence as persons, it is a basic (or primary) right. It is the right that enables us to think of ourselves as beings for whom it is meaningful and important to have personal and property rights. So, contrary to Thomson, he concludes that personal rights and property rights are derived from the right to privacy rather than the other way around. "Personal and property rights presuppose an individual with title to his existence—and privacy is the social ritual by which that title is conferred."[9]

I agree with Reiman that privacy is a basic or primary right in the sense that it is not derived from, and not reducible to, some other right or rights. But I reject his view that certain social practices and rituals both constitute the right to privacy and partially create personhood. In this regard, he does Scanlon one better. Scanlon claims that social conventions create only the right to privacy; Reiman claims that they create personhood as well.

Continuing, Reiman argues that consciousness cannot ground the right to privacy:

> That there are thoughts, images, reveries and memories of which only I am conscious does not make them mine in the moral sense—any more than the cylinders in a car belong to it just because they are in it. This is why ascribing ownership of my body to the mere connection with my consciousness begs the question. Ownership of my thoughts requires a social practice as well. . . . The contents of my consciousness become mine because they are treated according to the ritual of privacy.[10]

It appears that Reiman's legal background has too heavily influenced his philosophical outlook. His entire analysis of privacy and personhood, which claims to be philosophical, is couched in legal categories such as ownership and title. Reiman's central claim is that for me to be a self or a person, I must own my self and my body, and that this ownership is established by a social ritual and practice that constitute the right to privacy. There are two problems with this claim. The first concerns his view of ownership; the second concerns his view of the relation between social ritual or practice and the right to privacy.

As we saw in chapter 3 in discussing slavery, persons cannot be owned by others. By the same token, I cannot own my self or my body; I can only own things external to myself—my pen, my clothes, my car, my house, and so on. To clarify this point, let me briefly develop Gabriel Marcel's well-known distinction between being and having, although I do not follow what he says literally.[11]

I distinguish the terms *self*, *human person*, and *body*, which Reiman seems to equate.[12] As we saw in chapter 1, a self is any human person considered from the standpoint of I. My self is the ontological ground of self-consciousness. In this sense, it is literally true to say, I am my self. But it is false to say either that I have a self or that I own my self, because these statements presuppose that there is a more fundamental reality that either has or owns my self. But this is impossible. My self *is* my fundamental reality. As such, it is that which has and owns everything that I have and own. The most intimate reality I have is my body. It is so intimate that it is intrinsic to me. In this respect, it is true to say, I am my body. But this statement is only a partial truth, since it is also true to say that I have a body. In other words, the two statements, I am a body and I have a body, are partial truths about myself that must be stated simultaneously to correct each other.

The foregoing analysis implies that my self (or person) is not identical to my body. Since the body is material, a self or person is more than matter, more than a material and organic body. A self (or person), I contend, is constituted by an immaterial spiritual core. In this context, *I define a human person as embodied or incarnate spiritual selfhood.*[13] My body is the bridge or medium between my self and the world of objects and other persons. It is the medium by which I can own any object. Without a body, I could not own anything; my body is a necessary condition of ownership of external things. But the body itself cannot be owned by me. Reiman fails to adequately distinguish among what I am, what I have, and what I own; this failure mars his analysis of personhood and the right to privacy.

Another weakness in Reiman's analysis is that he does not distinguish between sensory consciousness and self-consciousness. Animals have sensory consciousness but that does not mean they have self-consciousness. As phenomenologists have emphasized, the structure of self-consciousness implies a distinction between the subjective and objective poles of consciousness. Reiman, of course, does not make this distinction. When he speaks of the contents of consciousness, this term denotes the objective pole of consciousness. When I reflect upon myself, I am conscious that I have many and various thoughts, feelings, memories, sensations, desires, goals, even fantasies. These are all contents of consciousness. As such, they are objects of consciousness. They are what I—my self—am conscious of or reflect upon. It follows, then, that a content or object of consciousness presupposes a subjective I or self that is conscious of and reflects upon—indeed, that has—this object or content of consciousness. This I or self constitutes the subjective pole of self-consciousness, and it is precisely this self that is the ontological ground of the right to privacy.

By contrast, it is the objective pole of self-consciousness that the psychological term *introspection* denotes. To introspect is to reflect upon an object or content of consciousness. In this sense, introspection is concerned only with the self as object, the objectified self. Introspection is not concerned with the subjective source or pole of self-consciousness, namely, the self as subject. Introspection is not concerned with the self *that* introspects, but only with *what* the self introspects. Sometimes self-consciousness and introspection are identified, but this identification is a mistake.

The second difficulty with Reiman's position concerns his claim that the right to privacy consists of a network of social practices and rituals. He denies that I am a person by virtue of my own nature and being; he denies an ontological conception of personhood. Rather, my personhood is created by a society conferring on me a right to privacy through a set of social rituals. Essentially, personhood is created by social and legal institutions. This may be fine for a legal conception of personhood, but it is scarcely adequate for a philosophical and ontological conception. Legally, a corporation is a person, but it does not follow that it is a real person, a person in an ontological sense.[14] There is a profound difference between the institutional and the ontological order of things. Society and its institutions ought to recognize and promote the right to privacy—and all other rights, for that matter. But social institutions do not thereby constitute the right to privacy; much less do they constitute personhood.

In contrast to Reiman, my own view is that the core of privacy consists of the inward subjectivity of self-consciousness. But since the self has a body that is intrinsic to its individual personhood, the domain of privacy likewise extends to our bodies. Since, however, the body is the medium between self and world, it is also public. The body has both a public and a private dimension. Through our bodies, the inward privacy of self-consciousness reveals itself in public speech, action, and communication. Thus, there is an essential relationship between the domain of subjective privacy and the domain of objective, public, social action. But this relationship also creates tension, which often produces unresolved conflict, as we shall see later.

Person, Subject, and Spirit

At this point, two serious objections can be raised against my position on privacy. First, my distinction between self as subject and self as object seems to reverse the order between subjectivity and objectivity that I developed in chapter 1 when I defined reason as the capacity for objectivity (primarily) and subjectivity (secondarily). Now I am saying that the self as subject (the subjective self) is more basic than the self as object (the objective self), since the former is the ground of the latter.

My answer is that the words *subjective* and *objective* are being used in two much different contexts and consequently have correspondingly different meanings. My definition of reason is essentially a definition of *knowledge*, which can occur on four levels of experience: thought, feeling, action, and communication. In the present context, I am analyzing the structure of consciousness and its ontological ground. This analysis, if rational, as I claim it is, produces knowledge, that is, knowledge of the real nature of selfhood. And to know that a self is constituted by a subjective self that grounds and "has" the objectified self of introspection is to achieve objectivity in knowledge by means of subjective self-reflection upon the nature of selfhood. Therefore, in the order of knowledge, how the self really is (objectivity) determines how we should think about the self (subjectivity), which implies that objectivity is primary and subjectivity is secondary. But in the order of *being* (the ontological order), the self exists primarily as *subject* and secondarily as *object* in the sense in which we have just explained these two words, which have a very different meaning from the terms *subjectivity* and *objectivity* in the definition of reason. There is no inconsistency in my usage of these four terms.

The second objection concerns my definition of a human person as embodied or incarnate spirit. The definition implies that the core of a human person is spirit, spiritual being. This view puts me at odds with Macmurray, and will be rejected, of course, by all materialists. I am concerned here with Macmurray's views. Macmurray categorically rejects the idea that human personhood consists of spiritual being that is independent of, and not reducible to, material being. For him, to affirm spiritual reality implies a dualism between spirit and matter, or between soul and body, and he rejects all forms of dualism. In Macmurray's view, the self as agent is inclusive of personhood, and an agent is wholly body. "As agent . . . the Self is the body. . . . As an agent I am a body, operative, material and existent. . . ."[15] One problem with this view is that it seems to contradict his statement, cited in chapter 1, that a person is *more than* an organism. But how can a person be more than an organism if she is identical to her body, which is precisely an organism?

To carry this analysis further, I introduce the term *person-body* to characterize Macmurray's position, since he identifies human personhood with body. For Macmurray, the essential difference between a person-body and an organism is that the former performs activities such as thought, action, and communication, and the latter does not. Nevertheless, the different essential activities of persons vis-à-vis organisms are ultimately reducible to the materiality of body. There are three kinds of bodies: person-bodies, organisms, and inorganic bodies, in descending order of inclusiveness of being. Each type of body is distinguished from the others by its degree of material complexity and organization, and corresponding level of activities. A person-body is a qualitatively or essentially higher kind of wholly material being than is an organism, just as an organism is a qualitatively or essentially higher kind of material being than is an inorganic body. We do not have to introduce a dubious notion of spirit (or mind) to explain the essential difference between person-bodies and organisms (and by implication, inorganic bodies). Matter is sufficient.

Of course, a person-body is still partially an organism with respect to its purely biological nature. In an even less-inclusive sense, a person-body has a physico-chemical structure and constitution that is similar to inorganic bodies. All bodies obey the laws of physics, and all are composed of molecules, atoms, and subatomic particles. In sum, a person-body transcends but includes organicity and inorganic materiality, just as an organism transcends but includes inorganic materiality.

The foregoing interpretation of Macmurray will perhaps raise eyebrows among Macmurrian scholars. True, he does not explicitly say all of the above. It is an attempt to interpret a problematic doctrine of his philosophy in a way that makes sense (at least to me). I contend, then, that the foregoing analysis represents Macmurray's implicit position. But is it adequate? I do not think so. If it were, then science, in principle, could completely explain the nature of personhood. Such a view would be incompatible with Macmurray's overall philosophy. At the very least, it would conflict with a central doctrine of his philosophy, namely, that religion (including morality), art, and science are the three major reflective activities of persons and that religion and art are more inclusive activities of personhood and of reality than is science.

Finally, what about God? As a theist and Christian, Macmurray affirms the existence of God as an infinite, universal Person. As person, He is also agent, Macmurray says. Does that mean that God is the infinite, universal person-*body*, and that He is wholly a material being, just as His creation is entirely material? Macmurray does not say. In the last analysis, there appears to be a serious incoherence in his thought regarding his apparent view that persons are wholly material.

However, my definition of human person as embodied spirit avoids the above difficulties. Moreover, the definition also avoids dualism. *Embodied spirit* implies spirit *in* matter, not spirit *and* matter (the formula for dualism). Spirit-in-matter constitutes one unified body. I prefer *spirit* to *mind*, because the latter term has an intellectualist and Cartesian connotation that is incompatible with my conception of human personhood. I use the term spirit in a kind of Hegelian sense, without, however, reducing matter to spirit, à la idealism.[16]

My definition implies, of course, that persons perform activities that are not, in principle, completely explainable by material reality. Although I cannot adequately treat this complex issue here, let me give one example of such an activity, namely self-consciousness itself. I present the following brief argument for the immateriality or spirituality of self-consciousness. It is based on what I call the *coincidentality* of self-consciousness, to coin a word. In self-consciousness, I am aware that I am the same identical self that performs all my many and diverse acts. In this experience, the I that is aware of itself as subject knows itself as the same I which is subject. Therefore, the I that knows itself as subject coincides with the I that exists as subject. This coincidentality also discloses the fundamental ontological simplicity of the self as subject. However, both coincidentality and ontological simplicity are foreign to the nature of matter. Material things are made up of parts, which are discrete from each other, since they are quantitative and extended or displaced in space. True, a material thing is what it is, but this tautology is obviously not what I mean by coincidentality. It follows, then, that the subjective pole of self-consciousness and its ontological ground, the self as subject, are immaterial or spiritual. Nevertheless, since the human person is an *embodied* spirit, the brain is a necessary condition for exercising self-consciousness (at least in this life).[17] But the brain is not a sufficient condition of self-consciousness; self-consciousness is not completely explainable by and reducible to brain activity.

This argument and the point of view it represents is rejected by materialism, of course. (By materialism I mean the philosophical view that all reality is reducible to some form of matter.) In a recent article, "The Mystery of Consciousness,"[18] several scientists and philosophers examine consciousness from the viewpoint of the new, emerging science of consciousness. All are materialists and most of them embrace scientism, the view that only science is knowledge. Central to this new science is a distinction between what it calls the Easy Problem and the Hard Problem. The Easy Problem involves distinguishing between conscious and unconscious mental activity, and correlating specific contents of each with specific elements of brain activity. Practitioners of this science claim that much progress has been made in this area, and that is all well and good. However, the Easy Problem is not relevant to our present problem, for the consciousness of the Easy Problem refers to introspection, the objective pole of consciousness (the self as object). The Hard Problem is what is relevant here. This problem consists in trying to explain the subjective pole of consciousness by brain activity, "[to] explain how subjective experience arises from neural computation."[19] It is this problem they call the mystery of consciousness, for they have not had much success in resolving it. Their difficulties, of course, do not surprise me. Science can no more provide an adequate explanation for the subjectivity of self-consciousness than it can prove or disprove the existence of God. Some questions are off limits to the sciences for a simple and obvious reason: not all questions are scientific ones. Science is not omnicompetent. Every discipline has its limits, defined by its method and subject matter.

Most of the participants in this article, however, are optimistic that the science of the brain will eventually be able to explain the subjectivity of self-consciousness. They believe this not so much because they are dedicated scientists, but because they affirm the doctrine of scientism. The problem, however, is that this doctrine is incoherent. Science cannot prove that only itself is knowledge. There is no legitimate scientific method that can verify or confirm the proposition that only science is knowledge, for the proposition is not a scientific hypothesis but a philosophical doctrine. But as a philosophical doctrine it contradicts itself. For, since the statement "only science is knowledge" is a philosophical one, and since the proponents of scientism obviously believe that this statement is true, then they believe there is at least one instance of a true philosophical statement. Therefore, they implicitly claim that *not* all knowledge is science, which contradicts their original claim that all knowledge is science (or, conversely, only science is knowledge).

To compound this incoherence, scientism commits two elementary fallacies: argumentum ad ignorantiam (argument from ignorance), and argumentum ad verecundiam (appeal to inappropriate authority). We encountered the first fallacy in the previous chapter. It consists of the following reasoning: something does not exist, because the thing cannot be proven to exist; or conversely, something does exist, because the thing cannot be proven not to exist. For example, the late Senator Joseph McCarthy in the early 1950s reasoned that certain persons called before his committee were Communists, because they could not prove they were not Communists. He was rightly censured by his senate colleagues for ruining many innocent lives based on this fallacious reasoning. Similarly, some proponents of scientism reason that God does not exist, since science cannot prove such a being exists. Likewise, when the participants in the above article reason that the subjectivity of self-consciousness cannot denote an immaterial or spiritual aspect of a person because science cannot prove the existence of such an entity, they commit this fallacy.

The argumentum ad verecundiam fallacy consists in the transference of authority from a field in which a person has competence or expertise to another field in which he does not. For example, if someone appeals to the authority of Einstein to settle a dispute in politics, economics, religion, or even philosophy, she commits this fallacy. Advertising testimonials, in which celebrities endorse a wide variety of products, commit this fallacy. By the same token, proponents of scientism commit this fallacy. They reason that because they are competent scientists, they have similar competence to judge difficult and complex philosophical issues—for example, does God exist, is there life after death, is a person immortal in some sense, and so on. They do not. They are perfectly entitled to their opinions on these matters, of course, just as everyone is. But they should not think that their opinions on these issues are any more valuable or true than anyone else's opinions on the grounds that they are good scientists. Indeed, in the above article, many of the comments made by the scientists display a profound ignorance of philosophy and religion.

The way for all proponents of scientism to avoid the doctrine's incoherence and companion twin fallacies is for them to adopt a healthy dose of skepticism and intellectual humility. That is, instead of them saying that something does not exist because science cannot prove it exists, they should say something like the following: science cannot prove this, but it may (or may not) exist, because (1) science in this case may have reached its limits; (2) there may be other valid forms of knowledge, for example, philosophy, that are relevant to the issue at hand; and (3) competence or expertise in a particular science does not extend beyond one's field of scientific specialization.

I conclude this section with three observations. First, my present definition of a human person as embodied spirit complements my earlier definition of a human person as a rational and communicative agent. Therefore, the two definitions can be combined: a human person, as an embodied spirit, is a rational and communicative agent. However, each definition is free-standing; they do not have to be combined.

Second, the partial or core spirituality of human personhood implies theism or a similar position concerning God and spirit, for example, Hegel's panentheism. I now modify a statement made at the beginning of chapter 1: persons, as embodied spirits, are created by a theistic God, who is infinite person/spirit. This statement does not conflict with science and evolution, for persons' bodies are subject to all the forces and conditions of nature.

Third, my view of personhood does not imply idealism. Spiritual reality or being is equally compatible with realism and idealism. As I indicated in chapter 1, my version of personalism is personalist realism. The primacy of objectivity in knowledge emphasized in chapter 1 is a realist position.

PRIVACY AND SOCIETY

I now consider how different types of society deal with privacy. I single out three kinds of society as models or archetypes for how particular societies can organize themselves. As models, they are ideals that an actual society more or less approximates. And precisely as ideals, they have ethical significance; they are not merely descriptive. Moreover, a particular society may embody elements of more than one of them, but one model may dominate its actual structure. The three models are the individualistic, the organic, and the personalist. The first two are taken up in this chapter and the third in chapter 8.

The Individualistic Society

An individualistic society rests on the doctrine of individualism. As we saw in chapter 1, according to individualism, individuals are constituted as persons in themselves, independently of their relations with other persons. Relations are external to personhood. Society is not an essential aspect of human nature. Humans are not by nature social beings. Society is formed by means of a contract. Prior to the formation of society, individuals live in a state of nature. Society is a loose collection or aggregate of fully constituted individuals in their own right. Individuality is primary, and relationality is secondary. Individualism overemphasizes individuality at the expense of relationality. As a consequence, its implicit view of the scope of privacy is too broad, as I will explain.

The social and political philosophy of libertarianism provides us with a paradigm of the individualistic society. No one has articulated and defended libertarianism more brilliantly than Robert Nozick, especially in his meticulously reasoned book *Anarchy, State, and Utopia*.[20] I now analyze and evaluate some of its major elements.

Nozick's theory has been strongly influenced by Locke, who combines individualism with theism and a doctrine of natural rights. God creates human beings as independent, individual persons in the state of nature and, in so doing, endows them with certain natural rights. In this state of nature, all individuals are, in Locke's words, "equal and independent, [and] no one ought to harm another in his life, health, liberty or possessions."[21]

Locke's natural rights are essentially negative rather than positive. A negative right is one that requires a person not to act in a certain way toward the holder of that right. Correlative to a negative right is a negative duty: a duty persons have not to violate a negative right. A positive right is one that requires a person to act in a certain way toward the holder of that right. Correlative to a positive right is a positive duty: a duty persons have to fulfill or satisfy a positive right. The Lockean right to life means that I have a right not to be killed or harmed by others, and others have a right not to be killed or harmed by me; all have a negative duty not to violate anyone's right to life. In this respect, Locke's right to health reduces to the right to life. If the right to health were positive, then persons would have a positive duty to provide healthcare to those who could not afford it on their own. But this would be totally foreign to Locke's thinking. For Locke, then, there are three basic natural and negative rights: life, liberty, and property.

Although Nozick does not accept Locke's theism, he accepts his individualism and theory of natural, negative rights. Consequently, the right to life means that persons have a right not to be killed or harmed by others. The right to liberty means that I have a right not to be interfered with by others in what I do. Persons have a right to do whatever they want to do, so long as they do not violate anyone else's rights to life, liberty, and property. The right to property means that I am entitled to whatever holdings I have acquired, and no one else has any right to them, provided I have acquired them fairly, that is, acquired them without violating anyone else's rights to life, liberty, or property.

Nozick's interpretation of the right to property produces a theory of distributive justice that he calls the entitlement theory. It consists of three principles. First, a person is entitled to a holding if he or she has acquired it fairly, as explained above. Second, a person is entitled to a holding if he or she acquires it fairly from another person who is entitled to that holding. And third, no person is entitled to any holding except in accordance with the first two principles.[22] Nozick does not work out the details of these three principles, but his general line of thinking is clear. It is not a legitimate moral function of the state, on the basis of a false theory of positive rights, to redistribute holdings—that is, to redistribute property in the form of wealth and income—by taking away some holdings from wealthier members of society and transferring them to poorer and needier members of society.

Such views lead Nozick to adopt a minimalist (or night-watchman) theory of the state. In this view, the state's moral legitimacy is limited to protecting everyone's natural, negative rights of life, liberty, and property. Thus, the state's basic functions are to protect its citizens against violence, force, theft, and fraud and to enforce all valid contracts among its citizens.[23] A more extensive activist or welfare state is morally unjustifiable, because it violates persons' natural rights of liberty and property. It taxes their property without their consent; it coerces them to do things they do not want to do. "Taxation of earnings from labor is on a par with forced labor," says Nozick.[24] The only taxes permitted are those required to support the basic, legitimate functions of the minimalist state with respect to protecting everyone's natural rights of life, liberty, and property. All government health, education, and welfare programs that are based on the notion of positive rights are forbidden. That includes such sacred cows as Medicare, Medicaid, Social Security, student loan programs, subsidies to special-interest groups, pork barrel legislation, Aid to Dependent Children, food stamps, and so forth. All taxes that support these programs are immoral. They are a form of legalized theft. Moreover, government paternalism is immoral. It is an infringement of personal liberty. The state has no right to pass laws that require actions that are supposedly good for oneself that do not violate the rights of others (e.g., seat belt laws) or to pass laws that forbid actions that are supposedly harmful to oneself but do not violate others' rights (e.g., drug laws or laws prohibiting voluntary euthanasia and assisted suicide). Finally, the state has no right to pass laws that restrict the liberty of consenting adults based on the claim that such laws are in the best interests of society or because such laws enjoy majority support (e.g., sodomy laws and cohabitation laws).

For libertarianism, justice is defined in terms of liberty; justice has no content independently of liberty. A person acts justly if he or she does not interfere with anyone else's natural rights of life, liberty, and property. Conversely, a person acts unjustly if he or she interferes with such rights. In this sense, Nozick's concept of justice is negative. Justice is defined in terms of what I may not do to others and what they may not do to me. Justice excludes any form of redistribution of wealth and income. How, then, does society take care of its poor, needy, and otherwise disadvantaged? Nozick's answer is volunteerism—voluntary charity. The affluent ought to be charitable and give to the poor. But the affluent have no obligation or duty in justice to give to them, and the poor have no right in justice to expect or demand anything from the rich. Hence, the state has no right to tax the rich to give to the poor. Nozick is convinced that voluntary charity can be sufficient to take care of society's poor and needy. So far, history has proved him wrong. For volunteerism to work, the rich and affluent would have to become much more altruistic and charitable than most have proved themselves to be. But that is beside the point, Nozick would say. His point is that society may not take care of its poor and needy through government programs, even if the absence of such programs produces much more poverty than otherwise would be the case. People's rights may not be violated to secure greater social utility. Nozick is strongly antiutilitarian. The end does not justify the means, and any means that would infringe on any person's natural, negative rights is apparently intrinsically immoral, an intrinsic violation of justice, and thus may never be performed.

During the Reagan-Bush era of American politics, volunteerism received a fresh impetus because of massive cutbacks in federal social welfare programs during the Reagan administration. This "new" volunteerism began in 1988 with presidential candidate George Bush's famous "thousand points of light" speech, and it proved to be politically popular. As a result, the Democratic administration of Bill Clinton continued the Reagan-Bush cutbacks and promoted the volunteerism theme, which culminated in the 1997 President's Summit for America's Future in Philadelphia, where Clinton and General Colin Powell touted the power (and not only the virtue) of volunteerism. In 2000, presidential candidate George W. Bush picked up his father's message, calling himself a "compassionate conservative," and pushing for "charitable choice," a provision in the 1996 welfare reform bill that allowed religious-oriented organizations to contract with the government to provide social services to the poor. Democratic presidential candidate Al Gore supported the bill, but less enthusiastically.

In an insightful article, "The Vanity of Volunteerism,"[25] Sara Mosle narrates the failure of this new volunteerism and identifies the reasons for its failure: a paucity of volunteers, especially regular volunteers; and not nearly enough money from private donations to compensate for the governmental programs that had been axed. Therefore, in my view, if we care about the poor and the needy more than we care about our taxes, and we are unwilling or unable to privately and directly meet their needs, then the types of governmental social programs that have been cut must be restored so that the federal government can fulfill its essential role with respect to distributive justice. Of course, volunteerism should continue, but in a supporting role. After George W. Bush was elected president in 2000, things went from bad to worse. He progressively abandoned his *compassionate* conservatism as he obsessively waged his disastrous Iraqi War.

The middle class has also suffered. During roughly the same period as Mosle surveys, there was a growing maldistribution of wealth and income between the rich and the poor/middle class. In 1983, the top 20 percent of households in the United States owned 81.3 percent of all privately held wealth, and the bottom 80 percent owned 18.7 percent. In 2001, these figures were 84.4 percent and 15.5 percent, respectively. When a comparison is made between the top 1 percent and bottom 99 percent, the maldistribution is even more glaring. In 1976, the bottom 99 percent held 80.1 percent of private wealth, and the top 1 percent owned 19.9 percent. By 1998, the former figure dropped dramatically to 61.9 percent, and the latter figure rose to an astounding 38.1 percent. A similar pattern occurs in comparing income. In 1982, the top 1 percent earned 12.8 percent, and in 2001, this figure had risen to 20 percent. In contrast, the bottom 80 percent of households earned 48.1 percent of income in 1982, which dropped to 41.4 percent in 2000. Most outrageous of all is a comparison between the incomes of CEOs and factory workers in the United States. The ratio of CEO pay to worker pay rose from 42:1 in 1960 to 531:1 in 2000 at the peak of the stock market, but declined to a still whopping 411:1 in 2005. By comparison, the European ratio is only about 25:1. From 1990 to 2005, American CEO pay increased by almost 300 percent (adjusted for inflation), and worker pay rose a meager 4.3 percent. The federal minimum wage actually declined by 9.3 percent when inflation is calculated.[26]

Since 2005, and especially since the Great Recession of 2008, the inequality of wealth and income in the United States has worsened. The top 1 percent now owns more wealth than the bottom 90 percent. Indeed, the top 1 percent owns 40 percent of the private wealth in America. They earn 25 percent of its income, and it is greater than the income of the bottom 50 percent. The ratio of CEO to worker pay has risen to 600:1. Forty-seven percent of households cannot raise $2,000 within thirty days. The poverty rate in the United States rose to 15.7 percent in 2011, the highest rate since 1965, and up from 13 percent about ten years ago, the highest rate of any developed nation. In 2010, the median net worth of an American family shrunk to $77,300, down from $126,400 in 2007, mostly because of the dramatic drop in housing prices. Between 1979 and 2007, the income of the top 1 percent of households increased by 275 percent (and for the top .01 percent, it rose by more than 400 percent); the income of the next 19 percent rose by 65 percent; income increased by slightly under 40 percent for the next 60 percent of households; and income rose by only 18 percent for the bottom 20 percent. The maldistribution of wealth and income in the United States is at its worst level since the onset of the Great Depression of 1929.[27]

The point of all these statistics is threefold. First, volunteerism by itself is utterly incapable of resolving these egregious inequalities of wealth and income. Second, a healthy economy depends upon a reasonable distribution of wealth and income so that everyone can have enough money to spend on the basic goods and services that stimulate economic growth. Third, severe inequalities of wealth and income are a serious threat to democracy. Since democracy is a form of government, I submit, in which political *and* economic power (which are inherently related) reside in the people, *all* the people, a flourishing democracy depends upon a reasonable distribution of wealth and income spearheaded by a prosperous middle class and a serious, concerted effort to reduce poverty. By this definition of democracy, libertarianism is antidemocratic, despite its emphasis on liberty. Because of libertarianism's absolutization of an essentially negative and legalistic conception of liberty wedded to a similar conception of property rights, the form of government that libertarianism is naturally oriented toward is oligarchic plutocracy, which will be brought about by the only form of economic system that libertarians favor, namely, laissez-faire capitalism, in which the economy is completely determined by the free-market system, by the law of supply and demand. The government is prohibited from regulating the market in any way whatsoever. There must be total free competition. Laissez-faire (unregulated) capitalism is the only economic system that is morally right, because it is the only system that adequately safeguards everyone's natural rights, especially liberty.[28] The problem here, however, is libertarianism's theory of rights. It has only three rights—life, liberty, and property—and they are negative. Such an impoverished theory of rights is highly inadequate for a true democracy.

For libertarianism, privacy can be seen as the obverse of liberty. Liberty is one's right to do anything one pleases, so long as one does not infringe on anyone else's rights. Obversely, privacy is one's right to act in a way that others, and especially the state, have no right to infringe on. Moreover, Nozick, like Locke before him, gives more attention to property rights than to other rights. And by property, he means, of course, private property. In the last analysis, the triple rights of liberty, privacy, and property intersect and determine the content of distributive justice. As a result, I contend that libertarianism overvalues all three and undervalues justice. In so doing, it has a deficient notion of community. To show this, I must now indicate several difficulties with libertarianism.

The fundamental error of libertarianism is that it rests on individualism. Individualism denies the inherently relational and social nature of human persons. The mythical self-sufficient individual, in his or her natural rights of life, liberty, privacy, and property, is glorified and exaggerated. The social contract that such individuals eventually form cannot constitute a true community, if only because the social contract lacks the inherent relationality of persons that is fundamental to community.

Nevertheless, I agree with Nozick that persons as such possess natural rights. I disagree with him on two counts: that these rights are exclusively negative and there are only three of them, and that they have no foundation. Let us take the latter point first. As Nozick concedes in his book, he does not give his natural rights any basis.[29] Unlike Locke, he does not hold that God endows persons with rights in the act of creating them. Nozick is not a theist. However, natural rights cannot come from society or the state either. They are not conferred or acquired rights, as Scanlon or Reiman might say. Whence, then, do they come? Since Nozick's entire theory depends on the validity of natural rights, we are entitled to ask why libertarianism should be accepted if the existence of natural rights cannot be rationally justified. By not accepting Locke's theism, Nozick deprives natural rights of their strongest foundation, perhaps their only rational foundation.[30]

A theory of exclusively negative rights severely curtails the scope of distributive justice. It makes impossible any theory of distributive justice that would redistribute wealth and income. Such a theory, of course, would require a modification of the Lockean and libertarian notion of property rights. I deal with this issue later when I develop the personalist society.

Libertarianism's entitlement theory of distributive justice creates a false dualism between distributive justice and the redistribution of income/wealth. Of course, it regards any redistribution to be inherently unjust. This dualism, however, is based on the false presupposition that at any given moment in a society the actual, de facto distribution of income/wealth is perfectly (or at least adequately) just and thus requires no redistribution. In the concrete, there is no such thing as a distribution of wealth/income that cannot be made more just in the light of an adequate conception of distributive justice, also taking into consideration changing economic and political conditions. The promotion and implementation of distributive justice continually requires some adjustment in terms of redistribution. Therefore, the idea of redistributive justice is valid; it is an essential component of distributive justice. They are two sides of the same coin of justice. That said, however, a people's basic aim or intention should be to create ab initio a society whose economic and political structure embodies an adequate idea of distributive justice so that the need for redistribution is minimized. For libertarianism, however, this need is maximized. The huge amount of inequality of wealth and income that would be generated by the type of laissez-faire capitalism that libertarianism advocates guarantees that a massive amount of redistribution would be required to rectify the resulting injustice. We have seen that volunteerism is inadequate in this regard. And even if it were adequate, an issue of justice would be transformed into a form of demeaning "charity," as doles and handouts. The basic problem of distributive injustice would not be addressed. As Sammy Davis Jr. once said, what we want is justice, not charity.

The final problem with Nozick's libertarianism that I want to mention concerns his idea of liberty. As a moral idea, it is severely limited. It certainly cannot cover the whole scope or content of freedom. Liberty is the right to do what I want to do, not what I ought to do. Nozick's liberty is the right to do what is immoral as much as it is the right to do what is moral—so long as I do not violate anyone else's rights. A billionaire has a right in liberty to keep all his money, even though masses of people around him are poor, hungry, homeless, and even starving to death. A person has a right in liberty to become a drug addict without any interference from the law. I now want to add three terms to Nozick's notion of liberty, which were briefly developed in chapter 2: free will, autonomy, and freedom in friendship. Free will, or absolute freedom, is a person's inherent power or capacity to make free choices, to act freely or voluntarily, to do this rather than that. Free will is the ontological ground of Nozick's liberty. In turn, autonomy is the rational and right exercise of one's free will and liberty, as it is in Kant's third formulation of the categorical imperative, the principle of autonomy. But the fullness of autonomy resides in friendship and community. This fullness of autonomy I call freedom in friendship. It is the ultimate moral end—just as autonomy in itself is the penultimate end—of Nozick's liberty, which is essentially a means of developing one's autonomy on the way to freedom in friendship and community. From the standpoint of an adequate moral philosophy, then, libertarianism's liberty cannot be an end in itself.

The Organic Society

As we saw in chapter 3, the organic society conceives the relation between society and the individual as analogous to that between an organism and its organs. It also tends to identify society with the state, or at least to hold that the state is the supreme expression of society. Just as the life of an organ is submerged to that of the whole organism and has no real purpose or individuality apart from the organism, so also, in an organic society, individual persons exist solely for the state or the social whole and have no individuality or purpose apart from the state. Relationality is overemphasized at the expense of individuality.

In the history of Western thought, the organic type of society has its roots in Plato's ideal state, the republic, which takes its name from the title of his most famous dialogue. Plato's state is modified and further refined in the *Laws*. In the republic, individuality, liberty, and privacy are severely restricted for the good of the state.

The republic represents the supreme and all-inclusive good, an embodiment of the absolute Form, or Idea, of justice. Consequently, all individuals are to subordinate themselves to the state, and in achieving its good, they ipso facto achieve their own good as well. Individuals exist for the state rather than the other way around, as in democracy.

Plato reduces the variety and diversity of individuals to four categories, which constitute the four stratified classes of the republic. These four classes represent a caste system. The highest class is the guardian or ruling class. It consists of philosopher-kings, who have absolute power. Only philosophers are fit to rule, since the best state should be governed by the wisest people; philosophers, by nature, are lovers and practitioners of wisdom. The second highest class is the auxiliary or military class. It performs the functions of soldiers, police, and civil servants. The auxiliaries execute and enforce the policies of the guardians. Just below the auxiliaries is the artisan class. It includes skilled workers and businesspeople, those who produce the economic goods of life. The fourth and lowest class is the class of slaves, who are not citizens. Although this class is not specifically mentioned in *The Republic*, it is nonetheless implied, for Plato, like Aristotle, simply accepted slavery as a fact of life, an economic necessity.[31] In general, slaves perform the unskilled labor in the republic. Since the republic is a caste system, there is generally no upward social mobility. Unlike democracy, the republic is a closed society. Plato did not think that the masses possessed the requisite knowledge and virtue to govern.

In Book Five of *The Republic*, Plato develops his famous community of wives and children proposal. Unlike Aristotle, Plato is surprisingly enlightened for his time concerning the difference between men and women. Aristotle held that just as some humans by nature are meant to be slaves, so women by nature are meant to be ruled by men.[32] Although Plato agrees with Aristotle's views on slavery, he has a totally different attitude toward women. There are only two differences between men and women in his view: they have different reproductive organs and functions, and men in general are physically stronger than women. Plato believes that all offices open to men are equally open to women. They are to receive the same education as men, and they are equally eligible to serve as guardians and auxiliaries. In effect, Plato believes in the principle of equal opportunity between the genders.

Beyond this principle of equal opportunity, however, Plato advocates several measures that involve extraordinary invasions of privacy and suppressions of liberty by the state. The guardians and the auxiliaries are not permitted to own property or to have families. Plato believes that ownership of private property and the raising of a family needlessly distract guardians and auxiliaries from their highest duty in life, that of serving the state. On eugenic grounds, the marriages of guardians and auxiliaries are to be strictly regulated by the state. The aim is to produce the best possible offspring for the state. Immediately after birth, the offspring are separated from their biological parents and raised in state nurseries. Also for eugenic reasons, the state determines when guardian and auxiliary couples can bear children. For women, it is between the ages of twenty-five and fifty-five. Plato even hints that any child born outside these prescribed limits, or any child who is the offspring of adultery committed by guardians or auxiliaries, will be destroyed.[33] Children of the two upper classes who are not fit for the life of those classes but are born legitimately are relegated to the artisan class. Likewise, soldiers who leave their post in battle or who commit any other act of cowardice are demoted to the artisan class.[34]

Similar proposals are presented in the *Laws*. There will be a committee of women to oversee marriages for ten years after their inception. If couples have no children during this period, they should obtain a divorce. Men must marry between the ages of thirty and thirty-five, and women between sixteen and twenty (later changed to eighteen). Violations of marital infidelity are punishable by the state. Men perform their military service between twenty and sixty. Women perform their military service after bearing children but before they are fifty. Men cannot hold political office until they are thirty, nor women until they are forty. If much of this sounds like an intolerable intrusion of state power on privacy and freedom, Plato supplies his justification for it: "The bride and bridegroom should consider that they are to produce for the state the best and fairest specimens of children which they can."[35]

The state's massive invasion of privacy is not limited to matters of sex, reproduction, and family life. Plato really has it in for atheists and heretics. Atheism and heresy, which he tends to identify, are criminal offenses that the state severely punishes. Depending on the seriousness of the case, the penalty for a first offense is five years to life imprisonment, and the death penalty is imposed for a second offense.[36]

That the state is everything is likewise reflected in Plato's idea of justice, which is the central theme of *The Republic*. The republic is the fulfillment of justice, the embodiment of absolute justice. As an aristocracy, it is the only perfect type of state.[37] No individual can be perfectly or absolutely just; only the state can be. Individuals can only more or less approximate justice; they can never completely embody it.

Nevertheless, the basic attribute of justice is the same, whether it exists in individuals or in the state. This attribute is harmony, or right order, and it places Plato's idea of justice in sharp contrast with that of libertarianism. As is well known, Plato's idea of justice is rooted in his tripartite theory of the human soul, which is divided into reason, the spirited part, and appetite—from highest to lowest. They are not parts in a literal or material sense, but three different active principles, or aspects, of the soul. Reason, as the power of thought, contemplates the perfect Forms or Ideas. This activity produces knowledge (or truth), as in philosophy and mathematics. When a person makes reason and knowledge a way of life, he or she acquires wisdom, the virtue characteristic of philosophers. In contrast, appetite denotes bodily (or physical) desires, impulses, and urges, such as hunger, thirst, and sex. Plato's explanation of the intermediate, or in-between, aspect of the soul is somewhat unclear. The Greek-derived word for it is *thumos*, which is usually translated as spirit, and referred to as the spirited part of the soul, in the sense in which we speak of a person or even a horse as spirited. In humans, spirit is usually, and ought to be, the ally of reason, but it sometimes sides with appetite. In the former case, a person does what is morally right; in the latter case, he acts immorally. Plato's spirit seems to foreshadow, mutatis mutandis, the later concept of will, although A. E. Taylor says it is a "blunder" to identify spirit with will.[38] Nevertheless, as a distinct principle of the soul, spirit has the power to either follow the true judgments of reason or to succumb to the physical desires of appetite.

In any case, Plato's spirit is quite different from my own concept of spirit, which denotes immaterial reality. Since thumos is also found in animals, it cannot be an immaterial aspect of the soul. In fact, Plato holds that only reason is immaterial and immortal. It is reason that distinguishes humans from animals and makes them akin to the divine. Thus, it is Plato's reason, not spirit, that corresponds to my own concept of spirit.

Plato's basic idea of justice is harmony of the soul in relation to its three parts or principles. A person's soul possesses harmony when spirit obeys the dictates or judgments of reason and subordinates the physical desires of appetite. When such harmony occurs, a person acts justly; if it occurs consistently or habitually, she acquires the virtue of justice. Conversely, if spirit obeys the appetites, which means that appetite and not reason rules the soul, there is disharmony or disorder in the soul, which constitutes injustice. Justice and injustice, then, characterize the soul as a whole and not merely one of its parts. A person is just when appetite is subordinated to spirit, and spirit is subordinated to reason. This subordination of the lower to the higher is harmony of the soul and constitutes justice.

Plato then extends this idea of justice as harmony to the state, and in particular to the republic. Justice characterizes the state as a whole and not merely one of its classes. The justice of the state consists of harmony or right order among its classes. This means that all individuals in a lower class must duly subordinate themselves to the class or classes above them. There must be no upward social mobility, nor any downward social mobility either. Every individual in each class must know and accept his or her place in the social hierarchy and perform his or her appointed task. An artisan cannot attempt to become an auxiliary or guardian, any more than a guardian or auxiliary can attempt to become an artisan. One's station in life is determined by the twin principles of heredity and eugenics. Any attempt at either upward or downward social mobility is ipso facto an act of injustice, for it disrupts the harmony of the state. Injustice consists of a restless and meddlesome spirit, of one class interfering with the business of another class.[39]

The suppression of individuality, liberty, and privacy in the name of justice is obvious. Whereas Nozick subordinates justice to liberty, Plato subordinates liberty to justice by effectively denying that any individual has a right to either liberty or privacy. A right to privacy in Plato's republic is inconceivable.

If Plato's republic were merely utopian, we could dismiss it as a flight of fantasy and merely study it as a historical curiosity. Unfortunately, this is not the case, for its similarities with twentieth-century totalitarianism—whether Communist or Fascist—cannot be ignored. Indeed, totalitarianism is the ultimate logical expression of the principle of social organization embodied in the republic and the organic state in general: the total subordination of the individual person to the good of the state.[40] (Today, North Korea, China, Iran, and Syria are important examples of organic societies.) Despite Plato's emphasis on justice, the republic actually produces injustice. Both Nozick and Plato have deficient theories of justice. This deficiency is overcome in a personalist society, to which I now turn.

8

THE PERSONALIST SOCIETY, COMMUNITY, AND JUSTICE

In the previous chapter, we saw that the issue of privacy and private property raises fundamental questions about the nature of justice, especially distributive justice. We saw, too, that the individualistic and organic models of society have inadequate conceptions of both justice and privacy. I turn now to a third model of society, the personalist. A personalist society is one that aims at becoming a community, one that practices the principle of community. A personalist society may be regarded as a synthesis of the individualistic and organic societies, which stand to each other as thesis and antithesis. In a personalist society, the good of all persons is directly intended by intending the good of their relations with one another, within which is intended the good of their individuality. The individual's good cannot be achieved independently of community, nor can community be achieved independently of any individual's good.

In its ideal positive fullness, then, a personalist society is a community. This means, to summarize what was explained in chapter 2, that all members of a society intend a personal relation of persons, which includes relative impersonal but excludes absolute impersonal relations. Personal relations are constituted by the values of freedom, equality, and justice and are motivated by love. Their supreme expression is friendship. Within the fullness of community, however, a personalist society will contain a system of institutions that organizes its economic and political life. The primary moral purpose of these institutions is the achievement of justice. On a national scale, the central

245

institution of society's economic and political order is the state, whose purpose is to administer and enforce a system of law that is an expression of justice. However, as the world continues to grow in the direction of one global society, international institutions of justice are becoming increasingly important and necessary.

The economic and political life of a personalist society will take the form of a democracy; it will have a democratic state. In its literal sense, from the Greek, democracy means government of the people, meaning ideally all the people, or in the immortal words of Abraham Lincoln, government of the people, by the people, and for the people. Since democracy, as I use the term, refers to a democratic state, I define democracy as a form of government in which political and economic power resides in the people.

Within this definition, there are different forms of democracy. Regardless of the form, however, the primary moral purpose of any democratic state is the establishment of an order of justice. A democratic state is one that habitually intends justice. A nondemocratic state lacks such an intention. The moral legitimacy of any state is measured by how well it intends and achieves an order of justice.

In this chapter, I examine two roughly similar conceptions of democracy: Macmurray's constructive democracy and Rawls's political liberalism. As historical background for these two theories, I sketch some ideas on justice of Aristotle, Aquinas, and Kant. From a liberal perspective, I analyze two ongoing political controversies in the United States. I conclude with a synthesis that connects justice with the principles of community and intentionality.

HISTORICAL BACKGROUND: ARISTOTLE, AQUINAS, AND KANT

Aristotle distinguishes between universal and particular justice.[1] The former covers the whole realm of virtue and is concerned with what is legal or lawful. Since universal justice does not indicate what is distinctive about justice, Aristotle is chiefly concerned with particular justice, which is related to universal justice as a part to a whole. Particular justice deals with what is fair as equal. In turn, it is divided into two major modes: distributive and remedial (or rectificatory).[2] The latter is the basis for what later thinkers develop into retributive justice, which I treated in chapter 6. Our present concern is with distributive justice. In distributive justice, the state divides the goods of society—wealth, honor—among its members according to merit. And merit implies equality of proportionality, not absolute equality. That is, a citizen's share of goods received from the state is exactly proportionate to his or her merit, recognizing that not everyone is equally meritorious. Unfortunately, Aristotle does not develop a theory of what constitutes merit.

In any event, he makes two major contributions to the idea of justice. First, Aristotle defines justice as an interpersonal virtue, as a virtue that regulates our dealings with others—unlike Plato's view, which defines justice as harmony of the soul, and which he extends to harmony of the state. In this regard, our Western tradition has largely followed Aristotle rather than Plato. When we speak of justice today, we generally mean something that refers to how we treat one another and not a quality or condition of a person's soul. However, Aristotle's idea denies that justice is an intrapersonal virtue. As we saw in chapter 3, he holds that no one can treat himself unjustly. This view puts him in conflict with some later noted philosophers, such as Rousseau, Kant, and Mill. In his classic work, *On Liberty*,[3] Mill argues that a person who sells herself into slavery commits an injustice against herself, for no one has a moral right to use her freedom to negate or annul her freedom. A person is not free not to be free.

Second, it is widely accepted that distributive justice is an important mode of justice. (Today, distributive justice is often called social and/or economic justice.) However, what is controversial is the standard or criterion of distribution. Aristotle claims it is merit, but this criterion has provoked much criticism. As a result, there has been an ongoing debate on what constitutes a right and reasonable standard of distribution. Aquinas follows Aristotle, but significantly modifies his theory in the light of Christianity. In his typical systematic fashion, he begins with a definition of justice: "Justice is a habit whereby a man renders to each one his due by a constant and perpetual will."[4] Justice is necessarily interpersonal; it is concerned only with our dealings with others, not with ourselves.[5] In justice, our will gives everyone his or her due, regardless of how we feel toward them. And by due, he means what is owed others as a matter of right, that is, what others have a right to claim or demand of me.[6]

After accepting Aristotle's distinction between general and particular justice, Aquinas somewhat departs from his classification by saying that the two modes of particular justice are commutative and distributive.[7] The first is concerned with what we owe each other in the direct relations of persons, especially in business transactions. The second is concerned with how society ought to distribute common goods among its members. The standard of commutative justice is arithmetic proportion, and the standard of distributive justice, as Aristotle held, is geometric proportion.[8] Since commutative justice involves primarily business transactions, arithmetic proportion simply means that buyer and seller exchange something of equal value. Aristotle held similar views about remedial justice. In distributive justice, a person's share of society's common goods is proportionate to the importance or prominence of his position in society. However, Aquinas does not tell us what this prominence consists of, except by making the empirical observation, as Aristotle had done before him, that different societies judge prominence differently, depending on whether a society is aristocratic, oligarchic, or democratic. But he does not commit himself to a specific position.

In another place, Aquinas appears to substantially modify Aristotle's theory by making need rather than merit the standard of distributive justice. Although he thinks that persons have a natural right to private property,[9] he also holds that it is lawful for a person to steal because of an urgent need. Since the basic purpose of material goods is the satisfaction of human needs, wealth that exceeds one's needs is owed in justice to those people whose wealth is deficient to satisfy their needs:

Things which are of human right cannot derogate from natural right or Divine right. Now according to the natural order established by Divine Providence, inferior things are ordained for the purpose of succoring man's needs by their means. Wherefore the division and appropriation of things which are based on human law, do not preclude the fact that man's needs have to be remedied by means of these very things. Hence whatever certain people have in superabundance is due, by natural law, to the purpose of succoring the poor.[10]

Aquinas's overall position on distributive justice appears to be this: Within a private property system, society distributes goods, especially wealth and material goods, in proportion to a person's merit, that is, the prominence of his or her position in society. But since such a distribution inevitably produces quantitative inequalities of wealth, so that the rich receive more than they need and the poor receive less than they need, and since distributive justice must be based on need in addition to merit, the rich are obligated in justice to give their excess wealth to the poor. It does not seem, however, that Aquinas has satisfactorily synthesized the Aristotelian standard of merit with his more Christian standard of need. If both are standards of distributive justice, which one is primary? In any case, it is clear that the need standard requires some sort of positive or activist state in order to transfer private wealth from the rich to the poor. The state has positive duties in justice to assist the poor and needy. Private property rights must be subordinated to need. It is my contention that an adequate theory of justice and of democracy must include positive rights as well as negative rights, and must have a conception of distributive justice that includes redistribution based on a theory of needs. I address this issue later.

Kant's idea of justice centers on a distinction between perfect and imperfect duties. A perfect (or narrow) duty is one whose omission is wrong (e.g., keeping a promise). An imperfect (or wide) duty is one whose performance is good but whose omission is not wrong (e.g., benevolence or charity). Perfect duties constitute the order of justice, and imperfect duties the order of virtue (or supererogation, as others might say).[11] Both perfect and imperfect duties involve duties to others and to oneself, but only perfect duties correspond to an order of rights. That is, I have a perfect duty in justice to keep a promise, and the other has a right to demand that my promise be kept. It seems, then, that perfect duties include both positive and negative rights. The right to freedom—the right not to be constrained by another's will—is a negative right, but a person's right to have a promise kept can be either a positive or negative right, depending on the nature of the promise. If I promise to do something for you, for example, take you to the dentist, you have a positive right against me that I show up on time, and I have a positive duty toward you to act accordingly. But if I promise to keep a secret you have entrusted to me, you have a negative right that I not speak in a manner that breaks the secret, and I have a negative duty to you to keep my lips sealed. Thus, Kant's perfect duties include both positive and negative duties.

It appears to be Kant's view that perfect duties also involve duties to oneself.[12] In this respect, he goes beyond Aristotle and Aquinas, who restricted justice to interpersonal relations. I have a perfect duty to myself not to commit suicide, just as I have a duty to others not to murder them. In the first case, I violate my own right to life; in the second case, I violate another's right to life.

Kant has a notion of distributive justice, but it is considerably different from Aristotle's and Aquinas's. He also calls it legal justice. Distributive justice constitutes the central difference between the state of nature and the social contract (i.e., civil society), between a nonjuridical state of affairs and a juridical state of affairs. It denotes how the courts of law in a nation administer justice with respect to property rights and other rights that come under the law, such as the right to life.[13] In Kant's view, distributive justice includes retributive justice, since courts must punish those who violate the rights of others. But distributive justice does not seem to involve any duty of the state to redistribute wealth, although Kant is silent on the subject. Nevertheless, because one of his main ideas of justice is that perfect duties include both positive and negative rights, and since distributive justice is required by civil society, his notion of distributive justice can be transformed into a theory in which the state has positive duties to redistribute wealth and to establish, as best it can, a just economy.[14] Such a theory is contained in Macmurray's idea of constructive democracy and Rawls's political liberalism.

MACMURRAY'S CONSTRUCTIVE DEMOCRACY

According to Macmurray, the fundamental moral distinction in states or governments is between democracy and totalitarianism. The basic moral principle of democracy is that the state is subordinated to the inherent dignity or worth of all persons. Consequently, in democracy, "political authority is limited."[15] There are areas or zones of personal life that fall outside the scope of political control. Totalitarianism is the antithesis of democracy. Its basic principle is that persons are subordinated to the state. Consequently, in totalitarianism, "political authority is unlimited."[16] There is no area of personal life, in principle, that is off-limits to the state. Both major forms of totalitarianism—communism and fascism—consist of an "apotheosis" of the state.[17] Justice is the central value that limits the state's authority over persons, thereby establishing a political order in which personal freedom is guaranteed and can flourish. Therefore, from a moral standpoint, the central function of the state is to intend justice. Democracy actually intends it; totalitarianism does not. Democracy is founded on justice, totalitarianism on injustice.

However, Macmurray makes a crucial distinction between two historical aspects of democracy: cultural and economic. The core of cultural democracy, according to him, is religious freedom. It is central to cultural democracy for two reasons. First, it establishes a major area of personal life that the government has no right to control. And second, religious freedom implies, in principle, that all cultural activity ought to lie outside of government control:

> It implies freedom of conscience, freedom of thought, freedom of learning and of art and literature—in a word, all that is involved in freedom of mind. The implications of religious toleration run through all our democratic liberties—freedom of speech, freedom of thought, freedom of the press, of cultural association, of public criticism, and propaganda.[18]

By contrast, the economic aspect of democracy consists of economic freedom: freedom of trade and freedom of the marketplace. The state has no right or authority to control economic activity. In this context, the state's sole function is the protection of Lockean property rights. A minimalist state is required. Economic activity is determined by private capitalists in accordance with the law of supply and demand. Thus, the economic aspect of democracy implies laissez-faire capitalism, or what Macmurray calls negative democracy. It is negative in both a descriptive and an evaluative sense. In the descriptive sense, it is negative because the government in fact does not control economic activity. Negative democracy, he says, is the traditional democracy of both Great Britain and the United States. Today, libertarianism is a paradigm of negative democracy. In an evaluative sense, it is negative because he claims that governmental noninterference in economic activity tends to destroy democracy rather than promote it. This is so because economic freedom has decreased cultural democracy, which, for Macmurray, is the positive essence of democracy.

The cultural and economic aspects of democracy, then, have proved to be historically incompatible. In the early growth of industrialization, material resources—wealth—were concentrated in the hands of a decreasing number of people (capitalists). The gap between rich and poor increased. There was a severe maldistribution of wealth throughout society. The wealthy few had the economic power to control cultural life. But in a true democracy, the cultural life of society can be controlled by neither the state nor a powerful wealthy elite, which itself tends to become exempt from political control. In practice, then, the economic aspect of democracy produces negative democracy—laissez-faire capitalism—which in turn generates oligarchy (or plutocracy)—rule by the wealthy—rather than real cultural democracy. In this respect, negative democracy is a practical contradiction. True democracy cannot coexist with laissez-faire capitalism. Macmurray observes that in recent years, democracy has been advancing in both Great Britain and the United States precisely as cultural freedom has been growing and governmental regulation of the economy has been increasing.

It is time, says Macmurray, that we make a full transition from negative to positive or constructive democracy. In such a democracy, the economy will come under the positive control and direction of the government in order to secure enough material resources for all members of society, considering that material resources are not only the means of life but also the means of a good life. In a word, democracy must adopt socialism. "Socialism, of one kind or another, is . . . inevitable. The demand for socialism is a democratic demand . . . Capitalist democracy is at an end. The socialization of industry and finance has become unavoidable."[19] Constructive democracy implies democratic socialism. Democracy and capitalism are incompatible. Socialism is required by a fully developed conception of distributive justice.

The full concept of constructive democracy can now be stated. Since democracy consists of the inherent limitation of the state's political authority over persons, and since cultural democracy is the positive essence of democrracy, the preservation of democracy requires that a society's cultural life remain off-limits to the government. But a society's economic life need not remain off-limits to it. On the contrary, the government must direct and control economic activity in order to preserve and promote cultural democracy. Consequently, the primary aspect of constructive democracy is cultural democracy, which consists of those basic personal rights and freedoms that Macmurray has enumerated. The secondary or subordinate aspect of constructive democracy is socialism.

Macmurray's enthusiasm for socialism was undoubtedly influenced by Marx, whose philosophy he thoroughly studied and about whom he wrote two books during the 1930s.[20] However, it would be a mistake to call Macmurray a Marxist. As a personalist, a theist, and a Christian, he naturally rejects several of Marx's basic ideas: atheism, and the view that religion is an inherently invalid form of human activity and experience; dialectical materialism; the reduction of person to organism; and the reduction of community to functional social organization.

With the collapse of socialism in Russia and to some extent in China, it is interesting to speculate on whether Macmurray's attitude toward it would be different if he were alive today (he died in 1976). Moreover, his idea of constructive democracy was sketched during the depths of World War II, but there is no evidence that he ever repudiated or modified his prosocialist and anticapitalist views. Still, to my knowledge, he never made such strong statements again about socialism in his published writings.

On the basis of the evidence, then, Macmurray held that socialism is the only economic system that is compatible with democracy. This view must be rejected as simplistic. Socialism is one way that a democratic society can organize itself economically. I agree with Macmurray that democracy and laissez-faire capitalism are incompatible, but it does not follow that all possible forms of capitalism are antidemocratic. Capitalism has proved itself to be a remarkably flexible and resilient economic system, and it has gone through several different historical stages. Society can structure capitalism so that it promotes democracy. John Rawls is one important contemporary philosopher who holds this view.

RAWLS'S POLITICAL LIBERALISM

John Rawls (1921–2002) is one of the most influential moral and political philosophers of the twentieth century. The combination of his originality and depth of thought, the nobility of many of his ideas, and the rigor and subtlety of his argumentation appeal to many philosophers and nonphilosophers alike who have a passion for justice and reason. In 1974, he served as president of the *American Philosophical Association*. In 1999, he was awarded the National Humanities Medal. At the time of his death, he was James Bryant Conant University Professor, Emeritus, at Harvard University. A university professorship is the highest honor Harvard bestows on a faculty member. Of his six books, the two most important ones are *Theory of Justice* and *Political Liberalism*. The former has two editions, the latter three.[21]

Over a writing career that spanned some fifty years, Rawls's thinking on justice constantly evolved. *Theory*, first published in 1971, is his first book and magnum opus. Almost its equal, *Liberalism* was published twenty-one years later. In between them, Rawls published several transitional articles that criticized certain ideas in *Theory*. Some of these papers were incorporated into *Liberalism*.[22] Most of this section is devoted to *Liberalism* rather than to *Theory*, for *Liberalism* is much more relevant to a personalist society. Nevertheless, since *Theory* is his first and most comprehensive book, all his later books draw on it in one way or another, and so we begin there.

Theory develops a social contract theory of justice in the tradition of Locke, Rousseau, and Kant (especially Kant), but carries it to a broader and higher level of abstraction in order to overcome the objections considered fatal to the traditional theory. Rawls calls his theory *justice as fairness* and characterizes it as "highly Kantian."[23] He presents it as a superior alternative to utilitarianism in providing a foundation for the basic structure of society as a constitutional democracy, especially regarding the basic rights and liberties of persons as free and equal citizens. Justice as fairness regulates this basic structure. At the very beginning of *Theory*, Rawls emphasizes the difference between his theory and utilitarianism: "Justice is the first virtue of social institutions. . . . Each person possesses an inviolability founded on justice that even the welfare of society as a whole cannot override. For this reason justice denies that the loss of freedom for some is made right by a greater good shared by others."[24] We noted in chapter 6 a similar weakness in utilitarianism's theory of punishment.

After the publication of *Theory*, Rawls gradually noticed a serious incoherence in it. The incoherence is reflected in a distinction he makes in *Liberalism*, and in some of his transitional articles, between a comprehensive moral, philosophical, or religious doctrine, on the one hand, and a political conception of justice, on the other hand.[25] This distinction was not made in *Theory*. Having made it, Rawls says that justice as fairness in *Theory* is a comprehensive doctrine, but in *Liberalism*, it is a political conception of justice. This distinction denotes the fundamental difference between the two books.

It is a distinction, however, that many people have found difficult to understand.[26] I explain it as follows. A comprehensive doctrine, either religious or secular, is a theory that aspires to cover the whole of life: the nature of the universe and humanity's place in it, the meaning and purpose of life, a theory of values and morality, and so on. Aristotle's philosophy as a whole is an example of a secular comprehensive doctrine; the Bible from the standpoint of a person of faith, is a religious comprehensive doctrine. Some comprehensive doctrines are a combination of religious, philosophical, and moral— for example, those of St. Augustine, St. Thomas Aquinas, Hegel, and John Macmurray, to give a few examples. Rawls says that *Theory* is only a "partially" comprehensive doctrine, because there are important moral questions it does not cover, for example, environmental issues, and animal rights and welfare. Nonetheless, as a comprehensive doctrine, it is much broader than a political conception of justice, whose sole purpose is to develop a theory of justice for the *basic structure* of society. This structure denotes society's "main political, social, and economic institutions, and how they fit together into one unified system of social cooperation from one generation to the next."[27]

In *Theory*, Rawls calls justice as fairness a liberal comprehensive doctrine. Kant's and Mill's moral philosophies are also liberal comprehensive doctrines, he says, inasmuch as the former's key idea is autonomy and the latter's is individuality. By the same token, in *Liberalism*, Rawls calls his political conception of justice liberal, and thus the title of the book. In *Liberalism*, Rawls takes *Theory*'s comprehensive conception of justice as fairness and transforms it into political liberalism as a political conception of justice. Rawls characterizes the relation between the two conceptions as "asymmetrical."[28] Despite their differences, their content has much in common.

The purpose of the foregoing distinction is to eliminate *Theory*'s incoherence, which is this: A modern constitutional democracy is pluralistic. It has a diversity of incompatible and irreconcilable comprehensive doctrines, religious and secular, reasonable and unreasonable. This pluralism is not merely an accident of modern democracy; it is a normal and natural expression of human reason functioning within the framework of the free institutions of democracy. In *Theory*, however, he developed the concept of a stable and well-ordered constitutional democracy as a society in which all citizens endorse justice as fairness as a comprehensive doctrine. Rawls came to realize that this well-ordered society is not only unrealistic but also contrary to the very idea of justice as fairness, which is supposed to be the moral basis for a pluralistic constitutional democracy. But in such a democracy, it is both inevitable and reasonable that some citizens will not endorse justice as fairness as a comprehensive doctrine. To remove this inconsistency, Rawls replaces justice as fairness (a comprehensive doctrine) with political liberalism as the common political conception of justice that unites all *reasonable* comprehensive doctrines, despite their differences. (Of the unreasonable doctrines, I shall speak later.) Clearly, then, his meaning of liberalism is considerably broader than its conventional meaning, as in the liberal/conservative ideological distinction. His is a philosophical expression of political liberalism, a conception that is also an intrinsically moral idea, as Rawls says. It is more abstract and more profound than ordinary liberalism.

The fundamental question of political liberalism (or of *Liberalism*) is this: how can a plurality of reasonable but often incompatible and irreconcilable comprehensive doctrines accept a common political conception of justice as the moral basis of a constitutional democracy, especially considering that the political conception will often conflict with some values and beliefs of these comprehensive doctrines? *Liberalism*'s purpose is to answer this question.

I now briefly examine the following key ideas of political liberalism that answer this question and are important to a personalist society: (1) distinction between reasonable and unreasonable comprehensive doctrines, (2) twofold foundation of political liberalism, (3) two principles of justice, (4) the original position, (5) the reasonable and its criterion of reciprocity, (6) a family of reasonable political conceptions of justice, (7) public reason, (8) a reasonable overlapping consensus, (9) political values and their ordering, (10) the fair value of basic political rights and liberties, (11) a property-owning democracy, and (12) the family.

1. Rawls makes a sharp distinction between *reasonable and unreasonable comprehensive doctrines*. Strictly speaking, a constitutional democracy consists of a reasonable pluralism; its essence includes only reasonable comprehensive doctrines. Of course, it will have within its borders a variety of unreasonable doctrines, some of which may be even mad, irrational, and aggressive.[29] But political liberalism does not address them, for an unreasonable comprehensive doctrine is one that does not accept a common political conception of justice as the essential moral basis of a constitutional democracy.

Rawls is quite explicit about these unreasonable doctrines. They may be religious or nonreligious. Unreasonable religious comprehensive doctrines include all forms of fundamentalism, and the divine right of monarchs. Many have a strong desire to have their whole truth enacted into law. Secular unreasonable doctrines include aristocracy, autocracy, and dictatorship. Many unreasonable doctrines may advocate violence as a necessary means to get their way, and so they must be contained by force. Rawls considers unreasonable doctrines in general to be threats to the stability of constitutional democracy. Nevertheless, they must be allowed to express themselves in a way required by political liberalism, for example, the freedom of speech requirement. Political liberalism is *impartial* toward all reasonable comprehensive doctrines, be they religious or secular (or nonreligious). It is a mistake, Rawls insists, to view political liberalism as secular, or hostile to religion. Political liberalism is not Enlightenment liberalism, which attacked orthodox Christianity.[30] In the last edition of *Liberalism* (expanded edition), he was much more concerned than in previous editions, or in *Theory*, to address the relation between political liberalism and religion. Included in his list of reasonable comprehensive religious doctrines are Roman Catholicism after Vatican II, and "much of" Protestantism, Judaism, and Islam.[31] Rawls does not consider these religious doctrines to be liberal, since their conception of truth is based on the divine authority of either a church and/or a sacred text, but a reasonable comprehensive doctrine need not be liberal to endorse a constitutional democracy. Only a political conception of justice must be liberal in Rawls's sense or its equivalent. What *equivalent* means here I shall explain later.

2. Political liberalism rests on a *twofold foundation*. First, there are certain intuitive ideas that are latent in the tradition and public culture of democracy. The overarching and fundamental idea is that society is "a fair system of cooperation between *free* and *equal* persons."[32] The second, interrelated foundation is a Kantian conception of personhood. It is a normative and moral conception. A person has two moral powers (or capacities): a capacity for a sense of justice, which is the capacity to be reasonable; and a capacity for a conception of the good, which is the capacity to be rational. A person also has intellectual powers connected with them, such as thinking, deliberation, and judgment. Because persons possess these powers, they are free. And as fully cooperating members of society, persons are equal.

3. On this twofold foundation, there are *two principles of justice* that determine the basic structure of constitutional democracy:

1. Each person has an equal right to a fully adequate scheme of equal basic rights and liberties, which scheme is compatible with a similar scheme for all; and in this scheme the equal political liberties, and only those liberties are to be guaranteed their fair value.
2. Social and economic inequalities are to satisfy two conditions: first, they must be attached to offices and positions open to all under conditions of fair equality of opportunity; and second, they must be to the greatest benefit of the least advantaged members of society.[33]

The two principles suppose that the basic structure of a constitutional democracy is divided into two parts. Roughly speaking, the first principle applies to its political part, and the second principle to its economic part. In *Liberalism*, the basic rights and liberties included under the first principle are as follows: "freedom of thought and liberty of conscience; the political liberties and freedom of association, as well as the freedoms specified by the liberty and integrity of the person; and finally, the rights and liberties covered by the rule of law."[34] Rawls's first principle of justice is quite similar in content to Macmurray's idea of cultural democracy.

Likewise, there is similarity between Rawls's second principle and the economic aspect of Macmurray's constructive democracy. Just as Macmurray's economic aspect is secondary, Rawls says that the first principle has priority over the second—economic—principle. This priority means two things. First, the basic rights and liberties guaranteed by the first principle may never be violated for the sake of anyone's economic benefit. For example, a more equal distribution of wealth and income is unjust if it infringes on the first principle. Second, inequalities of wealth and income, and differences in authority and responsibility belonging to organizational offices and positions, are justified only if they are to the greatest benefit of the least advantaged members and only if the principle of equal opportunity is complied with.

Since both principles affirm the fundamental moral importance of equality, political liberalism is egalitarian. However, Rawls calls the second part of the second principle the *difference principle*. Its first part he calls the *equal opportunity principle*. Although he does not give the first principle a formal name, I call it the *egalitarian principle*. The difference principle covers the traditional idea of distributive justice.

4. The two principles of justice are chosen in a hypothetical (and non-historical) situation Rawls calls the *original position* and its companion idea, the "veil of ignorance." This position corresponds to, but is not the same as, the state of nature in traditional social contract theory. It is different, because in the original position, society's background institutions and culture exist. But society is not yet governed by any principles of justice. Consequently, all members of society agree, for the first time, to choose the principles of justice that will regulate the basic structure of their society. All persons choose their principles as free and equal citizens who view society as a fair system of cooperation. The actual choice of principles is made by their representatives, who act as rational and reasonable agents in their behalf. They act as rational agents, because they choose the *best* principles from a relatively short list taken from the tradition of moral and political philosophy. The best principles are those they see as advancing persons' determinate conceptions of the good and as developing the exercise of their two moral powers, subject to certain constraints.

These constraints bring in the reasonable and the veil of ignorance. To guarantee that the representatives in their choice of principles will act as reasonable agents, their choice must be made behind a veil of ignorance, as it were. Since they act from a sense of justice, they must act impartially. This impartiality requires that they not know two kinds of facts about the persons they represent that would compromise their impartiality and inevitably mean that some representatives would gain a bargaining advantage over the others based on self-interested bias. First, the representatives cannot know persons' determinate conceptions of the good. Second, they cannot know any persons' contingent social facts: their social, economic, and natural differences pertaining to status, class, wealth, intelligence, strength (and other native abilities), race, religion, ethnicity, and gender. Without this knowledge, all representatives are "symmetrically situated." In this situation, they act as reasonable agents in their choice of justice principles, for their choice is based on the idea that society is a fair system of cooperation between free and equal citizens.

After the representatives choose the principles of justice, the persons they represent freely endorse them and agree to live by them now and into the future. In so doing, all persons act reasonably. The two principles of justice thereby chosen regulate the basic structure of society as a constitutional democracy.

There is another way, however, in which the representatives act rationally (as distinct from reasonably). It is connected with Rawls's idea of *primary goods*. The representatives know that all persons need certain things as social conditions and all-purpose means to effectively pursue their diverse conceptions of the good and to develop their two moral powers. These things are the primary goods: (1) the basic liberties, such as freedom of thought and liberty of conscience; (2) freedom of movement and of occupational choice; (3) powers of office and positions of responsibility; (4) income and wealth; and (5) the social bases of self-respect.

The original position, as purely hypothetical, is a device of representation. It is a device that models the principles of justice that actual citizens would choose here and now viewing society as a fair system of cooperation among free and equal citizens, and acting as rational and reasonable persons.[35]

5. For a constitutional democracy to be well-ordered, it must be effectively regulated by a liberal (or reasonable) political conception of justice.[36]

In such a society, all citizens act reasonably toward one another, as specified by the *criterion of reciprocity*. This criterion means that free and equal citizens propose fair terms of social cooperation according to what they consider to be the best conception of political justice for all, and thus they will abide by these terms and expect others to abide by them also. This expectation is based on others' autonomous consent, of course, not on manipulation or domination.[37]

6. Naturally, Rawls thinks his two principles of justice constitute the most reasonable conception of political justice. But not all reasonable citizens will agree. In the last edition of *Liberalism*, Rawls speaks of a *family of reasonable political conceptions of justice*. This family must include the following two features: (1) a list of basic rights, liberties, and opportunities characteristic of constitutional regimes, and the priority of these rights/liberties/opportunities to other values, especially those associated with the general good and perfectionism; and (2) measures guaranteeing that all citizens will have the all-purpose means, such as adequate income and wealth, to make effective use of these rights/liberties/opportunities.

Within this reasonable family are two kinds of political conceptions of justice other than Rawls's political liberalism. First and foremost perhaps, are those political conceptions of justice that accept political liberalism's two principles of justice but do not derive them from Rawls's original position. This is the view of a personalist society, which derives the two principles of justice from the principle of community, which is the supreme principle of morality, wherein justice is one of community's three essential values. Nevertheless, Rawls's original position with its veil of ignorance is an important heuristic device in the transformation of justice from a basic value to fully formed principles. The second group of reasonable political conceptions are those that do not accept Rawls's two principles of justice as such, but have a political conception that satisfies the above two conditions. "There are many liberalisms and related views."[38] In this group, Rawls mentions two examples: the Catholic idea of the common good (and solidarity), derived from Aristotle and St. Thomas Aquinas, providing this conception is expressed in political values that meet the above two conditions; and Jürgen Habermas's discourse conception of legitimacy. As another example, I would include Macmurray's idea of a constructive democracy. It seems that these other political conceptions must be morally equivalent to Rawls's two principles of justice and therefore be liberal in some important sense of the term. Otherwise, justice, as he understands it, would not be fulfilled.

The criterion of reciprocity excludes all nonliberal political conceptions of justice: aristocracy, corporate oligarchy, autocracy, and dictatorship. All nonliberal political conceptions are unreasonable. As Rawls observes: "The criterion of reciprocity is normally violated whenever basic rights are denied. For what reasons can both satisfy the criterion of reciprocity and justify denying to some persons religious liberty, holding others as slaves, imposing a property qualification on the right to vote, or denying the right of suffrage to women?"[39] No reasonable reasons.

7. The criterion of reciprocity functions within the domain of *public reason*. When citizens act reasonably as described above, they express themselves publicly to each other. They have a duty to give others public reasons for their political actions. Public reasons are reasons based on the commonly accepted political conception of justice of a constitutional democracy. Citizens must not give each other nonpublic (or private) reasons, namely, reasons based on their own comprehensive doctrines. Citizens constitute a public, and their reason is a public reason. Its subject is the public good, which consists of matters of fundamental political justice, as represented by Rawls's two principles of justice. Its content is also public: a family of reasonable political conceptions of justice.[40]

However, public reason has an important *proviso*, as Rawls calls it. This means that any comprehensive doctrine, religious or secular, can be introduced into public reason, providing that whoever does this also gives public reasons that are sufficient to support what is so introduced.[41] For example, Nicholas Wolterstorff complains that Rawls's political liberalism forbids him to bring into public reason biblical passages, such as Psalm 72 of the Old Testament, which have shaped his moral and political views on poverty. His complaint is mistaken, for immediately after citing Psalm 72, he supplies the public reasons for introducing it, and so he satisfies the *proviso*: "I interpret what I read in these passages, about justice to the widows, the orphans, the aliens, and the poor, as implying that involuntary avoidable poverty is a violation of *rights*. . . . A violation of the rights of the poor, *qua* poor. . . . To be a human being is to bear the unconditional natural right to fair and non-degrading access to the means of livelihood."[42] Likewise, Martin Luther King Jr.'s civil rights crusade fulfilled the *proviso*.

8. Public reason's family of reasonable political conceptions of justice consists of a *reasonable overlapping consensus* of comprehensive doctrines. Although each doctrine is different, what they all have in common, as reasonable, is a political conception of justice. This commonality, or consensus, is overlapping: it represents the area of intersection among all diverse reasonable comprehensive doctrines. This area of intersection binds together all reasonable comprehensive doctrines, despite their differences, in their support of a constitutional democracy. As a result, each comprehensive doctrine is required to exclude its *distinctive* values and principles from the common political values that make up the overlapping consensus.[43]

Political liberalism is neutral toward all reasonable comprehensive doctrines. In its aim or direct intention, it does not favor one reasonable doctrine over another. It is not, however, "morally neutral" in all respects, as some have charged. For example, Robert George interprets Rawls as holding "that law and government can and should be neutral with respect to competing conceptions of morality."[44] This criticism is inaccurate and misleading. George omits the crucial word *reasonable*. As we have seen, there are several levels of goods and values that political liberalism endorses and so in these areas it is not morally neutral. Let us summarize some of them: justice itself; persons as rational and reasonable beings having the two moral powers of a sense of justice and a conception of the good; the two principles of justice, and the priority (and therefore greater value) of the first principle over the second; society as a fair system of cooperation among free and equal citizens, which sets the framework within which persons can effectively pursue their determinate conceptions of the good; the five kinds of primary goods; the greater or higher value of a reasonable vs. unreasonable comprehensive doctrine; and the political values that constitute a family of reasonable or liberal political conceptions of justice. All of these values, of course, are moral; they have moral content; they are not merely political as if they were morally neutral.[45]

A reasonable political conception of justice is *free-standing* (or *self-standing*): it stands on its own ground, as it were; it is autonomous, and does not depend on any one reasonable comprehensive doctrine to the exclusion of the others.[46] As self-standing, it is a "module" that can be fitted into any one of them.

9. A reasonable political conception of justice consists of various important *political values*, which grow out of the public culture and traditions of a constitutional democracy and have their historical origin in the principle of religious toleration.[47] These political values are moral, of course, but not in the sense that they are distinctive moral values of a particular comprehensive doctrine. According to Rawls, the preamble to the United States Constitution provides a list of political values: a more perfect union, justice, domestic tranquility, the common defense, the general welfare, and the blessings of liberty for ourselves and our posterity. Other examples he lists are: equal basic liberties, equality of opportunity, and ideals concerning the distribution of income and taxation (and many others, he says).[48]

To be more specific about political values and how public reason orders them, Rawls briefly discusses the issue of whether women should have the right to abortion in the first trimester of pregnancy. Proponents of this right (including himself) can appeal to three political values: due respect for human life, the ordered reproduction of political society over time, and women as free and equal citizens. Since all political values relevant to a particular issue must be properly ordered, balanced, or prioritized, Rawls holds that at this early stage of pregnancy overriding weight must be given to the value of women as free and equal citizens, and so women have the right to abort in the first trimester.[49]

However, opponents of this right can equally make their case in public reason. Rawls mentions the case of the late Joseph Cardinal Bernadin, Archbishop of Chicago, who argued in public reason against first trimester abortion based on the political values of public peace, essential protection of human rights, and commonly accepted standards of moral behavior in a community of law.[50] Not all arguments in public reason will prevail, of course. Others may be fallacious or mistaken. An argument in public reason is not necessarily a sound argument. In any event, since those who have argued against first trimester abortion in the arena of public reason have not won their case, they must recognize this right as belonging to legitimate law and not resist it by blocking access to abortion clinics, for example. These unreasonable actions are an attempt to impose their comprehensive doctrine on others who do not accept it. (By the same token, environmental and animal rights activists who use similar tactics in their public demonstrations are equally trying to impose their comprehensive doctrines on others.) Opponents of first trimester abortion can continue, of course, to argue their views in the forum of public reason. Of all democratic institutions, Rawls holds that the Supreme Court is the exemplar of public reason, a standard, he laments, it has often failed to embody.[51]

10. I now take up Rawls's notion of *fair value*. It is based on two suppositions. First, the egalitarian principle has priority over the equal opportunity and difference principles precisely in the sense that all of its basic rights and liberties constitute a *family*, and no single one should be seen in abstract isolation from the others and absolute in itself. Otherwise, these rights and liberties become merely formal, and their concrete equality cannot be realized. Second, both the equality of opportunity and difference principles are necessary to promote the concrete equality of the egalitarian principle's basic rights and liberties. Fair value, then, denotes the concrete equality of these rights and liberties viewed as an interrelated family. As such, they must be "adjusted" to each other as new social circumstances arise.[52] I now offer three examples to illustrate the importance of fair value.

The first is Rawls's critique of Nozick's libertarianism. As we have seen, for Rawls a reasonable political conception of justice consists of political liberalism's two principles of justice or their moral equivalent. Therefore, a doctrine that rejects either or both of these principles or their equivalent is ipso facto unreasonable. In this regard, Rawls asserts that libertarianism (of which he takes Nozick's theory as a model) rejects the second principle of justice, and in particular, the difference principle. It also lacks the criterion of reciprocity and allows excessive social and economic inequalities as judged by this criterion. Rawls characterizes libertarianism as an "impoverished form of liberalism."[53] It is especially the difference principle that gives justice as fairness its "liberal, or social democratic, character."[54] Since libertarianism rejects the difference principle, the political liberties that it endorses in the first principle of justice remain purely formal and are not given their fair value, which requires a union of liberty and equality. The socioeconomic inequalities that libertarianism permits cannot produce an equal scheme of liberties for all in terms of the content of these liberties. The second principle of justice, then, is essential for the fair value of the political liberties in the first principle.

Based on my criticism of libertarianism in the previous chapter, it should be clear that I agree with Rawls's critique. Unfortunately, however, since the election of President Barack Obama in 2008, libertarianism has exercised an influence on the Republican Party that is inversely related to the small size of the Libertarian Party. In a sense, libertarianism has become a victim of its own success. It has provided the main theoretical basis for the economic and political ideas of the anti-government Tea Party movement and its allies, such as Christian fundamentalists, conservative evangelicals, and those who identify themselves with supply-side or "trickle-down" economics. Of course, the fundamentalists and evangelicals (and some conservative Catholics) have their own cultural/social agenda on issues such as abortion, same-sex marriage, and even contraception that they want to impose on the nation by translating their religious doctrines into law by sidestepping public reason, an agenda that is contrary to libertarianism. As an indication of this libertarian influence, the 2012 Republican nominee for vice president was an ardent admirer of Ayn Rand. In any case, all of the above groups have come to dominate a Republican Party that has become increasingly extreme and unreasonable. They reject the political cooperation necessary for the effective governance of a constitutional democracy. "Compromise" is seen as a vice or weakness. The Republican Party's basic approach to governance is not guided by the criterion of reciprocity.

In the second example, Rawls argues that the second principle's implementation of fair value will require the following institutions: (1) public financing of elections and political campaigns, and the public availability of information on political issues and policies; (2) fair equality of opportunity, especially in the areas of education and training; (3) a reasonable distribution of wealth and income insuring that all citizens have adequate means to utilize their basic freedoms intelligently and effectively; (4) the government as the employer of last resort to insure that all citizens have long-term security and the opportunity for meaningful work, the lack of which is destructive to their self-respect and sense of positive participation in society; and (5) universal healthcare.[55] Rawls is particularly insistent upon the moral necessity of publicly financed political campaigns in order to avoid "the curse of money."[56]

The third example is an illustration of the curse of money. In *Buckley v. Valeo*,[57] Rawls calls the Supreme Court's decision "dismaying." The Court ruled unconstitutional those provisions of the Election Act Amendment of 1974 that placed limits on political campaign expenditures with respect to individual contributions to a favored candidate, expenditures from a candidate's own funds, and total expenses of a political campaign. The Court held that these limitations are a violation of the First Amendment guarantee of free speech; the law cannot restrict the free speech of the wealthy to enhance the free speech of the non-wealthy. In disagreeing with the Court's decision, Rawls distinguishes between the regulation of free speech and its content. The free speech of some (e.g., the wealthy) may be regulated, he argues, to ensure that the fair value of everyone's free speech is promoted and equalized without restricting the content of anyone's free speech. As Rawls expresses it: "What is fundamental is a political procedure which secures for all citizens a full and equally effective voice in a fair scheme of representation. Such a scheme is fundamental because the adequate protection of other basic rights depends on it. Formal equality is not enough."[58] A basic political right is the right to run for and hold political office. It ought not to depend on huge sums of money. Otherwise, the United States in this respect is more of a plutocracy than a democracy. The problem will only worsen as the costs of political campaigns continue to escalate.

And indeed the problem has worsened in the aftermath of the US Supreme Court's corruptive 2010 decision, *Citizens United v. Federal Election Commission*.[59] The Court ruled that the First Amendment right of free speech prohibits the government from placing *any* limits on independent spending for political purposes by corporations and unions. In the 2012 presidential election, and in other elections, such as the Massachusetts Senate race, the decision led to the proliferation of so-called SuperPacs, organizations that can accept unlimited contributions from individuals, unions, and corporations in support of a political candidate. These SuperPacs were instrumental in raising record levels of money for the presidential candidates, much of it coming from a handful of multimillionaires and billionaires, particularly in support of the Republican nominee for president.

In the *Citizens United* case, the Court made two fundamental moral and constitutional errors. First, it effectively separated the right or liberty of free speech from equality. But freedom and equality are inherently related. The basic rights and liberties affirmed in the constitution and all its amendments (which roughly correspond to Rawls's egalitarian principle) must be viewed as equal among citizens. Second, the Court failed to see how the right of free speech is inherently connected with other constitutional rights, such as the right to hold political office. As a result, neither the right of free speech nor the right to hold political office have been given their fair value; neither has been concretely equalized. To compound the problem, most of the money is spent on negative-attack ads on TV. The citizenry is neither informed nor enlightened. The effect of *Citizens United* has been to further weaken our constitutional democracy in the direction of an oligarchic plutocracy.

11. In the revised edition of *Theory*, Rawls makes a sharper distinction between a *property-owning democracy* and a *welfare state* than he did in *Theory*'s original edition.[60] This distinction is at least partly motivated by Rawls's desire to answer conservative criticism of the welfare state.[61] This criticism is understandable in view of the fact that in the first edition he endorsed welfare-state capitalism. In the revised edition, he rejects a welfare state in favor of a property-owning democracy. The second principle of justice requires either a property-owning democracy or a *liberal socialist regime*, but it excludes a welfare state as such. Although his preference is for a property-owning democracy, that is, capitalism adequately democratized, a nation may choose a liberal socialist regime, that is, liberal democratic socialism, if the latter regime is more in accord with a nation's own history, traditions, and circumstances. Why this regime also excludes a welfare state will now be explained.

A property-owning democracy and a welfare state have one important similarity (unlike socialism): the means of production are privately owned; they are systems of private property.[62] There the similarity ends because each has a different aim or intention. In a property-owning democracy, the aim is to create a society over time that is a fair system of cooperation among citizens as free and equal persons or citizens. This aim is achieved by competitive markets dispersing wealth and capital throughout society through the widespread ownership of productive assets and human capital such as educated abilities and trained skills. In contrast, the basic aim of a welfare state is the redistribution of income to secure a decent standard of living for everyone, and to ensure that all receive protections against accidents and misfortune through unemployment compensation and medical care, for example. A welfare state is quite compatible with large inequalities of both income and wealth as well as a weak principle of equal opportunity. A small percentage of society's population directly controls the economy and indirectly its politics. Thus, Rawls suggests that a welfare state leads more to a benevolent oligarchy or plutocracy than to a true democracy. A welfare state fails to satisfy the second principle of justice. Since a liberal socialist regime is no oligarchy or plutocracy, it too is not a welfare state.

Certainly, a property-owning democracy, like a welfare state, aims at a decent standard of living for all its citizens and protects them against accident and misfortune. However, in a property-owning democracy, this aim is merely ancillary, not basic or fundamental, as it is in a welfare state. A property-owning democracy, once established, will require much less redistribution of wealth and income than in a welfare state. Rawls holds that justice as fairness, as a political conception, includes no natural right to private property in the means of production, although there does exist a right to personal property that is necessary to citizens' independence and integrity. There is also no natural right to worker-owned and -managed companies.[63]

Because these economic distinctions are made in *Theory*, it is not clear to what extent they apply to political liberalism. Political liberalism excludes all forms of oligarchy, and to the extent that a welfare state is oligarchic, it is incompatible with political liberalism. In the preface to the revised edition, written in November 1990, Rawls still uses the term *justice* as fairness to apply to a political conception of justice (as well as to his liberal comprehensive doctrine, of course). It seems reasonable to conclude, then, that in the economic sphere political liberalism implies either a property-owning democracy or a liberal socialist regime, preferably the former.

In my view, Rawls's concept of a property-owning democracy can be called *democratic capitalism*. I began this chapter by defining democracy as a form of government in which economic and political power reside in the people. In democratic capitalism the people's power is extended from the political sector, which is characteristic of traditional democracy, to the economic sector, which is more characteristic of socialism. However, in democratic capitalism, the democratization of economic power is achieved without the gargantuan government of state socialism (and to a lesser extent that of a traditional welfare state) through the universalization of educated abilities and skills, and worker ownership of the private means of production, distribution, and communication. Moreover, democratic capitalism, unlike traditional Lockean-type democracy, promotes the fair value of the basic rights and liberties of the political sector of society. Democratic capitalism is an inherent ideal of a personalist society.

12. In his later works, including the last edition of *Liberalism*, Rawls applies political liberalism to *the family*.[64] As a basic institution of society, the family is an essential part of society's basic structure. Since the basic structure of society is regulated by the two principles of justice, Rawls's chief concern is to explain how his principles of justice apply to the family.

The principles of justice apply only indirectly to the family, as they do to other associations of society such as churches and labor unions. They do not apply directly to the internal affairs of the family. The two principles of justice impose external constraints on the family. Husbands must treat their wives as free and equal citizens (and vice versa), which would not be the case if a husband did not allow his wife to vote, or denied her equal opportunity in society. On the other hand, the principles of justice do not require an equal division of labor between husband and wife within the family; who does what work is up to them to voluntarily decide. Similarly, the principles of justice do not require that priests and bishops of a church be democratically elected by the faithful.

It is clear that Rawls is not developing a complete moral theory of the family, which would be appropriate only for a comprehensive moral doctrine. In comparison, Macmurray's idea of the family as a community, referred to in chapter 2, is part of a comprehensive moral doctrine. Connecting these two ideas, we can say that the family as a community transcends and includes the family as an essential part of the basic structure of society. In a constitutional democracy, the principles of justice apply to the family only in the latter sense. They apply in the form of a reasonable political conception of justice, which is determined by public reason and consists of various political values. The family has five such political values: (1) the orderly production and reproduction of society and its culture from generation to generation; (2) the raising and caring of children, and ensuring their moral development and education into the wider culture; (3) the freedom and equality of women; (4) the equality of children as future citizens; and (5) freedom of religion.

Rawls asserts that no particular form of the family has a monopoly on promoting these values. Any form that promotes these values and does not violate any other political values ought to be legally permitted, including gay and lesbian families.[65] Even an appeal to monogamy as the one, true form of marriage is unjustifiable by a reasonable political conception of justice if the appeal is made to a comprehensive moral or religious doctrine. However, if it could be shown that same-sex marriage and polygamy violate any essential political value of the family, both would be unjustifiable in public reason, and the government would have a legitimate interest in prohibiting them, for example, "if monogamy were necessary for the equality of women, or same-sex marriages destructive to the raising and educating of children."[66] Rawls emphasizes that it is outside the realm of political liberalism to make these judgments.

LIBERALISM AND TWO POLITICAL CONTROVERSIES

Using Rawls's views as a starting point, I comment on two important political controversies in the United States: same-sex marriage and religious liberty versus government-provided contraception.

1. On same-sex marriage, I want to go beyond Rawls's views, and make two claims in public reason: (1) nonmonogamous forms of marriage ought not to be legal, and (2) same-sex marriage ought to be legal. I address primarily the second claim and indirectly speak to the first.

Same-sex unions can and do promote all five essential political family values. Many same-sex couples adopt children or have them from previous heterosexual unions, and the partners care for each other and their children just as much as in heterosexual families. Regarding the first value, same-sex couples can even fulfill the procreative end of marriage by using any one of several artificial reproductive technologies (ARTs), for example, artificial insemination (AI) and in vitro fertilization (IVF). ARTs have been very successful in treating infertility problems of heterosexual couples, and there is no good reason why they should not be made equally available to same-sex couples. Even in a gay union, one of the partners could donate his sperm to a surrogate mother who would then be artificially inseminated. Immediately upon birth, the neonate would become the child of the gay partners.

The main objection to these procedures is the same as the fundamental objection to same-sex marriage: Both are intrinsically immoral because they are unnatural. Same-sex marriage is based on homosexuality, which is unnatural and intrinsically immoral. There is only one type of natural and therefore morally good sex: penile-vaginal intercourse (without artificial contraception) between husband and wife.[67] This type of sexual activity is a natural means of fulfilling the natural, procreative end of sex and marriage. This argument is developed within a theory of natural law which, although not inherently Catholic, is largely associated with Roman Catholicism.[68]

Others oppose same-sex marriage on religious grounds. They appeal to certain passages in the Bible or the Koran, which they regard as the revealed Word of God. They see these passages as condemning homosexuality and by implication same-sex marriage. Still others argue that homosexual acts and same-sex marriage are unnatural because they violate biological evolution.[69]

The problem with these arguments against same-sex marriage is that they appeal to a comprehensive moral, philosophical, or religious doctrine. Therefore, they are not arguments in public reason, and so are not good or relevant reasons for opposing same-sex marriage.

However, some opponents of same-sex marriage appear to make an argument in public reason by reasoning that it cannot fulfill the common good of society and so ought not to be legal. As we have seen, some versions of the common good are a reasonable political conception of justice. When the argument is analyzed, though, it is clear that it reduces to the foregoing natural-law argument, for it holds that an essential aspect of the common good of marriage is procreation by penile-vaginal unobstructed intercourse, which rules out same-sex marriage. Therefore, this argument ultimately appeals to the Catholic-oriented theory of natural law, and so is not an argument in public reason.[70]

Moreover, heterosexual marriages do not always reproduce society in an orderly way, nor do they always promote the other four values. Many heterosexual families are dysfunctional; child abuse and neglect are common within them. As a result, many children are placed in orphanages and foster homes until they can be adopted by loving and caring parents. This is where same-sex marriage complements heterosexual marriage. Both types of marriage are needed for the fulfillment or realization of all five political values and the promotion of the common good of society.

I reject the claim that we should let the voters of the various states of the United States decide whether to legalize or prohibit same-sex marriage. In this regard, Rawls distinguishes between a procedural democracy and a constitutional democracy. "A procedural democracy is one in which there are no constitutional limits on legislation and whatever a majority (or other plurality) enacts as law." By contrast, in a constitutional democracy, "laws and statutes must be consistent with certain fundamental rights and liberties, for example, those covered by the first principle of justice. There is in effect a constitution (not necessarily written) with a bill of rights specifying those freedoms and interpreted by the courts as constitutional limits on legislation."[71] For Rawls, a procedural democracy is morally inferior to a constitutional democracy because, in the former, all its matters of political justice are determined by majority or plurality vote. But the most important matters of justice ought not to be so determined, for they are the subject of the fundamental rights and liberties of persons as citizens. Other, less important, matters of justice are determined by majority rule in a constitutional democracy. A personalist society wholly agrees with Rawls on this point.

Since the family is a basic institution of society, and indeed its most basic institution, marriage is a basic right. However, marriage here means monogamy, because polygamy in practice almost always means the unequal treatment of women and the unequal treatment of children as future citizens. But monogamy includes both heterosexual and same-sex marriages, since both are capable of promoting the above five political values of the family.

Therefore, there is no good, much less compelling, reason not to legalize same-sex unions, but there is a compelling reason against opposition to their legalization. Since marriage as monogamy is a basic right, or so I claim, same-sex couples are not treated as free and equal citizens if their unions are not legal. They are discriminated against on a ground that is irrelevant to a reasonable political conception of justice, namely, their sexual orientation. They are treated as inferior citizens. Marriage is not a privilege for heterosexuals. Since the United States and its several states are constitutional democracies and not procedural democracies, and since monogamous marriage is a basic right of citizens, and since monogamy ought to apply to same-sex unions as well as to heterosexual unions, it is illegitimate for any state (or the United States) to permit its citizens to decide by majority vote, as in a popular referendum, whether to ban same-sex marriage on the grounds that such a procedure is wholly democratic. It is not. Likewise, The Defense of Marriage Act of 1996 (DOMA) ought to be repealed.

There is growing support for same-sex marriage in the United States. In March 2012, a poll found that 58 percent of Americans support same-sex marriage, up from 36 percent in 2006. Just a few years ago, Massachusetts was the only state in the union in which same-sex marriage was legal. Today, nine states have legalized it, and also Washington, DC. The other eight are: Connecticut, Iowa, New Hampshire, Vermont, New York, Washington, Maryland, and Maine. Nevertheless, some thirty states legally prohibit same-sex marriage, some by constitutional amendment. Still, that is down from over forty a few years ago.

In November 2008, California voters passed Proposition 8, banning same-sex marriage. Opponents sued in federal court, claiming the measure to be unconstitutional. The US District Court in San Francisco decided the case on August 4, 2010. In a 136-page opinion, Judge Vaughn R. Walker ruled that California's Proposition 8 was unconstitutional because it violated the equal protection clause of the Fourteenth Amendment. Among his reasons for so ruling are: (1) there is no evidence that same-sex marriage harms society, children, or heterosexual marriage in any way, but overwhelming evidence that children of same-sex unions turn out equally well as children of heterosexual unions; (2) excluding same-sex couples from marriage is not rationally related to any legitimate state interest; (3) tradition alone cannot form a rational basis for a law; (4) moral disapproval, without any other asserted state interest, is not a rational basis for legislation and therefore an improper basis on which to deny rights to gay men and lesbians; and (5) Proposition 8 enshrines in the California Constitution the notion that opposite-sex couples are superior to same-sex couples.[72]

On February 7, 2012, a three-judge panel of the United States Ninth Circuit Court of Appeals upheld Judge Walker's decision. It ruled that Proposition 8 violates the US Constitution's equal protection clause by treating same-sex couples as inferior to their heterosexual counterparts without providing a legitimate reason why they should be so treated.[73] On June 5, 2012, the whole Ninth Circuit Court refused to hear the case. In December, the US Supreme Court agreed to hear appeals against both Proposition 8 and DOMA in separate cases. As I write, hearings have begun. A ruling is expected in June 2013.

2. The religious liberty versus contraception controversy raises, quite starkly, the distinction between reasonable and unreasonable arguments. As we have seen, a reasonable argument is one that is made in the forum of public reason and is based on the shared political/moral values of the reasonable overlapping consensus of a constitutional democracy. An unreasonable argument is presented in the political forum as if it were reasonable. But it is not, because instead of being based on political/moral values of the overlapping consensus, it appeals exclusively to a distinctive belief of one's own comprehensive doctrine, which is outside the overlapping consensus. As a result, an unreasonable argument winds up violating some of the values of the overlapping consensus. And so, it is unreasonable for members of a religion to claim (or argue) that their religious liberty and conscience are violated by a public law that, as they see it, requires them to act, or refrain from acting, in a way that is contrary to a religious belief of their comprehensive doctrine, when in fact what the law really does in its direct intention is to promote certain political/moral values of the overlapping consensus as determined by public reason. In this type of situation, the political/moral values of a constitutional democracy take precedence over any *distinctive* religious, moral, or philosophical belief, and so a claim of infringement of religious or moral conscience is bogus.

For example, in a pluralistic constitutional democracy, a pacifist cannot justly refuse to pay the portion of his taxes that support the military; Mormons must comply with monogamy statutes; home-schoolers are obligated to pay their local taxes that support public education; a religious cult that believes in animal sacrifice cannot be allowed to practice its belief; Catholic judges who routinely grant divorces, and a Catholic politician who is "pro-choice," do not violate their religious conscience even if they accept the official teachings of the Roman Catholic Church on divorce and abortion (the Catholic Church absolutely prohibits both acts); and an employer on moral grounds cannot refuse to comply with the federal minimum-wage law. In all these instances, there is a conflict between a moral or religious belief and some important political/moral value, or values, of the overlapping consensus, and so the particular belief must not be exercised in a way that contravenes the overlapping consensus. By contrast, the state cannot compel Christians to celebrate the Sabbath on a day other than Sunday; Catholics cannot be ordered to practice artificial contraception; the state cannot pass a law prohibiting artificial contraception, nor can it pass a law requiring women without their consent to have a transvaginal ultrasound probe prior to obtaining an abortion; and, of course, the state cannot establish a state religion, prefer one religion over another, or discriminate against non-Christians, atheists, or agnostics. In all these instances, the state would be violating political/moral values of the overlapping consensus and thus exceeding its just authority, and so a claim of a violation of religious liberty, or liberty of conscience, would be valid and serious. Indeed, the protection of religious liberty is a basic political/moral value.

In light of the foregoing considerations, it is somewhat surprising that a healthcare contraceptive rule proposed by the Obama administration in January 2012 created such a political firestorm. The rule was announced by Kathleen Sebelius, Secretary of Health and Human Services, as part of the Patient Protection and Affordable Care Act (a.k.a. Obamacare).[74] The proposed rule (it did not go into effect until August 1, 2012) would require all employers, including religious-affiliated employers such as Catholic hospitals, Catholic colleges and universities, and Catholic social-services institutions (e.g., Catholic Charities), to cover their employees with health insurance policies that include no co-pay contraceptive services. These organizations were given a one-year grace period until August 1, 2013, for compliance with the requirement. Churches were exempted from the rule. Twenty-eight states have similar statutes, although nine do not even have an exemption for churches. The United States Conference of Catholic Bishops quickly denounced the rule as a violation of religious liberty and conscience on the grounds that since the official Catholic Church believes that artificial contraception is intrinsically immoral, the government is compelling Catholic employers to act in a way contrary to the Church's teaching. Letters condemning the rule were read in Catholic churches at Sunday mass throughout the country. Specifically, the bishops objected that the Catholic-affiliated employers would be required to *pay* for the contraceptive portion of the policies. The bishops were supported by most Republican leaders and some Democrats. Even liberal Catholics joined the chorus of protest. One so-called liberal journalist called the administration's position "indefensible." On the contrary, as I shall continue to argue (even though I am a Catholic).

The bishops' (and others') claim of a violation of religious liberty (or conscience) is unreasonable and therefore unjustified, because the claim appeals exclusively to the Catholic Church's distinctive moral belief on artificial contraception, while completely ignoring the fact that the direct intention of the rule they oppose promotes an important political/moral value of the overlapping consensus, namely, that women are free and equal citizens, and as such have a legal and constitutional right to adequate healthcare (which, moreover, is a human right),[75] including a right to no-cost contraceptive services, supplies, and counseling, as essential elements of their healthcare. Consequently, the claimants ought not to be allowed to interfere with the promotion and implementation of this value.

A woman's right to contraception is firmly established by constitutional law and the Civil Rights Act of 1964. In *Griswold v. Connecticut* (1965),[76] the United States Supreme Court struck down a Connecticut statute that banned the sale of contraceptive devices. The law was on the books because of the powerful influence of the Roman Catholic Church in Connecticut at that time. However, it was not enforced, because the law lacked popular support. One could purchase condoms, for example, in any drugstore. However, since they were technically illegal, they were not openly displayed; they were sold behind the counter. A customer had to ask the pharmacist to make a purchase. Such is the hypocrisy of unreasonable and unjust laws. The *Griswold* case was a landmark decision. Not only did it declare unconstitutional state anti-contraceptive laws; it affirmed a general constitutional right to privacy that became the foundation of *Roe v. Wade*. In 2000, the US Equal Employment Opportunity Commission ruled that an employer's failure to cover contraception when it covers other prescription drugs and preventive care is sexual discrimination as prohibited by Title VII of the Civil Rights Act of 1964.

It must be emphasized that these Catholic-affiliated employers have primarily a secular and nondenominational purpose: they serve the general public and promote the common good of society. They receive considerable public monies for their worthy services. The proposed rule was supported by 64 percent of Americans, including 59 percent of Catholics. DePaul University, the largest Catholic University in the country, has had contraceptive insurance coverage for all its employees for some time. A large percentage of these organizations' employees are non-Catholic, and so do not accept the Catholic Church's moral teaching on artificial contraception. Nor do, in fact, most Catholic women. Ninety-nine percent of sexually experienced women in the United States have used contraception; the figure for Catholic women is 98 percent. There is no good reason why these women's moral and religious beliefs should be subordinated to the beliefs of those who oppose artificial contraception, especially since women have a legal and constitutional right to contraception in the first place.[77]

Despite the fairness and reasonableness of the rule, President Obama, out of political prudence, acted quickly to quell the political controversy. In February 2012, he announced a modified rule. All women would still be covered by insurance policies that included no co-pay for contraceptive services. However, the insurance companies would now be required to issue and pay for separate policies for contraceptive coverage. The coverage would lower insurers' costs, since the number of abortions, unwed pregnancies and births, and related health problems, would be significantly reduced. Catholic-affiliated employers in general supported the new rule, which is even more strongly supported by the public than was the original rule. Nevertheless, some American bishops and most Republican politicians and leaders were not satisfied. They still claimed a religious liberty violation.[78] At this point, their claim must be regarded as irrational as well as unreasonable. The confusion between a distinctive belief of a comprehensive doctrine and the political/

moral values of the reasonable overlapping consensus is now complete. This controversy is a paradigm of one that should not take place in a well-ordered constitutional democracy.

CONCLUDING SYNTHESIS

I have spent so much time on Rawls's theory of constitutional democracy (which he also calls deliberative democracy in the latest edition of *Liberalism*),[79] because I think it is the finest expression of the kind of democracy required by a personalist society. His political liberalism is superior to Macmurray's constructive democracy in two ways. First, its conception of justice is much more elaborated and articulated. Second, it does not require socialism. However, the two conceptions are fundamentally similar in content. Macmurray's intrinsic connection between democracy and socialism is a significant difference between him and Rawls, but not a major, much less a fundamental difference. Moreover, I do not accept Rawls's political liberalism as an immutable theory. That would be contrary to the theory's spirit. As we have seen, Rawls's theory of justice was continuously evolving, and he said it would always need adjustment and fine-tuning.[80] In this sense, I use Rawls's political liberalism as a flexible module for the basic structure—the political and economic system—of a personalist society. Aristotle, Aquinas, and Kant are seen as three moments in a historical movement leading up to Macmurray's constructive democracy and Rawls's fuller political liberalism. Rawls's well-ordered constitutional democracy is the justice component of the principle of community as realized in the basic structure of a personalist society.

Recall that beyond justice, the other two constituent values of community are freedom and equality. But community's freedom and equality are fuller than their counterparts in society's basic structure, where freedom and equality are strictly elements of justice. By contrast, community's freedom and equality transcend justice and democracy.

Therefore, the freedom and equality that are realized by democracy are incomplete, for the freedom it achieves is liberty (which obversely includes privacy), and the equality it achieves is a legal equality and an economic equality. The last is the subject of distributive justice and is determined by the second principle of justice. In themselves, the liberty and equality of democracy are components of a relative impersonal relation of persons. Consequently, for these two values to reach their full moral realization, they must become elements in a personal relation of persons—especially in friendship—in which freedom becomes the fullness of autonomy (freedom in friendship) and equality becomes what I have called intentional equality, whereby a person treats another as an equal *whole* person rather than as a citizen, which is a functional type of equality in an institutional setting. Moreover, in community, as in friendship and the family, persons are motivated by altruistic love toward each other. But in society's basic structure, the motive of justice is enlightened (or mutual) self-interest. Similarly, community's bonds of communion transcend, or are more inclusive, than the cooperative bonds of justice.

Before I close this chapter, I address the relation between the principles of community/intentionality and the two principles of justice. Since the principle of community is the supreme moral principle, the two principles of justice are subordinated to the community principle and so are indirectly derived from it in the sense that they are elaborations and articulations of the justice component of community. The intentionality principle, too, is subordinated to community, but in a different way. As we have seen, it is a procedural principle that regulates the application of the community principle to particular actions. Since the two principles of justice, like the community principle, are substantive, the intentionality principle likewise governs their application to particular situations.

I have presented the community and intentionality principles as the two main principles of a personalist comprehensive doctrine. If they are acted upon by persons in society, persons create the community of a personalist society. But since community necessarily includes a justice component, the reality of community in a personalist society cannot be achieved unless its institutions of justice are firmly established. There is no community without justice. But since community transcends justice, all four principles must be acted upon together.

9

THE MORAL
TREATMENT
OF ANIMALS

A t first sight, it may seem that a personalist philosophy can have nothing original or important to say about the moral treatment of animals, for according to traditional personalism (including Macmurray's), there is an essential or absolute difference between humans and animals: humans are persons, and animals are mere organisms. Correspondingly, the field of morality is restricted to persons. It consists of interpersonal (and intrapersonal) actions and relations. According to this view, our treatment of animals is not considered a significant moral issue. Indeed, Macmurray himself had no special regard for animals. But I have tried to develop a personalism in this volume that is broad and flexible enough to grapple with the great moral issues of our day. Since one of them, in my view, is humans' treatment of animals, I now apply my personalist theory to this issue.

That our treatment of animals has been abysmal is undeniable and well documented.[1] We have needlessly caused animals untold pain and suffering. In the United States alone, seven billion animals are killed annually in laboratories, for fur, by hunters, and in slaughterhouses. Ninety-five percent are killed for food. Our systematic and pervasive abuse of animals has led one author to lament that "in their behavior towards creatures, all men are Nazis."[2] True, some of the worst experiments have ended, thanks to efforts by animal rights and animal welfare advocates. Most reasonable people now oppose the use of animals for frivolous and painful experiments. Yet other practices remain controversial: high-tech factory farms, hunting and trapping, animal captivity for human entertainment, using animals for athletic competition, and the apparent necessity of using experimental animals for biomedical research.

The last practice poses a serious moral conflict between the right treatment of animals and the good of human welfare. For example, dogs were used to discover insulin, and monkeys to develop the polio vaccine. Pig heart valves are used to replace faulty human valves. Similarly, animals have been used to develop treatments for cancer, stroke, and various heart ailments. If we are going to substantially reduce heart disease and find a cure for cancer and AIDS, scientists tell us that many animal experiments will be necessary. In the area of organ transplants, animals are needed to supplement the paucity of human organ donors and to enable physicians to practice and perfect their transplantation skills. The complete cessation of animal testing would have serious adverse consequences for humans—or so we are told.

In the first section, I explain and critically evaluate the standard or conventional theories on the treatment of animals, all of which I find inadequate. Then I develop my own personalist theory, which incorporates important elements of the other theories; it is a synthesis of them.

WESTERN CIVILIZATION AND ANIMALS

There are four standard theories on the treatment of animals in Western religion and philosophy. Two are traditional, and two are contemporary. The two traditional theories are the no duties theory and the indirect duties theory. The two contemporary theories are different versions of the direct duties theory—the equal consideration theory and the equal status (or rights) theory.

The No Duties Theory

The no duties theory holds that we humans have no moral duties whatsoever to animals, because they lack any significant value and are made solely for our own pleasure and purposes. Morality is homocentric (or anthropocentric). It applies only to humans and their interpersonal and intrapersonal activity. It does not apply to human relations and actions with animals. Only humans have moral status.

This theory has its origin in Descartes' dualism. Everything in reality is either mind (mental substance) or body (material substance). Nature consists of a multitude of bodies. God, the creator of nature, is an infinite mind. Humans stand in between God and nature, having characteristics of each. Like God, humans have minds—indeed, they are minds. Unlike God's mind, which is infinite, the human mind is finite. In addition to their minds, humans have bodies, which interact with their minds and connect humans with the rest of nature. Only humans are a combination of mind and body. Everything else is either pure mind or pure body.

The essence of mind is thought, whereas the essence of body is extension in space. Minds are thinking, nonextended substances; bodies are nonthinking, extended substances. Mind is the source of all consciousness. Moreover, only a mind that interacts with a body—only a human being—has the capacity for *sentience*, the capacity for pleasure and pain. Consequently, since animals do not possess mind (or soul), they are lacking in thought, consciousness, and sentience. For Descartes, animals are essentially machines or automata. "The [animal] body is regarded as a machine which, having been made by the hands of God, is incomparably better arranged, and possesses in itself movements which are made more admirable, than any of those [machines] which can be invented by man."[3]

Since animals are machines, we cannot have any duties toward them. In a letter to the English Platonist and poet Henry More, Descartes writes that "his opinion is not so much cruel to animals as indulgent to men . . . since it absolves them from the suspicion of crime when they eat or kill animals."[4]

Although Descartes' view that animals are machines has been largely rejected, his moral conclusion has not been. For example, veterinarian F. S. Jacobs maintains that "domestic animals exist in this world because they fulfill man's needs. . . . Therefore it is meaningless to speak of their rights to existence, because they would not exist if man did not exist."[5]

Both Descartes' dualism and the no duties theory have been widely criticized. The dominant attitude toward Descartes' dualism is neatly summarized by Gilbert Ryle's famous remark "ghost in the machine."[6] Macmurray quips that the machine is as fictional as the ghost.[7] Furthermore, many philosophers who hold that a human person is more than his or her body—such as Aquinas[8]—likewise reject dualism, as I did in chapter 7.

One argument against dualism is the following: We humans experience our self as one self, as a unity of experience in self-consciousness. In whatever I do, I am the same self that eats, walks, thinks, loves, grieves, speaks, and so on. And I experience myself as the same self that is the source of these and many other diverse activities. If dualism were correct, I would experience myself as two selves: a mental self, which is the source of all my mental activity, and a material or bodily self, which is the source of all my physical activity. When I think, I would experience myself as a different self from the self that eats. But I do not experience myself in this manner, precisely because such an experience, *per impossibile*, contradicts the fundamental unity of self-consciousness.[9]

Descartes' view that an animal is a machine is a relic of the seventeenth century, with its mechanistic and clocklike view of the cosmos. With the subsequent rise and establishment of the biological sciences, and in particular the theory of evolution, Descartes' view that there is no basic difference between organisms and inanimate bodies, and between animals and plants, has been discredited. More recently, Descartes' mechanism has fallen into further disrepute based on mounting evidence that the intelligence of many animals is considerably higher than has been traditionally believed.

If, as is now widely believed, higher animals are conscious, sentient, and in some cases intelligent organisms, then the no duties theory does not seem to follow. Instead, animals would appear to have an important value that is worth protecting. They may even have moral standing.

Since Descartes' dualism and mechanism, and the no duties theory that springs from them, are so extreme, it is not surprising that they have generated a backlash in the form of a growing and vocal animal rights and animal welfare movement. Nevertheless, from my personalist standpoint, there is one element of Descartes' view that is true: humans are persons and other animals are not.

The Indirect Duties Theory

The indirect duties theory is the one to which Western civilization has traditionally paid lip service but not actually practiced. The dominant theory in practice has been Descartes' no duties theory. The indirect duties theory makes a sharp distinction between our direct duties and our indirect duties. Since only persons have rights, we have direct duties to them but not to animals. However, we still have indirect duties to animals. Because humans, as persons, are rational beings, they have a moral duty to treat animals rationally, in accordance with a person's rational nature. Wanton cruelty to and destruction of animals are irrational and, therefore, wrong. If we are cruel to animals, such conduct will tend to make us cruel persons, and we will be more inclined to be cruel to other persons. Our direct duty not to be cruel to persons, then, generates an indirect duty not to be cruel to animals. But we have no duty to the animals themselves not to be cruel to them.

This theory is implicit in the biblical doctrine of stewardship. In Genesis, God distinguishes between humans and lower creation. Humans are the pinnacle or apex of creation, for only they are made in the image and likeness of God. As a result, God gives humans dominion over the rest of nature, provided they put it to good use and take care of God's creation. Thus, they may eat animals for necessary food. Philosophically, this view is echoed in the thought of Aquinas and Kant.

Aquinas, in typical medieval fashion, emphasizes creation as a hierarchy and enunciates the principle that the lower level of creation is for the sake of the higher:

> Plants, which merely have life, are all alike for animals, and all animals are for man. Wherefore it is not unlawful if man uses plants for the good of animals, and animals for the good of man. . . .
>
> Now the most necessary use would seem to consist in the fact that animals use plants, and men use animals, for food, and this cannot be done unless these be deprived of life: wherefore it is lawful both to take life from plants for the use of animals, and from animals for the use of men.[10]

Since animals exist for the sake of humans, the morality of our treatment of animals is determined solely by its effect on humans. Thus, for example, "he that kills another's ox, sins, not through killing the ox, but through injuring another man in his property. Wherefore this is not a species of the sin of murder but of the sin of theft or robbery."[11]

Unlike Descartes, who thought of animals as machines, Aquinas, following Aristotle, sees animals as sentient organisms, capable of feeling pleasure and pain. At the same time, since the lower is for the sake of the higher, and since humans constitute the highest level of creation, animals have solely instrumental value. Their value is determined by the human ends or purposes for which God has created them. They lack any value in themselves, any intrinsic value. Still, animals may not be used for any human end whatsoever, but only for those that are grounded in rational and biological human nature.

Kant's position is similar to Aquinas's, except that, from a moral standpoint, he has only two levels of creation: humans and nonhumans. Humans are persons, and they constitute the higher level of creation. As we saw in chapter 3, for Kant, a person is a rational and self-conscious subject, capable of autonomy. As such, a person is an end in itself, having unconditioned (or intrinsic) value. Nonhumans include the rest of creation: animals, plants, and inanimate things. They are solely means to human ends and thus have merely instrumental value. Consequently, we have indirect duties to animals only insofar as they promote our direct duties to persons. As Kant writes:

> So far as animals are concerned, we have no direct duties. Animals are not self-conscious and are there merely as a means to an end. That end is man. . . . Our duties towards animals are merely indirect duties towards humanity. Animal nature has analogies to human nature, and by doing our duties to animals in respect of manifestations of human nature, we indirectly do our duty towards humanity. Thus, if a dog has served his master long and faithfully, his service, on the analogy of human service, deserves reward, and when the dog has grown too old to serve, his master ought to keep him until he dies. Such action helps to support us in our duties towards human beings, where they are bounden [i.e., direct] duties.[12]

Several criticisms have been leveled against the indirect duties theory. First, in common with the no duties theory, it holds that humans differ in kind and not merely in degree from animals. Both Aquinas and Kant agree that all humans and no animals are rational beings. Therefore, what essentially distinguishes humans from animals are characteristics such as thought, reasoning, concept formation, and the like. However, this view is challenged by a growing number of animal behaviorists and psychologists.

Second, although the indirect duties theory is more respectful of and humane toward animals, it agrees with the no duties theory that animals have only instrumental value. It denies that they have intrinsic value. This denial is perhaps the most basic and irreconcilable difference between the two traditional theories and the animal rights movement.

Third, animal rights advocates charge that the indirect duties theory accepts all the major practices they oppose: factory farming, hunting and trapping, and the use of laboratory animals for scientific research. This theory justifies these practices as promoting important human interests and needs. Still, those who support the indirect duties theory are more inclined to properly anesthetize animals prior to laboratory experimentation and to oppose the use of animals for frivolous research (e.g., for cosmetic purposes).[13]

In sum, the combination of the no duties theory and the indirect duties theory forms the theoretical basis of Western civilization's traditional attitude toward animals, which treats them as mere means to human ends. This attitude is rejected by both contemporary theories concerning the moral treatment of animals.

The Equal Consideration Theory

Broadly speaking, there is only one contemporary theory, the direct duties theory. It holds that we have direct duties to animals, just as we have direct duties to humans. However, this theory has two substantially different versions: the equal consideration theory and the equal status (or rights) theory.

The equal consideration theory has its origin in Jeremy Bentham. In an oft-quoted passage, he endows animals with moral status by declaring that "the question is not, 'Can they talk?' or 'Can they reason?', but 'Can they suffer?'"[14] Bentham rejects traditional ethics' homocentric conception of morality. The field of morality covers all sentient animals, human and non-human. All sentient animals are members of the moral community.

Bentham makes suffering central to morality because of the principle of utility, which he later calls the greatest happiness principle. As we saw in chapter 6, this principle of morality makes pleasure the supreme good and pain the ultimate evil. John Stuart Mill's statement of the principle, which is more succinct than Bentham's, would be accepted by him:

> The creed which accepts as the foundation of morals, "utility," or the "greatest happiness principle" holds that actions are right in proportion as they tend to promote happiness; wrong as they tend to produce the reverse of happiness. By happiness is intended pleasure and the absence of pain; by unhappiness, pain and the privation of pleasure.[15]

Unlike Mill, however, Bentham interprets pleasure and pain in a purely quantitative sense. All pleasures are qualitatively the same; they differ only in quantity. These quantitative differences are to be measured by what Bentham calls the hedonistic calculus, which includes such factors as a pleasure's intensity, duration, and certainty of occurrence. But he denies that some types of pleasures are higher than others. For example, it cannot be said that philosophical pleasure is qualitatively higher than pornographic pleasure, or that human pleasure is qualitatively higher than animal pleasure. Pleasures can be compared only individually and quantitatively by applying the hedonistic calculus.

On this point, Mill strongly disagrees. He holds that pleasures differ qualitatively as well as quantitatively. Some types of pleasure are higher than others. The pleasures that humans obtain from the exercise of their higher powers—intellectual, moral, and aesthetic—are superior to the pleasure they receive from the gratification of their lower, animal appetites. In a memorable passage, he writes:

> It is better to be a human being dissatisfied than a pig satisfied; better to be Socrates dissatisfied than a fool satisfied. And if the fool, or the pig, are of a different opinion, it is because they only know their own side of the question. The other party to the comparison knows both sides.[16]

As may be inferred from this passage, Mill does not share Bentham's moral concern for animals. It is shared, however, by Peter Singer, the most articulate and influential proponent of the equal consideration theory, which is an interesting combination of Bentham's and Mill's utilitarianism. In his seminal and controversial book, *Animal Liberation*, and in other writings, Singer holds that utilitarianism must be developed into an ethical theory that is as much concerned with animal welfare as it is with human welfare.[17] He then, in effect, transforms the principle of utility into the equal consideration of interests principle, which is the basic principle of morality. This principle asserts that we humans must give equal moral weight to the same interest of human and nonhuman animals, especially with respect to the most basic interest of all: pursuing pleasure and avoiding pain. All sentient animals, and only sentient animals, have interests, which are grounded in their capacity to experience pleasure and pain. To avoid being arbitrary and unfair, we cannot give human interests greater weight or consideration than animal interests just because they are human. To do so is to commit a form of discrimination that Singer calls *speciesism*, which is morally equivalent to racism and sexism.

Racism and sexism deny the fundamental equality of all humans by holding that some groups of people are inferior to others. Racism holds that some groups of people are inferior because of their race, religion, ethnicity, or nationality. Sexism holds that some people are inferior because of their gender. By the same token, speciesism holds that some animals are inferior because they are not human animals. Just as racism and sexism use claims of inferiority to justify mistreatment of their victims, we humans justify mistreatment of nonhuman animals on the same basis. Society has confronted the evil of racism and sexism because we deny the premise on which they are based: that some groups of humans are inferior to others. Similarly, if society is going to confront the evil of speciesism, we must affirm that animals are equal to humans.[18]

However, Singer makes an important distinction. Animals are the equal of humans only with respect to the basic moral reality: pain and suffering. A human's pain is not of greater moral importance than an animal's pain. Pain is the same, no matter who suffers it. In other respects, humans are superior to other animals, and to this extent, their interests are preferable to animal interests. In Singer's words:

> A rejection of speciesism does not imply that all lives are of equal worth. While self-awareness, intelligence, the capacity for meaningful relations with others, and so on are not relevant to the question of inflicting pain— since pain is pain, whatever other capacities, beyond the capacity to feel pain, the being may have—these capacities may be relevant to the question of taking life. It is not arbitrary to hold that the life of a self-aware being, capable of abstract thought, of planning for the future, of complex acts of communication, and so on, is more valuable than the life of a being without these capacities.[19]

In this passage, he sounds like Mill. When it comes to the question of pain, he follows Bentham. From these two aspects of his utilitarianism, he draws the following moral conclusion: The primary goal of the animal welfare movement should be the elimination of pain and suffering among animals, not the complete cessation of the taking of animal life. Singer does not oppose using and killing animals for urgently needed biomedical experiments, provided they are properly anesthetized. However, he opposes using animals for scientific research that is not related to any immediately discernible important human need. And of course, he opposes factory farming and hunting and trapping, because of the enormous pain and suffering they cause animals.

Several objections against utilitarianism in general were discussed in chapter 6, and I will not repeat them here. Suffice it to say that some of Singer's most vehement critics are proponents of the equal status theory, to which I now turn.

The Equal Status (Rights) Theory

A distinction should be made between the animal rights movement and the animal welfare movement. Singer's equal consideration theory is the theoretical counterpart of the animal welfare movement. The equal status theory is the theoretical counterpart of the animal rights movement. The fundamental premise of the equal status theory is what I call ontological egalitarianism: humans and animals are equal in nature or being. As one leader of the animal rights movement puts it: "There is no rational basis for separating out the human animal. A rat is a pig is a dog is a boy. They're all mammals."[20]

This view is basically supported and articulated by philosopher Tom Regan, the most able and influential proponent of the equal status theory.[21] Regan specifically calls his theory the "rights" view, in order to contrast it with Singer's utilitarianism. He develops his theory in three progressive stages,[22] which can be called ontological, axiological, and moral. The ontological stage determines the axiological, and the axiological determines the moral.

In the ontological stage, Regan holds that humans and animals are essentially equal, because each is an *experiencing subject of a life*, sharing certain functional characteristics:

> The really crucial, the basic similarity [between humans and animals] is simply this: we are each of us the experiencing subject of a life, a conscious creature having an individual welfare that has importance to us whatever our usefulness to others. We want and prefer things, believe and feel things, recall and expect things.[23]

For Regan, an experiencing subject of a life may be regarded as a mode of being. In the second, axiological, stage, it constitutes the ground of his important concept of *inherent value.* All beings who are experiencing subjects of a life possess inherent value. Regan's idea of inherent value is similar to the more conventional notion of intrinsic value, but they are not identical. Both denote the idea of value-as-end and are thus distinguished from instrumental value, which is value-as-means. But according to Regan, the concept of intrinsic value is associated with utilitarianism's valuation of pleasure, which Regan accepts. Pleasure, then, has intrinsic value. By comparison, an individual being, precisely as an experiencing subject of a life, possesses inherent value. Therefore, a human's or animal's possession of inherent value is distinct from whatever intrinsic value of pleasure it may or may not experience. Furthermore, all possessors of inherent value possess it equally. Inherent value does not come in varying degrees; an individual either has inherent value or lacks it. There is an absolute difference, or a difference in kind, between those beings that have inherent value and those that do not.

Finally, in the moral stage, Regan makes inherent value the basis of *rights*. All beings who possess inherent value, and only beings who possess inherent value, are the possessors of moral rights. Since inherent value is equal, humans and animals equally possess moral rights. Consequently, the speciesism inherent in our Western, homocentric tradition, common to both theism and humanism, must be rejected. "What's fundamentally wrong with the way animals are treated . . . is the system that allows us to view animals as *our resources*, here for *us*—to be eaten, or surgically manipulated, or exploited for sport or money."[24] Regan endorses the three major goals of the animal rights movement: the total elimination of factory farming, the total abolition of hunting and trapping, and the total cessation of experimentation on animals.

One question remains, however. Exactly which beings are experiencing subjects of a life, possessing equal inherent value and equal moral rights? Regan has not given a consistent answer to this question. In his book, *The Case for Animal Rights*, he holds that all normal mammals over one year old possess equal moral rights. Presumably, then, all normal mammals one year old or younger completely lack moral rights. Elsewhere, however, he maintains that such a sharp line cannot be drawn with certainty. Nor do we need to draw one. All we need to know is that the animals in our culture that are routinely eaten, hunted, and used in laboratories are experiencing subjects of a life.[25]

In another place, he seems to hold that an experiencing subject of a life is a *person*. After asserting that persons are the possessors of moral rights, he goes on to define a person in terms similar to that of an experiencing subject of a life:

> Persons are individuals who have a cluster of actual (not merely potential or former) abilities. These include awareness of their environment, desires and preferences, goals and purposes, feelings and emotions, beliefs and memories, a sense of the future and of their own identity.[26]

Most human adults, he observes, possess these abilities and are thus persons. But PVS individuals, for example, do not possess them and so are not persons.

Likewise, human infants and fetuses are not persons. And some persons are not humans. Some possibilities include the Christian God and intelligent extraterrestrial beings. But for Regan, the most important nonhuman persons are animals: all adult mammals possess the above abilities and hence are persons.[27]

We can now see the basic difference between Singer's utilitarian or equal consideration theory and Regan's equal status (or rights) theory. For Singer, the fundamental wrong in our treatment of animals is that we cause them pain and suffering. For Regan, the fundamental wrong in our treatment of animals is that we treat them merely as means to our ends, as beings who have only instrumental value. We thus violate their inherent value and moral rights.

Several objections can be raised against Regan's theory. First, his notion of person is unclear. Is it a synonym for an experiencing subject of a life? He describes them in similar, but not identical, terms. As it stands, his concept of person is too broad, too thin, too low. It includes characteristics it should not. To say, for example, that any being who has desires, preferences, and emotions is thereby a person is to make the concept of person so broad as to render it almost meaningless. I fail to see why a dog, a cat, and especially a rat is a person because it prefers one kind of food to another. With respect to personhood, it all depends on what desires, preferences, or emotions are at issue. There is a qualitative difference between the rational desire to know and the biological desire to eat, or between the emotions that are expressed in art and in love versus the emotions of anger, fear, and jealousy. In this context, a distinction should be made between higher and lower emotions, desires, and preferences. Personhood should be restricted to the higher level of these functions. At the same time, it is doubtful that some of his other characteristics of personhood can be shown to apply to all adult mammals—namely, a sense of the future and of their own identity.

Second, Regan's notion of an experiencing subject of a life appears to blur the distinction between *consciousness as such* and *self-consciousness*. Some critics say that he should at least distinguish between a lower level of sensory (or sentient) consciousness, characteristic of animals, and the higher level of self-consciousness, characteristic of humans. Such a distinction would yield a corresponding distinction between two levels or degrees of inherent value. Regan has not demonstrated why all inherent value must be equal, or why animals possess it equally to humans.[28]

Third, utilitarians, like Singer, would reject Regan's concept of inherent value while holding that only pleasure has intrinsic value. Consequently, our treatment of animals is immoral because we humans cause them pain and suffering, not because we violate their fictitious inherent value and illusory moral rights.

Finally, some environmentalists take issue with Regan's position that only experiencing subjects of a life possess inherent value and rights. They want to extend inherent value and rights beyond consciousness and sentience and apply them to the whole of nature, including nonsentient life (e.g., trees and flowers) and nonliving nature (e.g., streams, rivers, and mountains).[29]

Regarding the last objection to Regan's theory, he is correct in rejecting an extreme version of environmentalism: the holism and land ethic associated with Aldo Leopold.[30] According to Leopold, humans and sentient animals have no privileged moral standing in nature, no special rights. What has moral value are not individual beings but the whole biosphere. The biosphere is the totality of nature as an interrelated system in which all of its members are equal: humans, other sentient animals, nonsentient animals, plants, and inanimate nature. Human actions are right if they promote the integrity, beauty, diversity, and harmony of the biosphere. We must develop a land ethic to replace both the traditional homocentric ethics and the more recent mammalian-centered ethics, whether sentience based (Singer) or rights based (Regan). Animal liberation must be replaced by nature liberation. According to the land ethic, the moral community consists of water, soil, plants, and rocks, in addition to humans and animals.

Regan rightly denounces this view as environmental fascism.[31] It holds that the total biosphere counts for everything and the individual for nothing. The land ethic is ontological egalitarianism taken to its ultimate, absurd extreme. A person, dolphin, or chimpanzee has no more value than a rock. And since we are required to promote the diversity of the biosphere, humans and higher mammals can sometimes be expected to take a moral backseat to the rest of nature. As Regan observes, rare species of grasses contribute more to the biosphere's diversity than, say, the citizens of Cleveland. Therefore, if there is a conflict between them, the grasses take moral precedence over Clevelanders. However, any ethical theory that works to the detriment of human and animal well-being is contrary to the meaning and purpose of morality. The land ethic's conception of morality is so broad and diffuse that moral value and status are trivialized.

TOWARD A SYNTHESIS

I now sketch my own personalist theory on the moral treatment of animals. This theory may be regarded as a synthesis of the other four theories, for each theory, in my view, has some truth and some error. I explain this as I proceed.[32]

At the outset, I avoid a conventional and controversial distinction that is unhelpful: the superior/inferior distinction. It is unhelpful because it tends to generate two extreme and false positions, as thesis and antithesis, respectively. The thesis comprises the common element of the two traditional theories. This common element consists of four propositions: (1) humans are superior to animals (or conversely, animals are inferior to humans); (2) morality is homocentric (or anthropocentric); (3) humans transcend nature and are only superficially connected with it; and (4) animals have merely instrumental value and so can be used to satisfy a wide range of human ends or purposes. For the personalist theory, the second, third, and fourth propositions are false, and the first proposition needs reformulation. The two contemporary theories also assert, of course, that propositions two through four are false.

The falsity of the thesis engenders its antithesis. This antithesis rightly sees that propositions two, three, and four constitute the traditional Western moral attitude toward animals, which has led to their massive and systematic mistreatment. However, the antithesis sees these propositions as necessarily following from proposition one, and so it reasons that the only way to stop the traditional mistreatment of animals is to deny this proposition by replacing it with ontological egalitarianism, namely, that humans and other (sentient) animals are equal in nature or being. In sum, then, the antithesis is ontological egalitarianism.

However, the antithesis is likewise false. Thus, ontological egalitarianism cannot be a foundation for an adequate ethical theory on the treatment of animals. But ontological egalitarianism and the superior/inferior distinction do not represent a perfect disjunction, or a dilemma within which one must choose either the thesis or antithesis. I wish now to develop a third position, a tertium quid, between these two extremes. This tertium quid is a reinterpretation of the superior/inferior distinction, and it is the starting point of a synthesis. My synthesis rejects the second, third, and fourth propositions of the thesis.

There are at least three problems with the superior/inferior distinction. First, and foremost, it immediately suggests some kind of master-slave relation between humans and animals. But animals are not our slaves. Second, the distinction suggests a vertical hierarchy, like the stories of a building. This kind of thinking dominated ancient and medieval philosophy, but it is outmoded today. On this view, reality consists of higher and lower "levels" of reality that are separate or mutually exclusive. And third, the distinction is provocative and leads to an impasse. For instance, if one claims that humans are superior to animals because they have a more highly developed power of rational intelligence characterized by abstract and symbolic thought, the typical response will be that many animals are superior to humans in other ways, namely, in speed, strength, agility, the senses of sound and smell, instincts, and so on. Both statements are true. But what do they mean in terms of how humans should treat animals? If one tries to establish that the ways in which humans are superior to animals are activities in themselves which are superior to any activities of animals, the response is that throughout the animal kingdom all activities and skills are *contextual*, that is, they are acquired through evolution and enable the creature who possesses these activities and skills to effectively adapt to its particular environment and thus survive and flourish in it. But there is no such thing as a superior activity or skill as such, or a universally superior one, it is claimed, and so we have an impasse.

Accordingly, I replace the superior/inferior distinction with a distinction between a more-inclusive being and a less-inclusive being. A more-inclusive being is qualitatively fuller than a less-inclusive being, but part of its essential nature is similar to a less-inclusive being. In the present context, I apply this distinction to three kinds of beings: human persons, organisms, and inanimate beings. A human person is a more-inclusive being than an organism, and an organism is a more-inclusive being than an inanimate being. Their relationship can be visualized by three concentric circles where each outer circle includes and is more than each inner circle. This image emphasizes connectedness and a horizontal relation among them. As we have seen, a key doctrine of personalism is that a human person is more than an organism, but not completely other than an organism. As a *person*, he or she is more than its organic body. As *human*, he/she is an animal organism connected with nature and shaped by the forces of nature and evolution. By the same token, a human organism has an essential aspect that corresponds to an inanimate being. It has a skeletal structure, and is composed, like all material beings, of molecules, atoms, and subatomic particles.

More-inclusive and less-inclusive also replace the traditional distinction between higher and lower, respectively. In chapter 4, I spoke of higher and lower beings with reference to the concept of moral status. I have no objection to *higher* and *lower* so long as these terms are understood as referring to the more-inclusive/less-inclusive distinction rather than to superior and inferior.

From the standpoint of science, humans are completely organisms; the concept of organism denotes the totality of their being. But science has its limitations. Its data are confined to controlled observation and experimentation. Since a person is not reducible to such data, the concept of person is not a scientific concept, as everyone seems to agree. But unless one subscribes to scientism, there is no good reason for rejecting *person* as an ontological concept and insisting that organism is a sufficient and inclusive category for conceptualizing and understanding human beings.

We have developed three complementary (but free-standing) conceptions of human personhood: a person is a rational and communicative agent (chapter 1), a person is an embodied spirit (chapter 7), and a person is a free (or autonomous) moral agent endowed with the twin capacities for a sense of justice and for a conception of the good (chapter 8). I deny that other animals are persons in any of these three senses. Moreover, since personalism sees an inherent connection between personhood and rights, I also deny that animals have rights in the sense in which I have explained them. I reject, then, two central claims of Regan's theory: all adult mammals are persons, and they have rights that are equal to human rights.

That animals are not persons does not mean they are unimportant beings. On the contrary, I maintain that all sentient animals have moral status in the sense in which this concept was explained in chapter 4. In this regard, my position basically accords with the two contemporary theories. Since all sentient animals have moral status, they belong to the moral community. I replace a homocentric conception of morality with a sentientcentric conception. Therefore, humans must always take into consideration the interests and flourishing of all nonhuman sentient animals. The field of morality must be extended to include humans' dealings with animals in addition to their dealings with each other. On this point, I obviously disagree with the no duties theory and the indirect duties theory.

Since nonhuman sentient animals are not persons, they are inclusively organisms. As a result, the moral status of animals is less inclusive than that of humans. On this point, I part company with at least the equal rights theory, which holds that humans and animals have the *same* moral status. More-inclusive status means that a human person has a fuller value than the value of an animal, ceteris paribus. For example, if you could save either a child or a cat from a burning building (but not both), you ought to save the child. Singer, and the equal consideration theory, is somewhat unclear on this point. On the one hand, Singer says that humans and animals are morally the same when it comes to pain: pain is pain, and it does not matter who or what animal suffers the pain. Consequently, human pain, according to him, does not have a greater value than animal pain. On this point, I agree with Singer. True, there may be some kinds of psychological pain that animals do not experience, and this is where the second element of Singer's theory comes in. As we have seen, Singer holds that we are only equal to other animals with respect to sentience. But humans perform some higher, more complex activities that animals do not. This view, however, does not lead him to explicitly say that humans have a greater or higher moral status than do other animals, although he does conclude, as we saw, that animals can be used and killed for urgently needed biomedical experiments, provided they are properly anesthetized. Regan rejects Singer's conclusion.

Although sentient animals lack rights that are the equal of human rights, they do possess rights as an essential aspect of their moral status. To affirm that animals have moral status and deny they have rights would imply some sort of utilitarianism (such as Singer's, or the animal welfare position) that is inconsistent with my personalism. On this point, I am closer to Regan than Singer. Of course, since animals lack the full rationality of human beings as persons, they do not have the rights that flow from human rationality, for example, the rights of free speech, conscience, and religion. But as sentient organisms, they have those rights appropriate for such beings in their relations with humans, such as the right to life, the right not to be mistreated, and the right to the necessities of life, and others. The moral rights that sentient animals have are the foundation for the legal rights they ought to have.

When it comes to the moral treatment of animals, it is far more important that animals *have* moral status than it is that humans' moral status is fuller. Since nonhuman sentient animals have moral status, and since the principle of community is the supreme moral principle, it must be extended to include our dealings with them. However, because they are not persons, the principle applies to them analogously, just as it does to prepersonal fetuses (chapter 4). I extend the principle of community to nonhuman sentient animals as follows: a morally right action is one that promotes animal flourishing; a morally wrong action is one that needlessly and intentionally takes their lives, or needlessly and intentionally inflicts pain and suffering upon them. Acting on this principle would require the cessation of the following human activities: (1) commercial animal agriculture, (2) commercial and sport hunting and trapping, (3) keeping animals in captivity merely for human amusement and entertainment, (4) breeding and using animals for athletic competition, and (5) animal experimentation for unimportant or nonvital human ends. In all five activities, the enormity of the evil that we inflict upon animals far outweighs and overrides any slight good that humans receive.

Consider commercial animal agriculture. From birth until death, billions of farm animals in the United States are forced to endure an endless life of pain and misery for the sole frivolous gustatory value that humans like the taste of meat. As one author puts it: "No other human activity results in more pain, suffering, frustration, and death than factory farming and animal agribusiness."[33]

Adding to the enormity of this evil are several other major evils of the meat production business. First, it is bad for human health. Meat has high levels of artery-clogging saturated fat, which leads to heart disease and other serious ailments. The main nutritional benefit of meat is protein, which can be obtained from plants but in a healthier form without the saturated fat. If people stopped eating meat and ate a well-balanced vegetarian diet, there is no doubt that human health would dramatically improve. Second, meat production is a very inefficient usage of grain, the world's leading foodstuff. It takes eight pounds of grain to make one pound of meat. Third, animal production consumes huge quantities of water. It takes one hundred times more water to produce animal protein than the same amount of plant protein. Since at least 70 percent of Earth's fresh water is used by the agricultural industry, consumption of this precious resource would be drastically reduced by ending meat production. Fourth, animal agriculture substantially contributes to soil erosion. In the United States, the massive quantities of grain that are harvested for the meat industry require intensive agricultural methods that result in the loss of seven billion tons of topsoil annually. Fifth, commercial animal farming generates tremendous quantities of hazardous waste in the form of excrement. In the United States alone, 250,000 tons of excrement per second are produced by livestock animals. All this waste has a deleterious effect on rivers, streams, lakes, and estuaries. Its methane and nitrous oxide gases are leading causes of global warming.

In sum, there is no rational moral basis for supporting commercial animal agriculture, or any of the other four human activities listed above. The only human activity that intentionally kills animals that might be morally justifiable is urgent experimentation to promote vital human needs, providing the animals are properly anesthetized.[34] I do not hold this position as a firm judgment, but only as a moral possibility. The position conflicts with my view that sentient animals have a right to life. Therefore, the burden of proof rests on those who would claim or argue that the human need in question is so important that it overrides an animal's right to life.

All told, then, I have specified six types of situations relating to humans' treatment of sentient animals. Five have been judged to be immoral, and one might be morally permissible. If we consider all six situations together as a group or unit of human activity toward animals, Rule Five of the intentionality principle can be invoked. Let us recall this rule (in part): "If a direct intention has a good end and a bad means, the direct intention is significantly bad if the means is a prima facie immoral action." In the present context, the means consists of the six above institutional practices toward animals. Since one practice might be morally right, the means as a unit must be considered prima facie immoral rather than intrinsically immoral. In the sixth practice or situation, the goodness of the end might outweigh the evil of the means. That is, the good of vital human needs might outweigh the evil of using animals for biomedical research, providing such usage is necessary and providing the animals are properly anesthetized. But in the other five practices or situations, the evil of the practices themselves (which evil consists of the enormity of pain and suffering intentionally inflicted upon animals, and the billions of animals that are needlessly killed) far outweighs and overrides the slight good of the minor and sometimes frivolous human ends to which these practices are a means. Indeed, in these practices, the badness of the means outweighs the goodness of the end many times over. Consider some of the ends: liking the taste of meat; liking the look or status of a fur coat; liking the scent of certain colognes, aftershave lotions, perfumes, and deodorants; and feeling amused or entertained in watching animals in circuses, zoos, theme parks, or at race tracks.

A model for humans' treatment of all sentient animals should be how caring owners treat their pets in the sense that all are deserving of caring and respect. (This does not mean, of course, that wild animals should be adopted as pets, or that we should overlook the profound differences between domesticated and wild animals.) Yet, a typical dog owner in the United States thinks nothing of eating meat and how that meat got there on his or her plate. But what is the real, objective difference between a dog and a pig? Both are equally intelligent and sentient mammals. Americans are outraged, and rightly so, that in some Eastern cultures dogs are slaughtered for food. But such outrage should also be directed toward the whole animal agricultural industry and the millions of consumers who support it with their penchant for eating meat. There is no moral difference between killing dogs and pigs for food. If one is wrong so is the other.

AFFIRMATIVE ACTION AND JUSTICE

The concept of affirmative action is the product of recent political and legal history. In the United States, there have been several important laws and Supreme Court decisions relating to it.[1] Out of this legal and constitutional context emerged different moral positions and arguments on affirmative action. In this context, too, emerged several new terms and ideas, such as *affirmative action* itself. These terms, and the more traditional terms to which they are related, should be explained at the outset. Accordingly, in the first section, I define the key terms used throughout this chapter. In the next section, I sketch a brief legal and constitutional history of the affirmative action issue in the United States. Finally, I develop an ethics of affirmative action, focusing on the question of justice. I also critically examine several arguments that differ from my position.

DISCRIMINATION AND PREJUDICE

Two basic terms that arise in affirmative action discussions are *discrimination* and *prejudice*. In its most basic and literal sense, discrimination denotes the mental act of distinguishing between two or more objects. It occurs at various levels: perceptual, emotional, intellectual, and so forth. Perceptually, I discriminate between the skin color of a white person and that of a black person, or between a white car and a black car. Emotionally, I distinguish between love and hate. Intellectually, I distinguish between a sound and an unsound argument, and between a true and a false statement. In this sense, discrimination is an essential operation of rational thought and action, and there is nothing wrong or bad about it. But when we use the word *discrimination* in its usual legal and moral sense, it has a very different meaning, as when we speak of discriminating *against* someone. In this sense, I define discrimination as action that arbitrarily and irrationally favors some people and disfavors others in a morally important context. Discrimination may or may not be based on prejudice. It often is, but not necessarily. For the remainder of the chapter, I limit the term *discrimination* to its latter meaning and use words such as *distinction* for its former meaning.

Whereas discrimination denotes action, prejudice refers to an attitude.[2] It is an attitude by which a person makes a negative judgment about someone based solely on his or her group (or class) membership. The group or class in question is based on such factors as race, religion, gender, ethnicity, age, and sexual orientation. A prejudiced person irrationally judges the group to be inferior to other groups. As a result, an individual who belongs to one or more of these groups is judged to be an inferior person. Since attitudes generally produce their corresponding actions, prejudice usually leads to discrimination, especially if a prejudiced person has a position of power and authority over the persons of his or her prejudice. Discrimination, then, includes all prejudicial actions, all actions stemming from prejudice. Let us simply call this type of discrimination *prejudicial discrimination.* As I argue later, it is the worst kind of discrimination. It includes such standard subtypes as racism, sexism, homophobia, ageism, and the like.

As I said, however, there is no necessary connection between prejudice and discrimination. Prejudice may not lead to discrimination. A prejudiced person may be powerless over others and not have an opportunity to act out his or her prejudice. Moreover, a prejudiced person who is in a position of power or authority may keep it in check for fear of possible recriminations if he or she acts out of prejudice. Or a person may overcompensate for prejudice by irrationally favoring the persons of his or her prejudice over others. These cases may be rare, but they can happen. But more important, there may be a type of discrimination that is not based on prejudice. Instead, it is based on affirmative action, according to critics. Let us call this second type *affirmative action discrimination.* To explain the connection between affirmative action and discrimination, a distinction must be made between weak and strong affirmative action.

Thomas Nagel's descriptions appear to be adequate. Weak affirmative action refers "only to special efforts to *ensure equal opportunity* for members of groups that . . . [have] been subject to discrimination. These efforts include . . . public advertisement of positions to be filled, active recruitment of qualified applicants from the formerly excluded groups, and special training programs to help them meet the standards for admission or appointment."[3] As Nagel observes, this meaning of affirmative action is not controversial; most people generally support it. By contrast, strong affirmative action denotes "some degree of definite *preference* for members of these groups in determining access to positions from which they were formerly excluded. Such preference might be allowed to influence decisions only between candidates who are otherwise equally qualified, but usually it involves the selection of women or minority members over other candidates who are better qualified for the position."[4] Weak affirmative action is seen as an effort to fulfill the principle of equal opportunity, but strong affirmative action is viewed by many as violating this principle by practicing preferential treatment toward those groups historically discriminated against.

In turn, two subtypes of strong affirmative action are sometimes distinguished. I call them *rigid* and *flexible* strong affirmative action. Rigid denotes quotas, set-asides, timetables, numerical goals and percentages, and race norming. Flexible refers to preferential treatment in which race, ethnicity, or gender is one of several factors in an applicant's individualized and holistic assessment that compares him or her to all other applicants with respect to the same factors or criteria, without using quotas, set-asides, and so on. For example, in many college and university admissions programs, a minority applicant is given a plus in his or her file for race or ethnicity, but there is no two-track system: one for preferred groups and the other for disfavored groups. Rigid programs are sometimes interpreted as implying *proportionalism* (or *equal results*). These terms mean that minorities and women should be represented in all of society's institutions and occupations in the same percentage as these groups exist in society as a whole.

Since it is strong affirmative action—whether rigid or flexible—that is controversial, it is the main subject of this chapter. Strong affirmative action is controversial because it is based on preferential treatment, and such treatment, critics charge, involves discrimination. Preferential treatment treats the preferred groups as more than equal and the disfavored groups as less than equal. And since the contexts in which this treatment occurs are morally and socially important ones—employment, promotion, admission to institutions of higher education—preferential treatment satisfies the preceding definition of discrimination. Affirmative action discrimination, critics say, includes all forms and instances of strong affirmative action.

Nevertheless, a sharp distinction must be maintained between affirmative action discrimination and prejudicial discrimination. The former does not stem from prejudice as its motive. On the contrary, it springs from a good motive: caring for past or present victims of prejudicial discrimination. At least for this reason, then, affirmative action discrimination ought not (yet) to be condemned just because it is discrimination—unlike prejudicial discrimination, which is based on a malicious motive. By the same token, although some proponents of strong affirmative action concede that it does involve "reverse" discrimination against its disfavored groups, they contend that such discrimination is justifiable.[5] No reasonable person contends that prejudicial discrimination is ever justifiable. Consequently, whereas I can now assert that prejudicial discrimination is intrinsically immoral, my judgment does not include affirmative action discrimination. Its morality will be determined as I proceed.

In general, weak affirmative action does not involve a charge of discrimination, since it is not based on preferential treatment. There is one noteworthy exception to this generalization, however. Training programs for minorities may exclude disadvantaged whites, particularly white males. This exclusion is discrimination against them, according to critics. Accordingly, affirmative action discrimination includes primarily strong affirmative action and only secondarily weak affirmative action. Since most complaints about affirmative action discrimination involve strong affirmative action, for the remainder of the chapter I am concerned only with strong affirmative action.

AFFIRMATIVE ACTION AND THE LAW:
A HISTORY

As necessary historical background to the affirmative action issue in the United States, we must go back to the Civil War and the nation's struggle over slavery and racial injustice. President Abraham Lincoln signed the Emancipation Proclamation into law on January 1, 1863. This momentous act expressed Lincoln's intention that the primary purpose of the war was no longer only to preserve the union but to transform the nation into a union endowed with the higher moral purpose of ending slavery. After the war ended and Lincoln was assassinated on April 14, 1865, his Reconstruction program to improve the conditions of black people and to improve race relations between blacks and whites was carried on by President Andrew Johnson. For a short time, some gains were made. Three crucial amendments to the Constitution were passed: the Thirteenth Amendment in 1865, which abolished slavery; the Fourteenth Amendment in 1868, which, among other things, guaranteed blacks equal protection of the law; and the Fifteenth Amendment in 1870, which gave blacks the right to vote.

Unfortunately, this First Reconstruction period, as it is sometimes called, did not last long. President Johnson was weak and unpopular, and he barely survived an impeachment trial in the Senate. Southern racism against blacks soon reasserted itself, and it quickly eliminated any progress that had been made during this period. For example, to counteract the Fifteenth Amendment, Southern states passed poll taxes and literacy tests for voter eligibility. By the end of the century, Jim Crow laws, as they came to be called, were common. These laws required racially segregated schools and racial segregation in other public facilities.

Jim Crow laws were given constitutional sanction in the landmark 1896 case *Plessy v. Ferguson.*[6] In it, the Court enunciated its famous (indeed, infamous) "separate but equal" doctrine. Jim Crow laws were not unconstitutional, it ruled, so long as separate public facilities for blacks and whites were equal. The equal protection clause of the Fourteenth Amendment prohibited segregation only if the segregated classes were treated unequally, but the amendment, the Court said, did not prohibit segregation as such. In *Plessy,* the Court ruled that blacks were not treated unequally and so were not discriminated against.

Contrary to what the Court said, blacks were in fact treated unequally. Jim Crow laws were the products of prejudice, of prejudicial discrimination, against black persons. The reason that whites segregated blacks from themselves was that blacks were judged to be inferior to whites, and thus blacks were treated accordingly, in an inferior and discriminatory manner. In the words of Martin Luther King Jr.: "All segregation statutes are unjust because segregation . . . gives the segregator a false sense of superiority and the segregated a false sense of inferiority."[7] Sadly and outrageously, the highest court in the land put its stamp of approval on a legal system of discrimination against blacks that lasted into the mid-twentieth century.

In a stinging dissent to the *Plessy* decision, Justice John Marshall Harlan insisted that "our Constitution is color-blind, and neither knows nor tolerates classes among citizens." His color-blind metaphor has become a center of controversy in strong affirmative action programs.

It took until 1954 for Justice Harlan's minority-of-one opinion to become the Supreme Court's majority rule. In that year, the Court handed down its historic *Brown v. Board of Education* decision.[8] It struck down the separate but equal doctrine in public schools as a violation of the equal protection clause of the Fourteenth Amendment. In the words of Chief Justice Earl Warren: "Separate education facilities are inherently unequal." Thus, segregation as such is discrimination. The Court then quickly moved in a succession of cases to strike down Jim Crow laws in other arenas of public life. Legalized segregation was unraveling. The stage was set for the Second Reconstruction.

The Second Reconstruction began with the civil rights crusade of Martin Luther King Jr. in 1955. Despite Court rulings prohibiting legalized segregation, many Southerners deeply resented the intrusion of the federal government into their regional way of life. Decades-old patterns and habits of prejudicial discrimination proved resistant to change by legal means. It would not be until the 1960s, under the powerful and inspirational leadership of Dr. King, that the last vestiges of Jim Crow laws would finally disappear. In the meantime, other minorities, and women, were demanding full economic as well as political rights. The nation was developing a commitment to the principle of equal opportunity, which was seen as implied by the Fourteenth Amendment.

In 1961, President John F. Kennedy signed Executive Order 10925, which declared that federal contractors should take "affirmative action" to ensure that applicants are employed without regard to their race, creed, color, or national origin. The order meant weak affirmative action and so was not particularly controversial. Then in 1963, Congress passed the Equal Pay Act. It outlawed pay discrimination against women and required equal pay for equal work.

The following year, Congress passed the historic Civil Rights Act of 1964. Title VI and Title VII are the most important sections of the act. Title VI prohibited discrimination based on race, color, or national origin in any program or activity receiving federal financial aid. Title VII prohibited all forms of discrimination in employment based on race, color, religion, sex, or national origin. It applied to all employers, both public and private, with twenty-five (later amended to fifteen) or more employees. The act also stated that preferential treatment in the workplace based on race, color, religion, sex, or national origin (i.e., strong affirmative action) was not required. This provision was inserted into the act to placate Southern white legislators who otherwise would not have voted for it. Notice, though, that the act stopped short of prohibiting strong affirmative action. It merely did not require it. The door was left open to strong affirmative action.

In fact, the government's weak opposition to strong affirmative action did not last long. In 1965, after Congress passed the Voting Rights Act, President Lyndon Johnson issued Executive Order 11246. It required the Department of Labor to take race into consideration in awarding federal contracts to construction companies. Soon thereafter, he issued Executive Order 11375, which extended strong affirmative action to women. Gradually, the meaning of affirmative action shifted from weak to strong affirmative action. The former was seen as inadequate to correct imbalances in employment and education brought about by previous practices and patterns of discrimination.

In 1971, the US Supreme Court opened up the floodgates to strong affirmative action—at least in the workplace. In *Griggs v. Duke Power Co.* (9–0),[9] the Court ruled that Title VII prohibited both *disparate treatment* based on race, religion, gender, or national origin (i.e., prejudicial discrimination), and *disparate-impact discrimination*. The latter term refers to an employment test that was "fair in form" because its administrators did not engage in (directly) intentional disparate-treatment discrimination, but was "discriminatory in operation" (i.e., impact). The Court said that such a test could still violate Title VII. If a test or other seemingly race-neutral employee evaluation procedure has the effect of substantially favoring some racial groups over others, it is the employer's burden of proof to show why such a test or procedure is necessary. If she cannot show this, it is considered an instrument of disparate-impact discrimination and therefore illegal.

After the *Griggs* decision, employers tried to design testing and evaluation methods that were racially neutral in their impact (i.e., consequences). To assist employers in this task, the Equal Employment Opportunity Commission (created by the Civil Rights Act of 1964) devised the *four-fifths rule*: A racial group that passed a test less than 80 percent of the rate of another group put an employer in presumptive violation of Title VII. The *Griggs* decision cleared the way for a full-scale governmental promotion of strong affirmative action programs. The distinction between rigid and flexible strong affirmative action did not seem to matter to the Court.

In the wake of this decision, Congress passed the Equal Employment Opportunity Act of 1972, which amended the Civil Rights Act of 1964. Title VII now included a prohibition of disparate-impact discrimination. Both anti-discrimination and affirmative action laws were administered and enforced by the Equal Employment Opportunity Commission. Proportionalism now became the goal of government activity. This goal was to be achieved by quotas, timetables, and set-asides. The commission spelled out guidelines, or steps, for companies to follow in setting up affirmative action programs. One textbook aptly summarizes these steps:

> Firms must issue a written equal-employment policy and an affirmative action commitment. They must appoint a top official with responsibility and authority to direct and implement their program. . . . Firms must survey current female and minority employment by department and job classification. Where underrepresentation of these groups is evident, firms must develop goals and timetables to improve in each area of underrepresentation. They then must develop specific programs to achieve these goals, establish an internal audit system to monitor them, and evaluate progress in each aspect of the program. Finally, companies must develop supportive in-house and community programs to combat discrimination.[10]

Colleges and universities developed similar programs in their admissions policies.

As strong affirmative action programs increased in the 1970s, so did their critics. One frequent criticism of these programs was that, in their effort to eliminate the effects of past and present prejudicial discrimination, they simply replaced one form of discrimination with another: reverse discrimination against white males. But, continued the criticism, discrimination is wrong and illegal, regardless of who or what group is discriminated against. As the controversy grew, it was inevitable that the US Supreme Court would rule on the issue. It did in 1978 in the famous case of *Regents of the University of California v. Bakke*.[11]

In the early 1970s, the University of California, Davis School of Medicine set aside sixteen of its one hundred entrance seats for minority students. The entrance requirements for the sixteen minority seats were considerably lower than for the eighty-four regular seats. Alan Bakke, a white male, applied for admission to the Davis Medical School in 1973 and 1974. Both years he was rejected, even though his grades, placement-test scores, and other qualifications were higher than those of most minority applicants who were admitted. Bakke sued the university, charging that he had been discriminated against, in violation of the US Constitution and the Civil Rights Act of 1964. The university defended its quota system as constitutionally valid and necessary to increase the very small percentage of nonwhite physicians in society and to increase the number of nonwhite applicants to its medical school.

In a 5–4 vote, the Supreme Court ruled in Bakke's favor. In its decision, it rejected quotas and any form of rigid strong affirmative action. However, it approved of flexible strong affirmative action. The Court held that the admissions process could take race or ethnicity into account as one factor in evaluating an applicant. It used Harvard University's admissions program as a model. In such a program, race or ethnic background may be considered a plus in an applicant's file, but the plus does not insulate the applicant from comparison with all other candidates for the available seats. Moreover, the Court ruled that numerical goals or quotas are permissible when it can be proved that an institution has practiced discrimination. In general, though, the thrust of the Court's decision was to allow flexible strong affirmative action while striking down rigid strong affirmative action—at least with respect to admissions.

Nine years later, the Court took up the issue of gender. In *Johnson v. Transportation Agency, Santa Clara County*,[12] it ruled that gender was permissible as one factor in promoting Diane Joyce to the position of road dispatcher over a slightly more qualified male employee, Paul Johnson. Johnson was originally recommended for the promotion by his supervisors, but Joyce complained to the local affirmative action office. As her complaint was processed through the affirmative action system, an official eventually recommended that she receive the promotion. She did, even though it was never charged that the original promotion of Johnson discriminated against Joyce. But Joyce was the Transportation Agency's first female road dispatcher, and the agency had adopted an affirmative action program that called for an "equitable" representation of minorities, women, and handicapped persons in hiring and promoting.

Then in 1989, the Court, led by conservative justices appointed by President Ronald Reagan, struck a serious blow to strong affirmative action. In *Richmond v. J. A. Croson Co.*,[13] the Court invalidated a Richmond, Virginia, program called the Minority Business Utilization Plan. This plan, adopted by the Richmond City Council on April 11, 1983, required prime contractors with the city to subcontract at least 30 percent of the dollar amount of their contracts to minority business enterprises (MBEs). An MBE was defined as a company that was at least 51 percent owned by minority members, which included blacks, Spanish-speaking individuals, Asians, Indians, and Aleuts. Subcontractors could be located anywhere in the United States.

The Court ruled that the Richmond minority set-aside was unconstitutional, because it was a violation of the Fourteenth Amendment. At the same time, the Court set a strict standard for the permissibility of strong affirmative action programs. They had to be narrowly tailored to achieve a "compelling" government interest. Proponents of such programs had to prove that the minority groups included in the program were in fact being discriminated against. Statistical disparities by themselves did not constitute evidence of discrimination. In the *Croson* case, it was brought out in court that although 50 percent of Richmond's population was black, only two-thirds of 1 percent of its contracts had been awarded to minority businesses.

On June 12, 1995, the Court reaffirmed the earlier *Croson* decision. In *Adarand Constructors v. Pena*,[14] it extended the Croson standard to federal contractors, since the Croson decision applied only to state and municipal contractors. As a result, the Court ruled that all government contracts involving strong affirmative action are unconstitutional, except if they are narrowly tailored measures that promote a compelling government interest. In her majority opinion, Justice Sandra Day O'Connor wrote:

> [A] free people whose institutions are founded upon the doctrine of equality should tolerate no retreat from the principle that government may treat people differently because of their race only for the most compelling reasons. Accordingly, we hold today that all racial classifications, imposed by whatever Federal, state, or local governmental actor, must be analyzed by a reviewing court under strict scrutiny. . . . Such classifications are constitutional only if they are narrowly tailored measures that further compelling governmental interests.[15]

However, in separate concurring opinions, Justices Clarence Thomas and Antonin Scalia disagreed with O'Connor's exception. According to them, the Constitution prohibits all racial classifications. In Thomas's words: "I believe that there is a 'moral and constitutional equivalence' between laws designed to subjugate a race and those that distribute benefits on the basis of race in order to foster some current notion of equality."[16] For Thomas, strong affirmative action is as morally and constitutionally bad as prejudicial discrimination. Scalia agrees at least with the constitutional part of Thomas's statement. Under the Constitution, he says, there can be no such thing as either a creditor or a debtor race.[17]

Whatever one's views are on affirmative action, it is a serious error to equate it with prejudicial discrimination. Even if strong affirmative action is wrong, it is not nearly as bad as prejudiced discrimination. They have very different motives and direct intentions, as we shall see.

The *Croson* and *Pena* decisions set a stricter standard for the permissibility of affirmative action programs than the *Bakke* decision. Left unclear by the Court, however, was *Bakke*'s implicit distinction between rigid and flexible strong affirmative action, where only the latter is permissible in general. The Court's new strict standard seemed to apply to flexible as well as to rigid programs, although the phrase "narrowly tailored measures" seemed to favor flexible programs.

In view of this ambiguity, it is understandable that lower courts would interpret *Croson* and *Pena* as rejecting *Bakke*, even though their rulings may have gone beyond these twin decisions. In March 1996, the Fifth US Circuit Court of Appeals handed down a decision that contradicted the *Bakke* ruling. In *Hopwood v. State of Texas*,[18] the appeals Court ruled that the University of Texas Law School could not use race at all in its admission standards. Thus, it rejected *Bakke*'s distinction between rigid and flexible strong affirmative action. Cheryl Hopwood and three other white students were rejected by the law school. Hopwood's LSAT scores were high enough to qualify for the law school's pool of minority and disadvantaged applicants, but only sixty white students were accepted from the pool, a relatively small percentage. Exacerbating this problem was the fact that Hopwood fit the profile of a truly disadvantaged and talented student. For example, she had been offered a partial scholarship to Princeton but still could not afford to go there.

The appeals court observed that Hopwood was a good example of an applicant with a unique background whose circumstances would bring a different perspective to the law school. Although it held that a "diverse" student body is a valid goal for colleges and universities, diversity may not be achieved by resorting to racial classifications. However, a university may favor one applicant over another because of his or her ability to play the cello, relationship to alumni, or economic and social background. These preferences are permissible, according to the Court, because applicants are evaluated as individuals rather than by race. Some minority groups criticized this view by arguing that screening applicants for special skills or family connections is affirmative action for whites. I take up this question later. In response to the *Hopwood* case, the Texas state legislature passed a law called the "10 percent rule." The law guaranteed a seat in any public university to a student in the top 10 percent of his or her high school class, regardless of race, ethnicity, or gender.

The state of California passed, on Election Day 1996, Proposition 209. This referendum initiative prohibited strong affirmative action in public employment, education, and contracting. Its implementation, however, was quickly blocked by federal district court judge Thelton E. Henderson, who held that there was a strong probability that the measure was unconstitutional. He argued that Proposition 209 violated the equal protection clause of the Fourteenth Amendment, because it eliminated programs that benefit only minorities and women and not those that benefit other groups such as army veterans. On April 8, 1997, the Ninth US Circuit Court of Appeals in San Francisco overturned Henderson's preliminary injunction and upheld the constitutionality of Proposition 209, ruling that the voters have a right to prohibit preferential treatment based on race or gender.[19] After much legal wrangling it went into effect on August 29. Some time later, California passed its own version of Texas's 10 percent rule, called the "4 percent plan." This law guaranteed a seat at any campus of the University of California to a student who graduated in the top 4 percent of his or her high school class.

A major consequence of Proposition 209 has been a phenomenon known as *cascading.* Fewer blacks and Hispanics can meet the admissions standards of the most selective University of California schools such as Berkeley and UCLA, and so are sliding down the scale—cascading—to the lower-ranked UC schools such as Irvine, Davis, Santa Barbara, Santa Cruz, and Riverside. Cascading also exists at the University of Texas campuses. At Berkeley, the most selective of UC colleges, Hispanic enrollments fell 34 percent and black enrollments 57 percent in the two years after Proposition 209 was passed. During the same period, the least selective school, Riverside, saw Hispanic admissions jump 66 percent and black admissions 54 percent.

Proponents of strong affirmative action argue that cascading is evidence enough that strong affirmative action works and initiatives like Proposition 209 are a failure because they are exclusionary and therefore unfair. In an important book, *The Shape of the River,*[20] coauthored by William Bowen and Derek Bok, former presidents of Princeton and Harvard Universities, respectively, they presented powerful evidence that the more selective a college minorities attend the better they do for themselves and society. Minority students are more likely to become leaders, and take up positions of authority and responsibility in a variety of professions and institutions. Therefore, we must keep strong affirmative action in place so that minorities can have their fair share of America's highest opportunities and benefits, according to them.

Supporters of Proposition 209 counterargue that cascading is beneficial to minorities because it provides a more honest and realistic match between a student's abilities and a particular school than does the artificial prop of strong affirmative action. Moreover, if we focus on improving education from kindergarten through high school for all students, cascading will gradually diminish. I return to this issue later.

On June 23, 2003, the United States Supreme Court issued two long-awaited decisions involving the University of Michigan's strong affirmative action programs. The Court clarified its position on flexible and rigid affirmative action. In one case, *Grutter v. Bollinger*,[21] the Court ruled 5–4, in a majority opinion written by Sandra Day O'Connor, that the university's law school program was constitutionally valid for two fundamental reasons. First, it followed the Court's rulings set forth in the landmark *Bakke* case of 1978. In that case, as we have seen, the Court rejected racial quotas and other forms of rigid strong affirmative action. However, it approved of flexible strong affirmative action. In the *Grutter* case, Justice O'Connor implicitly held that the law school has a program of flexible strong affirmative action because it conducts an "individualized assessment" of all of its applicants. In this assessment, the race of underrepresented minorities, namely blacks, Hispanics, and American Indians, counts as one of several plus or positive factors in the law school's goal to achieve a diverse student body.

The second reason the Court declared the program constitutional is that it satisfies the standard laid down in the Court's *Pena* decision of 1995. In that decision, as we have seen, the Court ruled that "racial classifications" for affirmative action are constitutional only "if they are narrowly tailored measures that further compelling governmental interests." Justice O'Connor asserted that the government has a compelling interest in supporting the goal of colleges and universities to achieve a racially diverse student body defined by her as including a "critical mass" of underrepresented minorities. And since the law school's program to achieve this goal is based on an individualized assessment of all applicants, it is a narrowly tailored measure, unlike a quota or set-aside system. Therefore the phrase "narrowly tailored measure" excluded all forms of *rigid* strong affirmative action. The phrase permitted only flexible programs.

O'Connor offered several reasons why a racially diverse student body is a compelling government interest. Racial diversity among students has five substantial educational and social benefits. First, it promotes cross-racial understanding and helps to break down racial stereotypes, thus enabling students to better understand persons of different races. Second, classroom discussion is livelier, more spirited, more enlightening and interesting when students have the greatest possible variety of backgrounds. Third, diversity promotes learning outcomes and better prepares students for an increasingly diverse workforce and society, and better prepares them as professionals. Fourth, American businesses have made it clear that the skills needed in today's increasingly global marketplace can be developed only through exposure to widely diverse people, cultures, ideas, and viewpoints. And fifth, the strength and well-being of the military depend upon an educated, racially diverse force.

At the same time, the Court ruled that their approval of flexible strong affirmative action is only temporary. Twenty-five years from now, wrote Justice O'Connor, such programs should no longer be necessary. Hence, the Court envisioned in the next generation or so a color-blind society in which race will not matter.

The *Grutter* ruling implicitly rejected the *Hopwood* decision of the 5th US Circuit Court of Appeals. In this case, as we have seen, the Court ruled that the University of Texas Law School must stop classifying and evaluating applicants based on race. The *Hopwood* case rejected flexible as well as rigid strong affirmative action.

Justice O'Connor also rejected the 10 percent rule of the University of Texas and the 4 percent plan of the University of California. As we have just seen, these programs guaranteed a seat at any public campus of these two university systems if an applicant graduated in the top 10 or 4 percent, respectively, of his or her high school class. O'Connor noted that such programs are not based on individualized assessment, and do not take into consideration the large differences in academic quality among high schools. I comment on this ruling later.

In a stinging dissent to the *Grutter* decision, Justices Thomas and Scalia opined that "every time the government places citizens on racial registers and make race relevant to the provisions of burdens or benefits, it demeans us all." Both justices again equate affirmative action with prejudicial discrimination.

The other decision, *Gratz v. Bollinger*,[22] concerned a rigid strong affirmative action program of University of Michigan's undergraduate College of Literature, Science, and the Arts. In this program, the college automatically awarded 20 points on a scale of 150 to blacks, Hispanics, and American Indians, with 100 points guaranteeing admission. This practice is sometimes called race norming. In a 6–3 vote, the court ruled that the college's racial point system was unconstitutional because it constituted a racial *quota* in violation of the *Bakke* decision.

In sum, then, *Grutter* and *Gratz* collectively make two rulings. First, rigid strong affirmative action—quotas, set-asides, numerical goals and percentages, point systems—are unconstitutional. Second, flexible strong affirmative action is constitutional, providing it serves a compelling government interest such as a racially diverse student body, but only for twenty-five years. Expect a spate of lawsuits challenging strong affirmative action in twenty years or so.

Scalia called the Court's implicit distinction between flexible and rigid a "sham." According to him, both of the university's programs yielded similar results in terms of the percentage of minority students admitted. Even so, I would argue that the two programs are not thereby the same, for they have somewhat different direct intentions. Even if both programs have a similar end, they have different means. And since, on my view, the direct intention is the primary moral element of action, this difference in means is crucial.

On June 28, 2007, the Court ruled on affirmative action as it is practiced in public secondary and primary schools. In *Parents Involved in Community Schools v. Seattle School District No. 1* (5–4),[23] an increasingly conservative court declared that school districts cannot use race to assign a student to a particular school, or use it as a tiebreaker for admission in oversubscribed schools, in order to achieve diversity and integration. At the time of the decision, hundreds of school districts around the country had programs that used race in this way, although they involved only a small percentage of students. The plurality opinion was written by Chief Justice Roberts and signed by the other three conservative justices: Scalia, Thomas, and Alito. Justice Kennedy joined them in the voting but issued a separate opinion that partially disagreed with the plurality.

The decision overturned plans in Seattle and in metropolitan Louisville, Kentucky, which had been upheld in lower federal courts. The Louisville plan was covered by a companion case, *Meredith v. Jefferson County Board of Education*. Since the *Seattle* case had a lower docket number, the Court's decision bears its name, but it equally applies to the Louisville case. In the greater Louisville (or Jefferson County) plan, all schools in the district were required to maintain a population of between 15 and 50 percent black students. The US District Court of the Western District of Kentucky, following the precedent of the *Pena* and *Grutter* cases, upheld the plan because it is flexible and not rigid strong affirmative action. "The Plan . . . is sufficiently flexible to determine school assignments for all students by a host of factors, such as residence, student choice, capacity, school and program popularity, pure chance and race," and is "narrowly tailored" to meet the "compelling interest" of diversity.[24] The court denied the plan is a quota for two reasons. First, it does not have a precise target, such as mandating proportionality. It does not require that each school maintain a 34 percent black population, which is the county average. Second, no students are insulated from comparison with other students. The Sixth Circuit Court of Appeals found the lower court's decision "well reasoned" and affirmed its ruling.[25]

The Seattle district is 40 percent white and 60 percent minority, and its plan uses this racial composition as an approximate goal (but not as a precise target) of achievement for each of its schools. A school must not deviate more than 10 percent from this racial composition. Under the plan, all 46,000 students are allowed to apply to the school of their choice. If a school is oversubscribed (if it has more applicants than seats), a series of four descending tiebreakers are utilized, and in no case is a less-qualified minority chosen over a more-qualified white. The first tiebreaker gives preference to applicants who have siblings in the requested school. This tiebreaker accounts for 15 to 20 percent of high school assignments. The second tiebreaker is based on race. If a third tiebreaker is needed, it is the distance from a student's home to her requested school, with closer students admitted first. The fourth tiebreaker is a random lottery but is rarely needed. On October 20, 2005, the Ninth Circuit Court of Appeals upheld the plan as being consistent with the *Pena* and *Grutter* rulings. "We conclude that the district has a compelling interest in securing the educational and social benefits of racial (and ethnic) diversity. . . . We also conclude the district's plan is narrowly tailored to meet the district's compelling interests." [26] According to the court, then, the plan is one of flexible and not rigid strong affirmative action.

In overturning both plans, the Supreme Court rejected flexible as well as rigid affirmative action and put itself at odds with the *Bakke*, *Pena*, and *Grutter* decisions. In *Seattle*, the Court ruled that all race-conscious means to achieve diversity or any other goal are unconstitutional, because they violate the equal protection clause of the Fourteenth Amendment. The Constitution, it said, is color-blind; it forbids all racial classifications. "The way to stop discrimination on the basis of race is to stop discriminating on the basis of race,"[27] wrote Chief Justice Roberts. He claimed that the plurality opinion was more faithful to *Brown v. Board of Education* than were the dissenting opinions.

In a separate opinion, Justice Kennedy rejected Roberts's claim that all racial classifications are unconstitutional. In language reminiscent of *Pena* and *Grutter*, Kennedy argued that race can be used as one factor in achieving compelling governmental interests, such as equal educational opportunity and ending racial isolation, providing the usage of race consists of narrowly tailored programs to achieve these interests. Examples of such programs include drawing up school attendance zones, site selection of new schools, and additional resources to special programs. Kennedy also took issue with Roberts's interpretation of Justice Harlan's color-blind statement and his interpretation of *Brown*. According to Kennedy, Roberts has profoundly distorted their meaning by taking them out of their historical context. In *Plessy* and *Brown*, the meaning of *color-blind* was directed against prejudicial discrimination, against the racist segregation of Jim Crow and its legacy. Affirmative action, of course, was nonexistent then. It is fundamentally different from Jim Crow. Affirmative action, says Kennedy, historically fulfills the underlying purpose of *Brown* in creating an integrated society.

The principal dissenting opinion was written by Justice Stephen Breyer and signed by Justices Stevens, Souter, and Ginsberg. They argued that the kinds of programs invalidated by the Court are necessary tools of local communities to prevent the resegregation of public schools caused by segregated housing patterns. The desegregation mandate of *Brown* can be fulfilled only if the programs remain intact. Race-conscious means are sometimes needed to achieve racial diversity and integration, and the Constitution does not prohibit such action, according to them. Justice Breyer denounced the radicalism of the plurality opinion: "It is not often in the law that so few have so quickly changed so much."[28] And in a separate dissenting opinion, Justice Paul Stevens characterized the chief justice's appeal to *Brown* as a "cruel irony."[29]

The *Seattle* decision bitterly divided the Court. The decision is a substantial reversal of a pattern and scope of affirmative action's constitutional permissibility begun by *Bakke* and continuing through *Grutter*. Nevertheless, school district officials are encouraged by Justice Kennedy's partial rejection of the plurality opinion, which rejection forms part of the Court's majority decision. School districts will now be looking for race-neutral criteria to achieve diversity, such as income and socioeconomic status.

On June 29, 2009, the US Supreme Court issued a far-reaching decision on testing in the workplace that partially overturned the *Griggs* ruling. In *Ricci v. DeStefano* (5–4),[30] the Court ruled that the city of New Haven discriminated against twenty white firefighters (the plaintiffs in the case) by throwing out the results of a promotional exam for lieutenant and captain because the highest scoring applicants were white (including one Hispanic) and none were black. Although several black firefighters passed the exam, none scored high enough for promotion eligibility. The city feared a racial disparate-impact lawsuit from the black firefighters if it acted on the test results and promoted only whites. So the city promoted no one.

In overruling the lower courts, the Supreme Court said that test results cannot be set aside just because they have a disproportionate racial impact when there is no evidence that the test is racially biased. Statistical disparity is not enough to show discrimination.

In the *Ricci* case, the Court effectively scrapped the four-fifths rule, noted earlier. Instead, Justice Kennedy, who authored the majority opinion, said that the racial impact of tests can be taken into consideration at two stages: first, in the design of a test; and second, in "certain, narrow circumstances," employers may discard the results of a test if they can demonstrate "a strong basis in evidence" that using the test results would cause them to lose a disparate-impact suit. This higher, *strong basis-in-evidence* standard replaced the previous, lower, *good-faith* standard that grew out of the *Griggs* decision, which required that an employer show only that it acted in good faith in discarding test results. A basis-in-evidence claim requires an employer to show one of two things: (1) the test administered is not relevant to the position at issue; (2) other equally valid and less discriminatory tests were available but not used.

Both of these requirements make the new standard very difficult to meet. Consequently, it is now much harder for an employer to discard the results of a test, or for minorities to win a disparate-impact discrimination lawsuit. Once a test is given, all parties are pretty much stuck with its scores.

As a result, employers feel greater pressure to design racially neutral–impact tests, a pressure they have felt since 1971. New Haven paid a consultant $100,000 to design a racially neutral promotional exam. Written tests are especially vulnerable to disparate-impact scores: blacks as a group score lower than whites. As a consequence, some employers have abandoned written tests altogether in favor of other methods. One method gaining popularity occurs in an assessment center where applicants are evaluated on how they would handle simulated real-life situations they are likely to encounter on the job. Bridgeport, Connecticut, uses assessment centers, and its lieutenant and captain ranks of firefighters are approximately proportional to its black and Hispanic populations, unlike neighboring New Haven, whose fire department has a long history of minority underrepresentation.

The *Ricci* decision most directly affects public employers who use civil service exams and similar types of tests. Still, it applies to all employers, public or private, who use any form of testing procedure as a means of hiring and promotion.[31]

Ricci somewhat departs from the *Seattle* case because it permits strong affirmative action in exceptional instances, as specified by Justice Kennedy. In this regard, it is more in line with the *Bakke* through *Grutter* decisions.

AN ETHICS OF AFFIRMATIVE ACTION

I have discussed only the most important Supreme Court decisions on affirmative action. Except for the plurality opinion of the *Seattle* decision, they have enough unity and collective wisdom, in my view, to form a framework for a moral argument on affirmative action, especially bearing in mind that affirmative action programs operate within the basic structure of society as a constitutional democracy.

I develop a moral argument that supports the view that strong affirmative action is prima facie immoral. (Since weak affirmative action is not controversial, I do not consider it.)[32] Although my argument is explicitly developed within the context of employment and higher education, it also applies to secondary and primary education. In the light of this argument, I then critically examine several arguments for affirmative action. Because of space limitations, I select the strongest arguments, which enable me to amplify and refine my own argument.

Affirmative Action, Justice, and Intentionality: An Argument

My argument is based on three key ideas: the principle of community, the principle of intentionality, and the concept of justice as expressed by the two (Rawls's) principles of justice in chapter 8. As we have seen, community is the supreme moral principle. Intentionality is the procedural principle by which it is applied to various types of actions. An essential component of the community principle is justice. Justice constitutes the basic (or minimal) level of morality, and it applies to the basic structure of society. This means that justice is both a necessary and sufficient condition of a morally right action. It is a necessary condition because without justice an action cannot be morally right. It is a sufficient condition in the sense that if an action possesses justice, it is morally right even if it lacks other moral qualities that would make it better. Therefore, an unjust action is ipso facto an immoral action.

The principle of intentionality exhibits the moral structure of affirmative action with respect to its end, means (the two essential elements of direct intention), and motive. Moreover, since my argument claims that affirmative action is prima facie immoral, and since affirmative action is not primarily a single act but an institutional practice (and so a continuum of action), I apply Rule Five of intentionality to strong affirmative action. This rule states, in part (chapter 2): if a direct intention has a good end and a bad means, the direct intention is significantly bad if the means is a prima facie immoral action. I apply this rule to strong affirmative action as follows.

The end of affirmative action programs is good: racial, ethnic, and gender justice for members of groups that historically have been objects of substantial prejudicial discrimination, especially blacks, Hispanics, American Indians, and women. This end includes a more diverse and integrated society. Diversity and integration are two sides of the same coin of justice. Diversity means that persons of different race, ethnicity, and gender are represented in significant numbers throughout society's major institutions. The concept of diversity, however, does not emphasize the connectedness of these groups within the larger society. Integration does, by insisting that these same diverse peoples must be mainstreamed into society by acquiring positions of leadership and power, of authority and responsibility, in society's major institutions and professions. Diversity without the unity of integration tends toward balkanization and tribalism, which are contrary to the community of a personalist society. *E pluribus unum* expresses the reciprocity of diversity and integration, so long as this phrase is not interpreted (as it often is) as the bland, homogenous melting-pot metaphor, which is an effective denial of diversity. Indeed, the more diverse a society becomes, the more its citizens need to aim at the unity that binds them.[33]

The means of achieving affirmative action's end are the programs themselves. The programs consist of preferential treatment for the members of the aggrieved groups and thus disfavored treatment for members of the nonaggrieved groups, which consist mostly of white men. The former are treated as more than equal and the latter as less than equal. Therefore, in this respect affirmative action does not treat all persons equally. Furthermore, this unequal treatment occurs in morally and socially important contexts: in employment, promotions, and admission to higher education. For both reasons, in most cases (but not all) affirmative action programs violate the principle of equal opportunity. Therefore, these programs considered as *means* to the end of affirmative action have a significantly bad direct intention. It is not gravely bad because in some cases, to be specified, the programs are needed to promote the fair value of equal opportunity.

The motive of strong affirmative action is good: it is either noble or benign. It has a noble motive toward the aggrieved groups: a caring for these persons and a desire to render them justice. It has a benign motive toward the disfavored, nonaggrieved groups (primarily white males). For unlike prejudicial discrimination, the reason they are disfavored is not that they are judged to be inferior to the preferred groups; they are not objects of scorn, contempt, or hate. On the contrary, they are seen to be unfair recipients of benefits that are the result of prejudicial discrimination against the aggrieved groups, and so as having an undeserved superiority (or advantage) over them.

The combination of affirmative action's good end and good motive conflicts with the badness of its means. Since the means are bad, but not gravely bad, strong affirmative action programs have a significantly bad direct intention. Therefore, these programs are prima facie immoral—immoral in general. Consequently, there are some situations in which they are morally right. Insofar as these programs are immoral, the badness of the means outweighs the combined goodness of the end and motive. But insofar as these programs are morally right, the combined goodness of the end and motive outweighs the badness of the means. As immoral, strong affirmative action is unjust and discriminatory; as morally right, it is just and nondiscriminatory. As a result, affirmative action discrimination is a valid moral concept and is distinct from prejudicial discrimination. The latter is morally worse than the former. Prejudicial discrimination has a gravely bad direct intention and is intrinsically immoral.

In between the immorality of affirmative action discrimination and prejudicial discrimination is the immorality of *legacy preference*, the practice of giving admission preference to children of alumni. These practices are sometimes called "white affirmative action," since they primarily benefit white persons. At top colleges and universities, legacy preference is severe. At the University of Pennsylvania, the legacy acceptance rate is 41 percent compared to an overall rate of 21 percent; at Harvard University, the figures are 40 percent compared to 11 percent; at Princeton, 35 percent vs. 11 percent; and at Stanford, 25 percent vs. 13 percent.[34]

What is basically wrong about legacy preference is the *extent* to which it is practiced. The result is that large numbers of better-qualified applicants than the beneficiaries of legacy preference are disfavored and not admitted. This is prima facie unfair to them. Opponents of affirmative action are morally inconsistent in their opposition to all forms of strong affirmative action programs *and* in their unqualified support of legacy preference. To compound their inconsistency, they also morally equate strong affirmative action with prejudicial discrimination. If a society (e.g., the United States) practiced this inconsistency, it would be dominated by white men, who would possess a disproportionate amount of power and privilege, wealth and income, and positions of authority and responsibility. In this respect, we would have the United States for most of its history. It did not start to shift away from this white-male model until the 1960s, through the combined efforts of the civil rights and women's movements. In this context, affirmative action has played a key role in the shift away from the white-male social model.

The present practice of legacy preference must be regarded as morally worse than affirmative action discrimination for the following reason. Affirmative action programs have a good end: racial and gender justice. The apparent end of legacy preference is money: to ensure that alumni with children will continue their gifts to the institution. This is not a bad end, of course. It contributes to the financial health of the institution. What is wrong about legacy preference is its excessiveness or severity. Its end is not a noble one. Therefore, the end of affirmative action is morally superior to the end of legacy preference.

I must now specify the situations in which strong affirmative action is morally wrong and morally right. In general, rigid programs, such as quotas, are wrong, except perhaps those programs involving unskilled labor. Rigid programs do not sufficiently address the issue of variations or differences among persons regarding the mental and physical abilities, aptitudes, skills, and knowledge that are relevant to the positions/openings covered by an affirmative action program. Race, ethnicity, and gender as such are not abilities, aptitudes, skills, or knowledge. Therefore, they should not be overemphasized or used arbitrarily in the selection of applicants, as is done in rigid programs. Rigid programs do not promote the fair value of the equal opportunity principle. Nor do they satisfy the difference principle or the criterion of reciprocity. The extent of the above variations among individuals required by the difference principle would be significantly reduced by a rigid program, which has a kind of "leveling down" effect. Moreover, I do not think that free and equal citizens could reasonably propose a rigid program as fair terms of social cooperation that they would abide by, providing all others do so.

Consequently, all forms of rigid strong affirmation action (with the possible one exception noted above) are unjust and discriminatory toward the persons who are disfavored by such programs. Such discrimination is especially the case with proportionalism (equal results).

In contrast, some flexible programs are morally permissible. Flexible strong affirmative action programs are morally permissible when they meet the following eleven criteria: (1) the groups intended to be helped by the program have a history of being substantially discriminated against; (2) the same groups are substantially underrepresented in the fields covered by the programs; (3) there is only one pool of applicants for the positions/openings covered by the program, and no group of applicants is insulated from all the others; (4) race/ethnicity/gender is not given greater weight than any other criterion for selection; (5) all applicants are evaluated on several important criteria or qualifications relevant to a given position/opening; (6) the unqualified may never be chosen because of their race, ethnicity, or gender; (7) *disadvantaged* is a distinct category or criterion of evaluation, but is given no greater weight than any of the other criteria; (8) the programs are intended to be temporary and must be reviewed periodically to see to what extent their goals are being achieved; (9) the programs are only a door-opener; (10) there is vigorous enforcement of all antidiscrimination legislation; and (11) the best (or most qualified) candidates are chosen in accordance with the above criteria.

Programs that meet these criteria use race or gender in a positive yet reasonable and judicious way, and in a manner that promotes the fair value of the equal opportunity principle. Otherwise, we risk interpreting the principle in its formal and weak sense, as Shelby Steele does: "Entitlement by color is a dubious reward for being black. . . . I would . . . like to see affirmative action go back to its original purpose of enforcing equal opportunity—a purpose that in itself disallows racial preferences."[35] Of course, equal opportunity should be enforced. The question is how to adequately enforce it in all instances. Enforcing antidiscrimination laws is not enough. They must be supplemented by flexible strong affirmative action as specified above. We must promote the fair value of equal opportunity. Otherwise, it remains a purely formal principle.

All strong affirmative action programs have a significantly bad direct intention, as specified above. However, in immoral programs, this badness is aggravated by any number of factors or conditions (as explained above) to the degree that the badness of the program considered as means overrides the combined goodness of its end and motive, whereas in morally permissible programs this aggravation does not occur, so that the combined goodness of end and motive outweighs and overrides the badness of the means.

Some opponents of affirmative action complain that once these programs are established they become a permanent way of life. Thomas Sowell notes that as affirmative action programs have become entrenched in various countries around the world, they have increasingly served people they were never designed to serve and ought not to serve.[36] This is surely an abuse of affirmative action that no reasonable proponent of affirmative action supports. But the abuse of a thing is not a sufficient reason to oppose its legitimate use.

However, against my argument it may be objected that in strong affirmative action, discrimination against white men is morally permissible because such discrimination is not part of the means of the action but belongs to its indirect intention. According to this interpretation, the end of affirmative action is racial and gender justice, the means to achieve it is preferential treatment of minorities and women, and the indirect intention of the action—what is foreseen but unwilled—is discrimination against white men. And since in each instance of discrimination against white men, an equivalent benefit (or good) is directly intended for a minority person or woman, the evil of the indirect intention does not outweigh the goodness of the direct intention. Therefore, Rule Three of the intentionality principle is satisfied (chapter 2), and so strong affirmative action is always morally permissible.

This objection fails because it misapplies the principle of intentionality. A valid application of Rule Three presupposes an action whose means is really distinct from its indirect intention. But in strong affirmative action, there is no real, significant distinction between favoring minorities/women and disfavoring white men. Both are necessarily and reciprocally related; they are two sides of the same moral coin. It is impossible to directly intend favoring members of the one group without intentionally disfavoring members of the other. The disfavored treatment of white men is as willed as is the preferential treatment of minorities and women. Moreover, in affirmative action situations, the positions sought after are scarce; there are far more applicants than openings. Whoever is chosen for the job, promotion, or college seat excludes someone else who is not chosen. In this respect, strong affirmative action is a zero-sum game. As we also saw in chapter 2, a direct intention can include allowing just as much as doing. In strong affirmative action, the direct intention includes an active preferential choosing of a minority person or woman and allowing that a white man be disfavored.

Still, a policy or practice can have a direct intention that excludes preferential treatment of minorities or women but whose indirect intention disproportionately benefits them. In this instance, the policy or practice is not strong affirmative action—for example, Texas's 10 percent rule and California's 4 percent plan. Although these laws were foreseen as disproportionately benefiting blacks and Hispanics as groups by helping individual blacks and Hispanics with low test scores but high grades in less competitive high schools, the laws are not strong affirmative action because they did not make *race* a criterion of admissions; race is not part of the laws' direct intention. A student of any race or ethnic group can qualify for admission under the 10 percent rule or 4 percent plan. Whether the laws embody a completely adequate admissions standard is another issue. As we have seen, in the *Grutter* decision the Supreme Court struck down both programs because they were not based on "individualized assessment." In addition, they did not take into account the wide differences in academic standards among high schools.

Justice O'Connor certainly made a very good point about the variable academic quality of high schools. However, it is not enough reason to declare such programs unconstitutional or immoral. They are not racial or gender quotas, since they do not make race or gender part of the programs' direct intention. The programs do not *aim* at establishing race or gender as an essential factor in the admissions process. What they do aim at is replacing race and gender with the category of the *disadvantaged*. Consequently, the end of these programs is to help the disadvantaged by means of these programs. This end is good. The indirect intention includes a disproportionate benefit to blacks and Hispanics. Even if an opponent of affirmative action charges that the indirect intention is thereby bad, the action's direct intention as a whole is nevertheless good even if we factor into it the variation in academic quality among high schools. Consequently, these programs satisfy Rule One of the principle of intentionality: if the direct intention/consequences are good, the action is morally right, unless the badness of the indirect intention/consequences and/or motive outweighs the goodness of the direct intention/consequences. In fact, I do not think that the indirect intention is bad. But even if it were, the direct intention is good enough to outweigh the indirect badness. The really meritorious thing about these programs is that their direct intention replaces race/ethnicity/gender with disadvantaged. It is unfortunate that the Court struck down these programs.

I now turn to select arguments for affirmative action.

ARGUMENTS FOR AFFIRMATIVE ACTION

Reverse Discrimination Argument

This argument concedes that strong affirmative action programs generate reverse discrimination against white men and that such discrimination is an injustice against them. Nevertheless, this injustice is morally permissible because it is a necessary means to the end of achieving racial and gender justice, and the goodness of this end outweighs the badness of the means. According to Tom Beauchamp, reverse discrimination "is justified [but] only as a means to the end of ensuring nondiscriminatory treatment of all persons."[37] Similarly, Andrew Young concedes that "affirmative action is perhaps an individual injustice. But it might be necessary in order to overcome a historic group injustice or series of group injustices."[38]

I have two criticisms of this argument. First, it seems to hold that strong affirmative action's *disfavoring* of white men ipso facto *discriminates* against them. This identification is false. Strong affirmative action *always* disfavors white men, and in *most* instances this disfavoring implies discrimination, but not always, since strong affirmative action is prima facie immoral rather than intrinsically immoral. Therefore, in those cases where strong affirmative action is morally permissible, the disfavored white men are not discriminated against. *Discrimination* is an inherently moral term but *disfavored* is not.

Disfavored becomes immoral when it constitutes discrimination, as it generally does.

Second, injustice by its nature can never be intended as a means to a supposed end of justice, on the grounds that the justice of the end outweighs the injustice of the means. Justice is an inherent moral good; injustice is an inherent moral evil. Hence, injustice must always be avoided for its own sake, and justice must always be done for its own sake. Justice is not merely an instrumental good or value. The reverse discrimination argument, which is purely utilitarian, is mistaken in its instrumental interpretation of justice.

Compensatory Justice Argument

Unlike the previous argument, the compensatory justice argument claims that the whole direct intention of strong affirmative action is just: Both end and means are just. The end consists of racial and gender justice, and the means consists of compensatory justice. In this context, compensatory justice has the following meaning: Since minorities and women have been and are still being discriminated against in the important areas of employment, promotions, and higher education admissions (the third area generally does not apply to white women), society must now compensate them for their injuries by awarding them damages in the form of jobs, promotions, and seats in higher education. At the same time, since a racist and sexist society has undeservedly benefited white men precisely at the expense of women and minorities, it is not unjust to deny some white males jobs, promotions, and higher education seats while society transfers such benefits, as just compensation, to minorities and women.[39]

This interpretation of compensatory justice is a substantial departure from the traditional meaning of the term. According to the traditional meaning of compensatory justice, three conditions must be satisfied for compensatory justice to apply in a particular case: (1) there must be an identifiable injured party, (2) there must be an identifiable injurer who unjustly caused the injury, and (3) there must be a reasonable relation between the injury (or injustice) and the compensation. Compensatory justice may apply to groups as well as to individuals, and it may include both punitive and actual damages. For example, the US government has compensated Japanese Americans who were interned immediately after the outbreak of World War II. In the following example, the three conditions are satisfied: Suppose several people are conducting a peaceful and lawful demonstration in accordance with their First Amendment rights. A bystander does not like their message and destroys three of their signs. The protester who owns the signs sues the bystander for damages of $300, the amount he spent on the signs. In court, the judge rules against the bystander and orders him to pay $600 in compensation: $300 in actual damages, and $300 in punitive damage because of his malicious motive.

These three conditions are generally not satisfied in strong affirmative action's new interpretation of compensatory justice. In addition, the new interpretation commits two fallacies: division and composition. Thus, there are five difficulties with the new meaning of compensatory justice. First, it is usually not known or demonstrated that any of the compensated individuals are actual victims of discrimination in the sense of having incurred specific compensable injuries, such as having been denied a job because of their race. Second, even if some of them were known to be injured victims of discrimination, it is almost never the case that the white men who are denied jobs, promotions, and higher education seats were the perpetrators of the injury. In the name of "justice," they are being unfairly singled out as those who must pay for the sins of others, or so it is claimed. Ironically, it is they who become the real victims, the real injured parties. Third, even in the rare case in which the first two conditions are satisfied, it does not follow that an appropriate remedy—much less the only appropriate remedy—is to give the victim a job, a promotion, or admission to a college or university. The victim, precisely because he or she has been injured, may not be qualified for the position in question. In this case, the most appropriate or reasonable form of compensation may be money, which is generally the case under the traditional meaning of compensatory justice. Remedial programs under weak affirmative action may be appropriate for promising individuals.

Fourth, even if society or the community owes something to minorities and women under compensatory justice, it does not follow that any *individual* members of society owe anything. To say that they do commits the fallacy of division. According to this fallacy, one reasons that all the properties of the whole must likewise belong to the parts or individual members of that whole. For example, I commit the fallacy if I reason that since a large and complex machine is heavy in weight, each of its parts is therefore heavy in weight. In fact, of course, each of its parts is light in weight. Similarly, the fallacy is committed when affirmative action proponents argue that because society as a whole owes something to minorities and women, some individual white men therefore owe them their jobs. By the same token, the fallacy would be committed if one argued that since the US government owed compensation to the Japanese Americans who were wrongfully interned during World War II, individual Americans owed them compensation.

And fifth, if the new notion of compensatory justice is viewed from the standpoint of the original, valid meaning of compensatory justice, strong affirmative action commits the reverse fallacy, that of composition. According to this fallacy, one reasons that all the properties of the parts, or of individual members, must belong to the corresponding whole. For example, one commits this fallacy if one reasons that since each part of a machine is light in weight, the whole large and complex machine is therefore light in weight. In truth, the whole machine is heavy in weight. In the traditional meaning of compensatory justice, as in other modes of justice, the objects of justice are primarily individual persons. Justice applies to groups only in special cases, as I explained. But proponents of strong affirmative action reason that because justice applies to individual persons, it must likewise apply to the racial, ethnic, and gender groups of which they are members, or that since individuals possess rights, the groups to which they belong possess rights. This reasoning and notion of group rights commit the fallacy of composition. For all five reasons, the compensatory justice argument as it stands cannot support its claim that strong affirmative action programs across the board are morally permissible.

However, it may be objected that my own argument in justice, insofar as it supports affirmative action, is an argument based on compensatory justice. For am I not saying that persons who are members of the aggrieved groups are receiving a plus for their race, ethnicity, or gender as *compensation* for the historic (and perhaps still ongoing) injustices inflicted upon these groups? My answer is as follows. The justice reason for preferential treatment is not to rectify past injustices, which is virtually impossible. For either the persons treated unjustly are dead or else individual injustices cannot be identified. My justice reason does indeed recognize the existence and importance of these injustices, and in my argument it is the *origin* of preferential treatment. But the *justification* of preferential treatment is to create here and now and in the future a society that is more just than it has been with respect to these aggrieved groups. As my previous argument indicates, the end of strong affirmative action is racial, ethnic, and gender justice by creating a more diverse and integrated society, and not by trying to redress past injustices.

Antimerit Argument

According to this argument, traditional standards based on merit, on objective qualifications alone, are inadequate, for they may be biased in favor of white males, or they may be incomplete, or they may not be good predictors of success.[40] That being the case, there is nothing wrong or irrational in using race, ethnicity, or gender as one criterion or standard, especially since the traditional standards have worked against minorities and women. Furthermore, there are plenty of examples in white-male society of positions not being awarded on the basis of qualifications: nepotism, the old-boy network, and legacy preference. Therefore, preferential treatment based on race, ethnicity, or gender is morally permissible.

A weakness of this argument is that it does not sufficiently distinguish between the traditional merit standards and race/ethnicity/gender. I now attempt to do so.

First of all, reason demands that we have some sort of standards. Otherwise, there is no basis for comparing and judging the respective worth of individuals for society's multitudinous positions. Since it is rational to have standards, the standards themselves should be rational; they should have a rational content. But what standards are these? The apparent answer is: standards that are relevant to the position. Job qualifications and student admissions qualifications in general are relevant standards.

But can race, ethnicity, or gender be relevant to merit, or be a rational job-qualification or student-admission standard? To answer this question, we must distinguish three meanings of *relevant*. First, as we have indicated, in morally permissible programs of affirmative action, race, ethnicity, or gender is used as a criterion that *supplements* traditional job-qualifications and student-qualifications criteria. In this sense, race or gender is an external criterion to job-qualifications standards or student-qualifications standards. Therefore, in these situations, we are not saying that being black or female will make someone more qualified for a given position. On the contrary, we are saying that for other reasons we have indicated, such a person should be chosen for the position in spite of slightly lower qualifications, or better still, equal qualifications. But the unqualified should never be chosen. Second, race or gender can actually be a job- or student-qualification standard. For example, some African-Americans may feel more comfortable going to a black physician, just as many women feel more comfortable having a woman physician. A professor of Japanese linguistics and culture who herself is Japanese and thus was born and raised in Japan will probably have an edge over a non-Japanese person with a similar level of formal education in non-Japanese universities. In these cases, race, ethnicity, or gender is a *secondary* criterion of merit. The primary criteria must always be the job-qualifications or student-qualifications standards with respect to the abilities, aptitudes, skills, intelligence, knowledge, education, and physical abilities that are relevant to the positions or openings included within the affirmative action program. These primary criteria constitute the essence of a rational conception of merit. A primary criterion is a necessary condition that qualifies someone for a job or opening.

There is a third sense in which race or gender is job relevant, where one could even say it is a *primary* criterion. One must be Catholic to be a priest, Jewish to be a rabbi, or Protestant to be a minister, and so on. Again, it is perfectly appropriate—indeed, probably necessary—to have an African American minister for a black congregation. But these cases have nothing to do with affirmative action.

In place of the merit or qualifications-only standard, Ronald Dworkin proposes a utilitarian standard. By this standard, a job or student admissions qualification is relevant only if it is "publicly useful." Race or gender can be publicly useful, too. For example, a surgeon having black skin may be as publicly useful as another surgeon having quick hands. As Dworkin explains:

There is no combination of abilities and skills and traits that constitutes "merit" in the abstract; if quick hands count as "merit" in the case of a prospective surgeon, this is because quick hands will enable him to serve the public better. . . . If a black skin will . . . enable another doctor to do a different medical job better, then that black skin is by the same token "merit" as well.[41]

So Dworkin claims that race or skin color, by his publicly useful standard, can be as rational and meritorious as the traditional qualifications-only standard.

The claim has two difficulties. First, Dworkin needs to explain more clearly the relation between race or gender and the traditional qualifications standard. In terms of my threefold distinction concerning the relevance of race/ethnicity/gender to job qualifications, his example involves my second meaning of relevance. Regarding his example, race, ethnicity, or gender can count as a secondary criterion of merit but not a primary criterion. Dworkin, however, does make race a primary criterion of job qualification. If in a given case, an African American surgeon is more inclined than a white surgeon to serve poor black communities because he feels a kinship with and moral obligation toward black people, then his black skin is a secondary criterion of merit. The same could be said for my above example according to which some women feel more comfortable going to a female physician, or my Japanese professor example. Examples like these, however, in no way imply that race, ethnicity, or gender is a primary criterion of merit (or of job qualifications). In the case of being a skilled or competent surgeon, the primary criteria (or necessary conditions) include such attributes as manual dexterity (Dworkin's "quick hands"), high intelligence, good medical education, and others. But black, or any other skin color, or gender, is not one of them. Other black surgeons may choose not to go into poor black communities; they may choose to go into a predominantly white hospital. Conversely, some white surgeons may feel a moral duty to serve a poor black community, just as white civil rights workers went to the South in the 1960s to help register blacks as voters. And while many women feel more comfortable with a female physician, others choose a male physician, just as many men have female physicians. And one can be a competent professor of Japanese linguistics and culture without being

Japanese. In this context, there is no necessary connection between race, ethnicity, or gender and merit.

Second, it is misleading to reduce or translate *any* qualification into what is publicly useful. A skilled surgeon who is not hired because the market is saturated with surgeons, or another who is not hired because of his white skin (affirmative action discrimination), or still another who is not hired because of her black skin (prejudicial discrimination)—none of them ceases to be a skilled surgeon, even though, by definition, they are not publicly useful as surgeons. Of course, they are *potentially* publicly useful, and perhaps that is Dworkin's meaning. If so, he should be more clear about this.

On the other hand, it must be said, I think, that proponents of the traditional merit-only standard have a conception of merit that is not as rationally and reasonably meritorious as they claim. As we have seen, this traditional view seems perfectly comfortable with such unmeritorious factors as the old-boy network, cronyism, nepotism, and widespread legacy preference, all of which disproportionately and unreasonably favor wealthy white males. Money itself becomes a criterion or sign of merit. The danger is that this idea of merit will produce a meritocracy instead of a true democracy. Rawls presents an alarming sketch of meritocracy:

> A meritocratic society . . . follows the principle of careers open to talents and uses equality of opportunity as a way of releasing men's [i.e., persons'] energies in the pursuit of economic prosperity and political dominion. There exists a marked disparity between the upper and lower classes in both means of life and the rights and privileges of organizational authority. The culture of the poorer strata is impoverished while that of the governing and technocratic elite is securely based on the service of the national ends of power and wealth. Equality of opportunity means an equal chance to leave the less fortunate behind in the personal quest for influence and social position.[42]

In a constitutional democracy, the second principle of justice (both the equal opportunity and difference principles) does indeed imply a concept of merit, but a concept that is rational, reasonable, and fair to all persons in society as free and equal citizens. Operational definitions of merit must be periodically reviewed. A modest program of strong affirmative action, as I have proposed here, can play an important role in preventing merit from ossifying into meritocracy. If left unchecked, meritocracy will degenerate into oligarchy and plutocracy.

In sum, the antimerit argument does not sufficiently analyze the role race, ethnicity, and gender should and should not play in employment, promotions, and student admissions.

Cross-Time Wholes Argument

This argument is unique to Thomas Hill. He criticizes conventional arguments for affirmative action, because they communicate the wrong message about affirmative action to minority groups, women, and white men. Conventional arguments are one-sided: they are exclusively backward-looking or exclusively forward-looking. The former defend affirmative action by appealing to some form of justice, for example, reparations or compensatory justice, to rectify past injustices committed against blacks, other minority groups, and women. These arguments have two limitations. First, not all injustices can be rectified, for not all injuries are tangible. Many of the worst injustices suffered by blacks were psychological and intangible: "prejudicial attitudes damaged self-esteem, undermined motivations, limited realistic options, and made even 'officially open' opportunities seem undesirable. Racism and sexism were (and are) *insults*, not merely tangible *injuries*."[43] The second limitation is that these arguments do not focus on the future and what kind of society we want to create through affirmative action.

The forward-looking arguments are utilitarian. They emphasize the good consequences that affirmative action will produce, such as easing racial tensions, preventing riots, improving services in minority neighborhoods, reducing unemployment, removing inequities in income distribution, eliminating racial and sexual prejudice, and enhancing the self-esteem of blacks and women.[44] The message of these arguments is limited, too. They do not specifically address the real injustices inflicted upon blacks and women in the past, and how their rectification will shape the society we should have in the future.

Hill proposes that we undergird affirmative action with values that unite the past, present, and future. He calls these values cross-time wholes. In affirmative action, this means that race and gender relations should be governed by the values of mutual respect, trust, and fair opportunity for all within the context of a society that is a caring community. The right message we want to send to all concerned parties about affirmative action is one that embodies these three cross-time whole values.

Hill's argument has much to recommend it and agrees in several ways with my own concept of a personalist society governed by the principle of community. Despite the nobility of his message, I doubt it will satisfy white men, who see themselves as innocent victims of reverse injustice. Their resentment would probably be mitigated had Hill distinguished different types of affirmative action and indicated which programs are justifiable and which ones are not. That he did not do this must be regarded as a failing of his argument. For example, does his affirmative action message support racial and gender quotas in all areas of employment and education? His message is lacking in specifics.

The concept of justice in my own argument is, I contend, a cross-time whole value that includes past, present, and future. Insofar as my argument is against affirmative action, it holds that disfavored persons are the objects of injustice here and now, in the present. To the extent that my argument supports affirmative action, it originates in past injustices against aggrieved groups and terminates in achieving racial/ethnic/gender justice now and in the future.

11

COMMUNITY AND THE ENVIRONMENTAL CRISIS

Perhaps the most serious and urgent global problem facing humankind today is Earth's environmental crisis. It includes the problem of world hunger, poverty, and disease; and it is more fundamental than the problem of international terrorism, as I explain later. That it is a crisis cannot be reasonably disputed; the evidence to support it is overwhelming. Indeed, crisis may not be a strong enough word.[1] Yet, when it comes to Earth's health, far too many people are in a state of denial. They act as if Earth's limited resources will last forever. Materialism, greed, hedonism, and selfishness are the order of the day. Earth is unmercifully exploited for commercial and recreational gain. Since 1980, Earth has been in what ecologists call an "overshoot-and-collapse" mode: humanity's collective demands for the world's natural resources have exceeded Earth's capacity to regenerate them.[2] In 1999, this margin of excess was 20 percent, and it is widening by about 1 percent annually. Obviously, this trend must be reversed for the sake of Earth and all of its inhabitants, human and nonhuman. But to do so, humans must make significant changes in their lifestyles and values, and make them soon. Otherwise, the planet that we bequeath to future generations of humans will be so radically degraded that it will be unable to sustain civilization and human flourishing. Civilization will collapse.

The aim of this chapter is to show how the environmental crisis is rooted in ethics, that it is essentially a crisis of values created by how we *choose* to treat the natural environment compared to other conflicting values we hold dear. In order to understand the enormity of the crisis, I first sketch eleven dimensions of the environmental crisis. Then I explain how some traditional values and ethical ideas have brought it about, and critically examine the chief ethical theories that have been proposed for resolving the crisis. Since I find all these theories inadequate to the task, I conclude by briefly developing my own personalist theory, within which I sketch an idea of capitalism capable of overcoming the environmental crisis.

THE ENVIRONMENTAL CRISIS

Eleven dimensions of the environmental crisis are: (1) overpopulation, (2) global warming, (3) deforestation, (4) species extinction, (5) soil degradation/erosion, (6) water shortages/pollution, (7) collapsing fisheries, (8) air pollution, (9) urbanization/sprawl/trash, (10) poverty and public health, and (11) political instability and terrorism.[3]

Population Growth

Earth's population is now over 7 billion and has grown explosively in the last two hundred years.[4] Earth did not reach 1 billion people until 1804. Since then, Earth has taken progressively much less time to reach additional billions. World population passed the 2 billion mark in 1927, 3 billion in 1960, 4 billion in 1974, and 5 billion in 1987. Earth's population is expected to reach 9.1 billion in the year 2050. Exacerbating the population explosion is the fact that 90 percent of population growth is in the poorest countries. Increasing numbers of people need and devour more natural resources such as forests, fresh water, and oil, coal, and natural gas reserves, while at the same time they deplete and pollute the very resources needed to survive. For the well-being of the human race and the planet as a whole, world population growth must soon level off and indeed reverse itself. At the dawn of the agricultural age, the weight of all humans and their livestock and pets constituted only 0.1 percent of the weight of all vertebrates. Today, that percentage is an astounding 98 percent. As human population grows, the number of species with which we share the planet shrinks. Rapid and uncontrolled population growth is a disaster for biodiversity.[5]

Population growth, however, is spread very unevenly throughout the globe. The wealthiest and most developed nations have stable population rates. The highest rates are mostly in the Indian subcontinent and sub-Saharan desert, the poorest regions on Earth. Poverty itself is a major cause of environmental degradation. Rain forests dwindle because the poor cut trees for firewood and farming. The poor also erode their soil by overplowing and overgrazing land. In turn, these environmentally destructive practices exacerbate their poverty. Unless we stabilize world population, we cannot eliminate world poverty and hunger, and other measures we take to restore a healthy Earth will be unsuccessful.

Global Warming

Recently, no dimension of the environmental crisis has received as much attention as global warming.[6] There is good reason for all the concern. In the last few decades, Earth's average temperature has been rising at an alarming rate. Since 1970, it has risen nearly 1.4 degrees Fahrenheit, and in each decade the increase has been greater than the preceding one. Earth has experienced more than twenty-two of the warmest years on record since 1980.[7] The decade of 2000–2009 was the warmest one on record.[8] Globally, 2011 was one of the fifteen warmest years ever recorded. In the contiguous United States, 2012 turned out to be the warmest year recorded, according to the National Oceanic and Atmospheric Administration (NOAA).[9]

The major cause of this rapid rise in temperature is human activity that releases huge quantities of greenhouse gasses into the atmosphere. Greenhouse gases heat up Earth's atmosphere, thus causing global warming. The leading greenhouse gas is carbon dioxide (CO_2). The human activity that produces excessive levels of CO_2 is twofold: the burning of fossil fuels (petroleum, coal, and natural gas), and deforestation. The burning of fossil fuels releases tremendous amounts of CO_2 into the atmosphere, almost 32 billion tons annually. The principal cause of deforestation worldwide is the burning of trees (and related brush) for fuel and agriculture. Deforestation accounts for 20 percent of global CO_2 emissions.

Although the United States has slightly less than 4.5 percent of the world's population, it produces 25 percent of the world's CO_2 emissions,[10] 40 percent of which comes from heating, cooling, and powering office space. This fact alone underscores the urgency that the United States set a much better example than it has in substantially lowering emissions.

The amount of CO_2 in the atmosphere has increased substantially since the Industrial Revolution, when it was about 270 parts per million (ppm). In 2004, it was 377 ppm, far above any level in the last 740,000 years, with most of the rise coming after 1959. Since then it has increased every year. It is now approaching a level not seen in 55 million years, when the whole earth was a tropical planet with no polar ice caps and sea levels were 260 feet higher than today. Some experts predict it could reach 560 ppm by 2050 if current trends continue.[11] Environmental scientists consider 350 ppm the maximum "safe" level. Above that, we "threaten the ecological life-support systems that have developed in the late Quaternary environment, and severely challenge the viability of contemporary human societies."[12] In 2010, CO_2 concentrations exceeded 390 ppm for the first time, an increase of 2.1 ppm from 2009.[13]

Here is a short list of what has happened already because of global warming. Mountaintop glaciers (our so-called reservoirs in the sky) are rapidly shrinking. Coral reefs are dying as seawater warms. Drought is widespread in Africa and Asia. The Arctic permafrost is melting. Each year lakes and rivers are freezing later and melting earlier. Many plants and animals are shifting polewards and to higher regions.

Of particular concern are rising sea levels brought about by two factors. First, there is the recent accelerated melting of the polar ice caps, mountain glaciers, and Greenland ice sheet (the last is as much as 1.5 miles thick). Second, warmer water rises because of thermal expansion. In 2001, the Intergovernmental Panel on Climate Change (IPCC) projected that sea levels would rise during the century by 0.09–0.88 meters as a result of ice melting and thermal expansion.[14] For each one-meter rise in sea level, the shoreline retreats an average of 1,500 meters, almost a mile. At present rates of melting, a one meter rise is almost certain in this century. Such a rise would affect the following regions. One-half of Bangladesh's rice fields would be inundated (one of the world's most densely populated countries). The rice-growing floodplains of India, Thailand, Viet Nam, Indonesia, and China would also be drowned. More than a third of Shanghai (population 13 million) would be under water. In the United States, 14,000 square miles, mostly the Middle Atlantic and Gulf Coast states, would be submerged.

Rising Arctic temperatures are melting the tundra and its underlying permafrost. Besides damaging buildings, pipelines, and roads, this melting releases large amounts of CO_2 into the atmosphere. Scientists estimate that 350–400 gigatons (a gigaton is a billion tons) of carbon are locked up in the Arctic permafrost.[15]

Paradoxically, if the Greenland ice sheet continues to melt, it would cause dramatically lower temperatures in Europe by disrupting the warming effect of the Gulf Stream. The warm, lighter water of the Gulf Stream rides on the surface until it reaches Europe and releases its heat. On its return, the cold water sinks until it reaches the Gulf, warms up again, and repeats the cycle back to Europe. But vast amounts of melting freshwater from the Greenland ice sheet would dilute the saltwater, making it lighter. The lighter surface water would stall the Gulf Stream. This is just one example of how colder weather in some situations is consistent with overall global warming. For this reason, some scientists and others prefer the term *climate change*. Nevertheless, I still think that *global warming* is preferable because it is more accurate: it focuses on the overall breadth and long-term direction of the earth's climate change that has been going on for decades because of the various forms of human activity sketched in this chapter.

Two magnificent Arctic species whose very survival may be at stake are polar bears and ice-living seals. The latter are a basic food source for the Inuit. Two-thirds of the world's polar bears are expected to disappear by 2050— including the entire population of Alaska—because of thinning sea ice caused by global warming, according to a recent study by the US Geological Survey. In the Antarctic, rising temperatures threaten the penguins, who have evolved to survive in the cold.

The IPCC 2001 report predicted that Earth's average temperature would rise between 2.5 to 10.4 degrees Fahrenheit in this century. Even the lower figure would produce disastrous consequences: severe melting of glaciers (especially the Greenland ice sheet), shrinking polar and mountain ice caps, and rising seas would flood coastal areas, drown wetlands, contaminate estuaries, and pollute drinking water; severe inland droughts would create massive food shortages, forest fires, and wildlife extinction. Public health would drastically suffer due to many infectious, waterborne diseases such as malaria. Rising sea levels would contaminate drinking water with salt. Higher levels of urban ozone would increase respiratory ailments and make them more severe than now. Disease-carrying insects and rodents would increase substantially. Tropical storms would become much more frequent and severe. Storms like Hurricane Katrina would become commonplace. The complete melting of the Greenland ice sheet would raise sea levels by twenty-three feet (although this would not happen at the lower end of the temperature rise projection).

What must stop immediately are the current subsidies to the fossil fuel industry, which are costing world taxpayers $210 billion a year. The oil industry itself has a larger tax incentive relative to its size than any other industry in the United States. And what do taxpayers get for their money? Lester Brown tells us: "To subsidize the use of fossil fuels is to subsidize crop-withering heat waves, melting ice, rising seas, and more destructive storms."[16] Adding insult to injury are the record profits of the big oil companies.

Deforestation

Trees, especially densely packed trees in forests and woods, are among nature's most valuable ecological objects. They perform several vital environmental functions. Forests sequester carbon. They are storehouses of water, which they gradually release into the atmosphere by a process called evapotranspiration that provides needed rainfall for nearby croplands and grazing areas. Forests recharge aquifers. They prevent soil erosion, river silting, flooding, and landslides. In cities, trees trap particulate matter. They have a cooling effect in warm weather and climates, thus reducing the need for air conditioning. Forests contain the highest land concentrations of biodiversity. Tropical rainforests in particular are by far the richest areas of the biosphere, housing over one-half of Earth's species. The ecological services provided by trees are far more valuable than the lumber they provide, which some countries have discovered only too late, for example, Nigeria and the Philippines.[17]

At the beginning of the twentieth century, Earth's forested area stood at 5 billion hectares (a hectare equals 2.471 acres), and now it is 3.9 billion. The remaining forest cover is equally divided between the tropical/subtropical forests in developing countries and the temperate/boreal forests of industrial nations. Recent world forest loss is concentrated in the poor, developing countries. Since 1990, the loss in these nations has averaged 13 million hectares annually, about the size of Kansas. Overall, the developing world is losing 6 percent of its forests per decade. In contrast, the affluent industrial world is actually gaining about 3.6 million hectares of forestland a year because of abandoned farmland that is naturally regrowing and the spread of commercial forest plantations. This gain has occurred in Russia and New England. The latter's forested area has increased from a low of one-third two centuries ago to three-fourths today, about its original size. However, tree plantations are a far cry from old-growth forests. Only 40 percent of the world's remaining forests can be classified as *frontier forest*. This is defined as "large, intact, natural forest systems relatively undisturbed and big enough to maintain all of their biodiversity."[18] Since tree plantations are ecologically inferior to old-growth and frontier forests, what remains of them must be preserved.

What is particularly tragic is the rapid destruction of tropical rain forests. This deforestation is concentrated in three main areas of the developing world: Borneo, the Congo Basin, and the Brazilian Amazon. Brazil has already lost 97 percent of its Atlantic rainforest, and now it is destroying the largest rainforest on Earth. The Amazon rainforest was basically intact until about 1970 and was as large as Europe. Since then, 20 percent of it has disappeared.

Tropical forests that are clear-cut or burned off rarely recover; they turn to wasteland or scrub forest. Poverty is the principal cause of this destruction. Of the 3.34 billion cubic meters of wood harvested in 2003, over one-half was used for fuel. In poor, developing countries, firewood accounts for nearly three-fourths of the total. Foreign logging has also taken a heavy toll in these nations. A typical corporation, once it has harvested a country's trees, has no interest in renewing the land; it simply moves on to another poor nation.

Haiti, one of the poorest countries in the world, is a microcosm of what

CONTEMPORARY ETHICAL ISSUES

the planet will be like if deforestation continues. Haiti is a classic case of over-shoot and collapse. A country of 8 million people, it was once largely covered with forests. Now only 2 percent of its original forest cover remains. Most has been cut for firewood. With the trees gone, the topsoil has washed away. The land cannot support agriculture and grazing. Haiti survives on international food aid and economic assistance. Although once a tropical paradise, it has destroyed its economy by destroying the ecology that supported it.[19]

Species Extinction

Worldwide, species are disappearing one thousand times faster than they have evolved. Twenty-seven thousand species a year of flora and fauna are lost because of deforestation, poaching, and water pollution. The number of birds, mammals, and fish species that are at risk or in immediate danger of extinction is in the double digits: 12 percent of birds, 33 percent of mammals, and 46 percent of fish. Among mammals, 240 known species of primates are at risk.[20]

It is said that we are in the early stages of Earth's sixth great extinction. Earlier extinctions, however, were caused by natural forces. For the first time in Earth's long history of life and evolution, a species has evolved with the capacity to overturn evolution and extinguish itself along with much of life itself. Paleontology tells us that each of the earlier five great extinctions was a serious evolutionary setback for the whole biosphere. As is well-known, the last one occurred some 65 million years ago, when a six-mile-wide asteroid slammed into the waters off the now Yucatan peninsula with the force of over 10 million hydrogen bombs. The explosion spewed enormous amounts of dust and debris into the atmosphere, blocking out the sun and dramatically cooling the planet. The dinosaurs were extinguished along with more than 20 percent of all life forms on Earth. Are humans becoming the new asteroid?

As various life forms disappear, the biological functions that nature provides are diminished: pollination, seed dispersal, insect control, and nutrient cycling. The loss of species weakens the whole biosphere. Fewer species also means fewer potential sources of new foods and medicines.

The greatest threat to biodiversity is the loss of the tropical rainforests. As we burn off the Amazon rainforest, we are burning off a great library of genetic information. South of the Amazon basin is a huge savanna-like region called the *cerrado*. It is about the size of Europe. In both these regions, farmers and ranchers are opening up vast tracts of land. Farmers are growing soybeans for biodiesel and sugarcane for ethanol, replacements for fossil fuels. As world oil reserves dwindle and gasoline prices rise, and as motorists look for cleaner burning fuels, the rainforests are further threatened.

Species extinction is a profound and irreplaceable loss. E. O. Wilson calls every species a "masterpiece, exquisitely adapted to the particular environment in which it has survived for thousands to millions of years."[21] Environmental philosopher Holmes Rolston III has characterized species extinction as "superkilling" and we humans as the "super-killers."[22]

Soil Erosion/Degradation

"The thin layer of topsoil that covers the planet's land surface is the foundation of civilization."[23] The Agricultural Revolution ended humans' six-million-year nomadic existence as hunter-gatherers, preceded by an original arboreal, nonhunting, chiefly plant-eating lifestyle.[24] Agriculture meant a settled way of life that eventually led to the establishment of civilization. Without agriculture, civilization cannot exist.

Soil supports agriculture, grazing, grassland, and forests—in a word, all land plant life. Soil is the medium in which plants grow. In turn, plants protect soil from erosion. Human activity has been disrupting this relationship. In the last century, soil erosion began to exceed soil formation in large areas of the world.

Soil erosion is one form of soil degradation. Besides erosion, degradation includes nutrient loss caused by improper farming methods, desertification (the process of converting productive land into desert-like wasteland through overuse and mismanagement), and ruinous salt buildup in soil caused by irrigation. The last condition is one of several reasons dam building has become increasingly controversial. More than 40 percent of the world's agricultural soil is seriously degraded, and 67 percent is significantly damaged. Almost 50 percent of grasslands are lightly to moderately degraded, and 5 percent is severely degraded. Soil erosion is caused by overplowing, overgrazing, deforestation, and agricultural expansion onto marginal land.

Ten percent of Earth's land surface is cropland, and 20 percent is range-land. The latter is too dry, too steeply sloped, and not fertile enough to support crop production. This land supports the world's 3.2 billion cattle, sheep, and goats that support the 180 million people who make their living as pastoral-ists tending to these livestock. In other parts of the world, however, range-lands are exploited by large-scale commercial ranching, for example, the 95 million sheep in Australia.

The ultimate form of soil degradation is desertification. Dust bowls are perhaps its most visual expression. The 1930s dust bowl in the Great Plains was caused by overplowing. Dust bowls, once rare, are now commonplace. Not surprisingly, large-scale desertification is concentrated in the poorer regions of Earth, in Asia and Africa, which together contain about 5 billion of the world's over 7 billion people. China, with 1 billion people to feed, is being affected by desertification more than any other major country. In many countries around the world, the overplowing, overgrazing, and overcutting of trees that is driving desertification is accelerating because of the continuing growth of both human and livestock populations. Stopping desertification, then, depends on controlling both populations.

Water Shortages/Pollution

Only 3 percent of Earth's water is fresh, and potable water is becoming increasingly scarce. Human consumption of water has increased sixfold in the past century, double the rate of population growth. Although health is closely related to safe water, 1.1 billion people have water unfit to drink because of pollution from cities, farms, and factories. In developing countries, most sewage flows untreated into lakes, rivers, and streams. Three million people a year die from waterborne diseases.

Besides overpopulation, which figures into every dimension of the envi-ronmental crisis, water shortages are caused by aquifer overpumping and excessive irrigation. As water tables fall, the springs that feed rivers dry up and reduce river flows. Especially important here are the reservoirs in the sky, the masses of snow and ice in the mountains that store freshwater until it is fed into rivers during the dry summer season. However, global warming has turned some mountain snow precipitation into rain. This increased rainfall means more flooding during the rainy season and less snowmelt for rivers during the dry season.

Seventy percent of irrigation water is used for agriculture. It takes one thousand tons of water to produce one ton of grain. Irrigation means building dams and diverting rivers from their natural beds into vast reservoirs, which increase evaporation and destroy a river's natural ecosystem, including its fisheries. As river flows are reduced downstream and may even run dry, the lakes into which they normally empty shrink, and many eventually disappear. Lake Chad in central Africa, the Aral Sea in Central Asia, and the Sea of Galilee are three famous examples of disappearing bodies of water. The Colorado and Nile rivers rarely make it to the sea. Thousands of lakes worldwide exist only on half century-old maps. As more and more people live in cities, they increasingly siphon water from the world's farmers, who try to feed the 70 million people a year that are added to Earth's population. As a result, the gap between global water consumption and its sustainable water supply continues to widen. Each year, the drop in the water table is greater than the year before. In the future, both aquifer depletion and the diversion of water to cities will contribute to the growing irrigation deficit and so to a growing grain deficit in many water-short countries.[25]

Collapsing Fisheries

Ninety-seven percent of Earth's water is salt water. Unfortunately, its valuable fish stocks are being depleted rapidly because of disappearing coastal wetlands, sea grasses, and coral reefs. Fishing fleets are 40 percent larger than the oceans can support. The catch is declining for one-third of major commercial fish. Trawling destroys large areas of ocean floor. Warming water is killing coral reefs. Fertilizer and pesticide runoffs create dead zones in oceans.

After World War II, accelerating population growth and rising incomes drove the demand for seafood upward at a record pace. At the same time, advances in fishing technologies, including huge refrigerated processing ships, enabled trawlers to exploit distant oceans, as fisheries responded to growing world demand. Oceanic fish catches climbed from 19 million tons in 1950 to 93 million tons in 1997, five times more than population growth during this period. Per capita fish consumption has slightly declined from seventeen kilograms in 1988 to fourteen now. Today, 75 percent of fisheries are being fished at or beyond their sustainable capacity. Many are in decline and some have collapsed. Ninety percent of large ocean fish have become extinct in the last fifty years.[26]

Ninety percent of fish residing in the ocean rely on coastal wetlands, mangrove swamps, and rivers as spawning areas. Well over 50 percent of the original area of mangrove forests in tropical and subtropical countries has been lost. The disappearance of coastal wetlands in industrial countries is even greater. In Italy, for example, whose nurseries supply the Mediterranean Sea, the loss is 95 percent. Damage to coral reefs, which are breeding grounds for fish in tropical and subtropical waters, is also taking a hit. Between 2000 and 2004, the percentage of destroyed reefs worldwide increased from eleven to twenty. As the reefs deteriorate, so do the fisheries that depend on them.

Once again, governments are subsidizing the wrong industry. The global excess fleet capacity has been brought about by longstanding government loans for new boats and fishing gear. This policy was based on the erroneous assumption that fish harvests would indefinitely continue to grow.

If the worldwide demand for seafood is to be satisfied, it will be done by expanding fish farming (aquaculture). But putting fish in ponds and cages means they must be fed, which further strains land resources.

Air Pollution

Each year billions of tons of industrial emissions and toxic pollutants are released into the air. These include CO_2, sulfur, methane, nitrogen oxide, lead, mercury, and cadmium. Such massive pollution depletes the air's ozone layer, causes global warming, kills our forests and lakes with acid rain, and threatens human health. Although Western democracies have made significant progress in the last thirty years in reducing the level of some pollutants through lower motor vehicle and industrial emissions, the reverse is true for the rest of the globe. In some parts of the world, lung cancer is the leading cause of death.

Breathing air in some cities is equivalent to smoking two packs of cigarettes daily. Three million deaths a year worldwide are attributed to air pollutants, three times the number of traffic fatalities. Even worse, cigarette smoke kills 4.9 million people a year.[27]

The precious layer of ozone in the stratosphere shields Earth from the sun's harmful ultraviolet radiation. Greenhouse gases such as CO_2, methane, sulfur, and nitrogen oxides are destroying this vital barrier. So are chlorofluorocarbons (CFCs) used in refrigerants, air-conditioning, aerosol sprays, and Styrofoam containers—good reason why nations like the United States have taken measures to remove it from the market place. Although much progress has been made in reducing CFCs, Earth has lost between 2 and 3 percent of its ozone layer since 1969. In 1985, scientists discovered a huge hole in the ozone layer over Antarctica the size of the continental United States.

Air pollution is linked to acid rain, which is caused by the combination of fossil fuel emissions, sunlight, and water vapor. This combination produces clouds of nitric and sulfuric acids that can travel thousands of miles, where their poisonous compounds are washed back to earth in rainfall. The harmful effects of acid rain are enormous. It has killed all life in thousands of lakes and in many rivers. Acid rain has damaged ground water, soil, and buildings. More than 15 million acres of virgin forest in Europe, North America, and third world countries are thought to be dead or dying because of acid rain.

One of the most devastating effects of air pollution is *global dimming*, which has received much attention lately. As noted earlier, the direct effect of burning fossil fuels is the release of greenhouse gases such as CO_2 into the atmosphere, which causes global warming. The indirect effect of this burning is the production of visible pollutants such as sulfur dioxide, soot, and ash. Not only are these by-products harmful in themselves by causing problems such as smog, acid rain, and respiratory problems, they also cause the sun's light to be reflected back into space. Less sunlight reaches the earth, thus causing global dimming.

Global dimming has several harmful environmental effects. First, many scientists think that it led to the great famines in Northern Africa in the 1970s and 1980s. Less heat from the sun cooled waters in the Northern hemisphere, resulting in much less rain for the African Sahel region. Second, scientists predict that if global dimming is allowed to continue unabated, it will have a serious adverse effect on the Asian monsoons upon which 3 billion people—one half of Earth's population—depend. Third, global dimming is masking the full impact of global warming. Since less of the sun's heat is reaching the planet than otherwise would be the case, humans are causing more global warming than they realize. For example, a significant source of global dimming are *contrails*, the vapor from high-flying planes. After 9/11, when all commercial aircrafts were grounded for three days, scientists determined that the temperature rose by over 1 degree centigrade. If humans were to reduce air pollution worldwide without fighting global warming, the results of the greenhouse effect would be much more rapidly devastating to the environment. The message is clear, then. As we reduce the harmful effects of air pollution, it is all the more urgent and imperative that we effectively resolve the problem of global warming by immediately and substantially lowering the levels of greenhouse gas emissions.[28]

Urbanization/Sprawl/Trash

Urbanization, which includes suburban sprawl, has dominated population growth in the twentieth century. In 1900, 150 million people lived in cities. By 2000, it was 2.9 billion. Today more people live in cities than in rural areas. In 1900, only a few cities had one million inhabitants; today it is 408. Twenty megacities have more than 10 million residents. Tokyo leads the way with a population of 35 million, more than the whole of Canada. Almost all the population growth predicted by 2050 will occur in cities of developing countries.[29]

Cities and their metropolitan suburbs generate enormous amounts of human waste and trash. On average, each American generates 1,643 pounds of trash a year, which takes thirty tons of the earth's resources to produce. Not all of this trash is collected. Waste management collects 3.4 pounds of waste a day for every American, twice as much as in 1960 and ten times as much as 100 years ago. The United States discards 16 billion disposable diapers and 2 billion razors annually. Unfortunately, America recycles only 32 percent of its trash, although twice that of fifteen years ago. A large percentage ends up in landfills, which are serious environmental problems for the following reasons. Much of their content is nonbiodegradable plastic. Landfills take up vital space. They are hazardous to surface and underground water. Incinerating combustible waste produces gases that contribute to air pollution. The resulting ash must be treated and disposed of. Beyond landfills, the problem of nuclear waste is especially dangerous, and its radioactive effects can last thousands of years. Twenty percent of America's power plants are nuclear.

A growing concern of environmentalists is urban deforestation. In some US urban areas, deforestation has continued for the last twenty years at a pace of fifty acres a day for 365 days a year. As a result, temperatures in cities have been rising. In Atlanta, for example, where 380,000 acres were destroyed between 1973 and 1979, temperatures are five to eight degrees higher than in the surrounding wooded countryside. Happily, many cities in America are beginning to reverse deforestation. More than two thousand have long-term planting and preservation plans. Los Angeles will plant one million trees over the next thirty years. San Francisco has enacted laws that treat mature trees like historic buildings. A key factor in reversing urban deforestation is curbing Americans' penchant for oversized homes on mostly treeless lots.

Poverty and Public Health

As we have seen, poverty is both a cause and effect of environmental degradation. Poor people burn an inordinate number of trees and related brush, and they overplow arable land. As these activities go unchecked, the society eventually collapses ecologically and economically, and the poor become even more destitute (as, for example, in Haiti). Attacking poverty and restoring the natural environment are inextricably linked.

Poverty and poor health also go together and reinforce each other. A leading indicator of health is life expectancy. After World War II, it increased globally because of advances in vaccines, antibiotics, and food production. Today, the range of life expectancy among the various nations is wider than at any time in history. It ranges from a low of 33 in Swaziland and 37 in Botswana to a high of 82 in Japan and 81 in Iceland. Life expectancy in America is 77.

Unfortunately, the gap between the richest 1 billion and the poorest 1 billion people is growing. Worldwide, 1.2 billion people are undernourished, underweight, or often hungry. The poor suffer from infectious diseases related to water pollution, lack of vaccines, and weak immune systems. Not surprisingly, the HIV epidemic is concentrated in sub-Saharan Africa, the world's leading region of poverty. HIV was first discovered in 1981, and by 2004, 104 million people were infected. Infection rates are still climbing. Unless this disease is brought under control, one of the poorest regions of the world faces economic and ecological collapse. In contrast, the affluent have diseases and behavior related to aging and a hedonistic lifestyle, such as heart disease, cancer, obesity, smoking, diets rich in saturated fats and sugar, and exercise deprivation.

Lack of education is a major cause of overpopulation and its resulting poverty. Illiterate women generally have much larger families than do literate women. In Brazil, illiterate women on average have more than six children each, whereas literate women have only two. As education rises so does income and health. One of the most effective ways to stabilize population and eradicate poverty is to educate the poor, particularly poor women. In Lester Brown's words: "Educating women is the key to breaking the poverty cycle."[30] Education also improves health. As women's education rises, they take better care of themselves and their children as they learn the basics of healthcare and nutrition.

Political Instability and Terrorism

Since 9/11, terrorism is the number one global issue in the minds of many people. However, international terrorism and its companion problem of political instability are related to several aspects of the environmental crisis. Recently, the concept of the failed state has come to the fore. This concept denotes the politically unstable nations that emerged in postcolonial Asia and Africa, and from the later breakup of the Soviet Union. Basically, a failed state is a country that no longer has a central government. It is ruled by rival warlords or tribal chiefs, as in Somalia, for example. Such states become fertile grounds for spawning terrorism, which is directed against affluent and industrialized nations like the United States.

Foreign Affairs recently published a study ranking the top sixty failed or failing nations.[31] Nations were evaluated by twelve criteria. The three most important ones are: uneven development, loss of governmental legitimacy, and demographic pressure. The first means that wealth is concentrated within a small group, and the rest of society is poor. The wealthy rulers are usually corrupt. Civil conflicts between the rich and poor are common. The second criterion denotes the absence of a central government. The power vacuum is filled by factions loyal to rival warlords, tribal chieftains, or religious leaders. Demographic pressure refers to rapid population growth and its attending problems, such as diminishing croplands, dwindling water supplies, and lack of schools.

The highest state on the list is Côte d'Ivoire, followed, in order, by Democratic Republic of the Congo, Sudan, Iraq, Somalia, Sierra Leone, Chad, Yemen, Liberia, and Haiti. Next come Afghanistan, Rwanda, and North Korea. Also on the list are Saudi Arabia, Russia, Venezuela, Indonesia, and Pakistan. Some of these states are associated with terrorism. Many are poor.

Since a failed or failing state is ripe for terrorism, and since environmental degradation and its various causes have contributed to this failing, terrorism must be seen as deeply connected with the environmental crisis. Therefore, both issues must be addressed simultaneously.

ETHICS AND THE ENVIRONMENT

The global environmental crisis has its origin in the Industrial Revolution beginning in England in the late eighteenth century. Since then, humans have been busily mining fossil fuels to power it at a rate ten thousand times greater than the fuels were made and returning greenhouse gasses to the atmosphere at a corresponding increased rate over preindustrial times. Paralleling the Industrial Revolution is the population explosion mentioned earlier. The world population was less than one billion when the Industrial Revolution began, and now it is more than 7 billion. The revolution was accelerated and expanded by capitalism as its economic base—industrial capitalism, as I call it. After World War II, industrial capitalism, spearheaded by the United

States, took the form of what Lester Brown calls a "Plan A economy." It is based on fossil fuels, is automobile centered, and is a throwaway economy regarding consumer products.[32] As a result, industrial capitalism intensified its attack on the natural environment.

In turn, these combined forces were directed by a traditional ethics that is essentially anthropocentric (or homocentric), a human-centered ethics. This quartet of causes—the Industrial Revolution, the population explosion, industrial capitalism, and anthropocentric ethics—is, I contend, the central reason for the environmental crisis. As one environmental philosopher it: "Since the beginning of the industrial age our image of . . . [nature] has been that of a stockpile of resources and a sink for wastes."[33]

Anthropocentrism (Homocentrism)

Fundamental to this image of nature is anthropocentric ethics. Of the four causes, anthropocentric ethics is the basic one, for a society's ethics and values, whether religion-based or not, determines the nature of its economy, its attitudes toward population control, and the ends to which its technology is put. Since I examined homocentrism at length in chapter 9, I summarize it here. For homocentrism, only humans have moral status, and only interpersonal and intrapersonal activity has moral significance. Because humans have moral status, they have intrinsic value. The moral status and intrinsic value of humans is expressed in such well-known phrases as: All human life is sacred, every human being has worth and dignity, and all persons have rights. In contrast, all nonhuman nature lacks moral status and has merely instrumental value. Nonhuman nature can be used for whatever ends or purposes humans deem fit and rational. Homocentric ethics creates a separate-and-unequal relation of humans toward nature, a superior-inferior relation.

When anthropocentric ethics is combined with the Industrial Revolution and with capitalism, the results for the natural environment are devastating. The Industrial Revolution provides humans with an ongoing, spiraling technology that enables them to exploit the resources of nature and severely damage the environment, and anthropocentric ethics has no moral principles and values to restrain this burgeoning technological power. Accelerating the exploitation of nature is capitalism's twin values of production and consumption, a combination William Wordsworth called the "getting and spending ethic." Driven by the profit motive, capitalists are compelled to continuously increase production. This means that demand must continuously increase. Since genuine needs are relatively constant, a demand for frivolous and unimportant products and services must be created and sustained. This demand is sustained by the throwaway mentality. In turn, it is reinforced by the advertising industry, which, in the service of big corporations, helps them sell huge quantities of junk that are quickly discarded. Feeding this buying frenzy is another American institution, the shopping mall, with its slogan "shop 'til you drop." The United States has more shopping malls than high schools. Some are larger than many towns. Most consumers who frequent them buy on impulse, conditioned by a steady stream of advertising. Two-thirds of newspaper content consists of ads. The average American spends one year of his life watching television commercials. To ensure the steady growth of consumption-addiction, the advertising industry targets children at increasingly younger ages. This spiraling cycle of production and consumption creates a relentless destruction of the natural environment.[34]

This is not to say, of course, that only capitalist nations are major polluters and ravagers of the environment. Before the collapse of communism, the Soviet Union and its satellite nations were among the worst environmental offenders. But they learned from the West, and now that communism is gone, it can no longer be blamed for Earth's environmental ills. Capitalist nations must be concerned with much more than maximizing production. Capitalism must be modified so that it is equally concerned with a fair distribution of productive assets and with a mode of production in harmony with nature rather than exploitative of it. Such a modification is required by my concept of democratic capitalism, briefly discussed in chapter 8.

Sentient-Centrism

To reverse the cycle of exploiting nature for commercial and recreational gain, the conventional wisdom has been that we must first replace its ethical foundation, anthropocentrism, with an ethical theory that respects and cares for the natural environment. This has proved to be a long and difficult process, beset with its own problems. The first major Western philosopher to challenge anthropocentric ethics is Jeremy Bentham (1748–1832), who was discussed in chapter 9. As the philosophical forefather of the animal rights and welfare movement, let me recall his famous statement about moral status: the [moral] question is not whether beings can reason or talk but whether they can *suffer*.[35]

Bentham rejects the anthropocentric claim that reason is the standard of moral status. Instead, he makes sentience its standard: All beings that can suffer, that have the capacity for pleasure and pain, have moral status and are thus worthy of moral consideration and protection. Since many nonhuman animals are sentient, they too possess moral status. For Bentham, then, all sentient animals, both human and nonhuman, have moral standing, and are equal members of the moral community. Bentham replaces rational anthropocentrism with mammalian sentient-centrism. As we saw earlier, Bentham's views have been developed by Peter Singer, beginning with his landmark book, *Animal Liberation*.[36] Singer is generally regarded as the philosophical founder of today's animal rights and welfare movement.

Although environmentalists are gratified that the animal rights and welfare movement extends moral status beyond the realm of human beings, they consider the ethical theory upon which it is based to be woefully inadequate for a comprehensive environmental ethics. On Bentham's and Singer's view, all nonsentient nature—nonsentient animals, plant life, and inanimate nature—lacks moral status; it has merely instrumental value. For environmentalists, this sentient-centrism is unacceptable. Moral status must be extended to nonsentient nature. But how far? To what beings? Two different answers have been given: *biocentrism* and *ecocentrism*.

Biocentrism

Biocentrism contends that all biological beings have moral status. Environmental philosophers Kenneth Goodpaster and Paul Taylor are leading proponents of this theory. In Goodpaster's seminal article, "On Being Morally Considerable,"[37] he argues that all living beings are deserving of moral consideration and respect, because only a living being is conative (or teleological): only it has inherent tendencies or inclinations that enable it to survive, grow, and reach natural fulfillment, for example, Aristotle's observation that an acorn has an inherent tendency to grow into an oak tree. Therefore, according to Goodpaster, anyone who interferes with or destroys these tendencies engages in immoral action. In addition, Taylor emphasizes that all biological beings are equal in moral status.[38]

Three criticisms have been leveled against biocentrism. First, it cannot adequately protect endangered species. A living being facing extinction is no more teleological than one not facing extinction and so is deserving of no greater moral protection than the latter, a view that enrages many environmentalists. Second, since Goodpaster and Taylor do not distinguish different degrees or levels of moral status, critics charge that their theory is impractical for making environmental decisions in conflicts where one being must be given priority over another. Third, their concept of moral status is so broad that they have trivialized its meaning. For instance, does a weed or a cockroach have the same moral standing as a human, dolphin, or chimpanzee?

Ecocentrism

Widening the moral circle still further is ecocentrism, which is favored by a majority of environmentalists. On this view, the whole natural environment, inanimate as well as animate, has moral status. However, there are two quite different versions of ecocentrism: individualistic and holistic. For individualistic ecocentrism, the whole earth is a vast ecosystem, and all individual beings within it have moral status. A rock and a river have as much moral standing as a person. The second and third above criticisms of biocentrism apply to ecocentrism, but even more strongly. Since individualistic ecocentrism does not distinguish different levels of moral status, it is unable to say that one being takes priority over another when they are in conflict with each other; and the theory further trivializes the meaning of moral status by applying it to a far greater range of beings than biocentrism does.

To overcome these difficulties, many environmentalists adopt holistic ecocentrism. According to this theory, the primary possessors of moral status are species and ecosystems, not individual beings within them; and the ultimate possessor of moral value is the planet Earth considered as the all-inclusive eco-system. This theory is most associated with Aldo Leopold's groundbreaking work, *A Sand County Almanac*,[39] which has become a kind of bible of the environmentalist movement; with Arne Naess's deep ecology; and with ecological feminism (also called ecofeminism).

Leopold's Land Ethic

Leopold calls his theory a land ethic. "The land ethic simply enlarges the boundaries of the [moral] community to include soils, waters, plants, and animals, or collectively: the land."[40] The land is the whole earth, which he calls a "biotic community." It is ipso facto a moral community. Hence, an action is morally right when it promotes the integrity, diversity, harmony, and beauty of the biotic community; it is morally wrong when it does otherwise.[41] Within the biotic community, all species and ecosystems are equal. Humans and sentient animals have no privileged moral status in nature, no special rights. Humans, other sentient animals, nonsentient animals, plants, and inanimate nature are all moral equals. Any hierarchy of nature that distinguishes different classes of beings and arranges them in terms of higher and lower, superior and inferior, is a fallacious and harmful legacy of ethical anthropocentrism and must be rejected. Leopold replaces human liberation and Singer's animal liberation with nature liberation.

As we saw in chapter 9, animal rights philosopher Tom Regan has denounced Leopold's land ethic as "environmental fascism."[42] For on Leopold's view, biotic wholes—whether species or ecosystems—are morally analogous to totalitarianism's conception of the state. In both cases, individuals are completely subordinated to their respective wholes and have no value independently of them. Furthermore, since all biotic wholes are morally equal, and since humans are morally required to promote the diversity of the biotic community, humans and higher mammals can sometimes be expected to take a moral backseat to the rest of nature. To take Regan's example, rare species of grasses contribute more to the biotic community's diversity than do the citizens of Cleveland. Therefore, if there is a conflict between them, the grasses take moral precedence over Clevelanders, a conclusion Regan considers absurd.

Deep Ecology

Leopold is usually regarded as the father, or at least the forerunner, of holistic ecocentrism. One of its principal manifestations is the deep ecology movement. The term *deep ecology* was coined by Arne Naess, a Norwegian philosopher and environmentalist, in a 1973 article, "The Shallow and the Deep, Long-Range Ecology Movements."[43] More recently, deep ecology has been further articulated by environmentalists Bill Devall and George Sessions in their book, *Deep Ecology: Living as if Nature Mattered.*[44] Fundamental to the movement is its distinction between shallow and deep ecology. Deep ecologists like Naess and Sessions charge that conventional or establishment environmentalism is shallow ecology. It tries to resolve environmental problems in a piecemeal fashion by seeking accommodation with the anthropocentrism of society's reigning institutions, especially its politics and its corporations. Shallow ecology has no interest in developing a reflective philosophy of the environment and humans' place in it.

By contrast, deep ecology holds that we can effectively resolve our environmental problems only by articulating a metaphysical philosophy, a comprehensive vision of the whole of reality, based on asking searching questions about the meaning of life, society, and nature, in the long tradition of Western philosophy going back to Socrates. Such an approach will generate an ecological consciousness, which is fundamentally at odds with the dominant anthropocentric consciousness. A deep ecological consciousness consists of two ultimate values: self-realization and biocentric equality.[45] We can achieve self-realization as spiritual persons only by recognizing that we are connected with the rest of spiritual nature. We must then develop a harmonious relation with nature, achieving our own self-realization within the larger self-realization of nature as a whole. Biocentric equality affirms that all members of the biosphere have equal intrinsic value and equal moral standing. This includes not only living beings but also inanimate beings insofar as they are related to living beings. These twin values justify human intervention into nature only to promote nature's good and only to satisfy vital human needs. Forging an ecological consciousness enables us to get at the root causes of our environmental problems, two of which are individualism (or egoism) and consumerism. Furthermore, since deep ecology rejects compromising with the establishment, it has spawned groups that are quite politically and socially active, such as Earth First and the much more radical Earth Liberation Front. Critics charge these groups with "ecosabotage" and "ecoterrorism."[46]

Ecological Feminism (Ecofeminism)

A recent variation of ecocentrism is set forth by some feminist philosophers. It is called ecofeminism or ecological feminism.[47] A leading ecofeminist is Karen Warren, who has written extensively on the subject.[48] She agrees with deep ecology that we must uncover the root causes of environmental abuse. According to Warren and ecofeminism in general, there is only one basic cause of environmental problems: male supremacy, or male-centrism, which dominates and suppresses both women and nature. As she expresses it: "Ecological feminism . . . is the position that there are important connections . . . between the [male] domination of women and the [male] domination of nature, an understanding of which is crucial to both feminism and environmental ethics."[49]

Warren coins the term *naturism*,[50] which denotes male domination and oppression of nonhuman nature. It is morally equivalent to sexism, which is male domination and oppression of women. Both are based on a Western male form of thinking that she calls the logic of domination.[51] This reasoning consists of a three-step process. First, we identify differences between or among classes of beings. This act of thinking is valid in principle, although we sometimes make mistakes. On the one hand, she recognizes that each species possesses unique, objective differences from all other species. The human species, she suggests, is unique in its "conscious capacity to radically reshape . . . [its] social environment."[52] On the other hand, she says it is a mistake to distinguish between men and women, in a way influenced by Descartes, by asserting that men are inherently mental-rational beings and women are inherently natural-emotional beings.

In the second step, we infer that these differences denote superiorities and inferiorities between or among the classes of beings we compare. Once again, sometimes this inference is valid and sometimes it is not. It could be invalid even if the differences upon which the inference is based are true ones. For example, if one inferred, as a racist would, that whites are superior to people of color because of a difference in their skin color, his fallacious inference would be based on a true but irrelevant difference among these groups. In the case of men being mental-rational versus women being emotional-natural, the inference is that men are superior and women are inferior. Here the inference does not follow because the difference upon which it is based is false. In the above example concerning the difference between humans and other species, she says that the difference is probably true, but it does not necessarily follow that this difference is one of superiority to all other species. One would have to demonstrate this conclusion based on sound reasoning and clear and convincing evidence. Warren contends that Western man so far has been unable to prove that human differences from other species are differences of superiority.

In the third and final step, we infer that these differences of superiority justify superior beings dominating and oppressing inferior beings. Again, she says this inference does not follow. The superiority upon which it is based could be false, for example, that men are mental-rational and women are natural-emotional. But even if some beings are superior to others in some respects, it does not follow that the superior beings are morally justified in dominating and oppressing their inferiors. Tiger Woods is superior to almost everyone in golf-playing ability, and Albert Einstein was superior to most people in scientific intelligence, but it would be absurd to suggest that these superiorities give them any moral right to dominate and oppress others. Likewise, even if humans are superior to other species in some respects, the superiority would not justify Western man's traditional domination and oppression of nature.

A PERSONALIST SYNTHESIS

I now sketch my own environmental ethics, which is a synthesis of the preceding theories. It forms a framework for developing a new version of capitalism—*environmental capitalism*—to replace industrial capitalism. Environmental capitalism is implicit in democratic capitalism.

Moral Status, Ecological Value, and Aesthetic Value

Despite the considerable differences among the preceding theories, they all agree on one fundamental proposition: humans have moral status and their interpersonal and intrapersonal activity has moral significance.[53] This common agreement is their common strength and truth. Where the theories differ, as we have seen, is on which other beings possess moral status. This disagreement, in my view, produces a serious weakness or error in each theory. At the same time, each theory possesses an important element of truth.

On the question concerning what beings possess moral status, we must avoid two extremes. One extreme does not extend moral status broadly enough, so that some important beings are undervalued. This position characterizes anthropocentrism. It commits two mistakes: first, it holds that only humans have moral status; and second, that all nonhumans have merely instrumental value. Nevertheless, anthropocentrism's element of truth, in my view, is its claim that humans are higher than all other species, but not in the sense in which anthropocentrism claims.

The other extreme extends moral status too broadly, so that some beings are overvalued and the very meaning of moral status is diluted and ultimately trivialized. Biocentrism, I contend, dilutes moral status and ecocentrism trivializes it. Both theories extend moral status much too broadly. Moreover, they compound this error by maintaining that all beings having moral status possess it equally; they deny that there are different degrees or levels of moral status. In contrast, the common element of truth in biocentrism and ecocentrism is their view that nonsentient nature possesses intrinsic value. Still, this truth is mixed with an error; they identify intrinsic value with moral status.

Between these two extremes is sentient-centrism, standing somewhere in the middle as a moderate position. This suggests an important truth of sentient-centrism: all sentient animals, and only sentient animals, have moral status. In my view, sentient-centrism is correct in fixing the limit or circle of moral status at sentience, in holding that only beings with the capacity for pain and suffering have moral standing. However, sentient-centrism commits two errors, it seems to me: first, it holds that nonhuman sentient animals have the same moral status as humans, that they are morally equal to humans; and second, it holds that all nonsentient nature has merely instrumental value. I now develop my own position in a positive way by first addressing myself to these two errors.

As we saw in chapter 9, persons are more inclusive beings than are organisms. Therefore, the moral status of persons is more inclusive than that of sentient animals. Only persons are moral agents, having the capacity to act morally. Since nonhuman sentient animals are not persons, their less-inclusive moral status is based on sentience. Persons' moral status goes beyond sentience while still including it. In this context, then, I distinguish two modes of moral status: *person moral status* and *sentience moral status*. They may be regarded as higher and lower levels of moral status, so long as higher and lower are interpreted as more inclusive and less inclusive, respectively.

In environmental ethics, however, *environment* refers primarily to humans' treatment of nonsentient nature rather than to their treatment of sentient animals as individuals. Since I have fixed the limit of moral status at sentient animals, I deny that nonsentient nature has moral status. In chapter 1, I distinguished three basic modes of value: instrumental, aesthetic, and moral. In chapter 4, moral status was introduced as a version of moral value. Within this trilogy of values, I introduce the notion of *ecological* value. I claim that the central value of nonsentient nature is *ecological*. (Sentient nature, including human nature, has ecological value, but sentient beings also have moral status.) Ecological value is the core, essential value of ecosystems, of individual beings within them, and ultimately, of the whole planet Earth as a biosphere, that is, Earth and its surrounding air and moisture.

Ecological value is analogous to both moral value and aesthetic value: it is partially similar to and partially different from them. Like moral value, ecological value is relational; and like aesthetic value, it is both an intrinsic and nonmoral mode of value. As relational, however, ecological value is unlike aesthetic value, in which (as we saw in chapter 1) we value something as an *isolated* end-in-itself abstracted from its concrete relations with the other. And as a nonmoral mode of value, ecological value differs from moral value/status.

Once again, I use my distinction between more inclusive and less inclusive to explain the relation among moral status, ecological value, and aesthetic value. Moral status includes both ecological value and aesthetic value as limited but essential aspects, just as ecological value includes aesthetic value in a similar way. A tiger, for example, is a sentient being having moral status. As part of an ecosystem, however, a tiger possesses ecological value. And as an isolated end-in-itself, it surely possesses beauty. Likewise, nonsentient nature's total value is more inclusive than the value of art. A tree has ecological value, and it is beautiful; the Mona Lisa is beautiful but obviously lacks a tree's ecological value. Ecological value enables me to differentiate between the value of nature and that of art while avoiding the dubious assertion that nonsentient nature is the bearer of moral value/status.

For example, if someone needlessly cuts down a tree (or trees) on his or her own property, such an act is a violation of the tree's ecological and aesthetic values. But as an act against the tree itself, it is not an immoral act. The tree as such has no moral rights. Since trees lack personhood and sentience, and are completely devoid of consciousness, it is implausible to attribute moral status to them. However, tree cutting is immoral insofar as it indirectly harms humans and sentient animals, who do have moral status. This is certainly the case in deforestation.[54]

Vegetarianism and World Hunger

Because the distinction between person moral status and sentience moral status is relevant to the moral treatment of animals rather than to environmental ethics, the moral conclusions implied by this distinction were drawn in chapter 9. However, from the standpoint of environmental ethics, the conclusion recommending vegetarianism warrants further analysis, since it bears on the question of world hunger.

I begin by laying out the moral framework for this discussion. A person's access to a minimally nutritious diet is about as basic a right there is, since it is connected with life, health, and physical and mental flourishing. Therefore, both the principle of community and its implied principles of justice require that the affluent, industrialized nations of the world use their financial and technical resources to eradicate world hunger and poverty. A personalist society has a moral obligation not only to adequately feed its own, but the poor of other nations as well. Worldwide, 852 million people currently suffer from hunger, up from 820 million in 2000. The world must feed 70 million additional people a year by current growth rates.[55] These numbers put a tremendous strain on world food production and distribution. Nevertheless, the world's hungry and undernourished can be fed, especially if steps are taken to stabilize world population.

In affluent, industrialized nations, such as the United States, where people consume large amounts of meat and other livestock products, they would surely be healthier by switching to plant protein, or even if they moderately reduced their intake of livestock protein. The exception, of course, is skim milk and products made of skim milk, for example, yogurt. And for those people who adopt a vegetarian diet, which could include fish, there is no doubt that they would be healthier still. Moreover, as we have seen, it takes much more water to produce animal protein than plant protein, and water is becoming an increasingly scarce resource. Finally, in general the world's grain is used very inefficiently in meat production. If the rest of the world had America's eating habits, the current global grain harvest could feed a population of only 2.5 billion. For these reasons, affluent nations like the United States have a moral obligation to themselves and to the world to at least substantially reduce their consumption of meat and related products such as eggs, whole milk, and butter. Moreover, the international meat industry produces about 18 percent of the world's greenhouse gases, much of it in the methane and nitrous oxide emanating from animal manure. Methane's warming effect is 23 times greater than CO_2, while nitrous oxide's effect is 296 times greater.

However, it is doubtful that vegetarianism can be a worldwide model for overcoming world hunger and providing adequate nutrition.[56] It has a chance of succeeding only if it includes large quantities of fish from aquaculture. I say this for two reasons. First, animals vary widely in their efficiency to convert grain into protein. Second, plant protein production is relatively land inefficient. There is a third related point, namely, that some grains are thirstier than others.

With cattle in feedlots, it takes 7 kgs of grain to produce 1 kg of gain in live weight. For pork, the ratio is 4:1; for poultry, slightly more than 2:1; and for herbivorous species of farm fish (carp, tilapia, and catfish), the ratio is less than 2:1.[57]

Because of these ratios, and because plants require much more metabolic energy to produce high-quality (or complete) protein than to produce starch (complex carbohydrates), it can be more land- and water-efficient to produce animal protein from aquaculture and even from poultry than to produce plant protein from soybeans. An acre of land in Iowa can produce 140 bushels of corn or 35 bushels of soybeans. Feeding the corn to catfish or chickens will yield more high-quality protein than growing soybeans for direct human consumption, as in tofu. It does not seem possible to meet the global need for high-quality or complete protein by plant protein alone. Furthermore, animal feed has become much more efficient by mixing soybeans with grain. A combination of one part soybean meal with four parts of grain boosts the conversion efficiency of grain to animal protein by 100 percent. This fact accounts for the phenomenal rise in soybean production. In 2005, 220 million tons were produced, up from only 16 million tons in 1950. Of this total, 144 million tons of soybean meal are fed to cattle, pigs, chicken, and fish. Soybeans account for one of every nine tons of grain produced worldwide. Of the world's total grain harvest, 38 percent (730 million tons) is used to produce animal protein, and much of it is produced efficiently.[58]

A recent worldwide trend among environmentalists is raising beef cattle in rotational-grazing pastures. Among all animals that humans eat, feed-lot cows are the most environmentally harmful. They consume more energy-intensive feed than other livestock. The grain they eat, such as corn and soybeans, requires fossil-fuel-based fertilizers, pesticides, and transportation. Cows also produce more methane than other livestock animals do. However, if cattle are fed only grass in pastures where they are continually moving, not only is their carbon-footprint substantially reduced, it actually becomes carbon-negative.

The process works as follows. As the cows eat grass and move around, the blades they cut stimulate more growth, and their trampling of manure helps to convert it into a natural fertilizer that enriches the soil and prevents the manure from releasing its powerful methane into the atmosphere. And since the grasses' roots remain intact, they continue to store carbon dioxide. Moreover, cows are healthier, because they do not need the antibiotics that feed-lot cattle must have to prevent acidosis, which is caused by grain-feeding. Finally, the meat grass-fed cows produce is more nutritious. It has less saturated fat and more heart-healthy omega-3 fatty acids than does feed-lot beef. On the minus side, grass-fed beef is considerably more expensive than conventional beef. However, as rotational-grazing expands, the price is likely to drop. More importantly, the increased acreage devoted to grasslands will prevent soil erosion, keep water in the ground, and lower the level of global greenhouse emissions.[59]

We have seen that irrigation accounts for 70 percent of world water usage, and that it takes one thousand tons of water to produce one ton of grain. But the latter fact is just an average. Some grains use more water than others. Rice is thirstier than wheat. Since water is a scarce resource, I suggest that the nations of the world convert as much as possible to grains that are the most water-efficient, and to those animals that are the most efficient in converting grain to protein, namely farm fish and poultry, especially farm fish, as nations try to fulfill their moral obligation to provide everyone with a balanced, nutritious diet that includes adequate amounts of high-quality protein. Indeed, expanding aquaculture is probably the single best way to ensure that the world's population receives enough high-quality protein. China leads the way, with two-thirds of the world's aquaculture output, double that of its poultry production.

The poultry part of the above statement is at odds with my conclusion in chapter 9 that all commercial animal farming should cease (I did not intend to include the fish industry in this conclusion). I make three clarifying comments. First, for moral reasons, the world should try to fill global needs for protein by increasing aquaculture as much as possible. If fish farming is not enough to satisfy world need, then poultry must be treated as humanely as possible. This is not presently the case in factory farms.

Second, 180 million people worldwide make their living as pastoralists, tending cattle, sheep, and goats. Many of them are poor, and they depend on these animals for their protein needs. These pastoralists cannot be put in the same moral category as supporters of animal factory farms.

Third, if someone thinks I am placing too much emphasis on animal protein, it must be remembered that most grains are starch, not complete protein. And plant protein production is relatively land inefficient. A person cannot have an adequately nutritious diet by subsisting solely or largely on starch products, as the poorest 1 billion people in the world currently do. Protein deprivation partly accounts for their poor health.

Speaking of health, animal protein products differ considerably in their saturated fat and cholesterol content. Eggs are high in cholesterol. Pork has the most saturated fat (which raises cholesterol level), followed by beef, chicken (white meat has less fat than dark meat), turkey, and fish. Whole milk products are rich in saturated fat. From the triple perspectives of the moral treatment of animals, environmental ethics, and nutrition, a suggested ideal diet would include large amounts of fruits, vegetables, and whole grain products; potatoes in moderation (too many excessively elevate blood-sugar level); a combination of aquaculture fish, soybean products, and skim milk products; and oils without *trans* fat, such as olive oil, canola oil, and sunflower oil. Diets to be avoided are those of the planet's richest one billion and poorest one billion inhabitants. The former diet has excessive amounts of meat and other livestock products, whereas the latter consists largely of starches.

Community and Environmental Capitalism

The foundation of a global community and a flourishing civilization is a healthy Earth. To act in accordance with the principle of community and its principles of justice requires an economy that is capable of renewing and sustaining the world's natural resources instead of depleting and degrading them, as industrial capitalism has been doing. We must make a transition from industrial capitalism to environmental capitalism (or in Lester Brown's terminology, from Plan A to Plan B).

We have seen that the current state of industrial capitalism is based on fossil fuels, is automobile-centered, and is a throwaway economy. Environmental capitalism rejects these three attributes of current industrial capitalism. Environmental capitalism consists of a plan to overcome the eleven dimensions of the environmental crisis we sketched earlier. This plan consists of two parts: socioeconomic and ecological.

There are four goals of the socioeconomic part or sector: (1) stabilizing population growth and density through a program of reproductive health and planning services, (2) eradicating poverty and hunger, (3) establishing universal primary education and eliminating illiteracy, and (4) instituting universal basic healthcare (controlling infectious diseases and providing childhood vaccinations). These goals are required by distributive justice. Moreover, Earth's ecological health cannot be restored without their achievement. The ecological part also has four goals: (1) reforesting Earth and protecting bio-diversity, (2) protecting topsoils on croplands and restoring rangelands, (3) restoring fisheries, and (4) stabilizing water tables.[60] These goals are required by environmental justice. Both distributive and environmental justice are implied by the two principles of justice presented in chapter 8, which in turn are implicit in the principle of community.

For global society to achieve these goals, the three features of contemporary industrial capitalism (Plan A) must be replaced by corresponding features of environmental capitalism (Plan B). First, fossil fuels must be replaced by renewable sources of energy that do not pollute the air and cause global warming. These include wind power, solar power, and geothermal energy (and to a lesser extent, biomass fuel).

Second, instead of an automobile-centered culture, we must have a much greater reliance on alternative modes of transportation (especially in congested urban areas), such as light rail, buses, bicycles, and motor bikes. Our cities are much too crowded with cars, where they have become instruments of immobility. Cities today cater more to cars than to people. Many parking lots should be replaced by parks. Cars themselves must become more fuel efficient and environmentally friendly by replacing the conventional internal combustion engine with gas-electric hybrid cars (as is already occurring) and with all-electric cars. It has been estimated that if all cars in the United States were hybrid vehicles having a second battery with plug-in capacity for short trips powered by stored-up wind turbine energy, and were reduced in weight by replacing steel with advanced polymer components, America's automobile fuel consumption would drop by 85 percent.[61] This accomplishment would be a wonderful model for the rest of the world.

Third, instead of a throwaway economy, the new economy must be based on conservation and recycling across the board. To some extent, of course, this is currently being done, but it must become much more globally comprehensive. In developed nations, the leading cause of tree-cutting is paper production, and paper products dominate our throwaway economy. Recycling paper and replacing paper products with durable goods made of recyclable materials would greatly reduce trash disposal and preserve the world's forests.

There are many other changes that should be made. For instance, flush toilets should be replaced by dry, odorless composting toilets, whose material is eventually recycled. This change would eliminate the huge quantities of sewerage that are dumped into rivers, streams, and lakes, where they become the source of much disease. Composting toilets would save all the water lost in toilet flushing. Incandescent light bulbs should be replaced by compact florescent lamps (CFLs), which use only one-third as much electricity and last ten times longer. All household and business appliances, from refrigerators to computers, must become as energy efficient as possible.

One of the easiest important changes that can be made is replacing bottled water with safe tap water. The bottled water industry is huge and rapidly growing. In the United States alone, sales for 2006 were $10.8 billion, an increase of 9.5 percent over the previous year. The industry is very damaging to the natural environment. It takes much oil to create the plastic in bottled water containers and to fuel the trucks that transport them to market. Less than 25 percent of the containers are recycled; the rest end up in landfills. Perhaps even worse, the growing switch to bottled water creates the false impression that tap water is unsafe. Fortunately, some American cities are fighting back. New York City, for example, recently launched a $1 million campaign touting its well-deserved reputation for clean tap water.

The three essential differences between industrial and environmental capitalism are really values and not merely features. Since humans are persons with free will, and since we now have the finances and technology to make the transition to environmental capitalism, we must make a value choice between the old and the new, between destroying civilization and its ecological base or saving them. We freely chose to create this problem, and now we must freely choose to solve it or allow it to grow beyond the point of cure.

I emphasize the capitalist component of environmental capitalism. Unlike socialism, capitalism is based on a free market system, the law of supply and demand. The market system is more efficient than the central planning of socialism in allocating goods and resources, and in determining their realistic prices. To achieve this efficiency, though, the market must tell the whole truth, especially ecological truth, which industrial capitalism has not done. Historically, there are two fundamental defects of industrial capitalism: the exploitation and oppression of workers, and the exploitation and degradation of the environment. Marx emphasized the first, and environmentalism emphasizes the second.

Environmental capitalism would calculate the true environmental costs of products. For example, it has been estimated that the environmental costs of producing gasoline in the United States are $9 a gallon.[62] If this cost were added to current retail pump prices, a gallon of gas would cost about $13. The higher price would greatly increase demand for hybrid and all-electric cars, for lighter weight vehicles, and for cheaper modes of transportation. Environmental truth telling would require governments to end their subsidies to industries that harm the environment, such as the fossil fuel and commercial fishing industries (not aquaculture), and subsidize environmentally friendly industries, including the wind turbine and solar power industries. The world's taxpayers spend $700 billion a year to subsidize environmentally destructive activities, including fossil-fuel burning, overpumping aquifers, clear-cutting forests, and overfishing. It is totally irrational for humans to be subsidizing their own destruction. By contrast, if there is one industry that should be subsidized, it is the wind turbine industry. As Lester Brown notes, no other energy source has its environmentally ideal six attributes: it is abundant, cheap, inexhaustible, widely distributed, clean, and climate benign.[63] The United States has enough harnessable wind to supply all its energy needs (and not merely electricity needs).

Simultaneously, there must be a radical shift in tax policy, away from taxing income to taxing activities that damage the environment. A society could have a combination of carbon taxes, stump (tree-cutting) taxes, landfill taxes, excess automobile ownership and usage taxes, and so on. Germany made such a shift in 1999. Another recent proposal is *avoided deforestation*. According to this concept, poorer countries and businesses in developed nations would be provided with financial incentives to preserve the world's tropical rainforests.

There are several positive worldwide signs that a shift to environmental capitalism is already occurring. I mention six. First, wind farms in Europe are proliferating, especially in Germany. Europe's wind energy is expected to increase from a world-leading 34,500 megawatts in 2004 to 230,000 megawatts in 2030, enough to satisfy the electricity demand of half its population. Second, the demand for gas-electric (hybrid) automobiles in the United States is growing rapidly. Third, China has cut poverty from 648 million in 1981 to 218 million in 2001, the largest poverty reduction in human history. Fourth, in one generation Iran has dropped its population growth rate from one of the world's highest to one of the lowest in the developing world. It launched a family-planning program in 1989. Contraceptives such as the pill and sterilization were free of charge. All couples were required to take a class on modern contraception before obtaining a marriage license. Family size decreased from seven in 1987 to fewer than three in 1994. Iran's program is a model for all nations, which ought to aim at an average of two children per couple. In this context, moral education should teach the *virtue* of birth control by contraception (not by abortion). Fifth, South Korea's reforestation project is another model program. When the Korean War ended in 1953, the mountainous country was largely barren of trees. In 1960, a reforestation project was begun under the leadership of President Park Chung Hee. Today, forests cover 65 percent of the country, 8 million hectares. Sixth, there is Japan's world-leading program in solar rooftops. After companies commercialized solar roofing material, the government enacted its 70,000 Roofs Program in 1994, which subsidized the installation of solar roofs. The program is very successful.[64]

One final point. Relying on various studies, Lester Brown has calculated that it would cost the affluent nations of the world $161 billion annually to meet the above four socio-economic goals and four ecological goals of environmental capitalism (his Plan B). To put this figure in perspective, he notes that the 2006 military budget of the United States, including $50 billion for military operations in Iraq and Afghanistan, is $492 billion, and the world military budget is $975 billion.[65] For one-sixth of what they currently spend on weapons and war, the developed nations of the world can save the planet and civilization, restore hope, and address many of the underlying causes of terrorism and political instability. How can they not afford to do it?

12

THE MORAL TREATMENT OF CIVILIANS IN WAR
A Personalist Theory

In moral and legal theory, wartime civilians have a high level of moral protection not extended to combatants. Since civilians neither fight nor plan war, they possess a prima facie innocence that both gives them immunity from direct attack and places moral limits on indirectly attacking them. Crucial to the last statement is the distinction between *direct* and *indirect* attack, which will be explained later.

In the actual conduct of war, however, we often treat civilians very differently. What we say is not necessarily what we do. Throughout history, civilians have been routinely killed and even massacred. World War II was by far the costliest war in history, with 62 to 78 million persons killed, by latest estimates. Of these, 40 million to 52 million were civilians. World War II had one of the highest civilian-to-combatant death ratios in modern warfare. The massive mistreatment of civilians underscores the horrors and evil of warfare.

The purpose of this lecture is to explore the issue of the moral treatment of civilians in war. I shall attempt to give a defensible answer to two related questions raised by the major ethical theories of war. First, is it ever morally permissible to directly attack civilians? Second, to what extent, if any, is it morally permissible to indirectly attack them? In the first part of the lecture, I will briefly examine four theories of war and how they give different answers to these questions. The four theories are: *pacifism, nihilism* (including terrorism), *just war theory* (including Michael Walzer's important revision of it), and *utilitarianism*. Although I find much truth in these theories (except for nihilism), they also have defects. Consequently, in the second part of the chapter, I will develop my own personalist theory, incorporating elements from the other theories.

CONVENTIONAL THEORIES OF WAR

The Challenge of Pacifism

Pacifism is the theory that all war is immoral.[1] Everything about any war is evil. Therefore, all moral distinctions about war or in war are meaningless, including the distinction between combatant and civilian. This distinction implies that there are conditions under which it is morally permissible to attack combatants that are impermissible to attack civilians. But for pacifism, attacking combatants is as wrong as attacking civilians. Consequently, if pacifism is true, this entire chapter is pointless, an exercise in futility. For me to proceed in a rational way, then, I must answer and overcome the challenge of pacifism. I must show that pacifism is mistaken.

This challenge is made all the more formidable because of the compelling truth of pacifism: most wars are immoral (or so I think). In most cases, it is better not to fight than to fight. However, *most* is not *all*, and this is where pacifism errs, in my view. I will now argue that there are exceptional cases in which war is morally permissible, where it is better to fight than not to fight. The upshot of this argument is that it both invalidates (or falsifies) pacifism as it stands, and legitimizes the distinction between combatant and civilian as one of many necessary ways to contain and control the evil of warfare.

The first part of my argument against pacifism is embodied in a dilemma that faced John Macmurray as a longtime pacifist. To explain his dilemma, I sketch a narrative of the origin and genesis of his pacifism and its connection with his philosophy. The second part of my argument is developed later, as part of my personalist theory.

Macmurray retired from professional life in 1957 after teaching for many years at the University of Edinburgh, among other places. Over a writing career that spanned fifty years, he wrote some twenty books and many articles. Upon his retirement, Macmurray published a small semi-autobiography, *Search for Reality in Religion*,[2] in which he reflects upon his service in World War I and how the war profoundly changed him. Before the Great War began, he had strong pacifist leanings based on his Christian beliefs but felt a duty as a loyal British citizen to join the war effort against the Central Powers, principally Germany. He compromised by joining the Medical Corps and trained as a nursing orderly. This compromise, however, did not dim his enthusiasm for the war. As he puts it: "We went into war in a blaze of idealism, to save little Belgium and to put an end to war."[3] Macmurray believed (as most did at the time) that this would be the war to end all wars.

The grim realities of combat and trench warfare quickly disabused him of this naive idealism. He and his comrades became convinced that "war was simply stupidity, destruction, waste and futility."[4] By war's end, he had changed in three ways. First, he was a complete "realist" about war. The horrific reality of warfare excluded any idealistic thinking about it—any romanticization or glorification of it—and therefore any moral justification for it.

The second change in him was precipitated by a furlough back home midway through the war. At the Battle of Somme he severely sprained an ankle and was sent home for several months of sick leave. During this period, he was asked to preach in uniform at a church in North London. As a Christian, he spoke about the importance of avoiding the war mentality so that after the war Christians could begin the necessary task of reconciliation. The congregation took it badly. They reacted to his sermon with silent hostility, and no one spoke to him afterwards. As a result of this snub, he vowed on Christian grounds never again to join a Christian *church*. He now thought of organized or institutional Christianity as divided into the various national churches of Europe, with each church totally supporting the military policies of its nation. In this respect, he believed that organized Christianity did not understand the fundamental difference between religion and politics. For Macmurray, Christianity must transcend the politics of war. He followed the path of Kierkegaard, for whom the problem of becoming a Christian was existential, not organizational. Macmurray kept his promise never to join a church throughout his professional career. Upon his retirement, though, he joined the Society of Friends. His membership was the occasion for writing *Search for Reality in Religion*. It is clear that a major reason for his decision to join the Society is its fundamental commitment to peace and pacifism.

The third way in which the war changed Macmurray is that at war's end he vowed to dedicate the rest of his life to the elimination of war, whatever he did. When it was clear he would choose philosophy as a career, the elimination of war "became the underlying purpose of all my philosophizing."[5] The mature expression of this purpose is his theory of community, which is the culmination of his philosophy. For Macmurray, the creation and maintenance of community constitutes peace in the full, positive sense of the word. Community and war are incompatible. Therefore, the promotion of community implies pacifism. Moreover, as a Christian, Macmurray is convinced that real (or authentic) Christianity, which must be based first and foremost on the life and teaching of Jesus, is pacifist.[6] In Macmurray's mind, Christianity and philosophy converge and reinforce each other on the issue of pacifism.

By the 1930s, Macmurray was a well-established philosopher and a dedicated pacifist who addressed various Christian groups who shared his pacifist views. But along came Adolph Hitler and the rise of Nazism in Germany. Macmurray quickly understood that Nazism was the antithesis of everything he stood for.

After aggressive military acts in the Saarland, Rhineland, and against Austria and Czechoslovakia, Hitler began World War II by invading Poland on September 1, 1939. France and England immediately declared war on Germany. In 1940, the Axis Alliance (Tripartite Pact) was formed: Germany, Japan, and Italy. Between May 10 and June 21, 1940, Hitler invaded and conquered France and the lowland countries of northern Europe. Norway was invaded. Later that year, he attacked England by air. On June 22, 1941, he invaded the Soviet Union. On December 7, 1941, Japan attacked Pearl Harbor. The United States promptly declared war on Japan. In turn, Germany declared war on the United States. World War II was now fully on. Fighting the Axis powers were the Allies, principally the United States, the United Kingdom (mainly England), and the Soviet Union. Many other nations around the world joined either side. The global scale of World War II far exceeded that of the First World War. From the standpoint of the Allies, the war was being fought to save democracy, freedom, and civilization itself from the forces of Axis totalitarianism: the Nazism of Germany, the Fascism of Mussolini's Italy, and the militaristic fascism of Tojo's Japan.

For Macmurray, Hitler's Nazi regime was by far the most evil of the Axis powers.[7] Hitler was responsible for the large majority of the 62–78 million killed in World War II. Inherent in Nazi doctrine were the unspeakably evil genocidal policies toward Jews and other groups, which killed up to 17 million innocent civilians, chiefly in concentration camps. Hitler considered the Russian and Eastern European peoples subhuman, an attitude that led to the huge massacres of Russian and Slavic civilians during the war on the Eastern Front.[8] When Churchill visited President Roosevelt at the White House in late December 1941 to plan the course of the war, they decided, with the support of most of America's top military command, to devote the bulk of Allied military resources to the defeat of Germany. The war against Japan was secondary. Churchill writes that Hitler's victory over the Allies would mean that the whole world including the United States would sink into a new Dark Age. In a similar vein, John Rawls speaks of the "peculiar evil of Nazism."[9]

As a result of Macmurray's complete opposition toward totalitarianism in general and Nazism in particular, he supported the Allied war against the Axis, and in particular the war against Hitler's Nazism. Indeed, in private correspondence he goes so far as to say that had he been young enough to serve in World War II, "he would have fought to resist Hitler and all he stood for."[10]

This is an extraordinary statement for an avowed pacifist. "Fought" means bearing arms, being a soldier, a combatant, not just a nursing orderly, as he was in World War I. Was he simply being inconsistent and making a mistake, or did he now think that absolute pacifism is impractical and does not work in the real world? Based on both his published writings and his private correspondence, the answer is not clear. Eventually, he would reaffirm his pacifist views, as demonstrated by his joining the Society of Friends. Still, he never said he made an error in supporting the war against Hitler.

I suggest that Macmurray's dilemma—the conflict between his pacifism and fighting Hitler—is the ultimate case for testing the truth of pacifism.

The scope and magnitude of evil of Hitler's Nazism is so unprecedented in human history that if fighting against Nazi Germany cannot be morally justified, then war is never morally justifiable. But fighting Hitler, I contend, was morally right. Therefore, some war is morally permissible. That being the case, there may be other, less severe, wars that are morally right.[11]

The reason why Macmurray's story is compelling is that even as such a dedicated philosophical and religious pacifist, he felt it necessary to make an exception in the case of Hitler. This exception exposes a defect in pacifism. The defect is this. What pacifism proposes is that instead of a war of self-defense against an unjust aggressor nation, an attacked nation should adopt a systematic campaign of civilian resistance and noncooperation, which will make their nation ungovernable and cause the aggressors to leave, as the British did in 1947 when they left India in response to Gandhi's prolonged campaign of civil disobedience. Likewise, Gandhi, being a consistent pacifist, opposed the British Declaration of War against Germany in World War II. It is reported that Gandhi told the Jews in Germany that they should commit suicide rather than fight the Nazis.[12] Such advice is morally outrageous. It compounds one great evil with another and makes the Nazis' "final solution" much easier for them.

The success of nonviolent resistance, however, depends on the relative goodwill of the conqueror. This was true when Great Britain vacated India, but would not have been true of Hitler's aggression in Europe. His conquered peoples faced permanent oppression, enslavement, massacre, and even extermination. If Hitler had won the war, it would have been the end of democracy, community, freedom, equality, justice, and all the other great moral values of Western civilization. In truth, Hitler could not be allowed to win.

Nihilism and Terrorism

Nihilism is the theory that all war is hell (to use General Sherman's terse expression). Nevertheless, this hell has a supreme good: winning and vanquishing the enemy as quickly and expeditiously as possible, by whatever means necessary.[13] If one of the means is attacking and killing civilians, so be it: the end justifies the means. Like pacifism, nihilism believes that all moral distinctions in warfare are meaningless, including the distinction between combatant and civilian. Sometimes nihilism is euphemistically called *realism*, especially in political circles.[14] Pacifism and nihilism are the two extreme theories of war, at opposite ends of the moral spectrum.

Ironically, pacifism may unwittingly contribute to the support of nihilism. Since most people regard pacifism as a hopeless and unrealistic ideal to live by and thus reject it, and since nihilism and pacifism are united in their belief that all moral distinctions in warfare are meaningless (although for fundamentally different reasons), many see no reason to limit the hellishness of warfare on moral grounds.[15]

Terrorism may be regarded as the ultimate expression of nihilism. Michael Walzer's definition of terrorism is succinct and seems adequate. "Its [terrorism's] purpose is to destroy the morale of a nation or a class, to undercut its solidarity; its method is the random murder of innocent people."[16] Civilians are innocent people. Al Qaeda's attack against the United States on 9/11 is by definition an act of terrorism. The rejection of the distinction between combatant and civilian is *fundamental* to terrorism.

Just War Theory

In between the extremes of pacifism and nihilism are the two "moderate" theories of warfare: just war theory and utilitarianism. Since just war is the older theory, I consider it first. I now examine traditional and conventional just war theory, and then look into Michael Walzer's substantial revision of it.

Traditional/Conventional Just War Theory

Historically, there have been several versions of just war theory. It has its roots in early Christian thinkers such as St. Ambrose and St. Augustine;[17] was further developed in the Middle Ages by St. Thomas Aquinas;[18] and in its full development by later thinkers is divided into two parts: *jus ad bellum* (justice of war) and *jus in bello* (justice in war).[19] The first part sets forth the conditions of a just war in itself, and the second part specifies the conditions for the just prosecution of a war once it begins, regardless of whether the war itself is just or unjust. A just war can be rendered unjust, or be diminished in its original justice, by engaging in unjust practices, and an unjust war will become aggravated in its injustice by unjust practices.

The distinction between combatant and civilian (or noncombatant),[20] and how they are to be morally treated, falls under two conditions of *jus in bello*: the *principle of discrimination* and the *principle of double effect*. The discrimination principle makes a sharp conceptual and moral distinction between combatants and civilians. Combatants include not only military personnel but also persons engaged in close logistical support of the armed forces, such as munitions workers and transporters of munitions. When combatants surrender, they cease to be combatants and must be treated as civilians, except that they are held as prisoners of war (POWs). They cannot be tortured or mistreated in any way. All persons in a nation waging war who are not combatants are civilians. The principle of discrimination always forbids directly attacking civilians. To do so is considered murderous. By contrast, combatants may be directly attacked, providing it is done from a rightful motive, and the casualties inflicted upon the enemy combatants are not needless or excessive.

The distinction between direct and indirect attack, and the circumstances under which civilians may be indirectly attacked, are developed by the double effect principle. Since I examined this principle in detail in chapter 2, I now summarize it and apply it to warfare. Double effect is a procedural principle that applies to actions that have two morally conflicting effects (i.e., consequences, results, outcomes): the direct effect is good, and the indirect effect is bad (or evil). Because of this conflict, the moral permissibility of the action is in doubt, and the principle's purpose is to resolve this doubt.

The *direct effect* is intentional; it flows from an action's intention. The intention consists of an action's end and means. Therefore, the direct effect is intended (or willed) either as the end or means of action. According to double effect, for an action to be morally permissible, its intention must be good (or at least not bad) in both its end and means. An intention is bad if it has a good end but a bad means, even if the end is very good and the means is slightly bad. The direct effect is an action's primary effect (Rule One, chapter 2).

In contrast, the *indirect effect* is unintentional. It is the effect that is foreseen but unwilled as a secondary or side effect of the intention's execution.

Double effect holds that if the direct effect is good and the indirect effect is bad, the bad indirect effect is morally permissible if its badness is not greater than the good of the direct effect. This provision of double effect is called the *rule of proportionality* (Rule Three, chapter 2). If the evil of the indirect effect is greater (or weightier) than the goodness of the direct effect, there is a lack of proportionality between good and evil, and so the action is immoral.[21]

When the double effect principle is applied to warfare, its distinction between direct effect and indirect effect generates a corresponding distinction between directly attacking civilians and indirectly attacking them. Drawing from the discrimination principle, double effect affirms that directly attacking civilians is always immoral, since such action is intentional and civilians are innocent, nonwagers of war. However, double effect also affirms that it is morally permissible to indirectly attack them, providing the badness of the indirect civilian casualties (and also the badness of all other indirect effects, such as destruction of property, animals, and the natural environment) is not greater than the good of a military operation (means) in relation to the good of the war's just end (as determined by the conditions of justice of war), minus the costs of the military operation (principally combatant casualties and monetary costs). In military circles, indirect bad effects are called *collateral damage*. Since a bad indirect effect is permissible if it accords with the rule of proportionality but a bad direct effect is always impermissible, the double effect principle clearly gives greater moral importance to directly attacking civilians than to indirectly attacking them.

The proportionality rule is particularly used to determine whether bombing raids are morally justifiable. If a bombing attack aims at destroying a strategic military target in the prosecution of a just war, the direct effect is generally considered good. The moral question then shifts to indirect effects (or collateral damage) primarily in terms of civilian casualties: how many are likely to be killed and injured? The level of indirect civilian casualties will determine if the bombing raid is morally justifiable. For example, in the Allied bombing in 1943 of the German ball-bearing factory at Schweinfurt and the nearby Messerschmitt aircraft factory in Regensberg, both plants were considered vital military targets. However, because the bomb sights lacked pinpoint accuracy and the weather was somewhat cloudy, there were a significant number of nearby civilian casualties, judged, at the time, not to be at a level that outweighed the good of the direct effect, even though, from a military standpoint, the bombing mission was only partially successful and Allied losses were high—sixty Allied bombers and their crews were shot down. Such losses today would be unacceptable.

The proportionality rule does not apply, of course, to bombing operations that directly attack civilians, either by targeting an entire city or by indiscriminately bombing large population centers. This was the case in much of the Allied bombing campaign in World War II in Germany and Japan, and especially in the atomic bombings of Hiroshima and Nagasaki. These bombing missions have a bad direct effect, a bad intention, and thus violate both the principle of discrimination and Rule One of double effect.

Just war theory has proven to be very influential partly because of it comprehensiveness. Both justice of war and justice in war have several well-developed principles. Just war is the reigning theory of war today in international legal circles, although its conditions are often not practiced, especially by rogue nations and sometimes even by superpowers. The US invasion of Iraq in March 2003 was a clear violation of just war theory. It violated the *principle of just cause* under *jus ad bellum* as well as some of its other principles.[22] As the war continued, there were violations of the principle of discrimination. POWs were mistreated, even tortured, and Iraqi civilians were directly attacked.[23]

Walzer's Revision Theory

Michael Walzer has developed a heavily revised and updated version of just war theory. He makes five "revisions" of *jus ad bellum*,[24] and two "modifications" of *jus in bello*.[25] The two modifications are to the principles of discrimination and double effect. Since these are the two principles of just war theory that deal with the moral treatment of civilians, I confine myself to an examination of his two modifications: the *minimization rule* and the *supreme emergency*.

The Minimization Rule. Walzer has a difficulty with double effect's proportionality rule. Let us recall the rule: An action that has a good direct effect but an evil indirect effect is morally permissible unless the indirect evil is greater (or weightier) than the direct good. Here is Walzer's reaction to this rule: "We have to worry . . . about all those [indirect] deaths, for their number can be large; and subject only to the proportionality rule—a weak constraint—double effect provides a blanket justification."[26] I think Walzer exaggerates how much indirect evil is allowed under the proportionality rule—it surely does not provide a *blanket* justification. Nevertheless, his main point is clear: double effect permits too much indirect evil.

For this reason, Walzer adds a second intention to double effect's single intention. This double intention, as he calls it, is embodied in his minimization rule (as I call it), which replaces the proportionality rule and modifies Rule One of double effect. His minimization rule can be stated as follows: When a person executes his main intention producing the good effect, he must also intend to minimize the evil of his indirect effect, accepting costs to himself.[27]

What does Walzer mean by the last phrase, "costs to himself?" Bear in mind that he formulates his rule in the context of war ethics; he is speaking of soldiers in battle. *Costs* mean that soldiers must take *due care* to protect the lives and safety of enemy civilians. Walzer discusses several examples to illustrate the concept of due care. I limit myself to the following case from World War I. A British soldier, Frank Richards, describes one of his battle experiences:

> When bombing [by hand grenades] dug-outs or cellars, it was always wise to throw the bombs into them first and have a look around them after. But we had to be very careful in this village as there were civilians in some of the cellars. We shouted down to them to make sure. Another man and I shouted down one cellar twice and receiving no reply were just about to pull the pins out of our bombs when we heard a woman's voice and a young lady came up the cellar steps. . . . She and the members of her family . . . had not left [the cellar] for some days. They guessed an attack was being made and when we first shouted down had been too frightened to answer.[28]

Walzer argues that double effect's rule of proportionality would have allowed Richards to throw the bombs down the cellar without asking first if anyone was there. For if he did this, and it turned out that civilians were killed, their deaths would have been an unintended and indirect effect justified by the direct good of the military importance of securing the village. However, the minimization rule required Richards to shout down the cellar first. This shows he had the intention of minimizing civilian casualties by taking due care of their lives and safety—at some risk to himself. German soldiers could also have been down there, and when Richards told the civilians to come up, they could have followed them firing their guns. Walzer denies that his rule requires soldiers to act heroically. "He [Richards] was acting as a moral man ought to act; his is not an example of fighting heroically, above and beyond the call of duty, but simply of fighting well."[29] In a recent essay, Walzer restates the minimization rule: "Conduct your war in the presence of noncombatants on the other side with the same care *as if* your citizens were the noncombatants."[30] This imperative might be called the *doctrine of the moral equality of civilians.*

Despite the significant difference between the proportionality and minimization rules, it is arguable that Walzer misinterprets the double effect principle in the preceding example. On Walzer's interpretation of double effect, *if* Richards threw live grenades down a cellar where civilians may have been hiding without shouting out first "who's there," he would have acted as follows: The end of his action is to secure the village (good); his means is to clear cellars by using hand grenades (morally indifferent); the indirect effect is the death or serious injury of persons hiding in the cellars, be they enemy combatants or civilians; and in this case, direct good outweighs and overrides indirect evil. In my view, this interpretation is implausible because it makes a substantial distinction between the action's means and its indirect effect when, in reality, they are one and the same; the act of clearing cellars is ipso facto the act of killing and injuring the persons down there.

I think that the correct interpretation of double effect in this hypothetical situation is: The soldier's end is to secure the village; his means is clearing the cellars of persons hiding in them, whether civilians or enemy combatants, by using hand grenades to directly attack them; *and* the action has no significant indirect effect. On my interpretation, the soldier's action is immoral, since his means involves a significant probability of directly killing or injuring civilians; he already knows that civilians are hiding in some cellars. As we saw in chapter 2, for double effect to work, we must always be able to make a real distinction between an action's means and its indirect effect.

The Supreme Emergency. The supreme emergency (a term Walzer borrows from Churchill) modifies the principles of discrimination and double effect. A supreme emergency exists in a nation when it faces a wartime crisis defined by two criteria: (1) the danger posed by an enemy aggressor nation is imminent so that its national survival is at stake; (2) the danger is of an unusual and horrifying kind. In such a crisis, Walzer contends that a nation is permitted to directly attack civilians of the enemy nation if such action is deemed necessary for its national survival. The supreme emergency constitutes a major exception to just war theory's absolute ban on directly attacking civilians.

Walzer argues that Great Britain had a supreme emergency in the early days of World War II from June 1940 (after the fall of France) to the summer of 1942. During this two-year period, Hitler's armies triumphed everywhere, he says, and Britain stood alone against the Nazi menace, thus making the danger imminent. And certainly the Nazi danger was both unusual and horrifying. As Walzer expresses it: Nazism was "evil objectified in the world, and in a form so potent and apparent that there could never have been anything to do but fight against it."[31] Consequently, Britain's decision to indiscriminately bomb German cities, including large civilian population areas, was morally permissible during this two-year crisis. Britain need not restrict its bombing to military targets.

Implicit in his two criteria are two subcriteria: (1) the military measures proposed are judged to be a necessary and effective means in fighting the enemy; and (2) from one's own perspective, the decision to directly attack and kill civilians is based on a reasoned judgment, that is, someone in authority has carefully studied the issue, considered all alternatives, listened to advisors and experts, and is not deciding on self-serving motives. Walzer claims that these two subcriteria were also met by Britain's decision to indiscriminately bomb German cities. The second subcriterion does not mean one must have strong or sufficient evidence to think that the military measures decided upon will be effective by some objective, scientific standard. That does not matter, according to Walzer, because a nation's back is up against the wall, and there is no other way to fight. The decision has the form of a bet. "I wager this determinate crime (the killing of innocent people) against that immeasurable evil (a Nazi triumph)"[32] and hope for the best.

Walzer insists that Britain's bombing of German cities should have ended in July 1942. By then, the Russians were fighting effectively against the Germans, and the United States had long since entered the war. Britain was not standing alone. A supreme emergency no longer existed. Walzer does not provide any other examples of a supreme emergency.

After July 1942, Walzer condemns the Allied bombing campaign of German cities as terrorism, and that was when most of the bombing occurred, directly killing between 300,000 and 600,000 civilians in cities such as Essex, Hamburg, Cologne, Bremen, Berlin (several times), Dortmund, and reaching its nadir in the infamous fire-bombing of Dresden in February 1945, in a cultural city having no military significance where 100,000 civilians perished at a time when the war was essentially over. Churchill later regretted the decision to bomb Dresden.[33] Walzer characterizes the bombing as terrorism because its end was to break the will of the German people in continuing the war by means of the saturation bombing of cities and thus random mass murder of civilians.

Walzer equally condemns America's saturation and obliteration bombing of Japan's cities toward the end of the Pacific campaign. Obviously, no supreme emergency existed in the United States then—or ever during the war. In February 1945, the XXI Bomber Command under General Curtis LeMay began fire-bombing a total of seventy-three Japanese cities. Japan's six largest cities were devastated. Most casualties were civilians. In March 1945, 100,000 civilians perished in a bombing raid on Tokyo. Atomic bombs were dropped on Hiroshima and Nagasaki on August 6 and 9, respectively, quickly killing up to 220,000 mostly civilians. Tens of thousands more would die in coming years from a variety of illnesses and diseases caused by radiation.

In one respect, Walzer considers the bombing of Japanese cities to be even morally worse than that of German cities, especially the atomic bombings. For the Nazis were a far greater danger to democracy, freedom, and civilization than Japan was. Therefore, although it was just for the Allies to demand unconditional surrender from Germany, the same demand from Japan was excessive and unjust. But it was precisely this demand that led to the decision to drop the atomic bombs.

America's very costly planned invasion of the Japanese mainland scheduled for 1946 was predicated on unconditional surrender. By one estimate, one million American soldiers would die. Japanese losses would be much higher.

Other estimates were lower. America's leaders argued that by dropping the bombs, the war would end and the very costly invasion would be avoided. And although the casualties from the atomic bombs would be very high, their numbers would be far less than those of a mainland invasion. On this utilitarian argument, the bombs were dropped and the war did quickly end.[34]

However, if conditional surrender terms had been offered, and especially if Japan was told it could keep the emperor, *both* the invasion and the atomic bombings might have been avoided.[35] The Japanese were told this anyway after the bombs were dropped, and they quickly surrendered. Indeed, the emperor had been seeking peace since March, after touring devastated Tokyo.[36] But militating against offering peace terms or conditional surrender to Japan was a nihilistic, war-is-hell mentality among America's top political leaders, including Henry Stimpson, Secretary of War; James Brynes, Secretary of State; Arthur Compton, chief scientific advisor to the government; and President Truman himself.[37]

I agree with Walzer's critique of Allied bombing policy during World War II, except that I do not accept his supreme emergency, for reasons that will be developed later.

Walzer's concept of supreme emergency does not apply to the other absolute prohibitions against directly attacking civilians (or noncombatants). POWs may not be tortured or otherwise mistreated. Ground soldiers may not shoot and kill civilians, as they did in the My Lai massacre during the Vietnam War. Women may not be raped, as the Russian soldiers did when they rolled into Germany in the Battle of Berlin.

Utilitarianism

Although utilitarianism is probably the dominant ethical theory in Anglo-American thought today, it does not have a comprehensive theory of war. It has, however, one central idea that parts company with just war theory. For utilitarianism, the morality of an action is primarily determined by its consequences, not by either its intention or its motive. Since just war theory's moral distinction between the direct and indirect attack of civilians is based on intention—direct attacks are intentional and indirect attacks are not—

utilitarianism rejects this distinction. What matters is not *how* civilians are attacked and killed but *that* they are. Indirectly attacking civilians is as morally bad as directly attacking them.

As a result, utilitarianism rejects the principle of double effect. But there is another reason for this rejection. Utilitarianism argues that there is no difference between the means of an action and its indirect effect. Indirect effect is always reducible to means. Therefore, ethical reasoning is always about means-end reasoning. Does the goodness of the end outweigh the badness of the means? If so, an action is morally permissible. If not, an action is morally impermissible. In the conduct of war regarding the moral treatment of civilians, the question comes down to this: In a military operation, is the evil of all civilian casualties less or greater than the good of the end of the operation itself, in relation to, ultimately, the good of the war's end or purpose? In this context, utilitarianism shares Walzer's concern that double effect allows too many so-called indirect civilian casualties.

A PERSONALIST THEORY

I turn now to my own theory on the moral treatment of civilians in war. It is based on three main moral ideas: the *principle of community*, the *principle of intentionality*, and the *concept of human rights*. As explained in chapter 2, community is the supreme moral principle (or standard), and intentionality is the main procedural principle for applying the community principle to individual situations. In turn, the community principle grounds human rights, and the intentionality principle governs the application of these rights to individual situations.

I divide this part of the chapter into four sections. In the first three, I apply each of my three moral ideas to select war issues. Then in section four, I develop a lengthy critique of Walzer's supreme emergency.

Community and Pacifism: Personal and Impersonal Relations

In chapter 2, I formulated the principle of community as follows: An action is morally right if it promotes a *personal relation* of persons, either intrapersonal or interpersonal, and morally wrong if it directly intends an *absolute impersonal relation* of persons. However, a serious pacifist objection immediately arises. Since the essence of war consists of enemy combatants directly attacking and killing each other, how can such relations *not* be absolutely impersonal? If they are, then my principle of community implies pacifism just as much as Macmurray's concept of community seems to. And why not, since my principle has been so heavily influenced by it? To answer this objection, I must revisit and refine the principle of community and apply its three types of relations—personal, relative impersonal, and absolute impersonal—to war itself, and not just to civilians in war.

If persons act in accordance with the community principle, they establish personal relations between or among the persons related, and community is thereby created. And to the extent that many persons collectively act on this principle as members of society, their society becomes a community, a personalist society, as I developed the latter concept in chapter 8. Now, friendship, we have seen, is community between two persons and as such the smallest type of community. Friendship is also the model, the archetype, the fullest expression of community between two persons and hence the fullness of a personal relation. But there are other, less full personal relations (chapter 2), and these are the ones that are especially relevant to the morality of war.

The ideal of a personal relation, as in friendship, has the following characteristics. First, it is holistic: persons treat each other as whole persons and not as limited, specific functions or roles, which is the characteristic of impersonal relations. Second, the three constituent values of community are freedom, equality, and justice. Justice is the basic (or lower) value, and freedom and equality are its higher or primary values. Third, the motive of community is love; we care about the other for his or her own sake. And fourth, the fruition of community is peace, the harmony of persons in the fullest and most positive sense of harmony. These values and ingredients of friendship exist less fully in other types of personal relations.

Because of the necessities of social life, with its institutions, laws, and division of labor dictated by persons' economic needs and desires, many relations between or among persons are impersonal. These relations do not involve the whole person; they are limited and functional, for example, institutional, business, and legal relations. These relations are morally justifiable providing that an impersonal relation of persons is subordinated to a personal relation. When this occurs, an impersonal relation is *relative*. If such subordination does not occur, if an impersonal relation is directly intended for its own sake, then an impersonal relation is *absolute*, as in slavery, to take an extreme example. The principle of community shares a similarity with Kant's second formulation of the categorical imperative (often called the principle of respect for persons): Treat every person, including oneself, as an end and never merely as a means.[38] End corresponds to personal relation; means (without the qualifier merely) corresponds to relative impersonal relation; and merely as a means corresponds to absolute impersonal relation. The community principle is a reinterpretation of Kant's principle.

War is waged between nations and declared by states. The political and military leaders who run the war, and the combatants who fight them, are related to each other and to the enemy with respect to the roles they play in the war. Therefore, the relations that constitute war are functional and impersonal. From the standpoint of the principle of community, then, the moral question is whether the impersonal relations of warfare can ever be relative, or are they always (intrinsically) absolute? Insofar as they are relative, they are morally right; insofar as they are absolute, they are morally wrong.

I need to clarify what I mean by morally right and morally wrong in this context. As I stated, justice is the basic value of community. This means that justice is the minimal and necessary requirement for morality. For an action to be morally right, it must at least possess justice. An action that fails in justice is unjust and ipso facto immoral. Now, a relative impersonal relation is subordinated to a personal function. As a result, a relative impersonal relation is morally right. Second, it is lower than, has less moral value than, a personal relation. And since justice is the basic (or lower) value of community, justice is the essential value of a relative impersonal relation. For example, a contract, in a business or legal relation, is an instrument of justice. If the contract is honored, justice is served, and the impersonal relation is to that extent for the sake of a personal relation; if it is not honored, injustice is committed, and the impersonal relation becomes absolute by not being subordinated to a personal relation. Since absolute impersonal relations lack justice, they are inherently immoral.

However, a qualification is in order. I am not implying a dualism between justice, on the one hand, and freedom and equality, on the other. On one level, justice is constituted by freedom and equality, as in "equal justice under the law," or in Rawls's first principle of justice, which, as we have seen, states that all persons, as citizens, are entitled to the fullest amount of liberty (or freedom) that is compatible with an equal amount of liberty (or freedom) for all other citizens. As I explained in chapter 8, justice for all citizens, as constituted by freedom and equality, is the idea of justice that belongs to a society that is a constitutional democracy. But as I also explained (in chapter 2), there are different meanings of *freedom* and *equality*. To simplify matters for the present context, I distinguish two levels of freedom and equality: a lower level that defines justice, and a higher level that transcends justice. In the latter sense, as the primary values of community, freedom and equality are fuller expressions of personhood than they are as the two essential elements of justice, because the higher level of freedom and equality engage the whole person, whereas their lower level counterparts engage a limited aspect of personhood, that aspect covered by justice. Friends treating each other as equal persons is a fuller expression of equality than is equal justice under the law. Likewise, the mutual self-revelation and self-expression of freedom in friendship is a fuller expression of freedom than is political liberty.

Since the essence of war against the enemy consists of impersonal relations, and since the moral rightness or wrongness of these relations is a matter of justice, the morality of war is defined in terms of justice. This is the fundamental truth in just war theory. Therefore, for any war relation against the enemy to be just, a relative impersonal relation must be possible. If so, pacifism is false. Conversely, if all impersonal relations against the enemy in war are inherently absolute, a just war is impossible and pacifism is true. Accordingly, we must try to determine if we can have a relative impersonal relation with the enemy in war. Or, to reframe this as a question in the most forceful way: Since relative impersonal relations are subordinated to personal relations, can we ever treat the enemy in war in such a way that it makes sense to say that we also have a personal relation with him, even though we may be directly intending to kill him/her, which is normal for warfare? I now argue that such treatment is possible.

Since justice is the essential moral value of a relative impersonal relation and the basic (lower) moral value of a personal relation, if we can treat the enemy in war justly, then we establish a relative impersonal relation with him and in doing so also establish some sort of a personal relation. The personal relation would not have the fullness of friendship, of course, but as we said there are different kinds of personal relations. Regarding the question of justice, I contend that if a nation waging a war complies with all the provisions, principles, and rules of just war theory, as modified by my moral trilogy of community, intentionality, and human rights (some of these modifications will be explained later), then both enemy combatants and civilians are treated justly. In my view, just war theory in general is a valid elaboration of the justice component of the community principle insofar as justice applies to war, so when we act in accordance with the theory (as modified by my personalist theory), we establish a relative impersonal relation with an enemy thereby also establishing a *barely minimal personal relation* with him/her. I say "barely minimal" for good reason, for after all, combatants are required, if necessary, to directly attack and kill enemy combatants. But if they do so justly, they maintain a personal relation in the sense that enemy combatants treat each other with the respect that is due persons under the extreme conditions of war.

At this juncture, we face another objection. In the context of war, are we not effectively making a relative impersonal relation indistinguishable from a personal relation? If so, we are undermining the principle of community itself, which depends upon a real difference between personal and impersonal relations. The answer is that in general the two relations are not independent of each other. Instead, the impersonal relation is a *dimension* of the personal relation. For example, on one level, my relations with my students are impersonal, since they are institutional. As institutional, they are defined by the role or function of teacher-student, and I have a duty to be just to all my students with respect to their course performance. At the same time, I recognize that they are persons and treat them accordingly, with the respect due persons. I treat them with equality, as equal persons. I treat them with freedom, as rational and free beings who are responsible for their actions, who ought to want to freely and critically think for themselves, and who can make their own free choices as I attempt to educate them. The personal relation defines our relation as a whole, and since the impersonal relation is a dimension of it, the impersonal relation is subordinated to the personal relation.

It will be argued, however, that my education example is implausible for war, because war and education have contrary direct intentions. In education, the teacher intends the growth and development of his students as persons, as rational beings. In war, we intend the opposite: the death or destruction of the enemy.

Despite this major difference, the two relations have something significant in common. War is not always about killing.[39] The ultimate goal of war ought to be the establishment of a just and lasting peace with the enemy. During a war, there are long periods of routine activity, even boredom. As one military expert puts it: "Combat is 99 percent sheer boredom and one percent pure terror."[40] And as we saw in chapter 1, action may be a single act, a continuum of actions, or a collective action of a group. An entire war is a continuum of collective action made up of countless individual actions, only some of which intend killing. As a collective action, the war is informed by what Macmurray calls a *general intention*.[41] In all their individual actions, combatants and their military and political leaders ought to maintain a general intention to recognize that the enemy they are fighting are *persons*, and this general intention is expressed in the particular intention of all their varied individual actions. As a result, enemies are to be treated as equal and free persons just as they themselves ought to be treated. I say free, because combatants have at least the freedom as persons to choose between treating the enemy with the respect that is due persons by obeying the principles and rules of *jus in bello*, or to follow the nihilistic doctrine that all war is hell. Likewise, they are free to choose between acting courageously or cowardly in battle. As free persons, as rational beings endowed with higher intelligence and free will, all are responsible for their choices and actions. Moreover, essential to a just and lasting peace with the enemy (at least ideally) is the establishment of a constitutional democracy, which is founded on principles of justice constituted by freedom and equality. And if one is waging a just war against the enemy, the likelihood is that one's own society is a constitutional democracy and the enemy is an outlaw regime so that one is fighting for freedom and democracy against the forces of injustice and wrongdoing, as in World War II. As Rawls repeatedly observes, constitutional democracies do not wage war on each other, a point that others have noted. Finally, all combatants are obliged to obey the doctrine of the moral equality of civilians. Ultimately, then, the values of justice, freedom, and equality separate a morally right war from a morally wrong war, in the treatment of both combatants and civilians, and these are the same values that separate a personal relation of persons from an absolute impersonal relation.

Even in times of actual combat, when the enemy has to be repelled with destructive force and killed if necessary, the above general intention is maintained. One still sees the enemy as a person, who, because of circumstances, has to be regretfully killed. Here the motive that supports and sustains the general intention is vitally important. We ought not to fight a war from motives of revenge, vindictiveness, or hatred. The enemy is not subhuman, as Hitler thought the Russians and Eastern European peoples were.

In conclusion, despite my defense of the possibility of a just war, war as such is so evil and destructive that a particular war is morally justified only if not waging it constitutes a greater violation of the community principle than waging it. This rarely occurs, however. Therefore, most wars are immoral. War as such is prima facie immoral. But directly attacking civilians in war is intrinsically immoral, since it is murderous.

Intentionality, Proportionality, and Minimization

As explained in chapter 2, the intentionality principle modifies and replaces the principle of double effect. I now summarize and refine intentionality, highlight its differences with double effect, and apply intentionality to the conflict between the proportionality and minimization rules in an attempt to synthesize them.

The principle of intentionality is based on four key moral elements of action: direct intention, indirect intention, motive, and consequences. In the present context, I formulate the intentionality principle as follows: Direct intention is the primary moral element of action, and indirect intention, motive, and consequences are its secondary elements.

Direct intention corresponds to what double effect simply calls intention. It consists of an action's end and means. It is what a person knowingly and willingly aims at in action. *Indirect intention* is defined as what a person foresees but does not will in action. (When I say *foresees*, I do not necessarily mean that it is actually foreseen; I mean what ought to be foreseen by a reasonably prudent person.) Indirect intention corresponds to what double effect calls indirect effect, but with two differences. First, we must distinguish between indirect intention and indirect effect. For what is foreseen and unwilled may not actually occur, or may occur differently, as an action is performed. Likewise, we must distinguish between direct intention and direct effect. There is no guarantee that any intention will produce its intended effect. Double effect does not sufficiently distinguish between an action's intention and its effect (or consequences). Second, double effect denies that the indirect effect is intentional. Proponents of double effect characterize it as "accidental," or "unintentional." This is a mistake, in my view. Since the indirect effect is the by-product or side effect of direct intention, it is intentional in some sense, but to a lesser degree than is direct intention. The indirect effect is significantly thought secondarily intentional. My distinction between direct intention and indirect intention grounds the distinction between directly attacking civilians and indirectly attacking them.

Motive denotes the reason for a direct intention—the emotion (or emotions) in which the intention originates and which sustain it in action. Motives are the springboards of action. Finally, *consequences* are the effects, results, or outcomes of action. Unless and until an intention (either direct or indirect) is completed and actualized, one must always distinguish between intention and consequences.

Direct intention is the primary moral element because it is the core or central element of action. It distinguishes human action from animal behavior. Behavior has motive and consequences but lacks intention. However, the motives of behavior are simpler and more biological than the higher, more complex motives of action. Direct intention is more important than indirect intention for three reasons. First, only direct intention is *willed* in the strict sense. Second, the indirect is the by-product of the direct. Third, not every action has an indirect intention, but every action must have a direct intention without which it would become behavior. Finally, intention has moral priority over consequences because an intention does not always produce its intended consequences. Nevertheless, the action's intention remains intact. In sum, then, the morality of an action lies primarily in its direct intention, which constitutes the moral "essence" of an action.

The intentionality principle can help resolve the conflict between the proportionality and minimization rules. I think Walzer is basically right about the minimization rule. However, he leaves one big question unanswered: What degree, amount, or magnitude of indirect evil is needed to override a good direct effect, especially considering that Walzer agrees with double effect that a direct effect is morally more important than an indirect effect? What if a person did not act to minimize indirect evil, but the magnitude of indirect evil is still less than the direct good of his action. Would Walzer say that the action as a whole is immoral? Or is it still morally permissible, but not as good as an action that minimized indirect evil? He does not say. If he logically answered these questions, I contend he would have to say what the proportionality rule says: Indirect evil must be greater than direct good to override it and make the action as a whole immoral. However, the intent of the proportionality rule is to specify the *maximum* allowable indirect evil, which is a level approximately equal to that of direct good. But this maximum level need not be allowed to occur, and this is where Walzer's minimization rule nicely complements the proportionality rule. There is a wide range between maximum and minimum.

I now propose a synthesis of these two rules as part of my intentionality principle. In this context, the major difference between intentionality and double effect concerns the moral status of *motive*. In both the traditional version and Walzer's version of double effect, the moral quality of an action's motive is not taken into account in weighing indirect evil against direct good. One reason is that, for just war theory, there is a tendency to confuse motive and intention. However, since the intentionality principle makes an explicit distinction between an action's motive and intention, the motive must be taken into account in the calculus between direct good and indirect evil. Therefore, a good direct intention can be overridden by the *combined* weight of a bad indirect intention and a bad motive. So if a bad motive is present in an action, the magnitude of indirect evil could be less than the direct good and still override it.[42] Furthermore, since the indirect effect is intentional in some sense although not as intentional as the direct effect, whereas the double effect principle denies altogether that the indirect effect is intentional, this is another reason to favor minimizing the amount of indirect evil committed in warfare. Since indirect effects are intentional, persons are morally responsible for committing them. Indirect effects are morally serious.

However, since double effect asserts that indirect effects are merely accidental (or unintentional), one may ask why it needs the proportionality rule at all, since a person is not morally responsible for any accidental consequences that may follow from his or her action. And if they happen to be evil, so be it. In truth, double effect has an ambivalent attitude toward indirect effects. On the one hand, the principle endows indirect effects with considerable moral weight by holding that indirect evil will morally invalidate an action if indirect evil outweighs an action's direct good; on the other hand, the principle deprives indirect effects of any moral significance by characterizing them as accidental or unintentional. The two claims are contradictory. To resolve this moral incoherence, one must affirm that indirect effects are intentional in some significant sense. This affirmation paves the way for my synthesis of the proportionality and minimization rules.

Accordingly, I propose to replace the proportionality and minimization rules with what I shall call the *rule of minimal proportionality*: Direct good is overridden by either (a) the combination of indirect evil and bad motive, or (b) indirect evil singly, if either (a) or (b) is greater than the direct good, recognizing (c) that in each and every situation we have a duty to minimize indirect evil, and in so doing to abide by the doctrine of the moral equality of civilians. This rule refines and amends Rule One of intentionality (chapter 2).

As an application of this rule, I briefly comment on the Obama administration's counterterrorism drone attack policy in the Mideast. There is controversy over how many civilians have been killed and how they have been killed. It is not clear whether the civilian casualties are direct or indirect. Is everyone being targeted within a widely defined terrorist zone, which includes non-terrorist civilians? If so, it would seem that the administration is directly attacking and killing civilians. If, however, only terrorists are being targeted, and the weapons have pinpoint accuracy, civilian casualties would be indirect and only occasional, and therefore probably not of sufficient magnitude to outweigh and override the good direct intention with respect to the value of the terrorist(s) being targeted. If the latter is true, it might also be the case that the Obama administration has a policy of minimizing civilian casualties. Only if it releases more information can we properly morally evaluate the policy. As of this writing, it has promised to do so.

Human Rights, Terrorism, and Humanitarianism

As we have seen, rights and their correlative duties constitute the field of justice, one of the three constituent values of community. Human rights are the most basic of rights. They are natural in origin and universal in scope. All humans, as persons, are naturally endowed with them.

Human rights are divided into negative rights and positive rights. In a *negative* right, persons have a right *not* to be treated in certain ways, and others have a correlative duty not to so treat them, for example, the right to life or the right not to be tortured. In a *positive* right, persons have a right to *be* treated in certain ways, and others have a correlative duty to treat them accordingly, for example, the right to the necessities of life, such as food and water, housing, clothing, energy, education, and medical care. The Universal Declaration of Human Rights, passed by the General Assembly of the United Nations on December 10, 1948, is one of the most famous and important documents of human rights. In a constitutional democracy, some human rights are stated in its constitution, as in our own Bill of Rights, and in other amendments, particularly the Thirteenth, Fourteenth, Fifteenth, Seventeenth, Nineteenth, Twenty-Fourth, and Twenty-Sixth Amendments. The history of the US Constitution is a history of extending human rights to increasing numbers and groups of American citizens. In general, constitutional rights are embodiments of human rights.

Based on the foregoing trilogy of moral ideas, I summarily reject nihilism and terrorism. Since both reject the distinction between combatant and civilian and hold that it is morally permissible to directly attack civilians on the other side in massive numbers as if they were enemy combatants waging an unjust war, both are contrary to the community principle, to the intentionality principle, and to human rights. So also is any usage of nuclear, chemical, and biological weapons—commonly called weapons of mass destruction (WMDs)—terrorism's ultimate tactic. Any use of WMDs is intrinsically irrational and immoral, an act of madness, for several reasons. First, the war in which they would be used is unwinnable. Second, their use would have uncontrollable consequences. Third, the magnitude and extent of their damage is unacceptable. And fourth, the weapons by their nature obliterate the distinction between directly attacking civilians and directly attacking military targets.

My emphasis on human rights significantly modifies a provision of *jus ad bellum* in conventional just war theory. This provision holds that each nation-state has basic rights of territorial integrity and political sovereignty, which must be respected by all other nation-states. No state can interfere in the internal affairs of another state by using military force that violates its territorial integrity or political sovereignty. Such interference is aggression—a war crime—and the attacked nation has a just cause for war. This provision was certainly violated in the United States–led coalition's invasion of Iraq (infra, n. 22).

However, my personalist theory's deep concern for human rights may in exceptional cases require that nations interfere in the internal affairs of others on humanitarian grounds, even by using force, providing it is not excessive. If human rights abuses in a nation are so grave and egregious that they rise to the level of a people or peoples being massacred or enslaved, then nations of goodwill must unite to stop the horrendous evil. In such a situation, even invasion may be morally justified, as it would have been in Rwanda in 1994 when the ruling Hutu regime slaughtered an estimated 800,000 to one million civilians, and no one intervened to stop the massacre. President Bill Clinton later regretted his inaction, but no other nations intervened, nor did the United Nations. By contrast, the human rights abuses in Iraq in 2003 were not nearly on the level or of the magnitude to justify an invasion.

On a lower or lesser scale of human rights violations than what occurred in Rwanda, if a nation's people have been politically and economically oppressed by a long-ruling dictator, and they mount a popular uprising against this regime in their desire to establish a democracy but are no match for the dictator's military force, and they ask for military aid from outside nations of goodwill, the aid should be supplied, especially if it does not involve the deployment of any outside ground forces, as in the very successful case of the United States and its NATO allies supporting the popular uprising in Libya against Moammar Gadhafi.[43]

The Supreme Emergency: A Critique

Walzer's supreme emergency is curious for three reasons. First, whereas the intent of his minimization rule is to reduce the level of evil in warfare, the supreme emergency goes in the opposite direction. It increases the amount of direct evil that is morally permissible in war compared to traditional/conventional just war theory. Second, he holds (as I do) that direct evil is morally worse than indirect evil. So the kind of evil he would allow to increase is of greater moral importance (to him) than the kind of evil he wants to decrease. Third, his supreme emergency tends to weaken his moral condemnation of the Allied saturation and obliteration bombing of German and Japanese cities in the latter part of World War II. For these reasons, I consider the supreme emergency to be contrary to my trilogy of moral ideas. Therefore, I must reject it. I now argue that his supreme emergency has five defects: (1) the time frame for its one example is too broad, (2) its criteria are insufficient, (3) it is conceptually incoherent, (4) it is too utilitarian, and (5) it rests on communitarianism.

Supreme Emergency's Time Frame

The supreme emergency's time frame is too broad; it should end in early December 1941, not in July 1942. On December 6, 1941, the Russians decisively repelled the Germans in the Battle of Moscow. The stunning defeat ended the Germans' long Russian campaign (Operation Barbarossa), begun in June. The Soviet victory showed the world, including Britain, that the Germans were not invincible; the mighty *Wehrmacht* could be beaten. Stalin and his new commanding general, Marshal Zhukov, emerged as effective military leaders. The next day, December 7, Japan bombed Pearl Harbor, and the United States finally entered the war. Churchill was jubilant. He now knew that with America's industrial might, the Allies would eventually win. Time was on their side. Because of these momentous twin events, a supreme emergency in Britain no longer existed, even if one accepts Walzer's concept and one example of a supreme emergency.[44]

If, then, Walzer were to narrow the time frame accordingly, he would strengthen his case for the supreme emergency. I still would not accept it, however, because of its other defects.

Supreme Emergency's Criteria

Walzer's supreme emergency needs a third criterion: There must be *strong evidence* to think that the military measures under consideration will be effective in achieving their objective.

The third criterion was not satisfied in Britain's bombing campaign of German cities. Britain's leaders had no real knowledge that bombing German cities would break the will of the German people to fight, any more than the German bombing of London demoralized British civilians. On the contrary, it strengthened British resolve to fight on. Britain's decision to bomb must be seen as basically a reflexive act of self-defense on the part of its leaders, with no evidence or ethical reasoning to support it. But even this justification is hard to understand. Britain was not about to be invaded by Germany, which lacked the naval resources for such a huge amphibious assault. Hitler's foolish plans for a naval invasion of England in 1940 (Operation Sea Lion) were quickly abandoned. At the same time, his air war against Britain was a disaster for the German *Luftwaffe*. And Roosevelt's lend-lease program was supplying England with much materiel, despite heavy losses from German U-boats. Even after Britain's supreme emergency ended, and the bombings intensified with "Thousand Bomber" raids, the campaign utterly failed to achieve its military objective of breaking the will of the German people. Some historians think that if the military assets used in the bombing campaign had been used in targeting the destruction of German military assets, the war in Europe would have ended considerably earlier, thus significantly reducing casualties on both sides and avoiding the widespread destruction of German cities.

At the time, the bombing proposal was controversial even among the

British people. A large percentage was opposed to it on moral grounds. Directly bombing large civilian population centers, they felt, would be crossing a moral line and stooping to the level of the Nazis, and would be contrary to the moral values of the long democratic tradition of England.

Supreme Emergency's Incoherent Language

In his book *Arguing about War*, Walzer describes the supreme emergency in language that not only reveals his deep moral discomfort about it but is incoherent, in my view. This discomfort was present in his earlier book *Just and Unjust Wars*, but not as deeply. Speaking of Britain's bombing campaign during the supreme emergency, he writes:

> It is enough to say flatly that the intention was wrongful, the bombing criminal; its victims were innocent men, women, and children. . . . But if there was no other way of preventing a Nazi triumph, then the immorality—no less immoral, for what can the deliberate killing of the innocent be?—was also, simultaneously, morally defensible.[45]

How can one and the same act be simultaneously *immoral* and *morally defensible*? Walzer calls it a "paradox"; I call it a contradiction. For the remainder of the chapter in which this citation appears, he tries to resolve the paradox. I do not think he succeeds. It remains, in my view, an incoherence or contradiction.

The problem is his use of *moral* and *immoral*. If the situation at issue is a moral one, which in this case it is, and if a proposed action is defensible or permissible, then it must be morally right in some significant sense of *moral*. Conversely, if an act is immoral, it must be morally indefensible and impermissible in that situation. To overcome this incoherent use of language, he could say something like this: In all cases except for the supreme emergency, directly attacking civilians is immoral. But in the supreme emergency, it is morally permissible to attack them. I still would not agree with him, but at least his so-called paradox would disappear.

Another way Walzer could resolve the paradox is by distinguishing between the right and the good, which I do. On my theory, a particular act can be simultaneously bad and (morally) right, for example, lying to save an innocent person's life. The act is bad because the essence or nature of lying is bad, since it is contrary to the good of truth and truth-telling. But in this extreme or exceptional situation, the good of an innocent person's life, which the prospective liar has the power to save, overrides the evil of lying because this good is so much greater than the evil, and so in this situation lying is morally right. If Walzer took this route, he could say something like the following about the supreme emergency: Directly attacking innocent civilians is a very great evil, but in the supreme emergency, this evil is overridden by the still greater good of defeating Hitler and the Nazi Third Reich, and so the supreme emergency is morally right.

The reason he would not take this route, however, which is also the reason for his incoherent use of language, is that he wants to avoid any element or appearance of utilitarian means-end reasoning. Walzer denies that the supreme emergency can be morally justified by means-end reasoning. Such reasoning, he says, has strict limits. We must now address these limits.

The Limits of Means-End Reasoning

I agree with Walzer that utilitarian means-end reasoning has a limited and subsidiary role in ethical theory and that it has no place in morally justifying the supreme emergency, much less in justifying the rest of the Allied bombing campaign against German and Japanese cities. In my theory, means-end reasoning is limited by the principles of community and intentionality and by the concept of human rights. Means-end reasoning is morally permissible so long as it does not violate any of these three primary moral ideas. The intentionality principle spells out when means-end reasoning is permissible and when it is not. I deny that means-end reasoning is inherently utilitarian, as Walzer seems to think. The problem with utilitarianism is that it places no limits on such reasoning.

Walzer's ethical theory tries to steer a middle or moderate course between utilitarianism and absolutism. Absolutism completely rejects the moral validity of means-end reasoning. Absolutism, he says, refers to rights theory. Walzer writes:

> The absolutism of rights theory . . . [holds that] innocent human beings can never be intentionally [directly] attacked. Innocence is their shield, and though it is only a verbal shield, a paper shield, no defense at all against bombs and bullets, it is impenetrable to moral argument.[46]

According to Walzer, absolutism holds that all rights are absolute. Although he does not define an absolute right, I suppose he means a right that has no exceptions. However, it is inaccurate and unfair to characterize a rights theorist as necessarily an absolutist. I believe in human rights and in other kinds of rights. But probably only a few are absolute—but fundamental. The right not to be a slave is absolute, as is the right of a group of people not to be exterminated. But the right of free speech and a fortiori property rights are not absolute. I distinguish, then, between *absolute human rights* and *nonabsolute human rights*.

Is the right of civilians in war not to be directly attacked by the enemy absolute? I think so, providing one understands the proper meaning of *absolute*. I distinguish two possible meanings of absolute. (In this respect, I probably part company with traditional just war theory.) The first is illegitimate, in my view, and should be rejected as a serious ethical concept. It holds that there are no *possible* or *conceivable* exceptions to a right. To invalidate this meaning of absolute, all one has to do is think of a case in which the right does not seem to apply, no matter how implausible or preposterous the case may be. For example, if you claim that the right not to be tortured is absolute in this sense, does that mean you would not torture one person to prevent the deaths of one million people by some terrorist organization? If an absolutist answers no, his position is probably morally discredited in the minds of most people. If he answers yes, he contradicts himself and logically abandons his absolutism. He is impaled on the horns of a dilemma.

However, the horns of this dilemma can be escaped by defining a second meaning of absolute, which is more realistic and rational. In this sense, an absolute right is one that has no *legitimate* exceptions, where legitimate refers to plausible cases, cases that refer to the real world, not to cases that someone excogitates in some mental world of his own making. After all, the purpose of ethics is to formulate sound rational principles, rules, values, and virtues that apply to reality rather than to the fantastic examples of armchair philosophers. In this second meaning of absolute, which I accept, there must be an absolute ban on directly attacking enemy civilians in war with respect to our laws, treaties, conventions, and institutional policies and practices. Our legal and political institutions must absolutely prohibit such conduct. It is this meaning of absolute that was violated by the Bush-Cheney administration in its approval of torture, such as waterboarding.[47]

The violation of an absolute right produces an intrinsically immoral act, and the violation of a nonabsolute right produces a prima facie immoral act. Since civilians have an absolute right not to be directly attacked by an enemy nation, to do so is intrinsically immoral. Since intrinsically immoral acts are *always* immoral (e.g., slavery), means-end reasoning never applies to them. But since prima facie immoral acts are only immoral *in general* (e.g., lying and stealing), means-end reasoning does apply to them. However, as explained in chapter 2, only in exceptional cases of such acts will the goodness of the end outweigh and override the badness of the means, that is, the badness of the prima facie immoral act itself, as stated in Rule Five of intentionality.

My distinction between intrinsically immoral acts and prima facie immoral acts constitutes another important difference between the intentionality and double effect principles. As we have seen, double effect holds that a morally right action must have a good means (or at least an indifferent means) in addition to a good end; it cannot have a bad means. For intentionality, a morally right action cannot have a bad means if the means is an intrinsically immoral act. But in exceptional cases, a morally right action has a bad means if the means is a prima facie immoral act. By contrast, for the double effect principle, it seems that all immoral acts by definition are intrinsically immoral. Since double effect is part of traditional/conventional just war theory, my distinction represents a modification of just war theory.

This distinction also ties in to Walzer's minimization rule and to my minimal-proportionality rule. For when double effect judges a war or a military campaign or operation to have a good intention because its end is good and its means is either good or not bad, such moral purity could justify high levels if indirect evil. On the other hand, for the intentionality principle, since a war or military campaign or operation can be occasionally good even though it has a bad means, this mixture of good and evil diminishes the moral goodness of the direct intention so that a lesser amount of indirect evil is permissible.

Since means-end reasoning does not apply to absolute rights, and since the right of civilians in war not to be directly attacked by the enemy is absolute, the limits of means-end reasoning would be exceeded by anyone who applied such reasoning to this right. But I contend that these limits were exceeded in Walzer's supreme emergency. For despite his efforts to explain and justify it in language that avoids means-end reasoning, at bottom his supreme emergency is really based on it. In his one example of supreme emergency, he essentially argues that the means, consisting of the great evil of directly bombing civilians in German cities, is overridden by the still greater good of the end, consisting of a Nazi defeat, and so his justification of the supreme emergency is too utilitarian. However, even if we grant Walzer's claim (which I do not) that the supreme emergency is not based on means-end reasoning, we are still driven back to his incoherent use of moral language in his effort to justify it. Either way, his concept of supreme emergency fails.

Of course, Walzer denies that the right of civilians not to be directly attacked by the enemy in war is absolute, and this denial opens the door for the supreme emergency. Obviously, I think his denial is false. Still, I consider this denial, coupled with his denial that the supreme emergency is based on means-end reasoning, to be puzzling, even odd. This double denial is at the root of his incoherent use of moral language.

Since my absolute ban on directly attacking civilians in war is the same position held by traditional/conventional just war theory, how is my position original? Its originality lies in its foundation: my moral trilogy of community, intentionality, and human rights, and how they are interconnected and reinforce each other. By comparison, traditional just war theory is based on the moral theory of natural law; conventional just war theory is based on international law. Walzer's supreme emergency is based on his version of communitarianism, to which I now turn as my fifth and final criticism of the supreme emergency.

Communitarianism and Community

For Walzer, his communitarianism is the ultimate foundation of the supreme emergency. In chapter 2, I touched on this theory. It is time now to speak of it in some detail.

I suppose it would be fair to say that a communitarian holds that community is the supreme good and therefore the supreme standard of morality. Walzer seems to think so. For he holds that the survival and freedom of political communities are the highest values of international society.[48] Walzer frequently makes such statements about community. Therefore, when the survival and freedom of a community are at stake under the conditions specified by the supreme emergency, it is morally permissible to directly attack and kill enemy civilians. However, since I hold that the principle of community is the supreme moral standard, why cannot I likewise accept the supreme emergency?

The answer is that communitarianism and a personalist theory have quite different conceptions of community. As I stated in chapter 2, communitarianism's concept of community is that of an organic society. For a personalist theory, the organic model is a false conception of community, for reasons I explained in some detail in chapter 7. In contrast, a personalist society is a true community, and all of chapter 8 was devoted to laying out my conception of a personalist society. Communitarianism's idea of community is really a concept of *society*. This is indicated by the fact that when Walzer speaks of community it is usually as *political* communities. But a political group as such is a society, not a community. Walzer does not sufficiently distinguish between community and society. The following description of community is typical:

> The value of the community . . . isn't only individuals who are represented [in the community] but also the collective entity—religious, political, or cultural—that the individual compose and from which they derive some portion of their character, practices, and beliefs.[49]

This definition (or description) would seem to apply to any society, even an outlaw society.[50] But for a personalist theory, community is a society that is inherently morally good; it stands for a society that has noble moral ideals and aspirations and is intending their actualization into the key communal values of justice, freedom, and equality.

From a personalist standpoint, the combination of *political* and *community* is a confusing and ultimately incompatible combination of words, since a political group as such is a society for reasons explained in chapter 8. It is not thereby a community. However, if a political society embodies the values of community of which we spoke, it becomes a community and a personalist society. It is no longer merely a political society. A community, as in a personalist society, necessarily has a political structure that is essential to its societal dimension, but a community is more than or greater than a society as such, both morally and ontologically. A community is still a society, but *society* does not define its whole reality. Or as Macmurray succinctly puts it: "Every community is a society, but not every society is a community."[51] Individualistic and organic societies (chapter 7) are not communities in the personalist sense. Indeed, an individualistic society is not a community in any sense.

Communitarianism's conception of community is a version of the organic society because it is based on the whole-part analogy. By this analogy I mean that a whole is more than, or greater than, the sum of its parts. For communitarianism, the community as a whole is greater than the sum of its individual members, just as an organism as a whole is more than the sum of its member organs and other physical parts. Although Walzer says he is unsure about the whole-part analogy,[52] his descriptions of community belie his uncertainty; they display a robust whole-part thinking, as does the above citation. For my personalist theory, however, any organic model fails as an adequate or comprehensive description of both community and society.

It fails as an adequate description of community because persons as such, in their wholeness as persons, are not parts of anything, in the strict and literal sense of parts. Persons are wholes unto themselves (chapter 2) who are oriented toward other whole persons in community to fulfill their nature as persons. In this sense, community may be regarded as a *megawhole*, to coin a word, which I explain as follows. In the part-whole analogy, each part is subordinated to the whole. Such heteronomy, however, does not characterize community: each person in community is an autonomous and equal whole in relation to the other members of community, since they are all related as whole persons. In friendship, for example, it would be absurd to say that each friend is a part of the whole friendship and as such is subordinate to it. The friendship, as a community, consists of the free, equal, just, and loving way both friends are related to each other. By contrast, in society (or in the societal dimension of a personalist society), it makes sense to say that each individual's good is subordinated to the common good of society.

As the antithesis of an organic society, an individualistic society, such as libertarianism, does hold that the social whole is the sum of its individual member-parts. In this respect, individualism is based on a mathematical-type model. This is basically why libertarianism advocates a minimalist government and a laissez-faire capitalist economy. A personalist conception of community, however, transcends both the organic and mathematical models of thought.

The organic model also fails as an adequate description of society. Even though persons in society (as distinct from community) are related to each other as limited functions, they cannot be characterized *merely* as parts of the social whole. To make this point, we must distinguish between *person* and *individual*.[53] A person as a whole person is a member of community, as explained. A person as individual is a member of society, as a system of interrelated institutions and laws. In turn, two kinds of relations can exist between individuals and society. The first is adequately described by the whole-part analogy and is covered by the Aristotelian-Thomistic idea of the common good. In this respect, each individual is part of the social whole, part of the national society, and we all have a responsibility to work for the common good of society. This is the truth in communitarianism and in JFK's famous inaugural remark: "Ask not what your country can do for you, ask what you can do for your country." The whole-part analogy is not valid, however, when we speak of individual *rights*, especially constitutional and civil rights, unless one were to say that the idea of common good necessarily includes all the rights of individuals, which the traditional view does not. Insofar as individuals have rights, they do not have a responsibility to society but a claim against it, and so society has a responsibility (or duty) to individuals in justice to respect and promote their rights. This is why a society has a moral duty to provide universal healthcare to its citizens, for example. Healthcare is a human right.

It should be noted that when we consider limited aspects of personhood, the organic whole-part analogy is valid in a myriad of human relationships. As physic-chemical beings, we are parts of the whole cosmos; as organisms, we are parts of the whole planet earth as a mega-ecosystem; as team players, we are parts of the whole team, be it a military unit, a sports team, a business company (whether a corporation, a partnership, or a company owned by one individual), and so on. But as whole persons who are oriented toward community and find their self-realization in community, persons transcend all these relationships.

Since a personalist theory has a different idea of community than does communitarianism, it is not logically committed to the supreme emergency. By contrast, since Walzer's communitarian conception of community is actually that of an organic society, the good of the whole community is more than or greater than the good of its individual citizens, and so in the supreme emergency, the good of a nation-state overrides and justifies the evil of directly attacking some civilians of an enemy nation. The principle of community forbids this.

I close this chapter with an observation. Kant once said that if justice perishes, it is no longer worthwhile for humans to live upon the earth.[54] We might say something similar about peace. If peace perishes, either we will have, in the words of Hobbes, "the war of all against all,"[55] or else a universal totalitarian regime against which war can always erupt. In either case, it would be a life unworthy of humans, a life in which it would be true to say, in the legendary words of Santayana, "only the dead have seen the end of war."[56]

NOTES

1. PERSON, REASON, AND VALUE

1. On the naturalistic fallacy, see G. E. Moore, *Principii Ethica* (Cambridge: Cambridge University Press, 1903), p. 10.

2. How the principle of utility applies to individual cases differs, of course, depending on whether one is an act utilitarian or a rule utilitarian. For two good collections of different views of utilitarianism, see Jonathan Glover, ed., *Utilitarianism and Its Critics* (New York: Macmillan, 1990), and J. J. C. Smart and B. Williams, *Utilitarianism: For and Against* (New York: Cambridge University Press, 1973).

3. Jeremy Bentham, *An Introduction to the Principles of Morals and Legislation*, with an introduction by Laurence J. Lafleur (New York: Hafner, 1948), pp. 2–3 (emphasis in original).

4. Cf. Walter G. Jeffko, "A New Model of Reason as Standard of Value," in "Essays on John Macmurray's Post-Modern Philosophy: The Primacy of Persons in Community," ed. Harry Carson, unpublished manuscript.

5. John Macmurray, *Persons in Relation* (London: Faber & Faber; New York: Harper & Row, 1961; reprint, with an introduction by Frank G. Kirkpatrick, Amherst, NY: Humanity Books, 1991), p. 46. Page numbers from this and other works by Macmurray that have been reissued by Humanity Books are from the Humanity Books edition.

6. On Macmurray's description of the mutuality of the personal, see *Persons in Relation*, pp. 12, 69.

7. W. Norris Clarke, *Person and Being* (Milwaukee: Marquette University Press, 1993), pp. 58–59 (emphasis in original).

8. On the distinction between self and other, see John Macmurray, *The Self as Agent* (London: Faber & Faber; New York: Harper & Row, 1957; reprint, with an introduction by Stanley M. Harrison, Amherst, NY: Humanity Books, 1991), p. 106.

9. The term *activity* refers indifferently to action and to reflective (or secondary) thought. However, when I use the term *act*, it refers to action unless otherwise indicated.

10. Behaviorism would reject Macmurray's distinction between action and behavior. See, for example, B. F. Skinner, *Science and Human Behavior* (New York: Free Press, 1953).

11. On Macmurray's notion of absolute freedom, see *Conditions of Freedom* (London: Faber

& Faber, 1950; reprint, with an introduction by Walter G. Jeffko, Amherst, NY: Humanity Books, 1993), p. 2.

12. Macmurray's theory of the relation between action and reflective thought is a major theme in *Self as Agent*. Cf. Walter G. Jeffko, "Thought, Action, and Personhood," *Modern Schoolman* 52 (March 1975): 271–83.

13. Macmurray's evaluation of pragmatism is contained in his "The New Materialism," in *Marxism*, ed. J. Middleton Murray et al. (London: Chapman & Hall, 1935), pp. 54–58. On the differences between pragmatism and Macmurray, see Errol Harris, "Thought and Action," review of *The Self as Agent*, by John Macmurray, *Review of Metaphysics* 12, no. 3 (1959): 450–51.

14. Maurice Blondel, *L'Action* (Paris, 1983; reprint, Paris: Presses Universitaires de France, 1950); and *L'Action*, 2 vols. (Paris, 1936–37; reprint, Paris: Presses Universitaires de France, 1949 and 1963). Although both works bear the same title, they are quite different. The first is a phenomenology of action, the second an ontology or a metaphysics of action. For a brief and clear survey of Blondel's thought, see Henri Bouillard, "The Thought of Maurice Blondel: A Synoptic Vision," *International Philosophical Quarterly* 3, no. 3 (September 1963): 392–402.

15. For Macmurray's views on communication, see *Persons in Relation*, pp. 12, 34, 51, 59–60, 63, 67, 69, 76. Of related interest, see Robert O. Johann, "Freedom and Morality from the Standpoint of Communication," in *Freedom and Value*, ed. Robert O. Johann (New York: Fordham University Press, 1976), pp. 45–60, and Louis Roy, "Interpersonal Knowledge According to John Macmurray," *Modern Theology* 5, no. 4 (1989): 349–65. See also Walter G. Jeffko, "Are 'Person' and 'Agent' Coextensive? Reflections on John Macmurray," *American Benedictine Review* 44, no. 4 (December 1993): 352–70. I am indebted to Jürgen Habermas's remarkable work, *The Theory of Communicative Action*, vol. 1, *Reason and the Rationalization of Society*, trans. Thomas McCarthy (Boston : Beacon Press, 1984).

16. A salient feature of Macmurray's concept of reason is that it cannot be identified with intellect, with the capacity to think. Unlike most of the Western tradition, he argues that reason must be expanded to include our feelings and emotions. Otherwise, a false dualism is created between reason and emotion. See John Macmurray, *Reason and Emotion*, 2nd ed. (London: Faber & Faber, 1961; reprint, with an introduction by John E. Costello, Amherst, NY: Humanity Books, 1992). Psychology has become interested in the concept of emotional intelligence, as distinguished from the traditional, intellectual concept of intelligence as IQ. See, for example, Daniel Goleman, *Emotional Intelligence* (New York: Bantam, 1995).

17. On Macmurray's concept of self-transcendence, see his *Conditions of Freedom*, 54–59, and "Science and Objectivity," in *The Personal Universe: Essays in Honor of John Macmurray*, ed. Thomas E. Wren (Atlantic Highlands, NJ: Humanities Press International, 1975), p. 23. See also Walter G. Jeffko, introduction to *Conditions of Freedom*, pp. xii–xvi, and "A Personalist Concept of Human Reason," *International Philosophical Quarterly* 14, no. 2 (June 1974): 161–80. For two theories of reason that differ from Macmurray's, see Michael Slote, *Beyond Optimizing: A Study of Rational Choice* (Cambridge: Harvard University Press, 1989), and Robert Nozick, *The Nature of Rationality* (Princeton, NJ: Princeton University Press, 1993).

18. Several noted thinkers have attacked scientific realism. For a rigorous—and vigorous—defense of scientific realism, see James Robert Brown, *Smoke and Mirrors: How Science Reflects Reality* (New York: Routledge, 1994).

19. See Emmanuel Mounier, *Personalism* (New York: Grove Press, 1952).

20. In general, the philosophical influences on Macmurray's thought are not obvious. Moreover, his philosophy is influenced as much by his interpretation of Christianity as an expression of the Hebraic tradition of religion as it is by other philosophers. See his *The Clue to History* (London: Student Christian Movement Press, 1938). See also one of Macmurray's last publications, *The Philosophy of Jesus* (London: Friends Home Service Committee, 1973). The following philosophers appear to have exercised the most positive influence on Macmurray's thought: Plato, from whom he learned that feelings and emotions just as much as thoughts can be true or false; Aristotle, from whom he gets his basic realism and conception of a person as a rational being; Aquinas, who continues the Aristotelian tradition of rational realism in a religious context, and who provides Macmurray with a theory on the relation between faith and reason; Kant, who provides him with the primacy of practical over speculative reason and the principle of community as a kingdom of interrelated ends, and whose transcendental logic is a major influence on Macmurray's concept of logical forms; Hegel, whose dialectical thinking instills in Macmurray a passion for triads, and who teaches him that pure being apart from all determinations is equivalent to nothing; Marx, from whom he acquires the idea of the primacy of the practical over the theoretical in all human activities and a thoroughgoing opposition to idealism in religion; Kierkegaard, who teaches Macmurray that authentic Christianity must be defined existentially rather than institutionally; and Buber, whose I-Thou conception is similar to Macmurray's mutuality of the personal. Macmurray and Buber met once. After three hours of conversation, Buber reportedly said: "I see no point on which we differ. It is simply that you are the metaphysician and I am the poet." Costello, introduction to *Reason and Emotion*, p. xix. See Macmurray's semiautobiography, *Search for Reality in Religion* (London: George Allen & Unwin, 1965). A wealth of information about Macmurray's life is found in John E. Costello, *John Macmurray: A Biography* (Edinburgh: Floris Books, 2002).

21. Paul Weiss, "Man's Existence," *International Philosophical Quarterly* 1, no. 4 (December 1961): 548.

22. The relation I have just expressed among reason, rationality, and irrationality is one application of Macmurray's logical form of the personal that makes sense to me. He defines this form as a positive that includes, subordinates, and is constituted by its own negative. I have slightly amended the form by inserting the word *partially* before *constituted*. See Walter G. Jeffko, "John Macmurray's Logical Form of the Personal: A Critical Exposition" (PhD diss., Fordham University, 1970). See also D. D. Raphael, critical study of *The Self as Agent*, by John Macmurray, *Philosophical Quarterly* 9, no. 36 (1959): 267–77, and review of *Persons in Relation*, by John Macmurray, *Philosophical Quarterly* 15, no. 58 (1965): 74–76.

23. See Walter G. Jeffko, "Action, Personhood, and Fact-Value," *Thomist* 40, no. 2

(January 1976): 116–34. Compare my definition of value with John Rawls's definition of good-ness: "The good is the satisfaction of rational desire." *A Theory of Justice*, rev. ed. (Cambridge: Harvard University Press, Belknap Press, 1999), p. 80.

24. Cf. Macmurray, *Self as Agent*, p. 140. Or again, "without valuation action is incon-ceivable, since in any action the end sought is ipso facto designated as good." John Macmurray, Beaconsfield, England, to Walter G. Jeffko, Worcester, MA, May 25, 1967.

25. Henry Veatch, for example, rejects the validity of the naturalistic fallacy. See his *Rational Man* (Bloomington: Indiana University Press, 1962), pp. 188–203.

26. Macmurray, *Persons in Relation*, p. 178.

27. Martin Heidegger, *Being and Time*, trans. John Macquarrie and Edward Robinson (New York: SCM Press, 1962). For a development of this theme, see Don Ihde, *Existential Technics* (Albany: State University of New York Press, 1983).

28. For a trenchant critique of scientism that does not downgrade science, see Tom Sorell, *Scientism: Philosophy and the Infatuation with Science* (New York: Routledge, 1991).

29. On nature as the bearer of aesthetic value, see William Godfrey-Smith, "The Value of Wilderness," *Environmental Ethics* (1979): 309–10, reprinted in *Contemporary Moral Problems*, 2nd ed., ed. James E. White (New York: West, 1988), pp. 351–59; and Mark Sagoff, "On Preserving the Natural Environment," *Yale Law Journal* 84, no. 2 (December 1974): 167–205, partially reprinted in *Today's Moral Problems*, 2nd ed., ed. Richard A. Wasserstrom (New York: Macmillan, 1979), pp. 613–23.

30. Bertrand Russell, *Human Society in Ethics and Politics* (London: Allen & Unwin, 1954), p. viii.

31. Herbert Simon, *Reason in Human Affairs* (Palo Alto, CA: Stanford University Press, 1983), pp. 7–8.

32. David Hume, *A Treatise of Human Nature*, with an introduction by A. D. Lindsay (New York: Everyman's Library, 1911), 2:128.

33. For a critique of the Humean position on reason, see Nozick, *Nature of Rationality*, 133–40. For a theory of reason that applies it to both the ends and the means of moral life, see David Schmidt, *Rational Choice and Moral Agency* (Princeton, NJ: Princeton University Press, 1994).

2. MORAL VALUE, INTENTIONALITY, AND COMMUNITY

1. See Philippa Foot, "The Problem of Abortion and the Doctrine of the Double Effect," *Oxford Review* 5 (1967): 5–15, reprinted in *Moral Problems: A Collection of Philosophical Essays*, 2nd ed., ed. James Rachels (New York: Harper & Row, 1975), pp. 59–70. The makings of the principle are found in Aquinas's thought. St. Thomas Aquinas, *Summa Theologica*, trans. Fathers

of the English Dominican Province, 3 vols. (New York: Benziger Brothers, 1947), 2–2.64.7. All citations from this work are from this translation. Cf. Bentham's distinction between directly and obliquely intentional consequences in *Principles of Morals and Legislation*, p. 84. For additional literature on double effect, see Judith Thomson, "Killing, Letting Die, and the Trolley Problem" and "The Trolley Problem," in her *Rights, Restitution, and Risk* (Cambridge, MA: Harvard University Press, 1986), pp. 78–116; Warren Quinn, "Actions, Intentions, and Consequences: The Doctrine of Double-Effect," *Philosophy and Public Affairs* 18, no. 4 (Fall 1989): 334–51; Warren Quinn, "Actions, Intentions, and Consequences: The Doctrine of Doing and Allowing," *Philosophical Review* 98 (July 1989): 287–312; Frances Kamm, "Harming Some to Save Others," *Philosophical Studies* 57 (1989): 227–60; H. M. Malm, "Killing, Letting Die, and Simple Conflicts," *Philosophy and Public Affairs* 18, no. 3 (Summer 1989): 238–58; and Matthew Hanser, "Why Are Killing and Letting Die Wrong?" *Philosophy and Public Affairs* 24, no. 3 (Summer 1995): 175–201. For a good Internet reference on double effect, see Alison McIntyre, "Doctrine of Double Effect," *Stanford Encyclopedia of Philosophy* (Fall 2011 ed.), ed. Edward N. Zalta, http://plato.stanford.edu/archives/fall 2011/entries/double-effect/ (accessed June 18, 2012). For a typical textbook treatment of double effect and its four rules, see Austin Fagothey, *Right and Reason: Ethics in Theory and Practice*, 4th ed. (St. Louis: C. V. Mosby, 1967), pp. 97–100.

2. Foot, "The Problem of Abortion and the Doctrine of Double Effect."

3. John Macmurray, *Persons in Relation*, (London: Faber & Faber; New York: Harper & Row, 1961; reprint, with an introduction by Frank G. Kirkpatrick, Amherst, NY: Humanity Books, 1991), p. 120.

4. Cf. Walter G. Jeffko, "Processive Relationism and Ethical Absolutes," *American Benedictine Review* 26, no. 3 (September 1975): 283–97, reprinted in *Readings in Moral Theology No. 1: Moral Norms and Catholic Tradition*, ed. Charles E. Curran and Richard McCormick (New York: Paulist Press, 1979), pp. 199–214. In this context, "intrinsically" has a somewhat different meaning from the earlier meaning of "intrinsic" when I spoke of aesthetic values as intrinsic values.

5. For a detailed analysis of doing and allowing and a critical evaluation of different interpretations of the doctrine, see Frances Howard-Snyder, "Doing vs. Allowing Harm," *Stanford Encyclopedia of Philosophy* (Winter 2011 ed.), ed. Edward N. Zalta, http://plato.stanford .edu/archives/win2011/entries/doing-allowing/ (accessed June 18, 2012).

6. Thomson, "The Trolley Problem."

7. For Aristotle's and Aquinas's views on the voluntary and involuntary, see Aristotle, *Nicomachean Ethics*, in *The Basic Works of Aristotle*, ed. with an introduction by Richard McKeon (New York: Random House, 1941), 3.1–2.1109b.30–1115a; and Aquinas, *Summa Theologica*, 1–2.6.

8. In this context, "will" means free will and so to avoid repetition, I shall simply say "will."

9. Macmurray, *Persons in Relation*, p. 119. Macmurray interprets Kant's concept of

kingdom of ends as implying a principle of community: "Act always as a legislating member of a kingdom of ends." Ibid. However, Macmurray criticizes Kant's principle as being too legalistic. This is probably a fair criticism, inasmuch as Kant has no distinction between rules and principles, unlike rule utilitarianism, in which the former are subordinate to the latter and derive their ultimate validity from them. If Kant had made such a distinction, he might have been able to avoid the charge of absolutism, which is frequently leveled against his ethics. This distinction could be incorporated into Kant's ethics and improve its objectivism by making it more flexible. At least some rules could then be formulated as having reasonable exceptions built into them. All this could be done without someone thereby becoming a utilitarian.

10. On freedom in friendship as the fulfillment of relative freedom, see Macmurray, *Conditions of Freedom*.

11. Macmurray, *Persons in Relation*, p. 198.

12. Ibid., p. 43.

13. Ibid.

14. Ibid., p. 158.

15. Ibid., p. 159. See also ibid., p. 163.

16. Macmurray, *Conditions of Freedom*, p. 61.

17. For a sympathetic critique of Macmurray's concept of community, see Errol E. Harris, feature review of *Persons in Relation*, by John Macmurray, *International Philosophical Quarterly* 2, no. 3 (September 1962): 479–82. For two sympathetic books on Macmurray's theory of community and friendship, see Frank G. Kirkpatrick, *Community: A Trinity of Models* (Washington, DC: Georgetown University Press, 1986); and Philip Mooney, *Belonging Always: Reflections on Uniqueness* (Chicago: Loyola University Press, 1987). See also Kirkpatrick's later works, *The Ethics of Community* (Malden, MA: Blackwell Publishers, 2001); and *John Macmurray: Community beyond Political Philosophy* (Lanham, MD: Rowman & Littlefield, 2005). See also A. R. C. Duncan, *On the Nature of Persons* (New York: Peter Lang, 1990); Philip Conford, *The Personal World: John Macmurray on Self and Society* (Edinburgh: Floris Books, 1996); and *John Macmurray: Selected Philosophical Writings*, ed. with an introduction by Esther McIntosh (Exeter: Imprint Academic, 2004). For an anthology of essays on Macmurray's thought, see *John Macmurray: Critical Perspectives*, eds. David Fergusson and Nigel Dower (New York: Peter Lang, 2002).

18. Cf. Macmurray, *Persons in Relation*, p. 186.

19. Carol Gilligan, *In a Different Voice: Psychological Theory and Women's Development* (Cambridge, MA: Harvard University Press, 1982).

20. Lawrence Kohlberg, *Essays in Moral Development*, 2 vols. (New York: Harper & Row, 1981 and 1984); Rawls, *Theory of Justice*.

21. Gilligan, *Different Voice*, p. 174. Cf. Annette Baier, "The Need for More than Justice," *Canadian Journal of Philosophy*, supplementary vol. 3, ed. Marshal Haven and Kai Nielsen (Calgary: University of Calgary Press, 1988), reprinted in *Applying Ethics*, 4th ed., ed. Jeffrey Olen and Vincent Barry (Belmont, CA: Wadsworth, 1992), pp. 39–46.

22. Gilligan also emphasizes that the female ethics of caring is nonviolent. Similarly, Macmurray's ethics of community is pacifistic.

23. See Amitai Etzioni, *The Spirit of Community* (New York: Crown, 1993).

24. On Macmurray's distinction between community and society, see, for example, *Persons in Relation*, pp. 127–65. I develop this distinction in chapters 7 and 8, when I distinguish among three types of society: personalist, organic, and individualistic. Only the first is a community.

25. On the difference between teleological and deontological theories, see Rawls, *Theory of Justice*, pp. 21–27, and William K. Frankena, *Ethics* (Englewood Cliffs, NJ: Prentice-Hall, 1963), pp. 13–14. For an impressive utilitarian interpretation of the right and the good, see Richard B. Brandt, *A Theory of the Good and the Right* (Amherst, NY: Prometheus Books, 1998).

3. SUICIDE AND THE RIGHT TO DIE

This chapter is based on my Harrod Lecture "Is Suicide a Human Right?" delivered at Fitchburg State College, October 24, 1979, and published in *The Harrod Lecture Series*, vol. 2 (Fitchburg, MA: Fitchburg State College Press, 1981), pp. 1–19.

1. Ludwig Wittgenstein, *Notebooks 1914–16*, ed. G. H. von Wright and G. E. M. Anscombe (Oxford: Basil Blackwell, 1961), p. 91.

2. Joseph Margolis thinks that a definition of suicide must be culturally relativistic. See his "Suicide," in *Negativities: The Limits of Life* (Columbus, OH: Charles E. Merrill, 1975), pp. 23–29, 34–35, reprinted in *Ethical Issues in Death and Dying*, ed. Tom L. Beauchamp and Seymour Perlin (Englewood Cliffs, NJ: Prentice-Hall, 1978), pp. 92–97.

3. Émile Durkheim, *Suicide: A Study in Sociology*, trans. John A. Spaulding and George Simson (New York: Free Press, 1966), p. 44 (emphasis in original deleted).

4. Ronald Maris, "Sociology," in *A Handbook for the Study of Suicide*, ed. Seymour Perlin (New York: Oxford University Press, 1975), p. 100.

5. Tom L. Beauchamp, "What Is Suicide?" in *Ethical Issues in Death and Dying*, p. 101.

6. Tom L. Beauchamp, "Suicide," in *Matters of Life and Death: New Introductory Essays in Moral Philosophy*, 2nd ed., ed. Tom Regan (New York: Random House, 1986), p. 83.

7. Beauchamp, "What Is Suicide?" p. 99 (emphasis in original).

8. Beauchamp, "Suicide," pp. 86–87. The English philosopher R. F. Holland thinks that Oates did not commit suicide. See his "Suicide," in *Talk of God*, vol. 2 (New York: St. Martin's Press, 1969), reprinted in *Moral Problems: A Collection of Philosophical Essays*, 2nd ed., ed. James Rachels (New York: Harper & Row, 1975), pp. 388–400.

9. Austin Fagothey, *Right and Reason*, 4th ed. (St. Louis: C. V. Mosby, 1967), p. 225 (emphasis in original deleted).

10. Augustine, *The City of God*, trans. Marcus Dods (New York: Modern Library, 1950),

1.21 (all subsequent citations of this work are from this translation); Thomas Aquinas, *Summa Theologica*, 3 vols., trans. Fathers of the English Dominican Province (New York: Benziger Brothers, 1947), 2–2.64.5.r.obj.4.

11. Augustine, *City of God*, 1.20.

12. Ibid., 1.21.

13. Ibid.

14. Cf. Antony Flew, "The Principle of Euthanasia," in *Euthanasia and the Right to Die*, ed. A. B. Downing (London: Peter Owen, 1969), reprinted in *Death and Society: A Book of Readings and Sources*, ed. James P. Carse and Arlene B. Dallery (New York: Harcourt Brace Jovanovich, 1977), p. 111. Flew makes the wry comment that a God inventing such unspeakable horrors as hell could not be expected to be concerned with justice.

15. See "Suicide," *Catechism of the Catholic Church* (paragraphs 2280–2283), http://www .newadvent.org/cathen/14326b.htm (accessed March 27, 2009). I refer to God as *He*, because the Catholic and Christian tradition uses the male pronoun. However, metaphysically speaking, the Christian theistic God cannot have a gender.

16. It may be objected that although Aquinas and Locke held that these two presuppositions are rationally justifiable, this is not the case with Kant, who rejected all possible proofs for God's existence. However, it must be remembered that after Kant rejected the traditional, speculative arguments for God's existence, he developed a moral argument for the existence of a theistic God. See Immanuel Kant, *Critique of Practical Reason*, trans. with an introduction by Lewis White Beck (New York: Liberal Arts Press, 1956), 128–36.

17. Aquinas, *Summa Theologica*, 2–2.64.5.

18. Cf. R. M. Hare, "What Is Wrong with Slavery," *Philosophy and Public Affairs* 8, no. 2 (Winter 1979): 103–21.

19. See C. De Vogel. "The Concept of Personality in Greek and Christian Thought," in *Studies in Philosophy and the History of Philosophy*, ed. J. Ryan (Washington, DC: Catholic University of America Press, 1963), 2:20–60.

20. Aquinas, *Summa Theologica*, 1.29.3 (emphasis in original).

21. Immanuel Kant, *Lectures on Ethics*, trans. Louis Infield (London: Methuen, 1930; reprint, with a foreword by Lewis White Beck, New York: Harper Torchbooks, 1963), pp. 153–54. Locke's version of this argument adds nothing to Kant's and Aquinas's versions. See John Locke, *Two Treatises of Government*, ed. with an introduction by Peter Laslett (Cambridge: Cambridge University Press, 1963), p. 289.

22. Aquinas, *Summa Theologica*, 2–2.64.5.

23. In an excellent article to which I am indebted, R. B. Brandt critically evaluates the injury against the community argument and most of the other arguments against suicide in this chapter. See his "The Morality and Rationality of Suicide," in *Moral Problems*, 2nd ed., pp. 363–87. This article is an expanded version of his earlier essay, "The Morality and Rationality of Suicide," in *Handbook for the Study of Suicide*, pp. 61–76. I discuss Hume's views on suicide later.

For a recent survey of the different aspects of suicide and analyses of various positions on them, see Michael Cholbi, "Suicide," *Stanford Encyclopedia of Philosophy* (Fall 2009 ed.), ed. Edward N. Zalta, http://plato.stanford.edu/archives/fall2009/ entries/suicide/ (accessed June 18, 2012).

24. Aquinas, *Summa Theologica*, 2–2.64.3.

25. Aristotle, *Nicomachean Ethics,* in *The Basic Works of Aristotle*, ed. with an introduction by Richard McKeon (New York: Random House, 1942), 5.11.1138a.4–12.

26. Jean-Jacques Rousseau, "The Social Contract," in *The Social Contract and Discourses*, trans. with an introduction by G. D. H. Cole (New York: E. P. Dutton, 1950), p. 8.

27. Aquinas, *Summa Theologica*, 2–2.64.5.

28. Immanuel Kant, *Foundations of the Metaphysics of Morals*, trans. with an introduction by Lewis White Beck (New York: Liberal Arts Press, 1959), pp. 39–40.

29. In his criticism of Aquinas's self-love argument, Glanville Williams makes this error. See Glanville Williams, *The Sanctity of Life and the Criminal Law* (New York: Knopf, 1957), p. 264. On Aquinas's natural law theory, see *Summa Theologica*, 1–2.94.

30. Kant, *Foundations*, p. 47.

31. Brandt, "The Morality and Rationality of Suicide," p. 367.

32. Ibid., pp. 373–74.

33. David Hume, "On Suicide" (Edinburgh, Scotland, 1777), reprinted in *Ethical Issues in Death and Dying*, pp. 105–109.

34. Ibid., pp. 109–10.

35. Thomas Szasz, "The Ethics of Suicide," *Antioch Review* 31 (Spring 1971): 7–17, reprinted in *Ethical Issues in Death and Dying*, pp. 137–38.

36. Jerome A. Motto, MD, "The Right to Suicide: A Psychiatrist's View," *Life Threatening Behavior* 2, no. 3 (Fall 1972), reprinted in *Death and Society: A Book of Readings and Sources*, ed. James P. Carse and Arlene B. Dallery (New York: Harcourt Brace Jovanovich, 1997), pp. 225–26.

37. Ibid., p. 228.

38. Ibid., pp. 228–29.

39. Ibid., p. 227 (emphasis in original).

40. Albert Camus, *The Myth of Sisyphus* (New York: Vintage Books, 1960), p. 3.

41. James Hillman, "Suicide as the Soul's Choice," in *Suicide and the Soul* (New York: Harper & Row, 1964), reprinted in *Death and Society*, p. 234.

42. Ibid., p. 236 (emphasis in original).

43. Irving M. Copi, *Introduction to Logic*, 7th ed. (New York: Macmillan, 1986), p. 113.

44. In an insightful essay, Joel Feinberg makes several important distinctions about rights. See his "Voluntary Euthanasia and the Inalienable Right to Life," *Philosophy and Public Affairs* 7, no. 2 (Winter 1978): 93–123.

4. ABORTION, PERSONHOOD, AND COMMUNITY

This chapter is based on my Harrod Lecture "An Ontology and Ethics of Abortion," delivered at Fitchburg State College, March 19, 1980, and published in *The Harrod Lecture Series*, vol. 3 (Fitchburg, MA: Fitchburg State College Press, 1981), pp. 1–25.

1. An exception to the generalization that, in the abortion issue, ontology significantly determines morality, is the seminal essay by Judith Jarvis Thomson, "A Defense of Abortion," *Philosophy and Public Affairs* 1, no. 1 (Fall 1971): 47–66, reprinted in *The Problem of Abortion*, 2nd ed., ed. Joel Feinberg (Belmont, CA: Wadsworth, 1984), 173–87. Thomson argues that even if the fetus is a person for the entire period of gestation, it does not follow that abortion is immoral, much less murder. For similar views, see Jane English, "Abortion and the Concept of Person," *Canadian Journal of Philosophy* 5, no. 2 (October 1975), reprinted in *Problem of Abortion*, pp. 151–60.

2. *Roe v. Wade* 410 U.S. 113, 93 Sup. Ct. 705 (1973).

3. Thomas Szasz, "An Ethics of Abortion," *Humanist* (1966), quoted in Louis P. Pojman, *Life and Death: Grappling with the Moral Problems of Our Time* (Boston: Jones and Bartlett, 1992), p. 69.

4. See H. Tristram Englehardt, "The Ontology of Abortion," *Ethics* 84 (April 1974): 217–34.

5. Joel Feinberg, "Abortion," in *Matters of Life and Death*, 2nd ed., ed. Tom Regan (New York: Random House, 1986), p. 256.

6. For a good survey of artificial reproductive technologies (ARTs), see Lucy Frith, "Reproductive Technologies, Overview," in *Encyclopedia of Applied Ethics*, 4 vols., ed. Ruth Chadwick (Boston: Academic Press, 1998), 3:817–27. See also Rosemary Tong, *New Perspectives in Health Care Ethics: An Interdisciplinary and Crosscultural Approach* (Upper Saddle River, NJ: Pearson Prentice-Hall, 2001), pp. 137–76. There are several variations on IVF, including gamete intrafallopian tube transfer (GIFT), where fertilization occurs in the woman's body; zygote intrafallopian tube transfer (ZIFT), which (along with GIFT) has a slightly higher success rate than IVF; surrogate (or gestational) motherhood, in which a woman other than the genetic mother carries the conceptus to birth and then transfers the neonate to her; and intracytoplasmatic sperm injection (ICSI), in which only the cytoplasm of a donor's eggs are used (the woman herself has no eggs or else has diseased or damaged eggs). See Soren Holm, "Embryology, Ethics of," in *Encyclopedia*, 2:39–45.

7. For an excellent summary of the biological evidence on fetal development, see Daniel Callahan, *Abortion: Law, Choice and Morality* (New York: Macmillan, 1970), pp. 371–77. See also Thomas L. Hayes, "Abortion: A Biological View," *Commonweal* (March 17, 1967), pp. 676–79. For a differing viewpoint that denies the zygote is an organism, see Paul Wilkes,

"The Moral Dilemma of Abortion," in Wilkes, *The Good Enough Catholic* (New York: Ballentine Books, 1996), reprinted in *Ethics for Modern Life*, 6th ed., ed. Raziel Abelson and Marie-Louise Friquegnon (Boston: Bedford/St. Martin's, 2003), pp. 262–67.

8. Michael Tooley, "Abortion and Infanticide," *Philosophy and Public Affairs* 2, no. 1 (Fall 1972): 37–65; Mary Anne Warren, "On the Moral and Legal Status of Abortion," *Monist* 57, no. 1 (January 1973): 43–61, reprinted in *Problem of Abortion*, 102–19; Richard Werner, "Abortion: The Ontological and Moral Status of the Unborn," *Social Theory and Practice* 3, no. 4 (1974): 201–22; and Englehardt, "Ontology of Abortion."

9. Warren, "Abortion," in *Problem of Abortion*, pp. 110–14.

10. Ibid., pp. 111–12.

11. John Macmurray, "Science and Objectivity," in *The Personal Universe*, ed. Thomas E. Wren (Atlantic Highlands, NJ: Humanities Press, 1975), p. 16.

12. Warren, "Abortion," in *Problem of Abortion*, pp. 110–16.

13. For a brief survey and evaluation of most of these theories, see Paul Ramsey, "The Morality of Abortion," in *Life or Death: Ethics and Options*, ed. Daniel H. Labby (Seattle: University of Washington Press, 1968), reprinted in *Moral Problems*, 2nd ed., ed. James Rachels (New York: Harper & Row, 1975), pp. 37–58.

14. John T. Noonan Jr., "An Almost Absolute Value in History," in *The Morality of Abortion: Legal and Historical Perspectives*, ed. John T. Noonan Jr. (Cambridge: Harvard University Press, 1970), pp. 51–59, reprinted in *Problem of Abortion*, p. 13.

15. Stephen D. Schwarz, *The Moral Question of Abortion* (Chicago: Loyola University Press, 1990); chapter 7, reprinted in *Do the Right Thing: A Philosophical Dialogue on the Moral and Social Issues of Our Time*, ed. Francis J. Beckwith (Boston: Jones and Bartlett, 1996), pp. 180–81.

16. Ibid., p. 180.

17. Ibid.

18. Ibid., p. 181.

19. Because of the identical-twin objection, one author maintains that personhood may begin at two weeks of gestation. Philip E. Devine, "The Scope of the Prohibition against Killing," in *The Ethics of Homicide* (Ithaca, NY: Cornell University Press, 1978), reprinted in *Problem of Abortion*, p. 42.

20. For Aristotle's views on the fetus, see *De Generatione Animalium* 2.3.736a24–737a17. Since he did not consider the fetus at its earliest stages to be a real human being, he thought that early abortions were morally permissible. Aquinas accepted Aristotle's view of the fetus, but remained silent on the morality of abortion. St. Thomas Aquinas, *Summa Theologica*, trans. Fathers of the English Dominican Province, 3 vols. (New York: Benziger Brothers, 1947), 1.118.2.r.obj.4; and St. Thomas Aquinas, *Summa Contra Gentiles*, trans. with an introduction by James F. Anderson, 5 vols. (New York: Image Books, 1956), 2.89.

21. Schwarz, *Moral Question of Abortion*, p. 183.

22. Germain Grisez, *Abortion: The Myths, the Realities, and the Arguments* (New York:

Corpus Books, 1970), p. 306 (emphasis in original). Cf. Austin Fagothey, *Right and Reason*, 4th ed. (St. Louis: C. V. Mosby, 1967), p. 231.

23. Donceel has written several articles supporting mediate animation and criticizing immediate animation. See Joseph Donceel, "Abortion: Mediate v. Immediate Animation," *Continuum* 5 (Winter/Spring 1967): 167–71; "A Liberal Catholic's View," in *Abortion in a Changing World*, vol. 1, ed. Robert E. Hall (New York: Columbia University Press, 1970), pp. 39–45, reprinted in *Problem of Abortion*, pp. 15–20; "Immediate Animation and Delayed Hominization," *Theological Studies* 31 (1970): 76–105; and "Why Is Abortion Wrong?" *America* (August 16, 1975): 65–67. On a personal note, it was my pleasure to be a student of Fr. Donceel in two graduate courses at Fordham University: Philosophical Anthropology and Transcendental Method in Metaphysics.

24. See Walter G. Jeffko, "Self-Consciousness and the Soul-Body Problem," *American Benedictine Review* 31, no. 3 (September 1980): 346–60.

25. See Alan Zaitchik, "Viability and the Morality of Abortion," *Philosophy and Public Affairs* 10, no. 1 (Winter 1981): 18–26, reprinted in *Problem of Abortion*, pp. 58–64.

26. "World's Youngest Preemie," *People*, March 12, 2007, http://www.people.com/people/archive/article/0,,20062960,00.html (accessed November 22, 2010). See also "Earliest Surviving Preemie to Remain in Hospital," *MSNBC.COM*, February 20, 2007, http://www.msnbc.msn.com/id/17237979/ns/health-kidsandparenting (accessed November 22, 2010).

27. Feinberg, "Abortion," p. 258.

28. John Macmurray, *Persons in Relation* (Amherst, NY: Humanity Books, 1991), p. 51.

29. Ibid., pp. 44–63. John Costello, Macmurray's biographer, reports the following conversation to me regarding Macmurray's views on abortion: "Mr. Reg Sayers, the founder of the JM [John Macmurray] Society in Toronto reports from his last meeting with JM in 1971 that JM stated with regard to abortion that the decision must be left to the woman who was pregnant." John Costello, Toronto, Canada, to Walter Jeffko, Fitchburg, MA, April 27, 1993.

30. Tooley, "Abortion and Infanticide"; and Michael Tooley, "In Defense of Abortion and Infanticide," in *Problem of Abortion*, pp. 120–34.

31. See Walter G. Jeffko, "Is the Fetus a Person?" *Commonwealth Review* 3, no. 1 (May 1990): 15–18.

32. I am using *parasitic* in a purely biological and descriptive sense, not in a pejorative sense.

33. Cf. Richard Wasserstrom, "The Status of the Fetus," *Hastings Magazine* (June 1975), reprinted in *Moral Problems*, 3rd ed., ed. James Rachels (New York: Harper & Row, 1979), pp. 118–29.

34. Cf. Roger Wertheimer, "Understanding the Abortion Argument," *Philosophy and Public Affairs* 1, no. 1 (Fall 1971): 67–95, reprinted in *Problem of Abortion*, p. 43. Cf. Joel Feinberg, introduction to *Problem of Abortion*, p. 3–4.

35. R. M. Hare, "Abortion and the Golden Rule," *Philosophy and Public Affairs* 4, no. 3 (Spring 1975): 201–22, reprinted in *Moral Problems*, pp. 151–73.

36. Jonathan Bennett, "Whatever the Consequences," *Analysis* 26 (1966), reprinted in *Moral Problems*, 1st ed., ed. James Rachels (New York: Harper & Row, 1971), p. 43.

37. Feinberg, "Abortion," in *Matters of Life and Death*, p. 281.

38. See Judith Jarvis Thompson, "Self-Defense," *Philosophy and Public Affairs* 20, no. 4 (Fall 1991): 283–310. She defends the view that it is permissible to kill both Innocent Threats and Innocent Aggressors. Her view is disputed by Michael Otsuka, "Killing the Innocent in Self-Defense," *Philosophy and Public Affairs* 23, no. 1 (Winter 1994): 74–94.

39. Warren, "Abortion," in *Problem of Abortion*, p. 116. Warren goes on to assert that since early abortion is statistically safer than childbirth, an early abortion of an unwanted pregnancy constitutes a woman's protection of her right to life. The premise is much too weak to support her conclusion.

40. On the importance of the natural environment for abortion decisions, see Ronnie Zoe Hawkins, "Reproductive Choices: The Ecological Dimension," *APA Newsletters* 19, no. 1 (Spring 1992): 66–73, reprinted in *Contemporary Moral Problems*, 6th ed., ed. James E. White (Belmont, CA: Wadsworth, 2000), pp. 186–98.

41. Lester R. Brown, *Plan B 2.0*, updated and expanded (New York: W. W. Norton, 2006), p. 128. See UN Population Fund (UNPA), *The State of World Population 2004* (New York, 2004), p. 39.

42. The number of annual abortions in the United States has been moderately declining since 1990, when it peaked at 1.61 million. In 1996, it had declined to 1.36 million and by 2002 1.29 million. In 2008, abortions further declined to 1.21 million. "Abortion in the United States: Quick Stats," *Guttmacher Institute*, http://www.guttmacher.org/media/presskits/abortion-US/statsandfacts.html (accessed June 4, 2012).

43. Don Marquis, "Why Abortion Is Immoral," *Journal of Philosophy* 86, no. 4 (April 1989), reprinted in *Contemporary Moral Issues: Diversity and Consensus*, ed. Lawrence M. Hinman (Upper Saddle River, NJ: Prentice-Hall, 1996), pp. 65–79; and "An Argument That Abortion Is Wrong," in *Ethics in Practice*, 2nd ed., ed. Hugh La Follette (Blackwell, 2002), pp. 119–27.

44. Rosiland Hursthouse, "Virtue Theory and Abortion," *Philosophy and Public Affairs* 20, no. 3 (Summer 1991), reprinted in *Social and Personal Ethics*, 5th ed., ed. William H. Shaw (Belmont, CA: Wadsworth, 2005), 139–46.

45. Aquinas, *Summa Theologica*, 1–2.96.2.

46. In a recent year, the following was the percentage breakdown of abortions performed in the United States by gestational age: up to eight weeks, 50.3 percent; up to twelve weeks, 90.5 percent; after twenty weeks, 0.8 percent; after twenty-two weeks, 0.3 percent; and after twenty-four weeks, 0.01 percent. Many opponents of abortion greatly exaggerate the incidence of late abortions.

47. *Webster v. Reproductive Health Services*, 492 U.S. 490, 109 Sup. Ct. 3040 (1989).

48. *Planned Parenthood of Southeastern Pennsylvania v. Casey, Governor of Pennsylvania*, 505 U.S. 833, 112 Sup. Ct. 2791 (1992).

49. The question of men's rights in abortion decisions deserves much more attention than has been given so far. However, I do not have the space to address this important issue. See Steven D. Hales, "Abortion and Fathers' Rights," in *Reproduction, Technology, and Rights*, ed. James M. Humber and Robert F. Almeder (Totowa, NJ: 1996), pp. 5–26, reprinted in *Analyzing Moral Issues*, 3rd ed., ed. Judith A. Boss (Boston: McGraw-Hill, 2005), pp. 117–25; and George W. Harris, "Fathers and Fetuses," *Ethics* 96 (1986), reprinted in *Contemporary Moral Issues*, ed. Hinman, pp. 80–88.

50. Joerg Dreweke, "Abortion Declines Worldwide, Falls Most Where Abortion Is Broadly Legal," *Guttmacher Institute*, October 11, 2007, http://www.guttmacher.org/media/nr/2007/10/11/index.html (accessed November 1, 2007).

51. See *New York Times*, March 21, 1997, sec. A, 1, 24.

52. *New York Times*, July 2, 2000, sec. 4, 1, 5. *Stenberg v. Carhart*, 120 Sup. Ct. 2597 (2000).

53. *Gonzales v. Carhart*, No. 05-380. See *New York Times*, April 19, 2007, sec. A, 1, 14.

54. "Push for 'Personhood' Amendment Represents New Tack in Abortion Fight," *New York Times*, http://www.nytimes.com/2011/10/26/us/politics/personhood-amendments-would-ban-nearl(accessed August 22, 2012).

55. New York Times, September 29, 2000, sec. A, 1, 16; Nancy Gibbs, "The Pill Arrives," *Time*, October 9, 2000, 41–49.

56. "Definition of IVF," *Medicine Net*, http://www.medterms.com/script/main/art.asp?articlekey=7222 (accessed December 6, 2007).

57. The information on ESC research is taken from the following sources: "California Gives Go-Ahead to Stem-Cell Research," *MSNBC*, November 3, 2004, http://www.msnbc.msn.com/id/6384390 (accessed November 3, 2004); Peter Dizikes, "Reluctance of Egg Donors Stymies Harvard Efforts," *Boston Globe*, June 7, 2007, sec. A, 18; Nancy Gibbs, "Stem Cells: The Hope and the Hype," *Time*, August 7, 2006, 40–46; Holm, "Embryology, Ethics of," in *Encyclopedia*, 2:39–45; Colin Nickerson, "Studies Cite New Process for Stem Cells," *Boston Globe*, June 7, 2007, sec. A, 1, 18; and Tong, *New Perspectives in Health Care Ethics*, pp. 138–40, 220–27.

58. Sheryl Gay Stolberg, "Bush Vetoes Bill Removing Stem Cell Limits, Saying 'All Human Life Is Sacred,'" *New York Times*, June 21, 2007, sec. A, 21.

5. EUTHANASIA: A REINTERPRETATION

This chapter is based on my Harrod Lecture "Euthanasia and Respect for Persons," delivered at Fitchburg State College, October 24, 1984, and published in *The Harrod Lecture Series*, vol. 6 (Fitchburg, MA: Fitchburg State College Press, 1985), pp. 3–40.

1. Some authors subsume suicide as such under euthanasia. See J. P. Moreland, "James Rachels and the Active Euthanasia Debate," *Journal of the Evangelical Society* 31 (March 1988), reprinted in *Do the Right Thing*, ed. Francis J. Beckwith (Boston: Jones and Bartlett, 1990), p. 239.

2. On the moral relation of abortion to infanticide, see Michael Tooley, "Abortion and Infanticide," *Philosophy and Public Affairs* 2, no. 1 (Fall 1972): 37–65; Michael Tooley, "In Defense Abortion and Infanticide," in *The Problem of Abortion*, 2nd ed., ed. Joel Feinberg (Belmont, CA: Wadsworth, 1984), pp. 120–34; and Mary Anne Warren, "Abortion," in *Problem of Abortion*, pp. 102–19.

3. On the dispute concerning the definition of euthanasia, see Jeffrey Olen and Vincent Barry, eds., *Applying Ethics*, 4th ed. (Belmont, CA: Wadsworth, 1992), pp. 213–24.

4. The term *patient*, as used here, usually implies a hospital or medical setting, but not necessarily.

5. A. D. Woozley, "Euthanasia and the Principle of Harm," in *Philosophy and Public Policy*, ed. Donnie J. Self (Old Dominion University Research Foundation, 1977), reprinted in *Moral Problems*, 3rd ed., ed. James Rachels (New York: Harper & Row, 1979), pp. 498–507. See also Richard Brandt, "A Moral Principle about Killing," in *Beneficent Euthanasia*, ed. Marvin Kohl (Amherst, NY: Prometheus Books, 1975), reprinted in *Applying Ethics*, pp. 244–49.

6. J. Gay-Williams, "The Wrongfulness of Euthanasia," in *Intervention and Reflection: Basic Issues in Medical Ethics*, ed. Ronald Munson (Belmont, CA: Wadsworth, 1979), pp. 141–43.

7. R. M. Hare, "Euthanasia: A Christian View," *Philosophic Exchange* 2, no. 1 (Summer 1975): 45.

8. James Rachels, "Euthanasia," in *Matters of Life and Death*, 2nd ed., ed. Tom Regan (New York: Random House, 1986), p. 38.

9. *In the Matter of Conroy*, Sup. Ct. NJ ADiv., A–2483–82 (July 8, 1983) (emphasis added).

10. James Rachels, "Active and Passive Euthanasia," *New England Journal of Medicine* 292, no. 2 (January 9, 1975): 78–80. See Rachels's other writings: "Euthanasia, Killing, and Letting Die," in *Ethical Issues Relating to Life and Death*, ed. John Ladd (Oxford: Oxford University Press, 1979), pp. 146–61; and "More Impertinent Distinctions and a Defense of Active Euthanasia," in *Social Ethics: Morality and Social Policy*, 3rd ed., ed. Thomas A. Mappes and Jane S. Zembaty (New York: McGraw-Hill, 1987), pp. 78–81. Most important, see Rachels's book *The End of Life: Euthanasia and Morality* (Oxford: Oxford University Press, 1986).

11. Rachels, "Active and Passive Euthanasia," p. 78.

12. See, for example, Thomas D. Sullivan, "Active and Passive Euthanasia: An Impertinent Distinction?" *Human Life Review* 3, no. 3 (Summer 1977): 40–46, reprinted in *Social Ethics*, pp. 65–70; Tom L. Beauchamp, "A Reply to Rachels on Active and Passive Euthanasia," in *Ethical Issues in Death and Dying*, ed. Tom Beauchamp and Seymour Perlin (Englewood Cliffs, NJ: Prentice-Hall, 1978), pp. 246–58; Philippa Foot, "Euthanasia," *Philosophy and Public Affairs* 6, no. 2 (Winter 1977): 85–112; Bonnie Steinbock, "The Intentional Termination of Life," in *Ethics in Science and Medicine* (Pergamon Press, 1979), pp. 59–64, reprinted in *Morality in Practice*, 3rd ed., ed. James P. Sterba (Belmont, CA: Wadsworth, 1991), pp. 187–92; and Raziel Abelson, "There Is a Moral Difference," in *Ethics for Modern Life*, 2nd ed., ed. Raziel Abelson and Marie-Louise Friquegnon (New York: St. Martin's Press, 1982), pp. 73–81.

13. Rachels, *The End of Life*; Moreland, "The Active Euthanasia Debate."

14. Paul Ramsey, *The Patient as Person* (New Haven, CT: Yale University Press, 1970), pp. 122–33.

15. This threefold distinction is gaining acceptance. See, for example, Rachels, "Euthanasia," in *Matters of Life and Death*, pp. 38–39; and Thomas A. Mappes and Jane S. Zembaty, eds., *Social Ethics*, 5th ed. (New York: McGraw-Hill, 1997), p. 556. Still others distinguish only voluntary and nonvoluntary euthanasia. See Olen and Barry, *Applying Ethics*, pp. 214–15.

16. Walter G. Jeffko, "Are 'Person' and 'Agent' Coextensive? Reflections on John Macmurray," *American Benedictine Review* 44, no. 4 (December 1993): 352–70. See also chapter 7 on the spirituality of personhood.

17. "Coma and Persistent Vegetative State," *HealthLink*, http://healthlink.mew.edu/article/921394859.html (accessed December 4, 2006).

18. *In the Matter of Karen Quinlan, an Alleged Incompetent*, Supreme Court of New Jersey, 70 NJ 10, 355 A. 2nd 647 (March 31, 1976).

19. Ibid.

20. For a position similar to mine, see F. M. Kamm, "A Right to Choose Death?" *Boston Review*, August 28, 2001, reprinted in *Ethics for Modern Life*, 6th ed., ed. Raziel Abelson and Marie-Louise Friquegnon (Boston: Bedford/St. Martin's, 2003), pp. 216–26.

21. Rachels, "Euthanasia," in *Matters of Life and Death*, pp. 35–36.

22. Ibid., pp. 49–54. Some authors, such as Rachels, use the principle of utility and Kant's principle of universalizability (the first formulation of his categorical imperative) to justify direct-active-voluntary euthanasia. Among ethicists, there is wide support for direct-active-voluntary euthanasia. See, for example, Dan W. Brock, "Voluntary Active Euthanasia," *Hastings Center Report* 22, no. 2 (1992), reprinted in *Social and Personal Ethics*, 5th ed., ed. William H. Shaw (Belmont, CA: Wadsworth, 2005), pp. 79–89; Margaret Pabst Battin, "The Case for Euthanasia," *Health Care Ethics*, ed. D. VanDeVeer and Tom Regan (Philadelphia: Temple University Press, 1987), pp. 58–95, reprinted in *Analyzing Moral Issues*, 3rd ed., ed. Judith A. Boss (Boston: McGraw-

Hill, 2005), pp. 199–207; Peter Singer, "Justifying Voluntary Euthanasia," in Singer, *Practical Ethics*, 2nd ed. (New York: Cambridge University Press, 1993), pp. 176–78, 193–200, reprinted in *Contemporary Moral Problems*, 6th ed., ed. James E. White (Belmont, CA: Wadsworth, 2000), pp. 218–24; Timothy E. Quill, "Death and Dignity: A Case of Individualized Decision Making," *New England Journal of Medicine* 324 (March 7, 1991), reprinted in *Do the Right Thing*, ed. Francis J. Beckwith (Belmont, CA: Wadsworth, 2002), pp. 284–88; and Gregory S. Kavka, "Banning Euthanasia," in *Contemporary Moral Issues: Diversity and Consensus*, ed. Lawrence M. Hinman (Upper Saddle River, NJ: Prentice Hall, 1996), pp. 136–44.

23. Some authors persuasively argue that in certain extreme conditions, we even have a duty to die. See John Hardwig, "Is There a Duty to Die?" *Hastings Center Report* 27, no. 2 (1997): 34–42, reprinted in *Analyzing Moral Issues*, 3rd ed., ed. Boss, pp. 212–18.

24. David T. Watts and Timothy Howell, "Assisted Suicide Is Not Voluntary Active Euthanasia," *Journal of the American Geriatrics Society* 40 (October 1992): 1043–46, reprinted in *Social Ethics*, 5th ed., pp. 89–94. For a different moral position on assisted suicide, see Dan W. Brock, "The Moral Justifiability of Assisted Suicide," in *Physician Assisted Suicide*, ed. R. Weir (Indiana University Press, 1997), reprinted in *Ethics for Modern Life*, 6th ed., ed. Raziel Abelson and Marie-Louise Friquegnon (New York: Bedford/St. Martin's, 2003), pp. 191–200.

25. Many ethicists oppose both direct-active-voluntary euthanasia and assisted suicide, which they see as morally the same. Daniel Callahan, "When Self-Determination Runs Amok," *Hastings Center Report* 22, no. 2 (1992), reprinted in *Social and Personal Ethics*, 5th ed., ed. Shaw, pp. 89–95; Callahan, "Aid-in-Dying: The Social Dimensions," *Commonweal*, August 9, 1991, reprinted in *Analyzing Moral Issues*, 3rd ed., ed. Boss, pp. 208–11; Callahan, "Killing and Allowing to Die," *Hastings Center Report* 19 (January/February 1989): 5–6, reprinted in *Contemporary Moral Problems*, 6th ed., ed. White, pp. 215–18; Callahan, "The Immorality of Assisted Suicide," in *Physician Assisted Suicide*, ed. Weir, reprinted in *Ethics for Modern Life*, 6th ed., ed. Abelson and Friquegnon, pp. 201–15; Kenneth L. Vaux, "The Theologic Ethics of Euthanasia," *Hastings Center Report* (January/February 1989), reprinted in *Contemporary Moral Issues*, ed. Hinman, pp. 118–23; Richard Doeflinger, "Assisted Suicide: Pro-Choice or Anti-Life?" *Hastings Center Report* (January/February 1989), reprinted in *Contemporary Moral Issues*, ed. Hinman, pp. 128–35; Sissela Bok, "Physician-Assisted Suicide," in *Physician Assisted Suicide*, ed. Weir, reprinted in *Ethics for Modern Life*, 6th ed., ed. Abelson and Friquegnon, pp. 227–34; Paul Chamberlain, "A Case against Physician-Assisted Suicide," in *Do the Right Thing*, ed. Beckwith, pp. 268–83; and Patricia Wesley, "Dying Safely: An Analysis of 'A Case of Individualized Decision Making' by Timothy E. Quill, M.D.," *Issues in Law and Medicine* 8, no. 4 (1993): 467–85, reprinted in *Do the Right Thing*, ed. Beckwith, pp. 289–301.

26. *Compassion in Dying v. Washington*, 64 U.S.L.W. 2553 (9th Cir., March 12, 1996).

27. *Quill v. Vacco*, 64 U.S.L.W. 2620 (2nd Cir., April 9, 1996).

28. *Cruzan v. Director, Missouri Department of Health*, 497 U.S. 261, 110 Sup. Ct. 2841 (1990).

29. *Washington v. Glucksberg*, No. 96–110, and *Vacco v. Quill*, No. 95–1858. See *New York Times*, June 27, 1997, sec. A, 1, 18, 19.

30. *Gonzales v. Oregon* (04-623) 368 F. 3rd 1118. On this decision, see Timothy Egan and Adam Liptak, "Fraught Issue, but Narrow Ruling in Oregon Suicide Case," *New York Times*, January 18, 2006, http://www.nytimes.com/2006/01/18/national/18oregon.html?ex =1295240400&en=18040 (accessed December 4, 2006); and "Washington v. Glucksberg: 1997," *History of the Supreme Court: Encyclopedia*, http://www.historyofsupremecourt.org/scripts/ supremecourt/glossary.cgi?term=w&letter (accessed December 4, 2006). Oregon's assisted-suicide law is called the Oregon Death with Dignity Act. To read and download a copy, see "Oregon Death with Dignity Act," *Oregon: Department of Human Services*, http://www.oregon .gov/DHS/ph/pas/ors.shtml (accessed March 28, 2007).

31. "Montana Becomes Third State to Permit Physician-Assisted Suicide—But Final Exit Network Asks, 'Is It Enough?'" *Final Exit Network*, http://www.ereleases.com/pr/montana-ere -permit-physician assisted-suicide-final-exit-netw. . . (accessed January 6, 2010).

32. Joseph V. Sullivan, *The Morality of Mercy Killing* (Westminster, MD: Newman Press, 1950), reprinted in part in *The Right Thing to Do*, ed. James Rachels (New York: Random House, 1989), pp. 204–205.

33. Foot, "Euthanasia," pp. 111–12.

34. Daniel Callahan, *Abortion: Law, Choice and Morality* (New York: Macmillan, 1970), p. 475.

35. I am indebted to Munson, *Intervention and Reflection*, p. 90, for the analysis of spina bifida.

36. Anthony M. Shaw and Iris A. Shaw, "Dilemma of Informed Consent in Children," *New England Journal of Medicine* 289 (October 25, 1973): 885–90.

37. On the Terri Schiavo case, see *New York Times*, March 19, 2005, sec. A, 1, 11; and April 1, 2005, sec. A, 1, 16, 17.

6. THE DEATH PENALTY AND PURPOSES OF PUNISHMENT

This chapter is based on my Harrod Lecture "Criminal Punishment and the Death Penalty," delivered at Fitchburg State College, March 26, 1986, and published in *The Harrod Lecture Series*, vol. 7 (Fitchburg, MA: Fitchburg State College Press, 1986), pp. 37–70. See also my other articles on the death penalty: "Capital Punishment in a Democracy," *America*, December 11, 1976, 413–14; "The Death Penalty: A Personalist Approach," *American Benedictine Review* 38, no. 4 (December 1987): 360–80; and "Should the Death Penalty Be Abolished?" *Commonwealth Review* 1, no. 1 (January 1988): 33–37.

1. Louis H. Gold, "A Psychiatric Review of Capital Punishment," *Journal of Forensic Science* 6 (1961): 465, quoted in Neil Vidmar and Phoebe C. Ellsworth, "Public Opinion and the Death Penalty," *Stanford Law Review* 26 (June 1974): 1245–70, reprinted in *The Death Penalty in America*, 3rd ed., ed. Hugo Adam Bedau (New York: Oxford University Press, 1982), pp. 80–81. When Americans polled are asked to choose between the death penalty and life imprisonment without parole for convicted murderers, support for the death penalty substantially drops. A May 2004 Gallup Poll found that 46 percent of respondents favor life without parole, and 50 percent favor capital punishment. "Deterrence News and Developments— Previous Years," *Death Penalty Information Center*, http://www.deathpenaltyinfo.org/article .php?&did=1705 (accessed December 27, 2006). See also "Death Penalty," *Gallup*, http://www .gallup.com/poll/1606/death-penalty.aspx (accessed June 4, 2012).

2. Thomas Hobbes, *Leviathan* (New York: F. P. Dutton, 1914), p. 65.

3. Augustine, *De libero arbitrio* 1.5.

4. John Macmurray, *Persons in Relation* (Amherst, NY: Humanity Books, 1991), p. 205.

5. See Jeffrie G. Murphy, "Marxism and Retribution," *Philosophy and Public Affairs* 2, no. 3 (Spring 1973): 217–43. See also Richard Dagger, "Playing Fair with Punishment," *Ethics* 103, no. 3 (1993), reprinted in *Contemporary Moral Issues: Diversity and Consensus*, ed. Lawrence M. Hinman (Upper Saddle River, NJ: Prentice Hall, 1996), pp. 182–95.

6. G. W. F. Hegel, *Hegel's Philosophy of Right*, trans. T. M. Knox (New York: Oxford University Press, 1952), pp. 69–70.

7. Cf. Herbert Morris, "Persons and Punishment," *Monist* 5 (October 1968): 475–501; and Edmund L. Pincoffs, *The Rationale of Legal Punishment* (Atlantic Highlands, NJ: Humanities Press, 1966), pp. 2–16.

8. See, for example, Michael D. Bayles and Kenneth Henley, eds., *Right Conduct: Theories and Applications* (New York: Random House, 1983), pp. 183–86.

9. Immanuel Kant, *The Metaphysical Elements of Justice*, trans. John Ladd (New York: Library of Liberal Arts Press, 1965), p. 101.

10. Sir William Blackstone, "Commentaries on the Laws of England" (1769), reprinted in *Right Conduct*, p. 193.

11. Cf. Burton M. Leiser, *Liberty, Justice, and Morals: Contemporary Value Conflicts*, 3rd ed. (New York: Macmillan, 1986), pp. 212–13.

12. J. R. Lucas, "Or Else," *Proceedings of the Aristotelian Society* (1968–69), reprinted in *Moral Problems*, ed. James Rachels (New York: Harper & Row, 1971), pp. 227–28.

13. Hegel, *Philosophy of Right*, p. 70.

14. "The First 'Humane' Execution?" *Newsweek*, December 20, 1982, 41.

15. Sissela Bok, "Ethical Problems of Abortion," *Hastings Center Studies* 2 (January 1974): 41.

16. *Universal Declaration of Human Rights*, http://www.un.org/en/documents/udhr/index .shtm (accessed July 6, 2010).

17. Jeremy Bentham, *An Introduction to the Principles of Morals and Legislation* (New York: Hafner, 1948), p. 170; authoritative edition by J. H. Burns and H. L. A. Hart, with a new introduction by F. Rosen (New York: Oxford University Press, 1996), p. 158. There are minor differences of wording between the two editions.

18. Ibid., pp. 170–71 n. 1; 158 n.a., Hafner ed. Cf. Hugo Adam Bedau, "A World Without Punishment?" in *Punishment and Human Rights*, ed. Milton Goldfinger (Rochester, VT: Schenkman Books, 1974), pp. 141–62, reprinted in *Ethics: Theory and Contemporary Issues*, 3rd ed., ed. Barbara MacKinnon (Belmont, CA: Wadsworth, 2001), pp. 331–39.

19. Richard B. Brandt, "A Utilitarian Theory of Punishment," in Brandt, *Ethical Theory: The Problems of Normative and Critical Ethics* (Englewood Cliffs, NJ: Prentice-Hall, 1959), reprinted in *Morality in Practice*, 3rd ed., ed. James P. Sterba (Belmont, CA: Wadsworth, 1991), pp. 488–89 (emphasis in original).

20. American Friends Service Committee, "Critique of Rehabilitation," in *Struggle for Justice: A Report on Crime and Punishment in America* (Hill and Wang, 1971), reprinted in *Moral Problems*, 3rd ed., ed. James Rachels (New York: Harper & Row, 1979), pp. 332–45.

21. William H. Shaw, "Punishment and the Criminal Justice System," in *Contemporary Ethics: Taking Account of Utilitarianism*, ed. Shaw (Malden, MA: Blackwell, 1999), reprinted in *Social and Personal Ethics*, 5th ed., ed. William H. Shaw (Belmont, CA: Wadsworth), p. 343.

22. For another attempt to synthesize retributivism and the utilitarian theory, see R. S. Downie, "The Justification of Punishment," in Downie, *Roles and Values* (London: Methuen, 1971), reprinted in *Moral Problems*, 3rd ed., pp. 321–31. Thomas Hurka attempts a synthesis based on a rights theory of punishment. "Rights and Capital Punishment," *Dialogue* 21 (1982), reprinted in *Right Conduct: Theories and Applications*, 2nd ed., ed. Michael D. Bayles and Kenneth Henley (New York: Random House, 1989), pp. 210–17. For a synthesis that makes utilitarianism primary and retributivism secondary, see, for example, John Rawls, "Two Concepts of Rules," *Philosophical Review* 64 (1955): 3–32. Hugo Adam Bedau forges a synthesis that makes the two theories coequal. See Hugo Adam Bedau and Erin Kelly, "Punishment," *Stanford Encyclopedia of Philosophy* (Spring 2010 ed.), ed. Edward N. Zalta, http://plato.stanford.edu/archives/spr2010/entries/punishment/ (accessed June 18, 2012).

23. Walter Berns, "The Morality of Anger," in Berns, *For Capital Punishment* (Lanham, MD: University Press of America, 1991), reprinted in *Contemporary Moral Issues*, ed. Hinman, p. 220.

24. Louis P. Pojman, *Life and Death: Grappling with the Moral Problems of Our Time* (Boston: Jones and Bartlett, 1992), p. 99.

25. "The Chilling Message Some Inmates Receive," *Boston Sunday Globe*, September 2, 1984, 16.

26. *Newsweek*, September 2, 1998, reprinted in *Contemporary Moral Problems*, 6th ed., ed. James E. White (Belmont, CA: Wadsworth, 2000), p. 295.

27. "Warden: Williams Frustrated at End," *CNN Law Center*, December 13, 2005, http://www.cnn.com/2005/LAW/12/13/williams.execution (accessed March 28, 2007).

28. Cf. Hugo Adam Bedau, "Capital Punishment," in *Matters of Life and Death*, 2nd ed., ed. Tom Regan (New York: Random House, 1986), p. 192.

29. Ibid., p. 198.

30. Hugo Adam Bedau, "The Death Penalty as a Deterrent: Argument and Evidence," *Ethics* 80 (1970): 205–17, reprinted in *Applying Ethics*, 4th ed., ed. Jeffrey Olen and Vincent Barry (Belmont, CA: Wadsworth, 1992), p. 285; and "Deterrence and the Death Penalty: A Reconsideration," *Journal of Criminal Law, Criminology and Police Science* 61, no. 4 (1971), reprinted in *Ethics for Modern Life*, 2nd ed., ed. Raziel Abelson and Marie-Louise Friquegnon (New York: St. Martin's Press, 1982), p. 217.

31. *Report of the Royal Commission on Capital Punishment*, para. 65, cited by H. L. A. Hart, "Murder and the Principle of Punishment: England and the United States," *Northwestern University Law Review* 52, no. 4 (1958), reprinted in *Moral Problems*, 2nd ed., ed. James Rachels (New York: Harper & Row, 1975), p. 275.

32. Thorsten Sellin, "The Death Penalty Relative to Deterrence and Police Safety," in *The Sociology of Crime and Punishment*, ed. Norman Johnsten, Leonard Savitz, and Marvin L. Wolfgang (New York: John Wiley, 1962), pp. 78, 83. See also Sellin's later writings: *Capital Punishment* (New York: Harper & Row, 1967); *The Death Penalty* (Philadelphia: American Law Institute, 1959); and *The Penalty of Death* (Beverly Hills, CA: Sage Publications, 1980).

33. Isaac Ehrlich, "The Deterrent Effect of Capital Punishment: A Question of Life and Death," *American Economic Review* 65 (June 1975): 398.

34. For some of the literature criticizing Ehrlich, see Deryck Beyleveld, "Ehrlich's Analysis of Deterrence," *British Journal of Criminology* 22 (April 1982): 101–23; Alfred Blumstein, Jacqueline Cohen, and Daniel Nagin, eds., *Deterrence and Incapacitation: Estimating the Effects of Criminal Sanctions on Crime Rates* (Washington, DC: National Academy of Sciences, 1978); Brian E. Forst, "The Deterrent Effect on Capital Punishment: A Cross-State Analysis," *Minnesota Law Review* 61 (May 1977): 743–67; Richard O. Lempert, "Desert and Deterrence: An Assessment of the Moral Bases of the Case for Capital Punishment," *Michigan Law Review* 79 (1981); Peter Passell, "The Deterrent Effect of the Death Penalty: A Statistical Test," *Stanford Law Review* 65 (November 1975): 62–64; and Hans Zeisel, "The Deterrent Effect of the Death Penalty: Facts v. Faith," in *The Supreme Court Review*, ed. Philip B. Kurland (1976), 317–43, reprinted in *Death Penalty in America*, pp. 116–38. See also Anthony G. Amsterdam, "Capital Punishment," *Stanford Magazine* (Fall/Winter 1977), reprinted in *Contemporary Moral Issues*, 6th ed., ed. White, pp. 284–96.

35. Jeffrey H. Reiman, "Justice, Civilization, and the Death Penalty," *Philosophy and Public Affairs* 14, no. 1 (Spring 1985): 115–48, reprinted in *Social and Personal Ethics*, ed. William H. Shaw (Belmont, CA: Wadsworth, 1993), p. 426.

36. Bedau, "Capital Punishment," in *Matters of Life and Death*, 198. Cf. Bedau, *Death Penalty in America*, p. 97. For a fuller list of the scientific literature on deterrence, see the writings of Bedau and Sellin listed in notes 29 and 31. See also Bedau, *Death Penalty in America*, pp. 93–103.

37. John Donahue and Justin Wolfers, "Uses and Abuses of Empirical Evidence in the Death Penalty Debate," *Stanford Law Review* 58 (2005): 791, in "News and Developments—Deterrence," *Death Penalty Information Center*, http://www.deathpenaltyinfo.org/newsanddev .php?scid=12 (accessed December 27, 2006).

38. John Donahue and Justin Wolfers, "The Death Penalty: No Evidence for Deterrence," *Economists' Voice* (April 2006), in ibid.

39. See the following writings of Ernest van den Haag: "On Deterrence and the Death Penalty," *Journal of Criminal Law, Criminology and Police Science* 60 (June 1969): 141–47, reprinted in *Applying Ethics*, pp. 273–80; "In Defense of the Death Penalty: A Legal—Practical—Moral Analysis," *Criminal Law Bulletin* 14, no. 1 (January–February 1978): 51–68, reprinted in *Death Penalty in America*, pp. 323–33; with Joseph P. Conrad, *The Death Penalty: A Debate* (New York: Plenum Press, 1983); "Refuting Reiman and Nathanson," *Philosophy and Public Affairs* 14, no. 2 (Spring 1985): 165–76; and "The Ultimate Punishment: A Defense," *Harvard Law Review* 99 (1986), reprinted in *Contemporary Moral Problems*, 4th ed., ed. James E. White (New York: West, 1994), pp. 209–14. More recently, Louis Pojman has continued Van den Haag's debate with Jeffrey Reiman on the death penalty. See Louis P. Pojman, "The Wisdom of Capital Punishment," in *The Death Penalty: For and Against*, ed. Pojman and Jeffrey Reiman (Lanham, MD: Rowman and Littlefield, 1998), reprinted in *Ethics for Modern Life*, 6th ed., ed. Raziel Abelson and Marie-Louise Friquegnon (Boston: Bedford/St. Martin's, 2003), pp. 272–81; Jeffrey Reiman, "The Folly of Capital Punishment," in *The Death Penalty*, ed. Pojman and Reiman, reprinted in *Ethics for Modern Life*, 6th ed., ed. Abelson and Friquegnon, pp. 282–91; and Jeffrey Reiman, "Why the Death Penalty Should be Abolished," in *The Death Penalty*, ed. Pojman and Reiman, reprinted in *Analyzing Moral Issues*, 3rd ed., ed. Judith A. Boss (New York: McGraw-Hill, 2005), pp. 272–78.

40. According to one study, there were twenty-five innocent persons executed out of seven thousand between 1900 and 1985. Hugo Adam Bedau and Michael Radelet, *Miscarriages of Justice in Potentially Capital Cases* (Cambridge, MA: Harvard Law School Library, 1985).

41. James Fitzjames Stephen, "Capital Punishments," *Fraser's Magazine* 69 (1864), 753, quoted in Hart, "Murder and the Principles of Punishment," in *Moral Problems*, 2nd ed., p. 278 (emphasis in original).

42. "Arbitrariness," *Death Penalty Information Center*, http://www .deathpenaltyinfo.org/ article.php?did=1328 (accessed January 4, 2007).

43. William J. Bowers and Glenn L. Pierce, "Deterrence or Brutalization: What Is the Effect of Executions?" *Crime and Delinquency* 26 (October 1980): 453–84.

44. George Schedler, "Capital Punishment and Its Deterrent Effect," *Social Theory and Practice* 4, no. 1 (1976): 47–56, reprinted in *Today's Moral Problems*, 2nd ed., ed. Richard Wasserstrom (New York: Macmillan, 1979), pp. 555–56.

45. Bedau, "Capital Punishment," in *Matters of Life and Death*, p. 199.

46. Van den Haag, "The Ultimate Punishment," in *Contemporary Moral Problems*, 213 n.

10, citing Phillips, "The Deterrent Effect of Capital Punishment: New Evidence on an Old Controversy," *American Journal of Sociology* 139 (1980).

47. Andrew Bridges, "Gov't: Executions, Death Sentences Decline," November 14, 2005, http://news.yahoo.com/slap (accessed November 17, 2005). See also "What's New," *Death Penalty Information Center*, http:// www.deathpenaltyinfo.org (accessed January 3, 2007); "1999 Year End Report: Executions Reach Record High, But Concern Also Grows," *Death Penalty Information Center*, http://www.deathpenaltyinfo.org/node/470 (accessed April 4, 2009); "Execution List 2011," *Death Penalty Information Center*, http://www.deathpenaltyinfo.org/execution-list-2011 (accessed June 13, 2012); and "Execution List 2012," *Death Penalty Information Center*, http://www.deathpenaltyinfo.org/execution-list-2012 (accessed August 7, 2012).

48. "Deterrence: States Without the Death Penalty Have Had Consistently Lower Murder Rate . . .," Death Penalty Information Center, http://www.deathpenaltyinfo.org/deterrence -states-without-death-penalty-have-had-consiste . . . (accessed June 4, 2012); "Murder Rates Nationally and By State," *Death Penalty Information Center*, http://www.deathpenaltyinfo.org/murder-rates-nationally-and-state (accessed March 22, 2013).

49. For an excellent introduction to phenomenology, see Quentin Lauer, *Phenomenology: Its Genesis and Prospect* (New York: Harper Torchbooks, 1965).

50. Camus has emphasized the horribleness of the premeditated aspect of the death penalty. Albert Camus, "Reflections on the Guillotine," trans. J. O'Brien, in *Resistance, Rebellion and Death* (New York: 1961).

51. *San Francisco Sunday Examiner and Chronicle*, April 24, 1983, sec. A, 2.

52. "The First 'Humane' Execution?" *Newsweek*, December 20, 1982, 41.

53. Kant, *Metaphysical Elements of Justice*, p. 104.

54. Ex. 21:23–25 New American Standard Bible. See also Lev. 24:17–21 and Deut. 19:21.

55. Matt. 5:38–39 NASB.

56. *Coker v. Georgia*, 433 U.S. 584, 97 Sup. Ct. 2866 (1977). The Court said that the death penalty is unconstitutional if its only point is "the purposeless and needless imposition of pain and suffering." It thus condemned revenge as a purpose of punishment.

57. *Locket v. Ohio*, 98 Sup. Ct. 2954 (1978).

58. *Tison v. Arizona*, 481 U.S. 137, 107 Sup. Ct. 1676 (1987).

59. *Kennedy v. Louisiana*, 554 U.S. 407 (2008). See also Linda Greenhouse, "Supreme Court Rejects Death Penalty for Child Rape," *New York Times*, http://www.nytimes.com/2008/06/26/washington/26scotusend.htm (accessed July 6, 2008).

60. *Furman v. Georgia*, 408 U.S. 238, 927 Sup. Ct. 2726 (1972).

61. *Woodson v. North Carolina*, 96 Sup. Ct. 2978 (1976).

62. *Gregg v. Georgia*, 428 U.S. 153, 96 Sup. Ct. 1756 (1976).

63. *McCleskey v. Kemp*, 481 U.S. 279, 107 Sup. Ct. 1756 (1987).

64. Anthony G. Amsterdam, "Race and the Death Penalty," *Criminal Justice Ethics* 7, no. 1

(Winter/Spring 1988): 82–86, reprinted in *Moral Controversies: Race, Class, and Gender in Applied Ethics*, ed. Steven Jay Gold (Belmont, CA: Wadsworth, 1993), pp. 267–72.

65. *Ford v. Wainwright*, 477 U.S. 399 (1986).

66. *Panetti v. Quarterman* (2007), *On the Docket, Northwestern University: U.S. Supreme Court News*, http://docket.medill.northwestern (accessed July 7, 2007); Ralph Blumenthal, "Justices Block Execution of Delusional Texas Killer," *New York Times*, June 29, 2007, sec. A, 21.

67. *Thompson v. Oklahoma*, 487 U.S. 815 (1988).

68. *Stanford v. Kentucky*, 492 U.S. 361 (1989).

69. *Atkins v. Virginia*, 122 Sup. Ct. 2242 (2002).

70. *Ring v. Arizona*, 122 Sup. Ct. 2428 (2002).

71. *Roper v. Simmons* (03-633), 112 S. W. 3rd 397.

72. *Miller v. Alabama*, 567 U.S. (2012).

73. Hill v. McDonough, 547 U.S. (2006).

74. *House v. Bell*, 547 U.S. (2006).

75. *Baze v. Rees*, 217 S.W. 3d 207, (2008).

76. *Wilkerson v. Utah*, 99 U.S. 130 (1878)

77. "What's New," *Death Penalty Information Center*, http://www.deathpenaltyinfo.org (accessed January 3, 2007).

78. "Facts on Post-Conviction DNA Exonerations," *Innocence Project*, http://www.innocence project.org/Content/Facts_on_PostConviction_DNA_Exonerations.php (accessed June 4, 2012).

79. James S. Liebman, Jeffrey Fagan, and Valerie West, *A Broken System: Error Rates in Capital Cases, 1973–1995* (New York: Justice Project, 2000). See also *New York Times*, June 12, 2000, sec. A, 1, 21.

80. Sidney Hook supports the death penalty for premeditated murderers who murder again after they have been sentenced to prison for the first murder. However, his essay was written before the rise of supermax prisons. Sidney Hook, "The Death Sentence," *New Leader* 44 (April 3, 1961), reprinted in *Applying Ethics*, 8th ed., ed. Jeffrey Olen, Vincent Barry, and Julie C. Van Camp (Belmont, CA: Wadsworth, 2005), pp. 278–82. Supermax prisons have come under fire for being inhumane because their inmates are totally isolated. "The Paradox of Supermax," *Time*, February 5, 2007, 52–54.

81. Bedau, "Capital Punishment," in *Matters of Life and Death*, p. 197.

82. Bedau, "Recidivism, Parole, and Deterrence," in *Death Penalty in America*, p. 180.

83. Ibid., n. 3.

84. Barry Nakell, "The Cost of the Death Penalty," *Criminal Law Bulletin* 14, no. 1 (January–February 1978): 68–80, reprinted in *Death Penalty in America*, pp. 245–46; and Robert Johnson, "This Man Has Expired: Witness to an Execution," *Commonweal*, January 13, 1989, 9–15, reprinted in *Moral Controversies*, pp. 272–81. See also Richard C. Dieter, "Secondary Smoke Surrounds the Capital Punishment Debate," *Criminal Justice Ethics* 13 (Winter/Spring

1994): 2, 82–84, reprinted in *Social Ethics*, 5th ed., ed. Thomas A. Mappes and Jane S. Zembaty (New York: McGraw-Hill, 1997), pp. 144–48.

85. Nakell, "Cost of the Death Penalty," in *Death Penalty in America*, p. 245, citing McGee, "Capital Punishment as Seen by a Correctional Administrator," *Federal Probation* 28 (June 1964): 13–14.

86. Cf. Jonathan Glover, *Causing Death and Saving Lives* (Harmondsworth, UK: Penguin Books, 1977), reprinted in part in *Social and Personal Ethics*, p. 404.

87. Robert S. Gerstein, "Capital Punishment—'Cruel and Unusual'? A Retributivist Response," *Ethics* 85, no. 1 (October 1974): 75–79, reprinted in *Contemporary Moral Problems*, 2nd ed., ed. James E. White (New York: West, 1988), p. 116.

88. This exception should be taken as seriously as Van den Haag's exception to his position. He tells us that if it could be shown conclusively that executions increase the murder rate, he would be an abolitionist, even though, as a retributivist, he would still hold that convicted murderers deserve the death penalty. Of course, Van den Haag denies that this can be shown. Van den Haag, "The Ultimate Punishment," in *Contemporary Moral Problems*, 4th ed., 213 n. 10.

89. Reiman, "The Folly of Capital Punishment," in *The Death Penalty*, reprinted in *Ethics for Modern Life*, 6th ed., p. 291.

7. PRIVACY, PRIVATE PROPERTY, AND JUSTICE

This chapter, and a small portion of the next chapter, are based on my Harrod Lecture "Privacy and Personhood," delivered at Fitchburg State College, March 22, 1989, and published in *The Harrod Lecture Series*, vol. 10 (Fitchburg, MA: Fitchburg State College Press, 1989), pp. 128–59.

1. Bork's side of the controversial nomination is presented in his book, *The Tempting of America: The Political Seduction of the Law* (New York: Simon & Schuster, 1990), pp. 267–321.

2. John Macmurray, *Persons in Relation* (Amherst, NY: Humanity Books, 1991), pp. 86–105.

3. Judith Jarvis Thomson, "The Right to Privacy," *Philosophy and Public Affairs* 4, no. 4 (Summer 1975): 295–314.

4. Thomas Scanlon, "Thomson on Privacy," *Philosophy and Public Affairs* 4, no. 4 (Summer 1975): 315–22.

5. Ibid., p. 318 (emphasis in original).

6. Jeffrey Reiman, "Privacy, Intimacy, and Personhood," *Philosophy and Public Affairs* 6, no. 1 (Fall 1976): 26–44. Reiman also criticizes an article by James Rachels, "Why Privacy Is Important," *Philosophy and Public Affairs* 4, no. 4 (Summer 1975): 323–33.

7. Reiman, "Privacy," p. 39 (emphasis in original deleted).

8. Ibid., p. 40.

9. Ibid., pp. 43–44.

10. Ibid., p. 43.

11. Gabriel Marcel, *Being and Having*, trans. Katherine Farrer (Westminster, UK: Dacre Press, 1949). See also S. Strasser, *The Soul in Metaphysical and Empirical Psychology* (Pittsburgh, PA: Duquesne University Press, 1957).

12. I say *human person* rather than *person*, since there may be other kinds of persons, most important, God.

13. Cf. W. Norris Clarke, *Person and Being* (Milwaukee: Marquette University Press, 1993), pp. 32–42. See also Walter G. Jeffko, "Self-Consciousness and the Soul-Body Problem," *American Benedictine Review* 31, no. 3 (September 1980): 346–60.

14. For differing views on the personhood status of corporations, see Thomas Donaldson, *Corporations and Morality* (Englewood Cliffs, NJ: Prentice-Hall, 1982); John R. Danley, "Corporate Moral Agency: The Case for Anthropological Bigotry," in *Business Ethics: Readings and Cases in Corporate Morality*, ed. W. Michael Hoffman and Jennifer M. Moore (New York: McGraw-Hill, 1984); John Ladd, "Morality and the Ideal of Rationality in Formal Organizations," in *Ethical Issues in Business: A Philosophical Approach*, 2nd ed., ed. Thomas Donaldson and Patricia Werhane (Englewood Cliffs, NJ: Prentice-Hall, 1983); Kenneth Goodpaster and John B. Matthews Jr., "Can a Corporation Have a Conscience?" *Harvard Business Review* 60 (January–February 1982): 132–41; Peter French, "The Corporation as Moral Person," *American Philosophical Quarterly* 16 (July 1979): 207–15; J. Angelo Corlett, "Corporate Responsibility and Punishment," *Public Affairs Quarterly* 2 (January 1988); and Manuel G. Velasquez, "Why Corporations Are Not Morally Responsible for Anything They Do," *Business and Professional Ethics Journal* 2 (Spring 1983).

15. John Macmurray, *The Self as Agent* (Amherst, NY: Humanity Books, 1991), pp. 91–92.

16. Stanley Harrison, a well-known Macmurrian scholar, makes a similar criticism of Macmurray and proposes a similar definition of person. See his article, "Macmurray and the Mind-Body Problem Revisited," in *John Macmurray: Critical Perspectives*, ed. David Ferguson and Nigel Dower (New York: Peter Lang, 2002), pp. 51–67. See also Walter G. Jeffko, "Are 'Person' and 'Agent' Co-Extensive? Reflections of John Macmurray," *American Benedictine Review* 44, no. 4 (December 1993): 352–70.

17. The phrase "at least in this life" implies the possibility of life after death.

18. Steven Pinker, "The Mystery of Consciousness," *Time*, January 29, 2007, 58–69.

19. Ibid., p. 61.

20. Robert Nozick, *Anarchy, State, and Utopia* (New York: Basic Books, 1974). For two penetrating critiques of this book, see Thomas Scanlon, "Nozick on Rights, Liberty, and Property," *Philosophy and Public Affairs* 6, no. 1 (Fall 1976): 3–25; and Barbara Field, "Wilt Chamberlain Revisited: Nozick's 'Justice in Transfer' and the Problem of Market-Based Distribution," *Philosophy and Public Affairs* 24, no. 3 (Summer 1995): 226–45.

21. John Locke, *Two Treatises of Civil Government*, introduction by W. S. Carpenter (New York: E. P. Dutton, 1924), p. 119.

22. Nozick, *Anarchy*, p. 151.

23. Ibid., p. 26. The government's duty to enforce contracts is a negative duty, for it is correlative to the negative right to own private property. If someone reneges on a contract, he violates another's property rights just as much as if he were to steal from that person. The state must then intervene to rectify the injustice, just as it does when it punishes criminals.

24. Ibid., p. 169.

25. Sara Mosle, "The Vanity of Volunteerism," *New York Times Magazine*, July 2, 2000, 22–27, 40, 52–55.

26. G. William Domhoff, "Wealth, Income, and Power," *Who Rules America?* updated December 2006, http://sociology.ucsc.edu/whorulesamerica/power/wealth.html (accessed January 10, 2007).

27. "Trends in the Distribution of Household Income between 1979 and 2007," *Congressional Budget Office*, http://www.cbo.gov/doc.cfm?index=12485 (accessed October 26, 2011); Paul Krugman, "Oligarchy, American Style," *New York Times*, http://www.nytimes.com/2011/11/04/opinion/oligarchy-american-style.html?_r=1&hp (accessed November 4, 2011); "Family Net Worth Drops to Level of Early '90s, Fed Says," *New York Times*, http://www.nytimes.com/2012/06/12/business/economy-net-worth-drops-to-level-of-early-90s-fed-says.html (accessed June 14, 2012); and "U.S. Poverty on Track to Rise to Highest Since 1960s," *HuffPost Business*, http://www.huffingtonpost.com/2012/07/22/us-poverty-level-1960s_n_169 2744.html (accessed July 23, 2012). Of course, the inequalities of wealth will always be greater than inequalities of income, because the larger the income, the greater the percentage of it that is kept and subsequently saved and invested. See Catherine Rampell, "Inequality Is Most Extreme in Wealth, Not Income," *New York Times*, http://economix.blogs.nytimes.com/2011/03/30inequality-is-most-extreme-in-wealth-not-in . . . (accessed June 4, 2012).

28. Milton Friedman, Capitalism and Freedom (Chicago: University of Chicago Press, 1962).

29. Nozick, *Anarchy*, p. 9.

30. On my view, theism is at least rationally arguable, as has been the case for most of the history of Western philosophy. Theism is not just a matter of religious faith, nor is it contrary to science.

31. For Plato's views on slavery, see *Laws* 6.776–78, 11–930. The *Laws* is his last dialogue, written when he was seventy years old. This shows that he did not renounce his acceptance of slavery. All references to Plato are taken from *The Dialogues of Plato*, trans. B. Jowett, with an introduction by Raphael Demos, 2 vols. (New York: Random House, 1937).

32. Aristotle, *Politics,* in *The Basic Works of Aristotle*, ed. with an introduction by Richard McKeon (New York: Random House, 1941), 1.4–5.1254a–1255a.

33. Plato, *The Republic* 5.461.

34. Ibid., 5.468.

35. Plato, *Laws* 6.783.

36. Ibid., 10.908–9.

37. Plato, *The Republic* 8.543–45.

38. A. E. Taylor, *Plato: The Man and His Work*, 7th ed. (London: Methuen, 1960), 282. Another major difference between Plato's thumos (spirit) and will is that the former has emotion, whereas will is usually interpreted as devoid of emotion. However, the interpretation I gave of will in the first two chapters as an aspect of an action's direct intention implies a close connection between will and feeling. For since every action and therefore every direct intention has a motive, and since motive and direct intention are essential elements of action, and since motive includes emotion or feeling, it follows that will cannot be interpreted as inherently emotionless. Furthermore, it seems a mistake to translate *thumos* as *passion*, as some authors do. For Plato holds that reason has its own desire or passion, a passion for the truth (or knowledge).

39. Plato, *The Republic* 4.434, 4.444.

40. K. R. Popper, *The Open Society and Its Enemies*, 4th ed., vol. 1 (London: Routledge & Kegan Paul, 1962).

8. THE PERSONALIST SOCIETY, COMMUNITY, AND JUSTICE

1. Aristotle, *Nicomachean Ethics*, in *The Basic Works of Aristotle*, ed. with an introduction by Richard McKeon (New York: Random House, 1941), 5.1–2.1129a–1131a.

2. Ibid., 5.2–4.1131a–1132b.

3. John Stuart Mill, *On Liberty* (London: John W. Parker and Son, 1859).

4. St. Thomas Aquinas, *Summa Theologica*, trans. Fathers of the English Dominican Province, 3 vols. (New York: Benziger Brothers, 1947), 2–2.58.1 (emphasis in original deleted).

5. Ibid., 2–2.58.2.

6. Ibid., 2–2.60.1.

7. Ibid., 2–2.60.1.

8. Ibid., 2–2.60.2.

9. Ibid., 2–2.66.1.

10. Ibid., 2–2.66.7.

11. Kant's distinction between justice and virtue constitutes the two formal parts of *The Metaphysics of Morals*.

12. Immanuel Kant, *The Metaphysical Elements of Justice*, trans. John Ladd (New York: Library of Liberal Arts Press, 1965), p. 46.

13. Ibid., pp. 68–71.

14. Although Kant apparently advocated some version of the minimalist state, such a state, I contend, is not implied by his theory of justice. For a further discussion of this point, see Allen D. Rosen, Kant's *Theory of Justice* (Ithaca, NY: Cornell University Press, 1993).

15. John Macmurray, *A Challenge to the Churches: Religion and Democracy*, introduction by Francis Williams (London: Kegan Paul, French, Trubner and Co., 1941), p. 9 (emphasis in original deleted).

16. Ibid., p. 10 (emphasis in original deleted).

17. John Macmurray, *The Self as Agent* (Amherst, NY: Humanity Books, 1991), p. 29.

18. John Macmurray, *Constructive Democracy* (London: Faber & Faber, 1943), pp. 11–12.

19. Macmurray, *Challenge to the Churches*, pp. 32, 53.

20. John Macmurray, *The Philosophy of Communism* (London: Faber & Faber, 1933); and *Creative Society: A Study of the Relation of Christianity to Communism* (London: Student Christian Movement Press, 1935).

21. John Rawls's six books are: *A Theory of Justice* (Cambridge: Harvard University Press, Belknap Press, 1971; rev. ed., 1999); *Political Liberalism* (New York: Columbia University Press, 1993; paperback ed., 1996; expanded ed., 2005); *John Rawls: Collected Papers*, ed. Samuel Freeman (Cambridge: Harvard University Press, 1999); *The Law of Peoples* (Cambridge: Harvard University Press, 1999); *Lectures on the History of Moral Philosophy*, ed. Barbara Herman (Cambridge: Harvard University Press, 2000); and *Justice as Fairness: A Restatement*, ed. Erin Kelly (Cambridge: Harvard University Press, Belknap Press, 2001). Page numbers I refer to in *Theory* and *Liberalism* are from their latest editions.

22. See, for example, John Rawls, "Justice as Fairness: Political not Metaphysical," *Philosophy and Public Affairs* 14, no. 3 (Summer 1985): 223–51; "The Priority of Right and Ideas of the Good," *Philosophy and Public Affairs* 17, no. 4 (Fall 1988): 251–76; and "Kantian Constructivism in Moral Theory," *Journal of Philosophy* 77 (September 1980): 515–72. For an excellent sympathetic and constructive critique of Rawls's political philosophy, see Thomas W. Pogge, *Realizing Rawls* (Ithaca, NY: Cornell University Press, 1989).

23. Rawls, *Theory*, p. xviii.

24. Ibid., p. 3.

25. On Rawls's distinction between a comprehensive doctrine and a political conception of justice, see *Liberalism*, pp. 13, 175.

26. See John Rawls, "*Commonweal* Interview with John Rawls (1998)," in *John Rawls: Collected Papers*, ed. Freeman, p. 617.

27. Rawls, *Liberalism*, p. 11.

28. Ibid., p. 490.

29. Ibid., p. 144.

30. Ibid., p. 486.

31. Ibid., p. 438. See also Rawls, "*Commonweal* Interview," pp. 616–22.

32. Rawls, "Justice as Fairness," p. 231 (emphasis added).

33. Rawls, *Liberalism*, p. 291.

34. Ibid.

35. Ibid., pp. 22–28, 304–10.

36. On Rawls's idea of a well-ordered society, see ibid., pp. 14, 35–40.

37. Ibid., p. 446.

38. Ibid., p. 450.

39. Ibid., p. 447.

40. Ibid., p. 446.

41. Ibid., pp. 462–46. Rawls, *"Commonweal* Interview," p. 619.

42. Nicholas Wolterstorff, "Why We Should Reject What Liberalism Tells Us about Speaking and Acting for Religious Reasons," in *Religion and Contemporary Liberalism*, ed. Paul J. Weithman (Notre Dame, IN: University of Notre Dame Press, 1997), pp. 162–81, reprinted in *Do the Right Thing: Readings in Applied Ethics and Social Philosophy*, 2nd ed., ed. Francis J. Beckwith (Belmont, CA: Wadsworth), p. 116 (emphasis in original).

43. Rawls, *Liberalism*, pp. 483–84.

44. Robert P. George, "Same-Sex Marriage and Moral Neutrality," in *Homosexuality and American Public Life*, ed. Christopher Wolfe (Dallas: Spence Publishing, 1999), pp. 141–53, reprinted in Beckwith, *Do the Right Thing*, 2nd ed., p. 653.

45. Rawls carefully distinguishes several kinds of neutrality. *Liberalism*, pp. 190–94.

46. Ibid., pp. 12, 144–45, 485.

47. Ibid., p. xxiv.

48. Ibid., p. 453.

49. Ibid., p. 243, n. 32. In the later two editions of *Liberalism*, Rawls comments that some readers of the original edition interpreted his remarks on a woman's right to abortion in the first trimester as constituting an argument in public reason for that right. In the later editions, he says that he was only giving his own "opinion" and an opinion is not an argument. *Liberalism*, pp. liii–liv, n. 31; p. 479, n. 80.

50. Ibid., p. liv, n. 32.

51. Ibid., pp. 231–40.

52. Ibid., pp. 356–59.

53. Ibid., pp. lvi, 262–65.

54. Rawls, *Theory*, p. xii, n. 1.

55. Rawls, *Liberalism*, pp. lvi–lvii.

56. Ibid., pp. 449–50.

57. *Buckley v. Valeo*, 424 U.S.1 (1976). Rawls, *Liberalism*, pp. 359–63.

58. Rawls, *Liberalism*, p. 363.

59. *Citizens United v. Federal Election Commission*, 558 U.S. 310, 130 S. Ct. 876 (January 21, 2010). On how this case affected the 2012 presidential election, see "Why Money Matters," *Time*, August 13, 2012, 35–45.

60. Rawls, *Theory*, rev. ed., pp. xiv–xvi.

61. Rawls, *Liberalism*, p. 22.

62. Rawls, *Theory*, rev. ed., p. xvi.

63. Ibid., p. xvi.

64. Rawls, *Law of Peoples*, pp. 157–64; *Justice as Fairness: A Restatement*, pp. 162–68; and *Liberalism*, pp. 467–74.

65. Rawls, *Law of Peoples*, p. 157, n. 60; *Justice as Fairness: A Restatement*, p. 163, n. 42; *Liberalism*, p. 467, n. 60.

66. Rawls, *Liberalism*, p. 457.

67. I borrow the term *penile-vaginal intercourse* from Angela Bolte. See her "Do Wedding Dresses Come in Lavender? The Prospects and Implications of Same-Sex Marriage," *Social Theory and Practice* 24, no. 1 (Spring 1998), reprinted in Beckwith, *Do the Right Thing*, 2nd ed., p. 661.

68. See John M. Finnis, "Law, Morality, and 'Sexual Orientation,'" *Notre Dame Law Review* 69 (1994): 1049–57, 1063–76, reprinted in *Analyzing Moral Issues*, 3rd ed., ed. Judith A. Boss (New York: McGraw-Hill, 2005), pp. 385–90; John Finnis, "Why Homosexuality Is Wrong," from the trial in Colorado on the constitutionality of Amendment 2, reprinted in *Contemporary Moral Problems*, 6th ed., ed. James E. White (Belmont, CA: Wadsworth, 2000), pp. 322–24; and Michael Pakaluk, "Homosexuality and the Common Good," in Wolfe, *Homosexuality and American Public Life*, reprinted in *Social and Personal Ethics*, 5th ed., ed. William H. Shaw (Belmont, CA: Wadsworth, 2005), pp. 219–25. Of course, there are many arguments against this argument, but they are not relevant to our present purpose.

69. Michael Levin, "Why Homosexuality Is Abnormal," *Monist* (Spring 1985), reprinted in *Applying Ethics*, 8th ed., ed. Jeffrey Olen, Julie C. Van Camp, and Vincent Barry (Belmont, CA.: Wadsworth, 2005), pp. 96–102.

70. Finnis and Pakaluk, in their articles cited in n. 67, reduce their common-good argument against same-sex marriage to its unnaturalness.

71. Rawls, *Justice as Fairness: A Restatement*, p. 145.

72. *New York Times*, August 5, 2010, sec. A, 1, 4.

73. "Court Strikes Down Ban on Gay Marriage in California," *New York Times*, http://www.nytimes.com/2012/02/08/us/marriage-ban-violates-constitution-court-rules.html . . . (accessed February 8, 2012).

74. On June 28, 2012, the US Supreme Court ruled in a 5–4 decision that the Patient Protection and Affordable Care Act was constitutional, including its most controversial element, the individual mandate. Chief Justice John Roberts provided the swing vote and authored its majority opinion. *National Federation of Independent Business v. Sebelius*, 567 U.S. 132 S. Ct. 2566 (2012).

75. Article 25 of the Universal Declaration of Human Rights states in part: "Everyone has the right to a standard of living adequate for the health and well-being of himself and of his family, including food, clothing, housing and medical care." *Fiftieth Anniversary of the Universal Declaration of Human Rights*, http://www.un.org/rights/50/decla/htm (accessed May 27, 2004).

76. *Griswold v. Connecticut*, 281 U.S. 479, 381 U.S. 479 (1965).

77. See "HHS Decision on Contraception as Preventive Care Resists Pressure for Overly-Broad Religious Exemption," *Media Center* (January 24, 2012), http://www.guttmacher.org/media/inthenews/2012/01/24/index.html (accessed February 9, 2012); and Adam Sonfield, "The Religious Exemption to Mandated Insurance Coverage of Contraception," *Virtual Mentor* 14, no. 2 (February 2012): 137–45, http://virtualmentor.ama-assn.org/2012/02/pforl-1202.html (accessed February 9, 2012).

78. A few Catholic-affiliated organizations are self-insured. The Obama administration is working on how best to deal with their religious objections.

79. Rawls, *Liberalism*, pp. 447–50.

80. Ibid., pp. xlvi–xlvii, n. 20.

9. THE MORAL TREATMENT OF ANIMALS

This chapter is based on my Harrod Lecture "Ethics, Science, and the Treatment of Animals," delivered at Fitchburg State College, January 26, 1994, and published in *The Harrod Lecture Series*, vol. 14 (Fitchburg, MA: Fitchburg State College Press, 1994), pp. 47–76. It is dedicated (as was the original lecture) to my late son, Walter Jr., who loved animals.

1. On the extent of animal abuse, see the following: M. T. Phillips and J. A. Sechzer, *Animal Research and Ethical Conflict* (New York: Springer-Verlag, 1989); Andrew Rowan, *Of Mice, Models and Men: A Critical Evaluation of Animal Research* (Albany: State University of New York Press, 1984); Richard Ryder, *Victims of Science: The Use of Animals in Research* (London: National Anti-Vivisection Society, 1983); and Peter Singer, *Animal Liberation* (New York: New York Review of Books, 1975; 2nd ed., New York: Avon Books, 1990).

2. Isaac Bashevis Singer, *Enemies: A Love Story*, quoted in Louis P. Pojman, *Life and Death* (Boston: Jones and Bartlett, 1992), p. 103.

3. René Descartes, *Discourse on Method*, in *The Philosophical Works of Descartes*, trans. Elizabeth S. Haldane and G. R. T. Ross, 2 vols., corrected ed. (Cambridge: Cambridge University Press, 1931; reprint, New York: Dover, 1955), 1:116.

4. René Descartes, *Philosophical Letters*, trans. and ed. Anthony Kenny (Oxford: Oxford University Press, 1970), p. 245. Descartes' no duties theory has also been extended to the environment in general. See Walter G. Jeffko, "Ecology and Dualism," *Religion in Life* 42, no. 1 (Spring 1973): 110–27.

5. F. S. Jacobs, quoted in Phillips and Sechzer, *Animal Research and Ethical Conflict*, p. 75.

6. Gilbert Ryle, *The Concept of Mind* (New York: Barnes & Noble, 1949).

7. John Macmurray, *The Self as Agent* (Amherst, NY: Humanity Books, 1991), p. 79.

8. St. Thomas Aquinas, *Summa Theologica*, trans. Fathers of the English Dominican Province, 3 vols. (New York: Benzinger Brothers, 1947), 1.75.

9. Walter G. Jeffko, "Self-Consciousness and the Soul-Body Problem," *American Benedictine Review* 31, no. 3 (September 1980): 346–60.

10. Aquinas, *Summa Theologica*, 2–2.64.1.

11. Ibid., r.obj.3.

12. Immanuel Kant, *Lectures on Ethics*, trans. Louis Infield (London: Methuen, 1930; reprint New York: Harper Torchbooks, 1963), pp. 239–40.

13. For a recent defense of the indirect duties theory, see Tibor R. Machan, "Do Animals Have Rights?" *Public Affairs Quarterly* 5, no. 2 (1991), reprinted in *Social and Personal Ethics*, ed. William H. Shaw (Belmont, CA: Wadsworth, 1993), pp. 168–74.

14. Jeremy Bentham, *An Introduction to the Principles of Morals and Legislation* (New York: Hafner, 1948), p. 311 n. 1.

15. John Stuart Mill, *Utilitarianism*, ed. Oskar Piest (New York: Library of Liberal Arts, 1957), p. 10.

16. Ibid., p. 14.

17. Besides *Animal Liberation*, cited in note 1, see the following works of Peter Singer: "Animals and the Value of Life," in *Matters of Life and Death*, 2nd ed., ed. Tom Regan (New York: Random House, 1986), pp. 338–80; *In Defense of Animals*, ed. Peter Singer (New York: Blackwell, 1985); and *Practical Ethics*, 2nd ed. (New York: Cambridge University Press, 1993).

18. For a critique of Singer's speciesism, see, for example, Carl Cohen, "The Case for the Use of Animals in Biomedical Research," *New England Journal of Medicine* 314 (1986): 865–69, reprinted in *Contemporary Moral Issues: Diversity and Consensus*, ed. Lawrence M. Hinman (Upper Saddle River, NJ: Prentice-Hall, 1996), pp. 478–86; and Bonnie Steinbock, "Speciesism and the Idea of Equality," *Philosophy* 53, no. 204 (April 1978), reprinted in *Contemporary Moral Problems*, 4th ed., ed. James E. White (New York: West, 1994), pp. 396–402.

19. Singer, *Animal Liberation*, p. 21.

20. K. McCabe, "Who Will Live, Who Will Die," *The Washingtonian* (August 1986), quoted in Pojman, *Life and Death*, p. 108.

21. Tom Regan has developed his views in many publications. See *All That Dwell Therein* (Berkeley: University of California Press, 1982); *The Case for Animal Rights* (Berkeley: University of California Press, 1983); "The Case for Animal Rights," in *In Defense of Animals*, pp. 13–26, reprinted in *Applying Ethics*, 4th ed., ed. Jeffrey Olen and Vincent Barry (Belmont, CA: Wadsworth, 1992), pp. 356–63; "Ethical Vegetarianism and Commercial Animal Farming," in *Agriculture, Change, and Human Values: Proceedings of the Multi Disciplinary Conference* (Gainesville, FL: Humanities and Agriculture Program, 1984), reprinted in *Contemporary Moral Problems*, pp. 403–17; and *The Thee Generation: Reflections on the Coming Revolution* (Philadelphia: Temple University Press, 1991). The last work is a collection of Regan's more recent essays.

22. Cf. Mary Anne Warren, "Difficulties with the Strong Animal Rights Position," *Between the Species* 2, no. 4 (Fall 1987), reprinted in *Contemporary Moral Problems*, pp. 417–23.

23. Regan, "The Case for Animal Rights," in *Applying Ethics*, p. 361.

24. Ibid., p. 156 (emphasis in original).

25. Ibid., p. 362.

26. Regan, "Ethical Vegetarianism," in *Contemporary Moral Problems*, p. 411.

27. Ibid.

28. Louis P. Pojman, *Life and Death: Grappling with the Moral Problems of Our Time* (Boston: Jones and Bartlett, 1992), p. 109.

29. Cf. William Godfrey-Smith, "Value of Wilderness," in *Moral Problems*, 2nd ed., ed. James E. White (New York: West, 1988), pp. 351–59; Mark Sagoff, "On Preserving the Natural Environment," in *Today's Moral Problems*, 2nd ed., ed. Richard Wasserstrom (New York: Macmillan, 1979), pp. 613–23; and Christopher D. Stone, "Should Trees Have Standing? Toward Legal Rights for Natural Objects," *Southern California Law Review* 45 (1972): 450–501, reprinted in part in *Social and Personal Ethics*, pp. 175–80.

30. Aldo Leopold, *A Sand County Almanac* (New York: Oxford University Press, 1949).

31. Regan, "Ethical Vegetarianism," in *Contemporary Moral Problems*, pp. 414–15.

32. Several authors have adopted positions that attempt to mediate among these four standard positions. See Martin Benjamin, "Ethics and Animal Consciousness," in *Social Ethics*, 3rd ed., ed. Thomas A. Mappes and Jane G. Zembaty (New York: McGraw-Hill, 1987), pp. 476–84; R. G. Frey, *Interests and Rights: The Case against Animals* (Oxford: Clarendon Press, 1980); Christina Hoff, "Immoral and Moral Uses of Animals," *New England Journal of Medicine* 302, no. 2 (January 10, 1980): 15–18, reprinted in *Moral Controversies*, ed. Steven Jay Gold (Belmont, CA: Wadsworth, 1993), pp. 582–86; and Gary E. Varner, "Prospects for Consensus and Convergence in the Animal Rights Debate," *Hastings Center Report* 24, no. 1 (January 1994), reprinted in *Contemporary Moral Issues*, pp. 487–95.

33. Mylan Engel Jr. "Why *You* Are Committed to the Immorality of Eating Meat," in *The Moral Life*, ed. Louis Pojman (New York: Oxford University Press, 2000), reprinted in *Social and Personal Ethics*, 5th ed., ed. William H. Shaw (Belmont, CA: Wadsworth, 2005), p. 184. See also James Rachels, "Vegetarianism and 'the Other Weight Problem,'" in *World Hunger and Moral Obligation*, ed. Aiken and LaFollette (Upper Saddle River, NJ: Prentice-Hall, 1977), reprinted in *Contemporary Moral Problems*, 6th ed., ed. James E. White (Belmont, CA: Wadsworth, 2000), pp. 523–32.

34. I exclude here, of course, the euthanizing of animals, for example, pets, who are put down to end their pain and suffering, which can no longer be effectively relieved. This practice is analogous to the euthanasia issue (chapter 5), and does not fall under the present issue.

10. AFFIRMATIVE ACTION AND JUSTICE

This chapter is based on my Harrod Lecture "Affirmative Action and Justice," delivered at Fitchburg State College, October 29, 1997, and published in *The Harrod Lecture Series*, vol. 16 (Fitchburg, MA: Fitchburg State College Press, 1998), pp. 45–78.

1. Many countries around the world have affirmative action programs. For a critical evaluation of them, see Thomas Sowell, *Preferential Policies: An International Perspective* (New York: William Morrow, 1991), and "Affirmative Action: A Worldwide Disaster," *Commentary* (December 1989), reprinted in *Today's Moral Problems: Classical and Contemporary Perspectives*, 2nd ed., ed. Daniel Bonevac (Mountain View, CA: Mayfield, 1996), pp. 566–82.

2. On the relation between prejudice and discrimination, see Gordon W. Allport's classic work, *The Nature of Prejudice*, abridged ed. (Garden City, NY: Doubleday Anchor Books, 1958).

3. Thomas Nagel, "A Defense of Affirmative Action," in *Moral Philosophy: A Comprehensive Introduction*, ed. Brooke Noel Moore and Robert Michael Stewart (Mountain View, CA: Mayfield, 1994), p. 603 (emphasis added). This article was originally testimony before the Subcommittee on the Constitution of the Senate Judiciary Committee, June 18, 1981.

4. Ibid.

5. See, for example, Tom Beauchamp, "The Justification of Reverse Discrimination," in *Ethical Theory and Business*, ed. Tom Beauchamp (Princeton, NJ: Prentice-Hall, 1988), reprinted in *Do the Right Thing*, 2nd ed., ed. Francis J. Beckwith (Belmont, CA: Wadsworth, 2002), pp. 438–48.

6. *Plessy v. Ferguson*, 163 U.S. 537 (1896).

7. "Letter from Birmingham Jail," April 16, 1963, in Martin Luther King Jr., *Why We Can't Wait* (New York: Harper & Row, 1963), p. 85.

8. *Brown v. Board of Education*, 347 U.S. 483 (1954).

9. *Griggs et al. v. Duke Power Co.*, 401 U.S. 424 (1971).

10. William H. Shaw and Vincent Barry, eds., *Moral Issues in Business*, 6th ed. (Belmont, CA: Wadsworth, 1995), p. 425.

11. *Regents of the University of California v. Bakke*, 438 U.S. 265 (1978). After Bakke filed his original suit in the Superior Court of California, the university filed a countersuit asking for a declaration that its quota system was constitutionally valid.

12. *Johnson v. Transportation Agency, Santa Clara County*, 480 U.S. 616 (1987).

13. *City of Richmond v. J. A. Croson Company*, 488 U.S. 469, 109 Sup. Ct. 706 (1989).

14. *Adarand Constructors, Inc. v. Pena*, 115 Sup. Ct. 2097 (1995).

15. Ibid.

16. Ibid.

17. See Antonin Scalia, "The Disease as Cure," *Washington University Law Quarterly* 1 (1979), reprinted in *Today's Moral Problems*, pp. 553–58.

18. *Hopwood v. State of Texas*, 78 F. 3d 932 (5th Cir. 1996).

19. For a good summary of the history of Proposition 209, see *New York Times*, April 9, 1997, sec. A, 1, 23. For an insightful article on Ward Connerly, the architect of Proposition 209, see Eric Pooley, "Fairness or Folly?" *Time*, June 23, 1997, 32–36.

20. William G. Bowen and Derek Bok, *The Shape of the River: Long-Term Consequences of Considering Race in College and University Admissions* (Princeton, NJ: Princeton University Press, 1999). See also Adam Cohen, "When the Field Is Level," *Time*, July 5, 1999, 30–34.

21. *Grutter v. Bollinger*, 539 U.S. 306 (2003) 288 F. 3d 732.

22. *Gratz v. Bollinger*, 539 U.S. 244 (2003).

23. *Parents Involved in Community Schools v. Seattle School District No. 1*, 551 U.S. 701, 127 S. Ct. 2738 (2007). For an analysis of this decision, see *New York Times*, June 29, 2007, sec. A, 1, 20–21, 25, 27; Jennifer Koons, "Parents Involved in Community Schools v. Seattle School District #1, et al.," *Medill News Service*, http://docket.medill.northwestern.edu/archives/003697.php (accessed July 2, 2007); and David Gialanella, "Meredith Crystal (next friend for McDonald, Joshua) v. Jefferson County Bd. of Education, et al.," *Medill News Service*, http://docket.medill.northwestern.edu/archives/003698.php (accessed July 2, 2007).

24. *Meredith v. Jefferson County Board of Education*, 330 F. Supp. 2nd 834 (2004).

25. *Meredith v. Jefferson County Board of Education*, No. 04-5897 (6th Cir. 2005).

26. *Parents Involved in Community Schools v. Seattle School District No. 1*, No. 01-35450 (9th Cir. 2005).

27. *Parents Involved in Community Schools v. Seattle School District No. 1*, 551 U.S. 701, 127 S. Ct. 2738 (2007).

28. Ibid.

29. Ibid.

30. *Ricci v. DeStefano*, 129 S. Ct. 2658, 2671, 174L. Ed. 2d 490 (2009).

31. See *New York Times*, June 30, 2009, sec. A, 1, 13, 19; *Boston Globe*, June 30, 2009, sec. A, 1, 10, 12; and *Time*, July 13, 2009, 20.

32. Cf. Louis P. Pojman, "The Moral Status of Affirmative Action," *Public Affairs Quarterly* (1992), reprinted in *Do the Right Thing*, 2nd ed., pp. 424–38. Pojman totally opposes both weak and strong affirmative action. His opposition to the former is based on a slippery slope argument. If we practice weak affirmative action, it will inevitably "slide into" strong affirmative action, which he views as inherently unjust and intrinsically immoral.

33. On the difference and relation between diversity and integration as ends of affirmative action, see Robert Fullinwider, "Affirmative Action," *Stanford Encyclopedia of Philosophy* (Spring 2005 ed.), ed. Edward N. Zalta, http://plato.stanford.edu/archives/spr2005/entries/affi (accessed February 27, 2007).

34. *Wall Street Journal*, May 14, 2003, A1–A2.

35. Shelby Steele, *The Content of Our Character* (New York: St. Martin's Press, 1990), reprinted in part in *Social and Personal Ethics*, ed. William H. Shaw (Belmont, CA: Wadsworth, 1993), p. 382.

36. Sowell, "Affirmative Action," in *Today's Moral Problems*, pp. 566–67.

37. Beauchamp, "Justification of Reverse Discrimination," in *Do the Right Thing*, 2nd ed., p. 445.

38. Andrew Young, *Atlanta Journal and Constitution*, September 22, 1974.

39. In support of the compensatory justice argument, see Judith Jarvis Thomson, "Preferential Hiring," *Philosophy and Public Affairs* 2, no. 4 (Summer 1973): 364–84; and Bernard Boxill, "The Morality of Preferential Hiring," *Philosophy and Public Affairs* 7, no. 3 (Spring 1978): 246–68.

40. In support of the antimerit or antiqualifications argument, see Ronald Dworkin, "Why Bakke Has No Case," *New York Review of Books*, November 10, 1977, reprinted in *Moral Philosophy*, pp. 615–21; Richard Wasserstrom, "A Defense of Programs of Preferential Treatment," *National Forum: The Phi Kappa Phi Journal* 58 (Winter 1978), reprinted in *Do the Right Thing*, pp. 326–29; and Richard Wasserstrom, "Racism, Sexism and Preferential Treatment: An Approach to the Topics," *UCLA Law Review* 24, no. 1 (February 1977). See also Wasserstrom's more recent articles, "One Way to Understand and Defend Programs of Preferential Treatment," in *The Moral Foundations of Civil Rights*, ed. Robert K. Fullinwider and Claudia Mills (Savage, MD: Rowman and Littlefield, 1986), reprinted in *Social and Personal Ethics*, 5th ed. (2005), pp. 399–405; and "On Racism and Sexism: Realities and Ideals," in *Morality and Moral Controversies*, 3rd ed. (Prentice-Hall, 1993), pp. 453–58, reprinted in *Ethics: Theory and Contemporary Issues*, 3rd ed., ed. Barbara MacKinnon (Belmont, CA: Wadsworth, 2001), pp. 251–58.

41. Dworkin, "Why Bakke Has No Case," in *Moral Philosophy*, p. 619.

42. John Rawls, *A Theory of Justice*, rev. ed. (Cambridge, MA: Harvard University Press, Belknap Press, 1999), p. 91.

43. Thomas E. Hill Jr., "The Message of Affirmative Action," *Social Philosophy and Policy* 8, no. 2 (1991): 108–29, reprinted in *Contemporary Moral Problems*, 6th ed., ed. James E. White (Belmont, CA: Wadsworth, 2000), pp. 473–74 (emphasis in original).

44. Ibid., p. 471.

11. COMMUNITY AND THE ENVIRONMENTAL CRISIS

This chapter is based on my Harrod Lecture, "Ethics and the Environmental Crisis," delivered at Fitchburg State College, October 30, 2001, and published in *The Harrod Lecture Series*, vol. 18 (Fitchburg, MA: Fitchburg State College Press, 2004), pp. 3–46.

1. The term *environmental crisis* is not new. It was mentioned in the 1970s. However, the crisis has considerably worsened since then. See William Blackstone, ed., *Philosophy and the Environmental Crisis* (Athens: University of Georgia Press, 1974).

2. Lester R. Brown, *Plan B 2.0*, updated and expanded (New York: W. W. Norton, 2006), p. 5. I am deeply indebted to this remarkable book.

3. There is a vast body of evidence and literature on the various dimensions of the environmental crisis. For an excellent recent survey of the problem with supporting scientific evidence, see United Nations Development Programme, United Nations Environment Programme, World Bank, World Resources Institute, *World Resources 2000–2001: People and Ecosystems: The Fraying Web of Life* (Washington, DC: World Resources Institute, 2000). For a good popular summary of this volume, see *Time Special Edition: Earth Day 2000*, April–May 2000. See also Brown, *Plan B*.

4. "U.S. & World Population Clocks," *U.S. Census Bureau*, May 31, 2012, http://www.census.gov/main/www/popclock.html (accessed July 3, 2012).

5. Brown, *Plan B*, p. 6.

6. Two authoritative reports on global warming were issued in 2001. The first report was released by the Intergovernmental Panel on Climate Change (IPCC), a group of top scientists in their fields representing many nations and diverse viewpoints: *Climate Change 2001: The Scientific Basis* (New York: Cambridge University Press, 2001). Their study was the result of over ten years of meticulous research and constituted then the latest and best scientific thinking on the subject of global warming. Still, the Bush-Cheney administration questioned the scientific validity of the report and requested that the National Academy of Sciences (NAS) review the IPCC's findings and issue its own report. The Academy quickly assembled a panel of eleven leading atmospheric scientists, including a previous long-time skeptic of global warming as human-made, Dr. Richard S. Lindzen of the Massachusetts Institute of Technology. In June 2001, the panel issued a twenty-four-page report. Not surprisingly, it completely confirmed the IPCC report. To quote the NAS: "Greenhouse gases are accumulating in the earth's atmosphere as a result of human activities, causing surface air temperatures and sub-surface ocean temperatures to rise. Temperatures are in fact rising." One of the panelists remarked that the Bush administration's questions might have been appropriate in 1990. But global warming science has made tremendous advances since then. On April 6, 2007, the IPCC released a 1,572-page report on global warming. It concludes with a 90 percent certainty that humans are the major cause of warming since 1950. See *New York Times*, April 7, 2007, sec. A, 1, 5. And on April 2, 2007, the Supreme Court ruled that greenhouse gases come under the Clean Air Act, and so the Environmental Protection Agency has the authority to regulate auto emissions. The Bush administration had argued the contrary position before the Court. *New York Times*, April 3, 2007, sec. A, 1, 14.

7. Brown, *Plan B*, p. 61.

8. "World Meteorological Organization and NOAA Both Report: 2000–2009 Is the Hottest Decade on Record," *Climate Progress*, http://climateprogress.org/2009/12/08/world-meteorological-organization-wmo-20005-war . . . (accessed February 12, 2010); and "State of the Climate, Global Analysis, Annual 2009," *National Oceanic and Atmospheric Administration:*

National Climatic Data Center, http://www.ncdc.noaa.gov/sotc/?report=global (accessed February 12, 2010).

9. "Climate Change, Extreme Weather Linked in Studies Examining Texas Drought and U.K. Heat," *HuffPost Green*, http://www.huffingtonpost.com/2012/07/10/climate-change -extreme-weather_n_1663014 . . . (accessed July 11, 2012); and "State of the Climate," National Oceanic and Atmospheric Administration, http://www.nede.noaa.gov/sote (accessed January 11, 2013).

10. "Global Warming," Time, April 3, 2006, 42. China has surpassed the United States in CO_2 emissions. See Jeffrey D. Sachs, "A Climate for Change," *Time*, March 19, 2007, 94.

11. Sachs, "A Climate for Change," *Time*, 94.

12. Bill McKibben, *Eaarth: Making a Life on a Tough New Planet* (New York: Times Books, Henry Holt, 2010), 16, quoting John Rockstrom et al., "A Safe Operating Space for Humanity," *Nature* 461 (September 27, 2009): 472–75.

13. "Climate Change, Extreme Weather Linked."

14. IPCC, *Climate Change 2001*.

15. Erik Stokstad, "Defrosting the Carbon Freezer of the North," *Science* 304 (June 11, 2004): 1618–20.

16. Brown, *Plan B*, p. 78.

17. Teresa Cerojano, "Decades of Illegal Logging Blamed for High Death Toll in Philippine Storm," *Associated Press*, December 1, 2004; and Nigel Sizer and Dominiek Plouvier, *Increased Investment and Trade by Transnational Logging Companies in Africa, the Caribbean, and the Pacific* (Belgium: World Wide Fund for Nature and WRI Forest Frontiers Initiative, 2000), pp. 21–35.

18. Forest Frontiers Initiative, *The Last Frontier Forests: Ecosystems and Economies on the Edge* (Washington, DC: WRI, 1997).

19. "Haitian Storm Deaths Blamed on Deforestation," *Environment News Service*, September 27, 2004.

20. Species Survival Commission, *2004 IUCN Red List of Threatened Species* (Gland, Switzerland, and Cambridge, UK: World Conservation Union-IUCN, 2004).

21. Edward O. Wilson, "Vanishing Before Our Eyes," *Time Special Edition: Earth Day 2000*, April–May 2000, 31.

22. Holmes Rolston III, "Duties to Endangered Species," in *Environmental Ethics: Duties and Values in the Natural World*, Holmes Rolston III (Philadelphia: Temple University Press, 1988), pp. 126–59.

23. Brown, *Plan B*, p. 84.

24. The earliest hominids were small and lived in trees for protection and may have built nests. They were omnivores and ate anything to survive. Although they were scavengers, they subsisted principally on plant food: tubers, fruit, and stalks. Because their brains were tiny compared to ours, they did not make tools and so were not hunters. Man's tool-making and

hunting existence did not evolve until about 2.5 million years ago. The protein in meat fueled the rapid growth of his brain.

25. Ibid., pp. 41–58, 66–68.

26. Ibid., pp. 91–94.

27. Ibid., p. 132.

28. Anup Shah, "Global Dimming," *Global Issues*, January 15, 2005, http://www.global issues.org/EnvIssues/GlobalWarming/globaldimming.asp (accessed September 8, 2007).

29. United Nations, *World Population Prospects, The 2004 Revision: Highlights* (New York: 2005), p. 1.

30. Brown, *Plan B*, p. 125.

31. Fund for Peace and the Carnegie Endowment for International Peace, "The Failed States Index," *Foreign Policy* (July/August 2005): 56–65.

32. Brown, *Plan B*, p. 4.

33. Stanley B. Carpenter, "Sustainability," in *Encyclopedia of Applied Ethics*, 4:284.

34. See Laura Westra and Patricia N. Werhane, eds., *The Business of Consumption: Environmental Ethics and the Global Economy* (Lanham, MD: Rowman & Littlefield, 1998); and Vandana Shiva, *Staying Alive: Development, Ecology, and Women* (Atlantic Highlands, NJ: Zed Books, 1988).

35. Jeremy Bentham, *An Introduction to the Principles of Morals and Legislation* (New York: Hafner, 1948), p. 311 n.1. Cf. Bryan G. Norton, "Environmental Ethics and Weak Anthropocentrism," *Environmental Ethics* 6, no. 2 (Summer 1984): 131–48.

36. Peter Singer, *Animal Liberation* (New York: New York Review of Books, 1975; 2nd ed., New York: Avon Books, 1990).

37. Kenneth Goodpaster, "On Being Morally Considerable," *Journal of Philosophy* 75 (1978): 308–25.

38. Paul W. Taylor, "The Ethics of Respect for Nature," *Environmental Ethics* 3, no. 3 (Fall 1981): 197–218; and *Respect for Nature: A Theory of Environmental Ethics* (Princeton, NJ: Princeton University Press, 1986).

39. Aldo Leopold, *A Sand County Almanac, and Sketches Here and There* (New York: Oxford University Press, 1949; special commemorative edition, with an introduction by Robert Finch, 1987). Page numbers are from the special commemorative edition.

40. Ibid., p. 204.

41. Ibid., pp. 224–25.

42. Tom Regan, "Ethical Vegetarianism," in *Contemporary Moral Problems*, ed. James E. White, 4th ed. (New York: West, 1994), p. 411.

43. Arne Naess, "The Shallow and the Deep, Long-Range Ecology Movements: A Summary," *Inquiry* 16 (Oslo: 1973), pp. 95–100. See also his book *Ecology, Community, and Lifestyle*, trans. David Rothenberg (New York: Cambridge University Press, 1989).

44. Bill Devall and George Sessions, *Deep Ecology: Living as If Nature Mattered* (Peregrine

Smith Books, 1985). See also Bill Devall, *Simple in Means, Rich in Ends: Practicing Deep Ecology* (Layton, UT: Gibbs Smith, 1988); George Sessions, ed., *Deep Ecology for the 21st Century* (Boston: Shambhala Press, 1995); and Rachel Carson, *Silent Spring* (Boston: Houghton Mifflin, 1962).

45. Devall and Sessions, *Deep Ecology*, pp. 7–11, 65–73.

46. Peter C. List, ed., *Radical Environmentalism: Philosophy and Tactics* (Belmont, CA: Wadsworth, 1993).

47. The term *ecofeminism* was apparently coined by the French feminist, François d'Eaubonne, in her book, *Le Feminism ou le Mort* (Paris: Horay, 1974).

48. See the following works by Karen J. Warren: *Ecological Feminism* (Boulder, CO: Westview, 1994); "Environmental Justice: Some Ecofeminist Worries about a Distributive Model," *Environmental Ethics* 21, no. 2 (Summer 1999): 151–61; "Feminism and Ecology: Making Connections," *Environmental Ethics* 9, no. 1 (Spring 1987): 3–20; "The Power and Promise of Ecological Feminism," *Environmental Ethics* 12, no. 2 (Summer 1990): 125–46; with Nisvan Erkel, eds., *Ecofeminism: Women, Culture, Nature* (Bloomington: Indiana University Press, 1997).

49. Warren, "Power and Promise," p. 126.

50. Ibid., p. 132.

51. Ibid., pp. 128–32.

52. Ibid., p. 128.

53. For a similar irenic approach to the different and conflicting theories of environmental ethics from the standpoint of a noted holistic ecocentrist, see the following works by J. Baird Callicot: *Beyond the Land Ethic: More Essays in Environmental Philosophy* (Albany: State University of New York Press, 1999); *In Defense of the Land Ethic: Essays in Environmental Philosophy* (Albany: State University of New York Press, 1989); and "The Search for an Environmental Ethic," in *Matters of Life and Death: New Introductory Essays in Moral Philosophy*, ed. Tom Regan, 2nd ed. (New York: Random House, 1986), pp. 381–424.

54. See Christopher D. Stone, "Should Trees Have Standing? Toward Legal Rights for Natural Objects," *Southern California Law Review* 45 (1972): 450–51, reprinted in part in *Social and Personal Ethics*, ed. William H. Shaw (Belmont, CA: Wadsworth, 1993), pp. 175–80.

55. UN Food and Agriculture Organization (FAO), *The State of Food Insecurity in the World 2004* (Rome: 2004), p. 6.

56. Kathryn Paxton George, "Ethical Vegetarianism Is Unfair to Women and Children," in *Earth Ethics*, 2nd ed., ed. James P. Sterba (Englewood Cliffs, NJ: Prentice-Hall, 1995), reprinted in *Morality in Practice*, 6th ed., ed. James P. Sterba (Belmont, CA: Wadsworth, 2001), pp. 484–92.

57. Brown, *Plan B*, p. 171.

58. Ibid., pp. 173–79.

59. *Time*, Jan. 25, 2010, 50-53.

60. Cf. Brown, *Plan B*, pp. 140, 158.

61. Amory P. Lovins et al., *Winning the Oil Endgame: Innovation for Profits, Jobs, and Security* (Snowmass, CO: Rocky Mountain Institute, 2004), p. 64.

62. International Center for Technology Assessment, *The Real Price of Gasoline*, report no. 3 (Washington, DC: 1998), p. 34.

63. Brown, *Plan B*, pp. 187.

64. Ibid., p. 266.

65. Ibid., pp. 257–58.

12. THE MORAL TREATMENT OF CIVILIANS IN WAR

This chapter is based on my Harrod Lecture, "The Moral Treatment of Civilians in War," delivered at Fitchburg State University, October 19, 2010, *The Harrod Lecture Series* (Fitchburg, MA: Fitchburg State University Press, in press).

1. The pacifism discussed in this lecture is sometimes called anti-war pacifism. There is a more radical form of pacifism, which holds that all force is immoral. I consider this version of pacifism to be wholly indefensible. For a good philosophical defense of anti-war pacifism, see Douglas Lackey, "Pacifism," in *Social and Personal Ethics*, 7th ed., ed. William H. Shaw (Boston: Wadsworth, 2011), pp. 315–22.

2. John Macmurray, *Search for Reality in Religion* (London: George Allen & Unwin, 1965).

3. Ibid., pp. 18–19.

4. Ibid., p. 19.

5. Ibid., p. 22.

6. John Macmurray, *The Philosophy of Jesus* (London: Friends Home Service Committee, 1973).

7. Some of Macmurray's views on Nazism are expressed in his book, *Conditions of Freedom* (London: Faber & Faber, 1950; reprint, with an introduction by Walter G. Jeffko (Amherst, NY: Humanity Books, 1993), pp. 37–41.

8. See Omar Bartov, *Hitler's Army* (New York: Oxford University Press, 1991).

9. John Rawls, *The Law of Peoples* (Cambridge: Harvard University Press, 1999); and "Fifty Years after Hiroshima," in *John Rawls: Collected Papers*, ed. Samuel Freeman (Cambridge: Harvard University Press, 1999), p. 569. For a development of this point, see Alan Bullock, *Hitler: A Study in Tyranny* (London: Oldham's Press, 1952).

10. John E. Costello, *John Macmurray: A Biography* (Edinburgh: Floris Books, 2002), p. 253.

11. James Sterba argues that pacifism and just war theory are much closer to each other than

is usually realized and on their best interpretation are virtually identical. See his "Reconciling Pacifists and Just War Theories," in *Morality and Practice*, 6th ed., ed. James P. Sterba (Belmont, CA: Wadsworth/Thomson Learning, 2001), pp. 572–84. In Sterba's view, pacifism is at its best when it makes the kind of exceptions Macmurray apparently made. In my view, however, once it makes exceptions it is no longer pacifism. Pacifism is a form of ethical absolutism.

12. Michael Walzer, *Just and Unjust Wars*, 4th ed. (New York: Basic Books, 2006), p. 332. For a strong argument against pacifism, see Jan Narveson, "Pacifism: A Philosophical Analysis," in *Moral Problems*, 3rd ed., ed. James Rachels (New York: Harper & Row, 1979), pp. 408–25. Gandhi made the remark about Jews committing suicide in 1938 in response to a question, according to Louis Fischer, as reported in his *Gandhi and Stalin* (New York: Harper & Brothers, 1947). For commentary on Gandhi's remark, see George Orwell, "Reflections on Gandhi," *Partisan Review* (January 1949).

13. I borrow this usage of *nihilism* from Rawls. However, he uses it more broadly than I do. See his *The Law of Peoples*, p. 103; and "Fifty Years after Hiroshima," in *Collected Papers*, p. 572.

14. See Walzer, *Just and Unjust Wars*, 4th ed., pp. 3–20.

15. This point is admirably argued by G. E. M. Anscombe, "War and Murder," in *Nuclear Weapons and Christian Conscience*, ed. Walter Stein (London: Merlin Press, 1961), pp. 45–62.

16. Walzer, *Just and Unjust Wars*, 4th ed., p. 197.

17. See Roland Bainton, *Christian Attitudes toward War and Peace* (Nashville: Abingdon Press, 1960).

18. St. Thomas Aquinas, *Summa Theologica*, trans. Fathers of the English Dominican Province, 3 vols. (New York: Benzinger Brothers, 1947), 2–2. 40.1.

19. See, for example, Joseph C. McKenna, "Ethics and War: A Catholic View," *American Political Science Review* 54 (1960): 647–58. Although just war theory is the product of Western thought, a considerable number of its ideas are expressed more informally in Eastern wisdom and especially in what is generally regarded as China's oldest and most profound military treatise, *The Art of War*, written in the sixth century BCE. It has been studied for centuries by Western military leaders, students, and scholars. See Sun-tzu, *The Art of War*, trans., with introductions and commentary by Ralph D. Sawyer (Boulder, CO: Westview Press, 1994).

20. In this chapter *civilian* and *noncombatant* are synonyms.

21. There are other uses of *proportionality* in just war theory. In *jus ad bellum*, there is the *principle* of proportionality: The *projected* costs of a war cannot exceed its good (or benefits). In *jus in bello*, there is a modified version of this principle: The *ongoing* costs of waging war cannot exceed its good (or benefits). Ongoing costs often far exceed original projected costs. The Vietnam and Iraqi Wars are widely held to have violated the latter principle.

22. President George W. Bush's main theoretical justification for the Iraqi invasion was his doctrine of preemptive strike. However, this doctrine goes far beyond anything allowable under just war theory. See his *The National Security Strategy of the United States of America*, September 17, 2002, excerpted in *Applying Ethics*, 8th ed., ed. Jeffrey Olen, Julie C. Van Camp, and

Vincent Barry (Belmont, CA: Wadsworth, 2005), pp. 350–52. The Iraqi War is now sometimes called Gulf War II. What we originally called the Persian Gulf War, begun in January 1991, is now sometimes called Gulf War I.

Even Bush's own doctrine of preemptive strike was grossly violated by the invasion. As things turned out, there was nothing to preempt. His main justification for the preemptive strike was his claim that Saddam Hussein had WMDs and had a connection with al Qaeda as the means for delivering them against the United States. Both claims proved to be false. Nor is regime change by itself a just cause of war. A motive for the invasion was a Platonic-type vision of the Good consisting of the democratization of the entire Mideast region. It was thought that if democracy could be established in Iraq it would spread on its own to other nations in the region. The Bush administration wrongly thought that the Iraqi people would welcome Americans as liberators. Instead, the invasion proved to be a lightning rod for homegrown, anti-American terrorism and insurgency attacks against American troops. The long Iraqi War finally ended on December 31, 2011. It cost the United States nearly $1 trillion to wage an unjust war. For a philosophical debate on the Iraqi War, see Burton M. Leiser, "The Case for Iraq War II," and James P. Sterba, "Iraq War II: A Blatantly Unjust War," in *Morality in Practice*, 7th ed., ed. Sterba (Belmont, CA: Wadsworth/Thomson Learning, 2004), pp. 619–35.

23. For a comprehensive analysis of how Gulf War II has violated several principles of just war theory, see Craig M. White, *The Moral Reckoning: Applying Just War Theory to the 2003 War Decision* (Blue Ridge Summit, PA: Lexington Books, 2010).

24. Walzer, *Just and Unjust Wars*, 4th ed., pp. 72–124.

25. Ibid., pp. 151–56, 251–68.

26. Ibid., p. 153.

27. Ibid., p. 155.

28. Ibid., p. 152.

29. Ibid., p. 154.

30. Avishai Margalit and Michael Walzer, "Civilians and Combatants," *New York Review of Books*, May 14, 2009, reprinted in *Social and Personal Ethics*, 7th ed., pp. 329–33. (Author's emphasis.)

31. Walzer, *Just and Unjust Wars*, 4th ed., p. 253.

32. Ibid., p. 259.

33. Martin Gilbert, *Winston Churchill: Never Despair*, vol. 8 (Boston: Houghton Mifflin, 1988), p. 259.

34. Americans had a low regard for the Japanese people during the war. They were never forgiven for their sneak attack on Pearl Harbor. As wrong as the attack was, at least its direct intention was restricted to military targets. Soon after the Pacific campaign began, loyal Japanese-American citizens were rounded up and put in internment camps out West. Americans everywhere called the Japanese people "Japs." Japanese soldiers were seen as fanatics, imbued as they were with the ancient samurai code of *bushido*, which taught that surrender

is dishonorable. During the war, there was a popular jingle in the United States, sung to the melody of a leading song in the movie, *Snow White and the Seven Dwarfs* (1938): "Whistle while you work, Hitler is a jerk, Mussolini is a weeny, but the Japs are worse." That the Japanese are worse than Hitler and the Nazis is patently false. But if they are, then it helps to explain why American public opinion so strongly supported the dropping of the atomic bombs. They deserved it! According to noted historian David McCullough, Truman referred to the Japanese people as "beasts" believe that they should be treated as such. See McCullough, *Truman* (New York: Simon and Schuster, 1992), p. 458.

35. Some historians think that the bomb was also dropped to scare Stalin into being more agreeable to America's and Britain's peace terms for the reconstruction of Europe. See Gar Alperovitz, *Atomic Diplomacy: Hiroshima and Potsdam* (New York: Penguin Books, 1985). We now know that Stalin already knew about the bomb from Russian spies in America when Truman told him about it at Potsdam, which is why Stalin reacted so nonchalantly to Truman's remark. However, this fact does not necessarily alter Truman's motive for telling him.

36. See Barton Bernstein, "The Atomic Bombing Reconsidered," *Foreign Affairs*, 74:1 (January–February 1995); and Gerhard Weinberg, *A World at Arms* (Cambridge: Cambridge University Press, 1994).

37. Walzer, *Just and Unjust Wars*, 4th ed., pp. 263–68. In this context, Rawls emphasizes that political leaders must be statesmen and not mere politicians. "Statesmen are presidents or prime ministers or other high officials who, through their exemplary performance and leadership in their office, manifest strength, wisdom, and courage." *Law of Peoples*, p. 97. The politician looks to the next election; the statesman looks to the next generation. Washington and Lincoln, he says, were statesmen; Bismarck was not.

38. Immanuel Kant, *Foundations of the Metaphysics of Morals*, trans. with an introduction by Lewis White Beck (New York: Liberal Arts Press, 1959), p. 47.

39. The way that soldiers bond with each other on the battlefield is, of course, legendary. Such bonding clearly consists of personal relations. Yet impersonal relations still exist, which are defined by the military role each soldier plays within the organization. When the war is over, their unit disbands and the impersonal relations cease. Still, they may remain friends for life, as often is the case. However, our main concern here is with the relations between combatants and enemy combatants. See Stephen E. Ambrose, *Band of Brothers* (New York: Simon and Schuster Paperbacks, 1992).

40. Lt. Col. Dave Grossman with Loren W. Christensen, *On Combat: The Psychology and Physiology of Deadly Conflict in War and in Peace*, 3rd ed. (n. p.: Warrior Science Publications, 2008), p. 52.

41. John Macmurray writes the following about a general intention: "Whatever he [the agent] does is morally right if the particular intention of his action is controlled by a general intention to maintain the community of agents, and wrong if it is not so controlled. Such a general intention is a unifying intention. . . . It is this that enables us to define morality by

reference to maintaining community in action." *Persons in Relation* (London: Faber & Faber; New York: Harper & Row, 1961), reprinted, with an introduction by Frank G. Kirkpatrick (Amherst, NY: Humanity Books, 1991), pp. 119–20.

42. Part of what I mean by a good (or rightful) motive in war can be described as follows. A nation ought to be motivated by a desire to establish peace based on an order of justice, stability, and economic security in the defeated nation. A war must not be motivated by hatred or revenge, or by the pride and vainglory of its potential leaders. The enemy must not be demonized or dehumanized. Economic self-interest by itself is not a good enough motive to wage war.

43. See David Luban, "Just War and Human Rights," *Philosophy and Public Affairs* 9 (Winter 1980): 160–81.

44. Rawls accepts Walzer's supreme emergency, but differs from him on when its time frame should end. "This period extended, at least, from the fall of France in 1940 until Russia had already beaten off the first German assault in the summer and fall of 1941, and showed that it would be able to fight Germany until the end." *The Law of Peoples*, pp. 98–99. Perhaps Walzer's choice of July 1942 as the end date for the supreme emergency is based on the following set of facts. After the German defeat at Moscow, Hitler launched another military campaign against the Soviet Union in the spring of 1942 and regained much of the territory the Germans lost when they retreated from Moscow in December 1941. In July 1942, however, Hitler fatefully decided to split his forces and to send much of them in two directions to the south: one group would seize the rich Russian oil fields in the Caucuses, and the other would capture Stalingrad. In the end, the entire German Sixth Army was annihilated in the Battle of Stalingrad. After that, the Germans were in full retreat on the Eastern Front. However, the German catastrophe at Stalingrad really began in July 1942, since the campaign was doomed from the start.

45. Michael Walzer, *Arguing about War* (New Haven: Yale University Press, 2004), pp. 34–35.

46. Ibid., p. 35.

47. For different views on torture within the context of capturing terrorist suspects, see Alan M. Dershowitz, "Make Torture an Option," *Los Angeles Times*, November 8, 2001, reprinted in *Applying Ethics*, 10th ed., ed. Julie C. Van Camp, Jeffrey Olen, and Vincent Barry (Boston: Wadsworth, 2011), pp. 344–45; David Luban, "Torture and the Ticking Bomb," *Georgetown Law* (Spring/Summer 2005): 48–51, reprinted in *Applying Ethics*, 10th ed., pp. 346–48; and Jeff McMahan, "Torture in Principle and in Practice," *Public Affairs Quarterly* 22, no. 2 (April 2008), reprinted in *Social and Personal Ethics*, 7th ed., pp. 334–41. For a powerful critique of the Bush-Cheney policy of torturing terrorist suspects, see Martin Henn, *Under the Color of Law: The Bush Administration's Subversion of U.S. Constitutional and International Law in the War on Terror* (Blue Ridge Summit, PA: Lexington Books, 2010).

48. See, for example, Walzer, *Just and Unjust Wars*, p. 254.

49. Walzer, *Arguing about War*, p. 42.

50. The Nazi idea of *volksgemeinschaft* (people's community) for the Third Reich is an extreme expression of community as an organic society.

51. Macmurray, *Persons in Relation*, p. 146. See also Frank Kirkpatrick, *John Macmurray: Community beyond Political Philosophy* (New York: Rowman & Littlefield, 2005), pp. 121–24.

52. Walzer, *Arguing about War*, p. 42.

53. On person and individual, see, for example, Jacques Maritain, *Scholasticism and Politics*, trans. Mortimer J. Adler (Garden City, NY: Image Books, 1960), pp. 61–89.

54. Immanuel Kant, *The Metaphysical Elements of Justice*, trans. with an introduction by John Ladd (New York: Library of Liberal Arts, 1965), p. 100.

55. Thomas Hobbes, *Leviathan* (New York: E. P. Dutton, 1914), p. 65.

56. George Santayana, *Soliloquies in England* (New York: Scribner's, 1924), p. 102. Some people have falsely attributed the remark to Plato. General Douglas MacArthur did so in his famous farewell address to the cadets at West Point in May 1962. The statement is attributed to Plato on the wall of the Imperial War Museum in London, as it also is at the beginning of the film, *Black Hawk Down*. Ever since MacArthur's speech, it has been popular among American soldiers.

SELECT BIBLIOGRAPHY

Abelson, Raziel, and Marie-Louise Friquegnon, eds. *Ethics for Modern Life*. 2nd ed. New York: St. Martin's Press, 1982. 6th ed. New York: Bedford/St. Martin's, 2003.

"Abortion in the United States: Quick Stats." *Guttmacher Institute*. http://www.guttmacher.org/media/presskits/abortion-US/statsandfacts.html (accessed June 4, 2012)

Allport, Gordon W. *The Nature of Prejudice*. Abridged ed. Garden City, NY: Doubleday Anchor Books, 1958.

Alperovitz, Gar. *Atomic Diplomacy: Hiroshima and Potsdam*. New York: Penguin Books, 1985.

American Friends Service Committee. *Struggle for Justice: A Report on Crime and Punishment in America*. New York: Hill and Wang, 1971.

Amsterdam, Anthony G. "Capital Punishment." *Stanford Magazine* (Fall/Winter 1977).

———. "Race and the Death Penalty." *Criminal Justice Ethics* 7, no. 1 (Winter/Spring 1988): 82–86.

Anscombe, G. E. M. "War and Murder." In *Nuclear Weapons and Christian Conscience*, edited by Walter Stein, 45-62. London: Merlin Press, 1961.

Aquinas, St. Thomas. *Summa Theologica*. Translated by Fathers of the English Dominican Province. 3 vols. New York: Benziger Brothers, 1947.

———. *Summa Contra Gentiles*. Translated and with an introduction and notes by James F. Anderson. 5 vols. New York: Image Books, 1956.

"Arbitrariness." *Death Penalty Information Center*. http://www.death penaltyinfo.org/article.php?did=1328 (accessed January 4, 2007).

Aristotle. *The Basic Works of Aristotle*. Edited and with an introduction by Richard McKeon. New York: Random House, 1941.

Attfield, Robin. *Environmental Philosophy*. Aldershot: Avesbury, 1994.

Augustine. *The City of God*. Translated by Marcus Dods. New York: Modern Library, 1950.

Bainton, Roland. *Christian Attitudes toward War and Peace*. Nashville: Abingdon Press, 1960.

Baitlin, Margaret Pabst. "The Case for Euthanasia." In *Health Care Ethics*, edited by D. Van De Veer and Tom Regan, 58–95. Philadelphia: Temple University Press, 1987.

Bartov, Omar. *Hitler's Army*. New York: Oxford University Press, 1991.

Bayles, Michael D., and Kenneth Henley, eds. *Right Conduct: Theories and Applications*. 2nd ed. New York: Random House, 1989.

Beauchamp, Tom, ed. *Ethical Theory and Business*. Princeton, NJ: Prentice-Hall, 1988.

Beauchamp, Tom, and Seymour Perlin, eds. *Ethical Issues in Death and Dying*. Englewood Cliffs, NJ: Prentice-Hall, 1978.

Beckwith, Francis J., ed. *Do the Right Thing: A Philosophical Dialogue on the Moral and Social Issues of Our Time*. Boston: Jones and Bartlett, 1996. 2nd ed. Belmont, CA: Wadsworth, 2002.

Bedau, Hugo Adam. "The Death Penalty as a Deterrent: Argument and Evidence." *Ethics* 80 (1970): 205–17.

———. "A World without Punishment?" In *Punishment and Human Rights*, edited by Milton Goldinger, 141–62. Rochester, VT: Shenkman Books, 1974.

———, ed. *The Death Penalty in America*. 3rd ed. New York: Oxford University Press, 1982.

———. *The Case against the Death Penalty*. Washington, DC: ACLU Publications, 1997.

———, ed. *The Death Penalty in America: Current Controversies*. New York: Oxford University Press, 1998.

Bedau, Hugo Adam, and Paul Cassels, eds. *Debating the Death Penalty*. New York: Oxford University Press, 2004.

Bedau, Hugo Adam, and Erin Kelly. "Punishment." *Stanford Encyclopedia of Philosophy*. Spring 2010 ed. Edited by Edward N. Zalta. http://plato.stanford.edu/archives/spr2010/entries/punishment/ (accessed June 18, 2012).

Bedau, Hugo Adam, and Michael Radelet. *Miscarriages of Justice in Potentially Capital Cases*. Cambridge, MA: Harvard Law School Library, 1985.

Bennett, Jonathan. "Whatever the Consequences." *Analysis* 26 (1966).

Bentham, Jeremy. *An Introduction to the Principles of Morals and Legislation*. With an introduction by Laurence J. Lafleur. New York: Hafner, 1948. Authoritative edition by J. H. Burns and H. L. A. Hart, with a new introduction by F. Rosen. New York: Oxford University Press, 1996.

Bernstein, Barton. "The Atomic Bombing Reconsidered." *Foreign Affairs* 74, no. 1 (January–February 1995).

Beyleveld, Deryck. "Ehrlich's Analysis of Deterrence." *British Journal of Criminology* 22 (April 1982): 101–23.

Blackstone, William, ed. *Philosophy and the Environmental Crisis*. Athens: University of Georgia Press, 1974.

Blondel, Maurice. *L'Action*. Paris: 1893; reprint, Paris: Presses Universitaires de France, 1950.

———. *L' Action*. 2 vols. Paris: 1936–37; reprint, Paris: Presses Universitaires de France, 1949 and 1963.

Blumstein, Alfred, Jacqueline Cohen, and Daniel Nagin, eds. *Deterrence and Incapacitation: Estimating the Effects of Criminal Sanctions on Crime Rates*. Washington, DC: National Academy of Sciences, 1978.

Bok, Sissela. "Ethical Problems of Abortion." *Hastings Center Studies* 2 (January 1974): 33–52.

Bolte, Angela. "Do Wedding Dresses Come in Lavender? The Prospects and Implications of Same-Sex Marriage." *Social Theory and Practice* 24, no. 1 (Spring 1998).

Bonevac, Daniel, ed. *Today's Moral Problems: Classical and Contemporary Perspectives.* 2nd ed. Mountain View, CA: Mayfield, 1996.

Bork, Robert. *The Tempting of America: The Political Seduction of the Law.* New York: Simon & Schuster, 1990.

Boss, Judith A., ed. *Analyzing Moral Issues.* 3rd ed. New York: McGraw-Hill, 2005.

Bouillard, Henri. "The Thought of Maurice Blondel: A Synoptic Vision." *International Philosophical Quarterly* 3, no. 3 (September 1963): 392–402.

Bowen, William G., and Derek Bok. *The Shape of the River: Long-Term Consequences of Considering Race in College and University Admissions.* Princeton, NJ: Princeton University Press, 1999.

Bowers, William J., and Glenn L. Pierce. "Deterrence or Brutalization: What Is the Effect of Executions?" *Crime and Delinquency* 26 (October 1980): 453–84.

Boxill, Bernard. "The Morality of Preferential Hiring." *Philosophy and Public Affairs* 7, no. 3 (Spring 1978): 246–68.

Brandt, Richard B. *Ethical Theory: The Problems of Normative and Critical Ethics.* Englewood Cliffs, NJ: Prentice-Hall, 1959.

———. *A Theory of the Good and the Right.* Amherst, NY: Prometheus Books, 1998.

Brennan, Andrew, and Lo Yeuk-Sze. "Environmental Ethics." *Stanford Encyclopedia of Philosophy.* Summer 2002 ed. Edited by Edward N. Zalta. http://plato.stanford.edu/archives/sum2002/entries/ethi (accessed March 24, 2007).

Brock, Dan W. "Voluntary Active Euthanasia." *Hastings Center Report* 22, no. 2 (1992).

Brown, James Robert. *Smoke and Mirrors: How Science Reflects Reality.* New York: Routledge, 1994.

Brown, Lester R. *Plan B 2.0.* Updated and expanded. New York: W. W. Norton, 2006.

Bullock, Alan. *Hitler: A Study in Tyranny.* London: Oldham's Press, 1952.

Bush, George W. *The National Security Strategy of the United States.* In *Applying Ethics,* 4th ed., edited by Jeffrey Olen, Julie C. Van Camp, and Vincent Perry, 350-52. Belmont, CA: Wadsworth, 2005.

"California Gives Go-Ahead to Stem-Cell Research." *MSNBC,* November 3, 2004. http://www.msnbc.msn.com/id/6384390 (accessed November 3, 2004).

Callahan, Daniel. *Abortion: Law, Choice and Morality.* New York: Macmillan, 1970.

———. "Killing and Allowing to Die." *Hastings Center Report* 19 (January/February 1989): 5–6.

———. "'Aid-in-Dying': The Social Dimensions." *Commonweal,* August 9, 1991.

———. "When Self-Determination Runs Amok." *Hastings Center Report* 22, no. 2 (1992).

Callicot, J. Baird. *In Defense of the Land Ethic: Essays in Environmental Philosophy.* Albany: State University of New York Press, 1989.

———. *Beyond the Land Ethic: More Essays in Environmental Philosophy.* Albany: State University of New York Press, 1999.

Camus, Albert. *The Myth of Sisyphus.* New York: Vintage Books, 1960.

Capaldi, Nicholas. *Out of Order: Affirmative Action and the Crisis of Doctrinaire Liberalism*. Amherst, NY: Prometheus Books, 1985.

Carse, James P., and Arlene B. Dallery. *Death and Society: A Book of Readings and Sources*. New York: Harcourt Brace Jovanovich, 1971.

Cerojano, Teresa. "Decades of Illegal Logging Blamed for High Death Toll in Philippine Storm." *Associated Press*, December 2004.

Chadwick, Ruth, ed. *Encyclopedia of Applied Ethics*. 4 vols. Boston: Academic Press, 1998.

Cholbi, Michael. "Suicide." *Stanford Encyclopedia of Philosophy*. Fall 2009 ed. Edited by Edward N. Zalta. http://plato.stanford.edu/ archives/fall2009/entries/suicide/ (accessed June 18, 2012).

Clarke, W. Norris. *Person and Being*. Milwaukee, WI: Marquette University Press, 1993.

Cohen, Adam. "When the Field Is Level." *Time*, July 5, 1999, 30–34.

Cohen, Carl. "The Case for the Use of Animals in Biomedical Research." *New England Journal of Medicine* 314 (1986): 865–69.

"Coma and Persistent Vegetative State." *HealthLink*. http://healthlink.mew.edu/article/92139 4859.html (accessed December 4, 2006).

Copi, Irving M. *Introduction to Logic*. 9th ed. New York: Macmillan, 1994.

Cornford, Philip. *The Personal World: John Macmurray on Self and Society*. Edinburgh: Floris Books, 1996.

Costello, John E. *John Macmurray: A Biography*. Edinburgh: Floris Books, 2002.

"Court Strikes Down Ban on Gay Marriage in California." *New York Times*. http://www.nytimes .com/2012/02/08/us/marriage-ban-violates-constitution-court-rules.ktml . . . (accessed February 8, 2012).

Dagger, Richard. "Playing Fair with Punishment." *Ethics* 103, no. 3 (1993).

"Death Penalty." *Gallup*. http://www.gallup.com/poll/1606/death-penalty.aspx (accessed June 4, 2012).

"Definition of IVF." *MedicineNet*. http://www.medterms.com/script/main/art.asp?articlekey =7222 (accessed December 6, 2007).

Dershowitz, Alan. "Make Torture an Option." *Los Angeles Times*. Reprinted in *Applying Ethics*, 10th ed., 344-45.

Descartes, René. *The Philosophical Works of Descartes*. Translated by Elizabeth S. Haldane and G. R. T. Ross. 2 vols. Corrected ed. Cambridge: Cambridge University Press, 1931; reprint, New York: Dover, 1955.

———. *Philosophical Letters*. Translated and edited by Anthony Kenny. Oxford: Oxford University Press, 1970.

"Deterrence: States Without the Death Penalty Have Had Consistently Lower Murder Rate. . . ." *Death Penalty Information Center*. http://www.deathpenaltyinfo.org/murder-rates -nationally-and-state (accessed June 4, 2012).

Devall, Bill. *Simple in Means, Rich in Ends: Practicing Deep Ecology*. Layton, UT: Gibbs Smith, 1988.

Devall, Bill, and George Sessions. *Deep Ecology: Living as if Nature Mattered.* Salt Lake City: Peregrine Smith Books, 1985.

Devine, Philip E. *The Ethics of Homicide.* Ithaca, NY: Cornell University Press, 1978.

DeVogel, C. "The Concept of Personality in Greek and Christian Thought." In *Studies in Philosophy and the History of Philosophy*, edited by J. Ryan, 2:20–60. Washington, DC: Catholic University of America Press, 1963.

Dizikes, Peter. "Reluctance of Egg Donors Stymies Harvard Efforts." *Boston Globe*, June 7, 2007, sec. A, 18.

Domhoff, G. William. "Wealth, Income and Power." *Who Rules America?* Updated December 2006. http://sociology.ucsc.edu/whorulesamerica/power/wealth.html (accessed January 10, 2007).

Donaldson, Thomas. *Corporations and Morality.* Englewood Cliffs, NJ: Prentice-Hall, 1982.

Donaldson, Thomas, and Patricia Werhane, eds. *Ethical Issues in Business: A Philosophical Approach.* 2nd ed. Englewood Cliffs, NJ: Prentice-Hall, 1983.

Donceel, Joseph. "Abortion: Mediate v. Immediate Animation." *Continuum* 5 (Winter/Spring 1967): 167–71.

———. "Immediate Animation and Delayed Hominization." *Theological Studies* 31 (1970): 76–105.

———. "A Liberal Catholic's View." In *Abortion in a Changing World*, edited by Robert E. Hall, 39–45. New York: Columbia University Press, 1970.

———. "Why Is Abortion Wrong?" *America*, August 16, 1975, 65–67.

Downie, R. S. *Roles and Values.* London: Methuen, 1971.

Dreweke, Joerg. "Abortion Declines Worldwide, Falls Most Where Abortion Is Broadly Legal." *Guttmacher Institute*, October 11, 2007. http:// www.guttmacher.org/media/nr/2007/10/11/index.html (accessed November 1, 2007).

Duncan, A. R. C. *On the Nature of Persons.* New York: Peter Lang, 1990.

Durkheim, Émile. *Suicide: A Study in Sociology.* Translated by John A. Spaulding and George Simson. New York: Free Press, 1966.

Dworkin, Ronald. "Why Bakke Has No Case." *New York Review of Books*, November 10, 1977.

"Earliest Surviving Preemie to Remain in Hospital." *MSNBC.COM*, February 20, 2007. http:// www.msnbc.msn.com/id/17237979/ns/health-kidsandparenting (accessed November 22, 2010).

"Earth Day 2000." *Time Special Edition*, April–May 2000, 1–96.

d'Eaubonne, François. *Le Feminism ou le Mort.* Paris: Horay, 1974.

Egan, Timothy, and Adam Liptak. "Fraught Issue, but Narrow Ruling in Oregon Suicide Case." *New York Times*, January 18, 2006. http:// www.nytimes.com/2006/01/18/national/18oregon.html?ex=1295240400&en=18040 (accessed December 4, 2006).

Ehrlich, Isaac. "The Deterrent Effect of Capital Punishment: A Question of Life and Death." *American Economic Review* 65 (June 1975): 397–417.

Engel, Mylan, Jr. "Why *You* Are Committed to the Immorality of Eating Meat." In *The Moral Life*, edited by Louis Pojman. New York: Oxford University Press, 2000.

Englehardt, H. Tristram. "The Ontology of Abortion." *Ethics* 84 (April 1974): 217–34.

English, Jane. "Abortion and the Concept of Person." *Canadian Journal of Philosophy* 5, no. 2 (October 1975).

Etzioni, Amitai. *The Spirit of Community*. New York: Crown, 1993.

"Execution List 2011." *Death Penalty Information Center*. http://www.deathpenaltyinfo.org/execution-list-2011 (accessed June 13, 2012).

"Execution List 2012." *Death Penalty Information Center*. http://www.deathpenaltyinfo.org/execution-list-2012 (accessed August 7, 2012).

Ezorsky, Gertrude. *Racism and Justice: The Case for Affirmative Action*. Ithaca, NY: Cornell University Press, 1991.

"Facts on Post-Conviction DNA Exonerations." *Innocence Project*. http://www.innocenceproject.org/Content/Facts_on_PostConviction_DNA_Exonerations.phb (accessed June 4, 2012).

Fagothey, Austin. *Right and Reason: Ethics in Theory and Practice*. 4th ed. St. Louis: C. V. Mosby, 1967.

"Family Net Worth Drops to Level of Early '90s, Fed Says." *New York Times*. http://www.nytimes.com/2012/06/12/business/economy-net-worth-drops-to-level-of-early-90s-fed-says.html (accessed June 14, 2012).

"Feeling the Heat: Special Report: Global Warming." *Time*, April 9, 2001, 22–39.

Feinberg, Joel. *Social Philosophy*. Englewood Cliffs, NJ: Prentice-Hall, 1973.

———. "Voluntary Euthanasia and the Inalienable Right to Life." *Philosophy and Public Affairs* 7, no. 2 (Winter 1978): 93–123.

———, ed. *The Problem of Abortion*. 2nd ed. Belmont, CA: Wadsworth, 1984; 3rd ed., 1997.

Fergusson, David, and Nigel Dower, eds. *John Macmurray: Critical Perspectives*. New York: Peter Lang, 2002.

Field, Barbara. "Wilt Chamberlain Revisited: Nozick's 'Justice in Transfer' and the Problem of Market-Based Distribution." *Philosophy and Public Affairs* 24, no. 3 (Summer 1995): 226–45.

Finnis, John M. "Law, Morality, and 'Sexual Orientation.'" *Notre Dame Law Review* 69 (1994): 1049–57, 1063–76.

"The First 'Humane' Execution?" *Newsweek*, December 20, 1982, 41.

Fletcher, Joseph. *Situation Ethics: The New Morality*. Philadelphia: Westminster Press, 1966.

———. *Moral Responsibility: Situation Ethics at Work*. Philadelphia: Westminster Press, 1967.

Flew, Antony. "The Principle of Euthanasia." In *Euthanasia and the Right to Die*, edited by A. B. Downing. London: Peter Owen, 1969.

Foot, Philippa. "The Problem of Abortion and the Doctrine of the Double Effect." *Oxford Review* 5 (1967): 5–15.

———. "Euthanasia." *Philosophy and Public Affairs* 6, no. 2 (Winter 1977): 85–112.

Forest Frontiers Initiative. *The Last Frontier Forests: Ecosystems and Economies on the Edge.* Washington, DC: WRI, 1997.

Forst, Brian E. "The Deterrent Effect on Capital Punishment: A Cross-State Analysis." *Minnesota Law Review* 6 (May 1977): 743–67.

Frankena, William. *Ethics*. Englewood Cliffs, NJ: Prentice-Hall, 1963.

Freidman, Milton. *Capitalism and Freedom*. Chicago: University of Chicago Press, 1962.

Frey, R. G. *Interests and Rights: The Case against Animals*. Oxford: Clarendon Press, 1980.

Fullinwider, Robert. "Affirmative Action." *Stanford Encyclopedia of Philosophy*. Spring 2005 ed. Edited by Edward N. Zalta. http://plato .stanford.edu/archives/spr2005/entries/affi (accessed February 27, 2007).

Fund for Peace and the Carnegie Endowment for International Peace. "The Failed States Index." *Foreign Policy* (July/August 2005): 56–65.

Gelbspan, Ross. *The Heat Is On: The Climate Crisis: The Cover-Up: The Prescription*. Updated ed. Cambridge, MA: Perseus Books, 1998.

Gerstein, Robert S. "Capital Punishment—'Cruel and Unusual?' A Retributivist Response." *Ethics* 85, no. 1 (October 1974): 75–79.

Gialanella, David. "Meredith Crystal (next friend for McDonald, Joshua) v. Jefferson County Bd. of Education, et al." *Medill News Service*. http://docket.medill.northwestern.edu/ archives/003698 (accessed July 2, 2007).

Gibbs, Nancy. "The Pill Arrives." *Time*, October 9, 2000, 41–49.

———. "Stem Cells: The Hope and the Hype." *Time*, August 7, 2006, 40–46.

Gilbert, Martin. *Winston Churchill: Never Despair*. Boston: Houghton Mifflin, 1988.

Gilligan, Carol. *In a Different Voice: Psychological Theory and Women's Development*. Cambridge, MA: Harvard University Press, 1982.

Glover, Jonathan. *Causing Death and Saving Lives*. Harmondsworth, UK: Penguin Books, 1977.

———, ed. *Utilitarianism and Its Critics*. New York: Macmillan, 1990.

Godfrey-Smith, William. "The Value of Wilderness." *Environmental Ethics* (1979): 309–10.

Gold, Steven Jay, ed. *Moral Controversies: Race, Class, and Gender in Applied Ethics*. Belmont, CA: Wadsworth, 1993.

Goleman, Daniel. *Emotional Intelligence*. New York: Bantam, 1995.

Goodpaster, Kenneth. "On Being Morally Considerable." *Journal of Philosophy* 75 (1978): 308–25.

Greenhouse, Linda. "Justices Say EPA Has Power to Act on Harmful Gases." *New York Times*, April 3, 2007, sec. A, 1, 14.

Grossman, Lt. Col. Dave, with Loren W. Christensen. *On Combat: The Psychology and Physiology of Deadly Conflict in War and in Peace*. 3rd ed. N.p.: Warrior Science Publications, 2008.

Haag, Ernest van den. "On Deterrence and the Death Penalty." *Journal of Criminal Law, Criminology and Police Science* 60 (June 1969): 141–47.

———. "In Defense of the Death Penalty: A Legal—Practical—Moral Analysis." *Criminal Law Bulletin* 14, no. 1 (January–February 1978): 51–68.

————. "Refuting Reiman and Nathanson." *Philosophy and Public Affairs* 14, no. 2 (Spring 1985): 165–76.

————. "The Ultimate Punishment: A Defense." *Harvard Law Review* 99 (1986).

Haag, Ernest van den, and Joseph P. Conrad. *The Death Penalty: A Debate.* New York: Plenum Press, 1983.

Habermas, Jürgen. *The Theory of Communicative Action.* 2 vols. Translated by Thomas McCarthy. Boston: Beacon Press, 1984.

"Haitian Storm Deaths Blamed on Deforestation." *Environment News Service*, September 27, 2004.

Harding, John. "Is There a Duty to Die?" *Hastings Center Report* 27, no. 2 (1997): 34–42.

Hare, R. M. "Abortion and the Golden Rule." *Philosophy and Public Affairs* 4, no. 3 (Spring 1975): 201–22.

————. "Euthanasia: A Christian View." *Philosophic Exchange* 2, no. 1 (Summer 1975).

————. "What Is Wrong with Slavery." *Philosophy and Public Affairs* 8, no. 2 (Winter 1979): 103–21.

Harris, Errol. "Thought and Action." Review of *The Self as Agent* by John Macmurray. *Review of Metaphysics* 12, no. 3 (1959): 450–51.

————. Feature review of *Persons in Relation* by John Macmurray. *International Philosophical Quarterly* 2, no. 3 (September 1962): 479–82.

Harris, George W. "Fathers and Fetuses." *Ethics* 96 (1986).

Hart, H. L. A. "Murder and the Principles of Punishment: England and the United States." *Northwestern University Law Review* 52, no. 4 (1958).

Hawkins, Ronnie Zoe. "Reproductive Choices: The Ecological Dimension." *APA Newsletter* 19, no. 1 (Spring 1992): 66–73.

Hayes, Thomas L. "Abortion: A Biological View." *Commonweal*, March 17, 1967, 676–79.

Hegel, G. W. F. *Hegel's Philosophy of Right.* Translated by T. M. Knox. New York: Oxford University Press, 1952.

Heidegger, Martin. *Being and Time.* Translated by John Macquarrie and Edward Robinson. New York: SCM Press, 1962.

Henn, Martin. *Under the Color of Law: The Bush Administration's Subversion of U. S. Constitutional and International Law in the War on Terror.* Blue Ridge Summit, PA: Lexington Books, 2010.

"HHS Decision on Contraception as Preventive Care Resists Pressure for Overly-Broad Religious Exemption." *Media Center* (January 24, 2012). http://www.guttmacher.org/media/inthenews/2012/01/24/index.html (accessed February 9, 2012).

Hill, Thomas E., Jr. "The Message of Affirmative Action." *Social Philosophy and Policy* 8, no. 2 (1991): 108–29.

Hillman, James. *Suicide and the Soul.* New York: Harper & Row, 1964.

Hinman, Lawrence M., ed. *Contemporary Moral Issues: Diversity and Consensus.* Upper Saddle River, NJ: Prentice-Hall, 1996. 4th ed. Boston: Pearson Education, 2013.

Hobbes, Thomas. *Leviathan*. New York: E. P. Dutton, 1914.

Hoff, Christina. "Immoral and Moral Uses of Animals." *New England Journal of Medicine* 302, no. 2 (January 10, 1980): 15–18.

Hoffman, W. Michael, and Jennifer M. Moore, eds. *Business Ethics: Readings and Cases in Corporate Morality*. New York: McGraw-Hill, 1984.

Holland, R. F. *Talk of God*. Vol. 2. New York: St. Martin's Press, 1969.

Hook, Sidney. "The Death Sentence." *New Leader* 44 (April 3, 1961).

Howard-Snyder, Frances. "Doing vs. Allowing Harm." *Stanford Encyclopedia of Philosophy*. Winter 2011 ed. Edited by Edward N. Zalta. http://plato.stanford.edu/archives/win2011/entries/doing-allowing/> (accessed June 18, 2012).

Hume, David. *A Treatise on Human Nature*. With an introduction by A. D. Lindsay. 2 vols. New York: Everyman's Library, 1911.

Hursthouse, Rosiland. "Virtue Theory and Abortion." *Philosophy and Public Affairs* 20, no. 3 (Summer 1991).

Ihde, Don. *Existential Technics*. Albany: State University of New York Press, 1983.

Intergovernmental Panel on Climate Change (IPCC). *Climate Change 2001: The Scientific Basis*. New York: Cambridge University Press, 2001.

International Center for Technology Assessment. *The Real Price for Gasoline*. Report no. 3. Washington, DC, 1998.

Jacobs, Lesley A. *Pursuing Equal Opportunities: The Theory and Practice of Egalitarian Justice*. Cambridge: Cambridge University Press, 2004.

Jeffko, Walter G. "John Macmurray's Logical Form of the Personal: A Critical Exposition." PhD diss., Fordham University, 1970.

———. "Ecology and Dualism." *Religion in Life* 42, no. 1 (Spring 1973): 110–27.

———. "A Personalist Concept of Human Reason." *International Philosophical Quarterly* 14, no. 2 (June 1974): 161–80.

———. "Thought, Action, and Personhood." *Modern Schoolman* 52 (March 1975): 271–83.

———. "Processive Relationism and Ethical Absolutes." *American Benedictine Review* 26, no. 3 (September 1975): 283–97. Reprinted in *Readings in Moral Theology No. 1: Moral Norms and Catholic Tradition*, edited by Charles E. Curran and Richard McCormick, 199–214. New York: Paulist Press, 1979.

———. "Action, Personhood, and Fact-Value." *Thomist* 40, no. 1 (January 1976): 116–34.

———. "Capital Punishment in a Democracy." *America*, December 11, 1976, 413–14.

———. "Community, Society and the State." *American Benedictine Review* 28, no. 1 (March 1977): 77–94.

———. "Redefining Death." *Commonweal*, July 6, 1979, 394–97. Reprinted in *Death: Current Perspectives*, edited by Edwin S. Shneidman, 2nd ed., 131–37. Palo Alto, CA: Mayfield, 1980.

———. "Self-Consciousness and the Soul-Body Problem." *American Benedictine Review* 31, no. 3 (September 1980): 346–60.

————. "The Death Penalty: A Personalist Approach." *American Benedictine Review* 38, no. 4 (December 1987): 360–80.

————. "Should the Death Penalty Be Abolished?" *Commonwealth Review* 1, no. 1 (January 1988): 33–37.

————. "Is the Fetus a Person?" *Commonwealth Review* 3, no. 1 (May 1990): 15–18.

————. "Are 'Person' and 'Agent' Coextensive? Reflections on John Macmurray." *American Benedictine Review* 44, no. 4 (December 1993): 352–70.

————. "A New Model of Reason as Standard of Value." In "Essays on John Macmurray's Post-Modern Philosophy: The Primacy of Persons in Community," edited by Harry A. Carson. Unpublished manuscript.

Johann, Robert O., ed. *Freedom and Value*. New York: Fordham University Press, 1976.

Johnson, Robert. "This Man Has Expired: Witness to an Execution." *Commonweal*, January 13, 1989, 9–15.

Johnsten, Norman, Leonard Savitz, and Marvin L. Wolfgang, eds. *The Sociology of Crime and Punishment*. New York: John Wiley, 1962.

Kamm, Frances. "Harming Some to Save Others." *Philosophical Studies* 57 (1989): 227–60.

————. "A Right to Choose Death." *Boston Review*, August 28, 2001.

Kant, Immanuel. *Lectures on Ethics*. Translated by Louis Infield. London: Methuen, 1930; reprint, with a foreword by Lewis White Beck. New York: Harper Torchbooks, 1963.

————. *Critique of Practical Reason*. Translated and with an introduction by Lewis White Beck. New York: Liberal Arts Press, 1956.

————. *Foundations of the Metaphysics of Morals*. Translated and with an introduction by Lewis White Beck. New York: Liberal Arts Press, 1959.

————. *The Metaphysical Elements of Justice*. Translated by John Ladd. New York: Library of Liberal Arts Press, 1965.

Kanter, James, and Andrew C. Revkin. "Scientists Detail Climate Changes, Poles to Tropics." *New York Times*, April 7, 2007, sec. A, 1, 5.

King, Martin Luther, Jr. *Why We Can't Wait*. New York: Harper & Row, 1963.

Kirkpatrick, Frank G. *Community: A Trinity of Models*. Washington, DC: Georgetown University Press, 1986.

————. *The Ethics of Community*. Malden, MA: Blackwell Publishers, 2001.

————. *John Macmurray: Community beyond Political Philosophy*. Lanham, MD: Rowman & Littlefield, 2005.

Kluger, Jeffrey. "The Paradox of Supermax." *Time*, February 5, 2007, 52–54.

Kohl, Marvin, ed. *Beneficent Euthanasia*. Amherst, NY: Prometheus Books, 1975.

Kohlberg, Lawrence. *Essays in Moral Development*. 2 vols. New York: Harper & Row, 1981 and 1984.

Koons, Jennifer. "Parents Involved in Community Schools v. Seattle School District #1, et al." *Medill News Service*. http://docket.medill .northwestern.edu/archives/003697.php (accessed July 2, 2007).

Krugman, Paul. "Oligarchy, American Style." *New York Times*. http://www.nytimes.com/2011/11/04/opinion/oligarchy-american-style.html?_r1&hp (accessed November 4, 2011).

Labby, Daniel H., ed. *Life or Death: Ethics and Options*. Seattle: University of Washington Press, 1968.

Lackey, Douglas. "Pacifism." In *Social and Personal Ethics*, 7th ed., edited by William H. Shaw, 315–22. Boston: Wadsworth, 2011.

Ladd, John, ed. *Ethical Issues Relating to Life and Death*. Oxford: Oxford University Press, 1979.

Lauer, Quentin. *Phenomenology: Its Genesis and Prospect*. New York: Harper Torchbooks, 1965.

Leiser, Burton M. "The Case for Iraq War II." Sterba, James P. "Iraq War II: A Blatantly Unjust War." In *Morality in Practice*, 7th ed., edited by James P. Sterba, 619-35. Belmont, CA: Wadsworth/Thomson Learning, 2004.

———. *Liberty, Justice, and Morals: Contemporary Value Conflicts*. 3rd ed. New York: Macmillan, 1986.

Lempert, Richard O. "Desert and Deterrence: An Assessment of the Moral Bases of the Case for Capital Punishment." *Michigan Law Review* 79 (1981).

Leopold, Aldo. *A Sand County Almanac*. New York: Oxford University Press, 1949; special commemorative ed., with an introduction by Robert Finch, 1987.

Levin, Michael. "Why Homosexuality Is Abnormal." *Monist* (Spring 1985).

List, Peter C., ed. *Radical Environmentalism: Philosophy and Tactics*. Belmont, CA: Wadsworth, 1993.

Locke, John. *Two Treatises of Civil Government*. Introduction by W. S. Carpenter. New York: E. P. Dutton, pp. 19–74.

———. *Two Treatises of Government*. Edited and with an introduction by Peter Laslett. Cambridge: Cambridge University Press, 1963.

Locy, Toni. "High Court: Tenn. Inmate May Use DNA Tests." *Yahoo! News*, June 12, 2006. http://news.yahoo.com/s/ap20060612/ap_on_go_su_co/scotus_death_penalty_dna;_ylt =A (accessed June 26, 2006).

Lovins, Amory P., et al. *Winning the Oil Endgame: Innovation for Profits, Jobs, and Security*. Snowmass, CO: Rocky Mountain Institute, 2004.

Luban, David. "Just War and Human Rights." *Philosophy and Public Affairs* 9 (Winter 1980); 160-81.

Lucas, J. R. "Or Else." *Proceedings of the Aristotelian Society* (1968–69).

Machan, Tibor R. "Do Animals Have Rights?" *Public Affairs Quarterly* 5, no. 2 (1991).

MacKinnon, Barbara, ed. *Ethics: Theory and Contemporary Issues*. 3rd ed. Belmont, CA: Wadsworth, 2001.

Macmurray, John. *The Philosophy of Communism*. London: Faber & Faber, 1933.

———. *Creative Society: A Study of the Relation of Christianity to Communism*. London: Student Christian Movement Press, 1935.

———. *Freedom in the Modern World*. Foreword by C. A. Siepmann. 2nd ed. London: Faber & Faber, 1935. Reprint, with an introduction by Harry A. Carson. Amherst, NY: Humanity Books, 1992.

————. "The New Materialism." In *Marxism*, edited by J. Middleton Murray et al., 54–58. London: Chapman & Hall, 1935.

————. *The Clue to History*. London: Student Christian Movement Press, 1938.

————. *A Challenge to the Churches: Religion and Democracy*. Introduction by Francis Williams. London: Kegan Paul, Trench, Trubner and Co., 1941.

————. *Constructive Democracy*. London: Faber & Faber, 1943.

————. *Conditions of Freedom*. London: Faber & Faber, 1950. Reprint, with an introduction by Walter G. Jeffko. Amherst, NY: Humanity Books, 1993.

————. *The Self as Agent*. London: Faber & Faber; New York: Harper & Row, 1957. Reprint, with an introduction by Stanley M. Harrison. Amherst, NY: Humanity Books, 1991.

————. *Persons in Relation*. London: Faber & Faber; New York: Harper & Row, 1961. Reprint, with an introduction by Frank G. Kirkpatrick. Amherst, NY: Humanity Books, 1991.

————. *Reason and Emotion*. 2nd ed. London: Faber & Faber, 1961. Reprint, with an introduction by John E. Costello. Amherst, NY: Humanity Books, 1992.

————. *To Save from Fear*. London: Friends Home Service Committee, 1964.

————. *Search for Reality in Religion*. London: George Allen & Unwin, 1965.

————. *The Philosophy of Jesus*. London: Friends Home Service Committee, 1973.

————. "Science and Objectivity." In *The Personal Universe: Essays in Honor of John Macmurray*, edited by Thomas E. Wren, 7–23. Atlantic Highlands, NJ: Humanities Press, 1975.

Malm, H. M. "Killing, Letting Die, and Simple Conflicts." *Philosophy and Public Affairs* 18, no. 3 (Summer 1989): 238–58.

Mappes, Thomas A., and Jane S. Zembaty, eds. *Social Ethics: Morality and Social Policy*. 3rd ed. New York: McGraw-Hill, 1987; 5th ed., 1997.

Marcel, Gabriel. *Being and Having*. Translated by Katherine Farrer. Westminster, UK: Dacre Press, 1949.

Margolis, Joseph. *Negativities: The Limits of Life*. Columbus, OH: Charles E. Merrill, 1975.

Margalit, Avishai, and Michael Walzer. "Civilians and Combatants." *New York Review of Books*, May 14, 2009.

Maritain, Jacques. *Scholasticism and Politics*. Translated by Mortimer J. Adler. Garden City, NY: Image Books, 1960.

McCullough, David. *Truman*. New York: Simon and Schuster, 1992.

McGibbon, Bill. *Eaarth: Making a Life on a Tough New Planet*. New York: Times Books, Henry Holt, 2010.

McIntosh, Esther, ed. *John Macmurray: Selected Philosophical Writings*. Exeter, UK: Imprint Academic, 2004.

McIntyre, Alison. "Doctrine of Double Effect." *Stanford Encyclopedia of Philosophy*. Fall 2011 ed. Edited by Edward N. Zalta. http:// plato.stanford.edu/archives/fall2011/entries/double -effect/ (accessed June 18, 2012).

McKenna, Joseph C. "Ethics and War: A Catholic View." *American Political Science Review* 54 (1960): 647-58.

McMahan, Jeff. "Torture in Principle and in Practice." *Public Affairs Quarterly* 22, no. 2 (April 2008).

Mill, John Stuart. *On Liberty*. London, 1859.

———. *Utilitarianism*. Edited by Oskar Piest. New York: Library of Liberal Arts, 1957.

Mills, Nicolaus, ed. *Debating Affirmative Action: Race, Gender, Ethnicity, and the Politics of Inclusion*. New York: Delta, 1994.

"Montana Becomes Third State to Permit Physician-Assisted Suicide—But Final Exit Network Asks, 'Is It Enough?'" *Final Exit Network*. http://www.ereleases.com/pr/montana-ere -permit-physicianassisted-suicide-final-exit-netw . . . (accessed January 6, 2010).

Mooney, Philip. *Belonging Always: Reflections on Uniqueness*. Chicago: Loyola University Press, 1987.

Moore, Brook Noel, and Robert Michael Stewart, eds. *Moral Philosophy: A Comprehensive Introduction*. Mountain View, CA: Mayfield, 1994.

Moore, G. E. *Principia Ethica*. Cambridge: Cambridge University Press, 1903.

Moreland, J. P. "James Rachels and the Active Euthanasia Debate." *Journal of the Evangelical Society* 31 (March 1988).

Morris, Herbert. "Persons and Punishment." *Monist* 5 (October 1968): 475–501.

Mosle, Sara. "The Vanity of Volunteerism." *New York Times*, July 2, 2000, 22–27, 40, 52–55.

Motto, Jerome A. "The Right to Suicide: A Psychiatrist's View." *Life Threatening Behavior* 2, no. 3 (Fall 1972).

Mounier, Emmanuel. *Personalism*. New York: Grove Press, 1952.

Munson, Ronald, ed. *Intervention and Reflection: Basic Issues in Medical Ethics*. Belmont, CA: Wadsworth, 1979.

"Murder Rates Nationally and By State." *Death Penalty Information Center*. http://www .deathpenaltyinfo.org/murder-rates-nationally-and-state (accessed June 4, 2012).

Murphy, Jeffrie G. "Marxism and Retribution." *Philosophy and Public Affairs* 2, no. 3 (Spring 1973): 217–43.

Naess, Arne. *Ecology, Community, and Lifestyle*. Translated by David Rothenberg. New York: Cambridge University Press, 1989.

Nakell, Barry. "The Cost of the Death Penalty." *Criminal Law Bulletin* 14, no. 1 (January– February 1978): 68–80.

Narveson, Jan. "Pacifism: A Philosophical Analysis." In *Moral Problems*, 3rd ed., edited by James Rachels, 408-25. New York: Harper & Row, 1979.

"News and Developments—Deterrence." *Death Penalty Information Center*. http://www.death penaltyinfo.org/newsanddev.php?scid=12 (accessed December 27, 2006).

Nickerson, Colin. "Studies Cite New Process for Stem Cells." *Boston Globe*, June 7, 2007, sec. A, 1, 18.

"1999 Year End Report: Executions Reach Record High, But Concern Also Grows." *Death Penalty Information Center*. http://www.deathpenaltyinfo.org/node/470 (accessed April 4, 2009).

Noonan, John T., Jr. *The Morality of Abortion: Legal and Historical Perspectives.* Cambridge, MA: Harvard University Press, 1970.

Nozick, Robert. *Anarchy, State, and Utopia.* New York: Basic Books, 1974.

————. *The Nature of Rationality.* Princeton, NJ: Princeton University Press, 1993.

Olen, Jeffrey, and Vincent Barry, eds. *Applying Ethics.* 4th ed. Belmont, CA: Wadsworth, 1992.

Olen, Jeffrey, Vincent Barry, and Julie C. Van Camp, eds. *Applying Ethics.* 8th ed. Belmont, CA: Wadsworth, 2005. 10th ed. Boston: Wadsworth, 2011.

"Oregon Death with Dignity Act." *Oregon: Department of Human Services.* http://www.oregon .gov/DHS/ph/pas/org.shtml (accessed March 28, 2007).

Orwell, George. "Reflections on Gandhi." *Partisan Review* (January, 1949).

Otsuka, Michael. "Killing the Innocent in Self-Defense." *Philosophy and Public Affairs* 23, no. 1 (Winter 1994): 74–94.

Passell, Peter. "The Deterrent Effect of the Death Penalty: A Statistical Test." *Stanford Law Review* 65 (November 1975): 62–64.

Perlin, Seymour, ed. *A Handbook for the Study of Suicide.* New York: Oxford University Press, 1975.

Phillips, M. T., and J. A. Sechzer. *Animal Research and Ethical Conflict.* New York: Springer-Verlag, 1989.

Pincoffs, Edmund L. *The Rationale of Legal Punishment.* Atlantic Highlands, NJ: Humanities Press, 1966.

Pinker, Stephen. "The Mystery of Consciousness." *Time,* January 29, 2007, 58–69.

Plato. *The Dialogues of Plato.* Translated by B. Jowett, with an introduction by Raphael Demos. 2 vols. New York: Random House, 1937.

Pogge, Thomas W. *Realizing Rawls.* Ithaca, NY: Cornell University Press, 1989.

Pojman, Louis P. *Life and Death: Grappling with the Moral Problems of Our Time.* Boston: Jones and Bartlett, 1992.

————. "The Moral Status of Affirmative Action." *Public Affairs Quarterly* 6 (1992).

Pojman, Louis, and Jeffrey Reiman, eds. *The Death Penalty: For and Against.* Lanham, MD: Rowman and Littlefield, 1998.

Pooley, Eric. "Fairness or Folly?" *Time,* June 23, 1997, 32–36.

Popper, K. R. *The Open Society and Its Enemies.* 4th ed. Vol. 1. London: Routledge & Kegan Paul, 1962.

"Push for 'Personhood' Amendment Represents New Tack in Abortion Fight." *New York Times.* http://www.nytimes.com/2011/10/26/us/politics/personhood-amendments-would-ban -nearl . . . (accessed August 22, 2012).

Quill, Timothy E. "Death and Dignity: A Case of Individualized Decision Making." *New England Journal of Medicine* 324 (March 7, 1991).

Quinn, Warren. "Actions, Intentions, and Consequences: The Doctrine of Doing and Allowing." *Philosophical Review* 98 (July 1989): 287–312.

———. "Actions, Intentions, and Consequences: The Doctrine of Double-Effect." *Philosophy and Public Affairs* 18, no. 4 (Fall 1989): 334–51.

Rachels, James. "Active and Passive Euthanasia." *New England Journal of Medicine* 292, no. 2 (January 9, 1975): 78–80.

———. "Why Privacy Is Important." *Philosophy and Public Affairs* 4, no. 4 (Summer 1975): 323–33.

———. *The End of Life: Euthanasia and Morality*. Oxford: Oxford University Press, 1986.

———. *Created from Animals: The Moral Implications of Darwinism*. New York: Oxford University Press, 1991.

———, ed. *Moral Problems: A Collection of Philosophical Essays*. New York: Harper & Row, 1971; 2nd ed., 1975; 3rd ed., 1979.

———, ed. *The Right Thing to Do: Basic Readings in Moral Philosophy*. New York: Random House, 1989.

Rampell, Catherine. "Inequality Is Most Extreme in Wealth, Not Income." *New York Times*. http:// economix.blogs.nytimes.com/2011/03/30inequality-is-most-extreme-in-wealth-not -in . . . (accessed June 4, 2012).

Ramsey, Paul. *The Patient as Person*. New Haven, CT: Yale University Press, 1970.

Raphael, D. D. Critical study of *The Self as Agent*, by John Macmurray. *Philosophical Quarterly* 9, no. 36 (1959): 267–77.

———. Review of *Persons in Relation*, by John Macmurray. *Philosophical Quarterly* 15, no. 58 (1965): 74–76.

Rawls, John. *A Theory of Justice*. Cambridge, MA: Harvard University Press, Belknap Press, 1971; rev. ed., 1999.

———. *Political Liberalism*. New York: Columbia University Press, 1993; paperback ed., 1996; expanded ed., 2005.

———. *John Rawls: Collected Papers*. Edited by Samuel Freeman. Cambridge, MA: Harvard University Press, 1999.

———. *The Law of Peoples*. Cambridge, MA: Harvard University Press, 1999.

———. *Justice as Fairness: A Restatement*. Edited by Erin Kelly. Cambridge, MA: Harvard University Press, Belknap Press, 2001.

Regan, Tom. *All That Dwell Therein*. Berkeley: University of California Press, 1982.

———. *The Case for Animal Rights*. Berkeley: University of California Press, 1983.

———. *The Thee Generation: Reflections on the Coming Revolution*. Philadelphia: Temple University Press, 1991.

———, ed. *Matters of Life and Death: New Introductory Essays in Moral Philosophy*. 2nd ed. New York: Random House, 1986.

Reiman, Jeffrey. "Privacy, Intimacy, and Personhood." *Philosophy and Public Affairs* 6, no. 1 (Fall 1976): 26–44.

———. "Justice, Civilization, and the Death Penalty." *Philosophy and Public Affairs* 14, no. 2 (Spring 1985): 115–48.

Rolston, Holmes III. *Environmental Ethics: Duties and Values in the Natural World*. Philadelphia: Temple University Press, 1998.

Rosen, Allen D. *Kant's Theory of Justice*. Ithaca, NY: Cornell University Press, 1993.

Rosenfeld, Andrew. *Affirmative Action and Justice: A Philosophical and Constitutional Inquiry*. New Haven, CT: Yale University Press, 1991.

Rousseau, Jean-Jacques. *The Social Contract and Discourses*. Translated and with an introduction by G. D. H. Cole. New York: E. P. Dutton, 1950.

Rowen, Andrew. *Of Mice, Models and Men: A Critical Evaluation of Animal Research*. Albany: State University of New York Press, 1984.

Roy, Louis. "Interpersonal Knowledge according to John Macmurray." *Modern Theology* 5, no. 4 (1989): 349–65.

Russell, Bertrand. *Human Society in Ethics and Politics*. London: Allen & Unwin, 1954.

Ryder, Richard. *Victims of Science: The Use of Animals in Research*. London: National Anti-Vivisection Society, 1983.

Ryle, Gilbert. *The Concept of Mind*. New York: Barnes & Noble, 1949.

Sachs, Jeffrey D. "A Climate for Change." *Time*, March 19, 2007, 94.

Sagoff, Mark. "On Preserving the Natural Environment." *Yale Law Journal* 84, no. 2 (December 1974): 167–205.

Santayana, George. *Soliloquies in England*. New York: Scribner's, 1924.

Sartre, Jean-Paul. *Existentialism and Humanism*. Translated by Philip Mairet. London: Methuen, 1948.

Scalia, Antonin. "The Disease as Cure." *Washington University Law Quarterly* 1 (1979).

Scanlon, Thomas. "Thomson on Privacy." *Philosophy and Public Affairs* 4, no. 4 (Summer 1975): 315–22.

———. "Nozick on Rights, Liberty, and Property." *Philosophy and Public Affairs* 6, no. 1 (Fall 1976): 3–25.

Schedler, George. "Capital Punishment and Its Deterrent Effect." *Social Theory and Practice* 4, no. 1 (1976): 47–56.

Schmidtz, David. *Rational Choice and Moral Agency*. Princeton, NJ: Princeton University Press, 1994.

Schwarz, Stephen D. *The Moral Question of Abortion*. Chicago: Loyola University Press, 1990.

Self, Donnie J., ed. *Philosophy and Public Policy*. Norfolk, VA: Teagle & Little, 1977.

Sellin, Thorsten. *The Death Penalty*. Philadelphia: American Law Institute, 1959.

———. *The Penalty of Death*. Beverly Hills, CA: Sage Publications, 1980.

———, ed. *Capital Punishment*. New York: Harper & Row, 1967.

Shah, Anup. "Global Dimming." *Global Issues*, January 15, 2005. http:// www.globalissues.org/ EnvIssues/GlobalWarming/globaldimming.asp (accessed September 8, 2007).

Shaw, Anthony M., and Iris A. Shaw. "Dilemma of Informed Consent in Children." *New England Journal of Medicine* 289 (October 25, 1973): 885–90.

Shaw, William H., ed. *Social and Personal Ethics*. Belmont, CA: Wadsworth, 1993; 5th ed., 2005. 7th ed. Boston: Wadsworth, 2011.

Shaw, William H., and Vincent Barry, eds. *Moral Issues in Business*. 6th ed. Belmont, CA: Wadsworth, 1995; 8th ed., 2001.

Shawl, Jeannie. "Supreme Court Allows Death Row Lethal Injection Challenge to Proceed." *Jurist*, June 12, 2006. http://jurist.law.pitt.edu/paperchase/2006/06/supreme-court-allows -death-row-lethal.php (accessed June 26, 2006).

Shiva, Vandana. *Staying Alive: Women, Ecology and Development*. Atlantic Highlands, NJ: Zed Books, 1998.

Shiva, Vandana, and Maria Miles. *Ecofeminism*. Atlantic Highlands, NJ: Zed Books, 1993.

Simmons, A. John. "Locke and the Right to Punish." *Philosophy and Public Affairs* 20, no. 2 (Fall 1991): 311–49.

Simon, Herbert. *Reason in Human Affairs*. Stanford, CA: Stanford University Press, 1983.

Singer, Peter. *Animal Liberation*. New York: New York Review of Books, 1975; 2nd ed., New York: Avon Books, 1990.

———. *Practical Ethics*. 2nd ed. New York: Cambridge University Press, 1993.

———, ed. *In Defense of Animals*. New York: Blackwell, 1985.

Sizer, Nigel, and Dominiek Plouvier. *Increased Investment and Trade by Transnational Logging Companies in Africa, the Caribbean, and the Pacific*. Belgium: World Wide Fund for Nature and WRI Forest Frontiers Initiative, 2000.

Skinner, B. F. *Science and Human Behavior*. New York: Free Press, 1953.

Slote, Michael. *Beyond Optimizing: A Study of Rational Choice*. Cambridge, MA: Harvard University Press, 1989.

Smart, J. J. C., and B. Williams. *Utilitarianism: For and Against*. New York: Cambridge University Press, 1973.

Sonfeld, Adam. "The Religious Exemption to Mandated Insurance Coverage of Contraception." *Virtual Mentor* 14, no. 2 (February 2012): 137-45.

Sorell, Tom. *Scientism: Philosophy and the Infatuation with Science*. New York: Routledge, 1991.

Sowell, Thomas. "Affirmative Action: A Worldwide Disaster." *Commentary* (December 1989).

———. *Preferential Policies: An International Perspective*. New York: William Morrow, 1991.

"Special Report, Global Warming." *Time*, April 3, 2006, 28–62.

Species Survival Commission. *2004 IUCN Red List of Threatened Species*. Gland, Switzerland and Cambridge, UK: World Conservation Union-IUCN, 2004.

"State of the Climate, Global Analysis, Annual 2009." *National Oceanic and Atmospheric Administration: National Climatic Data Center*. http://www.nede.noaa.gov/?report=global (accessed February 10, 2010).

Steele, Shelby. *The Content of Our Character*. New York: St. Martin's Press, 1990.

Steinbock, Bonnie. "Speciesism and the Idea of Equality." *Philosophy* 53, no. 204 (April 1978).

Sterba, James P., ed. *Morality in Practice*. 3rd ed. Belmont, CA: Wadsworth, 1991; 6th ed., 2001; 7th ed., 2004.

Stokstad, Erik. "Defrosting the Carbon Freezer of the North." *Science* 304 (June 11, 2004): 1618–20.

Stolberg, Sheryl Gay. "Bush Vetoes Bill Removing Stem Cell Limits, Saying 'All Human Life Is Sacred.'" *New York Times*, June 21, 2007, sec. A, 21.

Stone, Christopher D. "Should Trees Have Standing?" *Toward Legal Rights for Natural Objects.* Los Altos, CA: William Kaufman, 1974.

———. *Earth and Other Ethics.* New York: Harper & Row, 1987.

Strasser, S. *The Soul in Metaphysical and Empirical Psychology.* Pittsburgh, PA: Duquesne University Press, 1957.

"Suicide." *Catechism of the Catholic Church* (paragraphs 2280-283). http://www.newadvent.org/cathen/74326b.htm (accessed March 27, 2009).

Sullivan, Joseph V. *The Morality of Mercy Killing.* Westminster, MD: Newman Press, 1950.

Sullivan, Thomas D. "Active and Passive Euthanasia: An Impertinent Distinction?" *Human Life Review* 3, no. 3 (Summer 1977): 40–46.

Sumner, L. W. *Abortion and Moral Theory.* Princeton, NJ: Princeton University Press, 1981.

Sun-tzu. *The Art of War.* Translated with introduction and commentary by Ralph D. Sawyer. Boulder, CO: Westview Press, 1994.

Szasz, Thomas. "The Ethics of Suicide." *Antioch Review* 31 (Spring 1971): 7–17.

Taylor, A. E. *Plato: The Man and His Work.* 7th ed. London: Methuen, 1960.

Taylor, Paul W. "The Ethics of Respect for Nature." *Environmental Ethics* 3, no. 3 (Fall 1981): 197–218.

———. *Respect for Nature: A Theory of Environmental Ethics.* Princeton, NJ: Princeton University Press, 1986.

Thomson, Judith Jarvis. "A Defense of Abortion." *Philosophy and Public Affairs* 1, no. 1 (Fall 1971): 47–66.

———. "Preferential Hiring." *Philosophy and Public Affairs* 2, no. 4 (Summer 1973): 364–84.

———. "The Right to Privacy." *Philosophy and Public Affairs* 4, no. 4 (Summer 1975): 295–314.

———. *Rights, Restitution, and Risk.* Cambridge, MA: Harvard University Press, 1986.

———. "Self-Defense." *Philosophy and Public Affairs* 20, no. 4 (Fall 1991): 283–310.

Time Special Edition: Earth Day 2000. Time, April–May 2000.

Tong, Rosemary. *New Perspectives in Health Care Ethics: An Interdisciplinary and Crosscultural Approach.* Upper Saddle River, NJ: Pearson Prentice-Hall, 2007.

Tooley, Michael. "Abortion and Infanticide." *Philosophy and Public Affairs* 2, no. 1 (Fall 1972): 37–65.

———. *Abortion and Infanticide.* Oxford: Clarendon Press, 1983.

"Trends in the Distribution of Household Income between 1979 and 2007." *Congressional Budget Office.* http://www.cbo.gov/doc.cfm?index=12485 (accessed October 26, 2011).

United Nations Development Programme, United Nations Environment Programme, World Bank, World Resources Institute. *World Resources 2000–2001: People and Ecosystems: The Fraying Web of Life.* Washington, DC: World Resources Institute, 2000.

UN Population Fund (UNPA). *The State of World Population 2004.* New York, 2004.

"U.S. & World Population Clocks." *U.S. Census Bureau*, May 31, 2012. http://www.gov/main/www/popclock.html (accessed July 3, 2012).

Universal Declaration of Human Rights. http://www.un.org/en/documents/udhr/index.shtm (accessed July 6, 2010).

Varner, Gary E. "Prospects for Consensus and Convergence in the Animal Rights Debate." *Hastings Center Report* 24, no. 1 (January 1994).

Vaux, Kenneth L. "The Theologic Ethics of Euthanasia." *Hastings Center Report* (January/February 1989).

Veatch, Henry. *Rational Man.* Bloomington: Indiana University Press, 1962.

Walzer, Michael. *Arguing about War.* New Haven: Yale University Press, 2004.

———. *Just and Unjust Wars.* 4th ed. New York: Basic Books, 2006.

"Warden: Williams Frustrated at End." *CNN Law Center*, December 13, 2005. http://www.cnn.com/2005/LAW/12/13/williams.execution (accessed March 28, 2007).

Warren, Karen J. "Feminism and Ecology: Making Connections." *Environmental Ethics* 9, no. 1 (Spring 1987): 3–20.

———. "The Power and Promise of Ecological Feminism." *Environmental Ethics* 12, no. 2 (Summer 1990): 123–46.

———. *Ecological Feminism.* Boulder, CO: Westview, 1994.

———. "Environmental Justice: Some Ecofeminist Worries about a Distributive Model." *Environmental Ethics* 21, no. 2 (Summer 1999): 151–61.

Warren, Karen J., and Nisvan Erkel, eds. *Ecofeminism: Women, Culture, Nature.* Bloomington: Indiana University Press, 1997.

Warren, Mary Anne. "On the Moral and Legal Status of Abortion." *Monist* 57, no. 1 (January 1973): 43–61.

———. "Difficulties with the Strong Animal Rights Position." *Between the Species* 2, no. 4 (Fall 1987).

"Washington v. Glucksberg: 1997." *The History of the Supreme Court: Encyclopedia.* http://www.historyofsupremecourt.org/scripts/supremecourt/glossary.cgi?term=w&letter (accessed December 4, 2006).

Wasserstrom, Richard. "The Status of the Fetus." *Hastings Magazine*, June 1975.

———. "Racism, Sexism and Preferential Treatment: An Approach to the Topics." *U.C.L.A. Law Review* 24, no. 2 (February 1977).

———. "A Defense of Programs of Preferential Treatment." *National Forum: The Phi Kappa Phi Journal* 58 (Winter 1978).

———, ed. *Today's Moral Problems.* 2nd ed. New York: Macmillan, 1979.

Watts, David T., and Timothy Howell. "Assisted Suicide Is Not Voluntary Active Euthanasia." *Journal of the American Geriatrics Society* 40 (October 1992): 1043–46.

Weinberg, Gerhard. *A World at Arms.* Cambridge, England: Cambridge University Press, 1994.

Weiss, Paul. "Man's Existence." *International Philosophical Quarterly* 1, no. 4 (December 1961): 545–68.

Weithman, Paul J., ed. *Religion and Contemporary Liberalism*. Notre Dame, IN: University of Notre Dame, 1997.

Werner, Richard. "Abortion: The Ontological and Moral Status of the Unborn." *Social Theory and Practice* 3, no. 4 (1974): 201–22.

Wertheimer, Roger. "Understanding the Abortion Argument." *Philosophy and Public Affairs* 1, no. 1 (Fall 1971): 67–95.

Wesley, Patricia. "Dying Safely: An Analysis of 'A Case of Individualized Decision Making' by Timothy E. Quill, M.D." *Issues in Law and Medicine* 8, no. 4 (1993): 476–85.

Westra, Laura, and Patricia N. Werhane, eds. *The Business of Consumption: Environmental Ethics and the Global Economy*. Lanham, MD: Rowman & Littlefield, 1998.

"What's New." *Death Penalty Information Center*. http://www.death penaltyinfo.org (accessed January 3, 2007).

White, Craig M. *The Moral Reckoning: Applying Just War Theory to the 2003 War Decision*. Blue Ridge Summit, PA: Lexington Books, 2010.

White, James E., ed. *Contemporary Moral Problems*. 4th ed. New York: West, 1994. 6th ed. Belmont, CA: Wadsworth, 2000.

"Why Money Matters." *Time*, August 13, 2012, 35-45.

Wilkes, Paul. *The Good Enough Catholic*. New York: Ballentine Books, 1996.

Williams, Glanville. *The Sanctity of Life and the Criminal Law*. New York: Knopf, 1957.

Wittgenstein, Ludwig. *Notebooks 1914–16*. Edited by G. H. von Wright and G. E. M. Anscombe. Oxford: Basil Blackwell, 1961.

Wolfe, Christopher, ed. *Homosexuality and American Public Life*. Dallas: Spence Publishing, 1999.

World Meteorological Organization and NOAA both report: 2000-2009 is the hottest decade on record." *Climate Progress*. http://climateprogress.org/2009/12/08/world-meteorological -organization-wmo-20005-war . . . (accessed February 12, 2010).

"World's Youngest Preemie." *People*. March 12, 2007. http://www.people.com/people/archive/ article/0,,20062960,00.html (accessed November 22, 2010).

Zaitchik, Alan. "Viability and the Morality of Abortion." *Philosophy and Public Affairs* 10, no. 1 (Winter 1981): 18–26.

INDEX